T0211146

Lecture Notes in Computer Science

Lecture Notes in Artificial Intelligence   **14453**

Founding Editor

Jörg Siekmann

Series Editors

Randy Goebel, *University of Alberta, Edmonton, Canada*
Wolfgang Wahlster, *DFKI, Berlin, Germany*
Zhi-Hua Zhou, *Nanjing University, Nanjing, China*

The series Lecture Notes in Artificial Intelligence (LNAI) was established in 1988 as a topical subseries of LNCS devoted to artificial intelligence.

The series publishes state-of-the-art research results at a high level. As with the LNCS mother series, the mission of the series is to serve the international R & D community by providing an invaluable service, mainly focused on the publication of conference and workshop proceedings and postproceedings.

Abdulaziz Al Ali · John-John Cabibihan ·
Nader Meskin · Silvia Rossi · Wanyue Jiang ·
Hongsheng He · Shuzhi Sam Ge
Editors

Social Robotics

15th International Conference, ICSR 2023
Doha, Qatar, December 3–7, 2023
Proceedings, Part I

Springer

Editors
Abdulaziz Al Ali
Qatar University
Doha, Qatar

John-John Cabibihan ⓘ
Qatar University
Doha, Qatar

Nader Meskin
Qatar University
Doha, Qatar

Silvia Rossi ⓘ
University of Naples Federico II
Napoli, Italy

Wanyue Jiang ⓘ
Qingdao University
Qingdao, China

Hongsheng He ⓘ
The University of Alabama
Tuscaloosa, AL, USA

Shuzhi Sam Ge ⓘ
National University of Singapore
Queenstown, Singapore

ISSN 0302-9743   ISSN 1611-3349 (electronic)
Lecture Notes in Artificial Intelligence
ISBN 978-981-99-8714-6   ISBN 978-981-99-8715-3 (eBook)
https://doi.org/10.1007/978-981-99-8715-3

LNCS Sublibrary: SL7 – Artificial Intelligence

This Springer imprint is published by the registered company Springer Nature Singapore Pte Ltd.
The registered company address is: 152 Beach Road, #21-01/04 Gateway East, Singapore 189721, Singapore

Paper in this product is recyclable.

Preface

The 15th International Conference on Social Robotics (ICSR 2023) was held in Doha, Qatar as a face-to-face conference on December 3–7, 2023. It was the first time that the conference was hosted in Qatar and in the Middle East and North Africa (MENA) region. The theme of this year's conference is "Human-Robot Collaboration: Sea, Air, Land, Space and Cyberspace", which emphasizes on all physical and cyber-physical domains where humans and robots collaborate. The conference aims to bring together researchers and practitioners working on the interaction between humans and intelligent robots and on the integration of robots into the fabric of our society.

This book constitutes the refereed conference proceedings. Out of a total of 83 submitted manuscript reviewed by a dedicated international team of Senior Programme Committee and Programme Committee, 64 regular papers and 4 papers in Special Session: "Personalisation and Adaptation in Social Robotics" were selected for inclusion into the proceedings and were presented during the technical sessions of the conference.

ICSR 2023 also featured two keynote, workshops, and robot design competitions. The first keynote talk, titled "Robotics Meets AI & 5G — The Future is Now!", was delivered by Professor Bruno Siciliano, who is a Professor of Robotics and Control at the University of Naples Federico II and a Past President of IEEE Robotics and Automation Society. The second keynote talk, titled "Perspectives and Social Impacts of Humanoids as General Purpose Robots", was delivered by Professor Abderrahmane Kheddar, Director of Research at the Centre National de la Recherche Scientifique, France. He is a Titular Member of the National Academy of Technology of France and a Knight of the French National Order of Merits.

We would like to express our sincere gratitude to all members of the Organising Committee and volunteers for their dedication in making the conference a great success. We are also indebted to members of the Senior Programme Committee and the Programme Committee for the hard work for their rigorous review of the papers. Lastly and most importantly, we are grateful to the continued support to ICSR by the authors, participants and sponsors, without which the conference would not be possible.

December 2023

Abdulaziz Al Ali
John-John Cabibihan
Nader Meskin
Silvia Rossi
Wanyue Jiang
Hongsheng He
Shuzhi Sam Ge

Organization

General Chair

Ali, Abdulaziz Al   Qatar University, Qatar

General Co-chair

Cabibihan, John-John   Qatar University, Qatar

Local Arrangement Chair

Mukahal, Waled   Qatar University, Qatar

Finance Chair

Sagheer, Mohammad Al   Qatar University, Qatar

Web Chair

Jabbar, Rateb   Qatar University, Qatar

Program Committee Chairs

Meskin, Nader   Qatar University, Qatar
Rossi, Silvia   University of Naples Federico II, Italy

Competition Chair

Pandey, Amit Kumar   Rovial Space, France; Socients AI and Robotics, France

Sponsorship Chairs

Sadda, Mohammad Al   Qatar University, Qatar
Jaber, Faisal Al   Qatar University, Qatar

Workshop Chairs

Qidwai, Uvais   Qatar University, Qatar
Erbad, Aiman   Hamad Bin Khalifa University, Qatar
Celiktutan, Oya   King's College London, UK
Ortega, Elena Lazkano   University of the Basque Country, Spain

Exhibition Chairs

Jang, Minsu   Electronics and Telecommunications Research
                              Institute, South Korea
Chellali, Ryad   Moore Nanjing Robotics Institute, LLC, China
Staffa, Mariacarla   University of Naples Parthenope, Italy

Publication Chairs

He, Hongsheng   University of Alabama, Tuscaloosa, USA
Jiang, Wanyue   Qingdao University, China

Publicity Chairs

Belushi, Mariam Al   Qatar University, Qatar
Yafei, Ghusoon Al   Qatar University, Qatar
Rossi, Alessandra   University of Naples Federico II, Italy
Holthaus, Patrick   University of Hertfordshire, UK
Chandra, Shruti   University of Waterloo, Canada
Hart, Justin   University of Texas at Austin, USA
Taheri, Alireza   Sharif University of Technology, Iran
Shidujaman, Mohammad   Independent University, Bangladesh

International Advisory Committee

Kheddar, Abderrahmane	CNRS-AIST JRL, Japan and CNRS-UM LIRMM IDH, France
Tapus, Adriana	ENSTA-ParisTech, France
Wagner, Alan Richard	Penn State University, USA
Agah, Arvin	University of Kansas, USA
Cavallo, Filippo	University of Florence, Italy
Feil-Seifer, David	University of Nevada, USA
Williams, Mary-Anne	University of New South Wales, Australia
Salichs, Miguel Ángel	University Carlos III of Madrid, Spain

Standing Committee

Ge, Shuzhi	National University of Singapore, Singapore
Khatib, Oussama	Stanford University, USA
Mataric, Maja	University of Southern California, USA
Li, Haizhou	Chinese University of Hong Kong, China
Kim, Jong Hwan	Korea Advanced Institute of Science and Technology, South Korea
Dario, Paolo	Scuola Superiore Sant'Anna, Italy
Arkin, Ronald C.	Georgia Institute of Technology, USA

Associate Editors

Mabrok, Mohamed	Qatar University, Qatar
Holthaus, Patrick	University of Hertfordshire, UK
Fiorini, Laura	Università degli studi di Firenze, Italy
Andriella, Antonio	Pal Robotics, Spain
Rossi, Alessandra	University of Naples Federico II, Italy
Nuovo, Alessandro Di	Sheffield Hallam University, UK
Gómez, Marcos Maroto	University Carlos III of Madrid, Spain
Louie, Wing-Yue (Geoffrey)	Oakland University, USA
Esposito, Anna	Università della Campania "Luigi Vanvitelli", Italy
Hindriks, Koen	Vrije Universiteit Amsterdam, The Netherlands
Bodenhagen, Leon	University of Southern Denmark, Denmark
Palinko, Oskar	University of Southern Denmark, Denmark
Fazli, Pooyan	Arizona State University, USA

Kwak, Sonya S.	Korea Institute of Science and Technology, South Korea
Tafreshi, Reza	Texas A & M University, USA
Meskin, Nikan	Qatar University, Qatar
Qidwai, Uvais	Qatar University, Qatar

Reviewers

A. Fiaz, Usman
Abdelkader, Mohamed
Abou Chahine, Ramzi
Aitsam, Muhammad
Alban, Ahmad
Amirova, Aida
Amorese, Terry
Andriella, Antonio
Angelopoulos, Georgios
Assuncao, Gustavo
Azizi, Negin
Barik, Tanmoy
Baroniya, Rupesh
Bello Martín, Felipe
Beraldo, Gloria
Berns, Karsten
Bevilacqua, Roberta
Bodenhagen, Leon
Bossema, Marianne
Boumans, Roel
Bray, Robert
Chandran Nair, Nandu
Chehade, Zeina
Cabezaolías, Carmen María
Cabibihan, John-John
Carrasco-Martínez, Sara
Carros, Felix
Chandra, Shruti
Chidambaram, Vigneswaran
Cuciniello, Marialucia
De Graaf, Maartje
de la Cruz, Andrea
Di Nuovo, Alessandro
El Khalfi, Zeineb
Ebardo, Ryan

Effati, Meysam
Elsayed, Saber
Esposito, Anna
Etuttu, Mariam
Fazli, Pooyan
Fernández Rodicio, Enrique
Fiorini, Laura
Fracasso, Francesca
Ghoudi, Zeineb
Gaballa, Aya
Ganti, Achyut
Greco, Claudia
Hedayati, Hooman
Hellou, Mehdi
Hindriks, Koen
Holthaus, Patrick
Kaman, Zeittey
Kang, Dahyun
Khan, Imy
Kim, Jaeseaok
Kim, Boyoung
Kim, Sangmin
Kwak, Sonya S.
Lacroix, Dimitri
Lakatos, Gabriella
Lee, Hee Rin
Li, Jamy
Lim, Yoonseob
Louie, Wing-Yue (Geoffrey)
Love, Tamlin
Luperto, Matteo
Mabrok, Mohamed
Maroto Gómez
Marques-Villarroya, Sara
Maure, Romain

Meskin, Nader
Minguez Sánchez, Carlos
Mohamed, Chris
Moros, Sílvia
Nesset, Birthe
Noorizadeh, Mohammad
O'Reilly, Ziggy
Osorio, Pablo
Palinko, Oskar
Paplu, Sarwar
Perugia, Giulia
Pramanick, Pradip
Preston, Rhian
Qidwai, Uvais
Radwan, Ibrahim
Recchiuto, Carmine Tommaso
Rehm, Matthias
Reimann, Merle
Rhim, Jimin
Romeo, Marta
Rossi, Silvia
Rossi, Alessandra
Staffa, Mariacarla

Sabbella, Sandeep Reddy
Schmidt-Wolf, Melanie
Seifi, Hasti
Shahverdi, Pourya
Shrivastava, Manu
Sienkiewicz, Barbara
Sirkin, David Michael
Sorrentino, Alessandra
Story, Matt
Tafreshi, Reza
Taheri, Alireza
Tarakli, Imene
Thijn, Jorrit
Uchida, Misako
Vagnetti, Roberto
Van Minkelen, Peggy
Velmurugan, Vignesh
Vigni, Francesco
Vinanzi, Samuele
Wang, Shenghui
Xu, Tong
Zeinalipour, Demetris
Zou, Meiyuan

Contents – Part I

Contents – Part II

Special Session Papers

Regular Papers

Virtual Reality Hand Tracking for Immersive Telepresence in Rehabilitative Serious Gaming

Noaman Mazhar[1], Aya Gaballa[1], Amit Kumar Pandey[2], and John-John Cabibihan[1(✉)]

[1] Mechanical and Industrial Engineering Department, Qatar University, Doha, Qatar
john.cabibihan@qu.edu.qa
[2] Socients AI and Robotics, Toulouse, France

Abstract. Intelligent systems face an increasingly complex array of challenges in the rapidly evolving landscape of human-device interactions. To address these challenges, there arises a pressing need for the development of refined methods of information transfer, capable of capturing subtle nuances such as body language and tonal subtleties. The system presented in this paper is designed to highlight a novel method of refined human-device interactions and its potential impact on the medical domain. Leveraging the Oculus SDK in the Unity Game Engine alongside the Oculus VR headset, our system allows users to interact with virtual objects naturally, mirroring real-world hand movements while simultaneously promoting upper limb rehabilitation through engaging gameplay scenarios. The integration of haptic feedback enriches the immersive experience, enabling users to not only visualize but also feel their virtual interactions. The system accommodates varying levels of mobility, adapting its complexity to individual progress. Furthermore, our VR rehabilitation system has garnered positive outcomes from user assessments, demonstrating the system's effectiveness and user satisfaction. While limited in addressing severe upper limb impairments, the system's flexibility allows for modular improvements and broader clinical integration.

Keywords: clinical rehabilitation · serious gaming · visuo-haptic mixed reality

1 Introduction

The evolution of human-machine interaction throughout the progressive advancement of technology has paved the way for unprecedented possibilities. As humanity embarks on a new era of innovation marked by the integration of machines as necessary components of the social and economic fabric [1], the convergence of humanity and robotics rises to the forefront [2]. Recent months have witnessed the mainstream emergence of AI solutions [3], highlighting the imminent need for seamless human-robot interaction. As this trend continues, predictions point to a future where interactions transcend physical confines, transpiring within virtual or semi-virtual domains, such as the metaverse [4].

A. Al. Ali et al. (Eds.): ICSR 2023, LNAI 14453, pp. 3–12, 2024.
https://doi.org/10.1007/978-981-99-8715-3_1

In this context, a significant challenge lies in the existing limitations of mainstream human-device interactions [5], particularly as advanced intelligent systems continue to play a growing role in daily activities. Interactions with machines thus far have predominantly taken place through a computer screen, limiting the depth of information that can be conveyed. The necessity to develop refined methods of information transfer [6], that are able to encompass nuances like body language and tonal subtleties, becomes increasingly apparent as we approach an era where such interactions become integral to innovation [7,8].

This paper proposes a forward-looking approach to address these challenges by harnessing the latest developments in virtual reality technology to devise novel solutions in the medical domain. While considerable progress has been made to integrate technology into various sectors, the medical field has historically exhibited a measured pace of change [9,10]. The urgency to bridge this gap arises from the potential consequences of falling behind in an era of compounding technological advancement. Alternatively, seizing such opportunities could yield transformative impacts on our capacity to assist and effect positive change [11–14].

Specifically, we delve into the integration of serious gaming into rehabilitative procedures, targeting physical rehabilitation scenarios that often pose significant mental and physical barriers for patients. The immersive potential of serious gaming holds great promise in redirecting patients' focus towards rehabilitation goals, reducing perceived burdens, and fostering engagement through competitive elements. [15] By choreographing scenarios that align with therapeutic exercises, patients are prompted to perform the required motions within an immersive context.

Given the expanding sector of remote solutions, catering to enhanced accessibility and user comfort becomes a necessity [16]. Telepresence in the virtual environment enables the direct immersion of healthcare providers for monitoring and feedback [17], additionally, it facilitates the creation of group scenarios for collective rehabilitation and support.

Notably, current virtual reality serious gaming experiences rely on controllers or sensors affixed to the body to permit virtual interactions [18]. However, this reliance can hinder the natural flow of interactions, impeding immersion, and particularly posing challenges for elderly patients unaccustomed to gaming setups [19].

This paper proposes the integration of hand tracking technology as an avenue to alleviate these issues. By capturing the entirety of limb motion without the need for attached devices, we aspire to foster organic interactions, mirroring real-world experiences within virtual environments.

Throughout this paper, we aim to highlight new methods to refine human-device interactions and their potential impact on the medical domain [20]. We present the transformative potential of serious gaming in rehabilitation. Furthermore, we introduce the concept of hand tracking technology to enhance immersive telepresence and interaction fidelity as a means of promoting subsequent exploration and development in the field.

2   Methods

2.1   Sensing and Image Capture

The system relies on the Oculus Quest 2 device, featuring integrated cameras and sensors, for an immersive interaction experience. This device is connected to a Lenovo PC with an Intel Core i7 processor, Windows 11 OS, and GeForce RTX 3070 graphics card. An Arduino Nano is integrated into the system, along with two mini disc motors placed on each wrist attached with medical adhesive tape, providing vibrational feedback. Oculus SDK is used to capture hand, finger, and head positions via integrated hardware and software. The Unity3D game engine (v2020.3.41f1) in combination with C# is used for development.

This complete hardware and software setup, including the haptic feedback mechanism enhances the immersive experience and interaction by providing users with tactile feedback on every interaction in the virtual scenario.

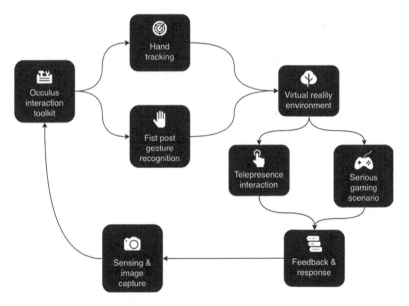

Fig. 1. A flowchart diagram detailing the relationships between each phase of building the system and demonstrating the performance feedback loop.

2.2   Oculus Interaction Toolkit

The Unity game engine, along with the Oculus Integration Asset (v46.0), is used for creating the virtual environment. The Oculus SDK is employed for implementing hand tracking within Unity. The system then uses those gestures as a means of interacting with objects in the virtual environment. While hand tracking is a built-in function of the Oculus headset and SDK, it was essential to tailor it to the specific needs of our framework.

2.3   Hand Tracking and Gesture Recognition

Within the Unity engine, the collated Oculus hand tracking data is combined with inherent gesture recognition capabilities. This facilitates the translation of users' real-world hand movements into the virtual environment (Fig. 1). Upon launching the serious game and wearing the Oculus headset, they are presented with a dynamic visual representation of their actual hand movements within the virtual environment.

2.4   Virtual Reality Environment

The virtual reality environment comprises two distinct scenes that encourage targeted upper limb movements to aid in rehabilitation. Users are immersed in a captivating prehistoric realm, assuming the role of a caveman. In the first scene, users engage in a task involving vertical shoulder motion by crushing virtual apples. The second scene involves chopping wood, requiring horizontal shoulder motion. By striking a virtual log repeatedly, users engage in a motion that enhances their shoulder's horizontal range of motion. Both scenes are carefully designed to target the relevant muscle groups and simulate real-world activities, enabling users to perform exercises aligned with clinical objectives.

2.5   Serious Gaming Scenario

The virtual gaming scenario is meticulously designed to align with users' clinical objectives. Drawing inspiration from established upper limb rehabilitation protocols, a captivating gaming environment is constructed. The activities include apple crushing and wood chopping. These two activities are deliberately designed to facilitate both vertical and horizontal shoulder motion exercises, effectively targeting the desired muscle groups.

It is important to note that training commencement relies on the execution of a power grasp to lift the club. This grasp mechanism was deliberately chosen from amongst the 33 possible hand grasps [21], due to the strength required to perform the grasp. Performing a power grasp is not contingent upon the presence of external forces [22], which eliminates the need for complex feedback control. Furthermore, the grasp choice stems from the predominance of the power grasp in performing in daily activities [23], and it's important for conducting routine object manipulation tasks [24].

Throughout the gaming scenario (Fig. 2), the training difficulty dynamically evolved. Informed by healthcare provider recommendations, training complexity advanced in accordance with the user's progress. The healthcare provider can customize the complexity by changing the target score for each scenario. This personalized approach fosters tailored rehabilitation experiences, resulting in optimized skill advancement within an engaging virtual context. For every instance of successful task execution, the user was rewarded with visible points displayed on a canvas within user's visual scope. Task completion was bound by a predetermined timeframe, which can be set by healthcare professionals,

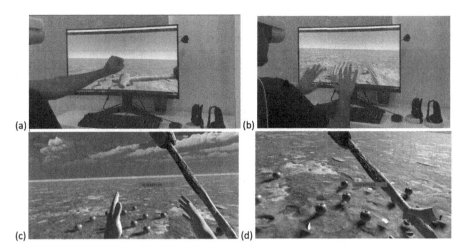

Fig. 2. Images showing hand tracking in virtual reality. (a) User grasping the virtual club by closing the hand. (b) User viewing hands simulated in virtual reality. (c) First-person view in the virtual environment. (d) First-person view of the user grasping the club in the virtual environment. The link to the full video is provided here: https://youtube.com/watch?v=qL-kFB6EHD8& si=dEg2OgyJVzCWDRTS

primarily physiotherapists. Once this timeframe elapsed, the points ceased to accumulation and the score was locked.

The score-based system serves a dual purpose. Firstly, it provides users with quantifiable performance feedback, allowing them to adapt their performance in real-time. This competitive element redirects the user's attention from the difficulty of the task to the excitement of succeeding in the game [25]. The psychological benefits of this have been proven to enhance performance incrementally over time. Secondly, the quantitative nature of the point system can be used to inform healthcare providers of the user's performance capability at varying stages of the rehabilitation process. Finally, the point system establishes a basis for telepresence applications, enabling in-game task execution for multiple users, whether collaboratively or competitively.

2.6   Telepresence Interaction

Tactile sensations, delivered via forearm-mounted miniature disc motors, enhance immersion by providing sensory cues during interactions. These motors are triggered when users grab a tool or strike an object, bridging the virtual and physical worlds. User movements seamlessly integrate into the virtual environment, creating an interactive loop (Fig. 1).

The system utilizes forearm-mounted miniature disc motors to assess object grasp and hand identification. It dispatches a 0.5-second vibrational signal through an Arduino to activate the respective forearm motor, as outlined in Algorithm 1. This dynamic feedback enhances virtual interactions.

Algorithm 1: Dynamic Haptic Feedback

---

1 **while** *interaction continues* **do**
2   **if** *object grab-event(fist) detected* **then**
3   Identify interacting hand holding the tool through Oculus SDK;
4   Send 0.5-second haptic signal indicating hand-held grab;
5   **else if** *user employs tool for environmental interaction* **then**
6   Send 0.5-second haptic signal indicating interaction;
7   Pause briefly for coherent haptic delivery;
8   **else if** *interaction event concludes* **then**
9   Reset haptic feedback status and hand information;

2.7   Performance Feedback and Assessment

Subjects and Sampling Method. Inclusion criteria enrolled individuals aged 18 and above proficient in VR device usage, while exclusion criteria excluded those with dizziness, cybersickness history, significant hand/wrist immobility, epilepsy, severe vision impairment. This ensured a group capable of meaningful engagement. 7 suitable participants were selected for the evaluation process.

Experimental Design. Prior to the commencement of the study, participants engaged in a brief 5-minute tutorial session designed to acquaint them with the immersive interaction and feedback system. Haptic feedback motors were then attached to participants' wrists using medical adhesive tape.

Following this tutorial, participants independently interacted with the system for 5 min. Subsequently, they provided feedback through the System Usability Scale (SUS), Simulator Sickness Questionnaire (SSQ), and Presence Questionnaire (PQ). These assessments gauged participants' impressions, comfort, and perceived presence in the virtual environment, offering valuable insights into the system's effectiveness and user experience.

User Experience Assessment. The evaluation process commenced with the collection of essential demographic information from participants, including their name, age, gender, relevant medical history, and explicit consent for their participation in the study.

To gauge the system's usability and user satisfaction, we employed the System Usability Scale (SUS) [26], a well-established metric. The SUS uses a 5-point Likert scale ranging from 1 (strongly disagree) to 5 (strongly agree) and consists of 10 questions addressing aspects of usability, adaptability, and user-friendliness. The resulting scores from the Likert scale were then transformed into percentages using basic mathematical operations.

For the assessment of potential cybersickness symptoms, we utilized the Simulator Sickness Questionnaire (SSQ) [27]. The SSQ evaluates 16 symptoms on a 4-point Likert scale, ranging from 0 (no symptoms) to 3 (severe), each with corresponding weights. It comprises three distinct subscales: Nausea (N), Oculomotor (O), and Disorientation (D), along with a total score. A higher SSQ score indicates a greater level of participant discomfort, with a total score exceeding 20 suggesting the presence of significant discomfort or severe cybersickness symptoms [27].

To assess users' sense of presence and immersion, we employed the Presence Questionnaire (PQ) [28]. This instrument focuses on user engagement and immersion within the virtual environment, consisting of 24 items rated on a 7-point Likert scale. Higher scores indicate heightened presence and immersion within the virtual space. The PQ has a maximum total score of 168 points, with higher scores indicating a higher level of presence. It assesses aspects such as involvement/control, naturalness, interface quality, and resolution following each system experience.

The procedures did not include invasive or potentially dangerous methods and were in accordance with the Code of Ethics of the World Medical Association (Declaration of Helsinki). Data were stored and analyzed anonymously.

3   Results

Following system testing, users began the training phase by wearing the Oculus headset. They were instantaneously immersed in the virtual environment. After providing participants with a thorough introduction to the system, they commenced their sessions. Upon the conclusion of each session, participants were asked to complete the provided questionnaires to record their feedback and suggestions. Their responses were subsequently analyzed and computed.

The participants' scores for each test were as follows: SUS (System Usability Scale) scores were 92.86 ± 2.19, PQ (Presence Questionnaire) scores were 149.14 ± 13.41, SSQ-N (Nausea) scores were 0.71 ± 0.95, SSQ-O (Oculomotor) scores were 0.85 ± 1.21, SSQ-D (Disorientation) scores were 0.85 ± 1.06, and SSQ-TS (Total) scores were 2.43 ± 1.62.

4   Discussion

The consistently favorable scores across all evaluation metrics underscore the system's commendable performance. In comparison to previous studies on similar systems [29–31], our system demonstrates equally high System Usability Scale (SUS) scores, reflecting users' contentment with usability. These high scores align with the immersive experiences indicated by the Presence Questionnaire (PQ) scores. Furthermore, our system exhibits lower Simulator Sickness Questionnaire (SSQ) scores, spanning Nausea (N), Oculomotor (O), and Disorientation (D) aspects, signifying users' comfort and resilience to simulator sickness. This observation suggests that our system outperforms or is at least on par with previous systems in terms of minimizing simulator sickness and maintaining a high level of usability.

The outcomes outlined in this paper demonstrate the framework's capacity to build on the documented success of rehabilitative serious gaming while enhancing personalized progression and collaborative engagement. The system is designed for clinical settings to operate under the supervision of licensed medical professionals and physiotherapists and to serve as a supportive tool within the broader spectrum of rehabilitative solutions. It is important to note that this framework is intended to supplement, not replace established methods [32]. By merging the benefits of increased engagement and immersion, it continues to enrich the training experience, motivating users towards improved adherence and participation.

4.1   Future Direction

During the next phase of the project, the goal is to continue refinement of the system with a focus on optimization for clinical settings [33]. To enhance its use alongside conventional clinical methods, future development will prioritize incorporating clinical monitoring features. Also, advanced telepresence and shared gaming are in planning, especially for remote users without the social aspect found in in-person mobility training at rehab clinics.

The upcoming phase also requires rigorous clinical validation. This involves testing the system with a larger cohort of patients from the target user group to optimize the training system's usability and efficacy within the clinical context. Validation trials must also be conducted with clinical rehabilitation experts and medical professionals to ensure that compatibility and efficacy extend to both the patient and the provider.

5   Conclusion

This study contributes to the field of virtual reality (VR)-based rehabilitation, specifically focusing on individuals with shoulder mobility limitations and post-stroke conditions. The study assessed the system's usability and feasibility, offering insights for future research. The results suggest positive aspects of the system's effectiveness, adaptability, and user-friendliness. This VR rehabilitation system has the potential to enhance the rehabilitation process for individuals facing specific mobility challenges.

Acknowledgements. This work was supported by a research grant from Qatar University under grant no. IRCC-2022-541. The statements made herein are solely the responsibility of the authors. The authors declare that they have no conflict of interest.

References

1. Ernst, E., Merola, R., Samaan, D.: Economics of artificial intelligence: implications for the future of work. IZA J. Labor Policy **9**(1) (2019)
2. Damiano, L., Dumouchel, P., Lehmann, H.: Towards human-robot affective co-evolution overcoming oppositions in constructing emotions and empathy. Int. J. Soc. Robot. **7**, 7–18 (2015)
3. Amin, M.M., Cambria, E., Schuller, B.W.: Will affective computing emerge from foundation models and general AI? a first evaluation on ChatGPT. arXiv preprint arXiv:2303.03186 (2023)
4. Chenna, S.: Augmented reality and AI: enhancing human-computer interaction in the metaverse. Available at SSRN 4324629 (2023)
5. Bonarini, A.: Communication in human-robot interaction. Curr. Robot. Rep. **1**, 279–285 (2020)
6. Xu, W., Dainoff, M.J., Ge, L., Gao, Z.: Transitioning to human interaction with AI systems: new challenges and opportunities for HCI professionals to enable human-centered AI. Int. J. Hum.-Comput. Interact. **39**(3), 494–518 (2023)
7. Urakami, J., Seaborn, K.: Nonverbal cues in human-robot interaction: a communication studies perspective. ACM Trans. Hum.-Robot Interact. **12**(2), 1–21 (2023)
8. Ham, J., Bokhorst, R., Cuijpers, R., van der Pol, D., Cabibihan, J.-J.: Making robots persuasive: the influence of combining persuasive strategies (gazing and gestures) by a storytelling robot on its persuasive power. In: Mutlu, B., Bartneck, C., Ham, J., Evers, V., Kanda, T. (eds.) ICSR 2011. LNCS (LNAI), vol. 7072, pp. 71–83. Springer, Heidelberg (2011). https://doi.org/10.1007/978-3-642-25504-5_8
9. He, J., Baxter, S.L., Xu, J., Xu, J., Zhou, X., Zhang, K.: The practical implementation of artificial intelligence technologies in medicine. Nat. Med. **25**(1), 30–36 (2019)
10. Sahija, D.: Critical review of mixed reality integration with medical devices for patientcare. **2022**, 10 (2022)
11. Snoswell, A.J., Snoswell, C.L.: Immersive virtual reality in health care: systematic review of technology and disease states. JMIR Biomed. Eng. **4**(1), e15025 (2019)
12. Davenport, T., Kalakota, R.: The potential for artificial intelligence in healthcare. Future Healthc. J. **6**(2), 94 (2019)
13. Kyrarini, M., et al.: A survey of robots in healthcare. Technologies **9**(1), 8 (2021)
14. Cabibihan, J.J., Javed, H., Ang, M., Aljunied, S.M.: Why robots? a survey on the roles and benefits of social robots in the therapy of children with autism. Int. J. Soc. Robot. **5**, 593–618 (2013)
15. Mantovani, F., Castelnuovo, G., Gaggioli, A., Riva, G.: Virtual reality training for health-care professionals. Cyberpsychol. Behav. **6**(4), 389–395 (2003)
16. Wang, M., Pan, C., Ray, P.K.: Technology entrepreneurship in developing countries: role of telepresence robots in healthcare. IEEE Eng. Manage. Rev. **49**(1), 20–26 (2021)
17. Dang, B.K., O'Leary-Kelley, C., Palicte, J.S., Badheka, S., Vuppalapati, C.: Comparing virtual reality telepresence and traditional simulation methods: a pilot study. Nurs. Educ. Perspect. **41**(2), 119–121 (2020)
18. Juan, M.C., Elexpuru, J., Dias, P., Santos, B.S., Amorim, P.: Immersive virtual reality for upper limb rehabilitation: comparing hand and controller interaction. Virtual Reality, 1–15 (2022)
19. McGloin, R., Farrar, K., Krcmar, M.: Video games, immersion, and cognitive aggression: does the controller matter? Media Psychol. **16**(1), 65–87 (2013)

20. Xie, B., et al.: A review on virtual reality skill training applications. Front. Virtual Reality **2**, 645153 (2021)
21. Cabibihan, J.J., et al.: Suitability of the openly accessible 3D printed prosthetic hands for war-wounded children. Front. Robot. AI **7**, 594196 (2021)
22. Zhang, X.Y., Nakamura, Y., Goda, K., Yoshimoto, K.: Robustness of power grasp. In: Proceedings of the 1994 IEEE International Conference on Robotics and Automation, vol. 4, pp. 2828–2835 (1994)
23. Bullock, I.M., Zheng, J.Z., De La Rosa, S., Guertler, C., Dollar, A.M.: Grasp frequency and usage in daily household and machine shop tasks. IEEE Trans. Haptics **6**(3), 296–308 (2013)
24. Demartino, A.M., Rodrigues, L.C., Gomes, R.P., Michaelsen, S.M.: Hand function and type of grasp used by chronic stroke individuals in actual environment. Top. Stroke Rehabil. **26**(4), 247–254 (2019)
25. Goršič, M., Cikajlo, I., Goljar, N., Novak, D.: A multisession evaluation of an adaptive competitive arm rehabilitation game. J. Neuroeng. Rehabil. **14**(1), 1–15 (2017)
26. Brooke, J.: SUS-a quick and dirty usability scale. Usability Evaluation in Industry, 189 (1996)
27. Kennedy, R.S., Lane, N.E., Berbaum, K.S., Lilienthal, M.G.: Simulator sickness questionnaire: an enhanced method for quantifying simulator sickness. Int. J. Aviat. Psychol. **3**(3), 203–220 (1993)
28. Witmer, B.G., Jerome, C.J., Singer, M.J.: The factor structure of the presence questionnaire. Presence: Teleoperators Virtual Environ. **14**(3), 298–312 (2005). https://doi.org/10.1162/105474605323384654
29. Zhou, Z., Li, J., Wang, H., Luan, Z., Li, Y., Peng, X.: Upper limb rehabilitation system based on virtual reality for breast cancer patients: development and usability study. PLOS ONE **16**(12), 1–16 (2021). https://doi.org/10.1371/journal.pone.0261220
30. Morizio, C., Compagnat, M., Boujut, A., Labbani-Igbida, O., Billot, M., Perrochon, A.: Immersive virtual reality during robot-assisted gait training: validation of a new device in stroke rehabilitation. Medicina **58**(12) (2022). https://www.mdpi.com/1648-9144/58/12/1805
31. Lee, N., Choi, W., Lee, S.: Development of a 360-degree virtual reality video-based immersive cycle training system for physical enhancement in older adults: a feasibility study. BMC Geriatrics **21**, 325 (2021). https://doi.org/10.1186/s12877-021-02263-1
32. Gentry, S.V., et al.: Serious gaming and gamification education in health professions: systematic review. J. Med. Internet Res. **21**(3), e12994 (2019)
33. Bellotti, F., Kapralos, B., Lee, K., Moreno-Ger, P., Berta, R.: Assessment in and of serious games: an overview. Adv. Hum.-Comput. Interact. **2013**, 1–1 (2013)

Human Perception of Emotional Responses to Changes in Auditory Attributes of Humanoid Agents

Zhao Zou[1]([✉]) [iD], Fady Alnajjar[2] [iD], Michael Lwin[1] [iD], Abdullah Al Mahmud[3] [iD], Muhammed Swavaf[2] [iD], Aila Khan[1] [iD], and Omar Mubin[1] [iD]

[1] Western Sydney University, Sydney, Australia
`19175225@student.westernsydney.edu.au`
[2] United Arab Emirates University, Abu Dhabi, United Arab Emirates
[3] Swinburne University of Technology, Melbourne, Australia

Abstract. Human-robot interaction has emerged as an increasingly prominent discourse within the domain of robotic technologies. In this context, the interaction of both visual and verbal cues assumes an essential role in shaping user experiences. The research problem of this study revolves around investigating the potential impact of auditory attribute alterations in humanoid agents, namely robots and avatars, on users' emotional responses. The study recruited a participant cohort comprising 14 individuals, aged 18 to 35, to engage in an experimental process of observing avatar videos with distinctive auditory attributes. These attributes encompassed two voice pitches, specifically alto voice and bass voice, as well as two speech styles denoted as frozen style and casual style. Through data collection, a repository of 13,600 data points was amassed from the participants, and subsequently subjected to rigorous analysis via the ANOVA methodology. The empirical findings demonstrate that users reveal sensitive, emotional responsiveness when faced with avatar videos characterized by varying auditory attributes. This pilot study establishes a foundational framework poised to guide future research undertakings aimed at inspiring user experiences through the deliberate manipulation of auditory attributes inherent in humanoid robots and avatars.

Keywords: Human-robot interaction · Auditory features · Emotion detection · User experience · Avatar

1 Introduction

The incorporation of artificial intelligence embedded agents into users' attitudes, emotions, acceptance, and behaviours constitute a highly stimulating topic. This phenomenon involves a diverse range of entities, including robotic animals, humanoid robots, AI-powered chatbots, virtual robots in the form of avatars, and mixed robots. These multifaceted agents find application in various practical contexts based on their visual appearances and functional attributes [1]. Humanoid robots are exceeding their practical functions to assume critical roles in fostering and cultivating social interactions with humans,

© The Author(s), under exclusive license to Springer Nature Singapore Pte Ltd. 2024
A. Al. Ali et al. (Eds.): ICSR 2023, LNAI 14453, pp. 13–21, 2024.
https://doi.org/10.1007/978-981-99-8715-3_2

including collaborators, educators, and more [2]. It is not hard to find that the increasing prevalence of humanoid robots is rooted in the facts that they can provide humans with companionship and good communication experience [3]. The interaction dynamics between humans and robots originate not solely from visual cues but also from verbal indicators [4]. After analyzing current literature, a research gap emerges regarding the impact of auditory traits in humanoid agents on user responses. While numerous studies delve into visual and interactive aspects, the auditory dimension, including speech patterns and intonation, remains understudied. As a result, this study aims to probe into the intricate dynamics of how auditory attributes of humanoid embedded agents exert influence over users' emotional responses.

The research scenarios employed for the study and the tasks assigned to the participants were initially tailored for the demographic of older adults. In preparation for the inclusion of older adults in a future experiment, a preliminary pilot study was conducted involving younger adults. The current paper reports the findings of the pilot study.

Functioning as an initial endeavor to assess human interpretations of avatars exhibiting varied auditory characteristics, this research is anticipated to enrich the body of scholarly work focused on the affective consequences stemming from spoken exchanges involving human-like entities such as robotic agents.

2 Literature Review

As an escalating field within the realm of artificial intelligence technology, human-robot interaction has attracted significant attention within both scholarly research and practical applications. A number of studies have hinted that emotion effect is a vital part in the field of human-robot interaction [5]. Moreover, it has been posited that humanoid robots possess the potential to evoke a spectrum of diverse emotional reactions [6]. Given that the interplay between humans and robots extends beyond the confines of text and visual elements, verbal attributes also assume a pivotal function in fostering effective human-robot interactions [2]. A study was conducted concerning chatbots, and the findings substantiate that when chatbots communicate messages in a cheerful tone, users are inclined to experience more favourable interactions [7].

The hypotheses posited within this study are twofold: Firstly, it is assumed that employing a casual speech style may elicit a greater prevalence of positive emotions, specifically evoking feelings of happiness, whereas the utilization of a frozen speech style is anticipated to evoke heightened negative emotions, particularly of an angry nature. Secondly, it is estimated that an alto voice will gather greater user preference, consequently engendering elevated emotions of happiness. Conversely, the utilization of a bass voice is envisaged to be associated with augmented feelings of sadness or anger.

3 Methodology

Western Sydney University Human Research Ethics Committee (HREC Approval Number: H15278) has approved the project. All procedures were conducted following appropriate guidelines and regulations. Prior implied consent was acquired by the first author from all participants and/or their legal guardians to both partake in the study and share information and images in an openly accessible online publication.

3.1   Scenario Design

We have produced four avatar videos, each exhibiting distinct auditory attributes. The auditory features are characterized by two elements: voice pitch and speech style. As indicated in Table 1, the voice pitch is represented by an alto voice and bass voice, where the former resembles an adult female's voice, while the latter matches an adult male's voice. As for the speech style, it encompasses casual and frozen styles. To ensure coherence, the avatars' appearances have been precisely tailored to correspond with their respective voice pitches.

Table 1. Auditory Features of Avatar Videos

No	Voice Pitch	Speech Style	Appearance
Avatar 1	Alto	Casual	Female
Avatar 2	Alto	Frozen	Female
Avatar 3	Bass	Casual	Male
Avatar 4	Bass	Frozen	Male

The videos entail the utilization of avatars to deliver instructions to the participants. The avatars, characterized by diverse voices and speech styles, are purposively designed to express these instructions. As demonstrated in Figs. 1 and 2, participants are anticipated to engage in a task involving the observation of two designated avatar videos, followed by the execution of tasks as directed by the avatar. The prescribed task entails a straightforward clock drawing activity on paper, encompassing the creation of a circle, twelve numerical clock markers, and two clock hands.

Fig. 1. Scenario Setting   **Fig. 2.** Demo of Participant's Task

Notably, as indicated in Table 2, the content conveyed through the avatars' frozen style and casual style speeches is semantically equivalent, despite their differing expressive characteristics.

In the context of the experimental session, the YOLOv5 emotion detecting model functions in parallel with the participants' involvement in task execution. This occurs while they attentively receive instructions from the avatar videos. The core purpose of

Table 2. Speech Scripts of Avatar Videos with Different Speech Styles

Casual Speech Style	Hello, my name is Fatima/Ahmed. I extend my sincere gratitude for considering participating in this research study. I will provide clear instructions for you to follow
	Now, you can see a paper in front of you. Please write down a time on the paper
	Great! Thanks for that. And my assistant will collect this paper
	Now, seems we can continue our task. You should now receive a new paper, right?
	Please draw a circle on the paper
	Please draw 1 to 12 clock numbers in the circle
	Now, please draw two clock hands
	And make sure the clock hands refer to the time you wrote before
	Well, seems everything is done now. Thanks for your time!
Frozen Speech Style	Hello, my name is Fatima/Ahmed. Thank you for considering participating in this research study. Clear instructions will be given for you to follow
	A paper is now in front of you. Write down a time on it
	Good. This paper will be collected by my assistant
	Task continues. You receive new paper now, yes?
	Step 1, Draw a circle on the paper
	Step 2, Draw 1 to 12 clock numbers in the circle
	Step 3, Draw two clock hands
	Make sure clock hands match the time you wrote before
	All tasks completed. Thanks

the emotion detecting model is to systematically capture and record the variations in participants' emotional states throughout the duration of the assigned tasks.

3.2 Emotion Detecting Model

The development of our emotion detecting model involved the implementation of the Python programming language. For this purpose, we opted to utilize the YOLOv5 model. YOLO model stands for "You Only Look Once" detecting model, and it is renowned for its real-time object detection capabilities and for striking a balance between speed and accuracy [8]. YOLOv5 relies on the PyTorch deep learning framework [9, 10] and was trained on the extensive AffectNet dataset [11]. The AffectNet dataset comprises approximately 400,000 images categorized into eight distinct emotion classes: neutral, angry, sad, fearful, happy, surprise, disgust, and contempt. Our study focused on five prominent emotions, namely sad, angry, happy, neutral, and surprise, for training our model. The training process employed 15,000 images. For a comprehensive evaluation of the model's performance, we refer readers to [12].

3.3 Participants

A sample size of 14 participants was drawn at random from the student at the United Arab Emirates University (UAEU) to take part in the study. These participants were requested to complete the experimental procedures in a controlled laboratory setting. A study found that the young adult demographic displays a higher tendency to accept and engage with the robots, as well as the underlying technology [13]. Additionally, it has been generally observed that younger adults tend to exhibit a greater preference towards interacting with robotic entities or avatars [14].

The participants were kept unaware of the ongoing emotion detection process to ensure their natural behavioural responses. However, upon completing the entirety of the experimental procedure, the researcher will provide a comprehensive explanation of the testing procedure and unveil the presence of the emotion detecting model. At this stage, the participants were allowed to provide their consent for utilising their data in subsequent experiments. If any participant declines to grant consent, all related documents and data pertaining to their involvement will be promptly removed. Upon obtaining voluntary consent from participants, strict regulations will be implemented to uphold their privacy, ensuring that their personal information remains anonymized and unidentifiable. The emotion detecting model will exclusively provide numeric data, comprising the percentages associated with each emotion detected. It is important to emphasise that the physical characteristics, including face details of the participants will not be recorded or retained in any form. Only the emotion data derived from the experimental sessions will be retained for subsequent analysis.

The participants will be subject to a randomized allocation into one of the four groups. The comprehensive procedure entails the participants' exposure to two distinct avatar videos, each with unique auditory attributes. The avatar videos presented within the four designated groups are shaped with distinct voice pitches and speech styles: avatar 2 and avatar 4 (G1), avatar 1 and avatar 3 (G2), avatar 1 and avatar 2 (G3), and avatar 3 and avatar 4 (G4). The auditory features of each avatar video are elaborated in Table 1.

4 Results

In our model, data points are automatically generated upon detecting participants' facial expression changes. Notably, there may be uneven distribution of data points across participants due to variations in emotional expression frequency. The dataset includes data points derived from four distinct groups, labelled as follows: G1 (n = 4863), G2 (n = 3754), G3 (n = 1653), and G4 (n = 3330). The collective dataset comprises 13,600 data points, which were sourced from 14 participants. Notably, the average contribution of data points from each participant falls within a range covering approximately 900 to 1500 points.

We conducted a repeated measures Analysis of Variance (ANOVA) to assess the comparability of measurements among participants across two distinct speech styles (Table 3) and voice pitches (Table 4). The ANOVA outcomes revealed the absence of statistically significant differences in user reactions pertaining to both the frozen speech style versus the casual speech style and the alto voice pitch versus the bass voice pitch.

Table 3. ANOVA Analysis of Speech Style

Emotion	Within Subject Effect: Speech Style
Angry	$F = 0.371, P = 0.554$
Happy	$F = 2.392, P = 0.148$
Sad	$F = 0.002, P = 0.965$
Surprise	$F = 1.509, P = 0.243$

Table 4. ANOVA Analysis of Voice Pitch

Emotion	Within Subject Effect: Voice Pitch
Angry	$F = 0.121, P = 0.734$
Happy	$F = 1.892, P = 0.194$
Sad	$F = 0.933, P = 0.353$
Surprise	$F = 1.140, P = 0.307$

This is evidenced by the p-values exceeding the threshold of 0.05, signifying the lack of a substantial effect.

Figure 3a, 3b, 3c, 3d illustrate the distributions of mean values for four primary emotions (i.e., happiness, sadness, anger, and surprise) within the context of the subject effect associated with speech style variations (specifically, frozen style and casual style). Regarding the emotion of "Happy", it is noteworthy that the frozen speech style yields substantially higher values in comparison to the casual speech style. In contrast, in relation to the emotion of "Surprise", the casual style exhibits higher values than the frozen style.

Figure 4a, 4b, 4c, 4d present the distributions of mean values pertaining to the four primary emotions (namely, happiness, sadness, anger, and surprise) within the context of the subject effect related to voice pitch variations (specifically, alto voice and bass voice). Notably, concerning the emotion of "Happy", the bass voice pitch yields higher values compared to the alto voice pitch. Conversely, in relation to the emotion of "Sad", the alto voice pitch exhibits greater values. It is important to mention that great differences in values are not notably detectible across other emotional domains.

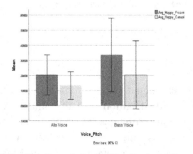

Fig. 3a. Speech Style Distribution-Happy

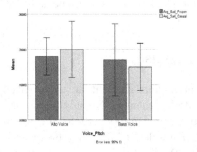

Fig. 3b. Speech Style Distribution-Sad

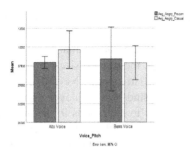

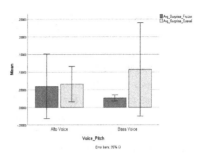

Fig. 3c. Speech Style Distribution-Angry   **Fig. 3d.** Speech Style Distribution-Surprise

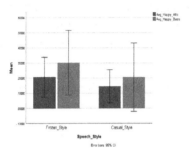

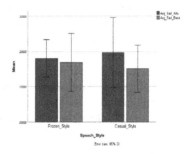

Fig. 4a. Voice Pitch Distribution-Happy   **Fig. 4b.** Voice Pitch Distribution-Sad

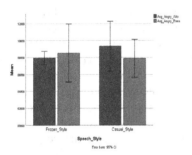

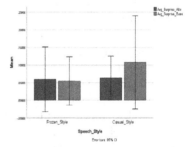

Fig. 4c. Voice Pitch Distribution-Angry   **Fig. 4d.** Voice Pitch Distribution-Surprise

5 Discussion

The findings derived from this study suggest that visible auditory distinctions inherent in embedded agents, such as avatars, exercise influence on the emotional responses exhibited by users. The empirical evidence underscores that within the confines of a consistent voice pitch, the adoption of the frozen speech style is more effective in eliciting sentiments of happiness among users. Furthermore, when avatars and robots adopt a casual speech style, it triggers a sensitive sense of surprise. This observation contradicts our initial assumption, suggesting a casual speech style preference. In maintaining an unchanged speech style, intriguing insights emerge regarding the influences stemming from varying voice pitches. According to the obtained data, the bass voice records a more pronounced efficacy in evoking feelings of happiness among users, while the alto voice engenders a sense of sadness.

It is worthwhile to acknowledge and address specific limitations that holds significance for prospective research undertakings. Foremost, the sample size employed in this study was relatively modest, including merely 14 participants. Nevertheless, we suggest that, as an introductory exploration, the present study contributes preliminarily to the domain of evaluating users' emotional responses to alterations in the auditory attributes of avatars and humanoid robots. Notably, it is noteworthy that each participant yielded a substantial volume of 8,000 to 10,000 data points. It is relevant to emphasize that the predominant target of this paper lies in embarking upon a preliminary analysis into this realm. Furthermore, the age range of participants was confined to individuals aged between 18 and 35, which potentially limits the extent of generalizability to a more expansive age demographic. Given the original design of the experiment's content catering to older adults, the relative simplicity of the tasks might be easy for younger participants, thereby potentially influencing their emotional responses. Additionally, the experiment was conducted in the UAEU. Consequently, the outcomes may be disposed to the culturally specific influences characteristic to this location. To augment the robustness and applicability of future inquiries, it is recommended that a broader participant pool encompassing older adults be integrated.

6   Conclusion

In summary, the primary objective of this pilot study was to separate the effects of humanoid embedded agents, encompassing robots and avatars, on users' emotional responses. Serving as an early undertaking to evaluate human perceptions of avatars possessing distinct auditory attributes, this study contributes to advancing literature concerning emotional impacts arising from verbal interactions with humanoid agents like robots. The findings revealed that users exhibit heightened emotional responsiveness when interacting with avatars and robots characterized by diverse voices and speech styles. Nonetheless, it is crucial to acknowledge that the study's constraints, including the restricted sample size, limited age demographic, and cultural influences, introduce restraints upon the generalizability of the results.

In a broader context, this pilot study lays the foundation for prospective research endeavours to enhance user experiences by manipulating auditory attributes of humanoid robots and avatars. A potential direction for future investigation could entail examining the potential effects of altered verbal cues in robot-assisted elderly care training on the emotions, acceptance levels, and cooperation dynamics among older age groups.

References

1. Tung, V.W.S., Au, N.: Exploring customer experiences with robotics in hospitality. Int. J. Contemp. Hosp. Manage. **30**(7), 2680–2697 (2018). https://doi.org/10.1108/IJCHM-06-2017-0322
2. Bartneck, C., Belpaeme, T., Eyssel, F., Kanda, T., Keijsers, M., Šabanović, S.: Human-Robot Interaction: An Introduction. Cambridge University Press, Cambridge (2020)

3. Mataric, M., Scassellati, B.: Socially Assistive Robotics. In: Siciliano, B., Khatib, O., Kroger, T. (eds.) Springer Handbook of Robotics, vol. 200, pp. 1973–1988. Springer, Berlin (2008)

4. Walters, M.L., et al.: Evaluating the robot personality and verbal behavior of domestic robots using video-based studies. Adv. Robot. 25(18), 2233–2254 (2011)

5. Shank, D.B., Graves, C., Gott, A., Gamez, P., Rodriguez, S.: Feeling our way to machine minds: People's emotions when perceiving mind in artificial intelligence. Comput. Hum. Behav. 1(98), 256–266 (2019)

6. Mathur, M.B., et al.: Uncanny but not confusing: Multisite study of perceptual category confusion in the Uncanny Valley. Comput. Hum. Behav. 1(103), 21–30 (2020)

7. Zhou, H., Huang, M., Zhang, T., Zhu, X., Liu, B.: Emotional chatting machine: emotional conversation generation with internal and external memory. In: Proceedings of the AAAI Conference on Artificial Intelligence, vol. 32, no. 1 (2018)

8. Mindoro, J.N., Pilueta, N.U., Austria, Y.D., Lacatan, L.L., Dellosa, R.M.: Capturing students' attention through visible behavior: a prediction utilizing YOLOv3 approach. In: 2020 11th IEEE control and system graduate research colloquium (ICSGRC), pp. 328–333. IEEE (2020)

9. Nepal, U., Eslamiat, H.: Comparing YOLOv3, YOLOv4 and YOLOv5 for autonomous landing spot detection in faulty UAVs. Sensors 22(2), 464 (2022)

10. Jiang, Y.: COTS recognition and detection based on Improved YOLO v5 model. In: 2022 7th International Conference on Intelligent Computing and Signal Processing (ICSP), pp. 830–833. IEEE (2022)

11. Mollahosseini, A., Hasani, B., Mahoor, M.H.: AffectNet: a database for facial expression, valence, and arousal computing in the wild. IEEE Trans. Affect. Comput. 10(1), 18–31 (2017)

12. Trabelsi, Z., Alnajjar, F., Parambil, M.M., Gochoo, M., Ali, L.: Real-time attention monitoring system for classroom: a deep learning approach for student's behavior recognition. Big Data Cogn. Comput. 7(1), 48 (2023)

13. Louie, W.Y., McColl, D., Nejat, G.: Acceptance and attitudes toward a human-like socially assistive robot by older adults. Assist. Technol. 26(3), 140–150 (2014)

14. Ezer, N., Fisk, A.D., Rogers, W.A.: More than a servant: Self-reported willingness of younger and older adults to having a robot perform interactive and critical tasks in the home. Proc. Hum. Factors Ergon. Soc. Ann. Meeting 53(2), 136–140 (2009). https://doi.org/10.1177/154 193120905300206

Leveraging the RoboMaker Service on AWS Cloud Platform for Marine Drone Digital Twin Construction

Mariacarla Staffa[(✉)] , Emanuele Izzo, and Paola Barra

Università degli Studi di Napoli "Parthenope", Naples, Italy
{mariacarla.staffa,paola.barra}@uniparthenope.it

Abstract. Drones and other robotic technologies enable us to explore and study the world without the need for human guidance. This enables us to interact with previously uncharted areas that pose a risk to human safety, including the underwater biosphere. A drone may encounter a variety of problems when operating in such an unpredictable and hazardous environment. In these contexts, creating a digital twin of a marine drone can provide several advantages, such as for example to enhance the management, maintenance, and performance of the marine drone through data-driven approaches, benefiting efficiency and safety. In this work, we present the development of a digital twin prototype, which is a virtual representation of a physical entity of a marine drone-type unmanned surface vehicle. ROS, Blender, and the AWS cloud platform were used to create the system. The three-dimensional model of the maritime drone was created in Blender, and the AWS Robomaker service was utilized for simulation testing and possible deployment of the robotic application without managing any infrastructure. The goal is to present the tools and architecture that were developed to collect data using non-invasive ways and generate a marine digital twin.

Keywords: digital twin of marine drones · USV · ROV · AUV · see monitoring

1 Introduction

The underwater environment is, to date, for most of the planet Earth, still a real unknown factor for human beings. The seabed has been mapped only for small land surface inventories, and it is very little known due to its inaccessibility to man. It is hazardous and complex to conduct work, whether environmental monitoring, sample collection, or mapping spaces and objects deposited on the seabed, but robotics can help us carry out dangerous activities. Unmanned Surface Vehicles (USV), are identical to real boats or even Remote Operated Vehicles (ROV) [4], are more complicated and are typically utilized in oil wells or deep oceans and can reach such high pressures that a pilot on board would perish. Also, several marine drones define the AUV (Autonomous Underwater Vehicle) as being capable of moving adequately according to the mission for which they

The Authors want to thank the GEAC group (Geology of Coastal Environments) of the University of Naples Parthenope (http://dist.altervista.org/geac/struttura.html), creator of the ARGO (ARcheological GeO application) marine drone.

A. Al. Ali et al. (Eds.): ICSR 2023, LNAI 14453, pp. 22–32, 2024.
https://doi.org/10.1007/978-981-99-8715-3_3

have been programmed [1]. Recently, there has also been a surge in interest in undersea projects and the development of AUVs dedicated to surveillance [2, 3].

For instance, authors in [15] used an innovative marine robotic instrumentation to reconstruct the landscape of the coast of an archaeological site near Campi Flegrei (Italy). The Unmanned Surface Vehicle (USV) used geophysical and photogrammetric sensors. In addition to reconstructing the underground city, the acquired data help document the underwater cultural heritage. In this regard, an Unmanned Surface Vessel (USV) with acoustic and optical sensors was also used to reconstruct the ancient Parthenope area, an area of the Roman coast between Pizzofalcone hill and Megaris islet, [16].

They enable us to perform things that would not be possible with any other vehicle, such as detecting wrecks, conducting scientific samples, and gathering data. Technological advancements and the associated software and hardware systems on the market are continually evolving, and how they are built and handled must also evolve. To do so, we need tools to match the new product realities brought about by digital breakthroughs. This is also where the Digital Twin comes into play. Michael Grieves used the term "digital twin" for the first time in 2001 [7].

Grieves described the digital twin as a physical product's virtual and digital equivalent. In his approach to PLM, Grieves highlighted a Mirrored Spaces Model referring to a highly dynamic representation, [18]; the actual dimension and the virtual dimension remained connected during the entire life cycle of the system, going through all the phases of creation, production, operation and disposal. Virtual replicas of physical products that provide a snapshot of the state of the product in real-time, digital twins allow you to deliver experience improvements without having to test them on the product itself. A product's digital twin is an invaluable source of information for engineers and operators. Information is obtained through combining multiple technologies, from the cloud to the Internet of Things to Artificial Intelligence.

The Digital Twin is connected to the physical product through various sensors. These produce data on different aspects of the physical object's performance, from temperature, energy used/produced, weather conditions, etc. The analysis of this data, combined with other sources of information, allows us to understand not only the product's behavior but also to predict how the product will behave in the future. This continuous flow of information allows the digital twin to run simulations, detect and analyze any product performance issues, and study possible improvements.

The purpose of the paper is to develop a digital representation of the marine drone known as ARGO (ARcheological GeO application) developed by the GEAC group (Geology of Coastal Environments) of the University of Naples Parthenope, Italy, by making use of ROS (Robotic Operating System), as well as of Blender 3D-modeling software and AWS cloud platform. ARGO marine drone was conceived to carry out coastal marine surveys aimed at the high-resolution reconstruction of the submerged coastal seabed.

The aim of this contribution is to highlight the benefits of utilizing AWS RoboMaker, a cloud-based simulation service provided by AWS (Amazon Web Services), that allows robotics developers to perform, scale, and automate simulations without having to worry about managing infrastructure. Through the use of virtual space and simulation, it will in fact be possible to evaluate the performance of the on-board sensors as well as foresee the use of additional sensors to improve both navigation and monitoring performance, testing their operation in simulation before mounting them on the real robot, thereby reducing downtime and maintenance costs. Additionally, operators can use the digital twin to simulate the intended flight path, check for obstacles, and assess how the drone will respond to various conditions. This reduces the risk of accidents and unexpected outcomes. Furthermore, the possibility of modifying the simulation environments as desired allows operators to test the performance of the drone in different environments and in different climatic conditions.

2   Related Work

A Digital Twin concept involves creating a digital simulation within an information platform, enabling real-time prediction, optimization, monitoring, control, and improved decision-making. This is achieved by integrating physical feedback data and complementing it with AI, machine learning, and software analysis. Numerous researchers from around the world have conducted research in the domains of air, land, and sea [9, 12, 17].

For instance, the authors in [11] integrated data from multiple sensor locations, using this information as inputs for the digital twin system, and combined it with simulation data to analyze the structural performance.

Meanwhile, Chen et al. [5] established a Digital Twin framework for submarine pipelines and highlighted the challenges in implementing it for design, construction, service life assessment, life extension, data collection, interpretation, sharing, and network security. The underwater environment presents unique complexities, and only a limited number of studies have explored the application of Digital Twin technology in this context.

In [10], the authors formulated a standardized method for recognizing a set of crucial system elements that require the creation of digital twins to support condition-based maintenance objectives. Although their initial application centred around an unmanned underwater vehicle (UUV), the procedure possesses sufficient generality for any system examining cost and reliability projections for implementing digital twin technology.

The research discussed in [8] employs a blended-wing-body underwater glider (BWBUG) to investigate the potential uses of high-fidelity digital models within the maritime domain. They introduce a digital twin technology developed using the Gazebo simulation platform. Their methodology encompasses the development of a high-fidelity model designed for underwater situations and includes the incorporation of a vehicle body with a range of sensors.

3   Planning and Development

The most important elements of the drone digital twin design flow will be examined in this section. We will focus on the specifications, the development libraries used, the building of the 3D robot model, the description of the mounted sensors and onboard thrusters, and its architecture.

AWS RoboMaker. AWS[1] is the world's most comprehensive and widely used cloud platform, offering a broad range of computing infrastructure services. In particular, *AWS RoboMaker* extends the most popular open source robotics framework, Robot Operating System (ROS), with connectivity to cloud services. This includes AWS machine learning services, monitoring services, and analytics services that enable a robot to transmit data, navigate, communicate, understand, and learn. AWS RoboMaker gives you access to gazebo, rqt, rviz, and terminal to interface with running simulations that can be easily customized.

UUV Simulator. UUV Simulator (Unmanned Underwater Vehicle Simulator) is a package set that includes plugins and ROS applications that allow the simulation of underwater vehicles in Gazebo [13].

Blender. Blender is a 3D graphics open-source software allowing the modelling and rendering of images in three dimensions using a professional work environment. It is a constantly evolving and updating program and is increasingly adopted in gaming, cinema, advertising, and architectural design.

Among other advantages, Blender offers native tools for creating animations and animated videos of projects, now increasingly in demand even in interior design and architectural design. Among others, we mention the possibility of inserting sounds, interactive paths and animated characters in the videos of the scenes.

In Fig. 1, we can see how the ARGO drone is visualized on Blender. On the right is the wire frame, and on the left is the preview with the materials used.

Unified Robot Description Format (URDF). For the development of the URDF model of the marine drone, extensive use was made of the constructs of the XACRO language (XML Macros), ideal for developing reusable macros. The description is organized in multiple files. The main file is *drone.xacro* from which the other files are loaded, and the macros are expanded:

- **base.xacro** contains the declaration of global constants and variables, model properties, global macro definitions, a path relative to the mesh file package, and the inclusion of external libraries and other files that make up the robot.
- **sensors.xacro** contains the definition of the various sensors and the relative names of the joints and links, the dimensions of the primitives used for the elements, the mass of the links, the limits of the joints, the offset of the reference systems of the visual, inertial and collision elements for the link reference, and the offsets of the joints for the link reference.
- **snippets.xacro** uses the macros for the definition of the *libuuv_thruster_ros_plugin.so* plugin of *uuv_simulator* allows the functioning of the thrusters, including the description of the dynamic systems and the conversion functions to be adopted.
- **actuators.xacro** contains the declarations of the macros used to create the thrusters.
- **gazebo.xacro** uses the macros for defining the *libuuv _underwater_object_ros _plugin.so* plugin of *uuv_simulator* providing the ability to buoyancy through the definition of the dimensions, volume and hull centre of the marine drone.

---

[1] Amazon Web Services. http://www.aws.amazon.com.

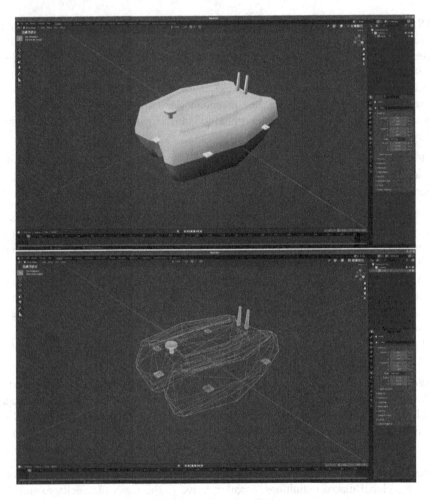

Fig. 1. Visualization of the 3D model of a marine drone in Blender. Up: Material preview: down: Wireframe.

3.1 Description of the Marine Drone

The drone is characterized by very compact dimensions (length of 120 cm and a width of 86 cm) with a maximum weight of 30 kg, such as making logistics handling easy. Its dimensions and the presence of electric motors powered by 12V DC allow a minimum impact on the sea and guarantee considerable operating autonomy (from 2 to 6 h) and excellent maneuverability in confined spaces typical of coastal and port environments, [6, 14].

On-Board Sensors. The drone digital twin has the same sensors mounted on board the physical robot, including:

- **GPS**: Acronym for Global Positioning System; it is an electronic device used to locate the exact position of a place, a person or an object through data triangulation.
- **Camera**: A portable electronic device that records images and sounds on an integrated storage medium.
- **Echo sounder**: It is a type of ultra-acoustic echo sounder instrument used to measure the depth of the sea through the transmission of sound pulses. To work, it uses sound waves, capable of measuring distances through sound. Echo sounder technology uses a transducer, transmitter and receiver/amplifier. It uses the same principle as radars to locate targets, from which it differs in speed propagation and wave type. The transducer receives the electrical energy and then transforms it into sound. The impulse is thus transmitted to the seabed. Once the target is hit, whether fish, seaweed or rocks, the sound is reflected back to the transducer and sent to the amplifier and then to the receiver so it can be viewed on the display.
- **Side scan sonar**: It is a particular instrument mainly used to research and map the seabed for underwater archaeology purposes. The name of this sonar derives from how the acoustic bases mounted on a small vehicle towed by a pilot ship are used. The acoustic bases emit pulses and identify the targets' echoes by scanning emissions and receptions only with beams directed sideways towards the bottom. It provides as a final product a resulting image of many stripes corresponding to signals received from the seabed following the sending of an impulse. The side scan sonar sends an acoustic signal towards the bottom of the sea from each of its sides at 90° to the course of the support vessel. The waves propagate through the water, and once they reach the bottom of the sea, they are reflected by the irregularities of the sea surface and by any object lying on it, returning to the receiver, which registers the body as a maximum reflector. The sonar amplifies the received signals and sends them to a data processing system and a display. Typical sonar applications result in grayscale recordings (sonograms), where strong reflectors are shown in the recording as bright areas. In contrast, a total lack of return signal results in a dark area. The main objectives of the side scan sonar are:
  - create nautical charts and the detection and identification of underwater objects.
  - search the bathymetric characteristics of the sites.
  - investigate the problems of marine archaeology.
  - helps locate and identify underwater manufactured artifacts.
  - to classify seabeds based on the type of deposit material.
  - detect items of debris and other obstacles on the seabed dangerous to navigation.
  - control seabed installations of the oil and gas industry.

  In Fig. 2, we can see how the side scan sonar is mounted on the drone, through the representation in Blender of the digital twin.
- **Forward scan sonar**: Besides the sensors already provided by the physical robot, we have the forward scan sonar, a device used during navigation to identify and avoid any bodies in front of the boat.

Thruster Configuration. The propulsion of the marine drone takes place via two thrusters. The *UUV Simulator* library is used to simulate the operation and configuration of these to the digital counterpart; it provides two modules: the dynamic model,

Fig. 2. Illustration of twin-mounted side scan sonar, used for research and mapping of the seabed for underwater archaeology purposes.

which describes the dynamics of the rotor and the conversion function, which describes the relationship between angular speed of the rotor and the thrust force produced. Below is an example of the macro that includes the thruster link, the joint and the Gazebo plugin containing the dynamic model and descriptions of the conversion function.

Architecture and Structure of the Control System Hardware. The drone control system hardware structure is shown in Fig. 3. The microcontroller gets the data from the computer and generates a pulse width modulation signal to the motors and servos. The onboard computer performs planned navigation, calculates control actions, runs the navigation system software and communicates with the remote control station.

4   Simulation

The simulation includes visualization of the digital clone in a marine environment to reconstruct the seabed through a scan by the side scan sonar mounted on it. The main simulation launch file *start_demo_pid_controller.launch* allows you to launch several nodes from a single configuration:

- *ocean_waves.launch* allows the generation of a virtual marine world made available by the *UUV Simulator* library.
- *upload_argo.launch* contains the description of the robot, the *robot_state_publisher* node to allow viewing of the robot and related information within *rviz*. It allows the generation of the simulation environment through Gazebo, (Fig. 4).
- *start_pid_controller.launch* contains a whole series of parameters for the correct functioning of the thrusters.

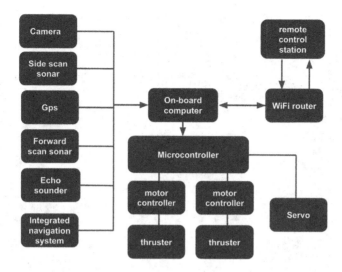

Fig. 3. Control system hardware structure diagram

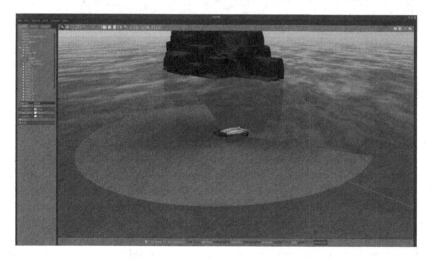

Fig. 4. Gazebo simulation execution.

In order for the robot model to activate the thrusters to carry out the navigation and reconstruction of the seabed in the simulated environment, a *geometry_msgs* message is published on the topic */thruster_manager/input/Wrench*. This is equivalent to generating a force in newtons along one of the x, y and z axes, which allows the drone's movement and, consequently, the side scan sonar to map the virtual seabed. Through a particular configuration of *rviz*, which allows the seabed to be displayed in the form of a point cloud, we obtained the result shown in Fig. 5:

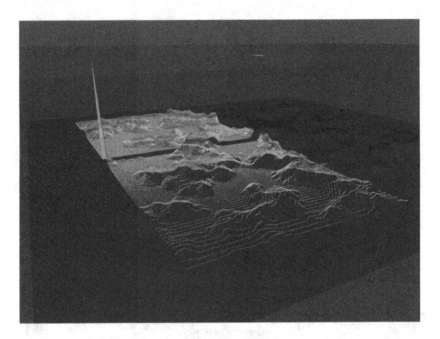

Fig. 5. Digital representation of the scanned seabed.

5   Conclusions

This work aimed to develop the prototype of a digital twin, a virtual representation of a physical entity, in our case, a USV-type boat. This system was created through ROS, Blender (a 3D graphics and modelling software that allowed the creation of the surface marine drone three-dimensional model), and the AWS cloud platform, specifically the AWS Robomaker service for simulation, testing, and possible deployment of the robot application without managing any infrastructure. By using cloud-based computing platforms to provide computational power, it has been possible to decouple robot hardware from its available functionalities in an always more promising RaaS approach. In a possible future development, new sensors could be integrated and tested for communication with the surrounding environment, developing navigation techniques that allow the achievement of a specific objective regardless of any environmental disturbances, such as wind and sea currents, through alternative simulators such as Gazebos that permit such circumstances. Finally, a potential work to be done is the connection of the digital twin to the physical product through various sensors or a possible distribution of the robot application to the physical robot through the features made available by AWS Robomaker.

Acknowledgements. We acknowledge support from the PNRR MUR project PE0000013-FAIR.

References

1. Allen, B., et al.: REMUS: a small, low cost AUV; system description, field trials and performance results. In: Oceans 1997. MTS/IEEE Conference Proceedings, vol. 2, pp. 994–1000 (1997). https://doi.org/10.1109/OCEANS.1997.624126
2. Allotta, B., et al.: Design of a modular autonomous underwater vehicle for archaeological investigations. In: OCEANS 2015 - Genova, pp. 1–5 (2015). https://doi.org/10.1109/OCEANS-Genova.2015.7271398
3. Bingham, B., et al.: Robotic tools for deep water archaeology: surveying an ancient shipwreck with an autonomous underwater vehicle. J. Field Robot. **27**, 702–717 (2010). https://doi.org/10.1002/rob.20350
4. Caccia, M., Bibuli, M., Bono, R., Bruzzone, G., Bruzzone, G., Spirandelli, E.: Unmanned marine vehicles at CNR-ISSIA. IFAC Proc. Vol. **41**(2), 3070–3075 (2008). 17th IFAC World Congress, https://doi.org/10.3182/20080706-5-KR-1001.00521, https://www.sciencedirect.com/science/article/pii/S1474667016394204
5. Chen, B.Q., Videiro, P.M., Guedes Soares, C.: Opportunities and challenges to develop digital twins for subsea pipelines. J. Mar. Sci. Eng. **10**(6), 739 (2022). https://doi.org/10.3390/jmse10060739, https://www.mdpi.com/2077-1312/10/6/739
6. Giordano, F., Mattei, G., Parente, C., Peluso, F., Santamaria, R.: Integrating sensors into a marine drone for bathymetric 3D surveys in shallow waters. Sensors **16**(1), 41 (2016). https://doi.org/10.3390/s16010041, https://www.mdpi.com/1424-8220/16/1/41
7. Grieves, M.: Origins of the digital twin concept, August 2016. https://doi.org/10.13140/RG.2.2.26367.61609
8. Hu, S., Liang, Q., Huang, H., Yang, C.: Construction of a digital twin system for the blended-wing-body underwater glider. Ocean Eng. **270**, 113610 (2023). https://doi.org/10.1016/j.oceaneng.2022.113610, https://www.sciencedirect.com/science/article/pii/S0029801822028931
9. Jin, B., Gao, J., Yan, W.: Pseudo control hedging-based adaptive neural network attitude control of underwater gliders. In: OCEANS 2017 - Aberdeen, pp. 1–5 (2017). https://doi.org/10.1109/OCEANSE.2017.8084963
10. Kutzke, D.T., Carter, J.B., Hartman, B.T.: Subsystem selection for digital twin development: a case study on an unmanned underwater vehicle. Ocean Eng. **223**, 108629 (2021). https://doi.org/10.1016/j.oceaneng.2021.108629, https://www.sciencedirect.com/science/article/pii/S0029801821000640
11. Lai, X., Wang, S., Guo, Z., Zhang, C., Sun, W., Song, X.: Designing a shape-performance integrated digital twin based on multiple models and dynamic data: a boom crane example. J. Mech. Des. **143**(7), 071703 (2021). https://doi.org/10.1115/1.4049861
12. Liu, Z., Chen, W., Zhang, C., Yang, C., Cheng, Q.: Intelligent scheduling of a feature-process-machine tool supernetwork based on digital twin workshop. J. Manuf. Syst. **58**, 157–167 (2021). Digital Twin towards Smart Manufacturing and Industry 4.0, https://doi.org/10.1016/j.jmsy.2020.07.016, https://www.sciencedirect.com/science/article/pii/S0278612520301266
13. Manhães, M.M.M., Scherer, S.A., Voss, M., Douat, L.R., Rauschenbach, T.: UUV simulator: a Gazebo-based package for underwater intervention and multi-robot simulation. In: OCEANS 2016 MTS/IEEE Monterey. IEEE, September 2016. https://doi.org/10.1109/oceans.2016.7761080
14. Mattei, G., Rizzo, A., Anfuso, G., Aucelli, P., Gracia, F.: A tool for evaluating the archaeological heritage vulnerability to coastal processes: the case study of Naples Gulf (Southern Italy). Ocean Coast. Manage. **179**, 104876 (2019). https://doi.org/10.1016/j.ocecoaman.2019.104876, https://www.sciencedirect.com/science/article/pii/S0964569119302789

15. Mattei, G., Troisi, S., Aucelli, P.P.C., Pappone, G., Peluso, F., Stefanile, M.: Sensing the submerged landscape of Nisida Roman Harbour in the Gulf of Naples from integrated measurements on a USV. Water **10**(11), 1686 (2018). https://doi.org/10.3390/w10111686, https://www.mdpi.com/2073-4441/10/11/1686

16. Pappone, G., Aucelli, P.P., Mattei, G., Peluso, F., Stefanile, M., Carola, A.: A detailed reconstruction of the Roman landscape and the submerged archaeological structure at "Castel dell'Ovo islet" (Naples, Southern Italy). Geosciences **9**(4), 170 (2019). https://doi.org/10.3390/geosciences9040170, https://www.mdpi.com/2076-3263/9/4/170

17. Wang, Y., Kang, X., Chen, Z.: A survey of digital twin techniques in smart manufacturing and management of energy applications. Green Energy Intell. Transp. **1**(2), 100014 (2022). https://doi.org/10.1016/j.geits.2022.100014, https://www.sciencedirect.com/science/article/pii/S2773153722000147

18. Zhang, L., Zhou, L., Horn, B.K.: Building a right digital twin with model engineering. J. Manuf. Syst. **59**, 151–164 (2021). https://doi.org/10.1016/j.jmsy.2021.02.009, https://www.sciencedirect.com/science/article/pii/S0278612521000455

Trust Assessment with EEG Signals in Social Human-Robot Interaction

Giulio Campagna$^{(\boxtimes)}$ ⓘ and Matthias Rehm ⓘ

Aalborg University, Aalborg, Denmark
giulio.campagna3@gmail.com, {gica,matthias}@create.aau.dk

Abstract. The role of trust in human-robot interaction (HRI) is becoming increasingly important for effective collaboration. Insufficient trust may result in disuse, regardless of the robot's capabilities, whereas excessive trust can lead to safety issues. While most studies of trust in HRI are based on questionnaires, in this work it is explored how participants' trust levels can be recognized based on electroencephalogram (EEG) signals. A social scenario was developed where the participants played a guessing game with a robot. Data collection was carried out with subsequent statistical analysis and selection of features as input for different machine learning models. Based on the highest achieved accuracy of 72.64%, the findings indicate the existence of a correlation between trust levels and the EEG data, thus offering a promising avenue for real-time trust assessment during interactions, reducing the reliance on retrospective questionnaires.

Keywords: Trust in Human-Robot Interaction · Social Robotics · Human-Robot Collaboration

1 Introduction

In social scenarios, trust is an important aspect of human robot collaboration because the level of trust of the human towards the robot can seriously affect the performance during the interaction. In other words, it can cause unbalance workload, inefficient monitoring of the robot, or even disuse of the system [4]. For example, socially assistive robots provide assistance to elderly people for improving their quality of life and independence [22] or serving as robot companions for activating and stimulating the users [27]. In such scenarios, fostering trust in the robot is crucial not only for the user but also for care personnel and relatives, ensuring a successful interaction.

Numerous attempts have been investigated to define the characteristics of trust as an emergent phenomenon in human-human as well as human-robot interaction (HRI). A meta-review of trust-related studies of human robot interaction [15] showed that the two main variants of trust are performance-based and relation-based, which in turn are related to specific domains of applications. Performance-based trust is mostly explored in manipulative robot systems in industrial contexts. By contrast, relation-based trust is more relevant for social scenarios focusing on communication rather than on manipulation of objects.

The work described in this paper was funded by the Independent Research Fund Denmark, grant number 1032-00311B.

To be able to use trust as a control parameter in the context of human-robot collaboration, evaluating real-time trust levels throughout the interaction becomes essential. As result, the behavior of the robot can be adapted to match the trust level of the user, increasing efficiency or preventing potentially dangerous situations. The current trust measurements are based on subjective, post-hoc questionnaires (e.g. [25,28]) that provide only summary information about the subjects' interpretation of the interaction but do not support a continuous trust assessment during the collaboration. For this reason, new methods must be developed for data-driven assessment of trust. Recent studies have shown some promising steps in this direction (e.g. [7,9,26,30]). For instance, Hu et al. [9] successfully experimented with electroencephalogram (EEG) signals as a real-time measurement of trust for a scenario based on performance-based trust. While their results are promising, the trust rating that was used for labeling the data was an oversimplification relying only on one question.

This paper proposes trust assessment based on **EEG signals** and **Machine Learning** (ML) within the context of relation-based trust. For the purpose of having a solid basis for labeling the EEG data, the *Multi-dimensional Measure of Trust* (MDMT) questionnaire [28] is used as the baseline measurement to infer the trust levels. The decision to opt for MDMT hinges on the necessity for a more in-depth comprehension of trust. Trust, being multifaceted, is thoroughly examined by MDMT across a spectrum of dimensions, allowing to gain a more holistic insight into trust-related constructs. The aforementioned approach allows for the automatic labeling of the data, facilitating the subsequent real-time analysis of the correlation between trust and physiological responses, thereby overcoming the limitations associated with questionnaire responses.

2   Related Work

Trust can be defined as the operator's perception of the competence of the machine where it is essential that the operator is confident that the system appropriately accomplishes its tasks [18]. A correlation is present between the operator's trust in the machine and his willingness to use it, i.e. the more the human trusts the system, the more he is likely to use it. In [18], Muir and Moray reported that the level of trust of the human subject in a machine was heavily affected by the machine's performance. As a matter of fact, trust is a relevant factor that could affect the acceptance of a robot as assistant, co-worker or companion in social scenarios [12,16]. Moreover, it can influence the human's perception of the capabilities of a robot [8,23].

In HRI, the concept of trust is a timely and relevant topic for various reasons. First of all, there is a lack of a general understanding of the dynamic nature of trust and the methodologies to study it [14]. Trust is not a static phenomenon: it can be built, repaired, adjusted and it changes over time according to events that occur. Secondly, trust is an essential feature of human decision-making in collaboration tasks and it becomes crucial when robots are closely working together with human users [29]. Thirdly, mismatches in trust towards a robot can lead to severe consequences, ranging from unbalance workload, to loss of expensive equipment or even human life due to inefficient monitoring [4,19]. Therefore, both under-trust and over-trust in robots have to be avoided.

Most trust assessments rely primarily on post-hoc questionnaires (e.g. [10,25]). Only a limited number of methods have endeavored to gauge trust through performance, with a primary emphasis on task success and efficiency. Floyd et al. [6], for instance, estimated the robot's trustworthiness based on observable performance which was calculated as a comparison between the number of successful task completions and failed or interrupted attempts. Xu and Dudek [30] proposed a data-driven approach to infer trust levels, focusing specifically on a performance-centric definition of trust, which evaluated success or failure in performing the task. A HRI trust scale was developed by Yagoda et al. [31] that is based on a list of item dimensions including HRI attributes: team configuration, team process, context, task, and system. Salem et al. [24] explored the factors that affect human perception and trust towards an erroneous robot.

The post-hoc questionnaires are not sufficient to promptly determine the change of trust level over time. Therefore, it is essential to track the unfolding of trust (and distrust) in HRI to define reliable, real-time measures of trust [9] with the goal of adapting the robot's behavior to the user's trust level. According to [21], the use of psycho-physiological signals could be a solution to sense trust level. Among the several psycho-physiological measurements, EEG is identified as a non-invasive and convenient method for capturing brain signals and observing brain activity in response to a specific event-related potential (ERP). Researchers have conducted studies on trust by means of EEG signals. Hu et al. [9] introduced an initial attempt to establish a connection between real-time physiological signals and human-machine trust. Regrettably, their trust measurement remains superficial as it solely relies on asking participants about their trust in the system. In a coin toss experiment that simulated trust and distrust [3], Boudeau et al. found that ERP components had different peak amplitudes for the several participants involved. Akash et al. [2] analyzed approaches to develop a classification model to sense human trust using EEG and galvanic skin response measurements.

3 Methodology

3.1 The Human Subject Study

To assess the trust level of the human subjects based on EEG signals, a social experimental scenario was designed. A human and *EZ-robot JD Humanoid*[1] played a collaborative game inspired by the board game Activity. As shown in Fig. 1, the game consisted of five sections where, depending on the section, the humanoid robot either mimed or vocally described a word among four options presented to the participant. Throughout the interaction, the participant had to guess which word the robot was presenting. In case of correct answer, the participant received a candy as reward; otherwise one candy had to be returned. Each section was composed of two trials where, for each trial, a different set of four words were presented by the robot. Furthermore, each section implemented a different trust strategy that determined how the robot would behave. The first two sections were used for building up trust. Section 2 showed some situation awareness, e.g. by commenting on the participant's cloth with the purpose to establish a relation. In

---

[1] https://www.ez-robot.com/.

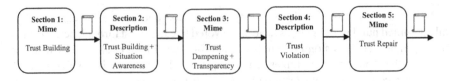

Fig. 1. Sequence of the sections with the different trust strategies associated.

section 3 the robot introduced the participant to some technical limitations of the system (trust dampening + transparency). Section 4 violated trust by a deliberate malfunction of the robot while section 5 was used to regain trust. In the end, between each section and after the last section of the experiment, the MDMT questionnaire was used to assess the average trust score. The participants were asked to rate on a 8-point scale (0–7) how well some trust-based descriptors applied to the robot. Finally, an average trust score was calculated over the several dimensions measured by the MDMT. To conclude, it is essential to emphasize that the initial three sections were employed to establish a solid foundation of trust between the participants and the robot prior to any violation of trust taking place. Consequently, Section 3 serves as a comprehensive synthesis, bringing together all the trust-related insights derived from the earlier stages.

The experiment protocols were in accordance with the *Declaration of Helsinki*. Ethical approval was obtained from the institutional review board prior to the study. Twenty-one participants were recruited, 9 male and 12 female with an average age of 28.3 ($SD = 9.94$). The sample size of 20 participants was chosen to initiate a preliminary assessment of trust levels, considering resource limitations and the exploratory nature of the study. Familiarity with robots was limited, three had previous practical experience with robots, while the remaining had only encountered them either in reality (12 participants) or through media (6 participants). The completion of the experiment required 30 min for each participant.

3.2 Experimental Setup

At the beginning of each session, a consent form and a description of the task were provided and, subsequently, the participant was equipped with an EMOTIV EPOC+ 14-Channel Wireless EEG Headset[2] connected to a computer to record brain waves with a rate of 128 Hz. To ensure a good contact quality, a saline liquid was applied to each electrode in order to have an efficient conductivity. A sensor map was used to check the location and contact quality of each sensor. The placement of the 14 electrodes is reported in Fig. 2 (left). Furthermore, participants were given instructions to avoid making pronounced movements to prevent any sensor shifts. The participant was seated on a chair facing a table with the robot (Fig. 2 right), which was controlled through the EZ-Builder software. In order to have a controlled data collection, a *Wizard of Oz* protocol was adopted, where the robot was manually controlled throughout the procedure. The participant remained unaware of this fact until the debriefing.

---

[2] https://www.emotiv.com/.

Fig. 2. Left: Placement of EEG electrodes. Right: Experimental scenario with the Humanoid Robot JD and the participant wearing the EEG headset.

3.3 Data Pre-processing

The EEG data was pre-filtered to remove the DC offset with 0.16 Hz high-pass cutoff. Before computing the *Fast Fourier Transform* (FFT), the EMOTIV Cortex API was used to *minimize artifacts* in the EEG signal. EEG waves can be affected by intrinsic artifacts (e.g. movements of the eye, eye blinks, bio-electric potentials from muscle and heart) and by external artifacts (e.g. environmental noise). Moreover, a *Hanning window* function was applied to obtain good frequency resolution and leakage protection with fair amplitude's accuracy. In order to analyze the alpha frequency band power, the continuous time series EEG data were transformed through FFT to assess the involved frequencies. Afterwards, the *power spectral density* was computed to determine the power of each band. Subsequently, the extraction of the power, expressed in μV^2, was performed from the following frequency bands: Theta (4–8 Hz), **Alpha (8–12 Hz)**, Low Beta (12–16 Hz), High Beta (16–25 Hz) and Gamma (25–45 Hz). Considering the nature of the task, the **alpha brain waves** were analyzed since previous studies have shown a strong correlation between **attention** and this typology of waves. In [13], it is reported that alpha suppression reflects attentional processes. The **hypothesis** is that if the robot committed errors during the performance, the human would less trust the robot, thus paying more attention in order to correctly guess the answer.

3.4 Data Analysis

For the trust assessment, the focus lay on the break point between section 3 and 4, where a trust violation occurs. Firstly, it was necessary to validate whether the trust scores from the MDMT were impacted by the trust violation. If that was the case, the data collected in sections 3 and 4 could be utilized for training a trust assessment model, incorporating the labels derived from the MDMT. A *Shapiro-Wilk test* revealed that the difference in average trust scores between section 3 and section 4 did not follow a normal distribution ($p = 0.001$). Therefore, instead of paired t-test, a *Wilcoxon Signed-Rank Test* was performed. The statistical test reported a significant difference in trust scores between section 3 ($M = 5.34$, $SD = 1.31$) and section 4 ($M = 4.64$, $SD = 1.79$). Specifically, the trust scores in section 3 ($Mdn = 5.45$) were significantly higher than those in section 4 ($Mdn = 5.07$), $W = 26$, $p = 0.002$. The results verified the usability of the trust scores for training the ML models.

Table 1. Features related to alpha frequency band power.

Features	Description
Mean Value	Average value of the power
Peak	Maximum value of the power
Standard Deviation	Dispersion of the power relative to its mean
Kurtosis	Sharpness of the peak

4 Trust Assessment

The categorization of the trust level was modeled as a **binary classification problem** (i.e. *high trust, low trust*). The ML models were based on features of the alpha frequency band power. For each participant, the contribution of the alpha frequency band power of each sensor was calculated and then averaged over the 14 channels. To **extract** the **features**, a *window size* of *1 s* (consisting of 128 data points) was defined. The initial features calculated on these windows were *mean, peak, median, standard deviation* and *kurtosis*. Based on the results of the MDMT questionnaire, the feature vectors were then labeled as one of the two classes, i.e. either as high or low trust. The labels were determined using the average of the results from the MDMT questionnaires as threshold for both section 3 ($M = 5.34$) and section 4 ($M = 4.64$). By applying *Univariate Feature Selection method*, the feature space was reduced by eliminating the median. The resulting features are summarized in Table 1. According to [17], classification algorithms are more suitable than regression models in brain computer interface applications. In this analysis, several supervised ML algorithms were selected to categorize the trust level of the participants. The adopted models were **Support Vector Machine** (SVM), **k-Nearest Neighbors** (kNN) and **Random Forest**. The data were normalized, shuffled and divided in 70% for the training set and 30% for the testing set. Tuning of hyperparameters was performed during the modeling phase. In the following, each algorithm is briefly presented along with the chosen evaluation metric (*classification accuracy*).

Support Vector Machine. With reference to [20], SVM is a suitable model to classify physiological data. It is a discriminative classifier whose purpose is to provide a hyperplane in a N-dimensional space (N corresponds to the number of features) that distinctly classifies the data points of a binary classification problem. Many hyperplanes can be chosen and the selection depends on the maximum achieved margin, which is the maximum distance between the support vectors, i.e. the data points of the two classes closer to the hyperplane. Maximizing the margins aims to provide a wider confidence interval for classifying new data points into one of the two regions in the space, based on their respective class memberships. To determine the optimal hyperplane (i.e. decision boundary), the hyperparameters must be computed through (1):

$$\min_{w,b,\xi} \frac{1}{2} w^t w + \frac{C}{n} \sum_{i=1}^{n} \xi_i \quad for\ i = 1,...,n \tag{1}$$

where w and b are hyperparameters, C is a tune parameter, n is the number of training samples and ξ_i is a variable that measures the extent of violation of constraint (2):

$$y_i(\langle w, x_i \rangle + b) \geq 1 - \xi_i \tag{2}$$

where x_i is the training set while y_i are the categories. To conclude, SVM robustly mitigates overfitting due to the margin maximization, support vector utilization and regulation parameter control. In this analysis, the two regions of the space represented respectively the high trust and the low trust categories of the participants. The *regulation term C* was assigned a value of *0.5* and the *radial basis function* was selected as the *kernel*. The algorithm performs with 63.20% accuracy.

k-Nearest Neighbors. kNN is a memory based classifier that exploits the similarity of the features between classes in order to predict the class of a new feature vector. kNN estimates the likelihood that a new data point belongs to a specific class (high or low trust) based on which class most of the data points closest to the new feature vector belong to. A distance function is used to determine the similarity between a new data point and its nearest neighbors [11], which is frequently the standard Euclidean distance (3):

$$d(x_i, y_i) = \sqrt{\sum_{i=1}^{d}(x_i - y_i)^2} \tag{3}$$

where x_i are the unclassified samples, y_i are the labeled data and d is the dimension of the feature space. kNN is considered robust to overfitting due to its local nature and lack of assumptions about data distribution. Additionally, the choice of the hyperparameter k (*number of neighbors*) helps prevent overfitting. A number of *seven* neighbors was determined through experimentation, which resulted in an accuracy of 68.86%.

Random Forest. Random Forest utilizes ensemble learning, a technique that combines many classifiers to make predictions. It consists of a large number of decision trees on various subsets of the given dataset. Each individual tree derives a class prediction and the class with the most votes is the output of the algorithm [5]. The robustness of Random Forest to overfitting is attributed to the random selection of features and sample subsets for each tree. This randomness ensures that no single tree have excessive influence over the ensemble, promoting generalization and reducing the risk of overfitting to unseen data. This model achieved the highest accuracy of 72.64% by utilizing *100 decision trees* and employing *Gini criterion* as the quality measure for evaluating splits in each tree.

5 Discussion

The data analysis indicated a statistically significant difference concerning the trust scores between the two analysed sections of the experiment ($p = 0.002$). Therefore, considering that each of the two sections had a distinct trust strategy (i.e. the robot's performance varied), it can be concluded that the robot successfully elicited a noticeable shift in trust among the participants. Thus, the hypothesis about perceptible variations in trust scores around the break point when trust violation occurred has been validated.

Table 2. Supervised learning models and performance indicators.

Supervised Learning Model	Accuracy	Precision	Recall	F1-score
Support Vector Machine	63.20%	0.63	0.63	0.63
k-Nearest Neighbors	68.86%	0.70	0.69	0.69
Random Forest	72.64%	0.75	0.73	0.72

Based on this, three different algorithms for trust categorization were examined. The analysis involved various performance indicators, namely *accuracy, precision, recall, F1-score*. The corresponding outcomes are presented in Table 2. The *Random Forest* model achieved a higher accuracy (72.64%), likely attributed to its ensemble nature, indicating a greater number of correct predictions compared to the other models. Its elevated precision suggested a lower incidence of false positives, which is essential for minimizing misclassifications. Moreover, the model demonstrated a higher recall value, signifying its ability to identify a larger proportion of actual positive instances, i.e. high sensitivity. The second-best performing model was *kNN*. Its competitive performance might be attributed to its simplicity and the absence of strong assumptions about the underlying data distribution. Lastly, *SVM* exhibited low performance possibly due to the complexity of the dataset and limited feature space. SVM's performance might improve with more diverse and higher-dimensional data. For instance, other features concerning alpha band could be peak-to-peak amplitude and alpha band reactivity.

In summary, the results highlighted the utility of EEG data in estimating trust levels in relation-based trust in human robot collaboration. Being able to classify trust based on sensor data has two main advantages over traditional trust evaluation through questionnaires. Firstly, questionnaire results do not always align with user behavior [1]. Trust assessment relying on sensor data becomes more objective, eliminating the need to rationalize the entire interaction with the robot. Secondly, while questionnaires offer summative evaluation after interaction, sensor-based trust assessment enables continuous evaluation, capturing trust dynamics as it develops during interaction. This facilitates the potential to react in real-time to over/undertrust by adapting the robot's interaction or communication behavior. The study's main limitation was the fluency of the robot's speech, which significantly influences human attention and trust in the robot's communication abilities. When a robot communicates smoothly, it appears more competent and reliable, leading to increased trust from humans. To further explore trust, the next step could involve increasing the risk for human participants during interactions to elicit stronger trust responses toward the robot.

6 Conclusion

This paper explored the correlation between robot performance and levels of human trust by leveraging EEG signals as input to trust assessment models. To this end, a scenario fostering social collaboration was designed, requiring the human to engage with a robot to successfully accomplish a game. Results show the successful manipulation of the participants' trust levels through the robot performance. Using the identified trust levels, a connection between the EEG data and trust was identified through ML models. These findings serve as the foundation for future research endeavors. As part of their ongoing work, the authors intend to delve into the effects of the trust repair section on the process of regaining trust from user participants following the robot's performance error. Additionally, sensor fusion techniques, incorporating EEG data, will be employed to enhance the robustness of trust level categorization.

References

1. Adamik, M., Dudzinska, K., Herskind, A.J., Rehm, M.: The difference between trust measurement and behavior: investigating the effect of personalizing a robot's appearance on trust in HRI. In: 2021 30th IEEE International Conference on Robot & Human Interactive Communication (RO-MAN), pp. 880–885. IEEE (2021)
2. Akash, K., Hu, W.L., Jain, N., Reid, T.: A classification model for sensing human trust in machines using EEG and GSR. ACM Trans. Interact. Intell. Syst. (TiiS) **8**(4), 1–20 (2018)
3. Boudreau, C., McCubbins, M.D., Coulson, S.: Knowing when to trust others: an ERP study of decision making after receiving information from unknown people. Soc. Cogn. Affect. Neurosci. **4**(1), 23–34 (2009)
4. De Visser, E.J., et al.: Towards a theory of longitudinal trust calibration in human-robot teams. Int. J. Soc. Robot. **12**(2), 459–478 (2020)
5. Edla, D.R., Mangalorekar, K., Dhavalikar, G., Dodia, S.: Classification of EEG data for human mental state analysis using random forest classifier. Procedia Comput. Sci. **132**, 1523–1532 (2018)
6. Floyd, M.W., Drinkwater, M., Aha, D.W.: Learning trustworthy behaviors using an inverse trust metric. In: Mittu, R., Sofge, D., Wagner, A., Lawless, W.F. (eds.) Robust Intelligence and Trust in Autonomous Systems, pp. 33–53. Springer, Boston, MA (2016). https://doi.org/10.1007/978-1-4899-7668-0_3
7. Hald, K., Rehmn, M., Moeslund, T.B.: Human-robot trust assessment using motion tracking & Galvanic skin response. In: 2020 IEEE/RSJ International Conference on Intelligent Robots and Systems (IROS), pp. 6282–6287. IEEE (2020)
8. Hancock, P.A., Billings, D.R., Schaefer, K.E., Chen, J.Y., De Visser, E.J., Parasuraman, R.: A meta-analysis of factors affecting trust in human-robot interaction. Hum. Factors **53**(5), 517–527 (2011)
9. Hu, W.L., Akash, K., Jain, N., Reid, T.: Real-time sensing of trust in human-machine interactions. IFAC-PapersOnLine **49**(32), 48–53 (2016)
10. Jessup, S.A., Schneider, T.R., Alarcon, G.M., Ryan, T.J., Capiola, A.: The measurement of the propensity to trust automation. In: Chen, J., Fragomeni, G. (eds.) Virtual, Augmented and Mixed Reality. Applications and Case Studies: 11th International Conference, VAMR 2019, Held as Part of the 21st HCI International Conference, HCII 2019, Orlando, FL, USA, 26–31 July 2019, Proceedings, Part II 21, pp. 476–489. Springer, Cham (2019). https://doi.org/10.1007/978-3-030-21565-1_32
11. Jiang, L., Cai, Z., Wang, D., Jiang, S.: Survey of improving k-nearest-neighbor for classification. In: Fourth International Conference on Fuzzy Systems and Knowledge Discovery (FSKD 2007), vol. 1, pp. 679–683. IEEE (2007)
12. Khavas, Z.R., Ahmadzadeh, S.R., Robinette, P.: Modeling trust in human-robot interaction: a survey. In: Wagner, A.R., et al. (eds.) ICSR 2020. LNCS (LNAI), vol. 12483, pp. 529–541. Springer, Cham (2020). https://doi.org/10.1007/978-3-030-62056-1_44
13. Klimesch, W., Doppelmayr, M., Russegger, H., Pachinger, T., Schwaiger, J.: Induced alpha band power changes in the human EEG and attention. Neurosci. Lett. **244**(2), 73–76 (1998)

14. Kok, B.C., Soh, H.: Trust in robots: challenges and opportunities. Curr. Robot. Rep. **1**, 297–309 (2020)
15. Law, T., Scheutz, M.: Trust: recent concepts and evaluations in human-robot interaction. In: Trust in Human-Robot Interaction, pp. 27–57 (2021)
16. Martelaro, N., Nneji, V.C., Ju, W., Hinds, P.: Tell me more designing HRI to encourage more trust, disclosure, and companionship. In: 2016 11th ACM/IEEE International Conference on Human-Robot Interaction (HRI), pp. 181–188. IEEE (2016)
17. McFarland, D.J., Anderson, C.W., Muller, K.R., Schlogl, A., Krusienski, D.J.: BCI meeting 2005-workshop on BCI signal processing: feature extraction and translation. IEEE Trans. Neural Syst. Rehabil. Eng. **14**(2), 135–138 (2006)
18. Muir, B.M., Moray, N.: Trust in automation. Part ii. Experimental studies of trust and human intervention in a process control simulation. Ergonomics **39**(3), 429–460 (1996)
19. Parasuraman, R., Riley, V.: Humans and automation: use, misuse, disuse, abuse. Hum. Factors **39**(2), 230–253 (1997)
20. Rani, P., Liu, C., Sarkar, N., Vanman, E.: An empirical study of machine learning techniques for affect recognition in human-robot interaction. Pattern Anal. Appl. **9**, 58–69 (2006)
21. Riedl, R., Javor, A.: The biology of trust: integrating evidence from genetics, endocrinology, and functional brain imaging. J. Neurosci. Psychol. Econ. **5**(2), 63 (2012)
22. Robinson, H., MacDonald, B., Broadbent, E.: The role of healthcare robots for older people at home: a review. Int. J. Soc. Robot. **6**, 575–591 (2014)
23. Rossi, A., Dautenhahn, K., Koay, K.L., Walters, M.L.: How the timing and magnitude of robot errors influence peoples' trust of robots in an emergency scenario. In: Kheddar, A., et al. (eds.) Social Robotics: 9th International Conference, ICSR 2017, Tsukuba, Japan, 22–24 November 2017, Proceedings 9, pp. 42–52. Springer, Cham (2017). https://doi.org/10.1007/978-3-319-70022-9_5
24. Salem, M., Lakatos, G., Amirabdollahian, F., Dautenhahn, K.: Would you trust a (faulty) robot? Effects of error, task type and personality on human-robot cooperation and trust. In: Proceedings of the Tenth Annual ACM/IEEE International Conference on Human-Robot Interaction, pp. 141–148 (2015)
25. Schaefer, K.E., Chen, J.Y., Szalma, J.L., Hancock, P.A.: A meta-analysis of factors influencing the development of trust in automation: implications for understanding autonomy in future systems. Hum. Factors **58**(3), 377–400 (2016)
26. Shayesteh, S., Ojha, A., Jebelli, H.: Workers' trust in collaborative construction robots: EEG-based trust recognition in an immersive environment. In: Jebelli, H., Habibnezhad, M., Shayesteh, S., Asadi, S., Lee, S.H. (eds.) Automation and Robotics in the Architecture, Engineering, and Construction Industry, pp. 201–215. Springer, Cham (2022). https://doi.org/10.1007/978-3-030-77163-8_10
27. Shishehgar, M., Kerr, D., Blake, J.: A systematic review of research into how robotic technology can help older people. Smart Health **7**, 1–18 (2018)
28. Ullman, D., Malle, B.F.: What does it mean to trust a robot? Steps toward a multidimensional measure of trust. In: Companion of the 2018 ACM/IEEE International Conference on Human-Robot Interaction, pp. 263–264 (2018)
29. Wu, J., Paeng, E., Linder, K., Valdesolo, P., Boerkoel, J.C.: Trust and cooperation in human-robot decision making. In: 2016 AAAI Fall Symposium Series (2016)
30. Xu, A., Dudek, G.: OPTIMo: online probabilistic trust inference model for asymmetric human-robot collaborations. In: Proceedings of the Tenth Annual ACM/IEEE International Conference on Human-Robot Interaction, pp. 221–228 (2015)
31. Yagoda, R.E., Gillan, D.J.: You want me to trust a robot? The development of a human-robot interaction trust scale. Int. J. Soc. Robot. **4**, 235–248 (2012)

Feasibility Study on Eye Gazing in Socially Assistive Robotics: An Intensive Care Unit Scenario

Alessandra Sorrentino[1](✉) ⓘ, Andrea Magnotta[1], Laura Fiorini[1,2] ⓘ,
Giovanni Piccinino[3], Alessandro Anselmo[3], Nicola Laurieri[3],
and Filippo Cavallo[1,2] ⓘ

[1] Department of Industrial Engineering, University of Florence, Florence, Italy
`alessandra.sorrentino@unifi.it`
[2] BioRobotics Institute, Scuola Superiore Sant'Anna, Pontedera, Italy
[3] ITEM-OXYGEN S.R.L., Altamura, Bari, Italy

Abstract. Recently, there has been an increasing interest in the adoption of socially assistive robots to support and alleviate the workload of clinical personnel in hospital settings. This work proposes the adoption of a socially assistive robot in Intensive Care Units to evaluate the criticality scores of bedridden patients. Within this scenario, the human gaze represents a key clinical cue for assessing a patient's conscious state. In this work, a user study involving 10 participants role-playing 4 levels of consciousness is performed. The collected videos were manually annotated considering 6 gazing directions and an open-source automatic tool was used to extract head pose and eye gazing features. Different feature sets and classification models were compared to find the most appropriate configuration to detect user gaze in this scenario. Results have suggested that the most accurate gazing estimation is obtained when the head pose information is combined with the eye orientation (0.85). Additionally, the framework proposed in this study seems to be user-independent, thereby encouraging the deployment of appropriate robotic solutions in real assistive contexts.

Keywords: Socially Assistive Robotics · Gaze Estimation · Machine Learning

1 Introduction

Socially Assistive Robots (SARs) emerged in recent years as potential tools to promote wellbeing and support mental health in children [1], older adults [2], and any person in need of assistance [3]. The major contribution of SARs is that they can aid the end user, while supporting and alleviating the professional caregiver's workload. Indeed, there is a growing trend in clinical settings to adopt SARs for therapy and stroke rehabilitation [4], for drug dispensation and delivery [5], as well for monitoring the mental states of patients [6]. Recent works support the idea that SARs could be also introduced in more critical settings, e.g. Intensive Care Units (ICUs) and surgical settings, where their presence could be beneficial to patients, staff, and hospitals [7]. In intensive care units, the greatest application of SARs regards telepresence [7], where the presence of the robot led to earlier interventions, reducing the response time and the mortality rates [7].

A. Al. Ali et al. (Eds.): ICSR 2023, LNAI 14453, pp. 43–52, 2024.
https://doi.org/10.1007/978-981-99-8715-3_5

This work investigates the role of SARs in monitoring the critical state of bedridden patients in intensive care units. A critical health state refers to a condition in which the patient's vital signs are unstable and outside of their normal limits, leading to an unconscious state. The idea is to adopt a social robot for stimulating verbal and motor capabilities of the patient, and for evaluating the patient's level of consciousness based on the responses to the proposed stimuli. Within this task, the robot could support the clinical personnel's workload, thereby guaranteeing a larger and more accurate screening during daily and nightly shifts; this may help to identify higher critical states earlier, thus reducing the intervention time. For the conscious state assessment, the clinical practice relies on the administration of two main scales, namely the Alert, Verbal, Pain, Unresponsive scale (AVPU) and the Glasgow Coma Scale. Both scales consider three aspects of responsiveness: eyes' activity, verbal and motor responses, which allow the elaboration of a specific associated score. In the present study, we will focus on the evaluation of the eye activity response, namely investigating the technical reliability of integrating an eye tracking framework over a socially assistive robot in the proposed scenario.

The gaze direction of a subject is determined by the combined effect of position and orientation of head pose and eyeball [8]. Despite representing a gross approximation, the head orientation is commonly used as gaze activity indicator in human-robot interaction (HRI) scenario [9]. More recent works include the pupil information in the eye gazing estimation, asking the subjects to wear eye-tracking glasses [10]. It represents an invasive solution, especially in the ICUs context. With the rise of deep learning techniques, there has been an increasing interest of assessing eye gazing in wild settings adopting advanced neural networks, such as GazeNet [11], RT-Gene [12] and Gaze360 [13]. Usually, each framework is trained on a dedicated dataset in which the subjects are requested to wear eye-tracking glasses or to look at specific portion of computers and tablets, to obtain validated gazing features. The main limitation of the current datasets is that the subjects are usually standing or sitting in front of the camera, which represents an unconventional posture for the target users we are dealing with. Due to the lack of a publicly available datasets of supine users, a dedicated dataset has been created in this study, in which the subjects were recorded while interacting with a SAR, lying over a bed. The data collected were then labeled in 6 eye gazing orientations, and gaze direction features have been extracted using a trained model. A data analysis was then performed, aiming at investigating the following research hypothesis (H):

1 H1: In the proposed scenario, the detection of gaze activity is more accurate when the position and the orientation of the head and of the pupil are known.
2 H2: In the proposed scenario, a robust gazing framework is user independent, thus it does not depend on the subjective activity of the target user.

2 Methodology

2.1 Application Scenario

To assess the conscious state of the ICU's patient, a dedicated interaction was designed for the robot, based on both the AVPU (Alert, Verbal, Pain, Unresponsive) scale [14] and Glasgow Coma Scale (GSC) [15], in collaboration with a team of clinical experts.

Both scales are widely used to measure the extent of impaired consciousness of a person. For this assessment, both scales consider three aspects of responsiveness: eyes' activity, verbal, and motor responses. The difference between the two scales is on the rating convention. The AVPU's score is expressed as A (*i.e.* the patient is awake and conscious), V (*i.e.* the patients responds verbally and with motor acts only to verbal stimuli), P (*i.e.* the patients does not respond to verbal stimuli by only to painful stimuli), and U (*i.e.* the patient is unresponsive, completely unconscious) score [14]. However, the Glasgow coma score is obtained by summing up the values of each aspect (*i.e.* eyes' activity, verbal, and motor responses), and it ranges from 3 ("no response") to 15 ("fully conscious state") [15].

Within this context, the robot is requested to continuously monitoring the conscious state of the patient, by stimulating verbal and motor capabilities of the patient and evaluating the responses to the proposed stimuli. The interaction has been designed in such a way that the robot asks the patient three questions (*i.e.* "What is your name?", "How old are you?", "Where are you now?"), and demands one motor activity ("Please, rise your arm"). During the interaction, the robot is requested to monitor verbal and motor responses, as well to track the gaze activity of the patients. Based on the stimuli's responses, the AVPU and GSC scores are computed and forwarded to the clinical personnel's station. The decision tree of the proposed application is shown in Fig. 1.

2.2 Robotic System

In the proposed scenario, the Mover-L robot (Co-robotics, Italy) has been used. Mover-L is a ROS-based robot, specifically designed to satisfy the scenario's requirement. From a hardware perspective, a 1920x1080px Resolution Intel Realsense Camera D435i is mounted on the robot at 0.70 m height, while two lasers are integrated on the bottom part (i.e. One on the front and one on the back). Additionally, two speakers for reproducing audio are present, as well as two touch screens. As shown in Fig. 2, the smaller screen is used to show the robot's face, while the larger screen is designed to display the patient's Information. To administer the clinical scale described in Sect. 2.1, the dialog of the robot has been structured as a Finite State Machine, where the transition from one state to another is triggered when the robot detects that its request has been satisfied or when the waiting time for the Response expires (C.A. 7 S). Before moving to the next one, each question is asked twice. The finite state machine has been implemented using the smach[1] ROS Library. The svox-pico text-to-speech (TTS) Engine[2] is used as a speech synthesizer, while the azure microsoft speech-to-text service[3] has been integrated to recognize the user's utterances. At the current state, the motion of the user is not detected, and the clinical score is not computed by the robot.

3 Data Acquisition

Our dataset consists of 2D recordings of people interacting with Mover-L robot while simulating different levels of conscious state.

---

[1] http://wiki.ros.org/smach.

[2] https://github.com/naggety/picotts.

[3] https://learn.microsoft.com/en-us/azure/ai-services/speech-service/index-speech-to-text.

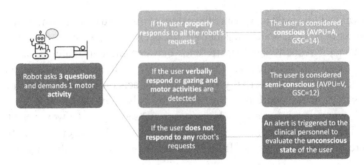

Fig. 1. Decision Tree of the designed interaction.

3.1 Experimental Setup

The user study was organized in one room of the Guest House at the BioRobotics Institute (Pontedera, Italy). The set-up for the user study is depicted in Fig. 2. A hospital-like environment was recreated with a bed and several pillows, where participants are instructed to lay down. The Mover-L robot was positioned diagonally to the right of the user and programmed to administrate the proposed clinical test reported in Sect. 2.2.

The experimental protocol was designed to test all the possible outcomes of the designed clinical test (described in Sect. 2.1), where the robot solicits verbal and motor stimuli to the participant. First, the participants were briefed on the purpose and the procedure of the study and signed the consent form. Then, they were asked to simulate a specific clinical condition in four different phases, namely:

1. C1-Conscious Phase: The participant is asked to positively react to the robot's requests, properly to answer to its questions (i.e. verbal response), to rise the arm when asked (i.e. motor response), and keep the eyes open (eye-opening response), as in Fig. 2(a)-(b).
2. C2-No motion Phase: The participant is asked to answer to the verbal requests (i.e. verbal response), but not to move the arm (i.e. no motor response). During this phase, the participant' eyes are open (i.e. eye-opening response), as in Fig. 2(a).
3. C3-No speech Phase: The participant is asked not to answer to the verbal requests (i.e. no verbal response), but to perform the requested movement (i.e. motor response), keeping the eyes open (i.e. eye-opening response), as in Fig. 2(b).
4. C4-Unconscious Phase: The participant is asked not to react, thus, neither to reply to any robot requests, and is asked to keep the eyes closed (no verbal, motor and eye-opening response), as in Fig. 2(c).

3.2 Dataset Coding

A total of 10 participants (4 female, 6 male, range age [25–30] years old) were involved among the researchers of the BioRobotics Institute (Pontedera, Italy). All participants completed the four conditions, but one condition of the last participant was not recorded properly (i.e. *C1*). Thus, a total of 39 videos were collected. Overall, the dataset comprises 63380 frames over 6550 s (109 min, 10 s), each depicting an RGB image containing the

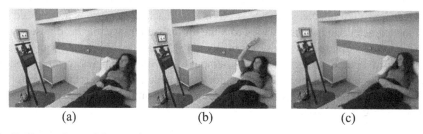

(a)   (b)   (c)

Fig. 2. Screenshots of the user in (a) conscious state, (b) answering to the motion requests, and in (c) unconscious state.

participants in the fixed camera view. On average, the *C1-Conscious state phase* lasted 2 min and 39 secs, the *C2-No motion phase* lasted 2 min and 12 secs, the *C3-No speech phase* lasted 3 min and 11 secs, and the *C4-Unconscious* phase lasted 3 min and 20 secs. The collected frames were manually annotated by two annotators, who were instructed to associate to the collected user behaviors into one of the following gaze directions, namely:

A. Left: user gaze points at the left side of the camera.
B. Right: user gaze points at the right side of the camera:
C. Up: user gaze points up with respect to the camera.
D. Down: user gaze points down with respect to the camera.
E. Center: user gaze points at the center of the camera.
F. Closed: user keeps the eyes closed.

The annotations were performed using the NOVA annotation tool [16], that generated per-frame annotation of the collected videos. Since no instructions were given on gaze during the experimental setup, the final dataset resulted quite imbalanced for each class, but quite distributed among the participants. The dataset is composed by the labeled recordings of all the phases together. The total samples belonging to each class are: 19580 for the Closed class, 14156 for the *Up* class, 11752 for the *Center* class, 9782 for *Left* class, 7819 for *Down* class, 291 for the *Right* class. Since the users were always keeping the eyes closed in *C4* phase, in the current work we discarded the *C4* recordings of 4 participants out of 10, reducing the instances of the Closed class to 13518.

4 Data Analysis

4.1 Gaze Estimation

Gaze orientation has been estimated by using the trained RT-GENE model [12]. RT-GENE model is an appearance-based deep convolutional neural network, that takes as input the image, and it returns the yaw and pitch angles of the head and of the eyes, respectively. While the yaw Angle (ϕ) describes the horizontal orientation (i.e. from left to right and Vice-Versa), the pitch angle (θ) describes the vertical orientation (i.e. related to up and down movements). To this aim, RT-GENE Model first detects the face along with the landmark points of the eyes, nose, and mouth corners with a multi-task cascaded Convolutional Networks (MTCNN). Then, each image face is normalized by using the extracted landmarks points. From the normalized image, the head pose of the user is detected using the methods described in [17], while the eye gazing's angles are extracted by a separate network that takes as input fixed-Size rectangles centered around the landmark points of the eyes [12]. Thus, for each image, the model returns a vector of 4 values: yaw and pitch angles of the head pose, and yaw and pitch angles of the pupils' orientation (Fig. 3).

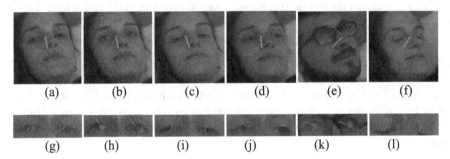

Fig. 3. Extracted gazing features. Example of head pose vectors in relation with (a) Center, (b) Up, (c) Down, (d) Left, (e) Right and (f) Closed classes. Extracted eye gaze vectors for the (g) Center, (h) Up, (i) Down, (j) Right, (k) Left and (l) Closed classes.

4.2 Classification

In this work, we performed intra- and inter-subjects' eye-gaze classification using only head pose information, only pupil orientation and all the features together. In the intra-subject case, the classification was performed on each subject individually. In the inter-subjects' classification, the features of all the users were merged and fed into the classifier. To minimize the bias, the 10-Cross Fold validation technique was applied in both classification modalities. Two common supervised algorithms were adopted and compared for the eye gaze classification, namely: K-nearest neighbors (KNN) and Random Forest (RF) algorithms. For these methods, we used the sklearn Python toolbox for Machine Learning. The effectiveness of each algorithm was estimated in terms of accuracy, precision, recall and F-measure. The same metrics were also used to compare the performance of the two algorithms on the different feature sets.

5   Results

In the intra-subject validation, the number of samples of the training and testing dataset depended on the number of frames recorded for each user. Considering the head pose's angles only, the RF and KNN algorithm got the same average accuracy of 0.75. As shown in Table 1, similar values were returned by both classifiers in terms of precision, recall and F-measure. When only the pupil orientation was considered, the average accuracy of the RF and KNN algorithm was 0.70. While the precision and F-measure score coincided in the two approaches (0.44), the KNN algorithm returned a recall of 1% higher than the RF algorithm. Merging the head pose information with the pupil orientation, the RF algorithm reached an accuracy of 0.86, while the KNN algorithm got an accuracy of 0.84. When all the features were present, the RF algorithm returned higher values of recall, precision, and F-measure than the KNN algorithm (see Table 1).

In the inter-subject classification, the number of samples belonging to each class corresponded to the values reported in Sect. 3.2. Considering the performances of the classification algorithm when only the head pose information is included, the average accuracy of the RF and KNN coincided (0.71). Slightly better performances were returned by the RF algorithm considering recall, precision, and F-measure metrics. When only the pupil orientation was used, the RF algorithm reached an accuracy of 0.53, while the KNN reached an accuracy of 0.54. Also in this case, recall, precision, and F-measure resulted slightly larger in the RF algorithm. Taking the four features as input, the classification performances of the RF reached 0.85, while KNN achieved an accuracy of 0.84. The precision, recall and F-measure are reported in Table 1.

To further analyze the classification performances of the best classifier (i.e. RF) in detecting gaze direction, the confusion matrices were computed for each dataset (i.e. head pose only, pupil orientation only, both information together), as shown in Fig. 4. While the RF correctly distinguished the classes Left, Right, and Center just considering only the head position, the pupil information seems to help in the detection of the Center class. In both cases, the larger mismatches concern the Closed class. As shown in Fig. 4(c), only by merging the two types of features, the algorithm could properly detect the gaze orientation, leading to better performances than the intra-subject classification (H2). Considering the last case, the large mismatches referred to some samples of Closed and Center classified as Up and some Closed and Up samples that were predicted as Center samples.

Table 1. Classification performances of the intra-subject (intra) and inter-subject (inter) analysis on the 3 datasets: head pose (Head), pupil orientation (Pupil) and all the features (All).

Algorithm	Features set	Accuracy		Recall		Precision		F-measure	
		Intra	Inter	Intra	Inter	Intra	Inter	Intra	Inter
RF	Head	0.75	0.71	0.57	0.63	0.54	0.61	0.55	0.62
	Pupil	0.70	0.53	0.58	0.44	0.55	0.42	0.56	0.42
	All	0.86	0.85	0.80	0.85	0.76	0.82	0.77	0.84
KNN	Head	0.75	0.71	0.59	0.65	0.54	0.62	0.55	0.63
	Pupil	0.70	0.54	0.59	0.43	0.55	0.41	0.56	0.41
	All	0.84	0.84	0.78	0.83	0.75	0.82	0.75	0.82

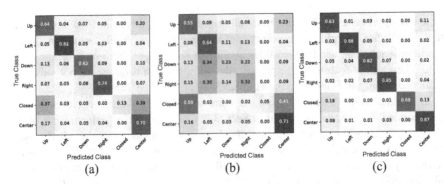

Fig. 4. Normalized Confusion matrices of the inter-subject classification with the (a) head pose features, (b) pupil features, and (c) merged features.

6 Discussion and Conclusion

The aim of this work was to investigate the performances of an automatic eye-gazing framework integrated in a socially assistive robot, for detecting the gaze activity of bedridden patients. While the gazing information is commonly used in HRI scenarios for predicting the intention and the attention of the involved users, here the gaze information is a fundamental clinical cue for assessing the conscious level of the patients in intensive care units. Within this aim, we created an ad-hoc dataset, composed by 39 video recordings of a socially assistive robot administrating an ad-hoc clinical test to young users role-playing different levels of consciousness. The users were lying over a bed, which is an uncommon configuration in eye-gazing datasets, and it may lead to poor gazing detection performances. The gazing detection results confirmed a good accuracy in detecting the 6 gaze directions of interest (*i.e.* Center, Up, Down, Right, Left and Closed) for the RF classifier, despite the other one.

The results highlighted that an accurate gazing detection is obtained considering both the head pose and the pupil orientation of the user (answer to H1). In detail, it seemed that the information on the pupil orientation improved the information carried in the head pose, improving the overall detection performance, as in other studies [9, 18]. Due to the nature of the proposed scenario, the user was mostly maintaining the head in stationary position, while moving the eyes in several directions. This led to a situation in which the stationary information of the head, which formed a predictable pattern in three cases (i.e., in Center, Left, and Right classes), is counterbalanced by the high sparsity of the pupil movements. As shown in Fig. 4(c), a more accurate gaze detection emerged by the head-eye interplay [8], since the less predictable class is the Closed condition, in which the head pose is clearly visible, while the pupils are not. As regards H2, the results highlighted that the accuracy of the inter-subject classification is comparable with the intra-subject classification. In the inter-subject classification, the higher number of samples in each class led the algorithm to properly learn the pattern underlined by the head pose features, with respect to the pupil orientation which varied a lot among the participants. A more precise classification of the proposed classes is achieved when both feature's types are present. In fact, the values of recall, precision and f-measure metrics were higher in the inter-subject classification than in the intra-subject one.

The proposed study validates the feasibility of adopting an eye-gazing framework for conscious state assessment application in intensive care unit scenarios. One limitation of this work is that the classification models have been tested in a controlled environment with healthy participants. As future work, we would like to evaluate this robot capability in the ICUs environments, to evaluate whether the accuracy reported in this study is also confirmed in a more challenging scenario, where the user's face may be occluded by the life support machines and there may be different environmental conditions (e.g. lighting). Future work will compare the gazing performances of different eye gazing feature extraction models (e.g. Gaze360 [13]). In this work, we mostly focus on monitoring eye-gazing activity, as first step on developing a SAR for ICUs. Further work will also investigate the development and integration of automatic tools for assessing motor and verbal responses to robot stimuli.

Acknowledgements. This work has been partially supported by European Union - Next Generation EU under Project: "A novel public-private alliance to generate socioeconomic, biomedical and technological solutions for an inclusive Italian ageing society" (Age-IT), CUP: B83C22004800006 and by Piano Nazionale per gli Investimenti Complementari PNC-PNRR Fit for Medical Robotics (Fit4MedRob), CUP: B53C22006950001.

References

1. Kabacińska, K., Prescott, T.J., Robillard, J.M. : Socially assistive robots as mental health interventions for children: a scoping review. Int. J. Soc. Robot. **13**, (2021). https://doi.org/10.1007/s12369-020-00679-0
2. Bemelmans, R., Gelderblom, G.J., Jonker, P., de Witte, L.: Socially assistive robots in elderly care. : A Syst. Rev. into Eff. effectiveness (2012). https://doi.org/10.1016/j.jamda.2010.10.002
3. Scassellati, B., Vázquez, M.: The potential of socially assistive robots during infectious disease outbreaks (2020). https://doi.org/10.1126/scirobotics.abc9014
4. Chang, W.H., Kim, Y.-H.: Robot-assisted therapy in stroke rehabilitation. J. Stroke **15**(3), 174 (2013). https://doi.org/10.5853/jos.2013.15.3.174
5. Rodriguez-Gonzalez, C.G., Herranz-Alonso, A., Escudero-Vilaplana, V., Ais-Larisgoitia, M.A., Iglesias-Peinado, I., Sanjurjo-Saez, M.: Robotic dispensing improves patient safety, inventory management, and staff satisfaction in an outpatient hospital pharmacy. J. Eval. Clin. Pract. 25, (2019). 10.1111/jep.13014.https://doi.org/10.1111/jep.13014
6. Jeffcock, J., Hansen, M., Garate, V.R.: Transformers and human-robot interaction for delirium detection. In: ACM/IEEE International Conference on Human-Robot Interaction (2023). https://doi.org/10.1145/3568162.3576971
7. Teng, R., Ding, Y., See, K.C.: Use of robots in critical care. Syst. Rev. (2022). https://doi.org/10.2196/33380
8. Ghosh, S., Dhall, A., Hayat, M., Knibbe, J., Ji, Q.: Automatic gaze analysis: a survey of deep learning based approaches. 1–24 (2021)
9. Admoni, H., Scassellati, B.: Social eye gaze in human-robot interaction: a review. J. Hum-Robot Interac **6**(1), 25 (2017). https://doi.org/10.5898/JHRI.6.1.Admoni
10. Wachowiak, L., Tisnikar, P., Canal, G., Coles, A., Leonetti, M., Celiktutan, O.: Analysing eye gaze patterns during confusion and errors in human-agent collaborations. In: RO-MAN 2022 - 31st IEEE International Conference on Robot and Human Interactive Communication: Social, Asocial, and Antisocial Robots (2022). https://doi.org/10.1109/RO-MAN53752.2022.9900589

11. Zhang, X., Sugano, Y., Fritz, M., Bulling, A.: Appearance-based gaze estimation in the wild. In: Proceedings of the IEEE Computer Society Conference on Computer Vision and Pattern Recognition (2015). https://doi.org/10.1109/CVPR.2015.7299081

12. Fischer, T., Chang, H.J., Demiris, Y.: RT-GENE: Real-time eye gaze estimation in natural environments. In: Lecture Notes in Computer Science (including subseries Lecture Notes in Artificial Intelligence and Lecture Notes in Bioinformatics) (2018)https://doi.org/10.1007/978-3-030-01249-6_21

13. Kellnhofer, P., Recasens, A., Stent, S., Matusik, W., Torralba, A.: Gaze360: physically unconstrained gaze estimation in the wild. In: Proceedings of the IEEE International Conference on Computer Vision (2019). https://doi.org/10.1109/ICCV.2019.00701

14. Romanelli, D., Mw, F.: AVPU Score. In: StatPearls (2020)

15. Jones, C.: Glascow Coma Scale. Am. J. Nurs. (1979)

16. Baur, T., Heimerl, A., Lingenfelser, F., Wagner, J., Valstar, M.F., Schuller, B., André, E.: Explainable cooperative machine learning with NOVA. KI - Künstliche Intelligenz 34(2), 143–164 (2020). https://doi.org/10.1007/s13218-020-00632-3

17. Patacchiola, M., Cangelosi, A.: Head pose estimation in the wild using convolutional neural networks and adaptive gradient methods. Pattern Recogn. 71, 132–143 (2017). https://doi.org/10.1016/j.patcog.2017.06.009

18. Palinko, O., Rea, F., Sandini, G., Sciutti, A.: A robot reading human gaze: why eye tracking is better than head tracking for human-robot collaboration. In: IEEE International Conference on Intelligent Robots and Systems (2016). https://doi.org/10.1109/IROS.2016.7759741

Clustering Social Touch Gestures
for Human-Robot Interaction

Ramzi Abou Chahine[1](✉), Steven Vasquez[2], Pooyan Fazli[3], and Hasti Seifi[3]

[1] University of East Anglia, Norwich, Norfolk NR4 7TJ, UK
r.abou-chahine@uea.ac.uk
[2] San Francisco State University, San Francisco, CA 94132, USA
svasquez7@sfsu.edu
[3] Arizona State University, Tempe, AZ 85281, USA
{pooyan,hasti.seifi}@asu.edu

Abstract. Social touch provides a rich non-verbal communication channel between humans and robots. Prior work has identified a set of touch gestures for human-robot interaction and described them with natural language labels (e.g., stroking, patting). Yet, no data exists on the semantic relationships between the touch gestures in users' minds. To endow robots with touch intelligence, we investigated how people perceive the similarities of social touch labels from the literature. In an online study, 45 participants grouped 36 social touch labels based on their perceived similarities and annotated their groupings with descriptive names. We derived quantitative similarities of the gestures from these groupings and analyzed the similarities using hierarchical clustering. The analysis resulted in 9 clusters of touch gestures formed around the social, emotional, and contact characteristics of the gestures. We discuss the implications of our results for designing and evaluating touch sensing and interactions with social robots.

Keywords: Social Touch · Touch Dictionary · Non-Verbal Communication · Crowdsourcing Study

1 Introduction

Social touch has been an active area of research for human-robot interactions (HRI) in the last decade. Social touch gestures refer to different ways that people use touch to communicate information or emotion and bond with other humans or robots [10]. For example, one may tap a robot's arm to get its attention or hug a robotic pet when stressed. A companion robot may stroke a user's hand to convey emotional support or guide the user's action by pushing their hand. Previous work has derived a set of social touch gestures and their definitions based on user interactions with robotic pets [28]. Others designed and evaluated touch interactions with humanoid robots [3,7]. The touch gestures from these studies have guided the development and evaluation of touch sensors for robots, helped examine user experience of robot-initiated touch, and informed the design of robot response to user touch.

© The Author(s), under exclusive license to Springer Nature Singapore Pte Ltd. 2024
A. Al. Ali et al. (Eds.): ICSR 2023, LNAI 14453, pp. 53–67, 2024.
https://doi.org/10.1007/978-981-99-8715-3_6

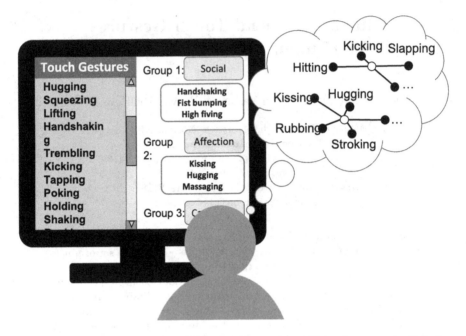

Fig. 1. In our study, users grouped social touch labels based on their perceived similarities (A). The resulting touch clusters can be used by robots to interpret and perform touch interactions with people (B).

Despite the abundance of interest in social touch communication, the semantic relationship(s) between various touch gestures remains unclear. Some gestures may be very similar or even identical in their contact characteristics (e.g., *tapping* vs. *patting*), while others may be similar considering the intended emotion or social context. People develop a mental structure for the semantics of touch gestures and their relationships. This mental structure shapes people's perception, interpretation, and use of touch [8]. Charting the relationship between social touch gestures can help HRI researchers select touch gestures for their studies (e.g., touch sensor evaluation) and develop robots that use touch in a socially intelligent manner. Yet, little data exists in the literature about how people perceive the relationships between social touch gestures.

As a first step toward addressing this gap, we asked how people perceive similarities of social touch labels (e.g., *stroking, hugging*). People can have unique styles in applying a touch gesture [12]. On the other hand, people often use natural language labels to refer to archetypal features of a touch gesture. The touch labels are also used in HRI studies to ask users to contact a robot (or a sensor) in a certain way [3,12] or to analyze user interactions with a robot [28]. The study of natural language labels for emotions has helped capture users' cognitive structure, leading to a circumplex model for affect [18]. Thus, as a first step, we investigated the semantic structure of social touch labels in the users' minds in this paper.

To chart the relationship between touch labels, we ran an online card sorting study with 56 users over Amazon Mechanical Turk (Fig. 1-A). The participant received the labels and definitions for 36 touch gestures from the literature, sorted them into 4, 8, and 12 groups successively based on their similarities, and provided descriptive names for each group. From this data, we identified 11 outliers by manually reviewing the data as well as analyzing the responses quantitatively. Then, we created a dissimilarity matrix for the 36 touch gestures with the data of the remaining 45 participants and applied agglomerative hierarchical clustering on the dissimilarity matrix. Furthermore, we analyzed the descriptive names that the participants had for their groupings using open codes (e.g., *social, aggressive*) and calculated the frequency of the codes for the gestures.

Based on the above analysis, we contribute 9 clusters for social touch gestures and the distribution of the top codes for each cluster. Using this data, we interpret the 9 clusters to capture the types of touch as follows: (1) social, (2) romantic affection, (3) caregiving affection, (4) hand contact, (5) aggression, (6) forceful press, (7) functional movement, (8) nervous contact, and (9) contact without movement (Fig. 1-B). Our results suggest that people primarily group touch gestures based on their social, emotional, and contact characteristics. These results provide the first data on cognitive structure(s) that people use to interpret and conceptualize social touch. We discuss how the results can help design and evaluate a robot to sense, interpret, and communicate via touch.

2   Related Work

2.1   Social Touch in HRI

The literature on social touch ranges from communication between humans to interactions between humans and robots. Hertenstein et al. studied how dyads use social touch gestures to communicate different emotions and found that people can decode the intended emotions with great accuracy when being touched [8]. Similar studies of human-human touch suggest that touchers can subtly but significantly vary contact attributes of their touch actions to communicate distinct messages [27]. HRI researchers have replicated Hertenstein et al.'s work to investigate how users and robots can use touch to communicate emotions. Some studies examined how humans communicate emotions to robots [11,28], while others examined whether a robot can communicate emotions to humans via touch [21,23].

Social touch gestures have also informed the development and evaluation of tactile skins for robots. Previous work in this area has proposed touch sensors with a novel working principle [5], sensors resembling the feel and structure of human skin [24], and low-cost do-it-yourself sensors for specific applications such as companion robots for children with autism [3]. To evaluate the sensor's efficacy, researchers select a set of social touch gestures and ask users to touch the sensor accordingly. Data from user contact with the sensor is then used to classify the gestures.

A variety of touch gestures are reported in the above studies. Yohanan and MacLean proposed a touch dictionary with labels and definitions for 30 gestures based on videos of user interactions with a furry lap-sized robot [28]. This dictionary has been widely used in social touch studies [3,11]. Others mentioned additional gestures for interactions with humanoid robots such as *fist bumping* [15–17], *handshaking* [2,17,26], or *kicking* [8,13,20]. To inform future work in this area, we collected common touch gestures from prior studies and examined how people conceptualize the relationship between these gestures.

2.2 Identifying Perceptual and Semantic Clusters

The psychophysics and interaction design literature has developed methods for estimating perceptual and semantic similarities of items through user studies. The pairwise rating method asks participants to rate the similarity of pairs of items in the set [1]. This method is effective for a small set of items (e.g., < 15) but it is prone to noise from local judgments and does not scale to large item sets [25]. The sorting methods, known as card sorting or cluster sorting, ask participants to group items into clusters based on their similarities. This process can be repeated with an increasing number of groups to obtain a fine-grained similarity matrix [22]. This method allows for collecting cognitive similarities of large item sets [18]. The similarity matrix is further analyzed using dimensionality reduction or clustering techniques [1,18]. Following this methodology, we used iterative cluster sorting and asked users to name their groups to obtain semantic clusters for social touch labels.

Natural language labels have been used to capture lay users' cognitive structure for sensory and emotional items. The circumplex model of affect by Russell [18] is based on a series of studies that use natural language labels for emotions. Also, studies of social touch often rely on user understanding of natural language labels for touch. In these studies, users receive labels for a set of social touch gestures (e.g., *tapping*, *stroking*) and are asked to touch the robot accordingly [3,11]. Similarly, studies on human-human and human-robot emotional communication sometimes provide a list of touch gesture labels for users to choose from, before applying the gestures [8,27]. The studies may also provide short definitions for each touch gesture e.g., from the touch dictionary by Yohanan and MacLean [28]. These studies rely on the users' knowledge of natural language labels for touch gestures. We follow a similar approach in our work to capture users' cognitive structure and similarities of social touch gestures.

3   Methods

To study how people perceive similarities of social touch gestures, we compiled a list of touch gestures from the literature, designed an online questionnaire for grouping the touch gestures, and ran a data collection study on MTurk.

Table 1. The 7 touch gestures that we added to the 29 gestures in Yohanan and MacLean's touch dictionary [28], resulting in 36 touch gestures for our online study.

Gesture Label	Gesture Definition
Finger Interlocking	Interlace fingers of one hand
Fist Bumping	Lightly tap clenched fists together
Handshaking	Shake clasped hands
High Fiving	Slap upraised hands against each other
Kicking	Strike forcibly with a foot
Picking Up	Take hold of and lift or move something
Squish	Press or beat into a pulp or a flat mass

3.1 Touch Gestures

We compiled 36 social touch gestures that are used for interacting with humans or robots. We focused our scope on gestures that are used in at least two publications in the social touch and HRI literature. Specifically, we included 29 touch gestures from the touch dictionary by Yohanan and MacLean [28]. Different subsets of these gestures are used in several other studies [11,12]. We removed *finger idly* from the touch dictionary as this gesture is not used in any other publication. We added seven other touch gestures that appeared in at least two publications including *finger interlocking* [8,9], *fist bumping* [15–17] *handshaking* [2,17,26], *high fiving* [6–8], *squishing* [4], *kicking* [8,13,20], and *picking up* [4,19,20].

We adapted the definitions provided in Yohanan and MacLean's touch dictionary by replacing the phrases related to their robotic pet (i.e., the Haptic Creature, or fur of Haptic Creature) with "something" in the definition. For example, we defined *lifting* as "raise something to a higher position or level." For the 7 actions that were not in the original touch dictionary, we created a definition with inspiration from sources such as the Britannica Encyclopedia. Table 1 shows the 7 newly added gestures and their definitions.

3.2 Questionnaire

We designed a Qualtrics survey to collect user demographics and data on the similarity of touch actions (Fig. 2). The first page of the survey asked users to enter their demographic information including their age, gender, and country where they grew up. The next three pages asked the users to divide the touch gestures into 4, 8, and 12 groups respectively. We call these 4 groupings, 8 groupings, and 12 groupings in this paper. Each page showed the list of touch gesture labels in a random order. The users could hover over a gesture's label to see its definition. The users were asked to group the touch gestures based on their likeness or similarity and provide a descriptive name for each group. Reasons for likeness were up to user interpretation. Having the users describe their groupings served multiple purposes. First, they helped us identify users' reasoning for the

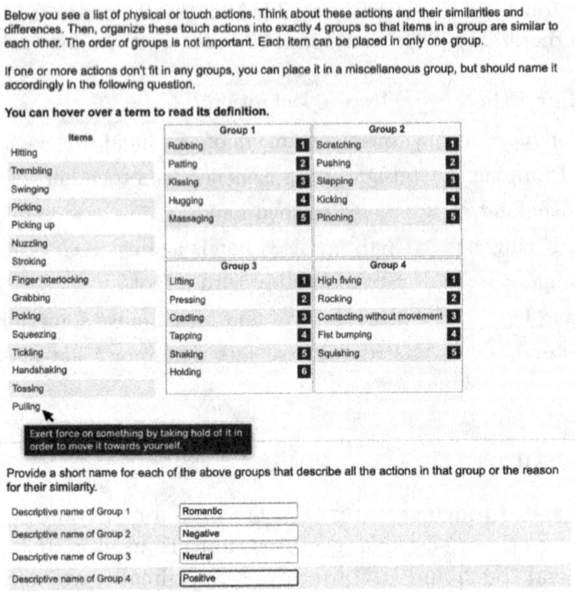

Fig. 2. A screenshot of the questionnaire for grouping the touch gestures in our study. The image shows touch gestures that are divided into four groups, the remaining list of gestures for grouping, and example descriptive names from one of the participants.

similarity of touch gestures. Second, the descriptive names served as an attention test and allowed us to detect those who did not do the task properly, e.g., if they organized the gestures into random groups.

We devised the above procedure based on common practices in studies of similarity perception and social touch gestures in the literature. First, the iterative cluster sorting method allowed us to collect users' holistic comparisons of the similarities of all 36 gestures. Second, following prior work on touch sensing and communication, the touch labels helped us abstract from a variety of styles that people use to apply the touch gestures (e.g., tapping one time or multiple times) to capture users' cognitive structure of the gestures.

4   Analysis and Results

We collected participant responses through MTurk. Eligible turkers were required to have at least 5,000 completed tasks with a minimum success rate of 97% and to speak English at the B2 level or higher. We analyzed their data in the following steps:

- **Identifying outliers.** We identified participants who did not follow the study instructions or appeared to group the touch gestures randomly (Sect. 4.1) and removed their data from the subsequent analysis. We also examined the effect of where participants grew up on their groupings.

- **Coding descriptive names for the groups.** To identify the themes behind the user groupings, we coded the descriptive group names from the participants. This step resulted in 25 codes (e.g., social, aggressive) to capture user logic for their groupings (Sect. 4.2).
- **Clustering touch gestures.** We calculated a dissimilarity matrix for the touch gestures based on the participants' groupings and identified semantic groups by applying hierarchical clustering on the dissimilarity matrix.
- **Interpreting the clusters.** Finally, we counted how many times a code from Step II was applied to the touch gestures in each cluster. The results helped us interpret and label each of the 9 social touch clusters (Sect. 4.3).

Below we detail these steps and their results.

4.1 Identifying Outliers

We marked and removed outliers who did not follow the study instructions or their groupings and descriptive names appeared random. One of the authors carefully examined all the responses from the 56 participants and marked potential outliers for further analysis. The author marked cases where no label was provided, the label was gibberish, or the description of group labels did not match with its gesture items. For example, if a participant grouped *kissing*, *nuzzling*, and *stroking* with *hitting* and labeled them as "fighting", we marked this as an unusual group. By the end of this step. 16 participants with several unusual groupings were marked as potential outliers.

Next, we calculated a similarity matrix where each cell showed similarity of the groupings provided by two participants (56×56 matrix). To obtain the best matching between groups from two different participants, we calculated the Jaccard Index values for all pairs of groups provided by them (e.g., 8 pairs for the 4 groupings) and averaged the highest Jaccard values as a measure of the similarity of the two participants.

We projected the participant similarities into two dimensions using a common dimensionality reduction technique known as non-metric Multidimensional Scaling (nMDS) and used clustering to assess outliers (Fig. 3). In addition, we conducted k-means clustering with a range of 2 to 10 clusters on the dissimilarity matrix. The value of the Gap Statistic suggested 3 as the optimal number of clusters (Fig. 3). Our analysis revealed that cluster 3 contained 11 out of the 16 participants that we had manually identified as potential outliers. Cluster 2 contained the remaining 5 potential outliers, as well as participants not considered to be outliers in our manual analysis. Thus, the two methods of manual and quantitative analysis of outliers largely overlapped and provided support that the cluster 3 participants either provided noisy data or judged similarities differently from the majority. Thus, we included the participants from clusters 1 and 2 ($n = 45$ participants) in further analysis.

The remaining 45 participants were from the United States (32), followed by India (7), Brazil (5), and Japan (1). They self-identified as man ($n = 29$), woman ($n = 16$), or nonbinary ($n = 0$). The mean age of the participants was

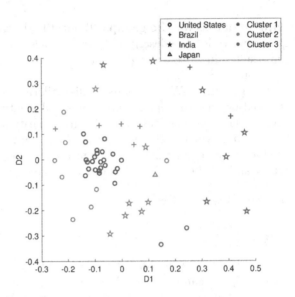

Fig. 3. MDS plot visualizing similarity of the 56 participants in grouping the gestures. Each mark represents one participant. The color and shape of the marks denote the clustering results and participant backgrounds, respectively. Participants in cluster 3 (red) were identified as potential outliers and were removed from further analysis. (Color figure online)

36.4 (±10.73) years and their ages ranged between 21–63 years. The participant background is denoted with the shape of the marks in Fig. 3. Participants who were not from the US are either in clusters 2 or 3. We analyzed this aspect further in our clustering results (Sect. 4.3).

4.2   Coding Descriptive Names for the Groups

To understand the reasoning behind group choices, we coded the descriptive names provided by the participants for each group. From 4 to 8 to 12 groupings, the codes became more complex as subgroups began to form. The process of identifying these codes was iterative. For example, when coding the descriptive names for 12 groupings, we used the codes identified from 8 groupings in the first iteration. If we found any new or more specific patterns, we added new codes and recorded the previous data accordingly. Upon completing the coding of all the groupings, we had a total of 25 codes. We found some descriptive names to be ambiguous and coded them as 'vague'. We also found that some names did not match the social touches they were assigned to, we coded these descriptive names as 'random'. In some cases, participants labeled a group as 'other' or 'miscellaneous'. Thus, we also coded these groupings as 'miscellaneous'. If a grouping contained only a single social touch, we coded it as 'single action'. The remaining 21 codes included: aggressive, annoying, caregiving, direction, fingers, force, friendly, full-body, functional, grief, hands, holding onto, massage, nervous, playful, rapid, repetitive, romance, slow, social, and squeezing.

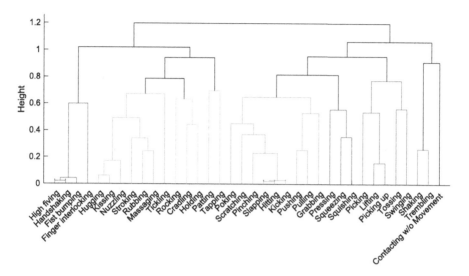

Fig. 4. Results demonstrating hierarchical clustering results for the social touch gestures. The Gap Statistic criterion suggested an optimal number of 9 clusters. The Cophenetic correlation coefficient is 0.85 suggesting strong correspondence with the dissimilarity matrix. Each color represents one cluster.

4.3   Clustering Touch Gestures

Using the grouping data of each participant, we created a similarity matrix of touch gestures following the same procedure described by Russell [18]. First, each pair of words was given a minimum similarity score of 1. If pairs of words were included in the same user-defined group, then their similarity score was increased by the number of groups being organized. For example, we increased the similarity score by 4 if a pair of words were in the same cluster for the 4 grouping mode for a participant. If a pair of words were included in the same group for 4, 8, and 12 groupings modes, then the words would have the maximum possible similarity of $1+4+8+12 = 25$. A single similarity matrix was calculated from the three grouping modes, and the matrix was subsequently normalized by dividing its entries by the maximum possible similarity value (i.e., 45 participants $\times$ 25 = 1125). We subtracted the normalized matrix from a matrix of ones to generate a dissimilarity matrix for all the gestures.

We applied clustering to the dissimilarity matrix and identified 9 clusters for the touch gestures. Specifically, we employed agglomerative hierarchical clustering using the unweighted pair group method with arithmetic mean (UPGMA) [14]. To determine the optimal number of clusters for hierarchical clustering, we utilized the Gap Statistic evaluation criterion with a range of 2 to 10 clusters.

Table 2. Our derived names and the top 5 codes with their percentages for the 9 clusters. All the single-item groups are coded as 'single action'.

C1	Social	social 50%	hands 14%	romance 14%	caregiving 4%	random 3%
C2	**Romantic Affection**	romance 33%	caregiving 11%	massage 6%	random 5%	vague 4%
C3	**Caregiving Affection**	caregiving 15%	romance 12%	vague 10%	functional 8%	random 6%
C4	**Hand Contact**	force 12%	hands 10%	social 9%	vague 9%	random 8%
C5	**Aggression**	aggressive 52%	functional 9%	random 5%	hands 5%	vague 5%
C6	**Forceful Press**	aggressive 18%	functional 12%	squeezing 12%	vague 9%	force 8%
C7	**Functional Movement**	functional 29%	vague 12%	aggressive 8%	random 8%	hands 5%
C8	**Nervous Contact**	nervous 30%	aggressive 14%	vague 11%	random 6%	force 5%
C9	**Contact w/o Movement**	single action 24%	miscellaneous 10%	social 10%	vague 7%	functional 6%

This analysis suggested 9 clusters (Fig. 4). The Cophenetic correlation coefficient was 0.85 for the 9 clusters, indicating a strong positive correspondence between the clusters and the original dissimilarity matrix. These clusters include:

– **Cluster 1:** *high-fiving, handshaking, fist bumping,* and *finger interlocking*
– **Cluster 2:** *hugging, kissing, nuzzling, stroking, rubbing, massaging,* and *tickling*
– **Cluster 3:** *rocking, cradling,* and *holding*
– **Cluster 4:** *patting* and *tapping*
– **Cluster 5:** *poking, scratching, pinching, slapping, hitting, kicking, pushing, pulling,* and *grabbing*
– **Cluster 6:** *pressing, squeezing,* and *squishing*
– **Cluster 7:** *picking, lifting up, picking up, tossing,* and *swinging*
– **Cluster 8:** *shaking* and *trembling*
– **Cluster 9:** *contacting without movement*

To test the effect of cultural background and English proficiency in our results, we repeated the above clustering analysis on data from 32 participants from the US. The analysis led to similar clusters with the exception that clusters 2 and 3 were merged into one cluster. Thus, we decided to continue with the above 9 clusters in our further analysis.

4.4   Interpreting the Clusters

We calculated the distribution of our codes for the descriptive names across these clusters to interpret the reason behind the groups. Table 2 presents the five frequent codes for the gestures in each cluster.

We named the clusters based on the distribution of their five top codes. For clusters 1 and 5, the majority of the codes ($\geq 50\%$) are 'social' and 'aggressive'. Thus, we call these clusters *Social* and *Aggression* respectively. Clusters 2, 7, 8, and 9 have one frequent code ($\geq 24\%$), followed by one or two codes with $\geq 10\%$ frequency. For cluster 2, the top code is 'romance' followed by 'caregiving', both of which reflect the affective nature of touch. Thus, we name this group as *Romantic Affection*. For cluster 7, the top code is 'functional', followed by 'vague'. This cluster includes a set of gestures that involve lifting and moving an object or person. Thus, we name it *Functional Movement*. Cluster 8 has a top code of 'nervous', followed by 'aggressive'. Thus, we call it *Nervous Contact*. Cluster 9 includes the single gesture of *contacting without movement*. This gesture was often put in a separate group by the participants and we coded it as 'single action'. Thus, we name this cluster as *Contact w/o Movement* to reflect its distinct nature in the participants' minds. Finally, clusters 3, 4, and 6 have a relatively flat code distribution. Cluster 3 has the same two top codes as cluster 2, representing affect, but in the reverse order. Thus, we name it *Caregiving Affection*. Cluster 4 has two codes of 'force' and 'hands' with more than 10% frequency. With two gestures of *patting* and *tapping*, we name this cluster as *Hand Contact*. The top codes ($\geq 10\%$) for cluster 6 are 'aggressive', 'functional', and 'squeezing'. Since the top labels indicate both the 'aggressive' and 'functional' aspects of the gestures in this cluster, we use a neutral label and call this cluster *Forceful Press*. Next, we discuss these clusters and their implications for HRI research.

5   Discussion

In this study, we present data on the user perception and description of touch gestures. Our findings indicate that users tend to assess the similarity of touch gestures based on their emotional and social connotations, in addition to the functional and contact characteristics. Specifically, cluster 1 includes touch gestures that are frequently annotated with 'social' names. Clusters 2 and 3 include gestures that are mainly coded with positive associations of 'romance' and 'caregiving'. Similarly, clusters 5 and 8 are coded with negative descriptors of 'aggressive' and 'nervous'. Finally, four clusters (i.e., 4, 6, 7, 9) seem to be mainly described based on the characteristics of the contact such as the body part (cluster 4), force (cluster 6), and whether the touch involved movement (cluster 7) or not (cluster 9). These clusters emerged without providing information on the context of interaction, suggesting that users have strong social, positive, negative, and functional associations with touch gestures even without context. Some clusters have a flat distribution of codes and show a notable mix of affective and functional interpretations (e.g., cluster 6 with *pressing*, *squeezing*, and *squishing*) suggesting that an individual's background or interaction context may notably shift their meaning. Interestingly *contacting without movement* was often regarded as different from the other gestures, which could be due to its neutral emotional content as well as the static nature of the touch.

These user-generated clusters are a step toward a framework for the analysis and understanding of social touch and can inform research on sensing, designing, and analyzing human-robot touch interactions. We anticipate the following use cases of the touch clusters for HRI:

(1) *Sensing touch from humans.* A desirable factor for robotic touch sensors is their ability to recognize a variety of gestures [11]. These clusters can aid researchers in selecting gestures that are different in their semantic and contact characteristics. For instance, the co-location of *stroking* and *rubbing* gestures in cluster 2 suggests that it might be appropriate to choose one of the two gestures. Relatedly, when evaluating the efficacy of a touch-sensing algorithm [3,5,11], HRI researchers can weigh misclassifications according to these semantic clusters. For example, misclassifying *stroking* with *slapping* should be penalized more than mistaking *stroking* with *rubbing* or *nuzzling*.

(2) *Interpreting and responding to touch from humans.* The proposed touch gesture clusters can aid robots in responding intelligently to human touch. These clusters can help robots identify the intention behind touch gestures. While the significance and purpose of social touch gestures may depend on the context, these clusters and their labels can help develop a probabilistic mental model for robots about a user's intent of a touch gesture. During an interaction episode, the robot can update these probabilities based on other contextual parameters and modes of communication such as the user's verbal utterances and body pose.

(3) *Touching people to communicate.* The semantic clusters can help design and evaluate robots that touch humans to communicate information or emotion [23]. Specifically, to evaluate the efficacy of a robot in using touch gestures, HRI researchers can determine the degree of dissimilarity between the intended touch gesture and the one identified by the human. Also, depending on the purpose of the interaction (e.g., social, emotional, or functional), the robot may use the clusters to select and use alternative gestures with similar connotations.

(4) *Analyzing human-robot touch interactions.* HRI researchers can use these clusters to code video recordings of touch interactions with a robot and aggregate touch interaction into higher-level themes. To support this, our work builds on the touch dictionary [28] by providing data on the relationship between touch gestures. Thus, these clusters provide an initial framework for the analysis of social touch interactions with robots.

6   Conclusion and Future Work

Our work is a first step toward charting the relationship of touch gestures for HRI. We anticipate that our results can pave the way for future work on designing and evaluating robots that use touch as a non-verbal communication channel.

We see several avenues for extending this work. First, the relationship between the user-generated clusters for touch gestures and signals produced by the gestures on different touch sensors is an open question. A good touch sensor should be able to create distinct signals for gestures that are in different clusters according to user perception. Also, robots should be able to create distinct sensations when touching users with gestures in different clusters.

Second, future work can examine the impact of presentation modality on the semantic relationship of touch gestures. In this paper, we presented text labels for social touch gestures, following the common procedure in user studies of touch sensing for social robots. This approach helped abstract different styles of applying the gestures and study the user's mental representations of archetypal touch gestures. Future studies can examine how people group the touch gestures using videos or by applying robot touch on the user's body and compare the results to the clusters we found in this work. These studies should capture a wide range of touch styles (e.g., contact, force) for each gesture to avoid biasing the results to a small sample.

Finally, the meaning of touch can vary based on contexts, cultures, and individuals. As a first step, we examined if any generalizable patterns could be found about the relationships between various touch gestures. Our study population primarily consisted of individuals that grew up in the United States. Participants from other cultures often fell into cluster 3 and around the borders of cluster 2. It is unclear whether this result is due to their lack of familiarity with touch labels or the difference in their cultural background. Future studies can examine how the clusters of social touch gestures differ across cultures by translating the text labels into different languages. A larger dataset can also allow future work to look into individual differences in perception of social touch.

References

1. Abou Chahine, R., Kwon, D., Lim, C., Park, G., Seifi, H.: Vibrotactile similarity perception in crowdsourced and lab studies. In: Seifi, H., et al. (eds.) Haptics: Science, Technology, Applications, EuroHaptics 2022. LNCS, vol. 13235, pp. 255–263. Springer, Cham (2022). https://doi.org/10.1007/978-3-031-06249-0_29
2. Ammi, M., et al.: Haptic human-robot affective interaction in a handshaking social protocol. In: Proceedings of the ACM/IEEE International Conference on Human-Robot Interaction (HRI), pp. 263–270 (2015)
3. Burns, R.B., Lee, H., Seifi, H., Faulkner, R., Kuchenbecker, K.J.: Endowing a NAO robot with practical social-touch perception. Front. Roboti. AI 86 (2022)
4. Burns, R.B., Seifi, H., Lee, H., Kuchenbecker, K.J.: Getting in touch with children with autism: specialist guidelines for a touch-perceiving robot. Paladyn J. Behav. Robot. **12**(1), 115–135 (2021)
5. Choi, H., et al.: Deep learning classification of touch gestures using distributed normal and shear force. In: Proceedings of the IEEE/RSJ International Conference on Intelligent Robots and Systems (IROS), pp. 3659–3665 (2022)
6. Cramer, H.S., Kemper, N.A., Amin, A., Evers, V.: The effects of robot touch and proactive behaviour on perceptions of human-robot interactions. In: Proceedings of the ACM/IEEE International Conference on Human-Robot Interaction (HRI), pp. 275–276 (2009)

7. Fitter, N.T., Kuchenbecker, K.J.: Analyzing human high-fives to create an effective high-fiving robot. In: Proceedings of the ACM/IEEE International Conference on Human-Robot Interaction (HRI), pp. 156–157 (2014)
8. Hertenstein, M.J., Holmes, R., McCullough, M., Keltner, D.: The communication of emotion via touch. Emotion **9**(4), 566 (2009)
9. Hertenstein, M.J., Keltner, D.: Gender and the communication of emotion via touch. Sex Roles **64**, 70–80 (2011)
10. Huisman, G.: Social touch technology: a survey of haptic technology for social touch. IEEE Trans. Haptics **10**(3), 391–408 (2017)
11. Jung, M.M., Poel, M., Poppe, R., Heylen, D.K.: Automatic recognition of touch gestures in the corpus of social touch. J. Multim. User Interfaces **11**(1), 81–96 (2017)
12. Jung, M.M., Poppe, R., Poel, M., Heylen, D.K.: Touching the void-introducing cost: corpus of social touch. In: Proceedings of the International Conference on Multimodal Interaction (ICMI), pp. 120–127 (2014)
13. Li, B., et al.: Human robot activity classification based on accelerometer and gyroscope. In: Proceedings of the IEEE International Symposium on Robot and Human Interactive Communication (RO-MAN), pp. 423–424 (2016)
14. Murtagh, F., Contreras, P.: Algorithms for hierarchical clustering: an overview, II. Wiley Interdiscip. Rev. Data Mining Knowl. Discov. **7**(6), e1219 (2017)
15. Pelikan, H.R., Broth, M., Keevallik, L.: Are you sad, cozmo? How humans make sense of a home robot's emotion displays. In: Proceedings of the ACM/IEEE International Conference on Human-Robot Interaction (HRI), pp. 461–470 (2020)
16. Prasad, V., Koert, D., Stock-Homburg, R., Peters, J., Chalvatzaki, G.: Mild: multimodal interactive latent dynamics for learning human-robot interaction. In: Proceedings of the IEEE-RAS International Conference on Humanoid Robots (Humanoids), pp. 472–479 (2022)
17. Rognon, C., et al.: An online survey on the perception of mediated social touch interaction and device design. IEEE Trans. Haptics **15**(2), 372–381 (2022)
18. Russell, J.: A circumplex model of affect. J. Personal. Soc. Psychol. **39**, 1161–1178 (1980). https://doi.org/10.1037/h0077714
19. Salter, T., Dautenhahn, K., te Boekhorst, R.: Learning about natural human-robot interaction styles. Robot. Auton. Syst. **54**(2), 127–134 (2006)
20. Salter, T., Michaud, F., Létourneau, D., Lee, D., Werry, I.P.: Using proprioceptive sensors for categorizing human-robot interactions. In: Proceedings of the ACM/IEEE International Conference on Human-Robot Interaction (HRI), pp. 105–112 (2007)
21. Seifi, H., Vasquez, S.A., Kim, H., Fazli, P.: First-hand impressions: charting and predicting user impressions of robot hands. ACM Trans. Hum. Robot Interact. (2023)
22. Ternes, D., MacLean, K.E.: Designing large sets of haptic icons with rhythm. In: Ferre, M. (ed.) EuroHaptics 2008. LNCS, vol. 5024, pp. 199–208. Springer, Heidelberg (2008). https://doi.org/10.1007/978-3-540-69057-3_24
23. Teyssier, M., Bailly, G., Pelachaud, C., Lecolinet, E.: Conveying emotions through device-initiated touch. IEEE Trans. Affect. Comput. (2020)
24. Teyssier, M., Parilusyan, B., Roudaut, A., Steimle, J.: Human-like artificial skin sensor for physical human-robot interaction. In: Proceedings of the IEEE International Conference on Robotics and Automation (ICRA), pp. 3626–3633. IEEE (2021)
25. Tsogo, L., Masson, M., Bardot, A.: Multidimensional scaling methods for many-object sets: a review. Multivar. Behav. Res. **35**(3), 307–319 (2000)

26. Wang, Z., Giannopoulos, E., Slater, M., Peer, A.: Handshake: realistic human-robot interaction in haptic enhanced virtual reality. Presence **20**(4), 371–392 (2011)
27. Xu, S., Xu, C., McIntyre, S., Olausson, H., Gerling, G.J.: Subtle contact nuances in the delivery of human-to-human touch distinguish emotional sentiment. IEEE Trans. Haptics **15**(1), 97–102 (2021)
28. Yohanan, S., MacLean, K.E.: The role of affective touch in human-robot interaction: human intent and expectations in touching the haptic creature. Int. J. Soc. Robot. **4**(2), 163–180 (2012)

Attainable Digital Embodied Storytelling Using State of the Art Tools, and a Little Touch

Unai Zabala[1], Alexander Diez[1], Igor Rodriguez[1], Agnese Augello[2], and Elena Lazkano[1(✉)]

[1] Computer Sciences and Artificial Intelligence, University of Basque Country (UPV/EHU), Manuel Lardizabal 1, 20018 Donostia, Spain
{unai.zabalac,e.lazkano}@ehu.eus
[2] Institute for High Performance Computing and Networking (ICAR-CNR), Via Ugo La Malfa, 153, 90146 Palermo, Italy

Abstract. How closely can a robot capable of generating non-verbal behavior approximate a human narrator? What are the missing features that limit the naturalness and expressiveness of the robot as a storyteller? In this paper we explore this topic by identifying the key aspects to effectively convey the content of a story and therefore by analysing appropriate methodologies and tools that allow to automatically enrich the expressiveness of the generated behavior. Lastly, we will explore some modifications to weigh up the gap between robot and human-like behavior. Demonstration videos reveal that albeit the communicative capabilities of the robot are appropriate, there is still room for improvement.

Keywords: storytelling robot · sentiment analysis · gesture generation · social robot

1 Introduction

The challenge of developing embodied storytelling agents itself is not new, it emerged almost two decades ago when robots with human traits and semi-natural talking abilities were rare. Since then, digital or embodied storytelling has been used for different uses ranging from pure entertainment [18] to more sophisticated applications such as children's therapy [21] or education [3,8]. Even some educational tools (Codi[1], TROBO[2]) have been commercialized as storytelling robots. However, storytelling robots do not show yet the communication expression we humans do.

Storytelling, independently of its goal, requires to emphasize expressiveness as the listener/public is intended to merge with the story and enter the imaginary world woven by the narrator. As highlighted in [9], the use of a robot

---

[1] https://www.pillarlearning.com/products/codi.
[2] https://www.kickstarter.com/projects/trobo/trobo-the-storytelling-robot/.

© The Author(s), under exclusive license to Springer Nature Singapore Pte Ltd. 2024
A. Al. Ali et al. (Eds.): ICSR 2023, LNAI 14453, pp. 68–79, 2024.
https://doi.org/10.1007/978-981-99-8715-3_7

in storytelling only has meaning when its communicative affordance is tapped. In short, a social robot in the role of a storyteller needs to be persuasive and requires performing or acting capabilities accordingly without loose of spontaneity. Unfortunately, as the literature reveals, the dramatic flair is not enough, we hitherto have not been able to reproduce the touch of intrigue, drama and mystery required [28].

In this work we confront the challenge of automatically generating a robot behavior closer to a human storyteller. Our test bed is the robot Pepper, a humanoid robot with restricted face expressiveness. This forces us to limit the behavioral aspects identified by Appel et al. in [1] (gestures, contextual head movements, eye gaze, and different voices) to the following two essential components to be materialized using contemporaneous software tools:

1. Expressive voice(s): It is essential the use of an emotional Text-to-Speech (TTS) tool that allows to annotate the text, emphasizing and changing the voice and modulating the generated audio accordingly.
2. Body gesturing: Voice must be accompanied by proper body gesturing. There is no doubt that embodied storytelling can take huge profit of the advances in the area of co-speech gesture generation. However, as highlighted in [20], the use of deep learning approaches has permitted a step forward in perceived naturalness, but also a step backwards in terms of communicative efficacy. We focus on the modulation of a hybrid body gesture generation module by the decisions of an emotion extraction system. We propose a hybrid gesture generation approach that combines an state of the art data-driven gesture generation [5] with a rule-based gesture insertion mechanism to emphasize the link between the body language and the spoken text.

Social robots in general and storyteller robots in particular must reflect emotions. Voice intonation as well as body posture are affected by the emotional state. To ensure this, we use the system proposed in [2] to automatically extract the proper emotion to tag specific pieces of the input text and to modulate the general behavior accordingly.

We show how the automatically produced storytelling behavior albeit appropriate, is far from being expressive enough. Still, a much more attractive behavior can be obtained by modifying some of the decisions taken by the automatic system. As a result, the credibility of the robot in its role is increased. This last step is done using a specially designed GUI. The results allows to visualize the attainable dramatization level, adding a little touch to the decisions made by current state of the art tools, and outlining the features that are still missing.

2   Related Work

As mentioned before, to enhance robots as storytellers, behavioral aspects such as gestures, contextual head movements, eye gaze, and different voices need to be considered [1]. Moreover, the fit of non-verbal displays of emotions and verbal information influences comprehension and prevents misunderstandings. Some of these behavioral aspects have been studied in the literature, many of them focusing mainly on voice features and facial expression or head movements, fewer studies pay attention to the importance of the body gesturing during storytelling. In any case, the behavioral aspects to be evaluated are mostly handcrafted.

In the early years, Mutlu et al. [17] evaluated the importance of a human-like gaze behavior and combined it with six predefined gestures to allow Honda's Asimo robot to act as an soryteller. Chella et al. presented an emotional story-teller Peoplebot robot, where the intonation of the robot's voice was modified according to the piece of the story [6]. In [14] also the emotional expressiveness of the TEGA robot's speech was explored, together with its effect in vocabulary learning by children. In a more recent work, Carolis et al. investigated the preferences of an audience of children regarding a (Pepper) storytelling robot by comparing a human versus a robotic voice. The robotic one received a higher rate according to their experiment described in [4]. Finally, Ham eta al. [11] studied how the combination of gazing and gesturing increases the persuasive power of a NAO robot acting as a storyteller qualifying head movements as gaze movements and limiting the body motion to a set of 21 gestures.

Focusing on body expression, gesturing is a crucial element of human non-verbal communication, and includes co-speech gestures by facilitating language comprehension. People use co-speech gestures to emphasize speech, communicate semantic information, draw the attention to others, or better describe and shape the concepts they are talking about [13]. Back to storytelling robots, in [29] the authors emphasize the need for a specific body gesturing in such tools and use a database of more than 500 gestural annotations to enact tales performed by two NAO robots.

Definitely, gestures must be modulated according to the story mood [30]. Xu et al. found that higher ratings were given by participants to a storytelling NAO robot if there was congruence between story mood and the robot's gestures. A set of parameterized co-verbal gestures was used to express mood. The gestures were manually selected for the sentences of the stories and manually aligned with the words in the sentences. In a similar vein, Paradeda et al. [22] found that there are significant differences between the setup of voice intonation and posture as well as an acceptable assertive robot's configuration using a combination of posture, pitch and speech rate. Tests were performed using EMYS robotic head[3]. Hendrik et al. [25] modeled a Reeti robot that tells a story in an exciting manner using emotional facial expressions and using only head movements. Haru proposed a personalized storytelling experience by adapting, in a preliminary attempt, the narrative style (voice pitch, emotion and action) [26].

We found some attempts to automatically select [23] or adapt [27] the stories to the user or public [10] or even to complete the stories in a collaborative storytelling context [19]. Nonetheless, as far as we know, there is no reference to the automatic behavior generation applied to embodied storytelling as the one described here.

---

[3] https://ww.emys.co.

3   Storytelling Behavior Generation System

The starting point to generate the non-verbal behavior that accompanies the speech of the robot is a story in raw text format. The core of the proposed approach can be summarized in three main steps: (1) sentence annotation, (2) voice generation and processing, (3) gesture generation.

In the first step, the raw text of the story is split into sentences, and each sentence is then processed with two goals. On the one hand, the lemmas of each word in the sentence are extracted. On the other hand, the prevailing emotion in each of the sentences is recognized, as well as its intensity. The output of this step is twofold: an emotionally annotated sentence; and the lemmatized sentence.

In the second step, the voice annotations made in the previous phase are used to generate the voice audio using an expressive TTS. Subsequently, the audio is processed using an automatic speech recognition (ASR) tool to extract the timestamps for each word in the sentence.

Finally, the gesture generation system produces the synchronized co-speech gestures using a generative model that takes as input the audio and the raw text of the story.

Next subsections describe those steps more in depth.

3.1   Expressive TTS

As it is remarked in [24], voice acting can improve narrative presence, making the robot more interesting. Thus, we need an expressive TTS tool. Two alternatives were considered: NVIDIA Riva TTS[4] and Google TTS cloud service[5]

Both tools support portions of Speech Synthesis Markup Language (SSML), allowing you to emphasize and to adjust pitch, rate, volume and pronunciation of the generated audio output. RIVA can be run locally. However, it requires GPU hardware and a not so easy installation process. Google's cloud service, on the other hand, offers for free only a limited number of bytes. Notwithstanding, the cloud option offers the choice to insert silences and to embed other audio chunks (for instance to insert onomatopoeic sounds), both vital properties in our context. Those features, together with the needless of specific hardware tipped the balance in favour of Google's TTS.

3.2   Gesture Generation

In a previous approach [31] a GAN based beat gesture generation module was used as the backbone of the gesturing system. The GAN was trained in the robot joint space obtained after transforming data collected while recording people using OpenPose-based motion capturing system. As this beat gesturing module did not take into account the audio itself (only its duration), the synchronization was not good enough.

---

[4] https://docs.nvidia.com/deeplearning/riva/user-guide/docs/tts/tts-overview.html.
[5] https://cloud.google.com/text-to-speech.

In the current approach, the model used to generate gestures is the state of the art co-speech gesture generation model presented in [5]. The model uses the Tacotron2 architecture as a backbone, which was originally designed for speech synthesis, with some adjustments to the architecture and training paradigm to perform co-speech gesture generation. The model takes as input the audio file, the transcription of that file and the identity of the speaker, represented by a number (in training samples this number corresponds to the actual speaker and in inference, any speaker identity can be used) and it outputs a bvh[6] file of the joint representations of the head, neck, spine, legs, hips and arms, but not of the hands. The audio processing uses mel-spectrograms, MFCCs and prosodies, all of which are normalized and concatenated before being passed to the model. The text features are extracted from the transcription and converted into embeddings, to which two additional dimensions are added to represent whether the corresponding audio frame is silent and whether any laughter is present. The audio and text features are concatenated by aligning them frame by frame and fed into the model.

To translate the gestures to the robot's configuration space, we extract the angles of the relevant joints in each frame of the bvh file, then separately translate the angles of the head, hips, right arm and left arm into valid robot inputs and concatenate those inputs in the original frame order. Although most information is preserved in the aforementioned translation, due to slow motor motion, only every third frame of the bvh file is used to calculate the input for the robot. Furthermore, the robot has fewer degrees of freedom in its movement than the digital avatar (especially in the shoulder movement), thus some of the smaller details and nuances of the original motion are lost. Thankfully, it is not a very big loss, as the robot is not capable of executing such small movements anyway.

3.3 Mapping Words to Expression

To annotate the emotional content of the sentences we take the same approach as in [2]. The Synesketch tool [15] tags each sentence by giving the intensity (certainty) of each of the Ekman's basic emotions [7]: disgust, anger, fear, sadness, surprise and happiness. It computes numerical vectors representing emotional weights for each emotional category, indicating the intensity of emotions. These vectors are then utilized to identify the predominant emotional type (the one with the highest weight) and ascertain the overall emotional valence of a sentence (whether it is positive, negative, or neutral). When the vector approaches zero or is exactly zero, the sentence is considered emotionally neutral.

Due to the difficulties of showing subtle features with Pepper, we cluster the emotions into three sets: disgust, anger and fear are clustered as sadness; surprise is jointed with happiness; and neutral expression is chosen when no clear emotion is distinguished.

The obtained emotion must be expressed by the robot. Certainly, voice's tone, gesture and face display must be linked. Disengagements can occur if emotion

---

[6] BioVision Hierarchy (BVH) is a file format used for storing motion capture data.

is not coherent among them resulting in a bizarre robot behavior. Accordingly, three behavioral properties are affected by the emotion as explained here on.

How Is the Emotion Displayed in the Voice? As mentioned before in Sect. 3.1, Google's TTS supports the SSML to provide more advanced control over the generated speech. The <prosody> tag in SSML allows modification of the speech prosody, which refers to variations in pitch, rate, and volume that add expressiveness and naturalness to the synthesized voice: *pitch*, specifies the change in pitch from the baseline, where 0 means no change, and positive or negative values in semitones indicate raising or lowering the pitch, respectively; *rate*, controls the speaking rate of the text. A value of 100 represents the default rate percent, while values greater than 100 increase the speed, and values less than 100 decrease it; and *volume*, modifies the loudness of the speech. A value of 0 represents the default volume in decibels (dB), while values greater than 0 increase the volume, and values less than 0 decrease it.

To determine the values of the mentioned attributes, we map the intensity value obtained from Synesketch to the range defined for each attribute's maximum and minimum values. For Pitch (P) and rate (R) of complete sentences are adjusted according to Eq. 1.

$$P = I_{emotion} * (P_{max} - P_{min}) + P_{min}$$
$$R = I_{emotion} * (R_{max} - R_{min}) + R_{min} \tag{1}$$

How Is the Emotion Displayed in the Body? Likewise, the emotion is transferred to the pitch angles (θ) of both, the head and the hip (2). A higher intensity results in the straighter the hips and the more upright the head. On the other hand, a negative intensity leads to downward lean in both the hip and the head.

$$\theta_{head} = I_{emotion} * (\theta_{head_{max}} - \theta_{head_{min}}) + \theta_{head_{min}}$$
$$\theta_{hip} = I_{emotion} * (\theta_{hip_{max}} - \theta_{hip_{min}}) + \theta_{hip_{min}} \tag{2}$$

How Is the Emotion Expressed in the Face? Pepper is a robot that lacks eyebrows and mouth, but it includes several color LEDs in the eyes that can be used to show facial features.

Just like in the two aforementioned behavioral properties, the conversion from intensity into facial expression is done by changing the color of the eye LEDs. We adopt the same color configuration employed in the previous work ([31]). Sadness is displayed by a dark blue-greenish color, happiness is displayed by a yellow color, and neutral by a light blue-white color.

3.4   Robot Behavior

Two stories have been borrowed from Jara Sanchis[7], a professional storyteller with a YouTube channel where she narrates children's books: *The Enchanted Forest*, a tale with only a narrator character; and *The Sad Tree*, a story with multiple characters and more different emotional up and downs during the narration[8].

The performance of the robot as a storyteller can be appreciated in the following two videos. The first video[9] corresponds to the performance of the *The Enchanted Forest* story, while the second one[10] corresponds to *The Sad Tree*.

Both videos show a nice but inhibited behavior. It can be appreciated the effect of the expressive audio and how the rate and the pitch varies according to the emotion, reflected in the eyes as well. The intonation affects whole sentences, though there are no emphasized words. Emotion also affects the body posture coherently. However, the major issue is the grossly insufficient gesturing of the robot. It completely misses those raving gestures storytelling requires.

4   Adding Meaningful Gestures

According to [12] all kind of gestures have positive impact in the perception of the robot's performance as a narrator but deictic gestures significantly impact information recall. Neither deictic gestures nor metaphoric or iconic ones are noticeable in the output of the gesture generation system. None of the identities present in the training database [16] corresponds to a storyteller and the output gestures are rather restrained.

In order to enrich the communicative affordance, we complement the Tacotron2 gesture generation module with a semantic related gesture insertion system. The insertion process is performed as in [31]. Basically, we apply a rule-based approach. The lemmas extracted from each sentence are searched in a keyword database and associated gestures are selected using a probabilistic approach. The insertion point of a new movement is calculated obtaining the timestamps of the words by means of Whisper[11], an Automatic Speech Recognition (ASR) system. The new gesture replaces the automatically generated poses for the required duration.

The overall architecture of the behavior generation system is shown in Fig. 1.

---

[7] www.jaracuentacuentos.com.
[8] The different voices have been manually annotated in the SSML file.
[9] The Enchanted Forest Tacotron+Emotions: *https://youtu.be/J4iHMcz_ODg*.
[10] The Sad Tree Tacotron+Emotions: *https://youtu.be/CDirRQ8ccoo*.
[11] https://openai.com/research/whisper.

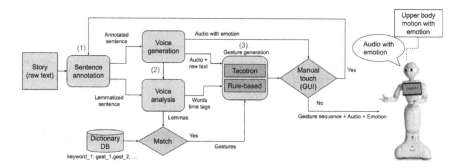

Fig. 1. The global system architecture

4.1   Robot Behavior

The newly generated behavior of the robot can be observed in the subsequent videos. The first video[12] corresponds to the performance of the *The Enchanted Forest* story, while the second one[13] corresponds to *The Sad Tree*.

The improved eloquence helps to better communicate the plot. The rule-based gestures associated to the meaning drive Pepper to become a more credible character. However, some issues arise. On the one hand, synchronization is not so good for large gestures, delays can be appreciated. As a consequence, the meaning of some gestures is lost. On the other hand, lemmatization shows some flaws. A tendency to reproduce gestures in non desirable moments comes out. Correct association between lemmas and gestures gets more complex the more the gestures present in the DB, but this is a requirement if a general system able to reproduce many tales is aimed.

5   The Little Touch

We have made an attempt to improve the behavior automatically produced by giving some brush-strokes to the tales. More precisely:

- The SSML files have been extra annotated for dramatization by adding silences and emphasizing some words by observing the original videos of Jara Sanchis.
- A few onomatopoeia have been added by inserting specific audios.
- Some of the decisions taken by the rule-based system according to lemmas have been corrected to remove not so coherent movements.
- The starting point (word) of some of the lemma-based gestures has been changed, improving synchronization.

---

[12] The Enchanted Forest Hybrid+Emotions: *https://youtu.be/ZVIPQV1ZcpQ*.
[13] The Sad Tree Hybrid+Emotions: *https://youtu.be/VyUY-jp2CFM*.

All this adjustments can me made through the GUI specifically designed for the storytelling context. Figure 2 shows an example of several sentences tagged using Synesketch. Each row corresponds to a sentence, together with its mapped pitch and rate values (green box). The columns in the red box show the detected emotion for the sentence and the corresponding led color. All the items displayed are editable allowing to apply the "magic" touch.

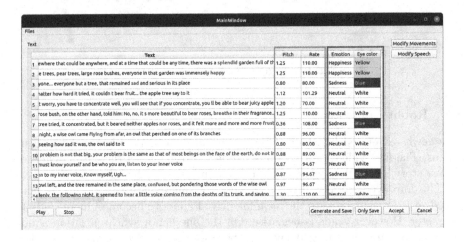

Fig. 2. Result of the interaction with Synesketch

5.1 Robot Behavior

The reader can see through the provided videos[14],[15] that the robot shows a rich performance for the two stories. The touch allows for a step forward in the reproduction of a thriving behavior by the robot. At a glance we are getting closer to the reference human model, but the gap is still there.

6 Conclusions and Further Work

The work described in this paper is an attempt to develop a full storytelling robot behavior generation system. We have used several state of the art tools to test what they can yield. Through manually adjustments of certain features, we obtained an improved and refined robot performance. However, we are still far from a fully automatic storytelling robot behavior generation system. There are some issues that, once solved, will enhance the system's output.

Regarding the audio generation, some common voice features, such as whispers are difficult to reproduce. Moreover, automatically adjusting the pitch can

---

[14] The Enchanted Forest Touch+Emotions: *https://youtu.be/zSvogw0OJT0*.
[15] The Sad Tree Touch+Emotions: *https://youtu.be/8hPEa_Ls0vY*.

confuse the audience since it is easy to fall in a completely different voice. Additionally, a method to automatize the use of multiple voices should be considered. Finally, concatenating audios to insert onomatopoeia is not the best option. Onomatopoeia are not detected by word parsers and thus, are ignored during any posterior analysis. This prevents to associate specific gestures with sounds.

Concerning the body language, hands are vital in message transmission and communication. The original database contains hand information but the Tacotron2 model does not take them into account. Hand motion should be integrated into the gesture generation system. Retraining the gesture generator with a specific database obtained from storytelling videos but adapted to include hands will be the next step.

We have not made any public performance yet since only a subjective questionnaire based evaluation would not bring any light at this development state. Once a completely automatic storytelling behavior generation is assessed, the "touched" behavior presented here will be used ground truth and make a comparison among the alternatives by exposing the robot to the public.

Acknowledgment. This work has been partially supported by the Basque Government, under Grant number IT1427-22; the Spanish Ministry of Science (MCIU), the State Research Agency (AEI), the European Regional Development Fund (FEDER) under Grant number PID2021-122402OBC21 (MCIU/AEI/FEDER, UE). Author Zabala has received a PREDOKBERRI research Grant from Basque Government.

References

1. Appel, M., Lugrin, B., Kühle, M., Heindl, C.: The emotional robotic storyteller: on the influence of affect congruency on narrative transportation, robot perception, and persuasion. Comput. Hum. Behav. **120**, 106749 (2021). https://doi.org/10.1016/j.chb.2021.106749
2. Augello, A., Pilato, G.: An annotated corpus of stories and gestures for a robotic storyteller. In: Third IEEE International Conference on Robotic Computing (IRC), pp. 630–635 (2019). https://doi.org/10.1109/IRC.2019.00127
3. Bravo, F.A., Hurtado, J.A., González, E.: Using robots with storytelling and drama activities in science education. Educ. Sci. **11**(7) (2021). https://doi.org/10.3390/educsci11070329
4. Carolis, B., D'Errico, F., Rossano, V.: Pepper as a Storyteller: Exploring the Effect of Human vs. Robot Voice on Children's Emotional Experience, pp. 471–480. Springer, Cham (2021). https://doi.org/10.1007/978-3-030-85616-8-27
5. Chang, C.J., Zhang, S., Kapadia, M.: The IVI lab entry to the Genea challenge 2022 - a tacotron2 based method for co-speech gesture generation with locality-constraint attention mechanism. In: Proceedings of the 2022 International Conference on Multimodal Interaction (ICMI 2022), pp. 784–789. Association for Computing Machinery, New York (2022). https://doi.org/10.1145/3536221.3558060
6. Chella, A., Barone, R.E., Pilato, G., Sorbello, R.: An emotional storyteller robot. In: AAAI Spring Symposium (2008)
7. Ekman, P.: Are there basic emotions? Psychol. Rev. **99**(3), 550–553 (1992). https://doi.org/10.1037/0033-295X.99.3.550

8. Glanz, I., Weksler, M., Karpas, E., Horowitz-Kraus, T.: Robofriend: An Adpative Storytelling Robotic Teddy Bear - Technical Report. arXiv e-prints arXiv:2301.01576 (2023). https://doi.org/10.48550/arXiv.2301.01576

9. Gomez, R., et al.: Exploring affective storytelling with an embodied agent. In: 30th IEEE International Conference on Robot and Human Interactive Communication (RO-MAN), pp. 1249–1255 (2021). https://doi.org/10.1109/RO-MAN50785.2021.9515323

10. Gray, C., et al.: This bot knows what i'm talking about! human-inspired laughter classification methods for adaptive robotic comedians. In: 31st IEEE International Conference on Robot and Human Interactive Communication (RO-MAN), pp. 1007–1014 (2022). https://doi.org/10.1109/RO-MAN53752.2022.9900634

11. Ham, J., Cuijpers, R.H., Cabibihan, J.J.: Combining robotic persuasive strategies: the persuasive power of a storytelling robot that uses gazing and gestures. Int. J. Soc. Robot. **7**, 479–487 (2015)

12. Huang, C.M., Mutlu, B.: Modeling and evaluating narrative gestures for humanlike robots. In: Robotics: Science and Systems (2013)

13. Kendon, A.: Gesture: Visible Action as Utterance. Cambridge University Press (2004)

14. Kory Westlund, J., et al.: Flat vs. expressive storytelling: young children's learning and retention of a social robot's narrative. Front. Hum. Neurosci. **11** (2017). https://doi.org/10.3389/fnhum.2017.00295

15. Krcadinac, U., Pasquier, P., Jovanovic, J., Devedzic, V.: Synesketch: an open source library for sentence-based emotion recognition. IEEE Trans. Affect. Comput. **4**(3), 312–325 (2013). https://doi.org/10.1109/T-AFFC.2013.18

16. Lee, G., Deng, Z., Ma, S., Shiratori, T., Srinivasa, S., Sheikh, Y.: Talking with hands 16.2m: a large-scale dataset of synchronized body-finger motion and audio for conversational motion analysis and synthesis. In: 2019 IEEE/CVF International Conference on Computer Vision (ICCV), pp. 763–772 (2019). https://doi.org/10.1109/ICCV.2019.00085

17. Mutlu, B., Forlizzi, J., Hodgins, J.K.: A storytelling robot: modeling and evaluation of human-like gaze behavior. In: 2006 6th IEEE-RAS International Conference on Humanoid Robots, pp. 518–523 (2006)

18. Nichols, E., Gao, L., Vasylkiv, Y., Gomez, R.: Collaborative storytelling with social robots. In: IEEE/RSJ International Conference on Intelligent Robots and Systems (IROS), pp. 1903–1910 (2021). https://doi.org/10.1109/IROS51168.2021.9636409

19. Nichols, E., Szapiro, D., Vasylkiv, Y., Gomez, R.: I can't believe that happened! : exploring expressivity in collaborative storytelling with the tabletop robot haru. In: 31st IEEE International Conference on Robot and Human Interactive Communication (RO-MAN), pp. 59–59 (2022). https://doi.org/10.1109/RO-MAN53752.2022.9900606

20. Nyatsanga, S., Kucherenko, T., Ahuja, C., Henter, G.E., Neff, M.: A comprehensive review of data-driven co-speech gesture generation. Comput. Graph. Forum (2023). https://doi.org/10.1111/cgf.14776

21. Ozaeta, L., Perez, I., Rekalde, I.: Interactive storytelling for the retelling of autobiographical memory in children: a social robotics approach. Glob. J. Inf. Technol. Emerg. Technol. **12**, 43–50 (2022). https://doi.org/10.18844/gjit.v12i1.7111

22. Paradeda, R., Ferreira, M.J., Martinho, C., Paiva, A.: Communicating assertiveness in robotic storytellers. In: Rouse, R., Koenitz, H., Haahr, M. (eds.) ICIDS 2018. LNCS, vol. 11318, pp. 442–452. Springer, Cham (2018). https://doi.org/10.1007/978-3-030-04028-4_51

23. Park, H.W., Grover, I., Spaulding, S., Gomez, L., Breazeal, C.: A model-free affective reinforcement learning approach to personalization of an autonomous social robot companion for early literacy education. In: Proceedings of the Thirty-Third AAAI Conference on Artificial Intelligence and Thirty-First Innovative Applications of Artificial Intelligence Conference and Ninth AAAI Symposium on Educational Advances in Artificial Intelligence (AAAI 2019/IAAI2019/EAAI2019). AAAI Press (2019). https://doi.org/10.1609/aaai.v33i01.3301687
24. Striepe, H., Donnermann, M., Lein, M., Lugrin, B.: Modeling and evaluating emotion, contextual head movement and voices for a social robot storyteller. Int. J. Soc. Robot. **13**(3), 441–457 (2019). https://doi.org/10.1007/s12369-019-00570-7
25. Striepe, H., Donnermann, M., Lein, M., Lugrin, B.: Modeling and evaluating emotion, contextual head movement and voices for a social robot storyteller. Int. J. Soc. Robot. **13**(3), 441–457 (2019). https://doi.org/10.1007/s12369-019-00570-7
26. Wang, H., et al.: Personalized storytelling with social robot Haru. In: Cavallo, F., et al. (eds.) Social Robotics: 14th International Conference, ICSR 2022, Florence, 13–16 December 2022, Proceedings, Part II, pp. 439–451. Springer, Cham (2022). https://doi.org/10.1007/978-3-031-24670-8_39
27. Weber, K., Ritschel, H., Aslan, I., Lingenfelser, F., André, E.: How to shape the humor of a robot - social behavior adaptation based on reinforcement learning. In: Proceedings of the 20th ACM International Conference on Multimodal Interaction (ICMI 2018), pp. 154–162. Association for Computing Machinery, New York (2018). https://doi.org/10.1145/3242969.3242976
28. Wicke, P., Veale, T.: Storytelling by a show of hands: a framework for interactive embodied storytelling in robotic agents. In: AISB - Artificial Intelligence and Simulated Behavior (2018)
29. Wicke, P., Veale, T.: The show must go on: on the use of embodiment, space and gesture in computational storytelling. N. Gener. Comput. **38**(4), 565–592 (2020). https://doi.org/10.1007/s00354-020-00106-y
30. Xu, J., Broekens, J., Hindriks, K., Neerincx, M.A.: Effects of a robotic storyteller's moody gestures on storytelling perception. In: International Conference on Affective Computing and Intelligent Interaction (ACII), pp. 449–455 (2015). https://doi.org/10.1109/ACII.2015.7344609
31. Zabala, U., Rodriguez, I., Lazkano, E.: Towards an automatic generation of natural gestures for a storyteller robot. In: 31st IEEE International Conference on Robot and Human Interactive Communication (RO-MAN), pp. 1209–1215 (2022). https://doi.org/10.1109/RO-MAN53752.2022.9900532

GERT: Transformers for Co-speech Gesture Prediction in Social Robots

Javier Sevilla-Salcedo[(✉)] [ID], Enrique Fernández-Rodicio [ID],
José Carlos Castillo [ID], Álvaro Castro-González [ID], and Miguel A. Salichs [ID]

RoboticsLab, Universidad Carlos III de Madrid, Madrid, Spain
{jasevill,enrifern,jocastil,acgonzal,salichs}@ing.uc3m.es

Abstract. Social robots are becoming an important part of our society and should be recognised as viable interaction partners, which include being perceived as i) animate beings and ii) capable of establishing natural interactions with the user. One method of achieving both objectives is allowing the robot to perform gestures autonomously, which can become problematic when those gestures have to accompany verbal messages. If the robot uses predefined gestures, an issue that needs solving is selecting the most appropriate expression given the robot's speech. In this work, we propose three transformer-based models called GERT, which stands for Gesture-Enhanced Robotics Transformer, that predict the co-speech gestures that better match the robot's utterances. We have compared the performance of the three models of different sizes to prove their usability in the gesture prediction task and the trade-off between size and performance. The results show that all three models achieve satisfactory performance (F-score between 0.78 and 0.86).

Keywords: Language Models · Social Robots · Deep Learning · Gesture Prediction · Multi-modal Interaction · Human-Robot Interaction

1 Introduction and Background

In recent years, robots have been integrated into multiple aspects of society and are now starting to be involved in tasks that include interacting with humans. For this to be possible, the robot should be seen as an appropriate interaction partner [21], and a way to achieve this is to make the robot have a lively appearance [3]. This can be done by giving it the ability to perform expressions[1] that seem intentional [22]. But this task can be difficult if the expressions accompany verbal messages (known as co-speech gestures), as the verbal and non-verbal

---

[1] In this work, we will use both expression and gesture indistinctively for any coherent combination of multimodal information aimed at achieving a particular communicative goal.

J. Sevilla-Salcedo and E. Fernández-Rodicio—The first two authors contributed equally to this work.

components of the robot's expressiveness should seek to achieve the same communicative goal and be adequately synchronised so they form a cohesive message.

Works focused on endowing robots with the ability to use co-speech gestures tend to follow one of two approaches: (i) generating the gestures dynamically from scratch based on the robot's speech (audio and/or transcription) and other factors (e.g., the identity of the user) [31], or (ii) selecting expressions from library of predefined gestures [20]). Generating expressions from scratch endows the robot's expressiveness with a higher variability while freeing roboticists from the burden of handcrafting the expressions. However, dynamically generated gestures might be more generic and transmit less defined messages than handcrafted expressions. This is the approach we have followed, which we will refer to as *co-speech gesture prediction*.

The literature shows more work in co-speech gesture generation than in co-speech gesture prediction, particularly among authors that work with humanoid robots. Kucherenko et al. [10] used representation learning in a co-speech gesture generation system that follows an encoder-decoder architecture using a Denoising Autoencoder. Yoon et al. [31] followed a similar approach and relied on an encoder-decoder architecture with a soft attention mechanism to generate motions for a humanoid robot by learning from a dataset of TED talks. Ginosar et al. [9] developed a method based on a convolutional network for generating co-speech gestures considering the speaker's gesticulation style. Ahuja et al. [1] and More recently, Liang et al. [13] proposed a method for generating semantic-aware upper body co-speech gestures by decoupling semantic-relevant information from irrelevant cues (beat information) from the speech, correcting the semantic misalignment of gestures and decoding beat and semantic gestures based on the information recovered. Chang et al. [4] added a locality constraint attention mechanism to the Tacotron2 architecture so the model learns the alignment between gestures and speech from local audio features.

Although most researchers have focused on gesture generation, others have opted for developing gesture prediction approaches. Chiu et al. [5] proposed a method that uses Conditional Random Fields to predict labels that indicate if the robot's speech should have or not gestures attached and then uses Gaussian Process Latent Variable Models (GPLVMs) to generate the motions. The same authors presented a year later the Deep Conditional Neural Field [6], a joint learning of deep neural networks and a second-order linear chain temporal contingency for predicting gesture labels. More recently, Pérez-Mayos et al. [20] proposed three methods for synchronisation of co-speech gestures: mapping symbolic gestures to keywords in the text and beat gestures to the rest, mapping only beat gestures to pitch peaks, and a combination of both that matches beat gestures to pitch peaks until a keyword appears and a symbolic gesture is performed. Kucherenko et al. [11] presented a work that, while focusing on gesture generation, used a temporal Convolutional Neural Network to predict certain gesture properties, such as the gesture type or its phase.

Natural language understanding has shown significant progress, thanks to a novel model: the *transformer*. A transformer is a Deep Learning (DL) model architecture based on the idea of self-attention that learns to focus on certain elements in the input data depending on their self-significance. By relying on self-attention alone, they outperform other solutions that have used the attention mechanism before [29]. The use of transformers for developing language models has led to a significant change in what current systems can achieve, such as new search tools using generative models [16], the generation of high-quality images following prompts [12], the development of more advanced speech recognisers [2], or more recently, applications of natural language processing (NLP) to social robotics [15,27].

A problem that the growth of DL has brought is the increasing amount of resources needed for training these models, requiring in some cases entire server rooms and gigabytes of information. New techniques have been developed to overcome these limitations and improve the results provided by the models. Among those, the one that is of interest for this work is *Fine-tuning*. This technique seeks to adapt a pre-trained model with a large dataset for a more general task to a new task by taking its weights and adjusting them without losing their learned features while keeping the main layers of the model frozen [24]. This work used this technique to take a model trained to understand the structure of a language and adapt it to labelling sentences with co-speech expressions that would suit them.

Among other tasks, transformers have been used for what is known as *token classification*. In this task, an input text is divided into a sequence of individually classified tokens. Two examples of this task are Part-of-Speech (PoS) labelling, where each word in a sentence is labelled with its corresponding PoS tag (verb, noun, etc.), and Named-Entity Recognition, where known entities that appear in a text are labelled with a category like *location* or *organisation*. We have framed the gesture prediction problem as a token classification task, where the labels represent the gestures assigned to the robot's speech. Following this approach, in this work, we present GERT, which stands for Gesture-Enhanced Robotics Transformer, three co-speech gesture prediction models that rely on BERT architecture [8] to predict the sequence of gesture labels that should be associated with the robot's speech. Using a custom dataset, we created three models fine-tuned from different variations of BERT for this task, and compared their performances.

The proposed method has been designed for embodied agents that perform real-world tasks, something that requires an analysis of other factors besides the objective performance of the models. Because robots tend to have constrained computational power, we should also seek to optimise the use of the available resources. Furthermore, inference time is a significant constraint, as research suggests that responses given to a user during an interaction should be conveyed in less than two seconds for the message to retain its meaning [17]. Other authors set this limit at one second [28]. Therefore, we also evaluated the resources used by the method proposed and the prediction time.

The remainder of the manuscript is structured as follows. Section 2 describes the models used in this work and the process followed for crafting the dataset we used for fine-tuning the models. The architecture of the gesture prediction module and the training process is presented in Sect. 3. Section 4 shows the results of the fine-tuning process and presents a comparison between the three models tested. Finally, Sect. 5 closes this manuscript by presenting the main conclusions extracted from our work.

2   Materials and Methods

This section presents the basic concepts behind the development of GERT, our model for gesture prediction. This includes a description of the transformer-based baseline models that have been fine-tuned for gesture prediction, a description of the dataset used for the training process, and the method followed to generate it.

2.1   Baseline Models

In recent years, many different models and architectures have appeared in NLP, with various performance levels depending on the task to complete. Among the existing architectures, encoder-based models are best suited for tasks that involve extracting information from an input text, unlike auto-regressive, decoder-based models (ChatGPT, Llama, PaLM-E,...), which are better suited for generation tasks. Also, encoder-based models tend to outperform autoregressive models in terms of inference time, which is a key feature for applications that will involve human-robot interactions. Because of this, we have decided to use encoder models as baselines for the development of GERT. Among those, one widely used (and has served as the baseline for many recent models) is the Bidirectional Encoder Representations from Transformers (BERT) [8] model. Its architecture consists of a multi-layer bidirectional Transformer encoder module that uses as input representation either a single sentence or a pair of sentences (understanding a sentence as a span of contiguous text that can include more than one linguistic sentence). This allows the model to handle a wide range of tasks.

Although most language models usually have been unidirectional (i.e. the model only considers the context that precedes or follows the target section of the text being evaluated), BERT was designed to consider both sides of the context. This was done by selecting two simultaneous pre-training objectives: (i) predicting masked words in sentences (*masked language modelling*); and (ii) predicting if two input sentences appeared together in the original text or not (*next sentence prediction*). Thanks to being able to train deep bidirectional representations, BERT can be fine-tuned for several tasks by adding just one extra output layer. Given its performance, BERT has become a baseline in many NLP works. For this reason, we have selected it as the baseline for our base GERT model.

In addition to the *base* model, we have developed two other GERT models based on two well-known variations of the BERT model: DistilBERT (baseline for the GERT *large* model) and RoBERTa (baseline for the GERT *small* model). This will allow us to test the effect of a model's size on its performance in the gesture prediction task by selecting a smaller (DistilBERT) and larger (RoBERTa) model.

DistilBERT [26] is a variation that seeks to reduce the size of the base BERT model in order to enhance its speed. This process is based on *knowledge distillation*, a method for training a compact model to reproduce the behaviour of a larger model or models. While maintaining the same architecture, DistilBERT reduces the size of the base BERT model by 40%, while increasing its speed by 60% and retaining 97% of the base model's performance on the GLUE benchmark [30]. RoBERTa (Robustly Optimized BERT pre-training approach), on the other hand, is a variation born from the finding that the original BERT had been significantly under-trained [14]. The authors sought to correct this issue by proposing a new paradigm for training BERT models: increasing the amount of data, the batch size, the number of training epochsm, and the length of the sentences used for training the model, removing the *next sentence prediction* training objective, and using a dynamic masking pattern during training. The authors reported that RoBERTa improved the state-of-the-art results for four of the nine tasks in the GLUE benchmark and matched the results for SQuAD and ReAding Comprehension from Examinations (RACE) tasks.

2.2   Dataset

We opted to represent the gesture prediction problem as a token classification task for two main reasons: (i) it would allow us to know directly the points in a sentence where gestures would have to start, and (ii) it would allow our model to attach a sequence of gestures to a sentence. We generated a dataset from scratch to fine-tune the models selected for the gesture prediction task. Each instance contains an utterance (one or several sentences forming a cohesive paragraph), the same text split into tokens, and a list of labels representing the type of gesture that should be associated with each token. These labels follow the IOB format, where the prefix indicates if a label is the beginning of an entity (B-) or if it is inside (I-) or outside (O-) of it. Since all tokens have an associated gesture, we only use the B- and I- prefixes.

To create the dataset, we extracted sentences from the Cornell Movie Dialogs Corpus [7]. The list of possible gesture labels was empirically determined based on an evaluation of the library of predefined expressions that our robots could use. For this, an annotator observed the robot performing each expression, grouped together the expressions perceived to convey a similar communicative message, and assigned a single label to each group. This resulted in 21 different gesture classes, like *greet* where the robot performs the gesture of greeting the user, *self* where the robot would perform a reflexive gesture towards itself or *thanks* where the robot would show a gesture of thanks to the user.

The final version of the dataset is composed of 2600 instances. Training, validation, and test splits have been created using 60%, 20%, and 20% of the instances, respectively. Moreover, these subsets ensure that all gesture labels are proportionally distributed between the three splits (that is, the training split would contain 60% of any given label).

Although the division ensured equal distribution of each label among the splits, we observed that some labels appeared in a significantly larger amount

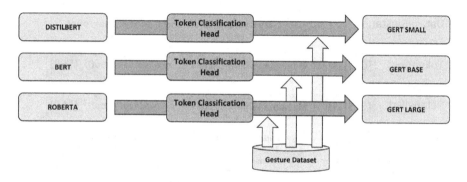

Fig. 1. Supervised Fine-Tuning Training Diagram of GERT variants.

of instances than others. This could induce the model to over-learn some labels while failing to recognise others, which significantly affects its performance. This was because some of the chosen labels applied to more generic situations while, in contrast, others were specific to specific situations that were connected to fewer sentences from the corpus. To evaluate the effect of this imbalance, we decided to prepare three versions of the dataset; on top of the original version that included the 21 original classes, two datasets were prepared by removing those classes that appeared in less than 100 instances for the first and 300 instances for the second, resulting on datasets with 9 and 5 classes, respectively. We did this by removing from the dataset any instance where one of the discarded classes was used. The 9-class dataset had 2195 instances, while the 5-class dataset had 1748. We have fine-tuned each model using all three datasets and evaluated how the number of classes affected the performance of these models. These datasets are publically available in HuggingFace[2]

3 Predicting Co-speech Gestures in the Robot Mini

In this section, we describe the approach followed to develop GERT and its integration into the social robot Mini software architecture.

3.1 The Gesture-Enhanced Robotic Transformer Model

As mentioned in Sect. 2, we have created three fine-tuned models from BERT-based models for gesture prediction in this work. We took versions for these models from HuggingFace (BERT base, RoBERTa, and DistilBERT) pre-trained on language modelling. We then adapted the original architecture by adding a new token classification head, as shown in Fig. 1 (a linear layer on top of the output of the hidden states). This layer will use the hidden states generated by the model to predict the classes assigned to each token.

---

[2] https://huggingface.co/qfrodicio.

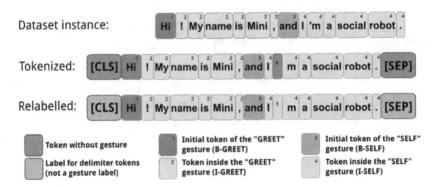

Fig. 2. Example of the co-speech gesture prediction dataset instances tokenizing and relabelling process.

Before training the models, we had to preprocess our dataset to correct two issues. First, the gesture labels we use are strings, while the models expect integer values, so we needed to map the list of labels to their integer values and apply this mapping to the entire dataset. Second, our models take a utterance and tokenize it internally. However, the tokens generated by the models might not match the original tokens from the dataset. We need to ensure that the number of tokens generated by the model matches the number of correct labels, while maintaining the label distribution of the original instance. For example, if one of the original tokens is divided into two tokens, we need to label both of them with the label of the original token. This preprocessing stage had to be applied to the dataset to fine-tune all three models tested. Figure 2 shows how the gesture label sequence is corrected for a dataset instance.

We have fine-tuned the three models using the preprocessed datasets, as shown in Fig. 1. We used the same hyperparameters for all three models, with a learning rate of $2 * 10^{-5}$, a weight decay of 0.01, and a batch size of 16. We fine-tuned the models for 10 epochs, and then kept the model from the best epoch, according to the model's validation loss. This happened around epochs 3–4 in most cases.

3.2   Gesture Prediction Module

For the inference phase, we have used the Transformers library provided by Huggingface to use our version of the model we want to deploy on the robot. The developed module receives the text to be classified as input, passes it through the model, post-processes the model's output to transform the prediction into the desired sequence, and returns this sequence.

An issue that DL models present is the high requirement of resources needed to run inferences. This is particularly pressing when working with embodied agents, as there are often more considerable hardware constraints. Also, because the gesture prediction model will be part of the pipeline for conveying messages

Fig. 3. Mini: a social robot developed for interacting with older adults with mild cognitive impairment.

to the user in every interaction the robot partakes in, we need to ensure that the inference times match the time constraints associated with human-human interactions. We deployed the model on an external server with specialised hardware to mitigate this problem. The robot sends the utterance to the server. Once the gesture sequence has been predicted, it is sent back to the robot.

3.3 Integration of the Gesture Prediction Module in a Real Robot

Mini is a social robot designed to assist older adults with mild cognitive impairment [25]. Mini has an anthropomorphic form (see Fig. 3), although its expressiveness capabilities are more constrained. The output interfaces of the robot include five degrees of freedom (two on the head, one on each shoulder, and another on the waist), OLED screens for eyes that can be used to display different gazes, a coloured LED heart that can change its colour, intensity, and heartbeat, a text-to-speech module, and a touch screen that can be used to display multimedia content, such as images and videos.

Regarding its software architecture, shown in Fig. 4, we have followed a modular approach using ROS [23]. In this architecture, skills are independent software modules that control specific tasks, such as reading the news to the user. A decision-making system controls which skill is active at any given time. Transversal to all skills, a series of modules provide all the robot's interaction capabilities, like extracting and processing information from the environment, interacting with users, and expressing a particular communicative message through its output interfaces. The Expression Manager module handles this last part, receiving requests to perform multimodal expressions. The gesture prediction module we have trained will interact with this last module. Whenever the Expression Manager receives a request to convey a message that contains only a verbal component, this is sent to the gesture prediction module running on the external

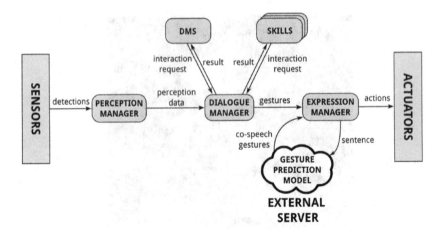

Fig. 4. Schematic vision of Mini's software architecture, with the external server where the gesture prediction model is deployed. Black arrows represent communication between ROS nodes, while red arrows represent the socket-based communication between the robot and the server (Color figure online)

server. Once the input text is processed, the predicted gestures are sent back to the Expression Manager, where they are loaded and executed. The following video shows the operation of the proposed system and a set of examples[3].

The server used in this work has been designed specifically for running deep learning models, and it has an Intel Core i9-10900K CPU running at 3.7 GHz, an NVIDIA GeForce RTX 3090 GPU, and 64 GB of RAM.

4   Evaluation

To evaluate the proposed co-speech prediction system, we have analysed three factors: (i) the metrics obtained during the fine-tuning process; (ii) the average inference time; and (iii) the number of resources (CPU and memory) that each model requires. In this Section, we first present the metrics that we have used for evaluating the performance of the models and then show the results obtained from the training and the deployment of the models in the robot.

4.1   Metrics

As mentioned in Sect. 2, we fine-tuned each model with the 21-class, 9-class, and 5-class datasets to see how this affects our results. The validation splits were used to evaluate the training process after each epoch, while the test splits were used to evaluate the models after the training. For this process, we decided to use the multi-label classification metrics provided by the Scikit-learn library [19]. These metrics measure each class's precision, recall, and F score and then compute

---

[3] https://youtu.be/lvQGwfu8J50.

Table 1. Results obtained from the training of the models. The best F-score for the three datasets have been highlighted in bold

Model	Classes	Precision	Recall	F1-Score
GERT Base	5	0.8578	0.8561	0.8533
	9	0.8365	0.8297	0.8281
	21	0.7954	0.7884	0.7827
GERT Small	5	0.8567	0.8555	0.855
	9	0.8144	0.8144	0.8095
	21	0.7925	0.7934	0.7875
GERT Large	5	0.8629	0.8628	**0.8619**
	9	0.8296	0.83	**0.8258**
	21	0.8189	0.8154	**0.8125**

average values. In particular, we have used the weighted average, where the number of class appearances weights each class's precision, recall, and F-score before computing the average value.

Although traditionally, the metric used for evaluating models for token classification is seqeval [18], the one we selected allows us to evaluate the partial matching of label sequences. This means that for a sequence that has seven tokens, if the first four should be labelled as *GREET* and the last three should be labelled *SELF*, a prediction where the labels are assigned to the first five and last two respectively would not result on an F-score, precision, and recall of 0 (like it would with seqeval), but instead on values that would better reflect how far or close from a perfect prediction our system is.

4.2   Model Evaluation

In this subsection, we present the model evaluation results, which can be seen in Table 1. When we compare the metrics obtained with the three models when fine-tuned with the same dataset, we observe that GERT Base and GERT Small present very similar results (for example, for the dataset with 21 classes, we can see that the accuracy of both models is 0.7884 and 0.7934, the precision is 0.7954 and 0.7925, the recall 0.7884 and 0.7934, and the F1 score is 0.7827 and 0.7875, respectively). We observed that the results also depended on the number of classes considered (GERT Base has a higher F1 score than GERT Small when fine-tuned with the dataset with nine classes, while the opposite happens on the other two tests). GERT Large, on the other hand, shows higher results for all metrics for all three datasets. When comparing the performance of each model depending on the dataset used, we observe that, as expected, all metrics improve when the amount of classes considered decreases.

4.3   Performance Evaluation

In addition to evaluating how well the different models can perform the gesture prediction task, we must also evaluate if they are usable in real-world situations.

Table 2. Resource usage, inference time, and complete time required for the complete process for all three models. The number in each cell represents the average value, plus-minus the standard deviation.

Model	GERT Base	GERT Small	GERT Large
Inference time (s)	0.0175 ± 0.0174	0.0132 ± 0.0153	0.0178 ± 0.0181
Total time (s)	0.1208 ± 0.1584	0.1272 ± 0.1836	0.1114 ± 0.1154
GPU usage (%)	1.6237 ± 0.7506	0.7332 ± 0.4209	1.7177 ± 0.6097
GPU memory (%)	3.1734 ± 0.0041	2.4407 ± 0.004	3.4247 ± 0.0038

As mentioned in the introduction, the number of resources used and the inference time are key features for a system designed to be integrated into an embodied agent with limited computational capabilities.

Table 2 shows the resource usage evaluation results. For this evaluation, we took the test split of the dataset (423 instances) and ran inferences for the sentences taken from those instances. The average length of these instances is 43.41 characters (with a standard deviation of 29.36. The shortest instances have 7 characters, while the longest have 229. The robot loads the instances and then sent to the external server where the gesture prediction models are deployed. During the trials, the robot and the server were connected to the internet via wifi. When the list of gesture tokens is obtained, the server sends it back to the robot. To evaluate possible delays due to the robot-server communication, we have measured the average time that passes since the sentence is sent to the server until the response is received (this is called total time in the table) and the inference time itself. We also evaluated the amount of GPU memory consumed (as a percentage of the available memory) and the percentage of time that at least one of the GPU's cores performs operations during the test. These resources have been measured at an interval of 0.5 s and averaged for the entire test duration.

Comparing the inference times, we see that GERT Base and GERT Large perform at a similar speed (inference times of 0.01753 and 0.01779, respectively). GERT Small, on the other hand, has a faster inference time (0.0132 s). Regardless, the tests show that the inference time is almost negligible compared to the latency introduced by the robot-server communication. GERT Large showed the best results, followed by GERT Base and then GERT Small (0.1114 vs 0.1208 vs 0.1272 s). While these results indicate that all three models are usable in real-world tasks (all of them abide by the *two-second rule*), in a few cases, the prediction time surpassed the two second threshold due to punctual connection issues between the server and the robot. This is a factor that will have to be taken into account when deploying the robot in real environments.

Regarding the number of resources needed for running the models, we did observe a difference between the three options, as GERT Small requires the least amount of GPU computing time and memory (0.73% and 2.44%, respectively), followed by GERT Base (1.62% and 3.17%, respectively) and then GERT Large

(1.72% and 3.42%, respectively). These results align with our expectations as GERT Small and GERT Large, as their names imply, represent the smallest and largest models, respectively.

Overall, the results obtained suggest the existance of a direct correlation between the size of the model and its performance on the task at hand, as well as the amount of resources consumed and the time required for generating inferences. While these results indicate that the best option would be to use GERT Large, if the hardware of the robotic platform allows it, they also show that for platforms with less resources, GERT Base and GERT Small can be solid alternatives.

5 Conclusions

In this work, we have created and evaluated GERT models' performance for predicting social robot co-speech gestures. Results showed that, while all three models achieved good metrics with an inference time that matches the time constraints in real-world interactions, the amount of computational power required for running these models limits their usability in platforms with hardware limitations.

The work described in this manuscript presents three main limitations. First, the objective metrics presented in this paper should be complemented with a subjective study that analyses how adding the predicted co-speech gestures affects users' perception of the robot. This is due to a sentence accompanied by the wrong gesture (as defined in the dataset) being objectively considered a prediction error; it could still be perceived as natural by the users and thus be regarded as a successful case. This study should also validate that the gestures used are being perceived by the user as we intended (this is, that the *greet* gesture is being perceived as a natural expression for greeting or saying goodbye to someone). Second, we identified an imbalance between the classes in the dataset because some were used in more common situations while others were more specific. Ideally, this should be corrected by adding more instances for the labels that appear less frequently to obtain a more balanced dataset. Finally, while the models presented in this manuscript can solve the issue of deciding which gestures should accompany the robot's speech, we still need a method that properly synchronises the verbal and non-verbal components. Both issues will be addressed in future works.

Acknowledgment. The research leading to these results has received funding from the grants PID2021-123941OA-I00, funded by MCIN/AEI/10.13039/501100011033 and by "ERDF A way of making Europe"; TED2021-132079B-I00 funded by MCIN/AEI/10.13039/501100011033 and by the European Union NextGenerationEU/PRTR. Mejora del nivel de madurez tecnologica del robot Mini (MeNiR) funded by MCIN/AEI/10.13039/501100011033 and by the European Union NextGenerationEU/PRTR. This work has been supported by the Madrid Government (Comunidad de Madrid-Spain) under the Multiannual Agreement with UC3M ("Fostering Young Doctors Research", SMM4HRI-CM-UC3M), and in the context of the V PRICIT (Research and Technological Innovation Regional Programme).

References

1. Ahuja, C., Lee, D.W., Nakano, Y.I., Morency, L.-P.: Style transfer for co-speech gesture animation: a multi-speaker conditional-mixture approach. In: Vedaldi, A., Bischof, H., Brox, T., Frahm, J.-M. (eds.) ECCV 2020. LNCS, vol. 12363, pp. 248–265. Springer, Cham (2020). https://doi.org/10.1007/978-3-030-58523-5_15
2. Baevski, A., Auli, M.: Robust speech recognition via large-scale weak supervision. arXiv preprint arXiv:2206.04541 (2022)
3. Bartneck, C., Kanda, T., Mubin, O., Mahmud, A.: Does the design of a robot influence its animacy and perceived intelligence? Int. J. Soc. Robot. 1, 195–204 (2009)
4. Chang, C.J., Zhang, S., Kapadia, M.: The IVI lab entry to the Genea challenge 2022-a tacotron2 based method for co-speech gesture generation with locality-constraint attention mechanism. In: Proceedings of the 2022 International Conference on Multimodal Interaction, pp. 784–789 (2022)
5. Chiu, C.C., Marsella, S.: Gesture generation with low-dimensional embeddings. In: Proceedings of the 2014 International Conference on Autonomous Agents and Multi-agent Systems, pp. 781–788 (2014)
6. Chiu, C.-C., Morency, L.-P., Marsella, S.: Predicting co-verbal gestures: a deep and temporal modeling approach. In: Brinkman, W.-P., Broekens, J., Heylen, D. (eds.) IVA 2015. LNCS (LNAI), vol. 9238, pp. 152–166. Springer, Cham (2015). https://doi.org/10.1007/978-3-319-21996-7_17
7. Danescu-Niculescu-Mizil, C., Lee, L.: Chameleons in imagined conversations: a new approach to understanding coordination of linguistic style in dialogs. In: Proceedings of the Workshop on Cognitive Modeling and Computational Linguistics (ACL 2011) (2011)
8. Devlin, J., Chang, M.W., Lee, K., Toutanova, K.: Bert: pre-training of deep bidirectional transformers for language understanding. arXiv preprint arXiv:1810.04805 (2018)
9. Ginosar, S., Bar, A., Kohavi, G., Chan, C., Owens, A., Malik, J.: Learning individual styles of conversational gesture. In: Proceedings of the IEEE/CVF Conference on Computer Vision and Pattern Recognition, pp. 3497–3506 (2019)
10. Kucherenko, T., Hasegawa, D., Henter, G.E., Kaneko, N., Kjellström, H.: Analyzing input and output representations for speech-driven gesture generation. In: Proceedings of the 19th ACM International Conference on Intelligent Virtual Agents, pp. 97–104 (2019)
11. Kucherenko, T., Nagy, R., Jonell, P., Neff, M., Kjellström, H., Henter, G.E.: Speech2properties2gestures: gesture-property prediction as a tool for generating representational gestures from speech. In: Proceedings of the 21st ACM International Conference on Intelligent Virtual Agents, pp. 145–147 (2021)
12. Li, R., Wang, Z., Wu, Y., Zhu, Y., Liu, C.L., Yang, Y.: Diffusion models beat GANS on image synthesis. arXiv preprint arXiv:2105.05233 (2021)
13. Liang, Y., Feng, Q., Zhu, L., Hu, L., Pan, P., Yang, Y.: SEEG: semantic energized co-speech gesture generation. In: Proceedings of the IEEE/CVF Conference on Computer Vision and Pattern Recognition, pp. 10473–10482 (2022)
14. Liu, Y., et al.: Roberta: a robustly optimized bert pretraining approach. arXiv preprint arXiv:1907.11692 (2019)

15. Martín Galván, L., Fernández-Rodicio, E., Sevilla Salcedo, J., Castro-González, Á., Salichs, M.A.: Using deep learning for implementing paraphrasing in a social robot. In: Julián, V., Carneiro, J., Alonso, R.S., Chamoso, P., Novais, P. (eds.) Ambient Intelligence-Software and Applications–13th International Symposium on Ambient Intelligence. LNNS, vol. 603, pp. 219–228. Springer, Cham (2023). https://doi.org/10.1007/978-3-031-22356-3_21
16. Microsoft: Bing chat (2023). https://www.bing.com/
17. Miller, R.B.: Response time in man-computer conversational transactions. In: Proceedings of the Fall Joint Computer Conference, 9–11 December 1968, Part I, pp. 267–277 (1968)
18. Nakayama, H.: seqeval: a python framework for sequence labeling evaluation. Software available (2018). https://github.com/chakki-works/seqeval
19. Pedregosa, F., et al.: Scikit-learn: machine learning in Python. J. Mach. Learn. Res. **12**, 2825–2830 (2011)
20. Pérez-Mayos, L., Farrús, M., Adell, J.: Part-of-speech and prosody-based approaches for robot speech and gesture synchronization. J. Intell. Robot. Syst. 1–11 (2019)
21. Powers, K.E., Worsham, A.L., Freeman, J.B., Wheatley, T., Heatherton, T.F.: Social connection modulates perceptions of animacy. Psychol. Sci. **25**(10), 1943–1948 (2014)
22. Rosenthal-von der Pütten, A.M., Krämer, N.C., Herrmann, J.: The effects of humanlike and robot-specific affective nonverbal behavior on perception, emotion, and behavior. Int. J. Soc. Robot. **10**(5), 569–582 (2018)
23. Quigley, M., et al.: ROS: an open-source robot operating system. In: ICRA Workshop on Open Source Software, Kobe, vol. 3, p. 5 (2009)
24. Radford, A., et al.: Improving language understanding by generative pre-training (2018)
25. Salichs, M.A., et al.: Mini: a new social robot for the elderly. Int. J. Soc. Robot. **12**, 1231–1249 (2020)
26. Sanh, V., Debut, L., Chaumond, J., Wolf, T.: Distilbert, a distilled version of bert: smaller, faster, cheaper and lighter. arXiv preprint arXiv:1910.01108 (2019)
27. Sevilla Salcedo, J., Martín Galván, L., Castillo, J.C., Castro-González, Á., Salichs, M.A.: User-adapted semantic description generation using natural language models. In: Julián, V., Carneiro, J., Alonso, R.S., Chamoso, P., Novais, P. (eds.) Ambient Intelligence—Software and Applications, ISAmI 2022. LNNS, vol. 603, pp. 134–144. Springer, Cham (2023). https://doi.org/10.1007/978-3-031-22356-3_13
28. Shiwa, T., Kanda, T., Imai, M., Ishiguro, H., Hagita, N.: How quickly should communication robots respond? In: 2008 3rd ACM/IEEE International Conference on Human-Robot Interaction (HRI), pp. 153–160. IEEE (2008)
29. Vaswani, A., et al.: Attention is all you need. Adv. Neural Inf. Process. Syst. **30** (2017)
30. Wang, A., Singh, A., Michael, J., Hill, F., Levy, O., Bowman, S.R.: GLUE: a multitask benchmark and analysis platform for natural language understanding. arXiv preprint arXiv:1804.07461v3 (2018)
31. Yoon, Y., Ko, W.R., Jang, M., Lee, J., Kim, J., Lee, G.: Robots learn social skills: end-to-end learning of co-speech gesture generation for humanoid robots. In: 2019 International Conference on Robotics and Automation (ICRA), pp. 4303–4309. IEEE (2019)

Investigating the Impact of Human-Robot Collaboration on Creativity and Team Efficiency: A Case Study on Brainstorming in Presence of Robots

Alireza Taheri[1]([✉]), Sean Khatiri[1], Amin Seyyedzadeh[1], Ali Ghorbandaei Pour[1], Alireza Siamy[1], and Ali F. Meghdari[1,2]

[1] Social and Cognitive Robotics Laboratory, Sharif University of Technology, Tehran, Iran
artaheri@sharif.edu
[2] Fereshtegaan International Branch, Islamic Azad University, Tehran, Iran

Abstract. The main objective of this research is to explore the impact of deploying social robots in team-based intellectual cooperation, specifically during brainstorming sessions. A total of 72 participants (36 females and 36 males) were involved, with groups of four participants (2 females and 2 males) engaging in brainstorming sessions. In nine sessions, three Nao robots were present; while in the other nine sessions, three human fellows participated instead of robots. The creativity of participants was assessed by measuring the average number of unique ideas generated using Bouchard and Hare's coding rules. The sessions with robots showed a significant increase in participant creativity. After the sessions, the participants completed a questionnaire, which revealed higher satisfaction, reduced production blocking, decreased free-riding, and increased synergy in sessions where robots were present. These findings were further supported by the video analysis. Future research can explore the long-term effects of interacting with social robots, including those equipped with artificial intelligence.

Keywords: Social Robots · Human-Robot Collaboration · Intellectual Cooperation · Brainstorming

1 Introduction

Computers and robots have been extensively utilized across various domains, including education, healthcare, etc. Presently, they are progressively integrating into social settings, transitioning from pre-programmed tools to entities capable of human-like thinking and behavior. In the recent years, robots have started to assume roles as educators [1, 2], therapists [3], entertainment tools [4, 5], impacting their work environment and colleagues, including emotional and social aspects. Moreover, computers have transformed interpersonal interactions and collaborative work dynamics. Hereby, an interesting subject of study is the impact of robots functioning as computer agents on intellectual cooperation within workplace as a team member.

© The Author(s), under exclusive license to Springer Nature Singapore Pte Ltd. 2024
A. Al. Ali et al. (Eds.): ICSR 2023, LNAI 14453, pp. 94–103, 2024.
https://doi.org/10.1007/978-981-99-8715-3_9

Brainstorming, introduced by Osborn [6], is an important intra-team intellectual cooperation which is widely used for enhancing creative idea generation in teams and organizations, and explored the optimal group size [7, 8]. Subsequent studies have examined its effectiveness and proposed additional techniques such as the nominal group technique and group passing technique [9, 10]. In [6], a new method in brainstorming has been presented that used computers as mediators during a session, so the members of the group could discuss and share ideas via them. This method, known as Electronic Brainstorming, has been studied several times and it could be still one of the most effective methods in brainstorming [7, 8].

However, human-robot collaboration may be different from human-computer interaction [11]. It means social robots may have different effects in comparison to computers. Therefore, the impacts of robots' presence in social environments must be discussed and examined [12]. Psychological studies have been conducted to measure how powerful these impacts can be [13]. One of the most important factors in a brainstorming session is creativity and how unique are the ideas. Studies have shown interacting with a social robot may enhance creativity [14, 15]. Alves-Oliveira et al. [16] have integrated established educational strategies that promote creativity with co-designing involving children as informants to develop the robot prototype, while some other studies examine the impact of various intellectual interaction scenarios on enhancing creativity.

Some recent studies estimate that doing creative works such as brainstorming with assistive social robots might be more beneficial than using other technologies. In a study based on storytelling in the presence/absence of a social robot called YOLO, Alves-Oliveira et al. [17] observed that using their robot led the participants to generate higher number of original ideas when the social robot actively supported creative thinking. Additionally, Ali et al. [18] reported that using a social robot called Jibo in facilitating figurative creativity, improved the uniqueness and productivity in the participants' performance in drawings compared to the tablet technology. In [14], Kahn et al. reported that in their study, the subjects have produced higher number of creative expressions when using a tele-operated robot compared to when animating presented via a PowerPoint file. In the mentioned three previous studies [14, 17, 18], the effectiveness of creative tasks and brainstorming with a social robot were compared with other technologies (rather than with human mediators). In [19], the authors have tried to fill the mentioned gap by comparing the results of using one Nao robot in brainstorming sessions with the situation in which a human mediator facilitates the brainstorming sessions. They observed that considering "productivity", there is no significant difference on the effect of using a social robot in brainstorming sessions (compared to having a human mediator in similar sessions).

This paper examines the impact of humanoid robots on intellectual collaboration during a brainstorming session. Specifically, it compares the creativity and number of ideas and solutions generated when social robots participate and contribute ideas versus when all participants are human. Additionally, participants' perceptions are assessed through a post-session questionnaire. The video recordings of all sessions are analyzed by two individuals, focusing on seven parameters (confirmation, distraction, observation of others, smiling, use of positive and negative verbs, and total verb usage per participant) for each of the 72 participants. The main research questions addressed in this study are:

1) Does the presence of social robots enhance participant creativity in brainstorming sessions? 2) What is the effect of social robots on satisfaction, free riding, production blocking, synergy, and sufficient time in brainstorming sessions?

2 Methodology

2.1 Procedure

The experiment involved 72 participants aged 18 to 20 (mean = 18.97, SD = 0.87). Half of the participants (n = 36) were in sessions with robots present (age mean = 18.94, SD = 1.01), while the other half were in sessions with only human members (age mean = 19.00, SD = 0.72). All participants were recruited from the Sharif University of Technology and were Persian natives. None of them had prior experience with social robots before participating in the experiment.

Participants were randomly assigned to groups of four individuals, consisting of two males and two females. The groups engaged in the brainstorming sessions, which were conducted in two different formats. In type A sessions, there were four individuals and three NAO robots. In type B sessions, all seven participants were human, with three of them being experimenters' colleagues, while the remaining participants were unaware of this fact.

2.2 Interview Script

At the beginning of every session, the participants were given a version of "Osborn's rules for brainstorming" and were asked to read it carefully in 5 min and follow the rules through the session. Then, the session manager answered the participants' questions about the session's rules. These rules were as follows: Be silent and listen to the ideas of others when you hear them, and even if it was the most ridiculous idea in the world, you should not comment on it. 1: you have to listen well to others' ideas so that you can get more ideas in the second round when it is time to give ideas based on others' ideas. 2: Be sure to think about your time and write down your ideas. 3: Do not use your phones during the session.

Two problems were discussed in each session. The first problem was "How to decrease depression among students?"; The second question was "Which features should be added to robots to make them more sociable?". After the first question was asked, every person would write their ideas on a sheet of paper in about 5 min. The Participants should not speak to each other during this period. After 5 min, the participants would express their ideas one by one. This section was called "round 1". After all 7 members finished this round, participants were given 5 more minutes to make new ideas, based on others' ideas or completely new ones. Then they would express new ideas like the previous part. We called this section "round 2" in a brainstorming session. During both rounds, the participants had to listen to each member expressing their ideas and they were not allowed to speak together. The second issue was discussed in the same way.

In the type A sessions, three Nao robots were part of the brainstorming sessions. When students entered the room, robots were present and greeted attendants to make a friendly atmosphere as well as to show that robots would be active members during the session. While every question was debated, robots said specific ideas in their place. They used body-language gestures while expressing ideas to make them more natural. The robots were controlled through the Wizard of Oz method, using Aldebaran's Choregraphe software.

In the type B sessions, the three experimenters' fellows (include 2 males and one female) would enter the room with other students and sit in the place of the robots. When it was their turn, they said the same specific ideas as robots would say in the type A sessions. The total number of members who attended each session was 7 because Osborn advocated using groups with 6 to 12 members [6].

In total, each session lasted for 30 min. After both of the issues were discussed, the manager of the session distributed the questionnaire. After the questionnaires were handed in, it was announced that the session had ended. In the type A session, after the experiment ended, the Wizards were introduced and participants would ask questions about robots and take photos with the robots.

2.3   Interview Environment

The sessions took place at the Social Robotics Laboratory at Sharif University of Technology, Iran. The experiment occurred in a distraction-free room with two cameras and a voice recorder, recording participants' verbal and nonverbal expressions. The room had two windows for natural light and a pleasant atmosphere. The Participants and robots were positioned around a large rectangular table (Fig. 1), with the session manager at one end. The robots were controlled from behind a concealed wall by our fellows, allowing the robots to express pre-determined ideas using appropriate body language.

Fig. 1. Positioning of the participants and the robots in a session

2.4 Assessment Tools

In this study we have used three assessment tools as follows:

The first assessment tool used is the number of unique ideas used in order to evaluate performance enhancement between the type A and type B sessions. Transcripts had produced by the participants were analyzed and the unique ideas has been identified based on the coding rules of Bouchard and Hare [20].

As the second tool, we have used the questionnaire by Dennis et al. [8]. The questionnaire analyzed the following parameters: Satisfaction, Production blocking, Freeriding (how much they became engaged in the session and generating ideas), Synergy and stimulation (how much they were stimulated to generate new ideas and work with others for more ideas), and Sufficient time. The rating was based on a 5 point Likert scale (1 the least to 5 the most). Table 1 shows the questions used for analyzing each parameter.

For the third assessment, the sessions were recorded, with participants being aware of the recording. Two video coders independently analyzed the recordings to identify the frequency of some variables include Confirmation (expressed through nodding, facial expressions, etc.), Distraction (cellphone usage during the session), Observing others (humans or robots), and Negative verb. The coders were unaware of the experiments' purpose; but were provided with the explanations for each variable. These parameters were used to confirm or reject conclusions from the questionnaire, serving as evidence of participants' honesty and accurate understanding of the questions. The coders tallied the occurrences of these parameters for each individual in each session.

Table 1. Sections of the Questionnaire and Its Related Questions

Section	Question
Satisfaction	How do you feel about the process by which you generate ideas?
	How do you feel about the idea proposed?
	All in all, how did you feel?
Production Blocking	When you thought of an idea, could you express it immediately?
	Did you express your ideas soon after you thought of them?
Free Riding	How much do you feel you participated in this idea generation session?
	How satisfied are you with your performance on this task?
Synergy and Stimulation	How stimulating did you find this task?
	How interesting was this idea generation task?
	How motivated were you to generate quality ideas?
Sufficient Time	For this idea generation session, did you have as much time as you needed?
	Considering all the ideas you thought of, did you Have time to express all your ideas?

3 Results and Discussion

The analysis revealed that sessions involving the robots resulted in a significantly higher number of unique ideas compared to sessions with only human participants. Additionally, in the type A sessions, the number of ideas generated per person exceeded that of the type B sessions (P-value < 0.001). Observations from the video recordings indicated that participants in the robotic sessions expressed beliefs that robots possess thinking and perception abilities through artificial intelligence. This suggests that the methodology for controlling robots was effective and credible. It should be noted that the coders' correlation was calculated to be at least 79% for each variable, and the average of their findings was considered the final value.

The presence of the social robots in sessions led to a significant increase in the number of unique ideas. This finding supports the main research questions regarding the positive impact of social robots on creativity, aligning with previous studies on enhancing children's creativity through interactive experiences with social robots [21]. Satisfaction significantly increased in sessions involving robots, indicating that participants felt more content when engaging in brainstorming sessions with both human and robot members, as opposed to sessions with only human members. Additionally, video analysis revealed that participants in robotic sessions exhibited more instances of laughter and used more positive language. However, there was no positive correlation between satisfaction reported in the questionnaires and the presence of smiles or positive verbs in the video analysis. This suggests that the participants may behave differently when responding to questionnaires compared to their actual session experiences. As social robots become more prevalent in society, ensuring people feel at ease when interacting with them becomes increasingly important [22–24].

According to the findings in Table 2, participants in robotic sessions were more motivated to generate novel ideas. Furthermore, video analysis revealed that participants in robotic sessions used a higher number of positive verbs compared to those in human-only brainstorming sessions. These observations align with previous research indicating that the presence of social robots enhances human stimulation and engagement in work [25]. However, in [19], the authors claimed that they observed no evidence of robot-assisted brainstorming sessions for the participants' productivity.

Based on the data presented in Table 3, production blocking was reduced in robotic sessions. This indicates that the participants in robotic sessions experienced fewer obstacles in expressing their ideas and displayed a greater inclination to actively participate. Additionally, video analysis revealed a higher frequency of smiles in the robotic sessions compared to the human-only brainstorming sessions. The decrease in production blocking aligns with the findings of previous research on virtual collaborator studies [26].

Based on the data presented in Table 3, freeriding was less prevalent in the robotic sessions compared to the human brainstorming sessions. There are several potential explanations for this finding, one of which could be attributed to the sense of competition that humans feel towards robots. Previous research has indicated that human participants often experience a heightened sense of competition with social robots [24], which can positively impact their active participation in brainstorming sessions by contributing more new ideas and reducing freeriding tendencies.

According to Table 4, video analysis revealed an increase in the use of positive verbs in robotic sessions. One possible explanation for this finding is the human perception that social robots are less intelligent than humans [23], which may reduce participants' apprehension about being evaluated.

Participants in the robotic sessions exhibited increased stimulation in generating ideas, indicating a higher level of synergy. This can be attributed to their heightened interest in the novel experience of robotic sessions. Notably, participants were given a 10-min period before the session to familiarize themselves with the robots.

All in all, it should be noted that the results observed/discussed in this study might be affected by the fact that all of the participants in the robotic sessions had their first experienced collaborating with social robots.

Table 2. The Result of Two-Sample T-test on the Number of Unique Ideas (Type A Verses Type B Sessions)

Item	Mean *(SD)*		P-Value
	Type A Sessions	Type B Sessions	
Number of unique ideas	22.11 (7.47)	8.56 (3.39)	**0.001**

Table 3. The results of two-sample T-test on the questionnaire scores (Type A verses Type B sessions)

Item	Mean *(SD)*		P-Value
	Type A Sessions	Type B Sessions	
Satisfaction	4.241 (0.426)	3.861 (0.548)	**0.002**
Production Blocking	3.750 (0.579)	3.361 (0.703)	**0.013**
Free Riding	3.875 (0.578)	3.375 (0.805)	**0.004**
Synergy and Stimulation	4.176 (0.583)	3.926 (0.829)	**0.144**
Sufficient Time	4.167 (0.396)	3.569 (0.776)	**0.001**

4 Limitations and Future Work

There were limitations to this study, such as the homogeneous sample of bachelor's students from Sharif University of Technology. It should be considered that this study is at an early stage. We need to have deeper studies on whether there is important effects in case the persons interacting face-to-face were different from the ones controlling the robots' behaviors. Future research could explore the impact of cross-cultural differences on human-robot brainstorming sessions and investigate whether participants' knowledge of the robots being controlled by humans affects the results. Additionally, the duration

Table 4. Results of one-way ANOVA on video coding scores (Type A verses Type B sessions)

Item	Mean *(SD)*		P-Value
	Type A Sessions	Type B Sessions	
Confirmation	2.344 (3.291)	1.167 (2.253)	**0.121**
Distraction	3.203 (3.282)	1.630 (1.707)	**0.029**
Looking at the others	20.97 (10.76)	10.48 (4.378)	**0.001**
Negative verb	6.407 (4.095)	3.661 (3.252)	**0.008**
Positive verb	68.02 (36.24)	46.84 (27.85)	**0.018**
Total verbs	78.22 (40.05)	52.86 (30.78)	**0.011**
Smile	17.64 (12.76)	6.165 (6.572)	**0.001**

of robot interaction (i.e., 10 min in this study) could be further examined for its impact on human creativity in robotic brainstorming sessions. These findings offer a new perspective on the effects of human-robot interaction, suggesting that users' awareness of the robot's nature may not significantly influence their behavior during the session.

5   Conclusion

This study aimed to compare idea creation in brainstorming meetings with and without social robots. The results indicated that participants exhibited different traits when interacting with the NAO robots, including increased creativity, agreeableness, openness, and extroversion compared to the human sessions. The level of creativity exhibited by the participants was evaluated by quantifying the average count of distinct ideas generated, employing the coding rules developed by Bouchard and Hare. Notably, the sessions involving robots exhibited a noteworthy and statistically significant enhancement in participant creativity. Subsequent to these sessions, participants were requested to complete a questionnaire, which unveiled meaningful heightened levels of satisfaction, a reduction in production blocking, a decrease in free-riding tendencies, and an increase in collaborative synergy during sessions where robots were present. These findings were further corroborated by conducting a thorough analysis of the recorded videos.

Acknowledgement. This study was funded by the "Dr. Ali Akbar Siassi Memorial Research Grant Award" and Sharif University of Technology (Grant No. G980517).

References

1. Ghorbandaei Pour, A., Taheri, A., Alemi, M., Meghdari, A.: Human–robot facial expression reciprocal interaction platform: case studies on children with autism. Int. J. Soc. Robot. **10**, 179–198 (2018)
2. Esfandbod, A., et al.: Fast mapping in word-learning: a case study on the humanoid social robots' impacts on children's performance. Int. J. Child-Comput. Inter. **38**, 100614 (2023)

3. Taheri, A., Shariati, A., Heidari, R., Shahab, M., Alemi, M., Meghdari, A.: Impacts of using a social robot to teach music to children with low-functioning autism. Paladyn, J. Behav. Robot. **12**(1), 256–275 (2021)
4. Meghdari, A., Alemi, M., Pour, A.G., Taheri, A.: Spontaneous human-robot emotional interaction through facial expressions. In: Agah, A., Cabibihan, J.-J., Howard, A.M., Salichs, M.A., He, H. (eds.) ICSR 2016. LNCS (LNAI), vol. 9979, pp. 351–361. Springer, Cham (2016). https://doi.org/10.1007/978-3-319-47437-3_34
5. Alizadeh Kolagar, S.A., Taheri, A., Meghdari, A.F.: NAO robot learns to interact with humans through imitation learning from video observation. J. Intell. Rob. Syst. **109**(1), 4 (2023)
6. Osborn, A. F. (1953). Applied imagination
7. Isaksen, S.G., Gaulin, J.P.: A reexamination of brainstorming research: Implications for research and practice. Gifted Child Quart. **49**(4), 315–329 (2005)
8. Dennis, A.R., Valacich, J.S.: Computer brainstorms: More heads are better than one. J. Appl. Psychol. **78**(4), 531–537 (1993)
9. Al-Samarraie, H., Hurmuzan, S.: A review of brainstorming techniques in higher education. Thinking Skills creativity **27**, 78–91 (2018)
10. Lynch, A.L., Murthy, U.S., Engle, T.J.: Fraud brainstorming using computer-mediated communication: The effects of brainstorming technique and facilitation. Account. Rev. **84**(4), 1209–1232 (2009)
11. Zhen, R., Song, W., He, Q., Cao, J., Shi, L., Luo, J.: Human-computer interaction system: a survey of talking-head generation. Electronics **12**(1), 218 (2023)
12. Rosenthal-Von Der Pütten, A.M., et al.: Investigations on empathy towards humans and robots using fMRI. Comput. Hum. Behav. **33**, 201–212 (2014)
13. Siino, R. M., Chung, J., & Hinds, P. J. (2008, Aug). Colleague vs. tool: effects of disclosure in human-robot collaboration. In RO-MAN 2008-The 17th IEEE International Symposium on Robot and Human Interactive Communication (pp. 558–562). IEEE
14. Kahn, P. H., Kanda, T., Ishiguro, H., Gill, B. T., Shen, S., Ruckert, J. H., & Gary, H. E. (2016, Mar). Human creativity can be facilitated through interacting with a social robot. In 2016 11th ACM/IEEE International Conference on Human-Robot Interaction (HRI) (pp. 173–180). IEEE
15. Gordon, G., Breazeal, C., Engel, S. (2015, Mar). Can children catch curiosity from a social robot. In Proceedings of the tenth annual ACM/IEEE International Conference on Human-Robot Interaction (pp. 91–98)
16. Alves-Oliveira, P., Arriaga, P., Paiva, A., & Hoffman, G. (2017, June). Yolo, a robot for creativity: a co-design study with children. In Proceedings of the 2017 Conference on Interaction Design and Children (pp. 423–429)
17. Alves-Oliveira, P., Arriaga, P., Cronin, M. A., Paiva, A. (2020, Mar). Creativity encounters between children and robots. In Proceedings of the 2020 ACM/IEEE International Conference Human-Robot Interaction (pp. 379–388)
18. Ali, S., Park, H.W., Breazeal, C.: A social robot's influence on children's figural creativity during gameplay. Int. J. Child-Comput. Interact. **28**, 100234 (2021)
19. Geerts, J., Witde, J., Rooijde, A.: Brainstorming with a social robot facilitator: better than human facilitation due to reduced evaluation apprehension? Frontiers Robot. AI **8**, 657291 (2021)
20. Bouchard Jr, T. J., & Hare, M. (1970). Size, performance, and potential in brainstorming groups. J. Appl. Psychol., **54**(1p1), 51
21. Alves-Oliveira, P., Arriaga, P., Hoffman, G., & Paiva, A. (2016, Mar). Boosting children's creativity through creative interactions with social robots. In 2016 11th ACM/IEEE International Conference on Human-Robot Interaction (HRI) (pp. 591–592). IEEE
22. GraafDe, M.M., Allouch, S.B.: Exploring influencing variables for the acceptance of social robots. Robot. Auton. Syst. **61**(12), 1476–1486 (2013)

23. Alimardani, M., Qurashi, S.: Mind perception of a sociable humanoid robot: a comparison between elderly and young adults. In: Silva, M.F., Luís Lima, J., Reis, L.P., Sanfeliu, A., Tardioli, D. (eds.) ROBOT 2019. AISC, vol. 1093, pp. 96–108. Springer, Cham (2020). https://doi.org/10.1007/978-3-030-36150-1_9

24. Anzalone, S.M., Boucenna, S., Ivaldi, S., Chetouani, M.: Evaluating the engagement with social robots. Int. J. Soc. Robot. **7**, 465–478 (2015)

25. Marti, P., Pollini, A., Rullo, A., & Shibata, T. (2005, Oct). Engaging with artificial pets. In ACM International Conference Proceeding Series (Vol. 132, pp. 99–106)

26. Siemon, D., Strohmann, T., & Robra-Bissantz, S. (2019, June). Towards the conception of a virtual collaborator. In Proceedings of the workshop on designing user assistance in intelligent systems, Stockholm, Sweden. KIT, Karlsruhe

A Set of Serious Games Scenarios Based on Pepper Robots as Rehab Standing Frames for Children with Cerebral Palsy

Leila Mouzehkesh Pirborj[1], Fady Alnajjar[2]([⊠]), Stephen Mathew[3], Rafat Damseh[2], and Muthu Kumar Nadimuthu[3]

[1] Western Sydney University, Sydney, Australia
[2] College of Information Technology (CIT), UAE University, Al Ain, UAE
fady.alnajjar@uaeu.ac.ae
[3] Al Noor Training Centre for Persons With Disabilities, Dubai, UAE

Abstract. One of the major issues in pediatric rehabilitation practices relates to children refusing to participate in or perform associated exercises targeted to improve their physical condition. Technology and serious games are effective approaches to engage and motivate children and assist therapists in rehabilitation exercises. This Paper tries to elicit from children's requirements for the objective of designing efficient serious games scenarios that facilitate the rehabilitation procedure. A novel set of six rehabilitation game scenarios on standing frame for robotic assistance involving children with cerebral palsy is presented. We discuss the use of serious games on a standing frame in terms of humanoid robot limitations and capabilities. The scenarios have been developed based on specialists' observations and in situ consultations with therapists at a pediatric rehabilitation center. Our findings are expected to help in future research tailored toward studying the effectiveness of adding humanoid robots to rehabilitation games to increase children's motivation, engagement, and enjoyment.

Keywords: Human-robot Interaction · Motivation · Rehabilitation · Scenario

1 Introduction

Children with physical disabilities often have limited play experiences compared to their peers without disabilities [1]. Most Cerebral Palsy (CP) therapy interventions aim to improve limb coordination, control, and range of motion through improved motor function [2]. Parents and therapists believe motivation is a significant component of motor and functional outcomes for children with Cerebral Palsy [3]. Various aspects of human intentions and activities are thought to contribute to motivation, according to study [4]. Children with neurodevelopmental disorders appear to benefit little from the application of serious games, at least according to the existing clinical evidence [5]. Participating children in a study [6] that developed an application on a tablet designed for children (preparing for radiotherapy) suggested the application could have been more interactive if it had been designed as a game. For children with cerebral palsy, virtual games have had limited applications, and none have offered an option for personalization within the session [7]. However, technology, such as virtual environments, can motivate repetitive motor rehabilitation exercises, therefore improving their effectiveness [8]. The study [9] developed a serious game system that included locomotion training exercises for the musculoskeletal system in real time. A growing number of human robot collaboration researchers are interested in working with people with disabilities [10]. A wide range of compelling reasons exist for using robots in therapeutic play scenarios, from increasing the capabilities of children with motor impairments to stimulating children with developmental disorders [11]. Social robots seem to be much more appealing to children, for reasons that are not fully understood [12]. IROMEC project aims to explore how robotic toys can become social mediators for children with special needs, encouraging them to discover a range of styles of play, from solitary to collaborative [13]. According to the preliminary results of study [14], the robot had a positive effect on children. This study measured joint attention, attitudes, and follow-up instructions as indicators of interaction. Study [15], which employed a Nao robot, a system was used to help therapists measure patients' performances and progress as well as reduce therapy risks. In study [16] using therapist consultation and observation, four specific roles were determined for the SAR (Social Assistive Robot) to function effectively as a therapeutic aid in rehab: demonstrator, motivator, companion, and coach. The results of IROMEC project were based on consultations with experts (therapists, teachers, parents) who provided advice on the play needs of the various groups of children with disabilities and helped investigate how robotic toys could be used to assist these children. In this paper, we aim to elicit requirements for designing effective rehabilitation game scenarios. Each game scenario is designed to address specific movements, challenges, and goals relevant to the rehabilitation needs of children with cerebral palsy. Rehabilitation standing frames are generally intended for children with high-level disabilities of the lower limb (mostly levels 4 and 5 GMFCS: Gross Motor Function Classification System). By integrating serious games tailored for this equipment, we can design interventions specifically for a group that is frequently overlooked in game design because of their extensive support requirements. As far as we know, no serious games scenarios have been developed on rehab standing frames using humanoid robots. This can be due to the difficulty of using humanoid robots in public spaces by non-specialists in robotics (since there are few commercial applications of pediatric rehabilitation games on humanoid robots). In addition, obtaining ethics approval for a study involving children with high levels of disabilities is challenging and require more time. In this context, we have outlined specific research questions and hypotheses that can be considered for future experimental studies:

Research Question: In rehabilitation games on the Standing Frame, what effects does include a humanoid robot have on motivation, engagement, and enjoyment for children with cerebral palsy? Adding a humanoid robot (human size) to a standing rehabilitation game system poses what technical challenges?

Hypothesis

- Compared to sessions without a humanoid robot, children with cerebral palsy are more motivated to play rehabilitation games on standing frames when accompanied and encouraged by the robot.

- When children with disabilities interact with humanoid robots during therapy sessions on standing frames, their engagement levels will significantly increase.
- With the introduction of a humanoid robot, children with cerebral palsy will be more likely to enjoy rehabilitation games on standing frames with their new interactive companion.

1.1 Using Robotics and Serious Games in Pediatric Context

The Effectiveness of Serious Game. The term "serious games" is becoming increasingly popular today. A serious game is one that runs on a computer or video game console that is designed for training, advertising, simulation, or education [17]. Games for mobile devices and virtual reality are the most frequently used gamification techniques [18]. In fact, there are many aspects to concepts such as engagement, immersion, flow, as well as other terms used to motivate using games as an alternative to more traditional didactic training [19]. There have been previous studies showing that serious games are beneficial to pediatric healthcare. Serious games for sensory processing disorders (SPDs) can combine vision, auditory, and vestibular stimulation because of the nature of multisensory stimuli and the multimodality of digital technologies [20]. There is evidence that digital games can reduce depressive symptoms, anxiety, and nausea after chemotherapy treatment in cancer patients [21]. It has been shown that children with visual impairments have a poorer self-concept and lower psychosocial well-being than peers without impairments. According to study [22], children with VIs who played the serious game See scored significantly higher on their academic self-concept than children who played care-as-usual (CAU).

Using Humanoid Robot in Pediatric Rehabilitation. Children's engagement and motivation can be enhanced by incorporating motivational expressions and emotions through humanoid robots such as Pepper or Nao in rehabilitation serious games. The use of humanoid robot-like Pepper in serious games can enhance pediatric rehabilitation in a number of ways, including engagement, motivation, enjoyment, and communication [23]. With Pepper's interactive nature and human-like attributes, children's engagement can be increased, which is not found in most rehabilitation serious games currently available. When the robot participates in games as a motivator and encouragement, exercise becomes more enjoyable and engaging for children instead of them having to do the rehabilitation game alone.

A *humanoid robot has artificial intelligence applications* that can recognize a child's facial expressions during a game and provide feedback that will motivate the child to keep playing. With Pepper's adaptability, real-time, personalized encouragement increases motivation far beyond a traditional serious game [24]. The humanoid form and ability of Pepper to mimic human behaviors and expressions create a sense of companionship and social presence [25]. It is difficult to replicate such a social dynamic in serious games without humanoid robots. Furthermore, Pepper can play cooperatively or competitively. By stimulating extrinsic motivation through gamified competition and cooperation, the robot can be further motivated to perform well. While serious games already engage and motivate children, humanoid robots like Pepper can take these features to the next level by offering adaptive encouragement, a social presence, and gamified competition [26].

Enhanced Data Collection with Pepper robot. Humanoid robots like Pepper can greatly improve the precision of data collection during serious games in pediatric rehabilitation. The integrated sensors in Pepper enable real-time monitoring of children's interactions and reactions. Unlike traditional therapeutic exercises, in which therapists must manually observe and record data, Pepper's automated data collection allows for more accurate assessment. Further, Pepper's ability to recognize children's emotional states during therapy provides unique insights into their emotional state.

Limitations of the Pepper Robot. In partnership with SoftBank Robotics Corp., Aldebaran Robotics SAS has developed a human-like social robot named Pepper. The robot is equipped with WiFi or Ethernet ports for connecting to the Internet, the NAOqi operating system controls Pepper [27]. Japanese influences can also be seen in the design, such as the manga-like big eyes and Pepper's hip joint that enables her to bow to someone when she meets them. In order to avoid stereotyping, the shape was designed to be gender neutral (without explicitly defining gender characteristics) [28]. In terms of its limitation, it is not possible for Pepper robot to understand the nuances of a user's speech. It is difficult for Pepper to hear (recognize the voice of the user who is talking to Pepper) in noisy environments. Although the therapy room isn't a crowded area (for standing frame game, 1 child works with 1 therapist), the game's background music may cause problems. However, because the game background music has no dialogue, when the background music is not loud, Pepper robot seems to be able to hear the short dialog (from child with Pepper). During the game, Pepper will talk more than the child who is playing, as most of Pepper's speech is motivating and encouraging. The user will be able to communicate with Pepper if he or she makes an utterance that is easy to understand. The age of our users (5 to 9 years old) makes it unlikely that they will use complex sentences, especially when playing games.

Physical Environment Consideration. From a design perspective, adding a humanoid robot into a serious games rehabilitation in pediatric context requires an understanding of the limitations of the robot and matching it with the needs and behavior of the target users. The humanoid robot Pepper has an excellent voice dialogue system, high emotion recognition accuracy, and a high degree of freedom of movement [29]. In the case of Pepper humanoid robot, the children in the targeted age group (aged 5 to 9) should be able to play the games with Pepper robot standing in front of them when their feet fixed to rehab standing frame. Our observation has shown that children's average height and that of the Pepper robot are strikingly similar when standing on the rehabilitation standing frame. As a result, the child and robot are able to interact and communicate better at eye level due to this height similarity.

It is possible for children interacting with humanoid robots to exert force on the robots, affecting their position or stability in uncontrolled environments (wild). In the context of Happy Rehab games, however, children with lower severity disabilities are safely fixed to a standing frame. By maintaining an appropriate distance between the child and Pepper, potential physical disruptions during their interactions are prevented. We can optimize the successful implementation of humanoid robots in pediatric rehabilitation centers by considering these physical environmental factors. The standing frame rehab game is designed to accommodate children with disabilities in both the left and right sides of their body. Therapists will adjust the game session and timing to accommodate the child's needs. The Fig. 1 shows the changes that occur when we add humanoid robot Pepper to the Happy rehab system game.

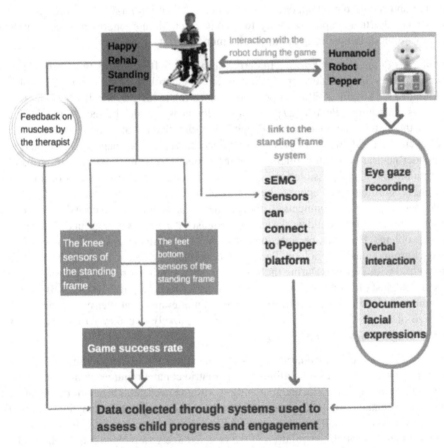

Fig. 1. How Pepper robot can affect rehabilitation standing frames is explained as part of the system's demonstration; green parts highlight the changes that will occur after Pepper robot is added to the system (The Pepper robot platform and rehab game system can be linked using touch sensors such as sEMG).

1.2 Current Happy Rehab Game Scenarios

With cerebral palsy, children cannot play with toys like other kids because of their motor disabilities, as a gaming interaction, sensory stimulation might be a better approach [30]. The study focused on the 2019 version of Happy Rehab standing frame game. This standing frame consists of sensors for knee and foot buttons to get children's muscles reaction for playing rehab game. After the therapist fixes the child's feet and back on the frame, he or she begins playing different games according to the child's therapy schedule. Each game environment is designed to accommodate different movements of the child's knees and feet. This study discusses five different rehab games that children with Cerebral Palsy (lower limb) can play on this standing frame.

An Airplane in the Desert: Two minutes at the beginning and two minutes at the end of the session: The airplane catches the stars as it flies in the desert. There is no effort required from kids as it is automatic. Standing frame pedals move kids' feet joints gently at this time. During this part of rehab game session, the goal is to warm up the child's body for the next game, which can be challenging for them. Background music is very calm, similar to airplane flight movements.

Red Racing Car: In Red Racing, four minutes are required: This game requires kids to move their knees and bottoms of their feet to control a racing car on a road. In general, the game design and background music are motivational. The kids are playing the role of race car drivers here. In order to control the car on the road, they need to move their knees and feet.

A Small Car in a Village: Children need to move their feet muscles in this four-minute game to drive a small slow car in a setting with trees, rocks, and other objects. In some situations, kids couldn't finish the game because this small car was stuck between trees, rocks, or roads. For passing trees and other obstacles, viewing the car was a bit high.

A Fast Airplane Shooting Crabs: It takes around 2 min for children to play this game by moving their knees. The background music for this game was exotic, and airplane movement seemed exciting. Knee movements allow children to kill purple crab-like creatures in the sky.

A Coin Moves on the Screen to Appear a Picture: This game lasted around two minutes. Pressing the bottom of the child's feet moves a coin on the screen and causes a picture to appear.

Game of Balance: In this four minutes' game, children do not need to move their feet and knees specifically. In the button on the screen, there was a rectangle that the child could move by moving his/her trunk. The child must move his/her trunk left and right to catch the circles that come from up to down of the screen.

1.3 Materials and Methods

We used a qualitative approach consisting of interviews (therapist consultations) and participant observation for gathering data and insights. Participants are observed and interviewed with therapists to understand their needs and preferences for creating appropriate game scenarios with humanoid robots.

Intervention: Happy-rehab game *rehab standing frame.* Standing frames for pediatric rehabilitation are therapeutic devices for children who have mobility impairments Fig. 3. Standing frames like the Happy Rehab system integrate interactive serious games specifically for rehabilitation purposes. With the Happy Rehab system, the user stands on movable foot pedals, and the games are controlled by plantar-/dorsiflexion movements of the ankle joint. The user plays computer games designed to activate specific muscle groups in the lower extremities through specific movements. For the development of future scenarios in pediatric rehabilitation games on standing frame, we conceptualized adding Pepper robots to this system for engaging and motivating children with disabilities.

Specialist Pane: Assembled a panel that included two therapists with experience employing the rehab standing frame, and the teacher for the ICT class (one main teacher and two assistants). We selected therapists and teachers based on their expertise and experience working with children with disabilities, including cerebral palsy.

1.4 Target User Group (Participants)

Children between the ages of 5 and 9 with cerebral palsy. Children with cerebral palsy at GMFCS level 3, GMFCS level 4, and GMFCS level 5 [31]. Our target group is limited to these levels based on observations and consultations with children's therapists. Children with disabilities that use rehab standing frames are shown in Fig. 2. We used to obtain the parents' informed consent.

Two therapists who work with children on the rehab standing frame were on the specialist panel, as well as the head therapist and the teachers for the ICT (computer lab) rehab center class.

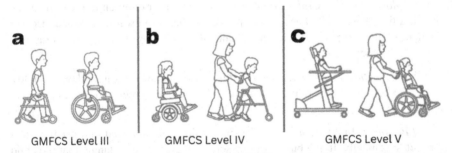

Fig. 2. Subjective explanations according to the GMFCS system in this study. a) Children walk using a hand-held mobility device in most indoor settings. They may climb stairs holding onto a railing with supervision or assistance. b) Children use methods of mobility that require physical assistance or powered mobility in most settings. c) Children are transported in a manual wheelchair in all settings. Children are limited in their ability to maintain antigravity head and trunk postures and control leg and arm movements.

Inclusion Criteria: The participants must be between the ages of 5 and 9 years old, diagnosed with cerebral palsy, and classified as level 3, 4, or 5 on the GMFCS. Furthermore, the specialist panel chosen for answering the questionnaire should include therapists with experience with rehab standing frames for children and physiotherapy in pediatric context.

Exclusion criteria: Children whose ages do not fall within the specified range (no children between five and nine years of age), as well as children whose diagnoses do not include cerebral palsy. Exclusion from the study also occurs when parents or guardians do not provide informed consent.

1.5 Ethical Approval

This study was conducted under the supervision and coordination of Al Noor Rehab Training Center. Research was conducted with the center's permission. This aspect of the study did not need ethics approval because the observation did not directly involve children or capture their personal data.

1.6 Data Collection

Rehab standing frame room and ICT class (computer lab for children's games) et al. Noor training rehab center observed for data collection. We observed 5 children with Cerebral Palsy while playing games on a standing frame and children with CP in the ICT class (computer classes in rehab centers). A rehab game on standing frame session for each child lasted 20 min and consisted of 6 different game environments. During an ICT class, children between the ages of 5 and 9 spend 30 min playing games on a computer or tablet, depending on their disabilities and ages. ICT class games differ from standing frame games in the use of different parts of children's bodies. When playing standing frame games, therapy sessions focus on lower limb exercises, but in ICT class, hand functions are essential during serious games. However, at both places, we saw the children's interaction when playing rehab serious games and their communication with their therapists when doing their rehab tasks. By taking notes, the researcher collected children's verbal and non-verbal feedback during the rehab game, also their game achievement and their communication with their therapist during playing the game was noted. Also, Teachers and therapists at the rehab center who work with the children were interviewed in situ. Before answering the questions, the project's aims and concept are explained to the children's therapists by the Al Noor rehab center. As a result of meticulously observing and gathering data from the interactive sessions and interviews, a set of specific needs was identified.

Need Identified. Height and Positioning Need: Adapt interactions for children who cannot stand unassisted (GMFSC Levels 3–5). - > Rationale: Ensuring effective communication with the Pepper robot, which has a fixed height.

Use of Robot's Tablet Need: Diverse interaction modes with the robot's tablet (touch/no-touch). - > Rationale: In standing frame situations, it is suitable for a variety of rehab games exercises and target movements without requiring direct touch.

Physical Interaction Safety Need: Ensure a safe distance between the robot and the child during interactions. - > Rationale: Children with both upper and lower limb disabilities need to be protected from unintended contact due to poor control.

Usage of External Tablets Need: Tablets can be used in an engaging and safe manner during therapy sessions without compromising the focus on exercise. - > Rationale: Therapists utilize tablets for encouragement and distraction during painful or challenging exercises (also for physiotherapy rooms), needing a balance between entertainment and safe exercise performance.

Monitoring and Adapting to Child Progress (Therapist's Interaction During Game Sessions) Need: Streamlined transitions and preparation between different game sessions during standing frame exercises. - > time to check equipment, monitor the child's condition, and prepare the next game session without causing unnecessary delays or interruptions in the child's engagement.

Motivation and Encouragement in ICT Classes Need: Consistent motivational strategies and encouraging interactions from teachers during ICT class sessions. - > and sustaining children's motivation throughout ICT class tasks and games, facilitating improved engagement and productive involvement.

Differentiated Game Environments for Varied Abilities Need: Children's disabilities, ages, and diagnosed body parts can be accommodated in game scenarios to ensure inclusive engagement. - > Rationale: Recognizing the wide-ranging requirements and capacities of children with cerebral palsy in ICT classes, varying in age and disability level, necessitating diversified and adjustable game scenarios and tasks.

1.7 Analysis Data

Based on the collected materials, this study used a thematic analysis [32], since this method does not require theoretical boundaries, it is a good choice for finding patterns that are not necessarily bounded by theory. Thematic analysis aims to identify and analyze patterns or themes within data. Based on the type of technology interaction, children's abilities, and observed impacts, a theme may be developed. Researchers manually coded the data.

In each rehab session involving standing frames, ICT classes, and Physiotherapy room, the participation of the children and their parents, the following materials were analyzed: 1) observations of rehabilitation gameplay, 2) summary notes made after each session, and 3) interviews questionnaires. Data collected was coded.

The gathered data was analyzed to find the main themes and potential subthemes:

- *Main Theme 1: Sensory Preferences and Engagement* (Subtheme 1.1 Auditory Preferences over visual stimulation, Subtheme 1.2 Engagement through action rather than verbal communication)
- *Main Theme 2: Assistive Interaction and Motivation* (Subtheme 2.1: Transfer Assistance and Physical Support, Subtheme 2.2: Therapist Assistance and encouragement in game-activities, Subtheme 2.3: Emotional Response and Anticipation for future session.)
- *Main Theme 3: Communication and Verbal Expression* (Subtheme 3.1: limited verbal communication and slow repetition, Subtheme 3.2: use of Non-verbal expression and gestures)
- *Main theme 4: Enjoyment and Meaningful experiences* (Subtheme 4.1: engagement in different games, Subtheme 4.2: Satisfaction in accomplishing task with therapist encouragement, Subtheme 4.3: expression of desire and emotional response to future sessions).

ICT class data was analyzed to identify the main themes and potential subthemes:

- Main theme 5: Interaction Types (Subtheme: 5.1Eye gaze interaction - > Code: using eye gaze for typing and playing games, Code - > eye gaze control without physical touch), (Subtheme 5.2 Touch screen interaction, Code - > touching tablet screen or monitor for game-play, Code - > Simple puzzle games through touch screen), (Subtheme 5.3 Keyboard Interaction- > Code: Typing sentences on the computer from a provided paper, Code - > Varied difficulty of sentences and words based on student abilities, Code - > Typing random letters due to limited control).
- Main Theme 6: Student's Abilities (Subtheme 6.1 mobility challenges: Code - > use of wheelchair, Code- > limited hand functionality (grasping, reaching, fine control), (Subtheme 6.2 cognitive and sensory abilities, Code - > variation in concentration and mood), (Subtheme 6.3 age-related abilities, Code- > children younger than 7 years old).
- Main Theme 7: Impact of Interaction (Subtheme 7.1 Engagement, Code- > participation in different games environments, Code - > touching colorful background screen), (Subtheme 7.2 Enjoyment, Code - > sound effects augmenting interaction).

Regarding the demonstration of the current *Happy Rehab game* on the standing frame and the observation of children with cerebral palsy playing the game, the following behavior was coded:

- Visual and Auditory Preference: C1: Disinterested in watching TV, C2: Calming response to classical music rather than game background music, C3: Indiference to encouragement to look at the big screen C4: Ability to look at the TV screen.
- Hand Function and other support: C1: Adequate hand muscle strength, C2: Supportive use of wheelchair for legs.
- Interaction and Function: C1: Light smile and calm demeanor, C2: Limited verbal communication, C3: Satisfaction in completing the game, C4: Exploring desire to come back again, C5: Engagement in different games based on the game scenario and environments, C6: Focus on Knee and foot movements.

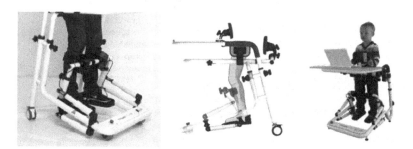

Fig. 3. Happy Rehab standing frame for playing rehab games.

1.8   Scenario Design Process

Human-Computer Interaction (HCI) research has been much less impacted by design, despite its strong presence in practice. It is necessary for the interaction design research contribution to constitute a significant invention [33]. It is important that the robot appears friendly to motivate subjects and create meaningful interactions with them [34]. Based on Happy Rehab serious games (2019) and researchers' observations and consultations with pediatric therapists, play scenarios (see Fig. 3) were developed. The researchers developed play scenarios based on observations of children with CP playing games on standing frames in physiotherapy and ICT classes, as well as comments from their therapists and teachers. In addition, they considered limitations, needs, and the range of interactions that Pepper robot facilitates (Fig. 4).

The main change, after adding the humanoid robot, is the greeting part (human features behavior), which will occur at the beginning and end of the rehab game session. While transferring the child from her/his wheelchair to the standing frame, Pepper robot can start a friendly conversation with her/him. Generally, during this time (when therapists are fixing child feet and trunk on the standing frame and bringing the game, they are busy, and children are waiting until their work is completed). Children's moods can be affected before playing the game, for example, Pepper robot encourages them to do their best when the game starts. Design the robot's gestures during key moments of the game to convey enthusiasm and motivation and to encourage children to do their rehab exercises. Scenarios might incorporate real-time feedback loops to maximize Pepper's interactive potential. As an example, Pepper may provide immediate positive reinforcement if a child successfully completes a game task with the correct foot movement.

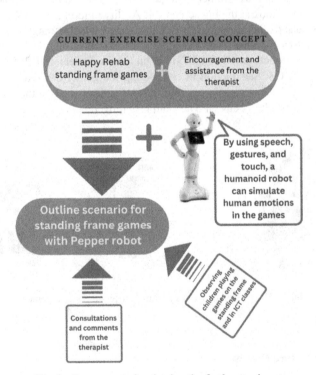

Fig. 4. Components for shaping the final scenario set.

Table 1. Standing frame rehabilitation games in two scenarios (without robot and with robot).

Happy rehab Current games scenarios	Game adaptation when Pepper robot is added
An airplane in the desert	It could serve as an emotional motivator. By cheering the children on and conversing with them, Pepper can create an emotional connection and further immerse them in the game
Red racing Car	As a racing coach, Pepper will offer tips and advice, and encourage them when they do well, and in times of struggle, reinforce them with positive reinforcement. Also, with the robot's dynamic gestures, driving can be mimicked
A small car in a village	It can guide children through the village, guiding them to avoid obstacles, just like in the racing game. In addition to creating short stories related to the game environment, the robot can enhance the game's interactive capabilities
A fast airplane shooting crabs	This game can be played with a robot as a mission commander, updating children on their progress and encouraging them to keep playing. The game can be made more realistic with robot gestures that mimic the shooting action
Game of balance	By providing real-time feedback, Pepper acts as a coach, guiding the child's movement to catch the circle. Additionally, Pepper can use its voice to instruct the child to move left or right, creating a more interactive experience
A coin moves on the screen to appear a picture	Pepper can encourage children's efforts to apply the right pressure by acting as an art enthusiast or museum guide. When the picture appears, Pepper can generate excitement by trying to guess what it is, thereby building suspense. In addition, Pepper can praise the children when the picture is fully revealed, for example, when they touch Pepper's head and Pepper starts laughing
Notes on General	The Pepper games enhance the child's rehabilitation experience by adding a layer of personalization and engagement A child's name, progress, likes, and dislikes should be remembered by the Pepper program

2 Discussion

Our paper focuses primarily on the design of serious game scenarios that could be applied to improve the rehabilitation process in children. A prototype of happy-rehab 2019 can be developed on Pepper robot platform based on engagement, enjoyment and motivations observed in ICT class (computer lab) and standing frame games played by children with cerebral palsy. The following approaches are considered after identifying is designed to provide emotional expression, encouragement, and positive reinforcement, making the child's environment nurturing and motivating. It is common for children with disabilities not to feel confident about their body, and boring and repetitive rehab exercises lead them to stop their muscle movement before their therapists expect them to.

There are three subthemes in the Assistive Interaction and Motivation theme; the example to explain them includes when therapists help children move their muscles in order to complete game tasks, or when therapists give them a Hi Five after a child has earned a good score. When the child was playing a game and completing rehab tasks, we captured therapist dialogue as encouragement. In addition, there were some emotional responses and anticipations from the child for future sessions, such as if I could come back tomorrow to play more rehab games?

Engagement is divided into two subthemes: auditory stimulation over visual stimulation and action over verbal communication. The graphic design of some games in the Happy Rehab game on standing frames was poor. This may be the main reason why children did not seem to be attracted to visual stimulation during the playing game. Because of more variety and more professional graphic design in games in ICT class, we didn't find the same results as standing frames. As a result of visual stimuli, children were more engaged in an ICT class than in a standing frame game. Finishing game tasks (through muscle movements) in action games such as racing a car and shooting airplanes was more satisfying than games with less action, such as driving a small car in the village. We noted limited verbal communication, slow repetition, and non-verbal expression and gestures under the Communication and Verbal Expression theme. A good example of an explanation is therapists' efforts to communicate verbally with children before, during, and after rehab games. Although it can also depend on other factors, such as the child's personality, children generally communicate verbally less than therapists.

We categorized the main theme Enjoyment and Meaningful experiences into three subthemes: engagement in different games environments, satisfaction with accomplishing tasks with therapist encouragement, and expression of desire for future sessions. However, since the general task for playing the rehab games was muscle movements (on a standing frame focusing on the feet muscles), the durations of playing the games and finishing them were not similar, matching this with facial expressions (happy face) and more emotional expressions (both verbal and gustatory), the difference in enjoyment level is apparent. An obvious indicator of a game's enjoyment is a child's desire to continue playing it more.

The safety of children during use of humanoid robots in pediatric rehabilitation is one of the most important aspects of humanoid robot use. It was also our priority from the beginning of the study, and we considered the appropriate place and situation for using Pepper, a humanoid robot. As a result, we focused on rehab games on standing frames. The interaction between a humanoid robot and a child with cerebral palsy can be utterly uncontrollable in this case. A therapist can fix the distance between the child and Pepper robot before the rehab game begins. Table 1. Contrasts the rehabilitation game scenarios before and after the humanoid robot Pepper can add to the rehab system in terms of human features.

3 Conclusion

Robot-assisted therapy appears to be an effective addition to conventional rehabilitation therapy for improving motor function in stroke patients according to study [35]. The results of a meta-analysis indicated that SARs could be effective in engaging children in therapeutic interventions [36]. Adding humanoid robot motivational expressions and emotions to the pediatric rehabilitation serious game can make it more immersive and engaging. As far as we know, no serious games have been developed on rehab standing frames using humanoid robots. It is necessary to conduct experimental studies in order to quantify the differences in Motivation, Engagement, and Enjoyment in different scenarios with and without humanoid robots when playing serious games.

Acknowledgments. Thank you to Al Noor, Management, Research and Training Department-Shameem, Department of Physiotherapy, all of which are located et al. Noor Training Centre for Persons with Disabilities in Dubai, UAE, for assisting us with this research. Also, this publication is supported by Digital Health CRC limited ("DHCRC"). DHCRC is funded under the commonwealth's Cooperative Research Centers (CRC) Program (Australia).

References

1. Miller, S., Reid, D.: Doing play: competency, control, and expression. Cyberpsychol. Behav. **6**(6), 623–632 (2003)
2. Henschke, M., Hobbs, D., Wilkinson, B.: Developing serious games for children with cerebral palsy: case study and pilot trial. In: Proceedings of the 24th Australian Computer-Human Interaction Conference, pp. 212–221 (2012)
3. Tatla, S.K., Sauve, K., Virji-Babul, N., Holsti, L., Butler, C., Van Der Loos, H.F.M.: Evidence for outcomes of motivational rehabilitation interventions for children and adolescents with cerebral palsy: an American Academy for Cerebral Palsy and Developmental Medicine systematic review. Dev. Med. Child Neurol. **55**(7), 593–601 (2013)
4. Ryan, R.M., Deci, E.L.: Self-determination theory and the facilitation of intrinsic motivation, social development, and well-being. Am. Psychol. **55**(1), 68 (2000)
5. Kokol, P., Vošner, H.B., Završnik, J., Vermeulen, J., Shohieb, S., Peinemann, F.: Serious game-based intervention for children with developmental disabilities. Curr. Pediatr. Rev. **16**(1), 26–32 (2020)
6. Engvall, G., Lindh, V., Mullaney, T., Nyholm, T., Lindh, J., Ångström-Brännström, C.: Children's experiences and responses towards an intervention for psychological preparation for radiotherapy. Radiat. Oncol. **13**, 1–12 (2018)
7. Tresser, S., Kuflik, T., Levin, I., Weiss, P.L.: Personalized rehabilitation for children with cerebral palsy. User Model. User-Adap. Inter. **31**(4), 829–865 (2021)
8. Koenig, A., et al.: Virtual environments increase participation of children with cerebral palsy in robot-aided treadmill training. In: 2008 Virtual Rehabilitation, pp. 121–126. IEEE (2008)

9. Tannous, H., Dao, T.T., Istrate, D., Tho, M.C.H.B.: Serious game for functional rehabilitation. In: 2015 International Conference on Advances in Biomedical Engineering (ICABME), pp. 242–245. IEEE (2015)

10. Arevalo Arboleda, S., Pascher, M., Baumeister, A., Klein, B., Gerken, J.: Reflecting upon participatory design in human-robot collaboration for people with motor disabilities: challenges and lessons learned from three multiyear projects. In: The 14th PErvasive Technologies Related to Assistive Environments Conference, pp. 147–155 (2021)

11. Howard, A.M.: Robots learn to play: Robots emerging role in pediatric therapy. Georgia Institute of Technology (2013)

12. Ros, R., et al.: Child-robot interaction in the wild: advice to the aspiring experimenter. In: Proceedings of the 13th International Conference on Multimodal Interfaces, pp. 335–342 (2011)

13. Robins, B., et al.: Human-centred design methods: Developing scenarios for robot assisted play informed by user panels and field trials. Int. J. Hum. Comput. Stud. **68**(12), 873–898 (2010)

14. Céspedes Gómez, N., Calderon Echeverria, A.V., Munera, M., Rocon, E., Cifuentes, C.A.: First interaction assessment between a social robot and children diagnosed with cerebral palsy in a rehabilitation context. In: Companion of the 2021 ACM/IEEE International Conference on Human-Robot Interaction, pp. 484–488 (2021)

15. Lara, J.S, et al.: Human-robot sensor interface for cardiac rehabilitation. In: 2017 International Conference on Rehabilitation Robotics (ICORR), pp. 1013–1018. IEEE (2017)

16. Martí Carrillo, F., et al.: Adapting a general-purpose social robot for paediatric rehabilitation through in situ design. ACM Trans. Human-Robot Interact. (THRI) **7**(1), 1–30 (2018)

17. Susi, T., Johannesson, M., Backlund, P.: Serious games: An overview (2007)

18. Adlakha, S., Chhabra, D., Shukla, P.: Effectiveness of gamification for the rehabilitation of neurodegenerative disorders. Chaos Solitons Fractals **140**, 110192 (2020)

19. Hookham, G., Nesbitt, K., Kay-Lambkin, F.: Comparing usability and engagement between a serious game and a traditional online program. In: Proceedings of the Australasian Computer Science Week Multiconference, pp. 1–10 (2016)

20. Hanan Makki Zakari, M.: A review of serious games for children with autism spectrum disorders (ASD). In: Minhua Ma, M. (ed.) SGDA 2014. LNCS, vol. 8778, pp. 93–106. Springer, Cham (2014). https://doi.org/10.1007/978-3-319-11623-5_9

21. Abd Majid, E.S., Garcia, J.A., Nordin, A.I., Raffe, W.L.: Staying motivated during difficult times: a snapshot of serious games for paediatric cancer patients. IEEE Trans. Games **12**(4), 367–375 (2020)

22. Lievense, P., Vacaru, V.S., Kruithof, Y., Bronzewijker, N., Doeve, M., Sterkenburg, P.S.: Effectiveness of a serious game on the self-concept of children with visual impairments: a randomized controlled trial. Disabil. Health J. **14**(2), 101017 (2021)

23. Winkle, K., Caleb-Solly, P., Turton, A., Bremner, P.: Social robots for engagement in rehabilitative therapies: Design implications from a study with therapists. In: Proceedings of the 2018 acm/ieee international conference on human-robot interaction, pp. 289–297 (2018)

24. Feingold-Polak, R., Barzel, O., Levy-Tzedek, S.: A robot goes to rehab: a novel gamified system for long-term stroke rehabilitation using a socially assistive robot—methodology and usability testing. J. Neuroeng. Rehabil. **18**(1), 1–18 (2021)

25. Rasouli, S., Gupta, G., Nilsen, E., Dautenhahn, K.: Potential applications of social robots in robot-assisted interventions for social anxiety. Int. J. Soc. Robot. **14**(5), 1–32 (2022)

26. Riedmann, A., Schaper, P., Lugrin, B.: Integration of a social robot and gamification in adult learning and effects on motivation, engagement and performance. AI & Soc., 1–20 (2022)

27. Cascone, L., Castiglione, A., Nappi, M., Narducci, F., Passero, I.: Waiting for tactile: robotic and virtual experiences in the fog. ACM Trans. Internet Technol. (TOIT) **21**(3), 1–19 (2021)

28. Pandey, A.K., Gelin, R.: A mass-produced sociable humanoid robot: Pepper: The first machine of its kind. IEEE Robot. Autom. Mag. **25**(3), 40–48 (2018)
29. Softbank, Product Specifications. https://www.softbank.jp/robot/consumer/products/spec/, Accessed 28 July 2018. (in Japanese)
30. Oliveira, E., Sousa, G., Tavares, T.A., Tanner, P.: Sensory stimuli in gaming interaction: the potential of games in the intervention for children with cerebral palsy. In: 2014 IEEE Games Media Entertainment, pp. 1–8. IEEE (2014)
31. https://cerebralpalsy.org.au/our-research/about-cerebral-palsy/what-is-cerebral-palsy/severity-of-cerebral-palsy/gross-motor-function-classification-system/
32. Braun, V., Clarke, V.: Using thematic analysis in psychology. Qual. Res. Psychol. **3**(2), 77–101 (2006)
33. Zimmerman, J., Forlizzi, J., Evenson, S.: Research through design as a method for interaction design research in HCI. In: Proceedings of the SIGCHI Conference on Human Factors in Computing Systems, pp. 493–502 (2007)
34. Sobrepera, M.: Social Robot Augmented Telepresence for Remote Assessment and Rehabilitation of Patients with Upper Extremity Impairment (Doctoral dissertation, University of Pennsylvania) (2022)
35. Chang, W.H., Kim, Y.H.: Robot-assisted therapy in stroke rehabilitation. J. Stroke **15**(3), 174 (2013)
36. Blankenship, M.M., Bodine, C.: Socially assistive robots for children with cerebral palsy: A meta-analysis. IEEE Trans. Med. Robotics Bionics **3**(1), 21–30 (2020)
37. Robins, B., Ferrari, E., Dautenhahn, K.: Developing scenarios for robot assisted play. In: RO-MAN 2008-The 17th IEEE International Symposium on Robot and Human Interactive Communication, pp. 180–186. IEEE (2008)

Can a Robot Collaborate with Alpana Artists?
A Concept Design of an Alpana Painting Robot

Farhad Ahmed[1], Zarin Tasnim[1], Zerin Tasnim[1], Mohammad Shidujaman[2]([✉]) [iD],
and Salah Uddin Ahmed[3]([✉]) [iD]

[1] Computer Science and Engineering, American International University, Bangladesh (AIUB),
Dhaka, Bangladesh
[2] FabLab, Department of Computer Science and Engineering, Independent University
Bangladesh (IUB), Dhaka, Bangladesh
shidujaman@iub.edu.bd
[3] School of Business, University of South-Eastern Norway, Notodden, Norway
salah.ahmed@usn.no

Abstract. The possibility of robots working along with Alpana artist is a developing field of research at the point of intersection between technology and traditional art. Alpana painters have the skill and creativity necessary for the delicate design process, but robots can execute these designs with greater accuracy and efficiency. In this kind of collaboration, artists would develop ideas for the Alpana, and robots would speed up the drawing. This combination makes sure that even when technology aids in the expression of Alpana art, its heart and soul remain human. Combining human creativity and robotic accuracy has the potential to produce a harmonious combination that embraces current achievements while retaining tradition. A growing natural process that respects tradition while embracing innovation is fostered by this mix of tradition and technology. The paper's contributions are its investigation of human-robot collaboration in Alpana art, its presentation of a conceptual Alpana painting robot, and its emphasis on maintaining cultural legacy while accepting technology progress.

Keywords: Human Robot Collaboration · Alpana Art · Human Robot
Interaction · Cultural Heritage · Robots Artists Collaboration

1 Introduction

For years, integrating art and technology has captured people's interest by bridging the gap between tradition and innovation. In the complex world of artistic expression, a new story is emerging, including a collaboration of robots and Alpana painters. The Alpana or Alpona art form, which is strongly based on cultural heritage and complex patterns, is a monument to the interplay of human creativity and regard for tradition [1]. Simultaneously, advances in robotics and automation have added new aspects to creative processes, offering extraordinary accuracy as well as effectiveness [2]. This research sets out to explore the unexplored areas where human creativity meets the potential of robotic help, all while preserving the authenticity of cultural narratives.

The Alpana art form, which originated in the cultural tapestry of the Indian subcontinent, has captured the essence of generations past via its intricate concepts and visually fascinating designs. These designs are not only beautiful, but they also have cultural importance, containing stories, rituals, and interactions between people [3]. Simultaneously, great advances in robotics have been made, giving the possibility of incorporating mechanical help into the creative process. This research explores the intersection of these seemingly different worlds, proposing a collaboration in which Alpana artists supply creative vision while robots contribute precision and efficiency in implementation.

The importance of this research lies in its ability to balance tradition and innovation in the context of artistic creativity. While robotic art is not a new phenomenon, incorporating robots into culturally rich and complex art forms such as Alpana provides a unique difficulty. This study's fundamental research question is: Can robots interact with Alpana painters in a way that speeds up design execution while respecting the authenticity of creative expression and cultural heritage? By exploring this subject, we hope to shed light on the collaboration and interactions between human artists and the robots as technical partners revealing the small details that affect the success of this collaboration.

Our research takes a cross-disciplinary approach to robotics, human-computer interaction, and human robot collaboration. This study intends to analyze the thoughts of Alpana artists and the obstacles they face in integrating robots into their creative processes through an analysis of robotic-assisted artistic outputs. We hope to provide a comprehensive understanding of the potential consequences, constraints, and benefits of incorporating robots into the Alpana art form by investigating both the aesthetic and technological sides of this collaboration.

This article attempts to contribute to the continuing discussion about the relationship between human creativity and technical growth by crossing the complicated structure of tradition, innovation, and visual art. Through a thorough examination of this unusual collaboration, we hope to provide insights that not only improve the field of art and technology but also encourage greater respect for the delicate relationship between tradition and innovation and the possibility of improving the collaboration by using the concepts of social robot [4]. This study illuminates the delicate balance between tradition and technological development through an interdisciplinary lens that includes human-robot interaction, aesthetic considerations, the difficulties of getting artists' acceptance, and enriching the conversation about the relationship between human creativity and technological advancement.

The rest of the paper is structured as follows: in Sect. 2.1, we present the historic background of Alpana and its current forms and usage. Section 2.2 provides some examples of how robots have been used in painting and art. Section 3 presents the concept design of a robot painter for Alpana painting. Section 4 discusses the issues and implications of using robot painter in painting Alpana, especially the challenges and the level of acceptance from the artists community. Lastly, Sect. 5 concludes the paper and gives a glimpse of our planned future work.

2 Background

2.1 Alpana

Alpana or Alpona paintings and the roles of Alpana artists provide views into cultural preservation within the context of creative legacy. In 2023 a paper by Mondal et al. expressed that Alpana is an ancient form of folk art primarily practiced by women in Bengal, where motifs, designs, and symbols are directly painted on the floor or wall using rice paste or colored dust [3]. Alpana is also known by different names in different parts of India, such as Aripana in Bihar, Mandana in Rajasthan, Rangoli in Gujarat and Maharashtra, Chowkpurana in Uttar Pradesh, and Kolam in South India (Figs. 1 and 2).

Fig. 1. Floor Art of Alpona in West Bengal   **Fig. 2.** Selection of colors of the Alpana represents the theme of the celebration.

Women in Bengal design Alpanas. This is part of a long-standing artistic tradition. They create these patterns by recalling what they have seen in the past and often occurring patterns. In order to symbolize abundance, Alpanas frequently feature commonplace items like flowers, leaves, fruits, and rice storage containers [5].

Ashraf et al. [6] mention the practice of painting Alpana or Aripan on the mud floor of the courtyards in Mithila as part of the Madhubani painting tradition. These paintings were done in white color with rice powder on cow dung plastered ground surfaces and were appreciated by visitors from the same village and nearby villages. The paintings were typically made by young girls of the family, and they would discuss the designs and patterns to be included in the painting. The girls would start making the Alpana in the afternoon and complete it by sunset, often singing in chorus while painting. However, due to the changing environment and the decline of joint families, there are now fewer courtyards and smaller canvases for Alpana paintings [6].

In Uttarakhand's Kumaon region, Alpana is known as Aipan which entails utilizing rice paste and a subdued crimson hue to create elaborate shapes and patterns on walls, paper, and garments. Aipan is primarily designed by women, who paint the artworks on the floors and walls of their homes using the last three fingers of the right hand. These arts are used in religious festivals such as Pujas and in ceremonies connected with birth, marriage, and death. Besides, they are also used in embellishing wedding invitations, Diwali artworks, and Kumaoni women's clothing [7].

Besides the religious connection, Alpana has been used in many social events as a symbol of art and decoration to increase the festivity and vibrance of the event. Minhus et al. [5] state that Alpana paintings is a well-known folk-art form in Bangladesh and its usage is noted in the realm of costume design and cultural celebrations. This form of art is connected to the way people dress and celebrate their heritage. White, red, yellow, orange and a particular shade of blue are some of the most significant and historically significant hues utilized in Alpana art. These colors are used in Bangladesh by people on festive occasions like Pohela Falgun, Pohela Boishak, International Mother Language Day. In these festival days, Bangladeshi people dress traditionally and adorn their skin with beautiful designs that resemble Alpana art. They don't just care about the art itself, but also about the colors and what they represent [8] (Figs. 3 and 4)

Fig. 3. Designing a street Alpana (Bangladesh)

Fig. 4. A street painted with Alpana in requires good labor from artists. Dhaka celebrating national day.

In current time in Bangladesh, Alpana is also widely used in different social events such as weddings, social gatherings, social awareness events, and observation of special significant days such as Independence Day, Victory Day etc. While religious festivals used rice flour and chalks or leaves and flours, the modern-day social events use paints for drawing Alpana. These arts are also bigger in shape and have less-complicated patterns and are used over a large open area where the focus is decoration and beautification while having cultural connection with the art forms and colors that relate to the region, heritage, and the vibe and theme of the occasion. Now-a-days, the Alpana is being used in different kinds of events which can include a simple family event such as wedding, a university orientation program, annual events organized by an institute or a company, sports events in schools or colleges or grand celebrations of national events of the country such as Victory Day, Independence Day, International Mother language day. Unlike the traditional Alpanas, where mostly women in the house participated, now participation from both genders – men and women, especially the young people from universities, colleges as well as any interested groups and volunteers from different organizations take part in the painting of modern days Alpana.

2.2 Collaborative Robots or Co-bots in Painting

Painting is a dynamic process where an artist's goals may change dynamically during the creative process. Schaldenbrand et al. discusses a concept known as FRIDA (Framework and Robotics Initiative for Developing Arts) [9]. It resembles a system that enables collaboration between humans and a painting robot. This robot can create canvas paintings from simple inputs like phrases or images. The approach developed by the authors enables the robot to continuously improve the painting. Because painting with a brush and paint is sometimes haphazard, this plan may vary. The robot continuously assesses how the artwork appears and modifies its strategy as necessary to improve it. The paper also discusses how unique maps and computer tools were used to create the appearance of realistic brush strokes on the artwork [9] (Fig. 5).

Fig. 5. FRIDA's embodiment and workspace.

The Busker Robot, a unique robot that can transform digital images into lovely watercolor paintings. This robot uses a computer program to assist it in making painting decisions. The computer program analyzes the image and creates a written plan for the robot to follow. To make the picture appear to have been done with watercolors, they employ unique techniques. To assist the robot in determining where to move its brush, they also use computer programs. They employ a robot that can move in 6 different directions and a programming language called UR Script Programming to control it [10]. Another paper describes the development of the collaborative robot known as Pictobot, which helps in the spray-painting procedure in cooperative settings. The idea is to speed up and simplify the process of painting. Using specialized sensors, the robot can operate the spray gun and choose how to paint. The robot also pays attention to the employee's suggestions for how to paint. By maintaining the spray gun at the proper distance and angle from the surface, Pictobot ensures that the paint is applied uniformly [11] (Fig. 6).

Fig. 6. Busker Robot painting at "Piccolo Teatro" (Milan, Italy, November 2017)

Fig. 7. A sample of artist and robot (co-bot) collaboration [12].

Co-bot technology could be used by Alpana artists to improve their work. Co-bots can be programmed, for instance, to help with the preparation of the traditional rice paste used in Alpana painting. Additionally, with the help of Co-bots, artists could experiment with using other colors and materials, and complete repetitive tasks faster with greater precision and efficiency.

3 Concept design of an Alpana painting robot.

In this section, we present a design for a robot that would be able to paint Alpana in the ground surface. It is important to note that its capabilities are limited to ground- level applications and it is not equipped to paint on vertical surfaces such as walls. From our experience of designing a wall painting robot Paintique [13], here we extend the design to make Alpana painter- the robot that would be capable of painting simple Alpana arts.

The Alpana Painter is powered by the Arduino Uno that organizes the robot's motions. It is propelled over the painting surface by a DC gear motor and wheels, and it has a servo motor that fine-tunes the nozzle pipe for precise paint placement. An LCD panel cover the Alpana Painter, enhancing the user experience by allowing users to select Alpana designs or patterns for the robot to perform. Safety and precision are vital, and the robot is outfitted with four IR sensors to detect obstacles and ensure optimal paint application. These sensors are critical in guiding the robot and ensuring precise painting strokes (Fig. 8).

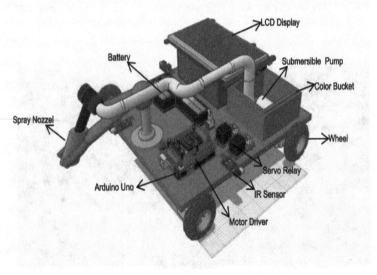

Fig. 8. 3D view of a Alpana painting robot.

Indeed, the Alpana artists can create sophisticated designs on traditional surfaces, and we have the ability to digitize these physical works of art. We can accurately dupli- cate these patterns in a digital environment by using Computer-Aided Design (CAD) technologies. This move allows us to more easily keep, edit, and distribute the designs while preserving their originality and historical significance. A well-established and widely used approach that can be used to assist the movement of the spray nozzle is by G-Code, a geometric code. G-Code is a generating algorithm that functions as a com- munication link between a computer design and the real-time movement of the spray nozzle [14]. By doing this robot can speed up the process of drawing and act as a helping hand. Artists will draw the design and we will convert those deign in digital format. So that we can use those design as input for the robot.

As Alpana designs move into digital formats, they will achieve extraordinary consistency and precision, ensuring precise duplication of even the smallest intricacies—a feat that may often be difficult for even the most skilled human artists. Furthermore, the robotic nature will allow for continuous work, resulting in a quick project completion. Furthermore, these digitally changed designs will be highly accessible, allowing for easy storage and sharing, bridging geographical divides, and boosting worldwide cooperation. This fusion of technology and traditional art forms will not only open the way for unique unions of historical and modern art forms but will also have substantial educational value, potentially captivating future generations [15].

4 Discussion

In the following section, we look at the various aspects of using robotic painters in the field of Alpana arts, examining both the benefits and drawbacks of this technological integration. The incorporation of robotic painters into the area of Alpana art creates new obstacles. One significant challenge is retaining the specific human touch that provides Alpana emotional depth and cultural importance. Another challenge is the wide variety of motifs and patterns that Alpana includes. For a simple robot, simpler designs might be doable but complex designs would require much more sophisticated robots with better precision and advanced algorithms for painting. Our proposed prototype also intends to draw only simpler designs. Indeed, if the robot's scope is confined to drawing simple designs such as leaves and flowers, the cost of developing such a basic robotic system might be relatively low. Robotic system complexity and cost are linked to the complexity of its capabilities.

Another challenge is the number of colors in the design of Alpanas. The more colors, the more complex the designing of the robot will be. Our proposed prototype is shown with only one-color bucket which would paint one color Alpana arts. For two or more colors, multiple color buckets will be needed. In that case, algorithm for selecting the right color bucket for the Nozzle will be needed. Another alternative is to have separate nozzles for separate color buckets. In either case, the complexity of the robot and its operating algorithm will fairly increase. For a primary simple prototype, an easier approach can be to reuse the same bucket with a second color after the completion of painting in the first color. But then precision of the positioning of the colors in the floor art will need precise detection of lines of the previously painted lines. As we can see the success of the art by the robot will depend largely on the precise technical design and accuracy of the painting algorithms including precise detection of lines, and precise movements of the robot.

On the positive side, the incorporation of robotic painters into Alpana art has the potential to attract the interest of university and college students in robotics and human-robot interactions. Students who participate in this creative form of art, and technology may gain a newfound interest in robotics research. Working together with robots may bridge theory with practical application, creating a desire to create and improve robotic systems. Social robots and co-bots can be an interesting in this domain where collaboration between artists and robots can be the focus of research agenda. Furthermore, through modernizing traditional art, Alpana may become more interesting and relevant to current students, encouraging a new wave of curiosity and learning at the meeting point of tradition and innovation.

Some artists may be hesitant in the beginning, worrying that the inclusion of robots may weaken the authenticity and emotional impact that human created Alpana designs possess. Ultimately, artists' acceptance will be determined by a variety of factors, including their desire to embrace technological progress, the benefits they receive from working with robots, and the wider cultural context in which these changes are happening. The artistic community will most certainly find methods to incorporate robotic help while keeping the authenticity of Alpana art as the advantages become obvious and the technology becomes more developed.

5 Conclusion

In conclusion, the relationship of digital Alpana designs with social robots brings in a new era for this classic art form. The combination of technology and tradition offers benefits that go beyond increased efficiency. Through digital conversion, it provides precision, consistency, and accessibility, while the integration of social robots adds an interactive and educative dimension. Instead of replacing human creativity, these advances magnify it, producing a harmonic collaboration that crosses generations and regenerates cultural narratives. This dynamic collaboration aims to keep Alpana art current and treasured while embracing digital-era innovations.

In this article we have presented an early-stage conceptual design. In the future, we hope to put our prototype robot to the test in the field. Our work with the Alpana Painter robot has great potential. We intend to conduct a survey to get artists' feedback, optimize the robot's algorithms for efficiency, experiment with real Alpana images to assess its capabilities, and constantly improve its functions. A detailed survey of artists' perspectives on the use of the Alpana Painter robot will provide essential insights into its acceptance and opportunities for improvement. Understanding their points of view is essential for improving the technology's integration with Alpana art. It will be essential to keep developing and fine-tuning the algorithms that power the Alpana Painter.

Optimizing the robot can result in increased efficiency, precision, and range, making it an even more beneficial tool for artists. Using the robot to experiment with Alpana photos will be an exciting step. It will help in assessing the robot's capabilities in real-world circumstances and providing useful feedback on its performance. By pursuing these future research activities, the Alpana Painter will be able to develop further, and incorporate better the requirements and expectations of artists while pushing the limits of what this technology can achieve in the domain of Alpana painting.

References

1. Mukherjee, S.: Evolution of alpana in Santiniketan was a venture into a secular aesthetic world. Get Bengal (2020). https://www.getbengal.com/details/Evolution-of-alpana-in-San tiniketan-was-a-venture-into-a-secular-aesthetic-world, (31 August 2023)

2. Syed, R., et al.: Robotic process automation: contemporary themes and challenges. Comput. Ind. **115**, 103162 (2020). https://doi.org/10.1016/j.compind.2019.103162

3. Mondal, M., Harry., Lalthanzama, S., Dhaka, N., Goswami, A.: Socio-religious and spiritual significance of symbols in the folk art of Bengal section. Eur. Chem. Bull. **12**(5), 4097–4107 (2023)

4. Yang, G.-Z., Dario, P., Kragic, D.: Social Robotics—Trust, learning, and Social Interaction. Sci. Robotics **3**(21) (2018). https://doi.org/10.1126/scirobotics.aau8839

5. Minhus, S.M., Hui, T., Huie, L.: Indigenous costume color of Bangladesh: A traditional context for cultural revival. Fibres Textiles Eastern Euro **30**(2), 123–132 (2022). https://doi.org/10.2478/ftee-2022-0015

6. Ashraf, A., Jha, S.: The madhubani metamorphosis: the intersection of art, ritual and gender roles. Inter. J. Culture History (EJournal) **6**(1), 1– 7 (2020). https://doi.org/10.18178/ijch.2020.6.1.141

7. Kaushik , A., Gupta, M.: Aipan creative art of Kumaon. Inter. J. Home Sci. **3**(2), 640–642 (2017)

8. Sarkar, A.: Drawing, migration and cultural memory; critical narrative of an artist. Mapping Memory, TRACEY J. (2012)

9. Schaldenbrand, P., McCann, J., Oh, J.: . Frida: A collaborative robot painter with a differentiable, real2sim2real planning environment. In: 2023 IEEE International Conference on Robotics and Automation (ICRA) (2023). https://doi.org/10.1109/icra48891.2023.10160702

10. Scalera, L., Seriani, S., Gasparetto, A., Gallina, P.: Busker robot: a robotic painting system for rendering images into watercolour artworks. Mech. Design Robot. 1–8,(2018). https://doi.org/10.1007/978-3-030-00365-4_1

11. Asadi, E., Li, B., Chen, I.-M.: Pictobot: A cooperative painting robot for interior finishing of industrial developments. IEEE Robot. Autom. Mag. **25**(2), 82–94 (2018). https://doi.org/10.1109/mra.2018.2816

12. Kaufman, S.L.: Artist Sougwen Chung wanted collaborators. So she designed and built her own AI robots. Article in The Washington Post Published on Nov 5 (2020). https://www.washingtonpost.com/business/2020/11/05/ai-artificial-intelligence-art-sougwen-chung/

13. Tasnim, Z., Ahmed, F., Tasnim, Z., Shidujaman, M., Ahmed, S.U.: Paintique: design and development of interaction model of a line following spray-painting robot. Culture Comput., 437–448 (2023). https://doi.org/10.1007/978-3-031-34732-0_34

14. Pan, J., Fu, Z., Xiong, J., Lei, X., Zhang, K., Chen, X.: Robmach: G-code-based off-line programming for robotic machining trajectory generation. Inter. J. Adv. Manuf. Technol. **118**(7–8), 2497–2511 (2021). https://doi.org/10.1007/s00170-021-08082-3

15. Chen, W., Shidujaman, M., Tang, X.: AiArt: towards artificial intelligence art. In: The 12th International Conference on Advances in Multimedia (2020)

Human-Robot Interaction Studies with Adults in Health and Wellbeing Contexts - Outcomes and Challenges

Moojan Ghafurian[1]([✉]), Kerstin Dautenhahn[1], Arsema Teka[1],
Shruti Chandra[1], Samira Rasouli[1], Ishan Baliyan[2], and Rebecca Hutchinson[3]

[1] Social and Intelligent Robotics Research Laboratory, Faculty of Engineering,
University of Waterloo, Waterloo, ON, Canada
moojan@uwaterloo.ca
[2] David R. Cheriton School of Computer Science, University of Waterloo, Waterloo,
ON, Canada
[3] Davis Centre Library, University of Waterloo, Waterloo, ON, Canada

Abstract. Social robots have great potential to support individuals' health and wellbeing. We did a follow up study based on previous work of a 2021 systematic review following PRISMA guidelines that identified 443 research articles evaluating social robots in health/wellbeing contexts with adult participants. In this paper we performed a new analysis that showed that while the vast majority of the articles reported positive outcomes related to the use of social robots in these contexts, only half of those articles supported the results by statistical tests and comparisons, highlighting a need for future studies with robust methodologies that can further study and inform the use of social robots for supporting adults in health/wellbeing. We discuss that different qualitative and quantitative methodologies are equally valuable, as long as the conclusions are based on the data collected. We also encourage publication of studies with well designed and executed methodologies that lead to neutral or negative outcomes. This is in line with other scientific research fields that emphasize the need to report on such results to avoid needless replication of studies that have already been done and could provide important lessons for the field, but never got published.

Keywords: Social robots · Health · Wellbeing · Study outcome · Systematic Review

1 Introduction

Social robots have been evaluated in many domains for supporting humans, showing different levels of success in a variety of user studies. Health and wellbeing contexts are one of such domains and hold great potential for the use of social robots in supporting individuals, as well as caregivers and health professionals. To better understand the benefits and potentials of social robots, it is informative to review past Human-Robot Interaction (HRI) studies and understand the

A. Al. Ali et al. (Eds.): ICSR 2023, LNAI 14453, pp. 130–142, 2024.
https://doi.org/10.1007/978-981-99-8715-3_12

outcome of such studies where social robots interacted with individuals, as well as to understand how they were evaluated.

There have been extensive studies of social robots for specific user groups, such as children with Autism or persons with dementia. Similarly, while there is a large body of reviews related to social robots and health and wellbeing, most of the review articles focus on a single type of user group or settings, such as in hospital settings [16], for supporting older adults (e.g., [5–7,18]), for supporting people with dementia (e.g., [14,19,20,22,33]), for mental health or psychological wellbeing interventions (e.g., [17,24,28]), from perspectives of non-patients who interacted with the robots (e.g., [15,27]), or focused on the robots as opposed to users' evaluations [4,10,21,25,32]. However, evaluation of HRI studies in the larger scope of health/wellbeing contexts has seen limited attention, perhaps due to the very large scope of the evaluation.

Recently, Santos et al. (2021) systematically mapped the literature relating to robotics and human care [26], covering 69 past studies in this domain to understand the types of tasks performed with the robot (e.g., personal assistant, object manipulation, human monitoring). A recent large-scale literature review conducted by the authors' research team covered 443 articles where social robots were evaluated in HRI studies with adult participants (including younger and older adults) [13]. The review presented the social robots used in the studies, the settings and situations in which HRI studies were conducted, type of data collected in the studies (i.e., quantitative, qualitative, or mixed), robot control (e.g., autonomous), and user groups and their health conditions [13]. Here, we expand on these findings and further analyze the data gathered in the search presented in [13]. The contributions of this review include (a) outcome of the past HRI studies, (b) presence of statistical analysis for supporting the outcome, and (c) distribution of number of articles contributed by different authors in the past studies as identified by our search.

2   Research Questions

This review article addresses the following research questions.

RQ1 What were the outcomes of the past HRI studies that evaluated social robots in health/wellbeing contexts with adult participants?

RQ2 How were the data used for reporting the outcomes of the studies analyzed? Specifically, we ask if the results of the articles were based on statistical analysis.

RQ3 How broad is the field in terms of the number of different researchers who have contributed to the publications in the reviewed context?

3   Methodology

This systematic review carefully followed the steps outlined by the Centre for Reviews and Dissemination [3], and the reporting follows the PRISMA 2020 guidelines [23]. In this section, we present a short summary of the methodology of the systematic review. A more thorough description of the methodology is presented in [13], where research questions beyond the scope of this article are addressed. As discussed earlier, in this paper, we expand on the results of the data collected in [13] to address new research questions that are presented here.

In this review, social robots are defined as robots that operate alongside humans and are capable of interacting in human-centric terms [8,9]. Health/wellbeing is defined as "the extent to which an individual or group is able, on the one hand, to realize aspirations and satisfy needs and, on the other hand, to cope with the interpersonal, social, biological and physical environments" [31]. A more thorough definition of the terminologies is presented in [13].

According to these definitions, our eligibility criteria required peer-reviewed studies that used and reported on social robots in a health or wellbeing context, where the participants interacted with the social robots.

3.1 Eligibility Criteria

Our inclusion and exclusion criteria were as below.
Inclusion Criteria:

- Studies with adult participants (18+ yrs old)
- Studies published in peer-reviewed conferences or journals
- Studies that involved participants who engaged with or evaluated a social robot in the context of health and wellbeing
- Studies on the use of social robots for a health or a wellbeing intervention, with related outcomes/evaluations
- Studies on the use of physically embodied robots, and robots that possess social skills, i.e., those that are considered social robots based on our definitions above
- Studies reported in English

Exclusion Criteria:

- Studies on the use of a purely robotic device (exoskeleton, sensors, artificial limbs etc.) without social attributes
- Studies on the use of robots in healthcare, where the robots did not exhibit a social behaviour (i.e., where the robot was not being operated/programmed to act as a social robot according to our above-mentioned definition)
- Studies with only children as participants
- Studies reported in a language other than English
- Studies that were not included in a conference proceeding or a journal (e.g., book chapters, technical reports, etc.)
- Studies that did not have any results related to health/wellbeing as defined above (e.g., studies that only evaluated general attitudes towards or acceptance of social robots without interactions with a robot or without considering a health context)

3.2 Information Sources and Search Strategy

Five databases were searched on February 6, 2021 to find relevant studies. MED-LINE via PubMed, PsycInfo via APA PsycNet, IEEE Xplore Digital Library, ACM Digitial Library and Scopus were chosen for their coverage of the health and/or technology literature. The initial search strategy was developed for PubMed in an iterative process by a librarian in computer science with input from the review team (see [13] for more information). See Table 1 for the search used in PubMed.

Table 1. PubMed Search

(((social*[tiab] OR sociable[tiab] OR companion*[tiab] OR humanoid[tiab] OR animal-like[tiab] OR human-like[tiab] OR humanness[tiab] OR animal assisted[tiab] OR pet therap*[tiab] OR pets[tiab] OR coach*[tiab] OR friends[mesh] OR Animal assisted therapy[mesh] OR pets[mesh]) AND (robot*[tiab] OR robotics[mesh:noexp])) OR (assistive robot*[tiab] OR robotic animal*[tiab] OR care robot*[tiab] OR personal robot*[tiab] OR interactive robot*[tiab])) AND English[Filter]

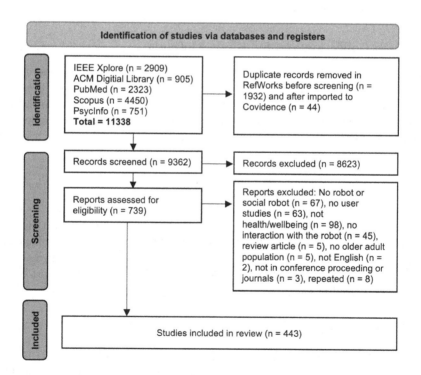

Fig. 1. Prisma flow diagram for systematic reviews

The main concepts searched in PubMed's MEDLINE were social AND robot and were selected based on the research questions. To cut down on the amount of irrelevant results found in the other databases (mainly on the development of social robots and their use outside of health), the concepts of participant AND health were added. To define the search terms, we reviewed relevant papers to ensure we captured the different keywords and vocabulary used by authors in both social robotics and health domains. After multiple iterations where different keywords were checked for their precision and recall of relevant articles, the search terms were defined for each database.

The databases returned a total of 11338 results. These results were exported into RefWorks [2] and 1932 duplicates were removed. The remaining 9406 were exported into Covidence [1] and 44 more duplicates were removed.

3.3   Selection Process

The 9362 unique articles were screened in Covidence by six members of the review team (two people per article) and disagreements were settled by discussion with at least two additional team members. 739 articles were included for full-text review. A full-text review (one person per article) was conducted afterwards. Full texts were checked again for eligibility at the time of data collection. Please see Fig. 1 for more details.

3.4   Data Collection and Synthesis Methods

The data items and extraction process were developed through discussion by a multidisciplinary team and tested by five of the reviewers. Five reviewers performed the data extraction (one person per article). Some studies did not include all the data points of interest and those were left blank in the chart (unless the missing information was required as a part of the inclusion criteria, in which case the article was removed).

4   Results

For a thorough summary of the country of authors of the reviewed articles and year of articles published see [13]. The majority of the articles were published by researchers in Japan and the United States; however, the search identified articles written by researchers in 44 different countries [13]. Below, we will report on the new results related to each of the above-mentioned research questions.

4.1   RQ1 - Study Outcomes

If the social robot had a positive influence on users (attitudes, behaviours, quality of lives, perceptions, etc.), the outcome was categorized as positive. It included instances where the robot improved various aspects of people's lives or moods,

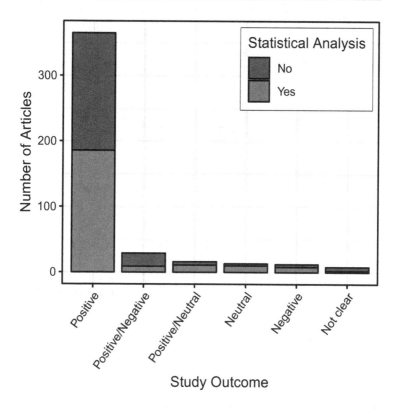

Fig. 2. Study outcomes

or was associated with positive attitudes. If it had a negative influence on participants, did not work as intended, or attitudes were negative, it was categorized
as negative. The negative category included instances in which participants displayed disinterest in using the robot or negative interactions were observed.
Some articles had more than one study with different outcomes, or in a single study, both positive and negative outcomes were reported. These cases are
shown with Positive/Negative. Similarly, neutral shows when no difference was
observed in the presence/absence of the robot, and positive/neutral shows the
cases were both observed in a paper, e.g., in two studies reported in the same
article. The "not clear" category shows instances where the effect of the robot
was indeterminable, or the study failed to yield conclusive results.

The social robots in the reviewed studies were used in many different roles,
such as for providing companionship, as therapeutic and rehabilitation robots
including animal therapy, for health data acquisition or diagnosis of different
conditions, for cognitive support, as health and exercise coaches, or for helping with fall detection/prevention. Different aspects of the social robots were
evaluated in the reported HRI studies, including their effectiveness and participants' attitudes toward the robots. The studies were conducted in a variety of

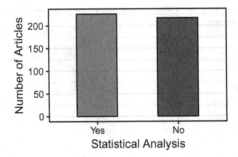

Fig. 3. The figure shows whether the articles reported the results based on statistical tests

settings, including research labs, participants' homes, care centres, and hospitals (see [13]).

Figure 2 shows the outcome of the reviewed papers. The vast majority of the articles(365 out of 443 articles) suggested a positive outcome of social robots on aspects of participants' attitude or health/wellbeing. As can be seen in Fig. 2, approximately in half of these cases, a proper data analysis method (i.e., statistical analysis) was performed.

4.2   RQ2 - Data Analysis

The presence of statistical analysis was assessed for the studies in the reviewed papers to investigate if the results or conclusions were drawn from those analyses. We acknowledge that statistical tests are not necessarily a requirement for all studies in the health and wellbeing contexts, but such tests can be meaningful in order to interpret the results. If a study conducted such tests and reported on any aspect of the analysis (e.g., even p-values only), it was classified in the "Yes" category (see Fig. 3).[1]. On the other hand, if a study did not conduct any statistical tests, it was categorized under the "No" category.

Figure 3 shows the number of articles that performed statistical analysis to support the reported outcomes. The others included studies where observations (in many cases with a few participants) motivated specific outcomes, by only reporting on what was observed. In other words, although those studies provided evidence that supported a specific outcome, they did not report on a thorough analysis to provide stronger evidence in favour of those outcomes.

4.3   RQ3 - Authors

We identified a total of 1406 unique authors in all the reviewed articles. Figure 4 shows the distribution of authors in terms of the number of articles published

---

[1] The specific statistical test used in the studies were also extracted, but are not reported here due to page limits.

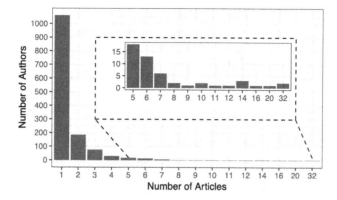

Fig. 4. Distribution of the number of articles contributed by authors based on our search.

based on our search and in the context of this paper. For example, this shows that over 1000 authors have contributed to one paper in our search, with 51 authors contributing 5 or more articles.[2]

5   Discussion, Gaps, and Future Directions

We revisited a review of 443 articles on social robots in health/wellbeing contexts for adults to better understand the outcome of Human-Robot Interaction (HRI) studies in these contexts, as well as to study how those outcomes were supported and to see the breadth of authors involved.

The vast majority of the articles (365 out of 443 articles) reported positive outcomes based on HRI studies, about half of which were supported by in-depth data analysis and statistical tests. These results are promising, supporting benefits of using social robots for supporting health/wellbeing.

However, the very high number of positive outcomes as compared with neutral and negative outcomes may be partly due to the fact that many researchers may not report on negative or neutral outcomes (while only in some of these cases such results may be due to methodological issues), due to a general bias of journals and conferences to focus on positive results. As HRI studies and generally user studies may be affected by many factors (e.g., participants are self-selecting, i.e. they have to self-enrol in the studies in order to meet requirements of institutional ethics boards), it is reasonable to expect that there exist more cases with neutral and negative outcomes that might have not been published. However, those reports could be very beneficial indeed, to better understand how social robots can be improved in this context and beyond. In other words, a well thought out methodology that did not lead to positive results could still inform

---

[2] Please contact us if you are interested to access the full list of all author names and corresponding number of papers based on our search.

the research community about different factors that may negatively affect outcomes and guide future research. This is also supported in other areas in science. For example, Teixeira da Silva (2015) argues that negative results can indicate what does not work and negative results are important in motivating scientific thoughts [29]. The author highlights a lack of a publishing channel for reflecting these negative results [29]. Furthermore, the general mindset in science that negatively perceives negative results could be the cause of why negative results are not published as often [29]. This emphasis on the importance of reporting negative results is not recent and dates back to many years ago in many scientific fields. For example, Smart (1964) argued for the importance of reporting negative results in research related to psychology, pointing out how negative results can inform researchers, and emphasized that negative results are often unpublished [30]. Fanelli (2012) argues how this can lead to a positive-outcome bias and may also affect how researchers treat their data and results [11].

Similarly, in HRI, we argue that the field could greatly benefit from learning about the negative outcomes of research, if the methodology is well thought out and executed. This could inform researchers about aspects of the robots (appearance, behaviour, etc.) that may not be desirable and/or be acceptable for users, including primary and secondary users. Additionally, these results could highlight user populations that may not have positive attitudes toward robots, or could point to methodologies or settings that may not work as well with social robots. A particular concern here is that researchers, students and faculty alike, who join the field of HRI for the first time, might unknowingly end up replicating unreported studies that previously gave neutral or negative results. Therefore, as HRI researchers, we need to be able to publish these negative or neutral results, as well as to see the value in such work when evaluating other researchers' work in the role of reviewers. But in order to succeed in this endeavour, conferences, journals, and funding agencies need to recognize the importance of reporting neutral or negative results, and mechanisms have to be in place to be able to publish and acknowledge those results, similar to publications with 'positive' results. Otherwise, generations of HRI research might replicate studies that were never published because the results were inconclusive or negative, which is counterproductive to advancing research in HRI.

Further, a lack of statistical comparisons might be in part due to the limited number of participants in many studies. As reported in [13], many of these studies have been based on relatively small sample sizes. Therefore, despite having many articles reporting on positive outcomes, only half of those that performed more in-depth data analysis such as using statistical tests (e.g., comparing experimental conditions, before-after studies, etc.) could provide strong evidence and support, while others are still valuable and informative. Future work based on larger sample sizes and methodologies that would allow for statistical tests and comparisons is needed to better understand the potential of using social robots in health/well-being contexts. This includes studies with multiple conditions with and without social robots, as well as studies where aspects of participants' health and wellbeing or attitudes are evaluated before and after using the social robots.

Those quantitative studies can complement other in-depth studies, including case studies, and other methodologies such as conversation analysis [12]. Ultimately, although in this review it was not possible to evaluate all data analysis methods and we only focused on statistical analysis (as the specific methods, especially related to qualitative analysis were not often reported in the reviewed articles), we acknowledge that statistical analysis is not a necessity in all HRI studies. Rather, the selection of methods should be decided based on the research questions addressed, the setting of the study, the number of participants that could be recruited realistically, etc. For example, in many of the reviewed studies that dealt with studying the effect of social robots on users' attitudes, moods, and other behavioural effects such as reducing depression, statistical tests comparing conditions with and without social robots would be required to provide evidence about positive effects of social robots. In the absence of such evidence, those studies can still be informative in terms of showing the impact the social robots can have, but then the claims need to be adjusted to be representative of the findings.

It is important to acknowledge that conducting long-term studies with social robots in health settings (similar to many other application-oriented settings), with specific user groups, and/or with a large number of participants can be highly challenging. Social robots introduced in many environments (e.g., hospitals, care centres) might be perceived as a novelty — depending on the location of the study — which may affect the number of participants who would be willing to join the research studies, or the number of facilities (hospitals, care centres, rehabilitation centres, etc.) that may approve such studies, depending on their attitudes towards robots as novel technology, as well as them considering the effort required in term of staff time and concerns such as interruptions to the operation of the unit.

Additionally, usually the number of social robots present in a lab that is running the study is limited — which is also affected by the cost of the robots — another factor that can affect recruitment of participants compared to the other types of technologies such as virtual agents and mobile applications that can become more widely available and used in parallel with multiple participants. Therefore, despite the need for long-term, large-scale studies with in-depth data analysis, there is definitely value in small-size studies that report on general observations with a small number of participants and based on shorter interactions. Especially studies conducted with a specific user group, in specific settings, etc., can act as a stepping stone for expanding these HRI studies to larger-scale future studies, for example by exposing different settings and user groups to social robots and reducing the hesitation that may be due to the novelty of social robots and general assumptions about them. Furthermore, while field studies in real-world settings such as hospitals and care centres are the ultimate goal in order to evaluate social robot technology in situ, lab based studies and their outcomes are still important as initial steps, to get prepared and ready (technically and methodologically), before going out 'into the wild'.

Limitations: This review had several limitations. We relied on authors' reports on the results and data analysis method. Therefore, our review did not identify the cases where the reported results were not supported by the study or where in-depth data analysis was performed but not reported in the articles. Also, although we had a large multi-disciplinary team who originally helped with the screening and data extraction steps, and despite carefully designing the search teams with direct involvement of an experienced librarian, we might have missed some of the related articles. Furthermore, for such a large scale review, some papers might have been missed due to human error during the screening stages, despite being screened in duplicates. This may specially affect the reported distribution of the number of papers contributed by different authors published before our cut-off date February 6, 2021. Finally, data analysis methods other than statistics may be as valuable, or more appropriate, depending on a study's research questions and context. Here, we had to only rely on statistical analysis reported in the papers as it was not possible to evaluate all approaches based on the information provided in the reviewed papers.

6 Conclusion

Social robots have great potential in health/wellbeing contexts and for supporting individuals. To better understand the results of HRI studies with social robots in this context, we reported on a large-scale systematic review, where we investigated the outcome of HRI studies in studies where a social robot was used in health/wellbeing contexts with adult participants. PRISMA guidelines were followed and the reported results expanded on another systematic review that was conducted on the similar set of articles, addressing other research questions. Here, we reported on the study outcomes and whether statistical tests were performed to support those outcomes. We also assessed the distribution of authors which showed a broad range of authors who have contributed to this field. A need for publishing studies with negative or neutral outcomes based on robust methodologies is identified, as well as a need for performing studies with a larger number of participants and robust methodologies. This would allow conducting data analysis that can help better understand and inform how social robots can assist people in health/wellbeing contexts. We also highlighted that different research methodologies, both qualitative and quantitative, including studies with small sample sizes, or studies with neutral or negative outcomes, can be important to advance HRI research in the context of supporting adults in health and wellbeing and beyond, as long as the findings of the studies match conclusions being made on the data.

Acknowledgement. We thank Garima Gupta for assisting with parts of the data extraction of the results related to this paper. We also thank Angelica Lim, Garima Gupta, Jimin Rhim, and Alexander M. Aroyo, who assisted in different steps of methodology development and data screening for a larger review article, further analysis of which led to the results and discussions in this paper. This research was undertaken, in part, thanks to funding from the Canada 150 Research Chairs Program.

References

1. Covidence - Better systematic review management. https://www.covidence.org/
2. ProQuest RefWorks. https://refworks.proquest.com
3. Akers, J., Aguiar-Ibáñez, R., Baba-Akbari, A.: Systematic reviews: CRD's guidance for undertaking reviews in health care. University of York, Centre for Reviews and Dissemination (2009)
4. Amirova, A., Rakhymbayeva, N., Yadollahi, E., Sandygulova, A., Johal, W.: 10 years of human-NAO interaction research: a scoping review. Front. Robot. AI. **8**, 744526 (2021). https://doi.org/10.3389/frobt.2021.744526
5. Araujo, B., et al.: Effects of social robots on depressive symptoms in older adults: a scoping review. Librar. Hi Tech. **40**(5), 1108–1126 (2022). https://doi.org/10.1108/LHT-09-2020-0244
6. Asgharian, P., Panchea, A., Ferland, F.: A review on the use of mobile service robots in elderly care. Robotics **11**(6), 127 (2022). https://doi.org/10.3390/robotics11060127
7. Asl, A., Ulate, M., Martin, M., van der Roest, H.: Methodologies used to study the feasibility, usability, efficacy, and effectiveness of social robots for elderly adults: scoping review. J. Med. Internet Res. **24**(8), e37434. https://doi.org/10.2196/37434
8. Breazeal, C., Dautenhahn, K., Kanda, T.: Social robotics. In: Siciliano, B., Khatib, O. (eds.) Springer Handbook of Robotics, pp. 1935–1972. Springer, Cham (2016). https://doi.org/10.1007/978-3-319-32552-1_72
9. Dautenhahn, K.: Socially intelligent robots: dimensions of human-robot interaction. Philos. Trans. R. Soc. B: Biol. Sci. **362**(1480), 679–704 (2007)
10. Esterwood, C., Robert, L.P.: Personality in healthcare human robot interaction (H-HRI) a literature review and brief critique. In: Proceedings of the 8th International Conference on Human-Agent Interaction, pp. 87–95 (2020)
11. Fanelli, D.: Negative results are disappearing from most disciplines and countries. Scientometrics **90**(3), 891–904 (2012)
12. Fischer, K.: Risk and responsibility in human-robot interaction. Risk Discourse Responsib. **336**, 172 (2023)
13. Ghafurian, M., et al.: Systematic review of social robots for health and wellbeing: a personal healthcare journey lens. (Under Review)
14. Ghafurian, M., Hoey, J., Dautenhahn, K.: Social robots for the care of persons with dementia: a systematic review. ACM Trans. Hum. Robot Interact. (THRI) **10**(4), 1–31 (2021)
15. Gibelli, F., Ricci, G., Sirignano, A., Turrina, S., De Leo, D.: The increasing centrality of robotic technology in the context of nursing care: bioethical implications analyzed through a scoping review approach. J. Healthcare Eng. (2021). https://doi.org/10.1155/2021/1478025
16. González-González, C.S., Violant-Holz, V., Gil-Iranzo, R.M.: Social robots in hospitals: a systematic review. Appl. Sci. **11**(13), 5976 (2021)
17. Guemghar, I., et al.: Social robot interventions in mental health care and their outcomes, barriers, and facilitators: scoping review. J. Mental Health. **9**(4), e36094. https://doi.org/10.2196/36094
18. He, Y., He, Q., Liu, Q.: Technology Acceptance in Socially Assistive Robots: Scoping Review of Models, Measurement, and Influencing Factors (2022). https://doi.org/10.1155/2022/6334732
19. Lee, H., Chung, M., Kim, H., Nam, E.: The effect of cognitive function health care using artificial intelligence robots for older adults: systematic review and meta-analysis. JMIR Ageing. **5**(2), e38896 (2022). https://doi.org/10.2196/38896

20. Lu, L.C., Lan, S.H., Hsieh, Y.P., Lin, L.Y., Lan, S.J., Chen, J.C.: Effectiveness of companion robot care for dementia: a systematic review and meta-analysis. Innov. Aging. **5**(2), igab013 (2021). https://doi.org/10.1093/geroni/igab013

21. Moyle, W., Murfield, J., Lion, K.: Therapeutic use of the humanoid robot, Telenoid, with older adults: a critical interpretive synthesis review. https://doi.org/10.1080/10400435.2022.2060375

22. Ong, Y.C., Tang, A., Tam, W.: Effectiveness of robot therapy in the management of behavioural and psychological symptoms for individuals with dementia: a systematic review and meta-analysis. J. Psychiatr. Res. **140**, 381–394 (2021). https://doi.org/10.1016/j.jpsychires.2021.05.077

23. Page, M.J., et al.: The Prisma 2020 statement: an updated guideline for reporting systematic reviews. Int. J. Surg. **88**, 105906 (2021)

24. Riches, S., et al.: Therapeutic engagement in robot-assisted psychological interventions: a systematic review. Clinic. Psychol. Psychother. **29**, 857–873 (2021). https://doi.org/10.1002/cpp.2696

25. Robaczewski, A., Bouchard, J., Bouchard, K., Gaboury, S.: Socially assistive robots: the specific case of the NAO. Int. J. Soc. Robot. **13**(4), 795–831 (2021)

26. Santos, N.B., Bavaresco, R.S., Tavares, J.E., Ramos, G.O., Barbosa, J.L.: A systematic mapping study of robotics in human care. Robot. Autonom. Syst. **144**, 103833 (2021)

27. Scerri, A., Sammut, R., Scerri, C.: Formal caregivers' perceptions and experiences of using pet robots for persons living with dementia in long-term care: a meta-ethnography. J. Adv. Nurs. **77**(1), 83–97 (2021). https://doi.org/10.1111/jan.14581

28. Scoglio, A.A., Reilly, E.D., Gorman, J.A., Drebing, C.E.: Use of social robots in mental health and well-being research: systematic review. J. Med. Internet Res. **21**(7), e13322 (2019)

29. Teixeira da Silva, J.A.: Negative results: negative perceptions limit their potential for increasing reproducibility. J. Negat. Results Biomed. **14**(1), 1–4 (2015)

30. Smart, R.G.: The importance of negative results in psychological research. Can. Psychol. Psychol. Can. **5**(4), 225 (1964)

31. Starfield, B.: Basic concepts in population health and health care. J. Epidemiol. Commun. Health **55**(7), 452–454 (2001)

32. Wang, X., Shen, J., Chen, Q.: How PARO can help older people in elderly care facilities: a systematic review of RCT. Int. J. Nurs. Knowl. **33**(1), 29–39. https://doi.org/10.1111/2047-3095.12327

33. Yu, C., Sommerlad, A., Sakure, L., Livingston, G.: Socially assistive robots for people with dementia: systematic review and meta-analysis of feasibility, acceptability and the effect on cognition, neuropsychiatric symptoms and quality of life. Aging Res. Rev. **78**, 101633. https://doi.org/10.1016/j.arr.2022.101633

Ethical Decision-Making for Social Robots in Elderly Care Scenario: A Computational Approach

Siri Dubbaka[1] and B. Sankar[2(✉)]

[1] Department of Mechanical Engineering, Indian Institute of Information Technology, Design and Manufacturing (IIITDM), Jabalpur 482005, Madhya Pradesh, India
2019248@iiitdmj.ac.in
[2] Department of Mechanical Engineering, Indian Institute of Science (IISc), Bangalore 560012, India
sankarb@iisc.ac.in

Abstract. As integrating social robots in elderly care scenarios becomes increasingly prevalent, the need for ethical decision-making frameworks to govern their actions is critically important. This paper presents a comprehensive computational approach using supervised machine learning algorithms to address the ethical considerations inherent in robot-assisted fetching tasks for the elderly. Drawing upon established ethical principles and novel moral dimensions specific to elderly care, we develop an intricate framework encompassing diverse entities and scenarios using a greet or beat approach. To validate the framework, we conducted a pilot study involving thirty participants experienced in caregiving. Through an interactive application, participants designed scenarios, decided whether the robot should fetch objects, and provided reasons for their choices. Their decisions were then compared with predictions generated by a set of machine learning algorithms trained on a dataset of various scenarios. Our results shed light on the diverse ethical perspectives in elderly care and the feasibility of automating ethical decision-making for social robots in this domain. This research contributes to the burgeoning field of roboethics, offering insights and tools to guide the responsible deployment of robots in assistive elderly care, ultimately promoting the well-being and ethical treatment of elderly individuals.

Keywords: Roboethics · Social Robots · Elderly Care · Supervised Classification Algorithms · Machine Learning

1 Introduction

The landscape of robotics has witnessed a significant evolution, culminating in the development of social robots - a category of robots designed to interact with humans and fellow robots in a manner that aligns with social norms. Breazeal and Scassellati's seminal work in 1999 [6] established the framework for social

A. Al. Ali et al. (Eds.): ICSR 2023, LNAI 14453, pp. 143–160, 2024.
https://doi.org/10.1007/978-981-99-8715-3_13

robots as entities that communicate intention perceptibly to humans and possess the capacity to pursue objectives alongside human and robot agents collaboratively [4]. Social robots are becoming increasingly integrated into human social environments, particularly in elderly care; socially assistive robots (SAR) or social robots (SR) are crucial assistants, enhancing well-being through social interactions and support [17].

The recent integration of socially assistive robots (SARs) represents a promising solution to enhance the well-being of the elderly and alleviate the caregiving burden on families [20]. SARs aim to enable independent living by assisting with essential tasks encompassing service and companion robots. These robots are essential for promoting social interaction, reducing stress, mitigating loneliness, and enhancing overall well-being, especially in elderly care [34]. However, the ethical considerations surrounding the use of social robots in elderly care scenarios emphasise the urgency of exploring these implications, given the evolving needs of the elderly population in a changing demographic landscape. Social robots are characterized by certain fundamental key attributes, such as autonomy, physical embodiment, perception, cognition, interaction and adherence to social norms, defined as ethics or roboethics [29]. These attributes emphasize the need for social robots to have a tangible form and the ability to engage with humans independently. Examining these ethics surrounding the deployment of these robots in sensitive caregiving contexts is essential to ensure alignment with the well-being and values of elderly individuals and their caregivers [18].

A fundamental challenge lies in the dual utility of robots, which can both assist and potentially misuse their capabilities, necessitating a careful ethical evaluation [9]. This discourse delves into critical ethical questions, including the delegation of decisions to autonomous machines, the distinction between human and robot decision-making, and the authorization of robots to make life-or-death determinations. Additionally, it addresses accountability in cases of harm caused by robots. The future trajectory of robotics is expected to encompass tasks crucial to human safety and well-being, making it essential to integrate ethical decision-making capabilities into software agents [7]. This approach allows computing systems to assess the ethical appropriateness of their actions, aligning with ethical and legal parameters. By integrating ethical and legal values into software systems, technology can be used conscientiously and ethically, ensuring its responsible and beneficial application in ageing and well-being.

Therefore, this paper elucidates fundamental ethical principles essential when elderly care-fetching robots interact with the elderly. We introduce a novel ethical computational framework designed to mitigate significant ethical concerns. The foundation of this framework lies in the incorporation of core principles from medical ethics, computer ethics, and machine ethics, all within social care ethics. This research explores the ethical dimensions of decision-making concerning social robots within elderly care scenarios. By examining the intricate interplay between technological innovation, social interaction, and ethical considerations, this study aims to contribute to the ethical framework essential for seamlessly integrating socially interactive robots into the care of the elderly populace. The present paper explores ethical considerations intrinsic to deploying social robots within elderly care scenarios, adopting a computational approach using machine learning techniques. The transformative demographic patterns and the ensuing challenges in elderly care underscore the urgency of this investigation, as it seeks to navigate the intricate web of ethical implications associated with the integration of technological solutions in addressing the evolving needs of the elderly population.

2 Background and Motivation

2.1 Social Robots: A Comprehensive Overview

The term "social robot" was introduced by Billard, Dautenhahn, and Breazeal, defining it as a robot endowed with social intelligence capable of engaging in communication and interaction with humans, understanding personal connections, and relating to individuals on a social level [6]. Breazeal further categorizes social robots into four classes based on their ability to support social models and the complexity of their interaction scenarios, ranging from socially evocative robots that elicit emotions through caregiving interactions to sociable robots that actively engage with humans to fulfil internal social aims [4]. Additional categorizations include socially situated robots, socially embedded robots, and socially intelligent robots, reflecting varying degrees of integration and awareness within social environments [24]. Notable examples of social robots include Sophia, Pepper, Nao, ASIMO, Jibo, Moxi, Kaspar, and Tiago, each contributing to the diverse landscape of machines designed for sophisticated social interactions and human-robot engagement.

2.2 Social Robots in Assisting the Elderly

Elderly care faces pressing challenges, including elder abuse, limited awareness of risk factors, nutritional concerns, social isolation, financial constraints, and the need for personalized care in a diverse ageing population [3]. Rather than solely relying on traditional elderly care facilities, a diversified and personalized approach is gaining prominence, with technology-driven in-home assistance fostering improved quality of life through enhanced patient-caregiver interactions [28]. Given the substantial increase in the global elderly population expected by 2050, social robots, particularly Social Assistive Robots (SARs), have emerged as a promising solution to address the escalating demand for elderly care services and improve health and social care quality [23]. SARs are intelligent robotic systems designed to assist with Activities of Daily Living (ADL), monitor physical conditions, and provide entertainment, contributing to the well-being and independent living of the elderly. They have advanced their ability to communicate with humans using diverse modes such as speech, gestures, and facial expressions, thanks to machine learning and pattern recognition [3].

2.3   Fetching Tasks by Social Robots for the Elderly

Social Assistive Robots (SARs) in elderly care serve dual roles as service and companion robots, each tailored to specific functions. Service robots assist elderly individuals with daily tasks like eating, health monitoring, reminders, and safety [17]. Mobile service robots, in particular, offer versatile capabilities, including object delivery, human and object detection, cognitive training, and entertainment, thereby enhancing the daily routines and overall quality of life for the elderly. Several notable examples of such robots include TIAgo, Pepper, Aethon, Temi Telepresence Robot, Relay robot, and Moxi [11]. While professionals in the care sector have shown receptivity to incorporating robots into their interactions with elderly residents, studies reveal differing views and concerns among staff and residents about the utility and acceptance of these robots. Research also indicates that older adults are open to engaging with humanoid robots for cognitive and physical activation but do not seek to replace human caregivers entirely [10]. The safety and security aspects of SARs have received positive feedback, although overall acceptance remains a topic for ongoing investigation. Additionally, existing research underscores the psychological benefits of SARs among elderly groups and emerging connections formed between the elderly and robotic animals. However, these studies have yet to comprehensively examine the ethical dimensions of SARs in elderly care, leaving an important area for future research [35].

3   Ethics in Social Robots

At its core, technology mirrors the values of humanity. As inherently moral beings, humans build their lives on these values, making ethics a vital component of responsible and morally upright technology use. The Principles of Robotics underscore that robots should adhere to existing laws, including privacy, and should be designed with safety and security in mind. Furthermore, it emphasizes the importance of identifying responsibility for the actions of robots.

3.1   Roboethics: Ethical Reflection on Robotics

Roboethics, as defined by [31], is the ethical reflection concerning the unique challenges that arise from the development and integration of robotic applications in society. It encompasses a wide array of considerations, including the dignity and integrity of individuals, their fundamental rights, and the intricate social, legal, and psychological aspects inherent in human-robot interactions [31]. Despite the significance of Social Assistive Robots (SARs) significance, [9] highlights a crucial gap in their ethical analysis. While they provide valuable Human-Robot Interaction (HRI) benchmarks for SARs' development, these benchmarks do not inherently incorporate ethical considerations. World-renowned robotics experts such as [6] and [26] foresee robots gaining the capacity to learn and comprehend human profiles, preferences, and habits. This evolution presents ethical quandaries concerning privacy, safety, and individual freedom [13].

3.2   Importance of Roboethics and Consequences of Neglect

The integration of Social Assistive Robots (SARs) into social care organizations, particularly in the context of elderly care, necessitates the establishment of a robust ethical framework. Failing to conduct ethical analysis when deploying SARs in elderly care settings can have detrimental consequences, given this population's inherent complexities and vulnerabilities [30]. Scholars like [25] have emphasized the importance of caution in the robotics community, highlighting that beyond physical safety concerns, vulnerable populations, including the elderly, can face psychological challenges arising from robot interactions. Acknowledging the potential risks associated with using robot carers for the elderly, such as reduced human contact, increased feelings of objectification, and threats to privacy and personal liberty, scholars like [32] and [27] emphasize the urgent need for guidelines and legal regulations, particularly concerning vulnerable groups like the elderly [1].

3.3   Ethical Considerations in Robot-Elderly Interaction

Human-robot interaction, especially within social robots, presents many ethical challenges, primarily in interactions' psychological, emotional, and social dimensions. One proposed ethical framework, derived from Bernard Gert's deontological rules, outlines ten guiding principles governing a robot's actions, irrespective of their consequences [19]. These principles involve preventing harm and upholding freedom and promises. Still, they can lead to ethical dilemmas, and as medical robots, social robots must also address concerns like attachment, deception, autonomy, privacy, and justice. Addressing these multifaceted ethical dimensions is paramount to ensuring responsible and morally acceptable human-robot interactions, particularly in assistive care contexts [14]. Social Robots in elderly care raise ethical concerns, including potential social isolation, deception, and loss of dignity, all rooted in human rights and shared values [2]. Balancing the empowerment of the elderly through technology with preserving their autonomy and privacy is crucial in addressing these ethical considerations.

3.4   Existing Approaches and Guidelines for Addressing Roboethics

Addressing ethical considerations in robotics and artificial intelligence involves two primary approaches: the bottom-up and the top-down approaches.

The bottom-up approach [33] involves designing machines capable of collecting information, predicting outcomes, making choices, and learning from experiences. This approach enables machines to discern right from wrong by learning from their actions and mistakes, allowing them to adapt their decision-making through experience. It is a self-modifying approach to ethical decision-making.

On the other hand, the top-down approach [33] encompasses two major ethical frameworks: Deontological Roboethics and Consequentialist Roboethics. Deontological Roboethics aligns with Asimov's Laws, which include principles like not harming humans, obeying human orders (unless conflicting with the first law), and self-preservation. Consequentialist Roboethics evaluates actions based on their outcomes, requiring robots to describe situations, generate alternative actions, predict outcomes, and assess situations in terms of their goodness or utility. The challenge lies in defining "goodness" and selecting criteria for assessing situations.

Implementing ethical guidelines in robotics, such as Asimov's Three Laws, presents computational challenges, particularly in real-time decision-making [19]. Roboethics involves maintaining human dignity, fundamental rights, ethical AI algorithms, and the potential for robots to make independent ethical decisions. Additional guidelines from HRI benchmarks and EPSRC rules emphasize safety, transparency, accountability, and legal adherence [5], collectively providing a framework for responsible robotics development.

In social robotic systems, adhering to specific ethical principles encompassing various dimensions: Human Dignity Considerations, Design Considerations, Legal Considerations and Social Considerations. The human dignity consideration encompasses the following principles essential in creating an ethical framework. a. Prioritize and respect individuals' emotional needs. b. Safeguard the right to privacy while considering design goals. c. Show utmost respect for human frailty, including physical and psychological aspects. These principles offer a structured framework to ensure responsible and ethical development of robotic systems while upholding human dignity, adhering to legal standards, and considering social implications. [8]

3.5   Developing an Ethical Framework for Assistive Care Scenarios

In the development of assistive technologies, particularly within the context of assistive care for the elderly, understanding the perspectives and requirements of the target groups is a crucial yet often neglected aspect of research in Human-Robot Interaction (HRI). While initial studies by [32] and [16] have shed light on the qualitative dimension of Socially Assistive Robots (SARs), a more profound comprehension necessitates practical investigations with direct input from elderly groups. This approach aligns with the principles of social care ethos, which emphasizes the importance of considering individuals' perspectives, attitudes, and dignity in care exercises. In elderly care, social care ethos interprets core medical ethical principles, particularly focusing on individual autonomy, beneficence, non-maleficence, and justice. However, applying these principles in caring for older individuals presents significant challenges due to differing perceptions about ethical matters among health professionals, patients, and their families. Consequently, there is a growing call for roboticists to develop a code of ethics, as advocated by [24], and proposals like the general code of ethics for robotics engineers by [15] aim to provide an ethical foundation for the field of robotics. Additionally, safety remains the paramount benchmark in HRI, as evaluating a robot's safety within its designated domain is critical to ensuring its ability to enhance the well-being of its users while neglecting safety considerations during the design process, which could potentially harm the very users it seeks to assist [21].

3.6   Research Objectives

The review of existing literature has revealed a significant gap between ethical considerations and the practical implementation of robotics, particularly concerning the assistance of elderly individuals. In essence, there is an absence of established roboethics frameworks that can offer guidance throughout the development and deployment of Socially Assistive Robots (SARs). This deficiency has resulted in a lack of ethical understanding and tools to facilitate effective communication between developers and potential users of SAR technologies.

In light of these findings, the following research aims and objectives have been identified:

- To investigate the current state of ethics in the development of SARs for elderly care and to identify potential limitations within existing practices.
- To propose a comprehensive computational roboethics framework encompassing human supervision schemes, HRI benchmarks, and ethical specifications for designing, developing, and utilising SARs in elderly care.
- To demonstrate the practical application of the proposed roboethics framework through case studies, thereby validating its effectiveness in real-world scenarios.

This research seeks to bridge the existing gap between ethical considerations and the practical deployment of SARs in assisting elderly groups, ultimately contributing to the development of responsible and ethically sound robotics technologies for elderly care.

4   Research Questions (RQ) and Methodology

The central inquiry of this study revolves around the feasibility of constructing an algorithmic framework for ethical decision-making tailored to care robots assisting the elderly. The overarching objective is to develop a framework that empowers an elderly care robot to navigate typical scenarios encountered by the elderly during their daily lives, assisting them in essential tasks. This framework aims to endow the robot with the capacity to make decisions guided by predefined ethical principles, ensuring the avoidance of ethical concerns, particularly in light of the heightened sensitivity surrounding elderly individuals.

RQ1. How do we design a generalized ethical framework for decision-making in elderly care social robots for fetch tasks? Is it possible to establish an algorithmic ethical decision-making framework for an elderly care robot capable of addressing the routine scenarios commonly encountered by elderly individuals in their daily lives while safeguarding against ethical concerns linked to the elderly's unique needs and sensitivities?

Methodology for RQ1: This research will adopt a multifaceted approach, beginning with an extensive literature review to identify prevailing ethical challenges and concerns associated with care robots for the elderly. Subsequently, a comprehensive set of ethical principles will be formulated, guided by established ethical frameworks and guidelines. These principles will serve as the foundation for the algorithmic framework.

The algorithmic framework's development will involve the integration of these ethical principles into the decision-making process of the care robot, enabling it to assess and respond to various scenarios with ethical considerations in mind. To validate the framework's effectiveness, practical case studies involving typical elderly care situations will be conducted, assessing the robot's decision-making performance in real-world contexts.

5   A Computational Approach for Ethical Decision Making

The primary objective of this research endeavour is to devise a comprehensive framework designed to address and accommodate the daily tasks and routines encountered by the elderly population. This framework aims for universal applicability, catering to the diverse needs of elderly individuals worldwide. It is grounded in a generalized scenario that encapsulates various facets of an elderly person's life, encompassing their social interactions, living conditions, essential daily activities, well-being practices, and health conditions. Moreover, this scenario considers domestic home settings and environments within elderly care facilities.

The ultimate goal of this research initiative is to furnish a versatile framework capable of guiding the decision-making processes of robots deployed to assist the elderly across many real-world scenarios. This framework, firmly rooted in a holistic understanding of the elderly's daily lives, aspires to enhance the quality of care and support provided to this demographic while adhering to ethical principles, thus bridging the gap between human intuition and robotic decision-making through a greet or beat approach.

5.1   Greet or Beat Approach

Ethical decision-making constitutes an inherent aspect of human cognition grounded in ethical intuition. However, integrating ethical considerations into the decision-making processes of robots necessitates the development of distinct rules and policies tailored specifically for these artificial entities. To illustrate this point, consider a scenario where a human and a robot are tasked with greeting or beating someone upon command. While a human may exercise ethical discernment and refrain from beating, a robot, devoid of such innate ethical intuition, may execute the command without hesitation. This stark contrast underscores the imperative need to imbue robots with the capability to make decisions that emulate human-like ethical judgment, distinguishing between permissible and impermissible actions in a given context. Our decision-making framework is designed to handle situations where a robot must decide whether to execute a given command. This decision is based on thoroughly analysing the scenario, particularly when sensitive ethical dilemmas arise. While there can be multiple possible reactions of the robot to a specific command, the primary focus in such delicate situations is determining whether to execute the command. To facilitate this yes or no kind of binary decision-making, the greet or beat approach is chosen. This research endeavours to contribute to creating ethically aware care robots tailored to the needs and sensitivities of the elderly while upholding a robust ethical decision-making framework that minimizes ethical concerns.

5.2 Comprehensive Ethical Framework for Elderly Care Robots

To establish an ethical framework for socially assistive robots (SARs) dedicated to elderly care, it is paramount to incorporate existing ethical principles and introduce novel ones tailored to the specific domain. The amalgamation of these principles serves as the foundation for a robust decision-making framework that addresses ethical concerns effectively. The core principles encompassed in this ethical framework encompass the following:

Existing Ethical Principles. *Asimov's Three Laws of Robotics*: These foundational laws emphasize the prohibition of causing harm to humans, the imperative to obey human orders (unless they conflict with the first law), and the mandate for self-preservation, as long as it doesn't contradict the prior two laws [19].

The Three Laws of Responsible Robotics: Extending beyond Asimov, these laws underscore the significance of systems safety, responsiveness in social interactions, and the seamless transfer of control during contextual disruptions [19].

Machine Ethics: This pertains to the ethical implications of artificial intelligence (AI) and autonomous systems. It involves formulating guidelines and frameworks to instil machines and AI systems with ethical behaviour, ensuring morally responsible actions, particularly in scenarios with ethical consequences [33].

The EPSRC Principles of Robotics: Encompassing compliance with laws, respect for human rights, and the establishment of transparency, these principles provide a fundamental ethical foundation [12].

Medical Ethics: Grounded in the Georgetown Mantra, medical ethics revolves around principles such as autonomy, beneficence, non-maleficence, justice, truthfulness, and dignity, all essential in elderly care [22].

Value-Sensitive Design: This approach seeks to integrate human values systematically throughout the design process, focusing on well-being, dignity, justice, welfare, and human rights [8].

In addition to these, the following ethical principles are newly proposed:
Relational Ethics: Given the frequent involvement of other individuals related to the elderly in caregiving scenarios, the principle of relational ethics emphasizes the ethical considerations associated with these relationships, factoring in the dynamics between the caregiver and the care recipient.

Self Ethics: Acknowledging the significance of personal ethical codes and principles, self-ethics encompasses the individual ethical standards and responsibilities that a person adheres to for their own well-being.

The Core Morals. With these ethical principles as the backdrop, the framework establishes five core morals that underpin the decision-making process for SARs in elderly care. These core morals act as guiding principles, mitigating ethical concerns during tasks related to the elderly:

Safety: Prioritizing the physical safety and well-being of the elderly by avoiding actions that may cause harm or pain, aligning with ethical considerations.

Hygiene: Upholding the elderly's hygiene and cleanliness, preventing the potential spread of germs or infections, is a critical ethical concern.

Privacy: Safeguarding the personal privacy of the elderly to ensure their mental comfort and well-being, addressing ethical concerns regarding intrusion.

Timely Awareness: Recognizing the significance of timely actions in the lives of the elderly, aligning with ethical responsibilities.

Situational Awareness: Ensuring the robot remains vigilant regarding the physical and mental state of the elderly, staying aware of their health conditions, and responding ethically.

The framework dictates that any command issued to the robot conflicting with these core morals will be rejected, thereby preventing ethical concerns and aligning the robot's actions with ethical principles.

5.3   Design of Ethical Framework

Our research tackles a seemingly straightforward yet ethically complex task: fetching objects by a robot for elderly individuals. To address the ethical intricacies associated with this task, we have meticulously crafted a scenario encompassing various elements of an elderly person's life, applicable to both regular home settings and elderly care homes. Moreover, we have categorized the involved entities into distinct classes based on potential ethical concerns, facilitating an algorithmic approach to our framework.

Entity Classification

- *Instructor*: These individuals command the robot to fetch objects for the elderly. They can be further subdivided based on "Relational ethics" into:
  - Elders: The elderly individuals who command for themselves.
  - Residents: First and second-level blood relatives of the elderly.
  - Personnel: Paid household helpers.
  - Visitors: Occasional visitors to the elderly.
  - Medics: Healthcare providers for the elderly.
- *Object*: The items instructed for fetching are categorized into subgroups such as medical items, unsafe items, hygiene-sensitive items, restricted access items, user-restricted items, personal items, shared items, and edible items.
- *Place*: The location where the elderly person resides while receiving the fetched object. This includes medical spaces, dining areas, lavatories, private rooms, and communal areas.

- *Time*: Different times of the day are classified based on the elderly's timely needs and habits, including early morning, morning, afternoon, evening, night, and sleep time.
- *Situation*: Represents the physical and mental state of the elderly during fetching, categorized as either emergency or normal situations.

Machine Learning Based Approach. A meticulous examination of all potential scenarios from combining these entity subclasses has been undertaken to address ethical concerns comprehensively. For example, a scenario involving a visitor instructing the robot to fetch an unsafe item for the elderly would violate our core moral of safety. An ethical framework has been developed based on these scenarios and hypotheses, with the robot programmed to abstain from fetching objects whenever there is a possibility of violating our five core morals: Safety, Hygiene, Privacy, Timely Awareness, and Situational Awareness. To operationalize this framework, a dataset containing all possible scenario combinations has been compiled, and machine learning classification algorithms such as Random Forest, Decision Tree, SVM, KNN, Naïve Bayes, Logistic Regression, Gradient Boosting, and Neural Networks have been trained. These models have been trained on a dataset divided into training and testing data (75% and 25%, respectively), and their accuracy has been evaluated using the testing data as shown in Fig. 1. In conclusion, the proposed ethical scenario framework and machine learning approach aim to ensure that assistance is provided to the elderly by robots in a manner that aligns with core ethical principles, safeguarding their well-being and dignity throughout the fetching process.

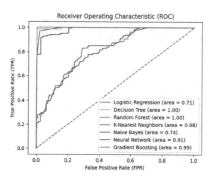

Fig. 1. Receiver Operator Characteristic (ROC) Curve for different ML algorithms

6   Pilot Study: User-Driven Evaluation Using the Computational Framework

The study design incorporates a user study facilitated by a purpose-built application encompassing essential entities and their respective sub-classes pertinent to the act of fetching. Participants are allowed to craft scenarios by selecting elements within these entities and determining whether, in their judgment, the robot should undertake the task of fetching. Furthermore, participants are encouraged to elucidate the rationale behind their decisions. Ultimately, participants can juxtapose their decisions with those generated by our trained computational model. This user-centric approach within the study design is a pivotal step in developing an ethical decision-making framework tailored for robot-assisted fetching, encompassing user perspectives and computational modelling to ensure the fulfilment of ethical imperatives in this context.

A pilot study was conducted with 30 participants, as shown in Fig. 2b in India, comprising twelve females and eighteen males, with an average age of 35. All participants had caregiving experience, and ethical committee approval was obtained for the study. Each participant spent an average of 10 min on the exercise.

6.1   Hypothesis Formulation

H1: *Hypothesis 1:* The decisions made by participants regarding whether the robot should fetch an object for the elderly will exhibit significant variance, reflecting diverse perspectives on ethical considerations in the context of elderly care assistance.

H2: *Hypothesis 2:* The computational model's predictions for the decision to fetch or not, based on participant-generated scenarios and rationales, will demonstrate a reasonable level of accuracy, indicating the feasibility of automating ethical decision-making in robot-assisted fetching tasks for the elderly.

6.2   Study Setup

Participants were provided with an isolated space to perform the exercise. An application named 'Ethical Decision Making in Elderly Care Robots: A Computational Approach' was developed using Python and PyQt6 as shown in Fig. 2a. The application's user interface featured five columns, each corresponding to entities related to fetching tasks, and offered layman examples related to sub-classes of these entities. Participants were allowed to choose whether the robot should fetch the object and were provided with a column to explain their decision. Additionally, a prediction column allowed participants to compare their decisions with those generated by our trained models.

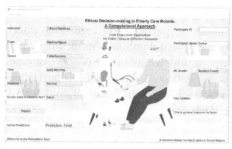

(a) Python Based User Evaluation Application

(b) Participant performing the study

Fig. 2. Study Setup

6.3 Procedure

The exercise followed these steps: Participants received an explanation of the columns' significance and clear definitions of each entity. Each participant received a unique ID. Participants began by entering their names. Participants created five scenarios for each algorithm, starting with Random Forest. After creating each scenario, participants decided whether or not the robot should fetch. Participants provided reasons for their decisions in the opinion column. Participants could check our trained model's decision by clicking the prediction option. The procedure was repeated for all eight algorithms.

6.4 Outcome Measures

A total of 765 samples were collected. After each participant completed the exercise, their choice data was recorded and saved in CSV files, including quantitative parameters such as 'Fetch' or 'Don't Fetch' choices for each entity in the scenarios, as well as qualitative data consisting of participants' opinions on the reasons behind their decisions in specific scenarios. This pilot study is a valuable step towards developing an ethical decision-making framework for elderly care robots, incorporating user perspectives and computational models to ensure ethical considerations are met during robot-assisted fetching tasks.

7 Results and Discussion

This study aimed to evaluate the feasibility of employing supervised learning classification algorithms to automate ethical decision-making for robot-assisted fetching tasks in the context of elderly care. Our analysis involved comparing the decisions made by human participants to those predicted by machine learning models, aiming to validate two primary hypotheses.

Validation of Hypothesis 1: Participant Decision Variance. Our first hypothesis posited that the decisions made by participants regarding whether the robot should fetch an object for the elderly would exhibit significant variance, reflecting diverse perspectives on ethical considerations in the context of elderly care assistance. To test this hypothesis, we collected data from 30 participants who were asked to create scenarios, decide whether the robot should fetch an object, and provide rationales for their decisions.

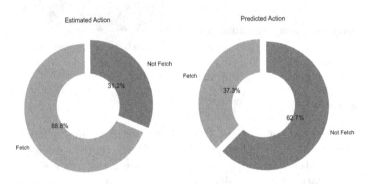

Fig. 3. Percentage of Fetch vs Non Fetch action in User Estimation and Model Prediction

The outcomes demonstrated substantial variability in participant decisions, as shown in Fig. 3. Each individual's unique perspective and judgment were evident in their choices. This result aligns with our hypothesis, reinforcing the idea that ethical decisions in elderly care scenarios can be multifaceted and subject to a range of considerations.

Validation of Hypothesis 2: Model Prediction Accuracy. Our second hypothesis aimed to assess the performance of machine learning models in predicting the decision to fetch or not based on participant-generated scenarios and rationales. Eight supervised learning classification algorithms were trained and tested using the dataset derived from the participant exercise. The accuracy of each model was measured using a testing dataset.

This analysis revealed varying levels of accuracy across the different machine learning algorithms, as shown in Fig. 4 and Fig. 5. Random forest and Decision Tree models demonstrated exceptional accuracy, both achieving 100%. Gradient Boosting and K-Nearest Neighbors (KNN) also performed admirably, with accuracies of 99 % and 98%, respectively. Other models, including Support Vector Machine (SVM), Naïve Bayes, and Logistic Regression, exhibited lower accuracies, ranging from 70% to 74%. Neural Network achieved an accuracy of 91%. These findings support our second hypothesis, indicating that computational models can reasonably predict ethical decisions. Random Forest and Decision Tree models emerged as the most suitable algorithms for creating an ethical framework for decision-making in robot-assisted elderly care tasks.

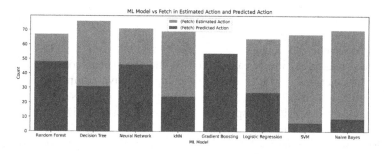

Fig. 4. Comparison of ML Models vs. Fetch Action

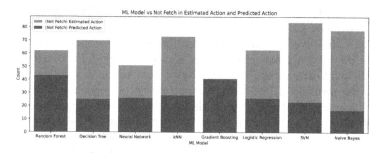

Fig. 5. Comparison of ML Models vs. Not Fetch Action

Moreover, a more detailed examination of the fetch and non-fetch decisions made by participants and the computational models offered valuable insights. The models consistently demonstrated a higher number of non-fetch decisions than the participants. This observation suggests that the models tend to err on the side of caution, opting to avoid fetching in scenarios where ethical concerns may arise. In contrast, participants preferred to fetch decisions in more scenarios, potentially indicating a more permissive approach. Additionally, when examining the differences between participants and the computational models, Random Forest, Decision Tree, and Neural Network displayed the least disparity in fetch and non-fetch decisions. This suggests that these algorithms closely align with participant perspectives and are more attuned to human-like ethical reasoning.

In conclusion, the results of our study affirm the feasibility of automating ethical decision-making for robot-assisted fetching tasks in the context of elderly care. The substantial variance in participant decisions highlights the complexity and subjectivity of ethical considerations in this domain. Furthermore, the success of the computational models, particularly Random Forest and Decision Tree, in predicting ethical decisions underscores their potential as tools for developing ethical frameworks in the field of social robotics for elderly care assistance. These findings contribute to advancing the responsible integration of technology into the care of elderly individuals, ensuring their autonomy and dignity are upheld.

8   Conclusion

This study endeavours to bridge the imperative gap between the increasing adoption of social robots in elderly care scenarios and the ethical considerations that underlie their actions. By introducing a comprehensive computational framework for ethical decision-making in the context of fetching tasks for the elderly, we have addressed a critical aspect of human-robot interaction that is particularly sensitive and complex. This framework incorporates established ethical principles, such as Asimov's Three Laws of Robotics, along with novel moral dimensions, including relational ethics and self-ethics, tailored to the specific needs and sensitivities of elderly care.

The pilot study conducted as part of this research demonstrates the feasibility and potential of automating ethical decision-making for social robots in elderly care. The diverse perspectives and decisions of experienced caregivers underscore the intricate nature of ethical choices in this domain. The comparison of participant decisions with those generated by machine learning algorithms highlights the promise of leveraging computational approaches to enhance the ethical behaviour of robots. As we continue to advance the capabilities and integration of robots into elderly care, the ethical dimension remains paramount. Our framework and pilot study serves as valuable contributions to the burgeoning field of roboethics, providing insights and tools to guide the responsible development and deployment of robots in assistive elderly care. By prioritizing safety, hygiene, privacy, timely awareness, and situational awareness, we can better ensure the well-being and ethical treatment of elderly individuals, promoting their autonomy and dignity in the process.

In summary, the ethical decision-making framework presented here represents a significant step towards realizing the full potential of social robots in elderly care while upholding the highest standards of care and respect for the elderly population. As we navigate the evolving landscape of human-robot interaction, an ethical compass will remain indispensable in fostering trust, acceptance, and positive outcomes for all stakeholders involved.

References

1. Tzafestas, S.G.: Roboethics: a navigating overview. Springer, Cham (2016). https://doi.org/10.1007/978-3-319-21714-7
2. The future of life institute's Asilomar principles (2017) introduced principles related to safety, transparency, responsibility, and alignment with human values for AI systems. Asilomar principles for beneficial AI (2017)
3. Amudhu, L.: A review on the use of socially assistive robots in education and elderly care. Materialstoday: Proceedings (2020)
4. Beer, J., Liles, K., Wu, X., Pakala, S.: Affective human-robot interaction. In: Emotions and Affect in Human Factors and Human-Computer Interaction, pp. 359–381. https://doi.org/10.1016/B978-0-12-801851-4.00015-X
5. Boden, M., et al.: Principles of robotics: regulating robots in the real world. Connect. Sci. **29**, 124–129 (2017). https://doi.org/10.1080/09540091.2016.1271400

6. Breazeal, C., Scassellati, B.: A context-dependent attention system for a social robot. In: Proceedings of the Sixteenth International Joint Conference on Artificial Intelligence, IJCAI 1999, pp. 1146–1153. Morgan Kaufmann Publishers Inc, San Francisco, CA (1999)
7. Bynum, T., Rogerson, S.: Computer ethics and professional responsibility (2003)
8. Davis, J., Nathan, L.P.: Value sensitive design: applications, adaptations, and critiques. In: van den Hoven, J., Vermaas, P., van de Poel, I. (eds.) Handbook of Ethics, Values, and Technological Design. Springer, Dordrecht (2021). https://doi.org/10.1007/978-94-007-6994-6_3-1
9. Feil-Seifer, D., Matarid, M.: Socially assistive robotics: ethical issues related to technology. IEEE, March 2011
10. Frennert, S., Aminoff, H., Ostlund, B.: Technological frames and care robots in eldercare. Int. J. Soc. Robot **13**, 317–325 (2011)
11. Gerłowska, J., Furtak-Niczyporuk, M., Rejdak, K.: Robotic assistance for people with dementia: a viable option for the future? Expert Rev. Med. Devices **17**, 507–518 (2020)
12. Gillon, R.: Medical ethics: four principles plus attention to scope. BMJ **309**, 184 (1994)
13. Hegel, F., Muhl, C., Wrede, B.: Understanding social robots. In: International Conferences on Advances in Computer-Human Interactions, pp. 169–174 (2009)
14. Huschilt, J., Clune, L.: The use of socially assistive robots for dementia care. J. Gerontol. Nurs. **38**(10), 15–19 (2012). https://doi.org/10.3928/00989134-20120911-02. pMID: 22998095
15. Ingram, B., Jones, D., Lewis, A., Richards, M., Rich, C., Schachterle, L.: A code of ethics for robotics engineers, pp. 103–104 (2010). https://doi.org/10.1145/1734454.1734493
16. Kidd, S., Henrich, C., Brookmeyer, K., Davidson, L., King, R., Shahar, G.: The social context of adolescent suicide attempts: interactive effects of parent, peer, and school social relations. Suicide Life-threatening Behav. **36**, 386–395 (2006). https://doi.org/10.1521/suli.2006.36.4.386
17. Logan, D., et al.: Social robots for hospitalized children. Pediatrics **144**, 20181511 (2019)
18. Martinez-Martin, E., Costa, A.: Assistive technology for elderly care: an overview. IEEE Access Pract. Innov. Open Solut. **9**, 92420–92430 (2021)
19. Murphy, R., Woods, D.: Beyond Asimov: the three laws of responsible robotics. IEEE Intell. Syst. **24**, 14–20 (2009). https://doi.org/10.1109/MIS.2009.69
20. Olatunji, S., et al.: Improving the interaction of older adults with a socially assistive table setting robot. In: Salichs, M.A., et al. (eds.) ICSR 2019. LNCS (LNAI), vol. 11876, pp. 568–577. Springer, Cham (2019). https://doi.org/10.1007/978-3-030-35888-4_53
21. Oruma, S., Gkioulos, V., Hansen, J.: A systematic review on social robots in public spaces: threat landscape and attack surface. Computers **11**(12), 181 (2022). https://doi.org/10.3390/computers11120181
22. Paola, I., Walker, R., Nixon, L.: Medical Ethics and Humanities. Sudbary, Jones and Bartlett Publisher (2010)
23. Qiu, R., et al.: The development of a semi-autonomous framework for personal assistant robots-SRS project. Int. J. Intell. Mechatronics Robot. **3**, 30–47 (2013)
24. Riek, L., Howard, D.: A code of ethics for the human-robot interaction profession. https://ssrn.com/abstract=2757805. Available at SSRN
25. Sharkey, A., Sharkey, N.: Children, the elderly, and interactive robots. IEEE Robot. Autom. **18**, 32–38 (2011)

26. Sharkey, A., Sharkey, N.: Granny and the robots: ethical issues in robot care for the elderly. Ethics Inf. Technol. **14**, 27–40 (2012). https://doi.org/10.1007/s10676-010-9234-6

27. Sharkey, N.E., Sharkey, A.J.C.: The crying shame of robot nannies: an ethical appraisal. J. Interact. Stud. **11**, 161–190 (2010)

28. Shishehgar, M., Kerr, D., Blake, J.: A systematic review of research into how robotic technology can help older people. Smart Health **7**, 1–18 (2018)

29. Aditya, U.S., Singh, R., Singh, P., Kalla, A.: A survey on blockchain in robotics: issues, opportunities, challenges and future directions. J. Netw. Comput. Appl **196**, 103245 (2021)

30. Veruggio, G.: Euron roboethics roadmap (2006)

31. Veruggio, G., Solis, J., Loos, M.: Roboethics: ethics apllied to robotics. IEEE Robot. Autom. Magaz. **18**, 21–22 (2011)

32. Wada, K., Shibata, T.: Social and physiological influences of living with seal robots in an elderly care house for two months (2008)

33. Wallach, W., Allen, C., Smit, I.: Machine morality: bottom-up and top-down approaches for modeling human moral faculties (2008)

34. Yin, J., Apuroop, K., Tamilselvam, Y., Mohan, R., Ramalingam, B., Le, A.: Table cleaning task by human support robot using deep learning technique. Sensors **20**, 1698 (2020)

35. Yuan, F., Klavon, E., Liu, Z., Lopez, R., Zhao, X.: A systematic review of robotic rehabilitation for cognitive training. Front. Robot. AI **8**, 605715 (2021)

Virtual Reality Serious Game with the TABAN Robot Avatar for Educational Rehabilitation of Dyslexic Children

O. Amiri[1], M. Shahab[1], M. M. Mohebati[1], S. A. Miryazdi[1], H. Amiri[2], A. Meghdari[1,3(✉)], M. Alemi[1,4], H. R. Pouretemad[5], and A. Taheri[1(✉)]

[1] Social and Cognitive Robotics Laboratory, Sharif University of Technology, Tehran, Iran
{meghdari,artaheri}@sharif.edu
[2] Quantitative Biosciences Institute, University of California, Berkeley, USA
[3] Fereshtegaan International Branch, Islamic Azad University, Tehran, Iran
[4] Department of Humanities, Islamic Azad University, West Tehran Branch, Tehran, Iran
[5] Institute for Cognitive and Brain Sciences (ICBS), Shahid Beheshti University, Tehran, Iran

Abstract. Emerging technologies such as social robotics and virtual reality have found a wide application in the field of education and tutoring particularly for children with special needs. Taban is a novel social robot that has been designed and programmed specifically for educational interaction with dyslexic children, who have various problems in reading despite their normal intelligence. In this paper, the acceptability and eligibility of a virtual reality serious game with the presence of the Taban social robot avatar was studied among nineteen children six of whom were dyslexic. In this game, children perform attractive practical exercises while interacting with the Taban avatar in a virtual environment to strengthen their reading skills; then the game automatically evaluates their performance and the avatar gives them appropriate feedback. The sense of immersion in the 3D virtual space and the presence of the Taban robot avatar motivates the children to do the assignments. The results of the psychological assessment using the SAM questionnaire are promising and illustrate that the game was highly accepted by both groups of children. Moreover, according to statistical analysis, the performance of children with dyslexia in the exercises was significantly weaker than their typically developing peers. Thus, this V2R lexicon game has the potential for screening dyslexia.

Keywords: Social virtual reality robots (*V2R*) · Educational technology · Learning disabilities. · Special Education · Phonological awareness

1 Introduction

Dyslexia, a common neurodevelopmental disorder, presents a significant challenge to children's acquisition of reading and language skills. It affects the fundamental ability to accurately and fluently recognize words, leading to reading difficulties that can persist into adulthood if not addressed early [1]. Dyslexic children often struggle with

A. Al. Ali et al. (Eds.): ICSR 2023, LNAI 14453, pp. 161–170, 2024.
https://doi.org/10.1007/978-981-99-8715-3_14

phonological processing, decoding words, and spelling, which can affect their overall academic performance and self-esteem [2]. The statistics surrounding dyslexia among children are staggering, underscoring the urgency of effective interventions. It is estimated that roughly one in ten children worldwide are dyslexic [3], and studies on Iranian children have reported a similar prevalence [4–6].

The rehabilitation and treatment of dyslexia and its associated symptoms involve a combination of strategies aimed at addressing learning difficulties and promoting academic success. These strategies range from assistive technologies such as text-to-speech [7] to more comprehensive approaches such as phonics instructions, multisensory structured language education, and individualized speech and language therapy [8–10]. Research suggests that effective intervention during early childhood can lead to substantial gains in reading and language skills [11, 12].

Computer games have offered a promising new avenue for the treatment of dyslexia in children, as well as in adults, by virtue of their engaging nature, multisensory components, repetition, immediate feedback, individualization, and anxiety-reducing features [13–17]. Gamification creates personalized interventions that can provide multisensory support, improve learning outcomes, and enhance functional skills. The game experience has been further enriched by the introduction of social robots with expressive behavior [18–21].

Furthermore, according to previous research, virtual reality (VR) technology is an effective tool in the rehabilitation of children with special needs, including those with autism spectrum disorder and cerebral palsy [22–24]. More recently, the idea of using VR game environments in the treatment of dyslexia has emerged, which leverages immersive and interactive virtual environments to amplify the efficacy of the gamification approach [25–28], sometimes supplemented with artificial intelligence [29, 30].

Maskati et al. study virtual reality's potential as a teaching tool for dyslexic students by combining education and entertainment to produce a more effective way of teaching. They proved that using a virtual reality application results in better learning outcomes, compared to conventional learning approaches [25]. Moreover, Maresca et al. illustrated that the attention spans, working memories, ability to process information quickly, and writing and reading skills of dyslexic children were all enhanced by virtual reality training [26].

Pérez-Quichimbo et al. developed Edufarmy, an interactive program that uses virtual reality to improve the reading and writing abilities of dyslexic children. Significant improvements are perceived in the study performed at a psychological facility, and the success is attributed to the sensory stimulation provided by virtual reality [27]. Guillen-Sanz et al. introduce DixGame, a virtual reality game tailored for dyslexic children. Through its gameplay, the study underscores the positive impact of VR games on skill development and emotional support for dyslexic children [28]. The use of VR games is a promising avenue for the rehabilitation, screening, and treatment of children with dyslexia.

Yeguas-Bolvar et al. suggested combining virtual reality and artificial intelligence to help dyslexic college students who struggle with learning. They utilized VRAIlexia, which contains a mobile app that uses virtual reality to gather data, along with AI-based software that analyzes the data and creates supportive teaching strategies specific to each student. According to the study, AI techniques have the potential to accurately predict the support resources and study techniques that dyslexic students will need, with an accuracy rate of about 90% [29]. Furthermore, Zingoni et al. also utilized the VRAIlexia project and its software platform that combines virtual reality and artificial intelligence. The significance of utilizing virtual reality for specialized educational assistance in the dyslexic community is highlighted by preliminary results from a sizable sample [30].

In this paper, by combining two emerging technologies including virtual reality and social robotics, we developed a novel Social Virtual Reality Robot (V2R) platform tailored toward dyslexic children and aimed at providing an immersive and engaging tool to enhance their literacy skills. The platform offers several types of expert-designed game challenges and incorporates an intelligent virtual social robot to accompany the children throughout the game experience. The robot is a virtual replica of Taban 2, a new generation of the Taban social robot that has been developed for educational interaction with dyslexic children [21]. As the main contribution, this study explores the potential of using V2R as a tool in situations where the Taban robot is not available for the rehabilitation of dyslexic children. Therefore, as the first step, we assess the acceptability of our VR game platform. By comparing the performance of dyslexic and typically developing children, we aim to determine whether V2R could be used as a supplementary method for the rehabilitation of dyslexic children.

2 Methodology

2.1 The Theories of Dyslexia Etiology

The Phonological processing deficit has substantial prevalence among dyslexics, and the phonological theory of dyslexia has been widely adopted by the research community [31, 32]. In this theory, dyslexic children's reading impairment is explained by the fact that learning to read in alphabetically written languages requires learning grapheme-phonemes correspondence (the correspondence between letters and their associated sounds), and if these phonemes are not well represented, stored, and retrieved, the foundation of reading in alphabetical writing languages will be impaired. Phonological processing is the use of phonetic structure while learning to decode (read) the written language. It is divided into three components: phonological awareness, phonemic access to vocabulary storage (rapid automatic naming), and phonological stimulus memory (verbal information) [33]. Phonological awareness is one's sensitivity to the structure of the oral language.

The games in this study have been designed to assess and improve the cognitive ability of dyslexic children, especially in the field of phonological awareness, by leveraging the unique capabilities of the Taban 2 social robot in a VR environment.

2.2 Game Design

We have designed an immersive VR experience environment, in which a player interacts with Taban (means "radiant" in Persian), a friendly socially expressive virtual reality robot (V2R) that instructs and guides the player through various games and scenarios.

The game was developed using the Unity engine for the Meta Oculus virtual reality headset. The various game levels were designed to immerse the players in the exercises, capture their attention, and motivate them to complete the levels and answer the questions. Each level consists of various 3D grabbable objects (e.g., animals, tools, etc.) and grabbable words presented on a table in front of the sitting player, with the intended gameplay mechanisms depending on the interaction required. The Taban virtual robot is also present as a guide.

The general design of the games is based on standard clinical interventions [34] used by professionals in learning disorder centers. After reviewing the interventions we finalized the game designs. The experience consists of nine levels with four unique designs, with each design targeting a different aspect of phonological deficit. The four designs were as follows:

2.2.1 Finding Objects with the Same Starting Phoneme

The goal of this mini-game is to familiarize the player with the overall experience by asking them to find the correct first phoneme of each given object's name. Taban tells the player to put the objects on the board with the correct first phoneme as its label.

2.2.2 Grouping Objects with the Same Starting Phoneme

In this game, we want the player to compare the first phonemes find out the objects with the same starting phonemes, and memorize them. Unlike the first scenario, the boards are not labeled and the players have to group the objects by themselves.

2.2.3 Finding Phonetic Pairs

The mini-game challenges the player's phonetic awareness by making them select and grab the 3D objects that are phonetic pairs, and then Taban tells the player to smash them together for an explosive effect that is very enjoyable.

2.2.4 Phonetic Substitution

This game design consists of recognizing the first phoneme and replacing it with a new one. Taban instructs the player to cut the words with a knife to separate the phonemes.

Although all the designs had at least two complete and game-ready levels, due to the limited time the children could wear the headset continuously (about 20 min) the headset was removed by the therapist to not to make them tired.

2.3 Game Mechanisms

The game's main constant environmental objects are the main table, the player, and the Taban model. Contents of the table change according to the levels. Each level design had its own programming, logic, and mechanism.

Taban plays a pivotal role and interacts with the player in various ways. At the beginning of each level, Taban explains the goal to the player and the steps they have to take to achieve the goal. Taban communicates with the player by utilizing body language such as animated hands, head, and face. Taban's facial expressions are animated and smoothly change during the dialogues. For example, when the player makes an incorrect move, Taban tells the player with a soft tone of voice and gentle facial expression (lowering its eyebrows) that he/she made a mistake; it also applauds the player when he/she completes a level and throws confetti on the table (Fig. 1a). Common dialogues have multiple versions that are randomly selected to make them less repetitive.

The player can interact with the objects using two controllers. Each controller can grab or select anything from a distance. For simplicity, the grab/select action is the only button that the player can use during the game.

Some levels utilize virtual magnets as a way of grouping and submitting the objects. The player should bring the object close to a magnet and let it go to make them stick together. During the game, the objects are represented as easily identifiable models. Some levels also have grabbable words that can be cut at the correct points using a virtual knife (Fig. 1b) and combined to create new words. In the game environment, there are some barriers to prevent objects from falling out of the player zone and becoming unreachable. Thus, the inaccessible objects automatically return to their initial position. Levels are automatically progressed when a challenge is complete. The level progression can be controlled manually by the operator/supervisor. Furthermore, there is also a menu for the player in the game, to change or repeat the levels individually. The game has an automatic logging system that records every player's action and headset or controller movement.

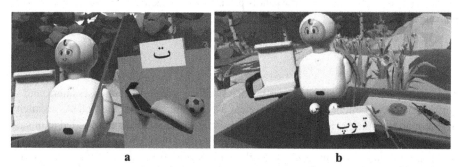

a **b**

Fig. 1. Screenshots of the game environment: a) Taban reacts to the player's choices based on their validity in design type one (The board is titled ت/t/ phoneme), and b) The cut-able words in the design type four, allows the player to use a knife to separate letters from words in order to combine them later (The word being cut is ball توپ /toop/ and the target word is soup سوپ/soop/).

2.4   Experimental Setup and Participants

Six children with dyslexia (Mean: 7.33, SD: 0.43 years old) and 13 typically developing (TD) children (Mean: 7.92, SD: 0.76 years old) between 7–8 years old participated in this study. Each participant was asked to put on an Oculus Quest virtual reality headset (Fig. 2). All participants were wearing it for about 20min (due to discomfort concerns). In the time allowed, the first 15 min were designated for playing the games. All participants were playing the same four types of games.

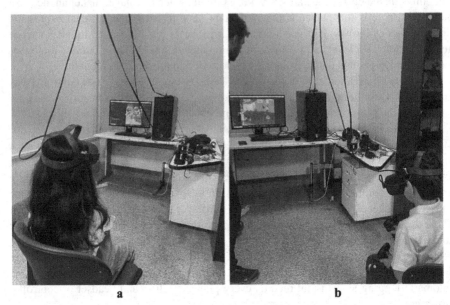

Fig. 2. Photos of the game session a) the participant is listening to the virtual Taban robot explaining the game rules. b) Another participant is playing the game's first level with the supervisor present.

2.5 Assessment Tools

Two assessment tools were utilized in this study: a psychological assessment and a performance assessment. The psychological assessment included the Self-Assessment Manikin questionnaire (SAM) [34] that used a smiley face scale from satisfied to unsatisfied and all items in the questionnaires were measured over a 5-point Likert scale. The SAM questionnaire was used to assess the child's sensed valance, arousal, and dominance rate when playing the games. The performance of the participants was assessed not only based on automatic game logs but also according to a therapist video coding evaluation using a prepared worksheet for each game. The criteria for both the automatic assessment and the video coding method were the participant's response time and the validity of their answers.

3   Results and Discussion

First, the participants' performances were evaluated during the VR games. The final score of each participant was evaluated afterward using their respective time and performance in answering the questions correctly the first time. The main goal of these games was to check whether there was a meaningful difference between the performances of the TD and dyslexic students in answering the questions.

According to Table 1. We observed that TD children scored significantly higher than dyslexic children in all of the four games design types (P-value < 0.05). This reflects the appropriateness of this approach for targeting phonological deficits, and highlights the high potential of this game platform and its associated assessment criteria to be used as an unbiased and rapid screening tool to identify children with dyslexia.

Table 1. The mean and standard deviation scores of the dyslexic and TD groups in different exercises and the T-value and P-values associated with the T-tests; P-value < 0.05 shows the 95% confidence interval.

No	Exercise	Score's mean out of 20 (SD)		T-value	P-value
		Dyslexia	TD		
1	Type 1	10.98(5.17)	16.87(2.53)	−2.65	**0.038**
2	Type 2	5.52(7.21)	17.90(1.87)	−3.39	**0.043**
3	Type 3	5.14(6.82)	18.60(0.94)	−4.4	**0.012**
4	Type 4	3.11(3.69)	16.70(2.21)	−6.09	**0.026**

In the second part of the experiment, the participants filled out the SAM questionnaire and determined their level of satisfaction with the game. By reviewing the results of the questionnaire, we can study whether there is a meaningful difference in the acceptance rate of the game between TD and dyslexic groups of participants (Table 2).

Table 2. The mean and standard deviation scores of the SAM questionnaire parameters and the T-value and P-values associated with the T-tests.

No	Item	SAM Questionnaire			
		Score's mean (SD)		T-value	P-value
		Dyslexia	TD		
1	Pleasure	4.66(0.51)	4.66(0.65)	0	1
2	Arousal	4.50(0.55)	4.84(0.39)	−1.33	0.22
3	Dominance	4.50(0.55)	4.50(0.80)	0	1

The questionnaires' results showed that both groups of children scored high in most assessment categories. The SAM questionnaire result for the games indicates an overall positive experience with pleasure, arousal, and dominance all scoring high on the Likert scale. This shows that for both groups of children, the games felt exciting and made them feel happy and in control of the experience. The implied high level of acceptability of this VR platform justifies and motivates the development of further game designs based on this platform. Moreover, the questionnaire results will help us improve the game and our future work.

3.1 Limitations and Future Work

The time duration of the sessions, which was a maximum of 20 min, and the number of participants were among the main limitations of this study; the participants could answer just a limited number of questions. The following step of this research line, given the high acceptance rate of the designed game, is to perform systematic educational interventions over at least 8 sessions on a group of children with dyslexia to evaluate the effectiveness of the *V2R*-based treatment with the use of virtual Taban robot and its training scenarios on the reading skills of participants.

4 Conclusion

The goal of this research was to evaluate the effectiveness of using a V2R serious game, which includes the virtual Taban robot in the role of tutor, as an assistant tool to comfort the learning process of dyslexic children. Using VR-based games also expands the possibilities for exercise designs that can be utilized in the game. This study focused on the design process of four different games and their following evaluation.

Two assessment criteria including the game performance and psychological scoring system were systematically used to evaluate the participants' performance, emotional response, and immersion. The results showed that the game designs have the potential to be used as a reliable screening tool for dyslexic children, while also giving them a fun and enjoyable experience and a high degree of acceptance.

In conclusion, the VR platform with a virtual reality robot (V2R) has shown promising results for dyslexic children and may be used as a valuable assistant tool for investigators, educators, and parents since it saves time, cost, and energy in comparison to a real robot. Additionally, by harnessing the immersive and interactive nature of VR, this approach can serve as a novel and effective means of improving reading abilities in dyslexic children.

Acknowledgment. This study was funded by the "Dr. Ali Akbar Siassi Memorial Research Grant Award" and Sharif University of Technology (Grant No. G980517). We would like to thank our friends Ms. Shabnam Tahbaz for recording the robot voices and Ms. Shakiba Ahmadi for her collaboration and aid during the acceptance sessions.

References

1. Lyon, G.R., Shaywitz, S.E., Shaywitz, B.A.: A definition of dyslexia. Ann. Dyslexia **53**(1), 1–14 (2003)
2. Peterson, R.L., Pennington, B.F.: Developmental Dyslexia. Annu. Rev. Clin. Psychol. **11**(1), 283–307 (2015)
3. Wagner, R.K., et al.: The prevalence of dyslexia: a new approach to its estimation. J. Learn. Disabil. **53**(5), 354–365 (2020)
4. Yavari, A., Valizadeh, A., Marofizadeh, S., Panahian, M.: Prevalence dyslexia among first to sixth grade Persian speaking students in Arak, Iran. Function Disability J. **2**(1), 100–104 (2019)

5. Pouretemad, H.R., Khatibi, A., Zarei, M., Stein, J.: Manifestations of developmental dyslexia in monolingual Persian speaking students. Arch. Iran. Med. **14**(4), 259–265 (2011)
6. Hakim, A., Ghorbanibirgani, A.: Prevalence of dyslexia among male students in primary schools and its relationship with obesity and being overweight in Ahvaz, Iran. Inter. J. Community Based Nursing Midwifery **3**(2), 116 (2015)
7. Nordström, T., Nilsson, S., Gustafson, S., Svensson, I.: Assistive technology applications for students with reading difficulties: special education teachers' experiences and perceptions. Disabil. Rehabil. Assist. Technol.. **14**(8), 798–808 (2019)
8. Habib, M., Giraud, K.: Dyslexia. Handb. Clin. Neurol.. Clin. Neurol. **111**, 229–235 (2013)
9. Nurul Anis, M.Y., Normah, C.D., Mahadir, A., Norhayati, I., Rogayah, A.R., Dzalani, H.: Interventions for children with dyslexia: a review on current intervention methods. Med. J. Malaysia **73**(5), 311–320 (2018)
10. National Research Council: Preventing Reading Difficulties in Young Children. National Academies Press, Washington, D.C. (1998)
11. van der Leij, A.: Dyslexia and early intervention: what did we learn from the Dutch Dyslexia Programme? Dyslexia **19**(4), 241–255 (2013)
12. Torgesen, J.K.: Recent discoveries on remedial interventions for children with Dyslexia. In: The Science of Reading: A Handbook, pp. 521–537. John Wiley & Sons, Ltd. (2005)
13. Pedroli, E., Padula, P., Guala, A., Meardi, M.T., Riva, G., Albani, G.: A psychometric tool for a virtual reality rehabilitation approach for Dyslexia. Comput. Math. Methods Med. **2017**, 7048676 (2017)
14. Broadhead, M., Daylamani-Zad, D., Mackinnon, L., Bacon, L.: A multisensory 3D environment as intervention to aid reading in Dyslexia: a proposed framework. In: 2018 10th International Conference on Virtual Worlds and Games for Serious Applications (VS-Games), pp. 1–4 (2018)
15. Fokides, E., Chronopoulou, M.-I., Kaimara, P.: Comparing videos and a 3D virtual environment for teaching school-related functional skills and behaviors to students with ADHD or developmental dyslexia, displaying challenging behaviors: a case study. Res. Pract. Technol. Enhanc. Learn. **14**(1), 22 (2019)
16. Peters, J.L., De Losa, L., Bavin, E.L., Crewther, S.G.: Efficacy of dynamic visuo-attentional interventions for reading in dyslexic and neurotypical children: a systematic review. Neurosci. Biobehav. Rev. **100**, 58–76 (2019)
17. Peters, J.L., Crewther, S.G., Murphy, M.J., Bavin, E.L.: Action video game training improves text reading accuracy, rate and comprehension in children with dyslexia: a randomized controlled trial. Sci. Rep. **11**(1), 18584 (2021)
18. Taheri, A., Shariati, A., Heidari, R., Shahab, M., Alemi, M., Meghdari, A.: Impacts of using a social robot to teach music to children with low-functioning autism. Paladyn, J. Behav. Robot. **12**(1), 256–275 (2021)
19. Ghorbandaei Pour, A., Taheri, A., Alemi, M., Meghdari, A.: Human–robot facial expression reciprocal interaction platform: case studies on children with autism. Inter. J. Soc. Robot. **10**, 179–198 (2018)
20. Belpaeme, T., Kennedy, J., Ramachandran, A., Scassellati, B., Tanaka, F.: Social robots for education: a review. Sci Robot. **3**(21) eaat5954 (2018)
21. Mokhtari, M., Shariati, A., Meghdari, A.: Taban: a retro-projected social robotic - head for human-robot interaction. In: 2019 7th International Conference on Robotics and Mechatronics (ICRoM), pp. 46–51 (2019)
22. Shahab, M., et al.: Utilizing social virtual reality robot (V2R) for music education to children with high-functioning autism. Educ. Inform. Technol., 1–25 (2022)
23. Shahab, M., Raisi, M., Hejrati, M., Taheri, A., Meghdari, A.: Virtual reality robot for rehabilitation of children with cerebral palsy (CP). In: 2019 7th International Conference on Robotics and Mechatronics (ICRoM), pp. 63–68. IEEE (2019)

24. Shahab, M., et al.: Social Virtual reality robot (V2R): a novel concept for education and rehabilitation of children with autism. In: 2017 5th RSI international conference on robotics and mechatronics (ICRoM), pp. 82–87. IEEE (2017)

25. Maskati, E., Alkeraiem, F., Khalil, N., Baik, R., Aljuhani, R., Alsobhi, A.: Using virtual reality (VR) in teaching students with Dyslexia. Inter. J. Emerging Technol. Learn. (iJET) **16**(09), Art. no. 09 (2021)

26. Maresca, G., et al.: Use of virtual reality in children with Dyslexia. Children (Basel) **9**(11), 1621 (2022)

27. Pérez Quichimbo, S.M., Barrera Quimbita, E.D., Navas Moya, M.P., López Chico, X.: Edufarmy: a multisensory educational software system that improves the learning of children with dyslexia using the orton-gillingham approach. In: Zambrano Vizuete, M., Botto-Tobar, M., Diaz Cadena, A., Durakovic, B. (eds.) CI3 2021. LNCSs, vol 511. Springer, Cham (2021). https://doi.org/10.1007/978-3-031-11438-0_36

28. Guillen-Sanz, H., Rodríguez-Garcia, B., Martinez, K., Manzanares, M.C.S.: A virtual reality serious game for children with Dyslexia: DixGame. In: De Paolis, L.T., Arpaia, P., Sacco, M. (eds.) Extended Reality. XR Salento 2022. LNCS, vol 13446. Springer, Cham (2022). https://doi.org/10.1007/978-3-031-15553-6_3

29. Yeguas-Bolívar, E., Alcalde-Llergo, J.M., Aparicio-Martínez, P., Taborri, J., Zingoni, A., Pinzi, S.: Determining the difficulties of students with dyslexia via virtual reality and artificial intelligence: an exploratory analysis. In: 2022 IEEE International Conference on Metrology for Extended Reality, Artificial Intelligence and Neural Engineering (MetroXRAINE), pp. 585–590 (2022)

30. Zingoni, A., et al.: Investigating issues and needs of dyslexic students at university: proof of concept of an artificial intelligence and virtual reality-based supporting platform and preliminary results. Appli. Sci. 11(10), Art. no. 10 (2021)

31. Vellutino, F.R., Fletcher, J.M., Snowling, M.J., Scanlon, D.M.: Specific reading disability (dyslexia): what have we learned in the past four decades? J. Child Psychol. Psychiatry **45**(1), 2–40 (2004)

32. Ramus, F., et al.: Theories of developmental dyslexia: insights from a multiple case study of dyslexic adults. Brain **126**(Pt 4), 841–865 (2003)

33. Anthony, J.L., Francis, D.J.: Development of phonological awareness. Curr. Dir. Psychol. Sci. **14**(5), 255–259 (2005)

34. Soleimani, Z.: Phonological awareness and effect of reading in 5.5 and 6.5 years old Persian children. Archives of Rehabilitation **1**(2), 27–35 (2000)

35. Bradley, M.M., Lang, P.J.: Measuring emotion: the self-assessment manikin and the semantic differential. J. Behav. Ther. Exp. Psych. **25**(1), 49–59 (1994)

Impact of Explanations on Transparency in HRI: A Study Using the HRIVST Metric

Nandu Chandran Nair$^{(\boxtimes)}$ ⓘ, Alessandra Rossiⓘ, and Silvia Rossiⓘ

Dipartimento di Ingegneria Elettrica e delle Tecnologie dell'Informazione, Università Degli Studi di Napoli Federico II, Naples, Italy
contact.nanducn@gmail.com, {alessandra.rossi,silvia.rossi}@unina.it

Abstract. This paper presents an exploration of the role of explanations provided by robots in enhancing transparency during human-robot interaction (HRI). We conducted a study with 85 participants to investigate the impact of different types and timings of explanations on transparency. In particular, we tested different conditions: (1) no explanations, (2) short explanations, (3) detailed explanations, (4) short explanations for unexpected robot actions, and (5) detailed explanations for unexpected robot actions. We used the Human-Robot Interaction Video Sequencing Task (HRIVST) metric to evaluate legibility and predictability. The preliminary results suggest that providing a short explanation is sufficient to improve transparency in HRI. The HRIVST score for short explanations is higher and very close to the score for detailed explanations of unexpected robot actions. This work contributes to the field by highlighting the importance of tailored explanations to enhance the mutual understanding between humans and robots.

Keywords: Social robotics · Explanations · Transparent HRI

1 Introduction

As robots become collaborative partners in various human-centered domains, researchers strive to facilitate clear understanding and control for people while enabling robots to interpret human cues, and accordingly adapt their behaviors [1,2]. This is particularly important because transparent communication between humans and robots fosters comfortable and effective collaboration [3,4]. While previous studies have examined different cues to make human-robot interaction more transparent [5,6], our focus is on verbal interaction and the role of explanations. Verbal communication is vital in enhancing the clarity and success of an HRI [7]. Our long-term goal is to explore strategies that empower effective communication between humans and robots both during activities performed in collaboration and not [8].

Focusing on evaluating the effectiveness of explanations in promoting transparency in HRI, we propose five different conditions of explanations that aim to

A. Al. Ali et al. (Eds.): ICSR 2023, LNAI 14453, pp. 171–180, 2024.
https://doi.org/10.1007/978-981-99-8715-3_15

evaluate the explanations based on the content and timing in which they are provided. We use the HRIVST (Human-Robot Interaction Video Sequencing Task) [9] measure to evaluate the legibility and predictability of very simple scenarios where a robot has "to fold" and "pick and place" some clothes. In this scenario, the robot may exhibit errors or have unexpected behaviors.

We recruited 85 participants and filtered the people in our quality check process. The outcomes indicate that the highest transparency score is attributed to providing short explanations in real-time. Notably, the second-highest score corresponds to situations where detailed explanations are provided upon a change in the robot's plan. In this study, we provide an evaluation of the multifaceted relationship between HRI explanations and transparency, and as a consequence, we identify which type of explanation contributes to improving people's trust in and understandability of robots through systematic experimentation and by using the HRIVST metric.

2   Related Work

Transparency allows humans to be aware of the state of a robot and assess the progress of tasks [10]. One way of providing transparent interaction is by using explanations. Explanations in HRI refer to a robot providing justifications or reasons for its decisions or actions. These explanations enhance user perceptions, justify the robot's reliability, and increase trust [11]. This paper addresses two main aspects of robot explanations: the content of the explanation and the timing of when the explanation is provided. It explores how the information conveyed in the explanation and the moment it is delivered impact the interaction between people and robots.

A relevant study [12] presented an experiment involving 366 participants to explore whether robots should provide explanations and examine the attributes of a desired explanation. These attributes encompass timing, the significance of engagement, resemblance to human explanations, and the act of summarization. The findings revealed a consensus among participants that robot behavior warrants explanation across the scenarios. It is to be noted that people's preferred mode of explanation aligns with how humans explain things in context. Participants appreciated concise summaries and preferred the robot to respond to only a limited number of follow-up questions.

While explanations alone may not significantly impact perceived competence intelligence, likeability, or safety ratings of the robot [11], they do contribute to the perception of the robot as more lively and human-like [11]. There are different types of explanations for HRI. One study evaluated the effectiveness of contrastive, causal, and example explanations in supporting human understanding of Artificial Intelligence (AI) in a hypothetical scenario [13]. Another study proposed a framework for generating explanations in autonomous robots focusing on presenting the minimum necessary information to understand an event [14]. Additionally, research on progressive explanations aims to improve understanding by limiting cognitive effort at each step [15]. Furthermore, human-like explanations based on the probability of success have been explored to make explanations more understandable for non-expert users [16].

Unlike prior research on robots explaining after being asked, this paper focuses on proactive explanations generated before actions are executed. The study investigates how these proactive explanations influence human-robot trust dynamics [17]. Prior work has shown that explanations, especially those of a complex nature, should be made in real-time during the execution of tasks. This helps spread the information to be explained and reduces the mental workload of humans in highly cognitively demanding tasks [18]. Moreover, the order in which the information is presented in an explanation or the progressiveness of the explanations can contribute to better learning and understanding [19].

3   Explanation Types

In this work, we want to focus on different explanation types based on the content size. In particular, we considered the following types of explanations to identify the most effective strategies for enhancing mutual understanding and trust between humans and robots:

- **Labeled Explanation**: Labeled explanations are presented as succinct labels, where each label corresponds to a specific robot action. For example, if a robot is observed moving towards a door, the accompanying labeled explanation would be "MOVE". This concise explanation encapsulates the essence of the robot's action in a single keyword, making it an easily graspable reference (see Fig. 1a).
- **Focused Explanation**: The focused explanation involves crafting sentences succinctly conveying the robot's actions while maintaining clarity and directness. For instance, if a robot is seen moving toward a door, the focused explanation would be, "Move towards the door". This approach provides a more detailed description than the labeled explanation while remaining concise and to the point (see Fig. 1b).
- **Comprehensive Explanation**: Comprehensive explanations represent a more elaborate form of communication. In this type, sentences are constructed to encompass not only the robot's action but also additional contextual information that aids in understanding the intent and purpose behind the action. For example, if a robot is observed moving toward a door, the comprehensive explanation would provide a detailed description: "Move from the room's right side to the left to open the red door." This in-depth narrative offers a holistic view of the robot's actions and underlying motivations (see Fig. 1c).

4   Methodology

For this study, we selected four videos where a robot performs a simple task. Each task consists of two or more actions. We use three videos in which the

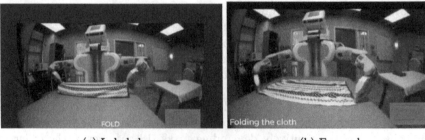

(a) Labeled   (b) Focused

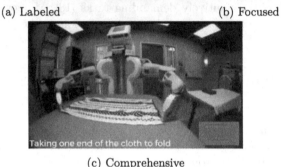

(c) Comprehensive

Fig. 1. Examples of explanation types for Video 4: (a) "Fold", (b) "Folding the cloth", and (c) "Taking one end of the cloth to fold".

robot picks and places a cloth and a fourth video in which the robot folds a cloth. Table 1 shows the description of the four videos.

Participants were tested with one of the following five different conditions:

- **No Explanation**: In this condition, the videos do not have any explanations. By observing participants' reactions and understanding when no explanation is provided, we establish a baseline for measuring the impact of explanations on transparency (see Fig. 2e).
- **Focused Explanation**: The second condition involves providing participants with short explanations accompanying the videos. These explanations are designed to succinctly describe the robot's actions while the actions are being performed. This real-time provision of information aims to enhance transparency by offering immediate insights into the robot's intentions and tasks (see Fig. 2a).
- **Comprehensive Explanation**: Participants will receive detailed explanations in this third condition. Similar to the above condition, these explanations will be delivered in real-time while the robot is engaged in its actions. The comprehensive nature of these explanations intends to provide a deeper understanding of the robot's actions, including contextual details that contribute to transparent communication (see Fig. 2b).
- **Alerted Focused Explanation**: The fourth condition introduces a novel element of explanation timing. Here, the focused explanations will be provided to alert the human observer about the robot's actions. This condition

Table 1. Description of each video

No.	Videos	Description
1	Video 1	A robotic arm moves to the right side of the table. The robot picks up the folded cloth and moves to the left side of the table. The robot places the folded cloth on top of another cloth.
2	Video 2	A robotic arm moves to the right side of the table. The robot picks up the folded cloth. The cloth gets unfolded. The robot stops and moves toward the human. The robot hands over the cloth to fold it up.
3	Video 3	A robotic arm moves to the right side of the table. The robot picks up the folded cloth very slowly without unfolding it. The robot carefully places the folded cloth on top of another cloth.
4	Video 4	A robot folds the cloth vertically and flats it. Then, it folds the cloth horizontally from the left side and right side. Then, it picks up the cloth and moves it to the other side of the room to put it into another table.

is especially relevant in scenarios involving robot failures or changes in plan of action. By focusing on the importance of explanations during these critical moments, we aim to ascertain the impact of timely explanations on transparency and overall human-robot interaction (see Fig. 2c).

- **Alerted Comprehensive Explanation**: The fifth condition also focuses on the timing of the explanation. However, comprehensive explanations are provided instead of focused explanations to alert the observer. This condition aims to validate by giving details of the robot's actions to understand the change of plan (see Fig. 2d).

4.1 Evaluation

We used the HRIVST to test if a robot's behavior is understandable to humans. The HRIVST metric is a subjective measure to evaluate the legibility of a robot's behavior by assessing individuals' capacity to discern goal-oriented actions [9]. The methodology involves segmenting the videos into several distinct clips, each corresponding to an action executed by the robot or the involved individuals during the interaction. Participants are prompted to view these video clips and arrange them in the order that reflects the chronological sequence of task actions. Participants could repeatedly watch the clips, enabling them to grasp the action sequence accurately and familiarize themselves with the task.

Participants were required to complete a brief questionnaire following each video clip to indicate the robot's intention, their expectation of the robot's actions, and their confidence level in attributing the robot's intention (i.e., whether it was difficult or easy).

The cumulative HRIVST score is derived from two components: the outcome of the logical sequence task, ranging from 0 to 6, and the responses provided

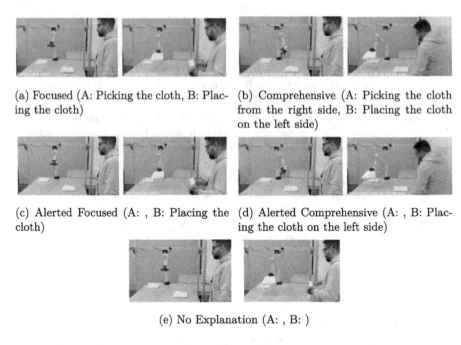

(a) Focused (A: Picking the cloth, B: Placing the cloth)

(b) Comprehensive (A: Picking the cloth from the right side, B: Placing the cloth on the left side)

(c) Alerted Focused (A: , B: Placing the cloth)

(d) Alerted Comprehensive (A: , B: Placing the cloth on the left side)

(e) No Explanation (A: , B:)

Fig. 2. Comparison of explanation in the five conditions for Video 2.

in the questionnaire, which also have a potential range of 0 to 2. These two components constitute the total HRIVST score for each video, yielding a possible score range of 0 to 8. The scoring mechanism for the logical sequence task is designed as follows:

– Both the first and last video clips are each assigned 2 points.
– For the others, if a participant correctly orders them in the sequence, they are awarded 2 points divided by the number of remaining clips.

For instance, in a video composed of 4 clips, the first and last clips would be worth 2 points each, while each centrally positioned clip would carry a potential value of 1 point if accurately sequenced.

5   Preliminary Results

The study was conducted online. The obtained participant distribution thus far is as follows: 30 participants in the "No Explanation" condition, 12 in the "Focused Explanation" condition, 21 in the "Comprehensive Explanation" condition, 10 in the "Alerted Focused Explanation" and 12 in the "Alerted Comprehensive Explanation" condition. Control questions were employed to ensure data quality. Consequently, participants providing incorrect responses were filtered out, resulting in the final participant counts of 21, 10, 14, 8, and 6 for the respective conditions. The final 58 participants included people of various nationalities.

Table 2. Descriptive Statistics of the HRIVST for different conditions. For each video, the highest value is reported in bold.

Conditions	Video 1	Video 2	Video 3	Video 4	Average
No Explanation Mean (SD)	6.23 (2.58)	7.00 (2.00)	6.71 (2.10)	6.57 (2.57)	6.63 (2.31)
Focused Mean (SD)	6.75 (2.10)	6.67 (2.13)	**7.50 (1.12)**	**7.86 (1.30)**	**7.19 (1.66)**
Comprehensive Mean (SD)	**6.76 (2.55)**	5.00 (2.35)	5.47 (2.03)	5.75 (2.61)	5.75 (2.38)
Alerted Focused Mean (SD)	5.5 (0.67)	5.2 (2.32)	6.67 (1.25)	6.45 (1.55)	5.95 (1.45)
Alerted Comprehensive Mean (SD)	6.58 (2.51)	**7.08 (2.03)**	6.38 (2.14)	6.86 (2.22)	6.73 (2.23)
Min - Max	0–8	0–8	1–8	1–8	

Table 3. T-Statistics for Videos

Video Pair	Mean Difference	SD Difference	T-Statistics	p-value
Video 1 vs Video 2	0.17	−0.43	0.34	0.74
Video 1 vs Video 3	−0.18	−0.18	−0.45	0.66
Video 1 vs Video 4	−0.33	−0.21	−0.80	0.44
Video 2 vs Video 3	−0.36	0.24	−0.63	0.54
Video 2 vs Video 4	−0.51	0.21	−0.89	0.39
Video 3 vs Video 4	−0.15	−0.03	−0.32	0.75

50.94 % of the participants have a Master's degree as an educational background. The participants are within the age group of 20 to 40 (avg. 26, st.dev. 4.98).

The HRIVST scores were computed for each video in all five conditions, as outlined in Table 2. Notably, the "Focused Explanation" condition yielded the highest HRIVST scores, indicating a higher level of legibility and understanding compared to the other conditions. However, the results are not statistically significant due to the limited number of participants. Hence, these findings provide only initial insights into the potential impact of different explanation strategies on transparency within HRI. Video 1 has a higher HRIVST score in "Comprehensive Explanation", Video 2 has a higher in "Alerted Comprehensive Explanation", Video 3, and Video 4 have higher HRIVST scores in the "Focused Explanation" condition.

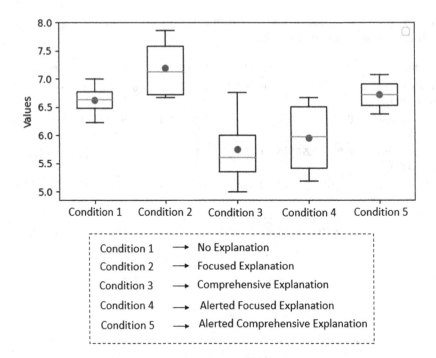

Fig. 3. Comparison of Different Explanation Types

By aggregating the evaluation of the different conditions for each video (see column Mean (SD) of Table 3), we can observe that Video 2 obtains the lower score using the HRIVST metrics and is evaluated as the less legible. The robot's actions in Video 2 are interrupted by an unexpected error, and it does not complete its task. This caused a certain uncertainty in understanding the final goal and made it less legible compared to other videos. The analysis suggests that while "Focused Explanations" are generally favorable, in the case of less legible behaviors, "Comprehensive Explanations" provided only at specific times could help transparency.

Figure 3 shows the aggregated averages for each condition. While we have a higher average for the Focused Explanations condition, all the p-values in our analysis are above the significance level ($\alpha = 0.05$), which means we do not have statistically significant evidence to reject the null hypothesis for any of the comparisons we performed.

Based on our results, providing a "Focused Explanation" while performing actions and a "Comprehensive Explanation" as the alert explanation can potentially improve transparency in HRI.

6   Conclusions and Future Work

Establishing transparent communication channels is crucial to successful interactions in a world where human-robot collaboration is gaining momentum. Our exploration into the impact of explanations on transparency within HRI sheds light on the significance of effective verbal communication. By delving into the nuances of explanation types and timings, we have gained valuable insights that contribute to the overarching goal of seamless collaboration between humans and robots. The findings from our study, supported by the HRIVST metric, highlight the influence of "Focused Explanations" on transparency and are in line with [12]. The increase in transparency scores when providing short explanations underscores the power of clear, concise communication. Additionally, we observed that "Comprehensive Explanations" accompanying changes in the robot's plan could contribute significantly in less legible cases.

As a future work, expanding the participant pool would provide a more comprehensive perspective on the effectiveness of different explanation strategies. Moreover, a qualitative analysis of participant feedback could provide deeper insights into the subjective experiences and preferences surrounding explanation-driven transparency.

Investigating the interplay between explanations and other cues, such as non-verbal gestures and visual displays, could unveil synergies that amplify the transparency achieved in HRI. Additionally, the influence of contextual factors, such as task complexity and familiarity, warrants exploration, as these aspects could impact the relevance and reception of different explanation strategies. By continuing to refine and expand our investigation, we aim to contribute to the ever-evolving understanding of how explanations can enrich human-robot interactions and pave the way for a future of harmonious collaboration.

Acknoledgment. This work has been supported by the Italian MUR and EU under the CHIST-ERA IV project COHERENT (PCI2020-120718-2) and Italian PON R&I 2014–2020 - REACT-EU (CUP E65F21002920003).

References

1. Rossi, S., Ercolano, G., Raggioli, L., Savino, E., Ruocco, M.: The disappearing robot: an analysis of disengagement and distraction during non-interactive tasks. In: 27th IEEE International Symposium on Robot and Human Interactive Communication (RO-MAN), pp. 522–527 (2018)
2. Raggioli, L., D'Asaro, F.A., Rossi, S.: Deep reinforcement learning for robotic approaching behavior influenced by user activity and disengagement. Int. J. Soc. Robotics (2023)
3. Sagheb, S., Gandhi, S., Losey, D.P.: Should collaborative robots be transparent? (2023). https://arxiv.org/abs/2304.11753
4. Hamacher, A., Bianchi-Berthouze, N., Pipe, A.G., Eder, K.: Believing in BERT: using expressive communication to enhance trust and counteract operational error in physical human-robot interaction (2016). https://arxiv.org/abs/1605.08817

5. Angelopoulos, G., Rossi, A., Napoli, C.D., Rossi, S.: You are in my way: non-verbal social cues for legible robot navigation behaviors. In: 2022 IEEE/RSJ IROS, pp. 657–662 (2022)
6. Matarese, M., Sciutti, A., Rea, F., Rossi, S.: Toward robots' behavioral transparency of temporal difference reinforcement learning with a human teacher. IEEE Trans. Hum.-Mach. Syst. **51**(6), 578–589 (2021)
7. Hayes, B., Shah, J.A.: Improving robot controller transparency through autonomous policy explanation. In: Proceedings of the 2017 ACM/IEEE International Conference on Human-Robot Interaction, pp. 303–312 (2017)
8. Rossi, S., Rossi, A., Dautenhahn, K.: The secret life of robots: perspectives and challenges for robot's behaviours during non-interactive tasks. Int. J. Soc. Robot. **12**(6), 1265–1278 (2020)
9. Rossi, S., Coppola, A., Gaita, M., Rossi, A.: Human-robot interaction video sequencing task for robot's behaviour legibility, July 2023. https://www.techrxiv.org/articles/preprint/Human-Robot_Interaction_Video_Sequencing_Task_for_Robot_s_Behaviour_Legibility/23696706
10. Patel, J., Ramaswamy, T., Li, Z., Pinciroli, C.: Transparency in multi-human multi-robot interaction (2021). https://arxiv.org/abs/2101.10495
11. Ambsdorf, J., et al.: Explain yourself! Effects of explanations in human-robot interaction (2022). https://arxiv.org/abs/2204.04501
12. Han, Z., Phillips, E., Yanco, H.A.: The need for verbal robot explanations and how people would like a robot to explain itself. ACM Trans. Hum.-Robot Interact. (THRI) **10**(4), 1–42 (2021)
13. Taschdjian, Z.: Why did the robot cross the road? A user study of explanation in human-robot interaction (2020). https://arxiv.org/abs/2012.00078
14. Sakai, T., Miyazawa, K., Horii, T., Nagai, T.: A framework of explanation generation toward reliable autonomous robots (2021). https://arxiv.org/abs/2105.02670
15. Zhang, Y., Zakershahrak, M.: Progressive explanation generation for human-robot teaming (2019). https://arxiv.org/abs/1902.00604
16. Cruz, F., Young, C., Dazeley, R., Vamplew, P.: Evaluating human-like explanations for robot actions in reinforcement learning scenarios (2022). https://arxiv.org/abs/2207.03214
17. Zhu, L., Williams, T.: Effects of proactive explanations by robots on human-robot trust. In: Wagner, A.R., et al. (eds.) ICSR 2020. LNCS (LNAI), vol. 12483, pp. 85–95. Springer, Cham (2020). https://doi.org/10.1007/978-3-030-62056-1_8
18. Zakershahrak, M., Gong, Z., Sadassivam, N., Zhang, Y.: Online explanation generation for human-robot teaming (2019). https://arxiv.org/abs/1903.06418
19. Zakershahrak, M., Marpally, S.R., Sharma, A., Gong, Z., Zhang, Y.: Order matters: generating progressive explanations for planning tasks in human-robot teaming (2020). https://arxiv.org/abs/2004.07822

The Effectiveness of Social Robots in Stress Management Interventions for University Students

Andra Rice[(⊠)], Katarzyna Klęczek, and Maryam Alimardani[ⒾⒹ]

Tilburg University, Tilburg 5037 AB, The Netherlands
{a.l.rice,k.a.kleczek,m.alimardani}@tilburguniversity.edu

Abstract. Stress affects many students, leaving them vulnerable to burnout. Social robots can provide personalized and non-judgmental support for individuals to engage in behavioral and cognitive therapy. This study investigated the effectiveness of a robot-assisted stress management intervention in reducing stress among university students. In a between-subjects design, students practiced a deep breathing exercise, either guided by a Pepper robot or using a laptop. To evaluate the effect of each technology, Galvanic Skin Response (GSR), Perceived Stress Questionnaire (PSQ) and the Unified Theory of Acceptance and Use of Technology (UTAUT) survey were collected. The results from PSQ and GSR showed no difference between the two technologies in reducing stress subjectively and physiologically. However, UTAUT reports indicated that participants in the Robot group were more inclined to use the robot in future practices, and that a more positive impression of the robot contributed to a stronger reduction of their self-reported stress levels.

Keywords: Social robotics · Mental health · Stress management · Breathing exercise · Galvanic Skin Response (GSR)

1 Introduction

Stress is known to have detrimental effects on our health and well-being [1]. University students are one demographic with high reports of anxiety, worry and stress [2]. Therapy is one way to reduce stress, but students may lack the necessary funds or time to pursue it. To solve these concerns, they can turn to technology for stress management. Chatbots [3, 4], virtual reality [5] and smartphone applications [6] can all be used to reduce stress. These tools, however, lack the sense of physical embodiment and social presence that a person provides during therapy sessions. Therefore, social robots can be used as embodied social companions that guide students through stress-relieving techniques [7].

While several studies have explored the potential of robots as physical activity coaches [8, 9], very little is known about the potential impact of social robots in mental well-being interventions [10]. For instance, Jeong et al. [11] used a Jibo robot as a positive psychology coach that delivered daily interventions to college students for more than a week. The study showcased an improvement of the students' well-being after the

A. Al. Ali et al. (Eds.): ICSR 2023, LNAI 14453, pp. 181–190, 2024.
https://doi.org/10.1007/978-981-99-8715-3_16

interventions, although no control condition was considered in this study. Another study by Spitale et al. [12] compared two robots (QTrobot vs. Misty) with coach personalities delivering positive psychology exercises over four weeks (one exercise per week). The results suggested the importance of robot form factors in how coachees perceived them; the smaller and less humanoid Misty robot was perceived more positively, whereas QTrobot received more criticism due to higher expectations. A major limitation of this study was that it only reported subjective perceptions of the robots and not their impact on the participants' mental states.

A recent review by Rasouli et al. [13] emphasized the gap that exists in the HRI literature for mental well-being support and listed different scenarios for social robots to be integrated in conventional therapies; one of which being mindfulness-based relaxation and stress reduction exercises. What is important to note is that previous research mostly suffers from methodological limitations such as uncontrolled experimental design (mainly due to interventions requiring days or weeks per individual) and the primary usage of subjective reports for stress measurement. To have a fair assessment of the effectiveness of social robots, the research in this field should go beyond exploratory investigations and employ controlled trials as well as sophisticated measures of stress. To achieve this, HRI researchers can turn to short but effective stress management techniques such as breathing exercises and employ wearable sensors such as Galvanic Skin Response (GSR) to objectively measure participants' physiological reactions.

Laptops are one of the technologies that are widely used by students for educational purposes [14], making them a suitable baseline technology for comparison in human-robot interaction (HRI) studies [15–17]. Therefore, this study aimed to examine the effectiveness of a social robot in guiding university students through a deep breathing exercise as opposed to a non-embodied technology (such as a laptop). Furthermore, the main novelty of this study is that, besides post-intervention questionnaires, we collected GSR signals during the intervention as an objective measure of each technology's impact on the users' physiological responses. Using this setup, we aimed to investigate the effect of the robot's physical embodiment and social presence on the success of stress management interventions and answer the following research questions:

– How do laptops and social robots compare in facilitating deep breathing exercise as a stress management technique for students?
– How do students perceive social robots as a tool for stress management interventions as opposed to a laptop?
– How does the students' perception of either technology influence their performance on the stress management exercise?

2 Methods

2.1 Participants

Data was collected from 44 university students between the ages of 17 to 38 (M_{age} = 21.34, SD_{age} = 3.64, 22 females, 21 males, 1 non-binary). All participants received information about the study and provided informed consent prior to participation. The study was approved by the Research Ethics and Data Management Committee of Tilburg University.

2.2 Experimental Conditions

The study employed a between-subjects design. Participants were randomly assigned to one of the experimental groups: Robot group vs. Laptop group. Each group experienced only one form of technology. The Robot group (n = 22) conducted the stress management task guided by a social robot providing vocal instructions and gestures whereas the Laptop group (n = 22) used a laptop technology that provided written instructions on the screen.

2.3 Instrumentation

The primary technologies used in this experiment were an Acer laptop, a Pepper robot (Softbank Robotics) and the Shimmer3 GSR + unit. GSR is a non-intrusive sensor that is worn on the wrist and fingers and monitors sweat response as a measure of stress (arousal) level (see Fig. 1A and B). The ConsensysBasic software (by Shimmer) was used to record the GSR data. The Montreal Imaging Stress Task (MIST) [18] was administered as a stress-inducing task before the intervention to induce stress in all participants (Fig. 1A). This task entailed performing arithmetic under the pressure of a timer and gave the participant increasingly less time to make the calculations.

The stress management exercise was a deep breathing exercise based on De Couck et al. [19] and included 5 s breathing in, 7 s breathing out, and one second of holding in between. To help participants with the breathing timing, an instructional video was created that was either displayed on the laptop screen or Pepper's tablet (Fig. 1B). The video displayed a circle that slowly expanded to indicate "inhale" and then shrank in size to instruct "exhale" timing (see Fig. 1C). Participants received explanations about the circle movement at the beginning of the video. Additionally, words of encouragement (e.g., "Very good, you are doing amazing", "Good job", and "Only 30 s left") were provided throughout the exercise, either in text (for the laptop group) or verbally spoken by Pepper (for the robot group).

2.4 Measurements

Three surveys were administered as part of the data collection. These included the Affinity for Technology Interaction scale (ATI) [20], a modified Perceived Stress Questionnaire (PSQ) [21], and the Unified Theory of Acceptance and Use of Technology (UTAUT) survey [22].

ATI was used to measure the participant's familiarity with technology and to compare the technological backgrounds between the two experimental groups. The PSQ acts as a subjective measurement of stress. The original PSQ was adapted to better fit this experiment by asking participants to report the stress they felt "at the moment" of taking the survey on a 5-point Likert scale. Participants' scores indicating their agreement with each statement (1 indicating complete disagreement and 5 indicating complete agreement) was totaled across all items with negative sentiments being reversed. The UTAUT was used to measure the participants' acceptance towards the technology they interacted with. The UTAUT constructs selected for this experiment were: Effort Expectancy, Performance Expectancy, Perceived Enjoyment, Satisfaction, Trust, Perceived Risk, and

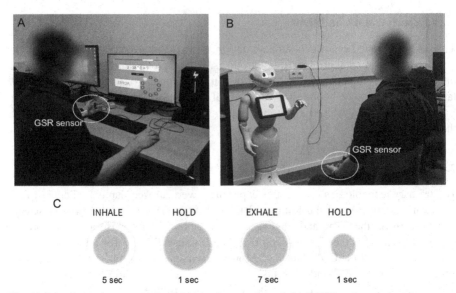

Fig. 1. Experiment setup. (A) Participants first conducted the MIST task to bring them to a comparable level of stress. (B) The stress management task was a deep breathing exercise that was guided by a Pepper robot for the experimental group as opposed to a laptop for the control group. (C) The timing of the breathing exercise was moderated by an instructional video shown on the Pepper's tablet or the laptop screen presenting a 5-s expanding and 7-s shrinking circle with 1-s holds in between.

Behavioral Intention. These constructs are scored on a 5-point Likert scale, providing insight into the participants' experience with and attitudes towards the technology they used, as well as their intention to use that technology again in the future.

2.5 Procedure

The experiment consisted of two groups: a control group who interacted with a laptop (Laptop group) and an experimental group who interacted with the Pepper robot (Robot group). Participants were randomly assigned to one of the two groups. Figure 2 presents the flow of the study. Upon receiving information and providing consent, participants first filled out the ATI questionnaire. Then the GSR sensor was affixed, and a baseline recording was collected. During baseline recording, participants stared at a fixation point on the screen and remained seated and still for a minute. Next, participants performed the MIST stress-inducing task, followed by the PSQ. The MIST lasted for approximately five minutes and served to bring participants to comparable levels of stress before the stress management exercise. After that, the groups conducted a single, three-minute-long stress management task either with Pepper or the laptop. GSR measures were recorded during the three-minute exercise. Once the exercise was over, participants completed the PSQ again, and filled out the UTAUT survey. Finally, they were debriefed, and the experiment ended.

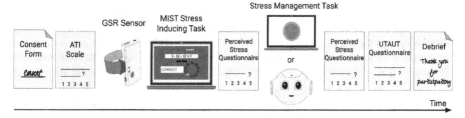

Fig. 2. Experimental procedure.

2.6 Data Analysis

Data from 6 participants was removed from analysis due to technical difficulties during the experiment and noise in GSR signals. This left 19 participants in each group after initial preprocessing.

The GSR signals were processed using pyEDA [23], an open-source tool for electrodermal activity analysis. Following signal processing, the average of the GSR values were calculated over the stress-inducing and the stress management tasks. To compare the physiological change during the breathing exercise, the mean GSR value during the first 20 s (i.e., the initial segment where explanation about the video was provided) of the stress management task was subtracted from the mean GSR during the remaining time for each participant. Similarly, the change in subjective stress level was measured by obtaining the difference in the total PSQ score before and after the exercise.

For the UTAUT survey, the scores given to items were summed per construct. If the questions had a negative sentiment attached to them, then the score was added with a negative value. The significance level for all tests were set at $a < .05$. First, a Shapiro Wilk test was conducted on data from Laptop and Robot conditions to determine normality of the data. Next, differences between groups were evaluated using a Welch Two Sample t-test for normally distributed data, or a Wilcoxon Rank Sum test, for non-normally distributed data. Where significant difference was observed, the effect size was determined by Cohen's d.

Finally, correlation tests were conducted between the total UTAUT score and each stress measurement (change in PSQ or GSR values). Since data was not normally distributed, Spearman's rank correlation was used to determine the relationship between the overall UTAUT scores with the GSR differences and the PSQ differences.

3 Results

The analysis of the ATI scores revealed no significant difference in technological affinity of participants in the Laptop ($M = 35.26$, $SD = 7.79$) and Robot ($M = 33.32$, $SD = 5.80$) groups ($t(33) = 0.87, p = .39$). This indicates that participants in both groups had relatively similar backgrounds in interacting with technology.

3.1 Laptops and Robots for Reducing Stress

The Shapiro-Wilk test confirmed a non-normal distribution of GSR mean values in both Laptop ($W = .82, p = .002$) and Robot ($W = .80, p = .001$) conditions. Therefore, a non-parametric Wilcoxon rank sum test was performed to compare the two groups (Fig. 3A), which determined a non-significant difference between the laptop and robot technologies in helping to reduce stress ($W = 167, p = .708$).

Similarly, following the Shapiro-Wilk test results, a Wilcoxon rank sum test was performed on the PSQ values (Fig. 3B), which indicated an insignificant difference between the Laptop and Robot groups ($W = 235, p = .115$). Thus, the subjective stress responses, taken through the PSQ, revealed no significant difference between the two technologies in facilitating the breathing exercise for stress reduction in students.

Taken together, both the objective GSR data and the subjective PSQ data showed no difference between laptops and social robots in reducing stress. Notably, as shown in Fig. 3A, the GSR signals showed an increase in arousal for some participants in the Robot group during the stress management exercise, which could be due to the novelty effect and excitement of interacting with the robot.

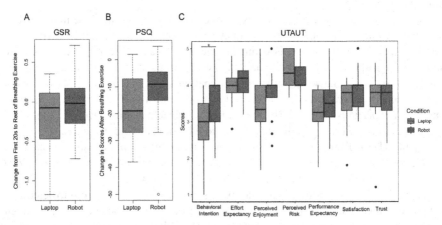

Fig. 3. Comparison between the Laptop and Robot groups in terms of (A) changes in GSR measurements, (B) changes in PSQ scores, and (C) the mean scores for each UTAUT construct, $* p < .05$.

3.2 Perception of Laptops and Robots

To analyze UTAUT scores, Shapiro-Wilk normality tests were applied to each construct. Out of all the constructs, only Effort Expectancy and Behavioral Intention scores were normally distributed in both groups. For these two constructs, the Welch Two Sample t-test was applied, and for the remaining constructs, the Wilcoxon rank sum test was employed. While the comparison of all other constructs yielded insignificant results, Behavioral Intention showed a significant difference between the Laptop and Robot groups ($t(36) = 2.1, p = .043$, Fig. 3C) with a moderate effect size (Cohen's d = 0.68, 95% CI [0.02, 1.33]), indicating a higher interest in using the robot again for the task among participants who experienced the exercise with the Pepper robot. The results also show that participants of the two groups had no considerable differences in their perceptions of the two technologies in regard to enjoyment, satisfaction, trust, etc.

3.3   Correlation between Technology Perception and its Stress Reducing Effects

To determine the relationship between participants' experience of each technology and the effect it had on their performance during the stress management task, correlation analyses were performed between the overall UTAUT scores and the change in GSR and PSQ values, separately. None of the tests yielded significant correlations, although there was a weak negative correlation between the UTAUT and PSQ values for the Robot group ($r(17) = -0.44$, $p = 0.061$) with people experiencing a more positive interaction with the robot reporting a larger reduction in their stress levels after the interaction.

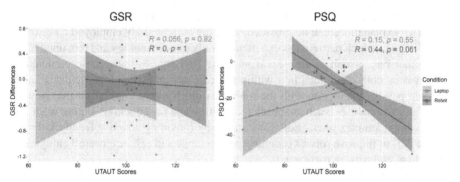

Fig. 4. The relationship between the overall UTAUT score and the GSR and PSQ differences.

4   Discussion

The current study investigated the effectiveness of social robots in facilitating mental well-being interventions such as stress-reducing exercises among university students. Previous literature [11, 12], while employing a longitudinal approach, suffered from an uncontrolled experimental design, and only relied on self-reported perceptions of stress or impressions of the robot. To address these shortcomings, this study compared a Pepper robot to a non-humanlike and non-social laptop device in a between-subjects experimental design and collected galvanic skin responses (GSR) for an objective evaluation of the participants' physiological responses during the stress-relieving task.

The results revealed no significant difference between the control and experimental groups; that is, both laptop and robot technologies yielded similar stress reduction effects and were perceived comparably by the participants. The only difference that was observed was a significantly higher Behavioral Intention reported by the Robot group indicating a greater inclination to employ the robot again for future stress management exercises, which could have been due to the novelty effect. Also, while non-significant, a notable negative relationship was observed between the overall UTAUT scores and PSQ changes in the Robot group, implying that the more positively the robot was perceived by the participants, the more effective it was at reducing subjective stress levels.

The outcome of this study differed from past research in three key areas in that we had a controlled design, objective stress measures, and a short-term interaction.

This contrasts with the study of Jeong et al. [11] who conducted a longitudinal study only with a Jibo robot (no control technology) and found an improved self-reported mood among participants after the interaction, and the study of Spitale et al. [12] who compared the impact of robot personalities on the intervention outcomes. Particularly, the short interaction with the Pepper robot in the current study could have impeded participants' high expectations stemming from the robot's humanlike appearance [12]. These differences in the study design might explain why our results do not immediately point to a benefit for social robots.

Unlike prior research that found social robots elicit more enjoyable interactions and greater trust compared to their non-social counterparts [15, 24], we observed no difference in the outcome of the UTAUT on Perceived Enjoyment, Satisfaction, and Trust. Two explanations can be provided; first, the current study employed a between-group design in which participants experienced only one technology and remained blind to the other one, which is different from most HRI studies that enable participants to experience both conditions in a within-subjects design. Second, participants had a short and passive interaction with the robot that did not give them a full overview of Pepper's functionalities, such as speech recognition and face tracking. Future work can create a more complex interaction, for instance by providing adaptive feedback during the task [25] to improve robot's coaching performance and enhance overall enjoyment, satisfaction, and trust in participants.

The primary novelty of this work was employment of wearable sensors such as GSR as an objective measure of the participants' mental states. Our results indicated that while most participants in the Robot group reported a reduction of stress in the PSQ, the arousal level for some had in fact increased over time. This discrepancy could be explained by the difference in the emotional valence that is accompanied by high arousal levels. In fact, a positive arousal is related to the experience of excitement and pleasure, which is different from negative arousal that is associated with frustrating or stressful situations. To provide more insight into participants' actual mental states, further exploration of neurophysiological responses such as brain activity [25–27] is required to determine the valence of their emotional experience throughout the task.

This experiment was limited in terms of the number of participants and duration of the interaction. Future research should attempt longitudinal studies to evaluate health benefits of technology-assisted mental well-being interventions over time, particularly when the robot novelty effect diminishes. Additionally, while the use of GSR provided a novel measurement of mental states in this experiment, future research should aim to employ more affective computing tools including EEG brain responses [27], in order to illuminate different dimensions of the participants' emotional experience such as valence and arousal. Finally, the robot behavior for this experiment was pre-scripted and relatively simple. Future work should attempt evaluation of more interactive and adaptive scenarios where robot behavior is adjusted according to the physiological responses of the participants extracted in real-time [26].

5 Conclusion

This current study investigated the effectiveness of social robots in delivering mental well-being interventions to university students. Our results from a controlled experiment, comparing two groups of students who interacted with either a Pepper robot or a laptop in a single stress management intervention, indicated no observable difference in terms of self-reported stress and physiological responses. However, we observed a positive relationship between participants' perception of the robot and the reduction of self-reported stress levels. Also, participants in the robot group indicated a significantly stronger desire to reuse the same technology for future interventions. Overall, these results show that while social robots might not have immediate effect in facilitating stress management tasks compared to other non-social technologies, they have the potential to engage users in the intervention and motivate them for continued usage of stress relieving exercises.

References

1. Dhabhar, F.S.: Effects of stress on immune function: the good, the bad, and the beautiful. Immunol. Res. **58**(2–3), 193–210 (2014). https://doi.org/10.1007/s12026-014-8517-0
2. Pascoe, M., Hetrick, E., Parker, A.: The impact of stress on students in secondary school and higher education. Int. J. Adolesc. Youth **25**(1), 104–112 (2020)
3. Boucher, E., et al.: Artificially intelligent chatbots in digital mental health interventions: a review. Expert Rev. Med. Devices **18**(sup1), 37–49 (2021)
4. De Nieva, J.O., Joaquin, J.A., Tan, C.B., Marc Te, R.K., Ong, E.: Investigating students' use of a mental health chatbot to alleviate academic stress. In: 6th international ACM incooperation HCI and UX conference, pp. 1–10. Association for Computing Machinery, Jakarta & Bandung Indonesia (2020)
5. Kluge, M.G., et al.: Development of a modular stress management platform (performance edge VR) and a pilot efficacy trial of a biofeedback enhanced training module for controlled breathing. PLoS ONE **16**(2), e0245068 (2021)
6. Lau, N., O'Daffer, A., Colt, S., Joyce, P., Palermo, T. M., McCauley, E., Rosenberg, A., et al.: Android and iphone mobile apps for psychosocial wellness and stress management: systematic search in app stores and literature review. JMIR Mhealth Uhealth **8**(5), e17798 (2020)
7. Scoglio, A.A., Reilly, E.D., Gorman, J.A., Drebing, C.E.: Use of social robots in mental health and well-being research: systematic review. J. Med. Internet Res. **21**(7), e13322 (2019)
8. Fasola, J., Matarić, M.J.: A socially assistive robot exercise coach for the elderly. J. Hum.-Robot Inter. **2**(2), 3–32 (2013)
9. Robinson, N.L., Connolly, J., Suddery, G., Turner, M., Kavanagh, D.J.: A humanoid social robot to provide personalized feedback for health promotion in diet, physical activity, alcohol and cigarette use: a health clinic trial. In: 2021 30th IEEE International Conference on Robot & Human Interactive Communication (RO-MAN), pp. 720–726. IEEE (2021)
10. Axelsson, M., Spitale, M., Gunes, H.: Robots as mental well-being coaches: Design and ethical recommendations. arXiv preprint arXiv:2208.14874 (2022)
11. Jeong, S., et al.: A robotic positive psychology coach to improve college students' well-being. In: 2020 29th IEEE International Conference on Robot and Human Interactive Communication (RO-MAN), pp. 187–194. IEEE, Naples, Italy (2020)

12. Spitale, M., Axelsson, M., Gunes, H.: Robotic mental well-being coaches for the workplace: An in-the-wild study on form. In: Proceedings of the 2023 ACM/IEEE International Conference on Human-Robot Interaction, pp. 301–310. Association for Computing Machinery, Stockholm, Sweden (2023)

13. Rasouli, S., Gupta, G., Nilsen, E., Dautenhahn, K.: Potential applications of social robots in robot-assisted interventions for social anxiety. Int. J. Soc. Robot. **14**(5), 1–32 (2022)

14. Curtis, F., Cranmer, S.: "Laptops are better": medical students' perceptions of laptops versus tablets and smartphones to support their learning. In: Proceedings of the 9th International Conference on Networked Learning 2014, pp. 67–75. (2014)

15. Bravo Perucho, A., Alimardani, M.: Social robots in secondary education: Can robots assist young adult learners with math learning? In: Companion of the 2023 ACM/IEEE international conference on human-robot interaction, pp. 355–359. Association for Computing Machinery, Stockholm, Sweden (2023)

16. van Ewijk, G., Smakman, M., Konijn, E. A.: Teachers' perspectives on social robots in education: an exploratory case study. In: Proceedings of the Interaction Design and Children Conference, pp. 273–280. Association for Computing Machinery, London, United Kingdom (2020)

17. Whelan, S., Kouroupetroglou, C., Santorelli, A., Raciti, M., Barrett, E., Casey, D.: Investigating the effect of social robot embodiment. In: Harnessing the Power of Technology to Improve Lives, pp. 523–526. IOS Press (2017)

18. Dedovic, K., Renwick, R., Mahani, N., Engert, V., Lupien, S., Pruessner, J.: The montreal imaging stress task: using functional imaging to investigate the effects of perceiving and processing psychosocial stress in the human brain. J. Psychiatry Neurosci. **30**(5), 319–325 (2005)

19. De Couck, M., Caers, R., Musch, L., Fliegauf, J., Giangreco, A., Gidron, Y.: How breathing can help you make better decisions: two studies on the effects of breathing patterns on heart rate variability and decision-making in business cases. Int. J. Psychophysiol. **139**, 1–9 (2019)

20. Franke, T., Attig, C., Wessel, D.: A personal resource for technology interaction: development and validation of the affinity for technology interaction (ATI) scale. Int. J. Hum.-Comput. Interact. **35**(6), 456–467 (2019)

21. Levenstein, S., et al.: Development of the perceived stress questionnaire: a new tool for psychosomatic research. J. Psychosom. Res. **37**(1), 19–32 (1993)

22. Venkatesh, V., Thong, J.Y., Xu, X.: Unified theory of acceptance and use of technology: a synthesis and the road ahead. J. Assoc. Inf. Syst. **17**(5), 328–376 (2016)

23. Aqajari, S.A.H., Naeini, E.K., Mehrabadi, M.A., Labbaf, S., Dutt, N., Rahmani, A.M.: Pyeda: an open-source python toolkit for pre-processing and feature extraction of electrodermal activity. Procedia Comput. Sci. **184**, 99–106 (2021)

24. Chen, Y.-C., Yeh, S.-L., Lin, W., Yueh, H.-P., Fu, L.-C.: The effects of social presence and familiarity on children–robot interactions. Sensors **23**(9), 4231 (2023)

25. Alimardani, M., Kemmeren, L., Okumura, K., Hiraki, K.: Robot-assisted mindfulness practice: Analysis of neurophysiological responses and affective state change. In: 2020 29th IEEE International Conference on Robot and Human Interactive Communication (RO-MAN), pp. 683–689. IEEE (2020)

26. Alimardani, M., Hiraki, K.: Passive brain-computer interfaces for enhanced human-robot interaction. Front. Robot. AI **7**(125) (2020)

27. Staffa, M., D'Errico, L., Sansalone, S. Alimardani, M.: Classifying human emotions in HRI: applying global optimization model to EEG brain signals. Front. Neurorobotics **17**(1191127) (2023)

Data-Driven Generation of Eyes and Head Movements of a Social Robot in Multiparty Conversation

Léa Haefflinger[1,2](✉) , Frédéric Elisei[1] , Béatrice Bouchot[2], Brice Varini[2], and Gérard Bailly[1]

[1] GIPSA-Lab, Grenoble-Alpes Univ., Grenoble, France
lea.haefflinger@gipsa-lab.grenoble-inp.fr
[2] Atos, 38130 Échirolles, France

Abstract. Given the importance of gaze in Human-Robot Interactions (HRI), many gaze control models have been developed. However, these models are mostly built for dyadic face-to-face interaction. Gaze control models for multiparty interaction are more scarce. We here propose and evaluate data-driven gaze control models for a robot game animator in a three-party interaction. More precisely, we used Long Short-Term Memory networks to predict gaze target and context-aware head movements given robot's communication intents and observed activities of its human partners. After comparing objective performance of our data-driven model with a baseline and ground truth data, an online audio-visual perception study was conducted to compare the acceptability of these control models in comparison with low-anchor incongruent speech and gaze sequences driving the Furhat robot. The results show that our data-driven prediction of gaze targets is viable, but that third-party raters are not so sensitive to controls with congruent head movements.

Keywords: Human-Robot Interaction · Gaze · AI · Head · Multiparty

1 Introduction

The importance of non-verbal cues in human conversations is no longer to be proven: authors of [4] consider that 60% of communication intents would pass through this channel. For a robot to interact with humans in the most natural way, it must be able to perceive, understand and generate such cues.

One of the most studied non-verbal cues for Human-Robot Interaction (HRI) is gaze [1]. And rightly so, it is a major social cue in face-to-face Human-Human interactions (HHI). Indeed, in addition to transmitting emotions, it is a powerful regulator of conversations [16,27]. This function is particularly important in multiparty conversations, for turn-taking management and role detection, such as who will be the next speaker, or who is the current addressee [13,32]. This impact of the gaze has also been emphasized in HRI. For example, the gaze control proposed by Multlu et al. [22] allowed their robot to signal the roles of participants in the conversation (bystander, overhearer, ...). In the same way, thanks to its gaze, a robot can influence turn-taking behaviors [30] and even regulate speaking times [10]. In addition to having an impact on the conversational regime, appropriate gaze behaviour increases participants' engagement in the conversation and positively impacts their perception of the robot [6,18,29].

All these studies confirm the importance of providing our robot with the most natural gaze control possible. This study introduces a unique method to control the robot gaze in a multi-party interaction by combining two Long Short-Term Memory (LSTM) models, one to predict the attention targets of the robot, and one to generate the corresponding head movements. We believe that the use of LSTM models will enable the generation of more subtle behaviours based on elements of the interaction context that the robot can perceive (who speaks, where the interlocutors look, ...) or related to its own intentions (who it is addressing, what it is talking about, ...). These models will first be evaluated objectively, then subjectively, through an online perception study, in order to compare them with a baseline model and ground-truth behaviours.

2   Related Works

Given the importance of gaze in HRI, a large number of gaze models have already been proposed and tested [1]. However, most of these models are developed for dyadic interactions and not for multiparty interactions as in this study. Two categories of models can be distinguished, models based on human interaction data, called data-driven, and those using rules extracted from human behavior, called heuristics. On the side of multiparty heuristic models, we can find the model proposed by Zaraki et al. [34], where each participant gets a coefficient of attention computed from multimodal cues, or the model proposed by Mishra et al. [20] for a robot playing a game with two humans. For data-driven models, Mutlu et al. [21] proposed a control to monitor roles of participants, Nakano et al. [23] built a model taking into account dominance in a conversation, and Shintani et al. [28] focused on gaze behavior during turn-taking. Some models use machine learning algorithms, as proposed by Stefanov et al. [31] who tested artificial neural networks using or not LSTM to model attention, or Huang et al. [12] who used Support Vector Machine (SVM) for their gaze prediction model.

Furthermore, beyond the prediction of gaze targets, this study also focuses on the generation of head movements that allow subtle control of head-eye coordination. Head-eye coordination has been extensively studied in humans [7,8,33]. For HRI head is mostly considered as a passive contributor of eye movements but not a component per se of the robot's communicative intentions [3,14,34]. However, Gillet et al. [10] were able to influence participants' speaking times by manipulating the head movements. Among the few studies that have implemented a context-aware control of head-eye coordination, are the model of Mishra et al. [20] where the contribution of the robot's head depends on the duration of fixation of the attention target, and the models proposed by [24,31] that predict both eye-gaze direction and head orientation.

Fig. 1. Setup for the RoboTrio data collection.

The two studies most similar to our method are those by Stefanov et al. [31] and Huang et al. [12] through the use of machine learning algorithms. However, Stefanov et al. [31] did not propose a subjective evaluation of their models and our study differs from that of Huang et al. [12] due to the roles being asymmetric in our interaction (robot plays game as animator), and their robot could not move its head and its eyes. Another major difference is that we use the robot's addressee as an input of our model. As shown in [11], the contribution of the head in the gaze depends on whether one or two people are addressed at a time.

3 Creating the Models

3.1 Gaze/Head Data Collection: Immersive Robot Teleoperation

To train and evaluate our models, we use multimodal data from three-party interactions in a collaborative game context [26], Fig. 1. The game is scored by finding the most quoted words for a given theme (previously played online by human players). E.g. for the "sea" theme, the words that would score the most are "ocean", "water", "beach", "mediterranean", "boat" and "fish".

The behavior we want to model is that of the game's animator. This animator is in fact an iCub robot [19] controlled by a human pilot through immersive teleoperation [5]. This setup allows to interact with two human players through the robot sensors and actuators. A tablet is placed in front of the robot so that the pilot can scan the information about the game in progress. The animator must report the themes, invites the players to propose words, and then reports the scores for the proposed words. **All head and eye movements of the pilot, including vergence, are reproduced in real time by the operated robot** (3+3 Degrees of Freedom, aka DoF). These gaze and head movements, as well as audio and video of the three-party interaction, are recorded as "the corpus". We use 11 recorded and annotated game sequences, with different pairs of players, but keeping the robot's pilot the same. This amounts to almost 4 h of recording, where each sequence lasts about 20 min. A sequence consists of 9 rounds (new theme word), and 5 collected answers per theme. While playing, the players collaborate to find the best answers and look/ask the robot at will. So there's a lot of interaction and social cues; thinking about the theme, sharing and gauging ideas on a potential answer, etc. The robot monitors them like its human pilot would do, and is included regularly in the conversation. **The corpus is therefore complex and rich in verbal and non-verbal content** for the players and the robot (mutual gaze, gaze aversion, speech overlap . . .).

3.2   Models Implementation

In order to make the attention control of our robot as natural as possible, we propose to generate both attention targets and head movements. For this purpose, we decided to cascade two models.

Tasks Definition. Our first model predicts gaze targets. To train this model, the gaze of the robot pilot was classified with Gaussian Mixture Models (GMM). After detection of the ocular saccades, the gaze was divided into 4 classes of attention; one for the leftmost player in the game *UserL*, one for the rightmost player *UserR*, one for the *Tablet* screened by the animator, and finally a class *Elsewhere*. To simplify the training of our model, the frames where the gaze is classified as *Saccade* or *Elsewhere* are grouped into an *Other* class. In addition, to filter out errors due to classification, fixations with a duration of less than 150 ms were merged with the preceding fixations. The distribution of gaze classes in the dataset is not completely balanced, with *UserL* and *UserR* representing 32.4% and 32.1% respectively, while *Tablet* represents 21.7% and *Other* 13.8%.

Then, the second model predicts the three DoF of the head: pitch (up/down), roll (tilt), yaw (left/right).
The outputs of both models are generated continuously at 60 Hz.

Input Multimodal Features. Multimodal features about the activity of the pilot and the players are given as input to both models. These features have been selected against others as they can be observed in real-time (targeting a future implementation with our Furhat robot [2]). Each feature, when composed of N classes, is decomposed into N channels, with only 0 or 1 values:

- 11 channels for **Robot pilot activity**:
  - *Speech:* whether pilot is speaking or not
  - *Speech Intent:* intent of the sentence, 7 different classes (ask for a proposition, give the score, the theme, an explanation or feedback,. . .)
  - *Addressee:* pilot's adressee(s) *UserL*, or *UserR* or *Both*, value is 0 for the three channels if the addressee is unknown
- 6 channels for **UserL and UserR activities**:
  - *SpeechL, SpeechR:* whether left (resp. right) user is speaking or not
  - *GazeL:* 2 classes, whether given user is looking at the other user, or at the robot. Value is 0 for both channels if the user is looking at elsewhere
  - *GazeR:* same as previous, but for the right user.

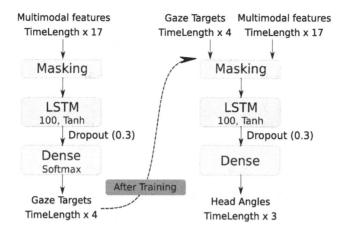

Fig. 2. Structure of the models, the one predicting gaze targets on the left, and the one generating head movements on the right.

In addition to these **17 input channels**, the model generating head angles also receives pilot gaze features, **adding 4 channels for a total of 21.**

Verbal features were annotated manually, while users gaze features were automatically annotated using GMM. The robot's addressee was annotated using the French pronouns "Vous" (*Both*) and "Tu" (*UserR/L*), see [11].

Models Training. To take into account possible temporal dependencies, the models use LSTM cells. Their input are temporal sequences, which have been cut to correspond to a whole game theme. The 11 interactions being composed of 9 themes, we obtain a total of 99 mini-batches. As the duration of the themes is variable and the input of the networks must be of fixed dimension, padding was applied to standardize the length of the sequences (TimeLength). The models have a many-to-many architecture; their output is a temporal sequence whose length matches the input. The structure and parameters of the two models are presented in Fig. 2. The masking layer is used for padding detection. The main differences between these two models are the input and output dimensions, and the use of a "softmax" activation function for gaze target classification. The networks are trained with 200 epochs, a batch size of 10, and an Adam optimizer [17] with a learning rate of 10^{-4}. For the gaze target classification model, the loss function is the categorical crossentropy, and for the head angle regression model the loss function is the Mean Squared Error (MSE).

Model Performances. To best evaluate the performance of our models, we used the K-fold cross validation method. For each training, the test dataset is composed of the n-th theme of each sequence (11 temporal sequences), and the training dataset of the 8 others (88 temporal sequences). The two networks are thus each trained and evaluated 9 times with different datasets (9 folds). The

Table 1. F1-score of the gaze classification model according to the interaction context.

Gaze Class	Pilot is Speaking	Pilot is Listening	No One is Speaking	ALL
UserL	0.50	0.54	0.51	0.52
UserR	0.52	0.59	0.51	0.55
Tablet	0.77	0.41	0.45	0.67
Other	0.05	0.01	0.03	0.03
Weighted F1-score	0.54	0.48	0.44	0.49

average accuracy of the attention target classification model is $52.9 \pm 1.4\%$. The average MSE of the head angle generation model is 7.93 ± 0.51.

In Table 1, the performance of the gaze classification model is analysed in detail, by calculating the F1-score for each class depending on the robot pilot's activity. First, we notice that the *Other* class is particularly badly predicted, which is not surprising as it does not correspond to a specific target and acts as a garbage collector. Moreover, contrary to the results presented in [12,31], the proposed model is better when the pilot speaks than when he listens. This can be explained by the pilot's role as the game animator who, when speaking, will often look at his tablet to consult the game information. Moreover, the model knows the verbal intention of the pilot, which is not the case when a user speaks.

Ablation Study. To study the influence of each input feature on model performance, we conducted an ablation study (Table 2). To do this, we trained separately our models under the same conditions as before (same parameters and 9-fold cross-validation) but removed selected input features (✗ in Table 2).

Removing the *Intent* feature has the biggest impact on gaze prediction, which can be explained by the importance of intentions in determining whether the robot should look at the tablet (theme announcement, scores) or specific/both players (ask for proposal, validation) when speaking. When all *Robot* features are removed, performance drops drastically, and the same applies to *Users* features. It therefore seems interesting to take into account both endogenous and exogenous information from the robot.

For head generation, *Robot_Gaze* is clearly the feature that provides the most information. Nevertheless, when all *Robot* features are removed, performance drops even further, assuming that the other *Robot* features are also important.

4   Subjective Evaluation

4.1   Method

Goal. The objective evaluation of model performance is not decisive. Indeed, it is not because the predicted target is different from the original target that this choice is less relevant or natural, and the same for the generation of head

Table 2. Results of the ablation study on input features.

Robot			Users		Gaze prediction:
Speech	Intent	Addressee	Speech	Gaze	**Accuracy**
–	–	–	–	–	52.9 ± 1.4%
–	✗	–	–	–	49.1 ± 0.8
–	–	–	–	✗	50.9 ± 1.3
–	–	–	✗	–	51 ± 1.2
–	–	✗	–	–	51.5 ± 1.8
✗	–	–	–	–	52.5 ± 1.1
✗	✗	✗	–	–	45.0 ± 1.7
–	–	–	✗	✗	47.9 ± 1.3

Robot				Users		Head prediction:
Speech	Intent	Addressee	Gaze	Speech	Gaze	**MSE**
–	–	–	–	–	–	7.93 ± 0.51
–	–	–	✗	–	–	13.48 ± 0.66
–	–	–	–	–	✗	8.26 ± 1.04
–	–	✗	–	–	–	7.97 ± 0.46
–	✗	–	–	–	–	7.96 ± 0.47
–	–	–	–	✗	–	7.92 ± 0.44
✗	–	–	–	–	–	7.91 ± 0.45
✗	✗	✗	✗	–	–	16.60 ± 0.57
–	–	–	–	✗	✗	7.88 ± 0.38

movements. A subjective evaluation is therefore necessary to validate the viability of our proposed attention control. To evaluate it, we predicted the gaze targets, for each frame (60 Hz), for all 11 sequences, and reused these predictions as input to the head generation model trained on ground-truth data (see Fig. 2). For each theme, the models used for prediction were those that were not trained with that theme. Finally, the predictions were filtered, removing gaze fixations shorter than 150 ms, and smoothing head movements with a Blackman filter. These attention behaviors are evaluated in this section.

Compared Attention Controls. We decided to compare our cascaded data-driven model with 3 other controls, to test both the prediction of attention targets, and the generation of head movements. To do so, we replay sequence of game interactions on a virtual Furhat robot [2] with different gaze and head behaviors. Between the different conditions, the verbal content is identical and is synthesized by Furhat, only the control of its eyes and head differs. The possible targets of attention are limited to *UserL*, *UserR* and *Tablet*. The different four models are listed below:

- **Lstm Model:** The proposed data-driven control that combines the two LSTM models described in this paper, that take into account the interaction context. All three angles of the head are controlled.
- **Heuristic Model:** This model focuses on the head movement generation, it is close to the observation model proposed by [14]. The robot looks at the same targets as the *LstmModel*, and the head movements are generated from these targets only, without taking into account the context (no pilot and players activities). The model calculates the distance between two fixations, if it is lower than a threshold value, the head does not move, otherwise it performs a defined percentage of the path. The percentages were set to be as close as possible to what was done by the pilot, 30% for the yaw angle and 45% for the pitch angle. For the calculation of the threshold value, and the trajectories of the head, we used the equations proposed by Itti et al. in [14]. Moreover an attraction-middline effect is also implemented for better realism [9]. This control uses only 2 DoF, pitch and yaw. The Table 3 shows the Root Mean Squared Error (RMSE) between the head angles of the control and those of *LstmModel*. Logically, the error is maximum on the Roll angle, this angle being equal to zero for this *HeuristicModel* control. The differences being not negligible, we hypothesized that they will be perceived during the perceptive study.
- **Simulated Ground Truth (GT):** *High_Anchor* This control corresponds to the original human behaviour of the pilot in the data collection, same attention targets, and same head movements (pitch, roll, yaw). In Table 3, RMSE between this control and the two previous ones are high, since targets of attention are not necessarily the same.
- **Shifted Ground Truth:** *Low_Anchor* This control is the same as the previous one, but uses data shifted in time. The robot will reproduce the same behavior as the pilot but 1 min ahead. The head movement corresponds to the current target of attention, but this target is incongruous. As sustained conversational states last several seconds, we chose a 1 min shift to get a close context without matching the original attention targets.

Table 3. Root Mean Squarred Error between (RMSE in degree) the head angles of the different controls.

Comparison	Pitch	Roll	Yaw	ALL
LstmModel vs *HeuristicModel*	1.73	2.56	3.61	2.63
LstmModel vs *SimulatedGT*	4.72	4.28	2.66	3.89
HeuristicModel vs *SimulatedGT*	4.85	5.00	4.49	4.78

Online Evaluation. For the perception evaluation, 21 clips of interaction were selected and extracted, 2 per game sequence plus 1 for the initial training example. These selections correspond to extracts where the head movements between

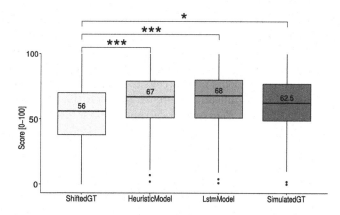

Fig. 3. Results of the online evaluation depending on the robot controls used. Each boxplot contains 600 points (number of subjects x number of clips). Significant p-values are indicated by * (<0.05), and *** (<0.001).

the conditions *HeuristicModel* and *LstmModel* differ the most. Each of these extracts of interaction result in 4 video clips of about 10 s, corresponding to the 4 controls to be compared. Only the virtual robot is visible on these videos, the players are perceived and differentiated using stereo audio, with the left (right) speaker using the left (right) audio channel. For the evaluation, we used the HEMVIP [15] method. On each page, the subjects compare 4 renderings of the same interaction segment. They must rate each video between 0 and 100. 20 web pages corresponding to the 20 extracts are presented in a random order, as well as the 4 videos of the different controls. The evaluation instruction given to the subjects was this: *"Rate the videos based on the relevance of the robot's behavior and gaze relative to the context"*. Before the experiment, the subjects are shown an explanation of the game and a picture of the scene being observed, so that they know what the targets of the robot's gaze are. At the end, they have to fill in a survey about their familiarity with the robots and their general feeling. We recruited 30 participants via the crowdsourcing platform Prolific[1], all native French speakers, with an equal representation of men and women.

4.2   Results

Figure 3 presents distributions of *rating_score* obtained by the 4 control policies. The significance of the results was tested by building a beta regression model, with *clips_Id* and *subject_Id* as random variables. A likelihood ratio test shows that the type of control significantly impacts the *rating_score* (chisq(3) = 16.511, p = 0.0008). Multiple pair-wise comparisons between the different controls resulted in the adjusted p-values presented in Fig. 3. The only significant differences were found between *ShiftedGT* and the other three controls. This

---

[1] https://www.prolific.co/.

confirms that the gaze target management proposed by our model is viable. Despite a small supportive bias for *LstmModel*, no significant difference was found between the proposed control *LstmModel* and the control *HeuristicModel*. The difference between the head movements generated by a context-aware model and a non-context-aware model is not perceived. Despite the scores obtained by *SimulatedGT*, there is no significant difference between this hypothesized high anchor and the two controls, *HeuristicModel*, and *LstmModel*.

4.3   Discussion

The subjective evaluation revealed that despite a moderate objective performance, the proposed control was rated as appropriate as the original behavior in the data set. However, even though no significant differences were found, it is surprising that the trend in the score of the *SimulatedGT* control is lower than that of the two controls *HeuristicsModel* and *LstmModel*. Indeed, this control is supposed to reproduce a human behavior, more subtle than the two others. A first comment is that subjects do hear but not see the two players. Their estimation of the addressee(s) of human partners is degraded. This lack of context may create a misunderstanding of the robot's behavior, which mimics the behavior of a knowledgeable human who was participating in the interaction. Secondly, although third-party evaluations have been shown to find similar results to those of internal participants in the interaction [25], it is possible that this evaluation method has limitations. This limitation would be especially valid when finely comparing controls. Finally, the subjective evaluation only focused on the question of appropriateness of the behavior, but other characteristics could have been interesting to evaluate, such as naturalness or engagement.

5   Conclusion

In this study, we introduced a data-driven gaze control for HRI multi-party interaction, where the robot is an animator of a collaborative game. The control is based on two cascaded LSTM networks trained on multimodal data, one for gaze target prediction, one for head movement generation. Using an online perception study, we showed that this control is viable, with attention target prediction comparable to human behaviour, but no advantage of context awareness was revealed for head movement generation. These promising modeling results need to be further developed. Future work will aim to identify the reasons for this non-perception of differences. Two approaches are envisaged: improving the models by using embedding or CNN layers, for example, but also conducting a new perception evaluation with raters facing the physical robot for checking the engagement hypothesis.

Acknowledgements. The RoboTrio corpus was supported by CNRS through a S2IH PEPS funding. This research is supported by the ANR 19-P3IA-0003 MIAI. The first author is financed by a CIFRE PhD granted by ANRT (2021/0836).

References

1. Admoni, H., Scassellati, B.: Social eye gaze in human-robot interaction: a review. J. Hum.-Robot Interact. Steering Committee **6**(1), 25–63 (2017)
2. Al Moubayed, S., Beskow, J., Skantze, G., Granström, B.: Furhat: a back-projected human-like robot head for multiparty human-machine interaction. Int. J. Humanoid Rob. **2021**, 1–11 (2013)
3. Aliasghari, P., Taheri, A., Meghdari, A.F., Maghsoodi, E.: Implementing a gaze control system on a social robot in multi-person interactions. SN Appl. Sci. **2**, 1–13 (2020)
4. Birdwhistell, R.L.: Background to kinesics. ETC Rev. General Semant. **13**(1), 10–18 (1955)
5. Cambuzat, R., Elisei, F., Bailly, G., Simonin, O., Spalanzani, A.: Immersive tele-operation of the eye gaze of social robots assessing gaze-contingent control of vergence, yaw and pitch of robotic eyes. In: ISR 2018–50th International Symposium on Robotics, pp. 232–239. VDE, Munich (2018)
6. Correia, F., Campos, J., Melo, F., Paiva, A.: Robotic gaze responsiveness in multiparty teamwork. Int. J. Soc. Robot. **15**, 27–36 (2022)
7. Freedman, E., Sparks, D.: Coordination of the eyes and head: movement kinematics. Exp. Brain Res. **131**, 22–32 (2000)
8. Fuller, J.H.: Comparison of Head Movement Strategies among Mammals. In: The Head-Neck Sensory Motor System. Oxford University Press (1992)
9. Fuller, J.H.: Head movement propensity. Exp. Brain Res. **92**, 152–164 (2004)
10. Gillet, S., Cumbal, R., Pereira, A., Lopes, J., Engwall, O., Leite, I.: Robot gaze can mediate participation imbalance in groups with different skill levels. In: Proceedings of the 2021 ACM/IEEE International Conference on Human-Robot Interaction, pp. 303–311. Association for Computing Machinery, New York (2021)
11. Haefflinger, L., Elisei, F., Gerber, S., Bouchot, B., Vigne, J.P., Bailly, G.: On the benefit of independent control of head and eye movements of a social robot for multiparty human-robot interaction. In: Kurosu, M., Hashizume, A. (eds.) Human-Computer Interaction. LNCS, vol. 14011, pp. 450–466. Springer, Cham (2023). https://doi.org/10.1007/978-3-031-35596-7_29
12. Huang, H.H., Kimura, S., Kuwabara, K., Nishida, T.: Generation of head movements of a robot using multimodal features of peer participants in group discussion conversation. Multimodal Technol. Interact. **4**(2), 15 (2020)
13. Ishii, R., Otsuka, K., Kumano, S., Yamato, J.: Predicting who will be the next speaker and when in multi-party meetings. NTT Tech. Rev. **13**, 07 (2015)
14. Itti, L., Dhavale, N., Pighin, F.: Photorealistic attention-based gaze animation. In: 2006 IEEE International Conference on Multimedia and Expo, pp. 521–524 (2006)
15. Jonell, P., Yoon, Y., Wolfert, P., Kucherenko, T., Henter, G.E.: HEMVIP: human evaluation of multiple videos in parallel. In: Proceedings of the 2021 International Conference on Multimodal Interaction, pp. 707–711. Association for Computing Machinery, New York (2021)

16. Kendon, A.: Some functions of gaze-direction in social interaction. Acta Physiol. (Oxf) **26**(1), 22–63 (1967)
17. Kingma, D., Ba, J.: Adam: a method for stochastic optimization. In: International Conference on Learning Representations (2014)
18. Kuno, Y., Sadazuka, K., Kawashima, M., Yamazaki, K., Yamazaki, A., Kuzuoka, H.: Museum guide robot based on sociological interaction analysis. In: CHI 2007, pp. 1191–1194. Association for Computing Machinery, New York (2007)
19. Metta, G., et al.: The iCub humanoid robot: an open-systems platform for research in cognitive development. Neural Netw. **23**(8), 1125–1134 (2010)
20. Mishra, C., Skantze, G.: Knowing where to look: a planning-based architecture to automate the gaze behavior of social robots. In: 2022 31st IEEE International Conference on Robot and Human Interactive Communication (RO-MAN), pp. 1201–1208. IEEE Press (2022)
21. Mutlu, B., Kanda, T., Forlizzi, J., Hodgins, J., Ishiguro, H.: Conversational gaze mechanisms for humanlike robots. ACM Trans. Interact. Intell. Syst. **1**(2), 1–33 (2012)
22. Mutlu, B., Shiwa, T., Kanda, T., Ishiguro, H., Hagita, N.: Footing in human-robot conversations: How robots might shape participant roles using gaze cues. In: Proceedings of the 4th ACM/IEEE International Conference on Human Robot Interaction, pp. 61–68. Association for Computing Machinery (2009)
23. Nakano, Y.I., Yoshino, T., Yatsushiro, M., Takase, Y.: Generating robot gaze on the basis of participation roles and dominance estimation in multiparty interaction. ACM Trans. Interact. Intell. Syst. **5**(4), 1–23 (2015)
24. Nguyen, D.-C., Bailly, G., Elisei, F.: Comparing cascaded LSTM architectures for generating head motion from speech in task-oriented dialogs. In: Kurosu, M. (ed.) HCI 2018. LNCS, vol. 10903, pp. 164–175. Springer, Cham (2018). https://doi.org/10.1007/978-3-319-91250-9_13
25. Pereira, A., Oertel, C., Fermoselle, L., Mendelson, J., Gustafson, J.: Effects of different interaction contexts when evaluating gaze models in HRI. In: Proceedings of the 2020 ACM/IEEE International Conference on Human-Robot Interaction, pp. 131–139. Association for Computing Machinery, New York (2020)
26. Prévot, L., Elisei, F., Bailly, G.: The robotrio corpus (2020). https://hdl.handle.net/11403/robotrio/v1, ORTOLANG (Open Resources and TOols for LANGuage) - www.ortolang.fr
27. Sacks, H., Schegloff, E., Jefferson, G.: A simple systematic for the organisation of turn taking in conversation. Language **50**, 696–735 (1974)
28. Shintani, T., Ishi, C.T., Ishiguro, H.: Analysis of role-based gaze behaviors and gaze aversions, and implementation of robot's gaze control for multi-party dialogue. In: HAI 2021, pp. 332–336. Association for Computing Machinery (2021)
29. Sidner, C.L., Kidd, C.D., Lee, C., Lesh, N.: Where to look: a study of human-robot engagement. In: Proceedings of the 9th International Conference on Intelligent User Interfaces, IUI 2004, pp. 78–84. Association for Computing Machinery, New York (2004)
30. Skantze, G., Johansson, M., Beskow, J.: Exploring turn-taking cues in multi-party human-robot discussions about objects. In: Proceedings of the 2015 ACM on International Conference on Multimodal Interaction, pp. 67–74. Association for Computing Machinery, New York (2015)
31. Stefanov, K., Salvi, G., Kontogiorgos, D., Kjellström, H., Beskow, J.: Modeling of human visual attention in multiparty open-world dialogues. J. Hum.-Robot Interact. **8**(2), 1–21 (2019)

32. Vertegaal, R., Slagter, R., van der Veer, G., Nijholt, A.: Eye gaze patterns in conversations: there is more to conversational agents than meets the eyes. In: Proceedings of the SIGCHI Conference on Human Factors in Computing Systems, pp. 301–308. Association for Computing Machinery, New York (2001)
33. Zangemeister, W., Stark, L.: Types of gaze movement: variable interactions of eye and head movements. Exp. Neurol. **77**(3), 563–577 (1982)
34. Zaraki, A., Mazzei, D., Giuliani, M., de rossi, D.: Designing and evaluating a social gaze-control system for a humanoid robot. IEEE Trans. Syst. Man Cybernet. A Syst. Hum. **44**, 157–168 (2014)

The Ambiguity of Robot Rights

Anisha Bontula[1], David Danks[2], and Naomi T. Fitter[1(✉)]

[1] Oregon State University (OSU), Corvallis, OR, USA
{bontulaa,fittern}@oregonstate.edu
[2] University of California San Diego, La Jolla, CA, USA
ddanks@ucsd.edu

Abstract. The prominence of robots as interdependent social agents continues to grow, leading to important conversations about legal and ethical considerations not just for humans, but also potentially for these autonomous agents (e.g., robot rights). Physical properties of the robot form factor have been shown to significantly impact human interactions with the system, including how law and policy-makers see and ascribe characteristics to it. For social robots in particular, an anthropomorphized or humanoid form factor can lead to assumptions about the robot's personhood, with potentially harmful ethical consequences. In this paper, we review current outlooks on social robots with regards to policy and personhood, particularly limits of current debates. We then provide a suggested redefinition of personhood for a robot with an emphasis on the dissociation of personhood from the humanoid form. We propose the treatment of robot personhood in terms of as interdependent group personhood rather than physical or anthropomorphic features, and suggest corresponding design principles and regulations about features such as system opacity.

1 Introduction

Debates surrounding robot rights are increasingly important in light of the exponential growth of autonomous robotic systems. The level of agency, nature of autonomy, and use case of robots are all factors that have played a role in not only defining the robot and its ethical obligations, but more controversially, informing the rights it should have. Much of this debate has focused on lethal autonomous weapons systems and other robots of war, as robot rights are relevant to whether a robot should be ethically or legally allowed to exercise lethal force. However, questions about robot rights are also important for robots in the personal, assistive, and commercial categories that are often thought to be less ethically problematic. Despite their more benign contexts, these robots can potentially act in ways that support or endanger human health, values, and interests, which thereby raises questions of both responsibility and rights. For example, a home healthcare robot might be tasked with ensuring that an elderly patient takes their medication; this type of ethically important interaction requires clarity about the rights and responsibilities, both ethical and legal,

A. Al. Ali et al. (Eds.): ICSR 2023, LNAI 14453, pp. 204–215, 2024.
https://doi.org/10.1007/978-981-99-8715-3_18

of both parties—patient and robot. Less obviously, as robots in these sectors function increasingly autonomously, questions naturally arise about permissible constraints or interference, and such questions can turn on the robots' rights. For example, it may soon be important (legally and ethically) to clarify the rights of an autonomous delivery robot, particularly as its actions may come into conflict with the wishes of various humans.

Historically, robot form has played a key role in discussions about robot rights in non-military sectors, perhaps most notably in the case of the robot citizen, Sophia. Sophia's capabilities are limited to that of a moderately intelligent chatbot, with attempts to expressively mimic human behavior. Sophia's humanoid form is the main differentiator, and so is presumably part of the reason that she was granted citizenship (though marketing and political reasons surely also applied). In general, anthropomorphism has been shown to have a strong impact on human acceptance, collaboration, and interaction with robots in the personal, assistive, and commercial categories. In contrast, the impact of anthropomorphism on robot *rights* has been relatively underexplored. Robot form has also been found to effect perceived robot intelligence, and personhood. At the same time, anthropomorphized terms used to describe a robot can lead to misunderstandings about the robot's function, role, and autonomy, all of which may be relevant to determining if a robot is deserving of rights. In this paper, we do not take a stand on substantive aspects of robot rights, but rather focus on the complex descriptive ("what is") and normative ("what ought") relationships between robot form factor, robot (potential) personhood, and possible robot rights, as well as the implications of those relationships.

We first argue that arguments about robot rights do and should depend partly on whether the robot has personhood. In particular, personhood (whether natural or artificial) has historically been understood to require a level of intelligence and rationality to justify relevant claims of autonomy, and those cognitive-emotional-social capacities thereby support the possession of certain key moral rights. In the specific case of robot rights, for example, robots that were tasked with making challenging decisions in a military context were given higher moral standing based on their ability to make ethically sound (and intelligent) decisions. We contend that considerations of personhood provide the bridge between intelligent capabilities and attributions of rights.

Robot form factor presents a challenge for this connection, however, as multiple studies have shown that form factor influences people's inferences about a robot's capabilities. Most importantly, humanoid robots are often inferred to have greater intelligence and capacity for suffering. That is, a robot's form factor can influence people's propensity to attribute it personhood, and therefore some rights, even though essentially no philosophical or legal theory of rights is grounded in physical form.

The possibility of these erroneous inferences implies a set of ethical constraints on robot design and implementation, particularly in the personal, assistive, and commercial sectors. For example, robot designers ought not use humanoid forms unless the robot's capabilities warrant the (likely) inferences about its personhood, and therefore rights. (Additionally, if attributions of personhood carry legal implications, then it might be pragmatically wise to avoid use of humanoid forms.)

We conclude by considering the importance in these debates of the widespread assumption that personhood necessarily involves "one body, one mind." We propose that robots are better understood as "one body, multiple minds," where the relevant minds include both robot and designers. We suggest that this more expansive view is both descriptively more accurate, and also normatively more defensible. Moreover, this broader view enables a more precise characterization of the conditions in which a robot should have moral and legal rights.

2   Descriptive Connections

The current treatment of robot rights is greatly informed by human rights and by regulations for evolving technology. A key concept in human rights literature is *personhood*; more precisely, the notion of 'personhood' captures the important characteristics of a being that allow (or require) their recognition as a legal "person." This concept thus characterizes those entities that receive strong(er) protective, legal, and moral rights, including humans and organizations alike. Historically, the context in which personhood gained mass popularity and widespread influence was highly problematic. Philosophers of personhood such as Plato, Locke, Kant, and Rawls all contended (or strongly suggested) that intelligence or rationality is a key determinant of personhood, thereby implying that one who possesses higher intelligence is arguably deserving of a higher moral status [7,13,15]. However, intelligence was often either associated with, or inferred from, physical European and masculine characteristics, thereby excluding women, people of color, children, and people with disabilities from personhood.[1] Although some degree of rational or intelligent capabilities is plausibly necessary for personhood, one must be careful not to thereby import socioculturally specific beliefs about signals or evidence of intelligence.

Previous work in the field of human-robot interaction has shown that such imports arguably occur, as perceptions of robot intelligence are influenced by form. In fact, form factor and morphology are used not just in everyday perceptions about robots, but also in current lawmaking and regulatory practices, even when form factor is unrepresentative of true robot function. As demonstrated by Graaf et al., the usage of anthropomorphic terms to describe the ability of a robot to exhibit human-like intelligence leads to the consequent assumption of the form of the robot in question [6]. This finding is indicative of many people's misrepresentation of humanoid robots as necessarily intelligent, and the more general, incorrect link between intelligence and human appearance. Humans are naturally associated with possessing moral agency, which expands their rights,

---

[1] Of course, these philosophers all had significantly more complex views than we have presented here. In particular, they all typically allowed that it was an empirical matter whether non-European, non-males had the requisite intelligence, and so they might have had different positions today.

compared to those of plants and animals, to include legal responsibility and liability. The instinct to associate moral agency to robots when they are humanoid, and to draw related parallels, is consequently unsurprising.

The tight link between form and perceived moral agency is interestingly less observed for robots in high-stakes situations, which are exactly those that might be expected to exhibit moral agency. In Gunkel's work investigating rights for war robots, the intelligence the robot displays in its decision-making is much more important than form factor when discussing its rights [9]. Robots that are tasked with making challenging decisions are given higher moral standing based on their ability to make ethically sound decisions, rather than whether they look like they are capable of doing so.

However, robots in the personal, assistive, and commercial domains are held to a different standard. Darling's work investigating care for robots showed that people cared more about robot abuse if the robot in question was one that depicted anthropomorphic properties. This point was further emphasized by elaborating on the known relationship between suffering and moral rights, which translates to the treatment of robot rights as well [5]. The field of human-robot interaction is greatly informed by human-human interactions, wherein human-human interactions often serve as a template for ideal fluid communication for robots. Human interactions, however, are not a sufficient template to inform how we treat and look at robots. Robots exhibit autonomous capabilities that can prompt designers and users alike to perceive them as more human, and less machine-like. They also can exhibit human-like form factors that lead to similar perceptions, even though this latter inference is not normatively warranted. Current robots can exist in a middle ground between simple machines and complex humans, and require unique regulatory policy grounded in clear ethical commitments.

3   Normative Commitments

The previous section focused on how people *do* attribute personhood and rights to robots; we turn now to the normative question of how they *should*, as that could obviously diverge from what they do. Our primary argument here is negative: theories of robot rights should dissociate personhood from robot form. One simple observation is that essentially no normative ethical theories include physical shape as a criterion for personhood, but rather all focus on cognitive, behavioral, phenomenological, and/or affective characteristics or capabilities. Of course, those theories might be wrong, but we think it is notable that no philosophical accounts of personhood (and subsequent rights) are grounded in the physical form of the thing.

We start, though, by considering pragmatic reasons to dissociate robot form and robot personhood. In particular, if there is a (legal) connection between form factor and perceived personhood, then companies and robot designers would have incentives to pursue unethical paths. An anthropomorphic form factor may be chosen by robot designers to aid in the robot's ability to be more socially accepted, even if that choice would yield unfair advantages to the designers or reinforce harmful biases. For example, Somaya and Varshney's work exploring the various aspects of intellectual property rights shows that a humanoid social robot with robot rights increases the perceived amount of humanness and the degree of intellectual property rights [24]. Parviainen and Coeckelbergh further emphasize the immense economic potential of animated and embodied robots, providing Sophia as their key example [19]. This gives robot designers incentive to acquire monetary gains by creating humanoid robots without appropriate functions that nonetheless benefit (in perceptions) from this morphology.

A distinct practical reason to not unnecessarily use human-like forms (and so dissociate personhood from form) is that inappropriate use of particular robot morphologies can reinforce stereotypes and biases (e.g., [12,26]). Persaud's work investigating the extension of human rights to robots is characteristic in stating that humans are the "ideal embodiment of cognition and ethics" [20]. As a result, robotics developers must be careful not to design their systems in ways that accidentally reinforce existing stereotypes, even if those would be pragmatically helpful (e.g., if a robot with lighter skin and a robot with darker skin are perceived as having different rights, and so designers opt for one on that basis).

Ethical concerns surrounding socially assistive robots are shared by several researchers (e.g., [3,11,23]). One particularly common worry is deception, where the population interacting with robots reports feeling deceived if the robot is unable to do a task that it is expected to do. Boada et al. show that deception is linked to perception, and can be used intentionally, although it is conceived as being morally wrong [3]. A direct link between deception and expectation is form factor. The general view of relational entities for robots presented by Tavani is a key example; the main relevant claim from this work is that there is no necessity to know if a robot possesses certain proprieties, as long as it appears like it can [25]. Hegel et al. present work studying the effects of anthropomorphization, and find that the more human a robot looks, the more human-like it is expected to be [10]. Mamak's work exploring the legal protection of robots presents a discourse with a key, often-overlooked statement: "robots are becoming increasingly human-like" [16]. This expectation of robots to look like humans (if they come under ethical considerations) extends culturally, as shown by Robertson [22]. In their work discussing robot rights in Japan, the authors explain coexistence by stating that it makes sense for a robot to have a human-like body if robots are to co-exist in human environments. The contrast between robot rights and human rights needs to be clearly defined, as morphology is currently an indicator of pre-existing biases towards robots, and even towards humans, who do not appear the same as others.

However, the likely risks associated with a humanoid form factor may clash with the potential convenience of choosing a human-like embodiment. That is, rather than decoupling form factor and rights, one might instead think that we should connect them, precisely to impose a "cost" on developers—namely, provision of appropriate rights—exactly when they gain a benefit solely by using that form factor. If we require legal considerations for robots that are most human-like, then we ensure that such robots (with their potentially deceptive form factor) have an appropriate level of moral agency. While this coupling is tempting, we contend that it should be resisted. The current legal system is insufficiently refined to provide rights in a fine-grained way to intelligent autonomous robots. While the law for software systems and existing AI may be a starting point, these laws are not inclusive of the unpredictability that embodiment brings in "open-world" contexts, and so they fail to cover the effects that misuse of robots could have. Moreover, the rights and legal protections that might be required for robots are quite different from those for humans. Existing legal frameworks for humans are not appropriately designed for robots, and so we ought not use them in that way (despite the temptation). In particular, the potential practical benefit of prompting robot developers to engage in more thoughtful design is insufficient to accord human-like rights on the basis of form factor. We should use other mechanisms to achieve that benefit.

More generally, human-like morphology can lead to harms such as concealing information, misuse of trust, and promoting biases unless there are clear explanations of robot functions and capabilities. For social robots in particular, it is challenging to not anthropomorphize robots due to the context in which they exist, but that anthropomorphization does not imply that we ought to afford rights to the robot. Robot morphology *is* used by people as a signal about its rights, but it *ought* not be used in this way.

We have focused on challenges and problems that can arise if we connect morphology with personhood, but there are also advantages to this dissociation, as it will (we suggest) lead to greater diversity of robot form factors. If personhood does not depend on form factor, then there is one less reason pushing robot designers and developers towards the same anthropomorphic forms. As a result, this dissociation can help to:

- Provide robot designers the freedom to explore more broadly varying robot morphologies.
- Expand the layperson's view of a robot.
- Promote a newly refined and better understanding of intelligence and personhood in the digital age.
- Enable people to view a robot as a moral agent on appropriate grounds, rather than parallels to human embodiment.

Of course, none of these potential benefits are *guaranteed* if we dissociate morphology and rights. Furthermore, the benefits themselves are largely practical and psychological, not legal or ethical. We agree, but we also emphasize that these benefits would largely accrue to the general public, and so are exactly the types of considerations that regulations should advance. More generally, robot designers and developers lose relatively little if we dissociate personhood and form factor, and potentially gain access and legitimacy for an expanded space of possibilities.

4   Prescriptive Guidance

If personhood is decoupled from form factor, then how ought we think about conditions for legitimate attribution of personhood to robots? We earlier noted that essentially all ethical theories use factors other than physical form, but we did not provide a positive account of the nature of personhood. Moreover, this issue connects directly with prescriptive guidance about norms, laws, and regulations that can help to ensure that appropriate criteria are used. We thus approach this problem by extracting commonalities from across relevant theories in fields that shape robot rights, namely philosophy, law, and human-robot interaction.

Personhood has played a significant role in shaping how the law recognizes persons and their rights. Ohlin presents a thoughtful piece showcasing the shortcomings and contradictions of personhood in great detail [18], which we summarize succinctly here. The rights that are ascribed to a being are based on whether they have personhood, non-personhood, or the "potential" of personhood. However, this approach in the law depends on clear lines to delineate these three states, which may not be forthcoming in complex cases. A very telling example is the personhood of someone suffering from multiple personality disorder (MPD). From a legal perspective [18], the personhood of one with MPD is quite unclear. On the one hand, one might claim that each personality is a "person" since those are what exhibit relevant psychological continuity. On the other hand, this approach would be legally problematic since a criminal act would be temporarily forgiven when other "persons" are present (i.e., other personalities at the fore) since they did not commit the crime, even though they are stuck in the same embodiment.[2] In practice, this debate has largely been resolved by treating individuals with MPD as a "group person," in a similar way to companies. This practice treats a person with MPD as one with several minds and one "body," just as legal group personhood for companies allows for specific departments within a company to be held more or less liable, while still receiving common representation. We suggest that this notion of group personhood can potentially be helpful in thinking about robot rights.

Group personhood also satisfies constraints emerging from focus on the reasons why legal personhood might be needed for robots. Avila Negri [2] has argued that personhood for a robot is (currently) only needed for the purpose of liability. That is, the proposal is that we only need to accord robots sufficient personhood and rights to hold them liable for harms and negative outcomes from their actions. However, this restricted focus not only fails to provide guidance about the nature of personhood, it also merely postpones difficult questions about robot rights and personhood that extend beyond liability (e.g., what are the intellectual property rights of works created by a robot?). We propose that any account of robot personhood and robot rights should provide guidance for multiple ethical and legal questions, not merely those relating to liability. The group personhood approach can clearly address liability questions, as shown by its use for issues of corporate liability. And in addition, many other legal and ethical issues can be usefully addressed using this framework, as shown by its successful application to cases of MPD.

---

[2] There are broader issues about the potential criminalization of a mental disorder rather than providing people with actual psychiatric help, but those would take us quite far afield from questions of robot rights.

A different feature of personhood arises in recent work of Arstein-Kerslake et al. [1], who argue that personhood requires consideration of an object's inter-actions. Historically, the law has struggled to recognize and evaluate impacts to legal objects, such as the environment; those impacts were typically deemed to be legally relevant only if they also affected the interests of legal subjects, such as persons. Legal subjects were characterized by intrinsic (mostly intellectual) features, and so anything without those features was legally and morally side-lined. However, there is a tight interconnectivity of legal subjects and objects, thereby calling into question the existence of a "bright line" distinction between the two. In particular, there is not necessarily a principled basis for distinguish-ing subjects from objects solely on the basis of intrinsic (rather than relational) features. We thus propose that we should broaden the notion of personhood to include any being that is interdependent with those in their surroundings.[3] The resulting conception—grounded in feminist theories of relational autonomy and Native American histories of connection to soil and trees—does provide a more expansive understanding of legal personhood, including many flora and fauna [14,21]. While this implication might be seen as an objection, we propose that lines for personhood should initially be drawn in a more expansive way, and scaled back in light of increased understanding. Such an approach is arguably an appropriate counterpart to the more general Precautionary Principle, as it would create legal protections (and barriers) as a default, with those weakened only in response to clear evidence and arguments.

Based on these various ideas, we propose to understand personhood for a robot as follows. First, robot personhood should be treated as group personhood (one body, several minds), where the robot necessarily acts on other objects and subjects as an independent representative of the company/designers who deployed it. Second, robots granted personhood are eligible to receive legal pro-tection and ethical consideration that a legal person can receive. Third, the robot's function, autonomy, and interdependency are the only factors that will determine its personhood. One immediate implication is that use of particular robot form factors and appearance should be justified by the designers solely on these bases (rather than other reactions that people might have). Robots are at the crux of interdependence in society, and this proposal ensures that social robots are appropriately understood as "persons" just when they exhibit the right characteristics, rather than when they happen to exhibit physical proper-ties of a human being.

We have deliberately not proposed or defended any particular set of neces-sary (for personhood) capabilities, capacities, or characteristics in this paper. Instead, we have aimed to develop insights and principles for robot personhood that are (largely) agnostic about the specific positive account of personhood writ large. We recognize the significant disputes and disagreements about whether, for example, the "capacity to feel pain" is a necessary feature for personhood.

---

[3] We emphasize that interdependence is necessarily an active, bidirectional relation-ship. The state of a rock can depend on the persons in its environment, but it is not thereby interdependent with those persons (and so not a legal subject).

And precisely because of those disputes, we have focused on developing guidance that is not dependent on the truth or acceptance of any particular list of characteristics, but rather can guide legal and ethical reasoning while further aspects of personhood are debated and resolved.

This understanding of robot personhood has immediate implications for regulations and legal practices, in particular the types of opacity that should be permitted. One standard approach [4,8] divides AI system opacity into three types: (1) companies making the system intentionally opaque due to potential outrage at the algorithm's biases or poor performance; (2) opacity due to the technical illiteracy of those interacting with the system; and (3) opacity due to complexity of the algorithmic model that is not fully understood even by programmers. Although these different types lead to different potential harm, they are currently all treated the same way under law. In particular, technical complexity (type (3)) is often used to escape liability, even if the opacity is actually of type (1) or (2). While AI systems are coming under increasing regulatory scrutiny around issues of opacity, the extension to intelligent robots requires a clear distinction between system opacity, system capability, and designer intent.

In particular, all three types of system opacity become more complex when embodiment is included. Intentional opacity can greatly increase and go undetected, and if a robot looks like a human, then the technical illiteracy and regulation of expectations also increases. If robot rights are grounded in appropriate system capabilities and interactions, then we can use those bases to inform regulation and liability, rather than relying on user, regulator, or developer understanding. We propose that regulations should ensure that system opacity and foreseeable complexity inform liability and protective rights. For example, if a social robot uses only its eyes to expressively communicate, then system complexity in terms of foreseeable harm due to misinterpretation is lower, and can be regulated accordingly. However, if the social robot uses speech, then the potential of harm due to misunderstanding increases, and needs to be regulated accordingly.

At the same time, social robots are in a distinctive position since they can become interdependent agents of their environments. Interacting fluently with humans is a compelling characteristic, but has also inadvertently limited social robots to a specific form factor. For example, Naneva et al.'s review paper on human-robot interaction focuses on attitudes and trust towards social robots, and showcases a key limitation through their definition of a social robot [17]: a "physically embodied artificial agent that mimics the features of a living being– usually a human." This definition is indicative of the general mindset towards social robots, with their intrinsic nature of being "social" directly related to anthropomorphism. In fact, they found no prior research on attitudes towards non-anthropomorphic or non-humanoid social robots, despite those being possible form factors. When assessing qualities of trust, anxiety, acceptance, etc., it is extremely important to be aware of the effect that form factor has, especially for agents such as robots that are extremely media-prominent. If robotics researchers themselves are subconsciously propagating the humanoid form factor in their research, then it can be anticipated for non-robotics researchers to do the same, narrowing their view of a robot in a social context. We propose that for the overarching discussion of robot rights, researchers must also focus on including the effect of form in their research, and broaden the current limiting aspects of social robots.

5 Discussion

Robots continue to grow increasingly prevalent in our daily lives, and with this growth comes many different concerns, impacts, and conversations. One such conversation is the proper status of robot rights, given their unique ability to be more of a moral agent than an animal, but not as morally aware as a human. Concerns regarding liability, accountability, and protection have arguably pulled in contradictory directions, as evidenced by the state of the current legal frameworks about robot rights. Primary discussions about robot rights have focused mainly on military robots and others with significant capabilities for harm. However, this focus has left little room for substantive discussion of potential rights for personal, assistive, and commercial robots. Which will arguably form the majority of robots with which the general public will interact. Public understandings of robot rights will thus likely be heavily shaped by these interactions, informing how we regulate robots and new technology in the future. A focus on personal and assistive robots is even more critical since they may interact with vulnerable populations, greatly increasing the risk of potential harm.

An underlying theme that has been observed in social robotics and the definition of their rights is the importance of the morphology of the robot. The humanoid form factor not only has an impact on how people interact with the robot, but also what they expect from it, the qualities associated with it, and the subsequent rights it can gain. If a robot simply possesses humanoid characteristics but not the adequate intelligence to make well-informed decisions, then deploying such a system has the potential to cause a great deal of harm, but without appropriate accountability since rights would be inappropriately attributed to it.

We have argued for a dissociation between robot morphology and robot personhood or rights, as the latter should be grounded in the robot's intelligence, sentience, and moral agency. This approach also provides practical benefits: (a) Designers and companies will have incentives to choose an appropriate robot morphology and transparency for the functions and purposes of the robot; and (b) There will likely be increased designer freedom, digital literacy, and a more holistic definition of personhood.

The solutions we present combine inspiration from several diverse fields that all have a unique influence on robot rights. We urge roboticists to include the impact of form in their analyses, and urge policy-makers to consider true capabilities of autonomous systems regardless of form factor. Robots fall in an uncommon niche that overlaps with not one, but rather many, domains. Robot designers and policy-makers must recognize this overlap when approaching an inherently challenging conversation, such as robot rights. Achieving the needed balance between fields may be difficult and time consuming, but is a necessary step. We encourage the much-needed conversation between representatives of those impacted by technology that can help bring unforeseen assumptions to light and aid in reaching a common understanding. From the discourse presented, we hope to increase the awareness of the impact of robot form and the potential harm of restricting acceptance to one sole form factor. With robots becoming more integral to society, it is important to recognize their unique advantage of possessing moral agency without having to draw parallels to their humanness. Robots are not human, and neither are their rights.

Acknowledgments. We thank Julie A. Adams for her guidance during the early stages of this work.

References

1. Arstein-Kerslake, A., O'Donnell, E., Kayess, R., Watson, J.: Relational personhood: a conception of legal personhood with insights from disability rights and environmental law. Griffith Law Rev. **30**(3), 530–555 (2021)
2. Avila Negri, S.: Robot as legal person: electronic personhood in robotics and artificial intelligence. Front. Robot. AI., 419 (2021)
3. Boada, J.P., Maestre, B.R., Genís, C.T.: The ethical issues of social assistive robotics: a critical literature review. Technol. Soc. **67**, 101726 (2021)
4. Burrell, J.: How the machine 'thinks': understanding opacity in machine learning algorithms. Big Data Soc. **3**, 1–12 (2016)
5. Darling, K.: Extending legal protection to social robots: the effects of anthropomorphism, empathy, and violent behavior towards robotic objects. In: Robot Law. Edward Elgar Publishing (2016)
6. De Graaf, M.M., Hindriks, F.A., Hindriks, K.V.: Who wants to grant robots rights? In: Companion of the ACM/IEEE International Conference on Human-Robot Interaction, pp. 38–46 (2021)
7. Dennett, D.: Conditions of personhood. In: Goodman, M.F. (ed.) What is a Person?, pp. 145–167. Springer (1988). https://doi.org/10.1007/978-1-4612-3950-5_7
8. Galaski, J.: AI regulation: present situation and future possibilities. https://www.liberties.eu/en/stories/ai-regulation/43740
9. Gunkel, D.J.: The rights of (killer) robots. Moral responsibility in 21st century warfare: Just war theory and the ethical challenges of autonomous weapon systems, pp. 1–21 (2020)
10. Hegel, F., Krach, S., Kircher, T., Wrede, B., Sagerer, G.: Understanding social robots: a user study on anthropomorphism. In: Proceedings of the IEEE International Symposium on Robot and Human Interactive Communication (RO-MAN), pp. 574–579 (2008)
11. Ienca, M., Jotterand, F., Vică, C., Elger, B.: Social and assistive robotics in dementia care: ethical recommendations for research and practice. Int. J. Soc. Robot. **8**(4), 565–573 (2016)
12. Jung, E.H., Waddell, T.F., Sundar, S.S.: Feminizing robots: user responses to gender cues on robot body and screen. In: Proceedings of the CHI Conference on Extended Abstracts on Human Factors in Computing Systems, pp. 3107–3113 (2016)

13. Kant, I., Schneewind, J.B.: Groundwork for the Metaphysics of Morals. Yale University Press, Ithaca (2002)
14. Karlan, P.S., Ortiz, D.R.: In a diffident voice: relational feminism, abortion rights, and the feminist legal agenda. Nw. UL REv. **87**, 858 (1992)
15. Locke, J., Perry, J.: Of identity and diversity (1975)
16. Mamak, K.: Whether to save a robot or a human: on the ethical and legal limits of protections for robots. Front. Robot. AI **8**, 712427 (2021)
17. Naneva, S., Sarda Gou, M., Webb, T.L., Prescott, T.J.: A systematic review of attitudes, anxiety, acceptance, and trust towards social robots. Int. J. Soc. Robot. **12**(6), 1179–1201 (2020)
18. Ohlin, J.D.: Is the concept of the person necessary for human rights? In: International Legal Personality, pp. 437–478. Routledge (2017)
19. Parviainen, J., Coeckelbergh, M.: The political choreography of the Sophia robot: beyond robot rights and citizenship to political performances for the social robotics market. AI Soc. **36**(3), 715–724 (2021)
20. Persaud, P., Varde, A.S., Wang, W.: Can robots get some human rights? A cross-disciplinary discussion. J. Robot. **2021**, 1–11 (2021)
21. RiverOfLife, M., et al.: Yoongoorrookoo. Griffith Law Rev. **30**(3), 505–529 (2021)
22. Robertson, J.: Human rights vs. robot rights: forecasts from Japan. Crit. Asian Stud. **46**(4), 571–598 (2014)
23. Sætra, H.S.: The foundations of a policy for the use of social robots in care. Technol. Soc. **63**, 101383 (2020)
24. Somaya, D., Varshney, L.R.: Embodiment, anthropomorphism, and intellectual property rights for AI creations. In: Proceedings of the AAAI/ACM Conference on AI, Ethics, and Society, pp. 278–283 (2018)
25. Tavani, H.T.: Can social robots qualify for moral consideration? Reframing the question about robot rights. Information **9**(4), 73 (2018)
26. Weßel, M., Ellerich-Groppe, N., Schweda, M.: Stereotyping of social robots in eldercare: an explorative analysis of ethical problems and possible solutions. In: Culturally Sustainable Social Robotics-Proceedings of Robophilosophy, pp. 239–246 (2020)

The Impact of Robots' Facial Emotional Expressions on Light Physical Exercises

Nourhan Abdulazeem$^{(\boxtimes)}$ ⬤ and Yue Hu ⬤

Active and Interactive Robotics Lab, Department of Mechanical and Mechatronics
Engineering, University of Waterloo, Waterloo, ON N2L3G1, Canada
{nourhan.abdulazeem,yue.hu}@uwaterloo.ca

Abstract. To address the global challenge of population aging, our goal
is to enhance successful aging through the introduction of robots capable of assisting in daily physical activities and promoting light exercises, which would enhance the cognitive and physical well-being of older
adults. Previous studies have shown that facial expressions can increase
engagement when interacting with robots. This study aims to investigate
how older adults perceive and interact with a robot capable of displaying
facial emotions while performing a physical exercise task together. We
employed a collaborative robotic arm with a flat panel screen to encourage physical exercise across three different facial emotion conditions. We
ran the experiment with older adults aged between 66 and 88. Our findings suggest that individuals perceive robots exhibiting facial expressions
as less competent than those without such expressions. Additionally, the
presence of facial expressions does not appear to significantly impact
participants' levels of engagement, unlike other state-of-the-art studies.
This observation is likely linked to our study's emphasis on collaborative physical human-robot interaction (pHRI) applications, as opposed
to socially oriented pHRI applications. Additionally, we foresee a requirement for more suitable non-verbal social behavior to effectively enhance
participants' engagement levels.

Keywords: facial expressions · emotions · collaborative robotic arms ·
social-physical human-robot interaction

1 Introduction

For the first time in history, the global population of individuals aged 6 and above
is projected to exceed the number of younger people. The decline in fertility
rates and the increase in life expectancy have resulted in a global phenomenon
of population aging [2]. This attracts researchers' attention to studying how to
enhance older adults' life quality and independent living.

We acknowledge the support of the Natural Sciences and Engineering Research Council
of Canada (NSERC), funding reference number RGPIN-2022-03857.

A potential enhancement for successful aging is introducing robots that can provide physical assistance with essential daily activities and promote light physical exercises. It has been proven that light physical exercise can be beneficial for older adults to maintain their cognitive and physical well-being [9]. As a consequence, this has drawn our attention to exploring what could contribute to a successful physical human-robot interaction (pHRI) [13].

Recent studies have demonstrated that, by bridging social human-robot interaction (sHRI) and pHRI, robots can physically interact with humans while also being socially acceptable [9]. One approach that has proven its effectiveness in enhancing robot perception and engagement is endowing robots with the ability to exhibit facial emotional expressions [19]. This has motivated us to explore the potential of facial emotional expressions in pHRI scenarios.

In this study, we adopt a light physical exercise scenario, as one of the potential applications for physically interactive robots in domestic environments, to investigate the impact of facial emotional expressions on users' perception of the robot and their level of engagement. We utilized Sawyer, a collaborative robotic arm developed by Rethink Robotics, for this purpose. Sawyer is equipped with a flat panel screen that allows us to display various facial expressions, as shown in Fig. 1. We anticipate that our results will be helpful for the research community toward the exploration of effective social skills for physically interactive robots.

Our research is founded upon two primary domains: sHRI and pHRI, which serve as the pillars of our investigation. Remarkable efforts were made to explore social-physical robots in various contexts such as hugging [4], touching in social and nursing scenarios [14], handshaking [12], and playing games [10]. However, only limited efforts involved the investigation of both domains with robots that possess high dexterity and manipulation capabilities [1] which are essential qualities for robots to efficiently engage in physical interactions. Even fewer studies have devoted their efforts to investigating facial emotional expressions, for those types of robots [10].

Some existing studies have relied on facial expressions to enhance the user's engagement with robots that possess high dexterity and manipulation capabilities in various pHRI scenarios, such as physical exercise [9], clapping/gaming, and teaching [1]. However, they did not investigate the impact of the robot's facial expressions on the interaction, unlike Tsalamlal et al. [18] and Fitter et al. [10]. Tsalamlal et al. [18] investigated how participants combine facial expressions and handshakes to assess the perceived emotions in robots. The findings indicated that participants assigned greater significance to facial expressions when evaluating Valence. Fitter et al. [10] assessed how participants' emotions were affected by a robot's responsive facial expressions compared to an unresponsive robot's facial expressions during a hand-clapping game. Participants perceived the interactive face as more pleasant, energetic, and less robotic than the unresponsive one.

However, none of the previously mentioned studies have investigated participants' perceptions of the robot's characteristics, such as its perceived intelligence. Furthermore, the influence of these facial expressions on users' performance remains unexplored. To address these gaps, our study seeks to investigate participants' perceptions of a physically interacting robot displaying facial expressions and examine the potential impact of these expressions on their performance during physical interactions.

2   Research Questions

Our study is designed to build upon the insights gained from existing literature. By rigorously exploring the effects of facial emotional expressions on older adults engaged in pHRI applications. As a result, the following research questions were formulated to lead this study:

- **RQ1**: Will facial emotional expressions impact an older adult's level of engagement and perception of a robot in a pHRI scenario?

The answer to the first research question will help us understand the importance of relying on facial expressions as a means of communication during pHRI with older adults. These findings will guide the research community towards investing further efforts in the development of facial emotional expressions for successful pHRI. Alternatively, they may prompt exploration of other social behaviors that could be better suited for typical pHRI scenarios.

To comprehend the impact of facial expression responsiveness, as well as the mere presence of a robot's face regardless of its responsiveness, on participants' perceptions of the robot's characteristics and performance, we pose our second research question:

- **RQ2**: Does a responsive robot's facial emotional expressions impact an older adult's level of engagement and perception of a robot, compared to an unresponsive robot, in a pHRI scenario?

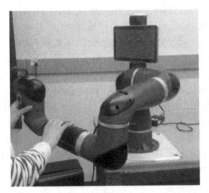
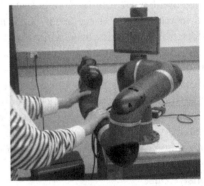

(a) Before performing a push and robot is in initial configuration

(b) After a push is performed and robot headlight blinks

Fig. 1. Participant exercising with Sawyer in the unresponsive social behavior condition

3   Method

3.1   Settings

To answer the proposed research questions, a user study, in the form of a light physical exercise game, was conducted in the Active & Interactive Laboratory at the University of Waterloo. The objective of the exercise is to perform the highest number of pushes possible, according to each participant's comfortable pace, against the robot's 4th joint as shown in Fig. 1. Further details of the game design are provided in Sect. 3.1.

A between-subject study design is considered and Sawyer from Rethink Robotics is used. Sawyer is a 7-degree-of-freedom torque-controlled manipulator equipped with a flat-panel screen and headlight, as shown in Fig. 1.

During participants exercising with the robot, 3 conditions of facial emotional expressions were considered:

1. **Inactive Facial Expression**: The robot displays its default screen, which features the Rethink Robotics logo [17].
2. **Unresponsive Facial Expression**: The robot showcases a happy face (as depicted in Fig. 2b).
3. **Responsive Facial Expression**: The robot exhibits varying facial emotional expressions in response to the user's performance.

In this paper, we will also refer to the unresponsive and responsive conditions together as the active conditions. In the responsive condition, the robot shows a neutral face (shown in Fig. 2a) at the beginning of the interaction. After the participant performs a set of successful pushes, the robot shows a happy face (shown in Fig. 2b) and after another set of successful pushes, the robot shows a surprised face (shown in Fig. 2c).

We opted to utilize Fitter and Kuchenbecker's established facial emotional expression set [8] due to its cross-cultural evaluation, a critical factor for conducting experiments in a Canadian societal context, as in our case. Fitter et al. [8] found that participants from the USA and India, similar to our participants (Caucasians and Southeast Asians), successfully identified their proposed set of the facial emotional expressions. Moreover, the study, which took place online, exclusively presented participants with Baxter's head. It's worth noting that Baxter's head is almost identical to Sawyer's head, as both robots are products of Rethink Robotics.

We considered using the safest rated facial emotions, according to Fitter and Kuchenbecker's results, as safety is the most crucial human factor in HRI [7]. Therefore, we decided to use the neutral, happy, and surprised faces for the responsive condition and the happy face, which is rated the safest among all faces, for the unresponsive condition. While the red and the purple colors were rated as the most energetic face colors, we chose to use purple for all conditions as red was, also, rated the least pleasant. Similarly, we aimed at using an arousing color as it contributes significantly to promoting the interaction. It should be noted that Sawyer's face color in Fig. 1 is purple, but it is shown blue due to the camera effect.

(a) Neutral Face   (b) Happy Face   (c) Surprised Face

Fig. 2. Sawyer facial emotional expressions [8] (Color figure online)

Physical Exercise Design. The exercise starts with Sawyer at its initial joint configuration, as shown in Fig. 1a. The participants stood upright and faced Sawyer's head. They are asked to perform the highest number of pushes possible according to their comfortable pace in 1 min against Sawyer's 4th joint as shown in Fig. 1. Further details about the instructions provided for the participants are indicated in Sect. 3.3. A push is only counted if a participant was able to push the joint to make an angle offset greater than a pre-defined threshold. Each time a push is counted, Sawyer's green headlight blinks as an indicator for the participant. Figure 1b shows the robot state, note the headlight, when a push is counted. Example of a participant exercising[1].

Robot Control. In order to physically exercise with Sawyer in a fully-autonomous mode, it is required to be under joint impedance control. The joints' initial configuration and stiffness are kept constant across all conditions, whereas Sawyer's facial expressions are adjusted according to the condition being examined.

In the responsive condition, to keep a consistent interaction experience with Sawyer across all participants and account for differences in participants' physical capabilities, each participant performed a trial session to determine their capability of pushing Sawyer's joints, i.e., baseline. Further details on how the trial session is conducted are in Sect. 3.3. Thus, we were able to predict each participant's total number of pushes during the actual session. Accordingly, we implemented our code to show a happy face after 25% of the baseline, and a surprised face after 75% of the baseline. Hence, each participant in the responsive conditions gets to experience all the facial expression alterations around the same phase in the experiment despite the expected diversity in participants' physical capabilities.

3.2 Participants

Twenty-seven participants were recruited in our study (17 female (F); 10 male (M), all older adults) from the University of Waterloo Research in Aging Participant Pool (WRAP), between the ages of 66 and 88 years (M = 76.52, SD =

---

[1] https://youtu.be/mZJcMLABNHg.

6.12). Out of the 27 participants, all 3 conditions were randomly assigned 9 participants each (ages: M = 76.78, SD = 7.31, 5 F, 4 M for the inactive condition, ages: M = 77.44, SD = 4.27, 6 F, 3 M for the unresponsive condition, ages: M = 75.33, SD = 6.18, 6 F, 3 M for the responsive condition).

Among the recruited participants for the experiment, the majority were right-handed. However, in the inactive condition, there were four exceptions: two left-handed individuals and two who identified as ambidextrous. Additionally, each of the two active conditions included one left-handed participant. Ethnically, the majority of participants identified as Caucasian, with two participants identifying as Southeast Asian. Notably, two participants of South Asian descent were assigned to each of the active conditions. Furthermore, all participants demonstrated good eyesight as confirmed by a brief eye test.

Initial survey results indicated that all participants displayed normal levels of depression, stress, and anxiety according to the Depression Anxiety Stress Scale 21 (DASS-21) [16]. Notably, depression levels were evaluated due to their established influence on activity motivation, a practice observed in prior similar experiments [9]. None of the participants had prior exposure to the Sawyer robot, as confirmed by a 5-point Likert scale. While some participants had encountered other robots before, over 50% of the assigned participants had no previous robotics experience across all conditions. During the trial session, participants demonstrated closely matched physical capabilities. Additionally, none of the recruited participants had upper or lower limb motion disabilities.

All our experiments received ethical approval from the University of Waterloo Human Research Ethics Board (protocol N. 45340) at the University of Waterloo, Ontario, Canada. Before the experiment, participants received proper information and gave informed consent to participate in the study.

3.3 Procedure

Each participant visited the laboratory and dedicated 20 to 30 min to complete the study. After obtaining participants' informed consent, they provided demographic information including age, gender, ethnicity, profession, and handedness. Following this, participants watched an instructional video[2] on how to exercise with the robot, without indicating the robot's capability of facial expressions, i.e., its screen is not shown. The decision to withhold information about the robot's facial expression capabilities prior to the experiment was intentional, aiming to prevent the formation of unrealistic expectations.

A short eye test was then administered to ensure participants' ability to see the robot's screen clearly. At the beginning of the setup, Sawyer's screen was turned away from the participant to prevent visibility of the screen. Participants were given the opportunity to perform 2 to 3 pushes to become accustomed to the robot's stiffness and determine their preferred distance from it. The experimenter ensured that participants performed the exercise correctly by ensuring they understood how the pushes were being counted.

---

[2] https://youtu.be/HxXZVLemShQ.

Next, a trial session lasting 10 s was conducted with Sawyer's screen still turned away. The purpose was to gauge each participant's physical capability. Upon successful completion of the trial, the robot rotated its screen to face the participant and proceeded to execute one of the three conditions detailed in Sect. 3.1. Participants conducted the trial session with the robot in the same state as depicted in the instructional video (Sawyer's screen not facing the participant). Participants performed the actual session for a duration of 1 min.

Following the task, participants completed robot perception and engagement questionnaires, detailed in Sect. 3.4. Subsequently, a debriefing session was held to address any questions or concerns. As a token of appreciation for their time, each participant received remuneration.

3.4 Measures

To evaluate robot perception, we employed the Robot Social Attribute Scale (RoSAS) [5]. RoSAS measured participants' perceived competence, warmth, and discomfort on a 9-point scale. Additionally, perceived safety was evaluated using the corresponding subscale from the Godspeed questionnaire [3] , which employs a 5-point scale. Perceived trust was assessed with a single-item questionnaire employing a 5-point Likert Scale. Participants indicated their level of trust by responding to the statement 'I trust the robot,' where 1 denoted 'strongly agree' and 5 denoted 'strongly disagree'. Items within each sub-scale are randomized.

For engagement assessment, we employed both objective and subjective evaluation methods. Participants indicated their level of engagement by responding to the statement 'I felt engaged with the robot during exercising' using a 5-point Likert Scale, where 1 represented 'strongly agree' and 5 represented 'strongly disagree'. The objective assessment (E_{obj}) involved determining the ratio between the actual number of pushes during the session (P_{actual}) and the expected number of pushes ($P_{expected}$) calculated from the trial session.

$$E_{obj} = \frac{P_{actual}}{P_{expected}}$$

Furthermore, we sought to understand the reasons behind the participants' responses to our quantitative measures by relying on open-ended questions. These questions included: "Did you enjoy the exercising session? Why or why not?", "What do you think about Sawyer as an exercising partner?", "What stood out to you the most about interacting with the robot?", "Do you think the robot can have more features that would make it more interesting? Suggest features.", and for the responsive condition, "Did you observe any changes in the robot's facial expressions? If so, how would you describe the changes in its facial expressions?" To ensure thorough and meaningful responses, we specifically asked participants to provide the reasoning behind their answers.

4 Results

To evaluate participants' perceptions of the robot, we calculated scores for competence, warmth, discomfort, and perceived safety by averaging individual items

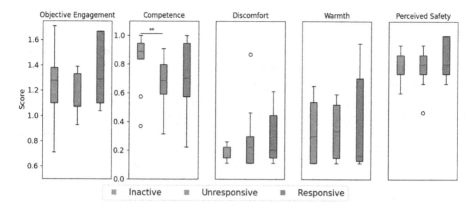

Fig. 3. Boxplots illustrate participants' perceived competence, discomfort, warmth, safety, and objective engagement. Each box plot features a line representing the median, with box edges indicating the 25th and 75th percentiles. Whiskers display the range up to 1.5 times the interquartile range, with outliers marked as 'o'. The ratio E_{obj} is represented as a value potentially exceeding 1. Competence, perceived safety, discomfort, warmth, and safety ratings are normalized to fall within the range of 0 to 1. Significance levels ($** := p - value < 0.01$) is indicated on lines between conditions.

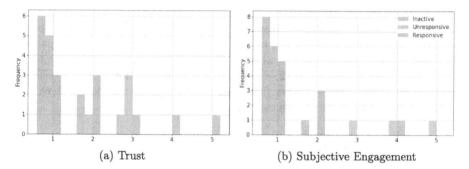

(a) Trust   (b) Subjective Engagement

Fig. 4. Bar plots illustrating participants' perceived trust and engagement for each condition on a 5-point Likert Scale (1 = highest, 5 = lowest).

within each sub-scale. Figure 3 illustrates participants' responses for each dimension across conditions. Notably, participants perceived the robot as more competent in the inactive condition compared to the active condition, showing relatively high ratings across conditions. Similarly, participants reported higher safety levels in the inactive condition compared to the active conditions, also displaying relatively high ratings overall. Ratings of discomfort remained consistently low across all conditions. Warmth ratings were comparable between the inactive and unresponsive conditions but were higher than the responsive condition, with relatively low ratings overall. Additionally, participants consistently expressed high levels of trust across all three conditions, as demonstrated in Fig. 4a.

Concerning engagement, participants consistently reported high levels across all three conditions, as shown in Fig. 4b. During the actual session, participants executed a higher number of pushes, in accordance with the instructions, compared to the expected count calculated from the trial session. The inactive and responsive conditions showed nearly equal ratios, while the unresponsive condition had lower values in comparison to the other two conditions. Objective engagement is presented in the leftmost section of Fig. 3. Objective and subjective engagement are presented in two separate graphs, as the former is continuous data and the latter is ordinal data.

To analyze significant differences between the three facial expression conditions, we employed Mann-Whitney U and Chi-Square (χ^2) tests. These non-parametric tests were chosen due to the smaller sample size in each condition ($n < 30$), which precluded a normality check. The selection of tests was based on the type of data being compared - continuous and ordinal. To mitigate false positives, we applied the Bonferroni Correction test. Effect size calculations were performed for significant differences.

There was a statistically significant difference in competence scores between the inactive condition ($\mu = 8.24, \sigma = 0.55$) and the unresponsive condition ($\mu = 6.07, \sigma = 1.50$), with a $p - value = 0.005$ and $W = 58$. This difference was associated with a substantial effect size of $r = 0.92$. No significant differences were observed for any other dimensions.

In conclusion, our findings in response to **RQ1** indicate that facial emotional expressions have a negative impact on older adults' perception of a robot, particularly in terms of competence. However, these expressions do not influence their level of engagement. As for **RQ2**, responsive robot facial emotional expressions, in comparison with unresponsive facial emotional expressions, do not have an impact on robot perception or engagement levels.

4.1   Correlation Analysis

To enhance our comprehension of the quantitative results, we employed Spearman's rank correlation coefficient (ρ) to identify correlations within the collected data. For a deeper understanding, we investigated whether gender exerts an influence on any of the dependent variables. To achieve this, we calculated the Rank- Biserial correlation coefficient (r_{rb}) and conducted Mann-Whitney U and χ^2 tests. However, no correlations or significant differences were found across conditions with respect to gender.

In the inactive condition, as depicted in Fig. 5a, it's apparent that individuals with lower stress levels tend to perceive the robot as safer, unlike those with higher stress levels. Conversely, increased engagement with the robot is associated with higher levels of anxiety.

Contrasting the inactive condition, the unresponsive condition reveals intriguing insights, characterized by a subset of robust correlations ($| \rho |> 0.8$) with an exceedingly low likelihood of arising by chance ($p-values < 0.005$). Illustrated in Fig. 5b, participants exhibiting heightened anxiety levels are inclined to perceive the robot as less competent, contrasting those with lower anxiety

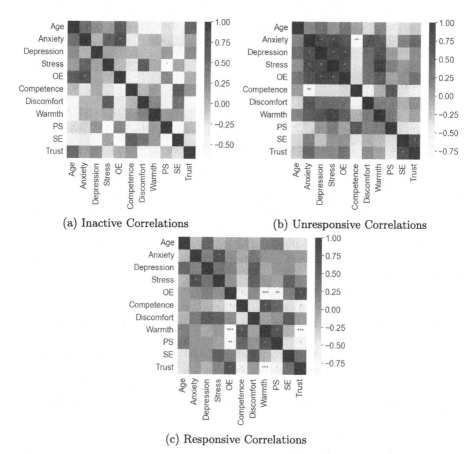

(a) Inactive Correlations   (b) Unresponsive Correlations

(c) Responsive Correlations

Fig. 5. Heatmap illustrates Spearman's correlations observed for each condition. Correlations marked with '*', '**', and '***' indicate a $p - value < 0.05, < 0.01$, and < 0.001 with a $| \rho | > 0.6$. Abbreviations: OE = Objective Engagement, SE = Subjective Engagement, PS = Perceived Safety.

levels. Additionally, individuals experiencing high stress levels are more inclined to perceive the robot as friendly and warm.

In contrast to the previously mentioned conditions, the responsive condition exhibited robust correlations($| \rho | > 0.8$) with dependent variables, demonstrating a high degree of statistical significance ($p - values < 0.001$). Participants who engage more intensively with the robot tend to perceive it as less warm than those who engage less. Similarly, participants reporting elevated levels of trust perceive the robot as less warm.

It's important to keep in mind that anxiety, stress, and depression levels are assessed prior to the experiment. This means that the measurements reflect participants' baseline levels in their everyday lives rather than during the course of the experiment itself. Furthermore, no significant differences in anxiety, stress, and depression levels were found between the conditions.

5   Discussion

We acknowledge that a larger sample size could have potentially revealed more statistically significant differences between dimensions, reducing the risk of Type II errors. However, due to the unique and challenging nature of recruiting older adults, obtaining a larger sample size was unfeasible. Our sample size is greater than previous studies involving robots and older adults, such as Nowak et al. [15], who could only recruit 7 participants, and Giorgi et al. [11], who recruited 17 participants to investigate perceived trust in a social robot across a wider age range (40 to 87 years). Moreover, the study's design, conducted as a between-subject experiment to mitigate issues highlighted in prior literature [10], unintentionally accentuated differences between conditions, reinforcing the need for a greater participant count.

Our findings demonstrate that participants perceived the robot as less competent when facial expressions were introduced, as opposed to when they were absent. This observation can be attributed to the non-social nature of the pHRI application—physical exercise—employed in our experiment. In contrast, previous literature has shown that incorporating facial expressions into pHRI applications with a social purpose, such as handshakes, led participants to perceive the robot's emotions more positively, as evidenced by Tsalamlal et al. (2015) [18]. Furthermore, this observation is supported by participants' responses to our open-ended questions, in which they referred to the robot as a "tool" or a "weight machine" in both active and inactive conditions. This underscores the importance of future investigations to enhance the robustness of these findings across various pHRI applications.

Moreover, it's worth considering the distinction between the physical interaction described in Tsalamlal et al.'s study [18], where a humanoid was employed, and our utilization of a collaborative robot like Sawyer, equipped with a screen. This contrast prompts a pertinent inquiry regarding how the type of robot employed in pHRI might influence robot perception. It's conceivable that people's preferences for engaging in physical interaction and communication could differ when interacting with a humanoid displaying facial expressions compared to a collaborative robotic arm with a screen conveying facial expressions. However, we believe that the context, whether social or collaborative, significantly influences user communication preferences.

Additionally, a notable recommendation arises to enhance the robot's facial features by incorporating elements such as cheeks or eyelids, aligned with the findings from Chen and Jia's study [6], thereby imparting a sense of maturity and user preference to the robot's appearance. This recommendation finds additional support through a considerable number of responses obtained from participants in our study's open-ended questions, wherein many participants suggested altering the robot's facial features. One participant even specifically mentioned the eyes. Implementing this adjustment holds the potential to cultivate a perception of Sawyer as more mature and visually appealing.

We anticipate that a comparison between the inactive and responsive conditions would likely unveil a significant difference in competence, given the availability of a larger sample size. Importantly, this observation extends to all other dimensions, underlining the pivotal role of conducting the study with a more substantial number of participants. Achieving this can involve augmenting the relatively hard-to-access population of older adults with a younger adult population. This augmentation naturally leads to the question of whether distinct age groups will perceive the robot's attributes in varying ways. Therefore, we plan to expand this research in the future by including younger adults, following the common practice in robotics studies involving older adults [15].

We speculate that the absence of a significant difference between the responsive and unresponsive conditions might be attributed to the abstract nature of the chosen set of facial expressions and the specific type of application employed in this experiment. This conjecture is supported by the fact that more than 50% of participants in the responsive condition reported not perceiving any changes in the robot's facial expressions, as their attention was directed towards activating the headlight blinks. This perspective gains further weight from one participant's response to the open-ended questions, where they suggested altering the facial expressions once the exercise was completed. This observation underscores the possibility that the nature of the application and its objective could have influenced participants' focus on facial expressions. It further implies that pHRI applications primarily centered around collaborative tasks, as opposed to sociability, such as engaging in physical exercises instead of handshaking, should consider incorporating facial features that are less abstract and more conspicuous.

The absence of a significant difference in participants' levels of engagement across all conditions suggests that facial expressions may not exert any influence on engagement during specific types of pHRI applications. However, an argument can be made that the robot's joint impedance control inhibited certain participants from executing a high number of pushes, as they waited for the robot's arm to return to its initial position after each push. In contrast, other participants proceeded without such hesitations. This divergence in exercise approaches highlights a potential limitation: the count of pushes might not have been the most suitable metric for assessing objective engagement in this context. Therefore, we encourage researchers to explore better-suited engagement measures.

Similarly, the lack of statistically significant differences in the subjective engagement measure bolsters the notion that facial expressions might not significantly impact participants' levels of engagement. This interpretation gains further support from the notable proportion of participants who recommended additional features like rhythmic music, encouraging phrases, visual timers, and verbal motivation. Collectively, these inputs suggest that facial expressions might not be the most suitable non-verbal social cue for enhancing engagement in collaborative pHRI applications.

There were no identifiable correlations between the conditions (each condition displayed different correlations), therefore the direct relationship between the correlations and the conditions remains uncertain. Nevertheless, the correlation analysis suggests that people's perceptions of a robot's attributes (safety, competence, friendliness, warmth) can be influenced by their anxiety, stress levels, engagement with the robot, and trust, and this could vary depending on the experimental condition. Notably, anxiety and stress levels significantly influence these perceptions. People with lower stress felt the robot was safer, while those with heightened anxiety perceived it as less competent. Engagement levels played a key role too. In the inactive condition, deeper engagement raised anxiety, while in the responsive condition, intense engagement led to a perception of reduced warmth. Trust further added complexity, as higher trust levels correlated with perceiving the robot as less warm, reflecting a more critical assessment.

These findings underline that emotions are not peripheral to pHRI; they are integral. However, a clear relationship between these findings and the distinct experimental conditions has yet to be established. To gain a more comprehensive understanding, additional research studies are necessary but out of the scope of the current paper.

6   Conclusion

Our research aimed to uncover the impact of facial expressions on a robot's perceived attributes and an individual's level of engagement within a collaborative pHRI application, with a particular focus on older adults. Our findings demonstrated that when robots display facial expressions during a collaborative pHRI application, people tend to perceive them as less intelligent compared to robots that do not exhibit any facial expressions. Interestingly, we observed that these facial expressions do not significantly influence the levels of engagement among older adults. We speculate that participants' perception of robots is intricately tied to the collaborative nature of pHRI applications we emphasized in our study, as opposed to socially oriented pHRI applications. Our results suggest the need for more appropriate non-verbal social behaviors to enhance participants' engagement levels. In the next experiments, we will also consider a larger number of participants by including younger adults, which will also allow us to investigate possible differences due to age groups, and further investigate the relationships uncovered by the correlation analysis with respect to the different conditions.

References

1. Abdulazeem, N., Hu, Y.: Human factors considerations for quantifiable human states in physical human-robot interaction. Sensors **23**, August 2023
2. Ageing: Global population. en. https://www.who.int/news-room/questions-and-answers/item/population-ageing

3. Bartneck, C., et al.: Measurement instruments for the anthropomorphism, animacy, likeability, perceived intelligence, and perceived safety of robots. Int. J. Soc. Robot. **1**(1), 71–81 (2009)
4. Block, A.E., et al.: In the arms of a robot. ACM Trans. **12**(2), 47 (2022)
5. Carpinella, C.M., et al.: The Robotic Social Attributes Scale (RoSAS). In: ACM/IEEE HRI. ISSN: 2167-2148, pp. 254–262, March 2017
6. Chen, C.H., Jia, X.: Effects of head shape, facial features, camera, and gender on the perceptions of rendered robot faces. Int. J. Soc. Robot. **15**(1), 71–84 (2023)
7. Coronado, E., et al.: Evaluating quality in human-robot interaction. J. Manuf. Syst. **63**, 392–410 (2022)
8. Fitter, N.T., Kuchenbecker, K.J.: Designing and assessing expressive open-source faces for the baxter robot. In: Agah, A., Cabibihan, J.-J., Howard, A.M., Salichs, M.A., He, H. (eds.) ICSR 2016. LNCS (LNAI), vol. 9979, pp. 340–350. Springer, Cham (2016). https://doi.org/10.1007/978-3-319-47437-3_33
9. Fitter, N.T., et al.: Exercising with Baxter. JNER **17**(1), 19 (2020)
10. Fitter, N.T., Kuchenbecker, K.J.: How does it feel to clap hands with a robot? Int. J. Soc. Robot. **12**(1), 113–127 (2020)
11. Giorgi, I., et al.: Friendly but faulty: a pilot study on the perceived trust of older adults in a social robot. IEEE Access **10**, 92084–92096 (2022)
12. Law, T., Malle, B.F., Scheutz, M.: A touching connection: how observing robotic touch can affect human trust in a robot. English. Int. J. Soc. Robot. **13**(8), 2003–2019 (2021)
13. Losey, D.P., et al.: A review of intent detection, arbitration, and communication aspects of shared control for physical human–robot interaction. Appl. Mech. Rev. **70**(1), 010804 (2018)
14. Mazursky, A., DeVoe, M., Sebo, S.: Physical touch from a robot caregiver. IEEE (RO-MAN), Napoli, Italy. IEEE, pp. 1578–1585, August 2022
15. Nowak, J., et al.: Assistance to older adults with comfortable robot-to-human handovers. In: CA, USA: IEEE ARSO, pp. 1–6, May 2022
16. Oei, T.P.S., et al.: Using the Depression Anxiety Stress Scale 21 (DASS-21) across cultures. Int. J. Psychol. **48**(6), 1018–1029 (2013)
17. Rethink   Robotics.   RethinkRobotics.   https://support.rethinkrobotics.com/support/solutions
18. Tsalamlal, M.Y., et al.: Affective handshake with a humanoid robot. In: 2015 ACII, pp. 334–340, September 2015
19. Urakami, J., Seaborn, K.: Nonverbal cues in human-robot interaction. ACM Trans., December 2022

Feasibility Study on Parameter Adjustment for a Humanoid Using LLM Tailoring Physical Care

Tamon Miyake$^{(\boxtimes)}$ ⓘ, Yushi Wang, Pin-chu Yang, and Shigeki Sugano

Waseda University, Tokyo, Japan
tamonmiyake@aoni.waseda.jp

Abstract. The increasing demand for care of the elderly, coupled with the shortage of caregivers, necessitates the introduction of robotic assistants capable of performing care tasks both intelligently and safely. Central to these tasks, especially those involving tactile interaction, is the ability to make human-in-the-loop adjustments based on individual preferences. In this study, our primary goal was to design and evaluate a system that captures user preferences prior to initiating a tactile care task. Our focus was on range-of-motion training exercises, emphasizing communication that demonstrates motion using the LLM approach. The system combines physical demonstrations with verbal explanations, ensuring adaptability to individual preferences before initiating range-of-motion training. Using the humanoid robot Dry-AIREC, augmented with the linguistic capabilities of ChatGPT, our system was evaluated with 14 young participants. The results showed that the robot could perform the range-of-motion exercises with tactile interactions while simultaneously communicating with the participant. Thus, our proposed system emerges as a promising approach for range-of-motion exercises rooted in human-preference-centered human-robot interaction. Interestingly, although there wasn't a significant shift in the overall positive subjective impressions when the tuning was performed using ChatGPT, there was an increase in the number of participants who gave the highest rating to the experience.

Keywords: Humanoid Robot · Large Language Model · Personalization for Caring Tasks · Human Robot Interaction

1 Introduction

1.1 Background

With the advancement of robotics, humanoid robots are expected to perform a wide range of service tasks to help a human in daily life. Humanoid robots exhibit striking resemblances to humans in terms of stature, physical appearance, and

This work was supported by JST Moonshot R&D, Grant No. JPMJMS2031.

degrees of freedom [19,22,35]. There is an optimistic outlook regarding their potential to undertake diverse tasks within the human living milieu, thereby enhancing their capacity to serve humans. This optimism is grounded in the alignment of these robots with human-centered design principles, as the everyday habitats are intricately tailored to accommodate human presence and activities.

In the domain of care robotics, the central concern pertains to human interaction, encompassing facets of both social and physical dimensions. This constituent stands as the focal point necessitating significant advancement. As for physical interaction, extensive research has been conducted. In [39], a robot joint based on clutches has been developed, thereby facilitating the realization of intrinsic safety. On the other hand, in [30], they proposed a sensor-less hybrid control system for robots using an H/sup infinity/ acceleration controller and reaction force estimation, successfully tested on a three-degree-of-freedom direct drive robot manipulator. However, these research endeavors have predominantly explored robots solely in terms of their utilitarian aspects. As we look toward the future, robots are anticipated to be sophisticated to coexist symbiotically with humans. In this context, the capacity to incorporate interaction to inform and shape their behavior emerges as a pivotal consideration. Numerous studies have been undertaken with a specific focus on interaction aimed at augmenting the assistive capabilities of robots, but usually no physical interaction was involved. For example [20,21,23,36], those robots are designed with animal-like appearances are intended to create a sense of familiarity or warmth, likely to enhance their interaction with humans. Contrary to robots designed primarily for companion roles, humanoid robots such as [27,28,41] are specifically engineered to provide physical assistance to humans. These robots excel in tasks such as lifting and transferring patients, aiding mobility, and handling objects in various environments. However, their primary design does not emphasize advanced semantic interaction with humans. Moreover, they are generally not equipped with the capability to discern and respond to individual human preferences.

In this study, our aim is to develop and evaluate the system obtaining preferences before starting to perform a physical caring task with communication involving the demonstration of motion. Thanks to the advancements in large language models (LLM), the viability of integrating semantic interaction via conversations has been made possible [37]. This advancement holds significant potential in augmenting the overall efficacy of assistance, particularly for addressing individualized human preferences. To validate the above idea, In this study, we chose to perform range-of-motion exercise by a humanoid robot. As daily opportunities for joint movement decrease, joint mobility can progressively worsen, creating a vicious cycle. To prevent joint contracture, regular range-of-motion exercises, prescribed by a physician, are highly recommended.

1.2 Related Works

There are many projects that focused on assistive robots, for example, DOMEO [4], KSERA [10], Cogniron [2], Companionable [3], SRS [12], Care-O-Bot [17], HERB [6]. They can be broadly categorized into two groups: physically assistive robots and socially assistive robots. Physically assistive robots, due to their direct interaction with users, necessitate high safety standards and a high degree of user tolerance or acceptance. A critical consideration for these robots is the careful selection of touch points, given the varying pain sensitivity across different regions of the human body [38].

Conversely, socially assistive robots are mainly focused on providing emotional and cognitive support. The Zora robot, a specialized version of the Nao robot, is designed to entertain and stimulate physical activity among residents in care facilities [18]. In a similar vein, PARO, fashioned to resemble a baby seal, serves as a therapeutic tool in multi-sensory behavioral therapy programs, proving especially effective in environments such as nursing homes, where it aids older adults with varying levels of dementia [42]. MARIO, another key player in socially assistive robotics, was developed to explore its impacts on the quality of life, depression levels, and perceived social support in individuals living with dementia [13]. Animal-like or anime-character-like [40] appearance offers more advantages in conveying emotions as a social robot. Although these robots are proficient in offering emotional comfort, entertainment, or health monitoring, their lack of physical interaction imposes certain limitations on their capabilities as care robots.

Contrary to socially assistive robots, physically assistive robots are engineered to engage in direct contact with users to fulfill tasks, such as transportation and rehabilitation. The use of humanoid robots in in-home nursing care scenarios has been proposed and is under active investigation [19,31,33]. Recent systems have started to incorporate the virtual presence of a therapist, aiming to facilitate both direct and indirect patient interaction [16]. However, this approach continues to rely on a therapist providing guidance from a remote location.

A noteworthy example of a physically assistive robot is RIBA, which boasts human-like arms designed for heavy lifting tasks that necessitate human contact. RIBA has demonstrated proficiency in tasks such as transferring a patient from a bed to a wheelchair and vice versa [27]. In this system, RIBA currently lacks the capability to independently plan its movement trajectory. In our previous work [25], the robot Dry AIREC can detect the human position and make the trajectory plan autonomously.

Personalization is crucial for human assistance robots since human perceptions and preferences are different among individuals. To our knowledge, the care robot obtaining preferences has not been established. The robot should learn user preferences to personalize the robot's action policy through human-robot interaction [26,29,32]. Communication robots are useful for human verbal interaction [24] or implicit intent indication of a robot to a human [34]. Language model enables robot to understand human intention [14,15]. However, it is difficult for us to verbalize preferences related to human physical perception. If the robot starts performing care tasks before adjusting the parameters of moving a human body, this motion can cause dissatisfaction in a user. In addition, high interpretation ability is necessary because the robot should not misunderstand human requests in the opposite way to avoid harming a user, although human speech patterns are diverse and sometimes ambiguous. Therefore, the function of obtaining preferences accurately before starting the care tasks is required.

2   System

Human-in-the-loop robotic system performing care tasks involving touch to a human with LLM is developed. The range-of-motion training, shown in Fig. 1(a), is the target task of the robot in this study. The robot touches and moves a human joint directly to maintain the range of motion of the joints while communicating with a human. The developed system adjusts the parameters of moving a human body with physical demonstration and verbal explanation to personal preference before performing the range-of-motion training movement. Figure 1(b) shows the overall developed system. LLM can generate text commands with high interpretation ability. LLM connects the audio system and the robot controller system, which forms the loop receiving the user's request and sending a text-style action flag to demonstrate to the user the robot's motion. ChatGPT, a transformer-based LLM developed by OpenAI [1], is a key component.

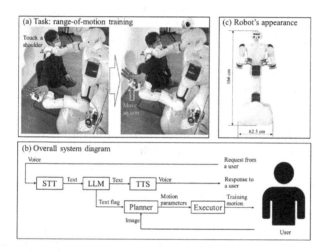

Fig. 1. Overall design of the system. (a) shows the target task in this study. (b) shows the overall system diagram. (c) shows the robot appearance used in this study.

2.1   The Used Robot

Figure 1(c) shows the humanoid robot "Dry-AIREC" used in this study, which is built by Torobo [7] (Tokyo Robotics inc., Tokyo, Japan). Dry-AIREC is a humanoid designed for various research applications. The vision for intelligent robots involves seamless and sophisticated interactions with the real world, and we view Dry-AIREC as a prime hardware platform for advancing robotics learning research. Notably, Dry-AIREC's head is equipped with three types of camera sensors and two usb microphone sensors, facilitating the capture of RGB-D and audio data. Moreover, the robot's neck and waist joints each possess three degrees of freedom-roll, pitch, and yaw-enabling the robot to assume human-like body postures. In addition, Dry-AIREC is equipped with one USB speaker (FOSTER 628421, Foster Electric Company Ltd., Tokyo, Japan.) in its head.

Each arm of the Dry-AIREC features 7 degrees of freedom, with torque sensors embedded in each joint. Even in unfavorable positions, the nominal arm load remains at 8 kg, allowing a wide range of daily objects to be handled with ease. The control mode, including options such as position, force, and impedance control, is highly adaptable to different work scenarios. Specific parameters such as damping and spring constants can be fine-tuned. Employing the compliance control mode empowers the robot arm to surmount local disruptions, execute intricate manipulations, and interact with humans in a secure manner. Furthermore, a four-finger robotic hand serves as an end-effector for each arm. Each finger is capable of exerting approximately 10N of force, while tactile sensors are thoughtfully integrated into the fingertips and palm. Rubber material was selected for the skin of the fingertips and palm to facilitate deformable and frictional contact. In terms of its physical dimensions, the Dry-AIREC's height of 1660 mm and trolley width of 625 mm are closely analogous to a human's. The robot can be maneuvered with the assistance of a trolley. On the software side, the Dry-AIREC is equipped with the ROS Noetic framework and the MoveIt motion planning tool, enabling control, movement, and data acquisition. A RealSense SR300 depth camera (Intel Corp Santa Clara, CA, USA) installed in the robot's head is used to obtain 3D information of an object.

2.2 Communication

An audio dialogue system is performed by Speech-to-Text (STT) services. Two USB microphones installed in a Dry-AIREC head obtain the user's voice (speech data). The library named speech-recognition (Python) is used to detect whether a user makes a speech or not. The data during the period between the start of sound input and the end of 0.5 s of input interruption is stored as speech data. If a speaker is used, any voice is not stored. The maximum duration of speech data was set as 2.5 s in the experiment explained in the following section. Faster-whisper is used to perform STT for processes in CPU. Faster-whisper [5] is reimplementation of OpenAI's Whisper model [8], which is a high-quality STT system based on a fast inference engine for Transformer. facilitate the conversion of a user's auditory input into a text-based format. This text is then passed to the ChatGPT model.

After receiving the transcription, ChatGPT is used to generate a text-based dialogue response. This process of response generation is achieved through the use of OpenAI's Application Programming Interface (API). When developing conversational systems, a robust architecture often requires the integration of multiple components for effective operation. The function-calling is used to generate the JSON-style output. The function-calling is a feature that allows Chatgpt to call external functions by teaching Chatgpt the format of the functions. Prompts for ChatGPT used in this study are shown in Table 1. Output parameters of ChatGPT included in JSON-type output are a flag of touch force, a flag of left arm movement velocity, and response text.

Table 1. Prompt using Function calling of ChagGPT. Original language was Japanese.

	Prompt
Role	You are an assistive humanoid robot designed to engage in conversation in Japanese and assist with people's rehabilitation, involving physical touch. Your parameters include touch, reaching, and response. While responding to user requests, adjust touch and reaching variables accordingly. Use the response to reply kindly and politely to help the user feel at ease
End flag	If there are further user requests, output Y. If the user doesn't have more requests, output N. Otherwise, output U
Touch force flag	Output touch information based on user requests. Output u to increase touch force, d to decrease it, and N for other cases
Movement velocity flag	Output movement velocity information based on user requests. Output Fa for faster movement, Sl for slower movement, and N for other cases
Response	Compose responses for user requests or conversations. Ensure to respond kindly and politely, avoiding asking questions. For example, if asked "Please touch harder," reply with "Understood. I will increase the touch force." If you don't understand, reply with "I don't understand

Finally, the text response received from ChatGPT is converted back into an audible format using a text-to-speech (TTS) service. The TTS service outputs audio data through the speaker (FOSTER 628421) of the robot. In this study, the open-source software of the synthetic TTS "VOICEVOX" is used [9]. Speaker ID 11 of the VOICEVOX, a voice like a calm voice of a young man, is used for the experiment explained in the following section.

2.3   Dual-Arm Manipulation

The dual-arm manipulation motion is generated based on the skeleton recognition proposed in the method [25]. The human pose is obtained by the library named Mediapipe developed by Google [11]. Due to the camera's limited view scope, only the head and shoulders are detected, but this is sufficient in our case. The 3D coordinates of the head and shoulders are obtained by combining pose information and depth information.

First of all, the robot clasps its right hand before starting the reaching motion to the human shoulder. Next, the robot holds out its left hand at a position just within reach of the human's outstretched arm. The robot starts reaching its right hand to the human's shoulder via a waypoint (higher point than the human's shoulder) with impedance control. The robot unclasps the right hand at the waypoint, and moves the hand down to touch the shoulder. Finally, the robot moves the human arm with its left arm in vertical direction. "Reaching trajectory of the arm is derived by solving inverse kinematics. The arm is moved with impedance mode."

2.4   Parameter Adjustment

Only verbal information is not enough to get human preference information because it is difficult for humans to explain their preferred values of the physical parameters quantitatively. Therefore, in this method, asking questions while demonstrating the motion is designed. The robot inquiries about the user's preferences and regulates parameters in a descending or ascending manner accordingly. The robot extracts the human's request from the response using the aforementioned communication system. The robot iteratively engages in a sequence of questioning, adjusting parameters, and demonstrating modulated movements as long as the user expresses preferences.

3   Experiment Method

14 young (20's) participants were recruited in the experiment (10 males and 4 females, age mean = 23.5, Standard Deviation (SD) = 1.59 year old). We started the experiment by obtaining the participants' consent. They were explained that they could stop the experiment whenever they wanted. The experiment was conducted based on approval from the Ethics Review Committee on Research with Human Subjects of Waseda University (No. 2021-429).

There were two conditions in this experiment. One condition was our proposal method, that is, performing range-of-motion training with the adjustment based on the ChatGPTcommunication system. The other condition was performing range-of-motion training without adjustment. The lists of parameters were shown in Table 2. The order of the trials was counterbalanced to reduce the effect of the order on the human impression.

Table 2. Prepared levels of velocity and joint impedance (shoulder) set heuristically. Movement velocity and impedance (touch force) were adjusted independently.

	Arm movement velocity m/s	Spring	Mass	Dumper
Level1	0.054	100	1.5	10
Level2	0.059	150	1.5	10
Level3	0.064	200	1.5	10
Level4 (default)	0.071	250	1.5	10
Level5	0.079	300	1.5	10
Level6	0.089	350	1.0	20
Level7	0.10	400	1.5	50

Figure 2 shows the flowchart of movement and dialog of the robot during the experiment. The participants sat on the bed in front of the robot during the trial. First, the robot held out its left hand and showed how to move its left arm during range-of-motion training. The robot obtained the participant's feedback about arm movement velocity just after the demonstration of left arm movement on the condition of using the proposed method. Next, the robot asked the participant to put his or her right hand on the robot's left hand and look at the robot's face. The robot estimated the shoulder coordinates of the participant and reached its right hand toward the participant's right shoulder. The robot obtained the participant's feedback about touch force while touching the shoulder on the condition of using the proposed method. Finally, the robot moves the participant's right arm between the horizontal position and a position approximately 1.2 m above it third times. The position of the robot's stance and the angle of its head were manually adjusted in order to facilitate interaction with the participants and to capture their body movements.

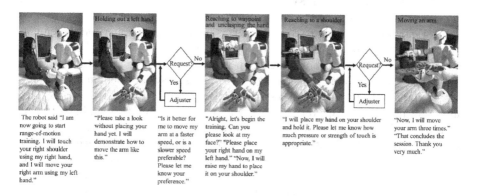

Fig. 2. Flow of movement and dialog of the robot during the experiment.

We evaluated the success rate of whether the developed communication system can obtain an action flag and change robot parameters from the human request in a single interaction. We did not count the cases when the voice is not inputted to the robot. In addition, the questionnaire was administered on a 7-point scale (1 strongly disagree - 7 strongly agree). First, the participants were asked whether the movement velocity and touch force of the robot were appropriate for them. Next, the participants were asked about their feelings of friendliness, safety, relief, reliability, and comfort towards the robot. Because the data distribution was non-parametric, the Wilcoxon signed-rank sum test was performed for significant tests. The statistical significance level was set as 0.05.

The proposed method enabled the robot (Dry-AIREC) to perform the range-of-motion exercise involving touch with a human while making verbal communication with the human. The movement velocity and touch force changed as the participants requested. As shown in Fig. 3, this system understood the requested content with a high probability in a single interaction. The mean success rates of understanding the movement velocity request, the touch force request, and the end of the request were 79%, 85%, and 94%, respectively. The ChatGPT-based recognition system demonstrated a high ability for interpretation. For example, understanding that the request was a decrease of the touch force through "too strong," "please touch me softly," "please touch me sofly" (that is a typo), and "please get weaken" (these were originally Japanese). There were no cases where the robot misunderstood the opposite meaning. However, the outputs of the action flags from ChatGPT sometimes changed even though the input was the same. In this case, the participants needed to repeat the same request to the robot. The number of repetitions of the request of their preference for the robot was 3 times at maximum and 1.2 times on average. Therefore, we consider that the proposed system is feasible for adjusting the parameters corresponding to user preference prior to initiating a caring motion.

4   Result and Discussion

Figure 4 shows the subjective score about the questions of whether the movement velocity and the touch force were appropriate or not. The subject score about the touch force was significantly higher (p-value was 0.042) in the condition with adjustment than without adjustment. The proposed system demonstrated efficacy in discerning user preferences regarding touch force during exercise. The number of people who answered strongly agree to the questions is higher in the condition with adjustment of parameters than in the condition without adjustment of parameters. Nonetheless, there were no significant differences between the trials with and without parameter adjustment for all subjective impressions, as shown in Fig. 5. We assume that this was because the default values already matched the preferences of some of the participants. Indeed, some participants did not require the adjustment, and the change in the levels of both movement velocity and touch force was just within 2 for the other participants.

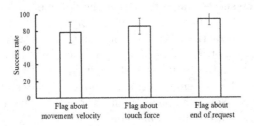

Fig. 3. Success rate in a single interaction

Not all participants deemed the adjusted parameters (move velocity or touch force) to be entirely suitable. A difference in physical appearance between a human and a robot could have contributed to lower scores. Some participants felt discomfort due to the robot's hand contact area differing from that of a human hand. In addition, the participants reported that their preferences changed during exercise due to changes in physical condition, such as fatigue. Even though the current system can adjust parameters during operation after starting the range-of-motion training movement, the parameters did not change once the movement started in this experiment since we did not expect that human preferences changed as time passes during movement. Modification after starting the movement would be integrated.

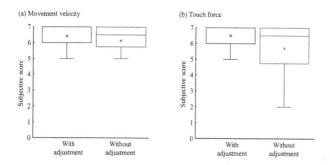

Fig. 4. Subjective score about the questions of whether the movement velocity and the touch force were appropriate or not. There was a significant difference in (b).

The Dry-AIREC's impedance control with ChatGPT's interpretation ability was effective in performing the range-of-motion training based on the user's preference. While the system demonstrated capabilities, there remain limitations regarding the accuracy of its responses to participants. Notably, several participants expressed diminished trust in the robot, citing instances where the dialogue content failed to align with the context. Future work should scrutinize the prompts provided to the LLM to facilitate more contextually appropriate responses. Integration of visual feedback is important in discerning both human and robot actions. By feeding the LLM system with real-time data on human movements corresponding to the robot's dialogue, we could potentially achieve more natural robotic responses. In addition, we plan to enhance the robot's listening system. This system currently doesn't allow for interruptions during speech. If participants talk to the robot before it completes its speech output, they are compelled to repeat their statements. Furthermore, there was a large difference in the number of male and female subjects in the experiment. Further investigation would be conducted in future work.

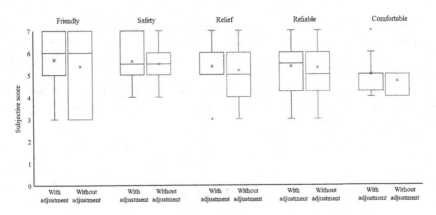

Fig. 5. Subjective score about positive impressions for the robot

5   Conclusion

The proposed system combines physical demonstrations with verbal explanations, ensuring adaptability to individual preferences before initiating range-of-motion training. Using the humanoid robot Dry-AIREC, augmented with the linguistic capabilities of ChatGPT, our system was evaluated with 14 young participants. The results showed that the robot could perform the range-of-motion exercises with tactile interactions while simultaneously communicating with the participant. The proposed system showed the feasibility of adjusting the parameters corresponding to user preference prior to initiating a caring motion.

References

1. Chatgpt. https://chat.openai.com. Accessed 21 Aug 2023
2. Cogniron project. https://www.cogniron.org/final/Home.php. Accessed 19 Aug 2023
3. CompanionAble project. http://www.robots-and-androids.com/CompanionAble-Project.html. Accessed 19 Aug 2023
4. Domeo project. http://www.aal-europe.eu/projects/domeo/. Accessed 19 Aug 2023
5. Faster Whisper transcription with CTranslate2. https://github.com/guillaumekln/faster-whisper. Accessed 1 Aug 2023
6. HERB project. https://robotsguide.com/robots/herb. Accessed 19 Aug 2023
7. HUMANOID ROBOT - TOROBO. https://robotics.tokyo/products/torobo/. Accessed 15 Aug 2023
8. Introducing Whisper. https://openai.com/research/whisper. Accessed 20 Aug 2023
9. Introduction of text-to-speech engine of VOICEVOX (in Japanese). https://blog.hiroshiba.jp/. Accessed 21 Aug 2023
10. Ksera project. https://ksera.ieis.tue.nl. Accessed 19 Aug 2023

11. Mediapipe. https://developers.google.com/mediapipe. Accessed 1 Aug 2023
12. SRS project. https://robotnik.eu/projects/srs-en/. Accessed 19 Aug 2023
13. Barrett, E.e.a.: Evaluation of a companion robot for individuals with dementia: quantitative findings of the mario project in an Irish residential care setting. Gerontological Nursing **45**(7), 36–45 (2019)
14. Bucker, A., Figueredo, L., Haddadin, S., Kapoor, A., Ma, S., Vemprala, S., Bonatti, R.: Latte: Language trajectory transformer. In: 2023 IEEE International Conference on Robotics and Automation (ICRA), pp. 7287–7294. IEEE (2023)
15. Cui, Y., Karamcheti, S., Palleti, R., Shivakumar, N., Liang, P., Sadigh, D.: No, to the right: online language corrections for robotic manipulation via shared autonomy. In: Proceedings of the 2023 ACM/IEEE International Conference on Human-Robot Interaction, pp. 93–101 (2023)
16. Jung, H., et al.: Towards extended virtual presence of the therapist in stroke rehabilitation. In: IEEE 13th International Conference on Rehabilitation Robotics (ICORR), pp. 580–586 (2013). 110.1109/ICORR.2013.6650345
17. Hans, M., Graf, B., Schraft, R.: Robotic home assistant care-o-bot: past-present-future. In: Proceedings. 11th IEEE International Workshop on Robot and Human Interactive Communication, pp. 380–385 (2002). https://doi.org/10.1109/ROMAN.2002.1045652
18. Huisman, C., Kort, H.: Two-year use of care robot zora in dutch nursing homes: an evaluation study. Healthcare **7**(1), 31 (2019)
19. Iwata, H., Sugano, S.: Design of human symbiotic robot twendy-one. In: 2009 IEEE International Conference on Robotics and Automation, pp. 580–586 (2009). https://doi.org/10.1109/ROBOT.2009.5152702
20. Jøranson, N., Pedersen, I., R.A.A.G.O.C.I.C.: Group activity with paro in nursing homes: systematic investigation of behaviors in participants. Int. Psychogeriatrics **28**(8), 1345–54 (2016)
21. Kanamori, M., Suzuki, M., Oshiro, H., Tanaka, M., Inoguchi, T., Takasugi, H., Saito, Y., Yokoyama, T.: Pilot study on improvement of quality of life among elderly using a pet-type robot. In: Proceedings 2003 IEEE International Symposium on Computational Intelligence in Robotics and Automation. Computational Intelligence in Robotics and Automation for the New Millennium (Cat. No.03EX694), vol. 1, pp. 107–112 (2003). https://doi.org/10.1109/CIRA.2003.1222072
22. Kanda, T., Hirano, T., Eaton, D., Ishiguro, H.: Interactive robots as social partners and peer tutors for children: a field trial. Hum.-Comput. Inter. **19**(1–2), 61–84 (2004)
23. Libin, A., Cohen-Mansfield, J.: Therapeutic robocat for nursing home residents with dementia: preliminary inquiry. Am. J. Alzheimer's Disease Other Dementias **19**(2), 111–116 (2004)
24. Matsuyama, Y., Akiba, I., Fujie, S., Kobayashi, T.: Four-participant group conversation: a facilitation robot controlling engagement density as the fourth participant. Comput. Speech Lang. **33**(1), 1–24 (2015)
25. Miyake, T., Wang, Y., Yan, G., Sugano, S.: Skeleton recognition-based motion generation and user emotion evaluation with in-home rehabilitation assistive humanoid robot. In: 2022 IEEE-RAS 21st International Conference on Humanoid Robots (Humanoids), pp. 616–621. IEEE (2022)
26. Moro, C., Nejat, G., Mihailidis, A.: Learning and personalizing socially assistive robot behaviors to aid with activities of daily living. ACM Trans. Hum.-Robot Inter. (THRI) **7**(2), 1–25 (2018)

27. Mukai, T., Hirano, S., Nakashima, H., Kato, Y., Sakaida, Y., Guo, S., Hosoe, S.: Development of a nursing-care assistant robot riba that can lift a human in its arms. In: 2010 IEEE/RSJ International Conference on Intelligent Robots and Systems, pp. 5996–6001 (2010). https://doi.org/10.1109/IROS.2010.5651735

28. Odashima, T., et al.: A soft human-interactive robot ri-man. In: 2006 IEEE/RSJ International Conference on Intelligent Robots and Systems, pp. 1–1 (2006). https://doi.org/10.1109/IROS.2006.282203

29. Ogata, T., Sugano, S., Tani, J.: Open-end human-robot interaction from the dynamical systems perspective: mutual adaptation and incremental learning. Adv. Robot. **19**(6), 651–670 (2005)

30. Ohishi, K., Miyazaki, M., Fujita, M.: Hybrid control of force and position without force sensor. In: Proceedings of the 1992 International Conference on Industrial Electronics, Control, Instrumentation, and Automation, vol 2, pp. 670–675 (1992). https://doi.org/10.1109/IECON.1992.254552

31. P. Deegan, e.a.: Mobile manipulators for assisted living in residential settings. Robot. Auton. Syst. **24**(2), 179–192 (2008)

32. Pantaleoni, M., Cesta, A., Umbrico, A., Orlandini, A.: Learning user habits to enhance robotic daily-living assistance. In: International Conference on Social Robotics, pp. 165–173. Springer (2022)

33. Pineau, J., Montemerlo, M., Pollack, M., Roy, N., Thrun, S.: Towards robotic assistants in nursing homes: challenges and results. Robot. Auton. Syst. **42**(3), 271–281 (2003)

34. Shrestha, M.C., et al.: Intent communication in navigation through the use of light and screen indicators. In: 2016 11th ACM/IEEE International Conference on Human-Robot Interaction (HRI), pp. 523–524. IEEE (2016)

35. Sugano, S.: Design of humanoid robot for human-robot interaction - waseda robots: wendy and wamoeba. In: 2005 IEEE International Conference on Robotics and Biomimetics - ROBIO, pp. 16–19 (2005). https://doi.org/10.1109/ROBIO.2005.246393

36. Wada, K., Shibata, T., Saito, T., Tanie, K.: Effects of robot assisted activity to elderly people who stay at a health service facility for the aged. In: Proceedings 2003 IEEE/RSJ International Conference on Intelligent Robots and Systems (IROS 2003) (Cat. No.03CH37453), vol. 3, pp. 2847–2852 (2003). https://doi.org/10.1109/IROS.2003.1249302

37. Wake, N., Kanehira, A., Sasabuchi, K., Takamatsu, J., Ikeuchi, K.: Chatgpt empowered long-step robot control in various environments: a case application. arXiv p. 2304.03893, April 2023

38. Wako, N., Miyake, T., Sugano, S.: 2020 8th ieee ras/embs international conference for biomedical robotics and biomechatronics (biorob), pp. 30–35 (2020). https://doi.org/10.1109/BioRob49111.2020.9224304

39. Wang, Y., et al.: Evaluation of series clutch actuators with a high torque-to-weight ratio for open-loop torque control and collision safety. IEEE Robot. Autom. Lett. **3**(1), 297–304 (2017)

40. Yang, P.C., et al.: Hatsuki: an anime character like robot figure platform with anime-style expressions and imitation learning based action generation. In: 2020 29th IEEE International Conference on Robot and Human Interactive Communication (RO-MAN), pp. 384–391. IEEE (2020)

41. Yi, J.B., Yi, S.J.: Mobile manipulation for the hsr intelligent home service robot. In: 2019 16th International Conference on Ubiquitous Robots (UR), pp. 169–173 (2019). https://doi.org/10.1109/URAI.2019.8768782
42. Šabanović, S., Bennett, C.C., Chang, W.L., Huber, L.: Paro robot affects diverse interaction modalities in group sensory therapy for older adults with dementia. In: 2013 IEEE 13th International Conference on Rehabilitation Robotics (ICORR), pp. 1–6 (2013). https://doi.org/10.1109/ICORR.2013.6650427

Enhancing Hand Hygiene Practices Through a Social Robot-Assisted Intervention in a Rural School in India

Amol Deshmukh[1]([✉]), Kohinoor Monish Darda[2], Mugdha Mahesh Mhatre[3],
Ritika Pandey[3], Aalisha R. Jadhav[2], and Emily Cross[1,4]

[1] University of Glasgow, Glasgow, UK
amol.deshmukh@glasgow.ac.uk
[2] ARISA (Advancement and Research in the Sciences and Arts) Foundation, Pune, India
[3] Fergusson College, Pune, India
[4] ETH Zurich, Zürich, Switzerland

Abstract. This paper discusses pilot deployment of a social robot "WallBo" that investigated the effectiveness in promoting and encouraging handwashing practices among children in a rural school in India. The results suggest an overall 85.06% handwashing compliance, 51.60% improvement from the baseline handwashing compliance and an overall ~ 50% knowledge improvement about handwashing. We also present students' perception about "WallBo" and feedback from the pupils and teachers.

Keywords: Handwashing · social robot · child—robot interaction · schools

1 Introduction

Social robots have the potential to positively impact children across various aspects of their development and well-being [1]. Previous research has investigated the use of interactive robots as educators and therapeutic tools, offering unique contributions to children's growth and improve children's motivation to learn and participate in classroom activities [2]. Social robots can act as engaging tutors and educational aids, making learning fun and engaging for children. However, most previous work in child-robot interaction research has been carried out in urban settings in developed countries [3]. Our research focuses on investigating how rural children from under-served communities in developing countries interact with social robots and addresses a real-world problem pertinent to their health and well-being: "hand hygiene".

Globally, nearly half a million children die every year due to diarrhea and respiratory diseases, and handwashing with soap can save 50% of these deaths [4]. During the COVID-19 pandemic handwashing was one of the most impactful public-health interventions to halt the spread of the virus [15]. Hand hygiene also plays a crucial role in preventing the spread of other diseases, especially in school environments where children interact closely with each other [5]. However, maintaining consistent handwashing practices among children can be challenging. This research aims to investigate the effectiveness of a social robot custom designed to promote and reinforce proper handwashing habits among children in schools. In this paper we discuss the results of using a social robot "WallBo" as an engaging and interactive tool to educate and encourage children to adopt and maintain healthy hygiene practices among rural school children in India.

2 Background

Introducing handwashing education in schools has proven to be a highly effective approach to reach children and instill the habit of handwashing from an early age [6] However, several handwashing intervention studies demonstrate that education alone may not be adequate to bring about lasting behavioral changes. Previous studies indicate that to effectively cultivate handwashing habits, it is essential to consider the physical and social environment surrounding the behavior [7]. This involves capturing children's attention, ensuring convenience in practicing handwashing, and reinforcing it as a positive social norm. However, barely any hand hygiene interventions have considered the use of interactive technology such as social robots.

Previous research in developed countries has shown that robots in education could motivate children to learn better [2]. Furthermore, scientific evidence strongly supports the idea that the presence of a physical robot has a more profound impact on human behavior compared to an agent displayed on a screen [1]. Our previous deployment with WallBo was performed in a school in Glasgow UK with urban children from privileged backgrounds [8] and in another Indian school in 2019 (pre-covid) [9, 14]. The results from those trails showed a positive impact on handwashing compliance. However, in this research we specifically wanted to investigate if incorporating social robots into handwashing interventions could potentially enhance children's engagement, and better understand the challenges of using social robots in rural contexts in developing countries.

3 Study Design

The study was carried out in a school in the slum area in the city of Pune, India (March 2023). The key research question we wanted to address was *"How do verbal/non-verbal actions from WallBo affect children's hand washing behaviour?"* This study employed a Wizard of Oz approach, where the researcher situated nearby, oversaw students at a handwashing station while controlling the robot's actions. The intervention was carried out over a period of 4 days.

During the first day, the pupils were asked to wash their hands at the handwashing station to record their baseline handwashing behaviour, and interviews were conducted to assess their knowledge about handwashing. On the second day, the robot was introduced by a facilitator (research team member) in the classroom and WallBo gave hand-hygiene education session to pupils. The pupils then washed their hands with the instructions provided from WallBo (verbal/non-verbal conditions) at the handwashing station. On the third day, WallBo was removed, and pupils were asked to wash their hands followed by interviews about their handwashing knowledge. On day 4 we also interviewed teachers to get their perspective on the intervention.

3.1 Physical Environment

The robot was set up at an outdoor communal handwashing station at the school (see Fig. 1). The Robot WallBo is a custom-built wall mounted/portable robotic platform robot designed with a hand-like shape to elicit a symbolic meaning relevant to the intervention (handwashing). The robot's eye movement enhances the *"Hawthorne effect"* [10], which means people change their behaviour when they know they are being watched. The robot has motorised eyes (yaw/pitch) and an animated mouth (on a small screen) with expressive animations e.g., "happy, "sad", "talking", "neutral" and Marathi speech (local language spoken in that region). The robot had a child-like voice, to make it relevant for that age group. The pre-recorded human utterances were post-processed using lower pitch to make it sound gender neutral to avoid any gender biases. The robot is built using off-the shelf electronics and 3D printing.

Fig. 1. From Left: handwashing station, a pupil with WallBo, WallBo robot.

3.2 Participants

The participating children (n = 28, 15 boys, 13 girls) were from underprivileged communities. The age ranged from 6–10 years and none of them, except one, had ever seen a robot before. The school authorities granted written consent for video recording handwashing sessions and audio interviews of participating children (parents authorized the school to act on their behalf in obtaining consent). Additionally, verbal agreement was obtained from pupils before interviews. The participants were assigned random IDs, ensuring anonymity and no collection of personal information. The class (Grade 1) of pupils had not been educated in hand hygiene before and were randomly selected by the school authorities. The study was approved by the ethics committee at the University of Glasgow (approval number 200200012).

3.3 Data Collection

Data collection occurred through: (i) audio-recorded interviews, and (ii) videos of handwashing on Day 2, 4 (pre/post, no WallBo) and Days 2–3 (During 1:1 intervention with WallBo). Video data was captured using a camera positioned above the handwashing station (see Fig. 1 for setup illustration). On Days 1 and 4 (prior to and after the intervention), pupils were interviewed to evaluate their handwashing knowledge. A previously validated questionnaire (*Bacterfree*) was improvised and translated into local language based on suitability for this study [11].

The questionnaire covered topics such as when to wash hands, the steps involved, soap's purpose, and handwashing enjoyment. Responses were scored based on use of specific keywords (e.g., soap, rub, water, germs). Post-intervention, students were asked about their perceptions of WallBo, including preferences and potential improvements to WallBo, its gender, whether it's seen as "alive, like a person," and if they want to see WallBo again. For a deeper understanding, questions were followed by asking, "Why do you think that?".

4   Results

4.1   Handwashing Compliance (HWC)

We assessed HWC, aligning with the 10 handwashing steps outlined by World Health Organization's (WHO) recommended handwashing technique[1]. Each handwashing video was given a score from 1–10 (one point for each of the handwashing step completed, 0 for incomplete step and 0.5 for uncertain step. Step 10 (*Dry your hands completely with a towel*) was omitted from the analysis as some participants went outside the camera frame for the annotator to assess a score. One annotator analyzed a total of 84 handwashing videos from 3 sessions (before/during/after the intervention) from 28 participants.

Handwashing Compliance Combined.   We observed a mere 50.17% average HWC for base-line handwashing technique, 85.06% during 1:1 session with WallBo and 70.45% after WallBo was removed. Overall, we observed an average percentage difference of **51.60% HWC improvement** during robot intervention from baseline/before and **33.62% retention/improvement** from baseline HWC after intervention. A **18.78% decrease** was observed from during WallBo and after WallBo was removed (See Fig. 2-left Combined results), further enforcing the fact the physical presence of the robot had a better influence during handwashing in-line with previous results with physically embodied agents [1].

Handwashing Compliance Gender Differences.   On average percentage difference, girls outperformed boys in handwashing compliance in all 3 sessions by 24.57% before, 8.22% during, and 18.61% after the intervention (See Fig. 2-left, boys/girls). This result is also consistent with prior research indicating that girls demonstrate greater motivation for practicing improved handwashing compared to boys [12].

Handwashing Conditions (Verbal/Non-verbal).   The study employed a between-subjects design, wherein pupils engaged with either a verbal or non-verbal WallBo. We did not see significant differences between conditions (Verbal Vs non-verbal conditions). The main difference between the conditions was, during verbal condition WallBo provided step-by-step instructions using speech and in non-verbal condition WallBo demonstrated the handwashing step displaying animation (without speech) on the small screen

---

[1] https://www.who.int/docs/default-source/patient-safety/how-to-handwash-poster.pdf.

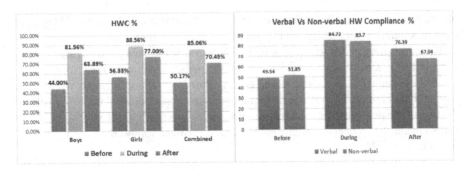

Fig. 2. Left-HWC, right- HWC conditions (Verbal/non-verbal)

on WallBo. This indicates that compliance remained higher irrespective of whether instructions were given verbally or non-verbally. (See Fig. 2 right).

Handwashing Steps Compliance. We observed from the average scores, pupils mainly showed a big improvement between pre/during WallBo intervention specially for steps 5–8, which involves rotational rubbing of the thumbs, rotational rubbing of both wrists and rotational rubbing of the fingertips on palm. Interestingly these are the common 3 handwashing steps missed by children according to a previous study [5]. We suppose that pupils were not aware about these handwashing steps from their prior knowledge about handwashing. (See Fig. 3).

Fig. 3. Handwashing steps compliance

4.2 Handwashing Knowledge

A single point was awarded for the accurate use of keywords for demonstrating their knowledge of the topic at least once in their response, out of a maximum score of 5 points. Q1 (*What is the best way of getting rid of germs from our hands?*) and Q4 (*Why do you use soap? What does soap do?*) - "soap", "clean", "wash", "germs" Q2 (*When should we wash our hands?*) and Q3 (*When you wash your hands, what do you do?*

What steps do you take?) - "eating", "play" "rub". There was **a 62.50% improvement** in Q2. When we should wash hands and **57.89% improvement** for Q3 On steps of handwashing. Also 8.57% and 21.74% improvement on Q1 best way to get rid of germs and Q4 what does soap do. No difference was observed on Q5 (*who taught you how to wash your hands?*). Overall significant improvement (~50%) was observed in their knowledge about handwashing (pre/post).

4.3 WallBo Perception

Overall. The interviews from the pupils were transcribed and analyzed thematically. The pupils seemed to really like WallBo and were keen to engage in sessions (and to speak to the researchers). There were numerous positive comments and curiosity about WallBo, and no signs of negative behaviours (e.g., aggression or sadness) around it. During the sessions, the children were very engaged, enthusiastic, and the majority listened well. Pupils were generally polite to WallBo and were trying to speak to WallBo between sessions (e.g., saying "hi", and trying to ask it things). Children were very curious about WallBo and were getting very close and trying to touch it (some consideration in the future should be given to put WallBo higher, or further away from pupils to avoid any potential damage to the device).

Understanding. *Q- Did you understand what WallBo was saying/asking you to do?*: All children reported that they could understand what WallBo was saying and wanted to see WallBo again. They also mentioned they wash their hands "better" when WallBo is around. When asked why they wanted to see WallBo again, they said that WallBo "helped them wash their hands" and "get rid of the germs". When asked why they wash "better" with WallBo, because WallBo was 1) watching them, 2) giving them the steps, or 3) showing them what to do (through videos).

Gender Perception- *Q-Do you think WallBo is a boy or a girl?*: There was an imbalance between whether WallBo was perceived as a boy (n = 18, 72%), or a girl (n = 5, 20%). An interesting point is that even though WallBo's voice was modulated to be gender-neutral, 9 out of 10 boys (90%) perceived WallBo as a boy, while only 4 out of the 14 girls (28.57%) perceived it as a girl. Similarly, only 1 boy (10%) thought WallBo to be a girl, while 8 of the 13 girls (61.14%) said that he was a boy. Out of the remaining two girls, one claimed that it was neither- "it is a hand" (n = 1, 4%), while the other believed it could be both- a girl and a boy (n = 1, 4%).

When asked why they thought it was a boy, most of the children said that "*he sounds like a boy / his voice is like a boy*" (n = 8, 32%) while others said he "*looks like a boy*" (n = 3, 12%), some of them said both, that he "*sounds and looks like a boy*" (n = 4, 16%). One of them even said that "*he is a boy even though he sounds like a girl because he looks like a boy*" (n = 1, 4%), while some others "couldn't say why" (n = 2, 8%) they thought he was a boy. When asked why they thought WallBo was a girl, the children commented that it was because it "*sounds like a girl*" (n = 3, 12%); One said that it was because she herself was a girl (n = 1, 4%), and another couldn't say why (n = 1, 4%). It was evident that the majority of boys associated WallBo with their own gender, whereas only a few girls expressed the same perspective.

Age. *Q-How old do you think WallBo is?:* When asked how old they thought WallBo was, some of the answers varied from ages 1–14, while others accounted for him looking either younger or older in reference to the children. $n = 5$ (21%) commented that WallBo was 10 years old, out of which 2 believed so because of his "face" or looks, 1 attributed it to his manner of talking, and one couldn't say why. $n = 8$ (32%) children indicated that WallBo was a child (age 5–9), out of which 4 couldn't say why, 2 (8%) believed that it was because WallBo seemed older than them, 1 said that it was because he was "small", and the one pupil ($n = 1$, 4%) said that it was because he was holding up 5 digits (fingers of his hand).

Interestingly, some children ($n = 2$, 8%) believed him to be a 1-year-old due to his small size, while 1 child also said that he looks like a 5-month-old, however the reason remains unclear. Out of the remaining children, $n = 4$ (16%) shared that WallBo was older to them, with reasons ranging from "because he seems older", "his hands are big", "he instructs us how to do things". Others, $n = 4$ (16%), believed that he was younger due to his small size, "seems like a child". Only 1 child couldn't answer this question. Children lacked awareness of their own ages, leading to a variety of responses, and consequently, they struggled to provide reasoned explanations for how old WallBo is.

Living. *Q- Do you think WallBo is alive, like a person?:* 76%, $n = 19$ children thought that WallBo was alive, out of which, $n = 13$ (52%) believed it was alive "like a person" while $n = 6$ (24%) acknowledged it to be alive but as a robot. The rest, $n = 6$ (24%), did not think it was alive. When asked why they thought WallBo was alive, most of the children commented that it was because WallBo could talk, ($n = 12$, 48%) while $n = 1$ couldn't say why they thought WallBo was alive. All the 6 children who said that WallBo was alive, but as a robot, attributed this to him talking, while $n = 2$ also mentioned his eye movements. When asked why they thought that he wasn't alive, $n = 4$ mentioned that it was because he was a robot, while the other 2 couldn't say why they thought so.

WallBo as a Friend/Classmate/Teacher. *Q- Do you think WallBo is a friend, classmate, or teacher?:* children were mixed in their responses. 44% ($n = 11$) thought that WallBo was like a friend because it was *"funny"*, *"helps"*, *"guides"*, and is *"friendly"*. 24% ($n = 6$) thought that WallBo was a classmate because it gives them "reminders", "teaches", is "nice", "fun" and is *"a bit shy and doesn't talk much"*. The latter point is interesting as it suggests that rather than being perceived as faulty or lacking capacity, a silent robot can be perceived as "shy". 24% ($n = 6$) thought that WallBo was like a teacher because it "teaches", "knows a lot", and because it "explains" or "tells" the child what to do. One child thought that WallBo was like a teaching assistant because they "teach" and are "funny". While the remaining children ($n = 7$, 28%) said that WallBo was a mix of a teacher and a friend, or a teacher and a classroom assistant.

Likes. *Q-What are some things that you like about WallBo?:* numerous kids enthusiastically reported that they liked WallBo. Main features for liking were- Moving eyes ($n = 7$); Voice ("cute", "funny") ($n = 7$); Eyes, movement, and expressiveness ($n = 8$); Mouth ($n = 13$); Song and singing / voice ($n = 5$); Hand shape ($n = 10$) Talking, instructing; Colour ($n = 4$); Everything ($n = 3$). Additional comments mentioned by some children were that they liked that WallBo "shows them how to wash their hands".

Suggested Improvements. *Q-Is there anything that you would change?:* Three children commented that they would change nothing about WallBo. The remaining children liked WallBo, and suggested further changes in his appearance- Mouth: n = 7, suggested changing the mouth colour, and some suggested for the mouth to be more humanistic, with lines to distinguish teeth. Eyes (n = 7), out of these, some children commented on a change in eye color, one of them said that his eyes could be bigger, while two of them suggested that WallBo should blink. Colour: (n = 5) some of the children shared their preferred colour pink (n = 4) and blue (n = 1). They suggested having more realistic facial features, for example having a nose, fingernails, and eyes that blink. While 24% (n = 6), one of them even commented on how he is shaped like a hand, but hands don't have eyes.

4.4 Teacher Interview Summary

In an interview with the teachers and head schoolteacher, they expressed that WallBo was a fun and interactive way for children to learn good handwashing practices. WallBo's resemblance to cartoons and his jolly manner of speaking were well received by the children. They had a positive response to the whole activity, including the approachable nature of the interviewers, who made the children feel very comfortable throughout the process.

When discussing keeping WallBo at school indefinitely, concerns regarding its safety were raised, but they concurred that placing him in a sealed case would help avoid possible damage. The teachers liked the idea of him delivering instructions once a week, so the children can act on it for the rest of the week, while the head schoolteacher mentioned that having monthly sessions could also help them maintain their practice. Everyone agreed that having an in-house teacher as a facilitator would be great, and the head schoolteacher added that they will be more than happy to have one of their team come by whenever available.

Suggestions about including some movements to make WallBo more cartoon-like and attractive were made to make him more engaging. It was observed that he appeared quite small, and his screen even smaller, when placed in a big area, so adjusting the same according to the dimensions of the classroom was discussed. They suggested having WallBo virtually demonstrate handwashing through the screen along with instructing, this could particularly help visual learners as well. Lastly, a teacher also suggested the involvement of more common English words/instructing the same in English as well, possibly to promote multilingual growth from a young age.

5 Conclusion

In this study we presented results from an intervention using a social robot WallBo as a tool to encourage and educate children in schools in context of handwashing. We observed an average 85.06% handwashing compliance during 1:1 session with WallBo a 51.60% improvement from the baseline handwashing technique and an overall ~ 50% knowledge improvement about handwashing. Conducting HRI research with these populations can help bridge the technology gap and provide equitable access to cutting-edge innovations. Also, social robotics research in diverse settings will contribute to a broader understanding of how rural communities from developing countries interact with social robots which is lacking in the HRI community.

Limitations: We recognize various uncontrolled variables stemming from the study's real-world context, including the coexistence of other pupils in the same environment as the handwashing station. Furthermore, the researchers' presence during the intervention may have influenced outcomes. While this trial doesn't definitively ascertain if students continued handwashing steps in their regular routines, or if compliance was maintained, we will delve into these aspects in the next long-term trial. The facilitator may have played a role in hyping the pupils up and driving attention and speaking enthusiastically to WallBo. It would be a subject for further investigation to tease apart how much the facilitator style influences the intervention outcome (and if a human facilitator is always needed). The facilitator of the sessions was also the research interviewer. As a result, many of the pupils built a rapport with that person, and they were more confident when answering questions.

Future Work: Our future work will focus on creating autonomous technology that precisely identify handwashing steps. Also, a behavior generation module with WallBo prompts behaviors automatically during handwashing. We intend to conduct a trial over a long-term period of 2–3 weeks to better assess changes in handwashing compliance and comprehend how these evolve over time. This extended timeframe allows measurement of sustainability and novelty effects stemming from the intervention [13]. Additionally, we would like to conduct a similar trial in a UK school to assess the cross-cultural differences between urban/developed country school children and rural/developing country school children. These trials will also help inform design decisions for WallBo and improve them iteratively through feedback obtained from consequent trials.

Acknowledgement. This work was funded by the ERC/UKRI Proof-of-concept funding and supported by IEEE Robotics and Automation Special Interest Group on Humanitarian Technology (RAS-SIGHT). We thank all the teachers, school authorities who supported our study and especially the children who participated in our study.

References

1. Belpaeme, T., Kennedy, J., Ramachandran, A., Scassellati, B., Tanaka, F.: Social robots for education: A review. Science robotics **3**(21), eaat5954 (2018)
2. Gordon, G., et al.: Affective personalization of a social robot tutor for children's second language skills. In: AAAI Conference on Artificial Intelligence, vol. 30, no. 1, March 2016
3. Baxter, P., Kennedy, J., Senft, E., Lemaignan, S., Belpaeme, T.: From characterising three years of HRI to methodology and reporting recommendations. In 2016 11th ACM/IEEE International Conference on Human-Robot Interaction (HRI), pp. 391–398, March 2016
4. Jamison, D.T., et al. (eds.). Disease control priorities in developing countries (2006)
5. Tengku Jamaluddin T.Z.M., Mohamed, N.A., Mohd Rani, M.D., et al.: Assessment on Hand Hygiene Knowledge and Practices Among Pre-school Children in Klang Valley. Global Pediatric Health. vol. 7 (2020). https://doi.org/10.1177/2333794X20976369

6. Dreibelbis, R., Kroeger, A., Hossain, K., Venkatesh, M., Ram, P.K.: Behavior change without behavior change communication: nudging handwashing among primary school students in Bangladesh. Int. J. Environ. Res. Public Health **13**(1), 129 (2016)
7. Biran, A., et al.: Effect of a behaviour-change intervention on handwashing with soap in India (SuperAmma): a cluster-randomised trial. The Lancet Global Health, pp. 145–154 (2014)
8. Deshmukh, A., Riddoch, K., Cross, E.S.: Assessing children's first impressions of "WallBo"-a robotic handwashing buddy. In: Interaction Design and Children, pp. 521–526, June 2021
9. Deshmukh, A., Babu, S.K., Unnikrishnan, R., Ramesh, S., Anitha, P., Bhavani, R.R.: (2019, October). Influencing hand-washing behaviour with a social robot: HRI study with school children in rural India. In: 2019 28th IEEE International Conference on Robot and Human Interactive Communication (RO-MAN), pp. 1–6. IEEE (2019)
10. Pfattheicher, S., Strauch, C., Diefenbacher, S., Schnuerch, R.: A field study on watching eyes and hand hygiene compliance in a public restroom. J. Appl. Soc. Psychol. **48**(4), 188–194 (2018)
11. Mohamed, N.A., Amin, N.N.Z., Isahak I Ramli, S., Salleh, N.M.: Knowledge, attitudes and practices of hand hygiene among parents of preschool children. J. Sci. Innov. Res. **5**, 1–6 (2016)
12. Ramseier, C.A., Leiggener, I., Lang, N.P., Bagramian, R.A., Inglehart, M.R.: Short-term effects of hygiene education for preschool (kindergarten) children: a clinical study. Oral Health Prev. Dent. **5**, 19–24 (2007)
13. Leite, I., Martinho, C., Paiva, A.: Social robots for long-term interaction: a survey. Int. J. Soc. Robot. **5**, 291–308 (2013)
14. Unnikrishnan, R., Deshmukh, A., Ramesh, S., Babu, S.K., Anitha, P., Bhavani, R.R.: Design and perception of a social robot to promote hand washing among children in a rural Indian school. In: 2019 28th IEEE International Conference on Robot and Human Interactive Communication, pp. 1–6 (2019). https://doi.org/10.1109/RO-MAN46459.2019.8956450
15. Alzyood, M., Jackson, D., Aveyard, H., Brooke, J.: COVID-19 reinforces the importance of handwashing. J. Clin. Nurs. **15–16**, 2760–2761 (2020). https://doi.org/10.1111/jocn.15313. Epub 2020 May 14. PMID: 32406958; PMCID: PMC7267118

Paired Robotic Devices with Subtle Expression of Sadness for Enriching Social Connectedness

Misako Uchida[1(✉)], Eleuda Nunez[1], Modar Hassan[1], Masakazu Hirokawa[2], and Kenji Suzuki[1]

[1] Institute of Systems and Information Engineering, University of Tsukuba, 1-1-1 Tennodai, Tsukuba, Ibaraki 305-8573, Japan
{misako,eleuda,modar}@ai.iit.tsukuba.ac.jp, kenji@ieee.org
[2] Data Science Laboratories, NEC Corporation, Kawasaki, Japan
hirokawa_m@ieee.org

Abstract. Various factors contribute to feelings of loneliness and compromised emotional well-being. One potential strategy to address this issue involves creating systems that enhance social connectedness between users at distance. In the literature, many of these systems utilize physically embodied devices and foster a sense of presence and intimacy. However, there has been limited exploration of targeting and sharing negative emotions. This study introduces a novel robotic device with a caricatured appearance named BlueBot, capable of subtle expressions of sadness. This study outlines the technical aspects and design principles underpinning touch-based non-verbal communication. Additionally, we present findings from a pilot test and in-the-wild field trial, describing users' responses and behaviors to investigate the impact on social connectedness. Our observations indicate that the developed system offers a nuanced approach that not only heightens awareness of the other individual's presence but also enhances emotional sensitivity. Several design insights for future similar studies are derived from our research.

Keywords: Social connectedness · Emotional communication · In-the-wild study · Social isolation

1 Introduction

Loneliness, distinct from simply being alone, encompasses negative emotions that arise from the disparity between desired and actual social connections [1]. Reduced interaction and communication contribute to the sense of loneliness, which in turn can potentially impact both physical and mental well-being. To address this issue, many researches have revealed that strengthening social connectedness can alleviate feelings of loneliness [2].

Social Awareness (SA) systems have emerged as a promising approach to maintaining these social ties by sharing awareness or social interaction that evokes the other's attention [3]. These systems facilitate positive emotions in terms of a sense of presence and intimacy by utilizing physical devices such

A. Al. Ali et al. (Eds.): ICSR 2023, LNAI 14453, pp. 254–263, 2024.
https://doi.org/10.1007/978-981-99-8715-3_22

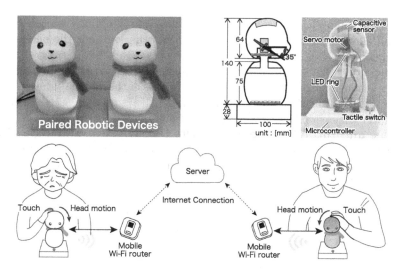

Fig. 1. (Top Left) Two identical devices, featuring a friendly appearance. (Top Right) Hardware overview, including dimensions and key features. (Bottom) Concept of Blue-Bot: users can engage in remote communication and share expressions.

as lamp-like structures [4,5] and displays [6]. However, there has been limited exploration of sharing negative emotions.

Negative emotions include sadness, fear, and disgust, but it has been suggested that sharing sadness not only opens doors for assistance but also nurtures a sense of intimacy [7]. In addition, social norms that discourage the expression of sadness can actually worsen negative emotions [8].

Taking these considerations into account, this study introduces a novel robotic device with a caricatured appearance that is capable of subtle expressions of sadness, named BlueBot. Then, using multiple BlueBot in paired configurations, we propose a new SA system for facilitating social connectedness between users at distance. To explore the effect on social connectedness, we conducted two field trials: a pair of friends and a mother-son dyad. We obtained the users' perceptions through questionnaires, interviews, and behavioral data analysis. Guided by these observations, we extracted design implications for a social awareness (SA) system endowed with the subtle expression of sadness.

2   Design of BlueBot

2.1   System Requirements

With a focus on the sustained application of the system in everyday settings, the subsequent set of system requirements was formulated.

1. **Casual Exchange of Non-Verbal Information:** While tools like telephones and emails facilitate verbal and explicit communication, the proposed

system is tailored for exchanging non-verbal and simplified expressions. It should allow users to keep awareness of each other without the necessity of exchanging messages with explicit content.

2. **Asynchronous Communication:** Designed for use in geographically distant relationships and throughout different times of the day, this system introduces a state transition model [3]. This model allows users to access messages whenever they choose, ensuring flexibility and convenience.

3. **Simple and Intuitive Operation:** With a focus on extended usage within everyday settings, simple touch-based operation is employed. Furthermore, a combination of visual cues seamlessly captures the user's attention.

4. **Friendly Design:** The robot's visual aesthetics incorporate curved surfaces to evoke a sense of familiarity. The simplified facial features encompassing round eyes and a mouth with upturned corners, were inspired by facial expressions commonly associated with likable robots [9].

2.2   System Configuration

An overview of the system is depicted in Fig. 1. This robot features a single degree of freedom (1 DoF) in the neck and color-changing capabilities. For optimal light dispersion, the robot's body is constructed using a translucent resin material. Inside both the body and the head, NeoPixel LEDs (NeoPixel Ring - 16×5050 and 12×5050 from Adafruit) were positioned to ensure even color distribution, illuminating the entirety of the robot's body. The head's pitch is controlled via a servo motor (SG92R, Tower Pro Pte. Ltd.), with a range of motion spanning $35°C$. Touch detection is achieved through a capacitive sensor (AT42QT1011, Sparkfun), with a 4 cm x 4 cm conductive sheet (ADFCS01, BitTradeOne) embedded within the robot's head, capable of reading input at a rate of 10 Hz. A tactile switch and a microcontroller (ESP32-DevKitC ESP-WROOM-32 development board, Espressif Systems Pte. Ltd.) are placed in the robot's base. The microcontroller contains a Wi-Fi module, and it establishes a client-server relationship through TCP/IP communication, by connecting to a mobile Wi-Fi router.

2.3   Expression of Sadness

BlueBot was designed to use color and head movements to convey expressions in a style that is intuitively understandable to the user as illustrated in Fig. 2. Previous research has demonstrated that the combination of color and motion provides the best cost-benefit ratio for conveying basic emotions [10]. Drawing from color psychology, blue is commonly linked with sadness, thus we used it for this purpose. Moreover, head motions and body postures have been used as a strategy to enhance emotional expression in robots [11].

2.4   State Transition

While our primary interest lies in assessing the impact of the sadness signal on social connectedness, having only a sadness signal has potential negative con-

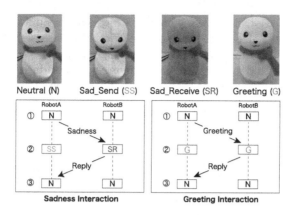

Fig. 2. State transition model

notations that might deter frequent usage of the system. Thus, we incorporated a more neutral signal option, a greeting signal, to give users more opportunities/motivations to interact with the robots. The state transition is illustrated in Fig. 2. Upon initialization, both robots default to a neutral state, represented by their bodies light up in white. Initiating a greeting signal requires one of the users to touch the tactile sensor on the robot's base. This prompts both the sender and receiver robots to perform two nods and light up in green, a color often associated with the emotion of calmness or neutrality [12]. To activate a sadness signal, a user needs to touch the robot's head, initiating the sad state. The sender and the receiver robots tilt their head downward and the only receiver illuminates in blue. Importantly, both robots return to the neutral state only after the receiver responds to the sadness/greeting signal. Signals can solely be sent while in the neutral state. Once sent, the state remains unchanged until a response is received.

3 Evaluation

3.1 Pilot Test

A pair of university student friends participated in this test. We installed BlueBot at their respective homes and asked them to freely communicate for 2 days. After the period, we collected their message log and conducted an interview to extract their impressions. For one of the participants (P1, age: 23, female), the experiment's purpose was deliberately withheld, but instead, we just explained the function of the robot. Conversely, the other participant (P2, age: 22, female) played the role of a confederate and was tasked with sending a sadness signal at a predetermined time.

Result. A total of 9 exchanges of messages were recorded during the test. P1 initiated 6 greetings and no sadness signal, whereas P2 initiated 2 greetings and conveyed sadness once. The messages and their corresponding replies were observed at various intervals, demonstrating asynchronous communication. During the interview, P1 shared, "Upon receiving a sadness signal, rather than instantly communicate by a phone call or message, I opted to communicate my presence at home. I did this by not only replying with a sadness signal but also by sending a greeting signal through the robot." P1 then elaborated, "Since I understand her sadness, I am receptive to what she might share when she reaches out."

3.2   Field Trial

Participants. For this study, our selection criteria involved participants who were well-acquainted with each other, lived apart and were experienced in remote communication with each other. A mother-son pair participated in the test. The son, aged 59, lives with his wife and two daughters. He commutes to work from Monday to Friday. The mother, aged 87, is a mother to three children who lives independently and seldom ventures outdoors. Every Wednesday, she goes shopping accompanied by a helper. They have face-to-face meetings only once a month. Communication is primarily through telephone conversations due to the mother's lack of mobile phone usage. On average, they use the phone about once a month, often making calls when they have specific information to convey. Most commonly, the son reaches out to his mother to inquire about her well-being.

Measurements. We collected data through a combination of questionnaires, interviews, and communication logs. To assess social connectedness in a quantitative manner, we utilized the Social Connectedness Questionnaire (SCQ) [13]. This questionnaire comprises two sets of questions: an overall level and an individual level. For the purposes of this study, we exclusively employed the individual-level questionnaire to gauge the connection between the two parties involved. Participants responded to each item using a 7-point Likert scale. This questionnaire prompted participants to evaluate their social connections with their partners over the past two weeks. The assessment encompassed five subdimensions: Relationship salience (RS), (dis)satisfaction with contact quality (CQ), Shared understandings (SU), Knowing each others' experiences (KE), and Feelings of closeness (FC). The Japanese-translated questionnaire was administered before and after the trial. Complementing this quantitative approach, we conducted semi-structured interviews to study the participants' experiences and to obtain deeper insights into their usage and perceptions of the system. Furthermore, communication logs described exchanges between the robots on the server. The timing and frequency of robot usage are quantitative measures of their interactions.

Procedure

- **Before the Trial.** We visited each household to install of the equipment, we requested participants to complete the SCQ. Subsequently, we introduced

Fig. 3. BlueBot at the participants' homes.

BlueBot as a communication interface capable of transmitting two distinct signals. Participants were encouraged to send these signals freely for two weeks, without constraints on the timing or frequency of use. Both participants positioned their robots in prominent locations within the living-dining areas of their homes. The son, opted to install the robot on a dresser, while the mother, chose to put it on a TV stand (see Fig. 3).

- **After the Trial.** We revisited each household to administer the questionnaires and conduct the interviews. Utilizing the observed behavioral patterns from the communication log, we formulated a set of interview questions. Subsequently, we proceeded to uninstall the system.

4 Results

The results of SCQ are illustrated in Fig. 4. It is categorized into a range of 1–7, 1 indicating low social connectedness and 7 indicating the highest. Both participants showed increases in the Relationship Salience (RS) dimension; however, the mother's overall score exhibited an upward trend, while the son's score showed a slight decline. Notably, the son's (CQ) considerably decreased following the utilization of BlueBot.

The distribution of messages per hour over the two weeks is depicted in Fig. 5. During the period, a total of 43 signal exchanges took place, with the greeting signal sent 39 times and the sadness signal sent 4 times. Among these exchanges, the son initiated the greeting signal 36 times (92.3%), while the mother initiated it 3 times. Additionally, the son sent the sadness signal 4 times, whereas the mother did not send any. Regarding response time, the son replied three times, with response intervals of 17, 21, and 23 s. On the other hand, the median of the mother's response time is 171 s. Detailed distribution of the mother's response times is provided in Fig. 5.

During the interviews, in terms of the usage of the sadness signal, the son remarked, "I pushed it when my favorite baseball team gave up a home run or when I felt tired, without thinking too much, I just wanted to let her know about it." In contrast, the mother noted, "I never felt sad, so I did not use it." The subsequent questions aimed to delve into how they felt upon receiving a sadness signal. The son, though not having experienced it himself, shared, "I did

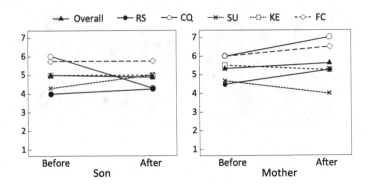

Fig. 4. Scores from the Social Connectedness Questionaire

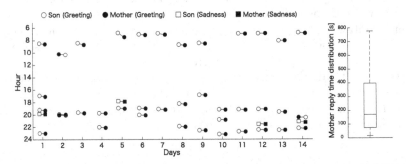

Fig. 5. (Left) Overview of all the messages exchanged during the 14-day trial. Markers on the left side of each link represent the senders and markers on the right side represent the respondent. (Right) Mother's reply time distribution [s].

not receive it, but I would think that my mother felt lonely." In contrast, the mother encountered the sadness signal from her son, but she did not attribute a negative significance to it. She explained, "I did not worry and just replied back. I think if he was really sad, he would call."

When we inquired about their feelings regarding having BlueBot at home, the mother responded, "Since we could communicate multiple times a day, I naturally felt more connected to him. Depending on the timing of his messages, I would imagine what he was up to at that moment." The son expressed, "The robot's movements in response to my mother's actions made me feel closer to her." Particularly, we discussed communication quality with the son due to the lower score for SCQ. He mentioned, "It often felt like one-way communication, with me initiating most of the contact." However, he added, "Even though I do not call her every day, receiving prompt responses through the robot was reassuring." In contrast, the mother, who scored higher, mentioned, "I do not usually call him frequently, and when I do, I keep it brief in case he is busy. With the robot, I could reach out every day somehow, and I found it enjoyable."

5 Discussion

Our focus is on creating an intuitive and engaging platform designed for sharing negative emotions. We believe this will not only deepen intimacy but also amplify the sense of social connectedness. Earlier research has indicated the importance of assessing these systems in real-world settings over extended periods [3]. Keeping this in mind, our goal was to create a system that is straightforward to operate and demands minimal supervision, allowing for seamless integration into users' daily routines. Following this approach, we conducted evaluation studies aimed at verifying the overall system performance and capturing user responses.

- **Sharing Sadness.** In the pilot test, although one of the participants did not use the sadness signal, she noted that the system helped her become more aware of her friend's emotions and prepare for embracing her sadness, but the situation was not deemed serious enough for her to reach out via phone. In the Field trial, users were able to differentiate the sadness signals from greetings due to their infrequent and unique nature, leading to quicker response compared to greetings (Fig. 5). The presence of sadness within greetings helps users to realize the other's emotional shift. For the sender, sending sadness did not necessarily signify that they were feeling sad, but rather that they wished to convey that sentiment and capture the recipient's attention. For the receiver, these signals did not carry a negative connotation; instead, we consider that they heightened the awareness of the sender in an emotionally impactful manner such as a sadness emoticon. An interesting finding is that in communicating daily greetings as well as the negative signal of sadness, both participants may have agreed that the proposed device communicates lighter emotions. We consider that, on the premise of being able to communicate verbally using the telephone, the proposed device could play a complementary role in enriching casual daily communication.
- **Accustomization.** In the field trial, the son, who was accustomed to various communication platforms, played a more active role by sending a greater number of messages and often taking the initiative. On the other hand, the mother, who primarily relied on phones for communication, could also grasp the purpose and role of the BlueBot. She mentioned that she was accustomed to responding to her son's messages, establishing a communication pattern that accommodated their routines. This dynamic was also reflected in the data. They typically communicated during mornings and evenings, with the son initiating communication more frequently, as depicted in the log (Fig. 5). This communication pattern is the same as their reported use of phones.
- **Increase the Feeling of "Being Together."** In relation to social connectedness, we carefully selected a tool that was most suitable for this context. The SCQ result exhibited noticeable changes after two weeks of interaction with BlueBots, with the dimension of relationship salience showing the most positive change (Fig. 4). In this regard, during the interview participants mentioned that the ability to communicate through the robot without disrupting each other's routines helped maintain a continuous awareness of one another

without requiring conscious effort. The presence of the always-on connection provided by the robots, coexisting within the same space as the users, seemed to foster a natural awareness of each other's presence and connection through ongoing interaction.

- **Contact Quality.** Certain scores exhibited a decline after the two-week period. Notably for the son, his perception of contact quality was negatively affected by his mother's limited initiative and more passive role. In the interview, he mentioned occasionally feeling like the communication was one-sided due to his mother's slower and infrequent responses (Fig. 5). This situation points to a potential downside of having a partner who is less responsive, which could impact the sense of social connectedness. Given the substantial impact of perceiving the robot as consistently unchanging, future research will explore methods to mitigate this effect.

5.1 Design Implications

We extracted key features for communication interfaces similar to BlueBot:

- **Subtle Expression.** Robot expressions intentionally lack specific information, inviting user interpretation. Their timing and frequency can prompt users to envision the other person's emotions or lifestyle. Responses are shaped by individual interpretations and relationship dynamics.
- **Easy Operation and Simple Interaction.** The system is designed to be user-friendly, even for those unfamiliar with new technologies. The combination of simple state transitions, touch-based controls, and intuitive, recognizable robot expressions has proven to be effective.
- **Actively Promote Interaction.** The negative impact of a partner's lack of responsiveness highlights the need for design strategies to mitigate this issue. One possible solution involves incorporating AI to stimulate user-initiated interaction by prompting messages during periods of reduced engagement.
- **Asynchronous and Synchronous Communication.** Adopting a state transition model that allows colored lights to persist over time after being sent facilitates asynchronous communication. Additionally, the colored lights and head motions of the robots enable synchronous communication, which is more immediate and necessitates both users to be actively engaged in the interaction simultaneously. Both forms of communication are equally relevant and serve distinct purposes, aligning with prior research findings [4].

6   Conclusion and Future Work

In this study, we outlined the technical aspects and design principles of Blue-Bots, a specialized robot designed to enhance social connectedness through sharing sadness. Through two trials, we documented users' reactions and behaviors, revealing seamless integration into their daily lives. Based on the participants' feedback, we have proposed design implications for future research. Regarding the question of whether the sadness signal can contribute to augmenting social connectedness, we must acknowledge that providing a definitive answer remains beyond our current scope. Nevertheless, our observations suggest that the signal has the capacity to evoke empathy by fostering an awareness of others' emotions. Furthermore, they provide an understated method for both fostering awareness of the other person's presence and heightening our own emotional awareness.

References

1. Martino, J., Pegg, J., Frates, E.P.: The connection prescription: using the power of social interactions and the deep desire for connectedness to empower health and wellness. Am. J. Lifestyle Med. **11**(6), 466–475 (2017)
2. Janssen, J.H., Ijsselsteijn, W.A., Westerink, J.H.: How affective technologies can influence intimate interactions and improve social connectedness. Int. J. Hum. Comput. Stud. **72**(1), 33–43 (2014)
3. Li, H., Häkkilä, J., Väänänen, K.: Review of unconventional user interfaces for emotional communication between long-distance partners. In: Proceedings of the 20th International Conference on Human-Computer Interaction with Mobile Devices and Services, pp. 1–10 (2018)
4. Gaver, W., Gaver, F.: Living with light touch: an autoethnography of a simple communication device in long-term use. In: Proceedings of the 2023 CHI Conference on Human Factors in Computing Systems, pp. 1–14 (2023)
5. Visser, T., Vastenburg, M. H., Keyson, D. V.: Designing to support social connectedness: the case of SnowGlobe. Int. J. Des. **5**(3) (2011)
6. Baecker, R., Sellen, K., Crosskey, S., Boscart, V., Barbosa Neves, B.: Technology to reduce social isolation and loneliness. In: Proceedings of the 16th International ACM SIGACCESS Conference on Computers, Accessibility, pp. 27–34 (2014)
7. Singh-Manoux, A., Finkenauer, C.: Cultural variations in social sharing of emotions: an intercultural perspective. J. Cross Cult. Psychol. **32**(6), 647–661 (2001)
8. Bastian, B., Koval, P., Erbas, Y., Houben, M., Pe, M., Kuppens, P.: Sad and alone: social expectancies for experiencing negative emotions are linked to feelings of loneliness. Soc. Psychol. Personality Sci. **6**(5), 496–503 (2015)
9. Kalegina, A., Schroeder, G., Allchin, A., Berlin, K., Cakmak, M.: Characterizing the design space of rendered robot faces. In: Proceedings of the 2018 ACM/IEEE International Conference on Human-Robot Interaction, pp. 96–104 (2018)
10. Löffler, D., Schmidt, N., Tscharn, R.: Multimodal expression of artificial emotion in social robots using color, motion and sound. In: Proceedings of the 2018 ACM/IEEE International Conference on Human-Robot Interaction, pp. 334–343 (2018)
11. Saunderson, S., Nejat, G.: How robots influence humans: a survey of nonverbal communication in social human-robot interaction. Int. J. Soc. Robot. **11**, 575–608 (2019)
12. Nijdam, N.A.: Mapping emotion to color. Book Mapping emotion to color, 2–9 (2009)
13. Van Bel, D.T., Smolders, K.C., IJsselsteijn, W.A., De Kort, Y.A.W.: Social connectedness: concept and measurement. In: Intelligent Environments, pp. 67–74. IOS Press (2009)

Explorative Study on the Non-verbal Backchannel Prediction Model for Human-Robot Interaction

Sukyung Seok[1,2] , Tae-Hee Jeon[1,2] , Yu-Jung Chae[1] , ChangHwan Kim[1] , and Yoonseob Lim[1(✉)]

[1] Korea Institute of Science and Technology (KIST), Seoul 02792, South Korea
`yslim@kist.re.kr`
[2] Korea University, Seoul 02841, South Korea

Abstract. Previous studies on backchannel prediction model have suggested that replicating human backchannel can enhance user's human-robot interaction experience. In this study, we propose a real-time non-verbal backchannel prediction model which utilizes both an acoustic feature and a temporal feature. Our goal is to improve the quality of robot's backchannel and user's experience. To conduct this research, we collected a human-human interview dataset. Using this dataset, we proceeded to develop three distinct backchannel prediction models: a temporal, an acoustic, and a mixed (temporal & acoustic) model. Subsequently, we conducted a user study to compare the perception of robot implemented with the three models. The results demonstarted that the robot employing the mixed model was preferred by participants and exhibited moderate frequency of backchannel. These results emphasize the advantages of incorporating acoustic and temporal features in developing backchannel prediction model to enhance the quality of human-robot interactions, specifically with regards to backchannel frequency and timing.

Keywords: Human-robot interaction · Backchannel prediction model · Non-verbal backchannel · Social robot

1 Introduction

Social robots are designed to interact with people in a way that resembles social interaction between humans. Many researchers have suggested that a natural and human-like communicative ability is crucial for social robots in order to effectively interact and engage with human users [1,6,8]. One way to obtain such communicative ability for robots is to replicate human's backchannel (BC), such as "mm, uh-huh", head nod, or laughter. BC is known for conveying information about the state of the communication, such as the listener's attention, comprehension, or acceptance, thereby making communication more efficient [26]. Studies have demonstrated that robots' or virtual agents' BC learned from human conversation can enhance rapport [7], engagement [12,29], and user preference [22,23] for robots or virtual agents.

Acoustic or visual cues from speaker has been widely used to develop a model for predicting the timing of robot's or virtual agent's BC. Acoustic cues such as pause, pitch, and spectral energy, as well as visual cues such as the speaker's gaze and head nods were considered as predictive features in BC prediction models [11,19]. Methodologically, rule-based [23,24], machine learning models such as LSTM [22], CRF [10], SVM [19], logistic regression [15], and Reinforcement learning [11] were explored.

Several studies on human-human interactions (HHI) have demonstrated the significance of a moderate frequency of BCs in intercultural communication [16, 17]. Furthermore, the frequency of BCs plays a crucial role in their application to robots. Poppe et al. (2013) [24] reported that a higher number of generated BCs does not necessarily increase the naturalness of BC behavior, and a reasonable number of BCs per minute typically falls between 6 and 12. These findings imply that BC frequency is closely related to communication quality, suggesting the existence of an desirable range for BC frequency. However, most previous studies on BC prediction models did not consider the frequency of BCs in human data. Therefore, in order to enhance the naturalness of BCs, this study found it necessary to incorporate frequency information into a BC prediction model.

In this study, we utilize the temporal feature of BC, specifically distribution of BC interval, to automatically adjust the frequency of BC and propose a real-time non-verbal BC prediction model that incorporates temporal feature and acoustic cue of BC in order to improve the naturalness and appropriateness of robot's BC and the perception of robot. For this purpose, we first build a HHI interview dataset with BC annotations. Using this dataset, we then construct three different BC prediction models, a *temporal model*, an *acoustic model*, and a *mixed (temporal & acoustic) model*. The temporal model uses the Erlang distribution of BC interval extracted from the HHI dataset as temporal feature of BC. The acoustic model is based on a traditional acoustic feature for speech processing, Mel-Frequency Cepstrum Coefficient (MFCC). The mixed model utilizes both temporal and acoustic features. Further, we compare the performance of the three different models through offline evaluation and conducted an HRI study to investigate the effect of BC prediction model on the perception of robot.

2   Backchannel Model Description

2.1   Interview Data Collection

We conducted dyadic casual interviews by referring to the questions presented in previous studies [21,27]. There were 10 closed-end questions and 7 open-end questions with casual and personal topics, such as hometown, family, favorite celebrities, etc. Before the interviews, the participants asked to prepare answers for the questions. After a preliminary interview session, two main interview sessions were conducted with a pair of participants taking turns as the interviewer and the interviewee. Three time-synchronized cameras captured the frontal view of each participant along with a lateral view. The two headset microphones for each participant were also time-synchronized with each other and the cameras.

Considering that there may be an influence between conversational context and BC [14], the interview format and questions of the interview data were used almost similarly in the subsequent user study.

32 participants (male = 16, female = 16) with a mean age of 26.9 (min = 21, max = 36) were recruited through e-mail at the Korea Institute of Science and Technology. Since the difference in the frequency of BC according to gender and gender pair has been studied [20], gender was pre-screened when applications were received to ensure a numerical balance of gender and gender pair. There were 8 same-gender pair (female-female = 4, male-male = 4) and 8 opposite-gender pair (female-male = 4, male-female = 4). In addition, considering the possibility that intimacy may affect BC generation, paired participants were controlled to see each other for the first time. The age group was controlled to be in the 20 s to 30 s. Each of the participants was paid roughly $ 12 USD for the interview. The interview was conducted with the approval of the Institutional Review Board of the Korea Institute of Science and Technology (KIST IRB: KIST-202209-HR-001).

The total amount of collected data was about 5.1 h. Two trained annotators annotated the non-verbal BCs (head nods) using video-annotation software ELAN [28] and achieved moderate and substantial levels of agreement (time-based kappa: 0.58, event-based kappa: 0.61) from interobserver agreement computing program Generalized Sequential Querier (GSEQ) [18]. Time-based kappa is obtained by aligning annotators' annotations to a certain time unit (100ms), and event-based kappa is obtained by counting as agreed events when the overlap between annotations is more than 60%. We also annotated pauses automatically by using speech sound analysis program Praat [2], which were then corrected by two experts on linguistics in case of annotation errors.

2.2   BC Prediction Model

We propose three methods for predicting the timing of non-verbal BC onsets in a robot, which involve temporal, acoustic, or a combination of both models. Details are described as follows:

Temporal Model. We apply Erlang distribution to model the interval of BC onset timing, since this distribution has been used for predicting the interval between two events [5] and also mentioned as an appropriate distribution for predicting the timing of BCs [24]. The Erlang distribution is defined by probability density function (PDF) as follows:

$$f(x; k, \beta) = \frac{\lambda^k x^{k-1} e^{-\frac{x}{\beta}}}{\beta^k (k-1)!} \quad \text{for } x \geq 0, \beta > 0 \tag{1}$$

The Erlang distribution $f(x; k, \beta)$ is characterized by time variable between BC onsets x, the number of BC onsets k, and the scale parameter β ($\beta = 1/\lambda$), where the λ denotes mean rate of BC onsets. In our study, β is obtained from the interview data ($\beta = 7.933$ s).

Acoustic Model. To represent acoustic property of a speech sound, we extract acoustic features based on 10th order mel-frequency cepstral coefficients (MFCCs) which is often used to represent the spectral characteristics of human voice. In MFCC, Fast Fourier Transform (FFT) is applied to convert the time domain into the frequency domain. Power coefficients are then obtained by a Mel-scale filter. Frequency h (in Hertz) is converted to Mel frequency m is given by:

$$m = 2595 \log_{10} \left(1 + \frac{h}{700} \right) \tag{2}$$

We apply Random Forest (RF) classifier to predict the timing of the BC onset based on the acoustic features. This classifier is an ensemble learning method based on multiple trees [3], and each tree is determined by nodes and branches using randomly selected features to deal with over-fitting. An objective function such as Gini Index is used to search for the best split in a tree.

In our work, the feature length was defined by 4 s to ensure a sufficient observation of the speaker's utterances, and the classifier was set by a total of 300 trees. We conducted Bootstrapping by randomly splitting the interview data into multiple balanced training and testing datasets and obtained 1,600 classifiers. We evaluated the classifiers by F1-score using the testing datasets, with a marginal time of 0.2 s applied as an error tolerance, in which the marginal time is the time difference between predicted BC and the ground truth annotated in the interview dataset. Finally, the classifier with a median F1-score was selected and applied to a robot.

Mixed Model. Mixed model utilizes both temporal and acoustic features. In this model, the acoustic model first predicts the timing of BC onset based on the MFCC of user's speech, and then the temporal model determines the validity of the interval between the predicted BC and the previous BC.

2.3   Model Implementation and Evaluation

We implemented BC prediction models based on ROS (Robot Operating System) Kinetic Kame in Ubuntu 16.04 LTS (Xenial Xerus). To apply these models to a robot, a minimum time constraint (1 s) is required to prevent the robot from generating a BC while executing a nodding motion. Additionally, we used WebRTC-based voice activity detection to apply the acoustic model while user speaks to the robot.

To evaluate how well the BC prediction models performed in predicting the timing of BC onsets, we selected the unseen data (318 s) from the interview data. Figure 1 partially shows the results with visual timelines indicating BCs that is produced by each BC prediction model during 40 s. The temporal model could not fit well with the ground truth and generated BCs sparsely. Meanwhile, the acoustic model with median F1-score performance seems to generate BCs frequently and aligned well with the ground truth (F1-score = 23.29%). The

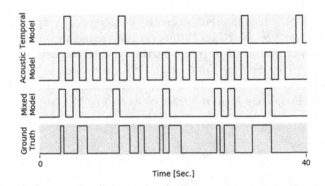

Fig. 1. Example traces of BC generated by temporal, acoustic, mixed model. Bottom trace in blue represents the ground truth of BC. (Color figure online)

timing of BCs predicted by the mixed model partially aligned with the ground truth, but the time interval and frequency were most similar to the ground truth. We used the same unseen data to evaluate the efficacy of the mixed model over 10,000 bootstrap iterations. The following results were found: F1-score (mean = 5.02%, SD = 3.8%)

3   User Study

We conducted a robot interview in which the robot acts as the interviewer and the user acts as the interviewee to investigate the user's perception of the robot implemented with our three BC prediction models: temporal, acoustic, and mixed model.

3.1   Participants

We recruited 36 participants (male = 18, female = 18) with a mean age of 26.0 (min = 21, max = 35) through e-mail at the Korea Institute of Science and Technology. As with interview data collection, gender was pre-screened when applications were received to ensure a numerical balance of gender. The age group was controlled to be in the 20 s to 30 s. Each of the participants was paid roughly $ 24 USD for the experiment. This experiment was conducted with the approval of the Institutional Review Board of the Korea Institute of Science and Technology (KIST IRB: KIST-202209-HR-001).

3.2   Experimental Setup

Our models were applied to the 'MyBom Mini' robot[1], as depicted in Fig. 2a. The robot was developed by Roaigen for social interaction in homes and measures

---

[1] https://roaigen.com.

a   b

Fig. 2. (a) Robot platform 'MyBom Mini' (b) An example of the robot interviews. Participants answered the questions focusing on the onset timing of nodding gesture (BC). They were instructed to continue to speak while the light is turned on.

184mm in width and 345mm in height. It comprises of an 8-channel audio board, one speaker, neck motors (2 DoF), a motor control board, and a PC with an i5-8259U processor and 8 GB of memory.

We design 5 nodding gestures using 3ds Max for expressing non-verbal BCs of the robot, and one of the gestures is randomly selected and executed during 1 s. We also use two facial expressions such as a smile and blinking to enhance natural interaction. The smile expression is triggered by predefined rules based on a script while speaking, and the blinking occurs simultaneously with the nodding gestures. The robot's speech was synthesized in a young female (Ha Eun) voice using Typecast's AI voice generator[2]. The robot produced BCs (nods) only in the speaking turns of the participants.

For the comparison of the three different models, temporal, acoustic, and mixed, we used within-subject design. Each participant takes part in an interview conducted by the robot with three different BC prediction models. The interacting order of the models was counter-balanced across participants. As a result, the subjects were divided into 6 groups which consists of 6 participants (3 males, 3 females).

Most of the robot interview questions in the user study were based on the same questions which were used in our human-human interview dataset. The question fell into 4 categories: *celebrity, narrative, vacation destination,* and *schedule.* The experimenter manually controlled the turn-taking of the robot. In turn, the robot asked the next question after a brief pause of 5 s.

3.3   Procedures

Before the main experiment, the participants responded to an online questionnaire which includes the questions used in the robot interviews. It was instructed to the participants that they should not focus on the nodding gesture itself, but the onset timing of the nodding gesture. We requested them to answer each question for at least 40 s. We turned off an electric light behind the robot after 40 s to

---

[2] https://typecast.ai/.

let the participant finish the answer (See Fig. 2b). A total of 3 robot interviews were conducted for the comparison of the 3 conditions. In each robot interview, the robot asked 4 questions which consist of the 4 different question types, celebrity, narrative, vacation destination, and schedule. The question types were presented in a random order, and each question was selected randomly without replacement. At the end of each robot interview, we requested the participant to fill out a questionnaire about the quality of BC timing of the model as a post survey. After the end of all robot interviews, we asked participants to rank the robot by the overall quality of the robot's BC as a final survey. Finally, we conducted an experimenter interview about the rank and the experiment overall.

3.4 Measurements

In the post survey, we constructed 6 questions for measuring the behavioral features of robot's BC and 6 questions for the functions of robot's BC. The survey used a 7-point Likert scale ranging from "Not at all" to "Very much". The questions on the behavioral features referred to the questionnaire items presented in previous HRI studies related to the BC model [10,13,19,22]. In addition, the questions on the functions also referred to the same previous HRI studies [10,13,22] and also considered the functions of the BC in a HHI study [4]. The questionnaire categories and items are listed in Table 1. The questionnaire items listed in each questionnaire category were presented in random order to avoid order effect.

In the experimenter interview, we asked the participants to rank the quality of each model in terms of the timing of BC to reconfirm the results of the post survey. We further calculated the frequency and interval of the BCs of each BC prediction model to investigate the relationship between perception of robot's BC and its function, and the actual BC generation pattern of the three BC prediction models. The frequency of BC was measured in times per a minute. The interval was calculated by subtracting the start time of the BC from the start time of the subsequent BC.

3.5 Results

The results of normality tests on the questionnaire items according to experimental conditions (BC model) showed that a normal distribution could not be assumed for all groups of each BC model on the questionnaire items (Shapiro-Wilk test $p < 0.05$). Therefore, we used a nonparametric statistical analysis, a Kruskal-Wallis test to verify the different effects among three BC models. All reverse-scored items (BF-Q4, BF-Q5) were reverse coded. Also, to remove outliers from the dataset, we employed the interquartile range (IQR) method, which involves identifying values outside the range of 1.5 times the IQR and removing them from the analysis.

There were statistically significant differences among the three BC model groups for the four out of the six questionnaire items evaluating the behavioral features of robot's BC (Naturalness (BF-Q1): $\chi^2 (2) = 8.91$, $p < 0.05$;

Table 1. Questionnaire categories and items

(Behavioral features (BF) of robot's backchannel)
BF-Q1 The robot's backchannels (nods) were natural
BF-Q2 The frequency of the robot's backchannels (nods) were appropriate
BF-Q3 The timing of the robot's backchannels (nods) were appropriate
BF-Q4 How often do you think the robot nodded at an inappropriate time?
BF-Q5 How often do you think the robot missed nodding opportunities?
BF-Q6 The robot's backchannel (nods) did not interrupt the conversation.
(Functions (F) of robot's backchannel)
F-Q1 The robot was listening carefully
F-Q2 The robot encouraged me to continue talking
F-Q3 The robot understood what I was saying
F-Q4 The robot sympathized with what I was saying
F-Q5 The robot agreed to what I was saying
F-Q6 The robot showed emotional response to what I was saying

Frequency appropriateness (BF-Q2): χ^2 (2) = 7.6, $p < 0.05$; Timing appropriateness (BF-Q3): χ^2 (2) = 17.8, $p < 0.001$; Perceived recall (BF-Q5): χ^2 (2) = 22.2, $p < 0.0001$) (Fig. 3a). Post-hoc tests using Dunn's test with Bonferroni correction revealed that there are statistically significant differences between temporal model and mixed model for all three items (BF-Q1, BF-Q2, BF-Q5: $p < 0.05$; BF-Q3: $p < 0.01$), and between temporal model and acoustic model for two items (BF-Q3: $p < 0.001$; BF-Q5: $p < 0.00001$). These results showed that participants rated the robot's BC behavior as more natural, appropriate in terms of frequency and timing, and better recall when using mixed model compared to temporal model. Also, participants evaluated that the robot's BC behavior had better timing appropriateness and perceived recall when implementing acoustic model than temporal model.

Further, there were statistically significant differences among the three BC model groups for the four out of the six questionnaire items evaluating the functions of robot's BC (Attentive listening (F-Q1): χ^2 (2) = 6.7, $p < 0.05$; Encouragement to talk (F-Q2): χ^2 (2) = 9.6, $p < 0.01$; Sympathy (F-Q4): χ^2 (2) = 7.4, $p < 0.05$; Agreement (F-Q5): χ^2 (2) = 21.8, $p < 0.0001$) (Fig. 3b). Post-hoc tests showed that there are statistically significant differences between temporal model and acoustic model for attentive listening, encouragement to talk, sympathy, and agreement (F-Q1, F-Q2, F-Q4: $p < 0.05$; F-Q5: $p < 0.001$), and between temporal model and mixed model for encouragement to talk and agreement (F-Q2: $p < 0.05$; F-Q5: $p < 0.0001$). These results imply that the participants rated the robot as listening more attentively, encouraging them to talk more, sympathizing more with their saying, and being more in agreement with their statements when implementing acoustic model compared to temporal

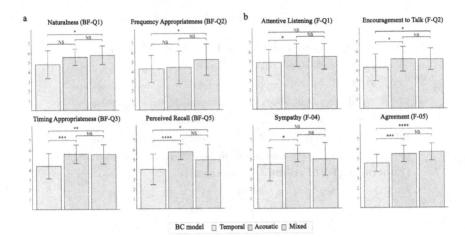

Fig. 3. (a) Survey result on the behavioral features of robot's BC. (b) Survey result on the function of robot's BC. Means and standard deviations are shown (NS p > 0.05, * p < 0.05, ** p < 0.01, *** p < 0.001, **** p < 0.0001).

Table 2. Descriptive statistics (Frequency and interval) of Predicted BC

BC prediction model	Mean Frequency (SD) (times per min)	Mean Interval (SD) (sec)
Temporal	3.96 (0.53)	10.70 (1.67)
Acoustic	12.30 (1.62)	3.42 (0.49)
Mixed	7.40 (1.17)	5.32 (0.64)

model, and as encouraging them to talk more and being more in agreement with their statements when using mixed model compared to temporal model.

In the final survey, the majority of participants (17/36, 47.2%) responded that the mixed model performed best, and more than 50 percent of them (21/36, 58.3%) answered that temporal performed worst. These results suggest that the overall quality of the robot's BC was better in the mixed model than the other two models.

Lastly, the frequency and interval of the BCs of each BC model are summarized in Table 2. Since we confirmed that a normal distribution could not be assumed for the BC frequencies and BC intervals of each model ($p < 0.05$), we used Kruskal-Wallis tests. The tests showed that there were statistically significant differences among the models in the BC frequency ($\chi^2 (2) = 94.3$, $p < 0.001$), and in the BC interval ($\chi^2 (2) = 97.9$, $p < 0.001$). Post-hoc tests using Dunn's test with Bonferroni correction revealed that there were statistically significant differences across the models in the frequency and interval ($p < 0.05$).

4 Discussions

We found that the acoustic model obtained better F1-score than the mixed model in the model evaluation. However, there was no statistically significant differences between the acoustic model and the mixed model in all questionnaire items from the post survey in the user study. These results were consistent with the result of Poppe et al. [24]. They found that when comparing various rule-based models the rule-based model with higher precision and recall did not necessarily obtain a higher human-likeness score.

Although we did not find the difference between the acoustic and mixed models from the post survey, more than half of them rated the mixed model as the best when participants were forced to rank the three models from the final questionnaire. We assumed that this result resulted from a moderate BC frequency of the mixed model. According to Poppe et al. [24], an increase in the number of BCs does not always lead to an improvement in the naturalness and appropriateness of BC. In addition, the mixed model was the only model whose frequency was in the range of reasonable number of BCs per minute (6–12) presented in Poppe et al. [24]. Overall, the mixed model achieved a moderate frequency of BCs, which suggests that applying the temporal feature of BCs could be an effective strategy to suppress excessive generation of BCs and adjust the BC frequency properly.

Lastly, it should be noted that we only focused on head nod, which is one type of non-verbal BC. However, there are other non-verbal BCs, such as facial expression and gaze, and verbal BCs as well. The effectiveness of the temporal feature on the BC prediction of other non-verbal BCs and verbal BCs should be validated. Furthermore, we only used an acoustic feature for the comparison purpose, which has been used in many previous studies of the BC prediction [11,30–32]. Several studies have shown that not only acoustic features but also visual, and linguistics features are important for the BC prediction [9,22,25]. Thus, more various features for the BC prediction need to be further explored with the temporal feature.

Acknowledgements. We would like to thank the two annotators (K.-H. Min & J.-I. Lim) who diligently supported our study for the interview data. This work was supported by the KIST Institutional Program (2E32282) and by the National Research Council of Science Technology (NST) grant by the Korea government (MSIP) (No. CAP21052-200).

References

1. Bartneck, C., Forlizzi, J.: A design-centred framework for social human-robot interaction. In: RO-MAN 2004, 13th IEEE International Workshop on Robot and Human Interactive Communication (IEEE Catalog No. 04TH8759), pp. 591–594. IEEE (2004)
2. Boersma, P., Weenink, D.: Praat (2023). https://www.fon.hum.uva.nl/praat/. Accessed 08 Feb 2023

3. Breiman, L.: Random forests. Mach. Learn. **45**, 5–32 (2001)
4. Cutrone, P.: A case study examining backchannels in conversations between japanese-british dyads. Multilingua **24**(3), 237–274 (2005). https://doi.org/10.1515/mult.2005.24.3.237
5. Erlang, A.K.: The theory of probabilities and telephone conversations. Nyt. Tidsskr. Mat. Ser. B **20**, 33–39 (1909)
6. Fong, T., Nourbakhsh, I., Dautenhahn, K.: A survey of socially interactive robots. Robot. Auton. Syst. **42**(3–4), 143–166 (2003)
7. Gratch, J., Wang, N., Gerten, J., Fast, E., Duffy, R.: Creating rapport with virtual agents. In: Intelligent Virtual Agents: 7th International Conference, IVA 2007 Paris, France, September 17–19, 2007 Proceedings 7, pp. 125–138 (2007)
8. Hegel, F., Muhl, C., Wrede, B., Hielscher-Fastabend, M., Sagerer, G.: Understanding social robots. In: 2009 Second International Conferences on Advances in Computer-Human Interactions, pp. 169–174. IEEE (2009)
9. Hjalmarsson, A., Oertel, C.: Gaze direction as a back-channel inviting cue in dialogue. In: IVA 2012 Workshop on Realtime Conversational Virtual Agents, vol. 9 (2012)
10. Huang, L., Morency, L.P., Gratch, J.: Learning backchannel prediction model from parasocial consensus sampling: a subjective evaluation. In: Intelligent Virtual Agents: 10th International Conference, IVA 2010, Philadelphia, PA, USA, September 20–22, 2010. Proceedings 10, pp. 159–172 (2010)
11. Hussain, N., Erzin, E., Sezgin, T.M., Yemez, Y.: Training socially engaging robots: modeling backchannel behaviors with batch reinforcement learning. IEEE Trans. Affect. Comput. **13**(4), 1840–1853 (2022)
12. Inden, B., Malisz, Z., Wagner, P., Wachsmuth, I.: Timing and entrainment of multimodal backchanneling behavior for an embodied conversational agent. In: Proceedings of the 15th ACM on International Conference on Multimodal Interaction, pp. 181–188 (2013)
13. Inoue, K., Lala, D., Yamamoto, K., Nakamura, S., Takanashi, K., Kawahara, T.: An attentive listening system with android ERICA: Comparison of autonomous and WOZ interactions. In: Proceedings of the 21th Annual Meeting of the Special Interest Group on Discourse and Dialogue, pp. 118–127 (2020)
14. Kim, S., Seok, S., Choi, J., Lim, Y., Kwak, S.S.: Effects of conversational contexts and forms of non-lexical backchannel on user perception of robots. In: 2021 IEEE/RSJ International Conference on Intelligent Robots and Systems (IROS), pp. 3042–3047 (2021)
15. Lala, D., Milhorat, P., Inoue, K., Ishida, M., Takanashi, K., Kawahara, T.: Attentive listening system with backchanneling, response generation and flexible turn-taking. In: Proceedings of the 18th Annual SIGdial Meeting on Discourse and Dialogue, pp. 127–136 (2017)
16. Li, H.Z.: Backchannel responses as misleading feedback in intercultural discourse. J. Intercult. Commun. Res. **35**(2), 99–116 (2006)
17. Li, H.Z., Cui, Y., Wang, Z.: Backchannel responses and enjoyment of the conversation: the more does not necessarily mean the better. Int. J. Psychol. Stud. **2**(1), 25–37 (2010)
18. Mangold International GmbH: Generalized sequential querier (GSEQ) (2023). https://www.mangold-international.com/en/products/software/gseq.html. Accessed 08 Feb 2023
19. Mao, X., Peng, Y., Xue, Y., Luo, N., Rovetta, A.: Backchannel prediction for mandarin human-computer interaction. IEICE Trans. Inf. Syst. **98**(6), 1228–1237 (2015). https://doi.org/10.1587/transinf.2014EDP7214

20. Marche, T.A., Peterson, C.: On the gender differential use of listener responsiveness. Sex Roles **29**, 795–816 (1993)
21. Mirheidari, B., Blackburn, D., O'Malley, R., Walker, T., Venneri, A., Reuber, M., Christensen, H.: Computational cognitive assessment: Investigating the use of an intelligent virtual agent for the detection of early signs of dementia. In: In ICASSP 2019–2019 IEEE International Conference on Acoustics, Speech and Signal Processing (ICASSP), pp. 2732–2736 (2019)
22. Murray, M., et al.: Learning backchanneling behaviors for a social robot via data augmentation from human-human conversations. In: Conference on Robot Learning, pp. 513–525. PMLR (2022)
23. Park, H.W., Gelsomini, M., Lee, J.J., Breazeal, C.: Telling stories to robots: the effect of backchanneling on a child's storytelling. In: 2017 12th ACM/IEEE International Conference on Human-Robot Interaction, pp. 100–108 (2017)
24. Poppe, R., Truong, K.P., Heylen, D.: Perceptual evaluation of backchannel strategies for artificial listeners. Auton. Agent. Multi-Agent Syst. **27**(2), 235–253 (2013). https://doi.org/10.1007/s10458-013-9219-z
25. Ruede, R., Müller, M., Stüker, S., Waibel, A.: Yeah, Right, Uh-Huh: a deep learning backchannel predictor. In: Eskenazi, M., Devillers, L., Mariani, J. (eds.) Advanced Social Interaction with Agents. LNEE, vol. 510, pp. 247–258. Springer, Cham (2019). https://doi.org/10.1007/978-3-319-92108-2_25
26. Sharifi, S., Azadmanesh, M.: Persian back channel responses in formal versus informal contexts. Linguist. Discov. **10**(2) (2012)
27. Tanaka, H., et al.: Detecting dementia through interactive computer avatars. IEEE J. Transl. Eng. Health Med. **5**, 1–11 (2017). https://doi.org/10.1109/JTEHM.2017.2752152
28. The Language Archive: Elan (2023). https://archive.mpi.nl/tla/elan. Accessed 08 Feb 2023
29. Türker, B.B., Buçinca, Z., Erzin, E., Yemez, Y., Sezgin, T.M.: Analysis of engagement and user experience with a laughter responsive social robot. In: Interspeech, pp. 844–848 (2017)
30. Truong, K.P., Poppe, R., Heylen, D.: A rule-based backchannel prediction model using pitch and pause information. In: Eleventh Annual Conference of the International Speech Communication Association. Citeseer (2010)
31. Türker, B.B., Erzin, E., Yemez, Y., Sezgin, T.M.: Audio-visual prediction of head-nod and turn-taking events in dyadic interactions. In: Interspeech, pp. 1741–1745 (2018)
32. Ward, N., Tsukahara, W.: Prosodic features which cue back-channel responses in English and Japanese. J. Pragmat. **32**(8), 1177–1207 (2000)

Detection of Rarely Occurring Behaviors Based on Human Trajectories and Their Associated Physical Parameters

Hesham M. Shehata[1]([✉]), Nam Do[2], Shunl Inaoka[2], and Trung Tran Quang[2]

[1] Asilla, Inc., 1 Chome-4-2 Nakamachi, Machida, Tokyo, Japan
hesham@asilla.jp
[2] Asilla Vietnam, 3F Hoang Linh Building, No. 6, Lane 82, Duy Tan,
Dich Vong Hau Ward, Cau Giay District, Ha Noi City, Vietnam
{namdo,inaoka,trungtq}@asilla.net

Abstract. The complexity of detecting rarely occurring behaviors through human trajectories is closely related to a lack of data, unclear behavioral characteristics, and complex variations in their related physical parameters (e.g., velocity and orientation angles, etc.). In this context, we propose a methodology to maximize the detection performance of rarely occurring behaviors in public places by investigating the data collection process, trajectory representation based on detected skeleton poses from videos, and the use of 2D (X, Y) trajectory positional data only versus its combination with their associated physical parameters as the input for trajectory learning models. In order to evaluate the proposed method, we studied a rare Japanese behavior in public places called UroKyoro, which is a combination of the two Japanese words Urouro and Kyorokyoro. This behavior includes aimlessly moving while frequently looking in both directions. Since there is a lack of related data from real-life cases, we hired professional actors to role-play the behavior alone or with normal pedestrians moving around. The learning system was trained using limited and augmented data. The trajectory learning system, trained with combined human trajectories and orientation angles following the proposed method, succeeds in detecting the studied behavior with an accuracy of 91.33%, outperforming the accuracy of the trained model using only human 2D (X, Y) trajectories by 4.33%. The results show the effectiveness of the proposed method to detect complex, rarely occurring human behaviors by training the LSTM classifier with a combination of human trajectories and physical parameters. However, the effectiveness of physical parameters on training performance may differ from one case study to another based on behavioral characteristics.

Keywords: Rarely Occurring Behaviors · Trajectory-Related Human Behaviors · Trajectory Learning · Trajectory Associated Physical Parameters · UroKyoro Behavior

A. Al. Ali et al. (Eds.): ICSR 2023, LNAI 14453, pp. 276–293, 2024.
https://doi.org/10.1007/978-981-99-8715-3_24

1 Introduction

In recent years, there has been a need for the use of security robots and autonomous security systems fitted with assistive devices (e.g., cameras and sensors), which are becoming increasingly popular to ensure high security in public places such as shopping malls. However, it is critical to thoroughly assess these systems' performance in recognizing anomalous behavior and maintaining public safety. A study conducted by [1,2] investigated the deployment of robots in public places and discovered that the level of autonomy granted to the robots can have a substantial impact on their capacity to recognize and respond to possible deviant actions. The authors suggested that the level of autonomy be carefully studied and adjusted in order for the robots to make real-time judgments while prioritizing public safety. Furthermore, it is crucial to consider the ethical and legal implications of using autonomous security systems in public spaces. A study by [3] investigated the ethical considerations of using security robots and concluded that it is essential to ensure that the robots are programmed to respect individual privacy and civil liberties. In conclusion, the use of robotic bodyguards in public spaces is a promising development for enhancing security measures. However, it is important to thoroughly evaluate and consider the level of autonomy, movement and action strategies, and ethical and legal implications to ensure that these systems provide a high level of security while also respecting public safety and individual rights.

On the other hand, the contribution of machine learning in the field of social behavior detection is promising and has increased rapidly. The basic information, including human trajectories and their associated physical parameters, should be precisely studied to detect the behaviors successfully. Recent studies rely on videos or sensors in order to extract or formulate trajectory information [4–6]. Usually, trajectory-related normal behaviors in public places can be detected using basic movement information (e.g., a person who is loitering while looking for a shop or waiting for a friend, etc.). However, for abnormal behaviors (e.g., shoplifting cases, etc.), it is difficult to capture and collect their data with high accuracy since they are rare to occur and require special permissions to acquire related information in public places. In addition, the detection process for such behaviors is challenging due to unclear characteristics, complex variations in their related physical parameters, and a lack of high-quality trajectories. In this context, we propose a method to successfully detect rarely occurring human behaviors using an appropriate representation of human trajectories and their associated physical parameters processed from video data. These parameters include human 2D position (X, Y), movement velocities, orientation angles, and other possible physical parameters (e.g., accelerations, deviations, etc.).

Therefore, we investigate the data collection process, trajectory representation based on detected skeleton poses from videos, and the use of trajectory positional data only versus combined positional data with physical parameters for trajectory-based learning approaches. The purpose of this research is to maximize machine learning detection performance of rarely occurring behaviors and to investigate the following research question: "How to achieve high-quality trajectories of rarely occurring behaviors from video data and maximize their detection performance through machine learning?". To answer this question, this study proposes a method to detect rarely occurring behaviors in real life. To implement the proposed method, we study the case of a rarely occurring Japanese behavior in public places called UroKyoro. A combination of Kyorokyoro (to move around restlessly) and Urouro (aimless wandering). Typically, shoplifter behavior is characterized by Kyorokyoro [7]. Security cameras should be equipped with AI software that automatically detects such suspicious activities. The results confirmed that training with combined human trajectories and their associated physical parameters can optimize the detection performance of rarely occurring behaviors.

The contributions of this work are:

- We propose effective analysis of human skeleton poses to precisely formulate human trajectories and confirm the accurate distribution of the physical parameters based on the overall body movements.
- We propose a simple yet effective method for detecting rarely occurring behaviors in public places and achieved a promising detection performance for a case study (UroKyoro behavior) by following a trajectory learning approach and considering the combined input of 2D (X, Y) positional data and their associated physical parameters.
- We apply an effective data augmentation, utilizing the data size through overlapping between samples, to enhance the overall detection performance.

The remaining sections are organized as follows: Sect. 2 discusses the background. Section 3 proposes the methodology for a successful trajectory learning approach for rarely occurring behaviors based on human trajectories and their associated physical parameters. Section 4 presents a case study of rarely occurring "UroKyoro" Japanese behavior. Section 5 shows the results following the proposed methodology. Section 6 discusses the findings of the study based on the results. Finally, Sect. 7 shows our conclusions.

2   Background

2.1   Human Trajectory and Machine Learning

Recent advancements in the field of detection and recognition of trajectory-related human behaviors have showcased the effectiveness of Long Short Term Memories (LSTMs) [8–14], Variational Recurrent Neural Networks (VRNNs) [15], and Gated Recurrent Units (GRUs) [16]. These neural network architectures have proven highly capable of sequence-to-sequence prediction tasks. For instance, in [4] Lee et al. employed RNNs to forecast future motion positions based on scene context and agent interactions. Su et al. [5] introduced a methodology utilizing LSTMs in conjunction with recurrent Gaussian processes to characterize crowd transitions and uncertainties in human trajectory prediction. Nevertheless, it's worth noting that this approach doesn't distinguish between pedestrians and exclusively considers the presence of surrounding pedestrians. These methodologies deviate from the traditional social force model, where social forces are calculated based on standard physical parameters [17–19]. Furthermore, they predominantly address normal behaviors, failing to account for abnormal behaviors or the potential benefits of integrating physical parameters with trajectory data. Only a limited number of research papers, such as App-LSTM [6], have explored models that generate an agent's trajectory towards a group of agents while considering orientation angles. Given this landscape, our research aims to fill the gap by developing models that not only excel at detecting rarely occurring behaviors based on movement trajectories but also leverage related physical parameters to enhance their predictive capabilities.

2.2 Social Behaviors and Machine Learning via Visual Approaches

In recent years, computer vision techniques, including those discussed in [20] by Wu et al., and supervised machine learning models, which leverage stand-alone Convolutional Neural Networks (CNNs) as presented in the work of Zamboni et al. [21] or combine them with Long Short-Term Memory networks (LSTMs) as demonstrated by Quan et al. [22] and Zhong et al. [23], have been extensively employed for learning social behaviors from human trajectories. These methods focus on detecting human trajectories effectively, building upon computer vision methodologies described in the works of Alahi et al. [8], Yi et al. [24], and Su et al. [5], who incorporated CNN architectures following the principles laid out in the computer vision literature [25, 26]. For instance, Yi et al. [24] utilized a CNN-based architecture to model pedestrian behavior, predicting their walking patterns and goals. Furthermore, various approaches have addressed the detection of abnormal behaviors in public spaces, such as fighting or kicking, by employing image processing from videos in conjunction with CNNs, autoencoders, and LSTM networks for behavior detection, as described in the works of Tay et al. [27], Ribeiro et al. [28], Ko et al. [29], Xu et al. [30], and Pennisi et al. [31]. However, these approaches do not delve into the strategies used to formulate trajectories, which is a challenging aspect due to the necessity of minimizing detection errors and enhancing trajectory representations based on overall body movement.

In addition to the above-mentioned methods, alternative approaches have been explored for behavior detection. Nater et al. [32] utilized the tracker tree method to specify actions at higher levels, while Lv et al. [33] employed the Pyramid Match Kernel algorithm for feature matching. Du et al. [34] proposed a recognition technique for low-moral behaviors, such as smoking or using mobile phones in public spaces, based on depth skeleton data obtained from Kinect sensors, achieving a maximum accuracy of 90%. Their approach focused on recognizing low-moral behaviors in public spaces by using depth data and extracted skeletons from Microsoft Kinect v2, conducting experiments with a group of 20 individuals aged between 22 and 54. Ko et al. [29] developed a CNN framework incorporating a Kalman filter to classify various behaviors. They fed images into the framework and transferred the output to another LSTM structure, primarily aiming to enable instant detection of risky behavior in video surveillance systems, specifically for socially disadvantaged groups like the elderly, using standard RGB images. Their models were trained on the "UT-Interaction-Data" dataset, containing video clips with multiple moving human subjects engaged in six different activities: "hand shaking,"' "hugging," "kicking," "pointing," "punching," and "pushing." The maximum reported recall and precision values were 0.95 and 0.97 for kicking behavior, respectively. Although these approaches studied the most common abnormal behaviors in public places, they did not investigate the quality of the skeleton data or the influence of their distributions on the physical parameters.

3   Methodology

Detection of rarely occurring behaviors in crowded public places is challenging due to complex variations in their trajectory-related physical parameters, a lack of high-quality trajectories, and unclear behavioral characteristics, e.g., loitering without clear intentions, shoplifting, etc. To achieve successful detection of these behaviors, the possible shortest detection duration should be considered for each sample. Hence, the tracking process should consider the results based on the continuously detected samples. A detection threshold should be tuned to confirm the abnormal behavior based on the detected number of samples within a specific duration. This helps to precisely identify and differentiate the abnormal occurrence from deviated normal behaviors on certain occasions or suspicious individuals who interfere with or align with normal people to use the same pattern of motion.

Human trajectory and their related physical parameters (e.g., positional noise, velocity, etc.) play an important role in achieving successful detection performance for rarely occurring human behaviors. Recent research studies have failed to propose efficient processing approaches to strengthen trajectory representation and minimize detection errors in video data. Hence, there is a need to investigate the effect of these parameters on the learning process. To solve these problems, we propose below steps and subsections to follow towards successful detection of rarely occurring behaviors based on the appropriate representation of human trajectories from video data and consideration of their associated physical parameters.

1. Collection of rarely occurring trajectory-related human behavior data from real life However, if it's difficult to collect related behavioral data, a role-playing experiment should be followed based on behavioral observations from real-life cases.
2. Strengthen trajectory representation and minimize detection errors by following proper processing of the collected data.
3. Deciding on an appropriate time series learning structure using 2D trajectory positional data along with the minimum possible sample size.
4. Maximize the detection performance of the rarely occurring behavior to be distinguished from normal behavior by considering combined input features

for training (2D trajectory positional data along with potential physical parameters).

5. Data augmentation by overlapping between samples to achieve the best possible performance of the trained model.

3.1 Collecting Data

Collection of rare human behavioral data should take place in real-world public areas using genuine cases. This is determined by a number of elements, including the likelihood of behavior occurring in public places, the ability to acquire reasonably large data sets, and the licenses to collect data in specified locations. If these conditions cannot be met, a potential alternate solution can include a role-playing experiment. The collecting method necessitates a proper choice of data collection location based on the desired behavior, an effective collection system, and precise observations for behavioral features in real life.

In a role-playing experiment, participants should be guided to act out the behavior based on the observed behavioral characteristics from real life while interacting freely with other pedestrians and obstacles in the environment (e.g., changing movement directions, slower or faster walking) based on the scenario or situation. In addition, to ensure that the data are as diverse as possible, the participants should be asked to change the starting point for each trial.

Human trajectories in two dimensions (X and Y) can be acquired using vision or non-vision tracking technologies. Non-vision-based tracking approaches address social privacy problems. However, in public settings, the related collection system using sensors, such as Li-DARs, might be complex and expensive to install. To overcome this problem, vision-based systems using cameras are cost-effective, and recent related identification algorithms can disguise the faces of each individual in the scene. The discovered data mostly consists of skeleton poses of people in the scene, which should be processed effectively in order to improve human trajectory representation. Figure 1 shows an example of detected skeleton poses from a moving pedestrian using Asilla product.

3.2 Strengthen Trajectory Representation

Reasonable human trajectory formulation based on collected videos via cameras is challenging due to detection errors, hidden poses on certain occasions (e.g., lower body poses because of sitting on chairs), etc. The detection performance via videos depends on the deployed algorithm, which detects and extracts human body poses. Hence, there is a need to strengthen the trajectory representation by considering the best possible distribution of associated physical parameters (e.g., positional noise, velocity, etc.) to reflect the actual overall body movement through clearly visible poses and minimize detection errors. In this context, there is a need to analyze formulated trajectories and their associated physical parameters based on different types of skeleton poses to confirm the best key point to formulate human trajectories.

Fig. 1. Example of detected skeleton poses using Asilla product

3.3 Learning Framework

The learning framework should be a fast, light model that can successfully learn sequence-to-sequence data. In this context, recurrent neural network architectures have proven highly capable in related prediction tasks. For instance, Long Short Term Memories (LSTMs) [8–14], Variational Recurrent Neural Networks (VRNNs) [15], and Gated Recurrent Units (GRUs) [16] have showcased the effectiveness in the field of detection and recognition of trajectories data. Then, the learning framework should be selected from these recent approaches. In addition, the number of layers and neurons should be minimized as much as possible while still showing promising detection performance.

3.4 Maximizing Detection Performance

To maximize the detection performance of rarely occurring behaviors, there is a need to learn behavioral-related features. Then, training data should include potential trajectory-related features closely relate to their physical parameters (e.g., velocity, orientation angle, etc.). These parameters should be fed to the learning framework along with basic trajectory information (2D of X and Y poses) to successfully detect complex hidden features (e.g., a person changing walking direction inappropriately while walking in crowded areas or continuously changing the moving pattern with unknown intentions). In addition, data augmentation by overlapping between samples can be a final step to achieving the best possible detection performance.

4   A Case Study of UroKyoro Behavior in Public Places

There is always a need to enhance public security by detecting abnormal behaviors at an early stage. To do so, we selected a rarely occurring Japanese behavior in public places called UroKyoro. The word itself is a combination of the other two Japanese words, Urouro (aimless wandering) and Kyorokyoro (to move around restlessly). The behavior involves a person moving around without a specific target or objective while behaving suspiciously by always changing the angle of view to different directions (i.e., looking in the right and left directions) and exploring their surroundings (i.e., loitering). It's considered an early stage of other suspicious behaviors (e.g., shoplifting) [7]. The studied behavior mostly occurs in public places (e.g., shopping malls), including normal pedestrians moving around the person who is behaving with the targeted behavior.

4.1 Data Collection

Due to the lack of UroKyoro behavior data from real-life cases, we conducted a field experiment in a closed environment as an alternative to a public place (e.g., a shopping mall) (as shown in Figs. 2 and 3) by hiring professional actors to role-play the behavior alone and with normal pedestrians moving around. Since the Asilla product is adapted for implementation on security cameras in public places, the collected data included recorded videos via similar setting for each scenario, with several trials lasting a total of twenty-four minutes, while every trial lasted for around two minutes. Different camera angles (e.g., 25, 30, and 40°) are considered so that we can ensure diverse trials as much as possible. Two professional actors were asked to play the role of UroKyoro behavior freely from different locations for every trial based on the behavior definition and their imagination about it, e.g., moving around while continuously changing the angle of view, stopping for a while rotating around the body, and loitering. Since our target is to distinguish UroKyoro behavior from normal pedestrians moving around, we also collected normal data for real pedestrians in a shopping mall (Tokyo, Japan) with the same size as the other class (normal class data is collected in two corridors with people moving in two opposite directions and includes straight-line movement, loitering, changing movement direction, slowing down, entering or exiting shops, etc.). The environment included familiar obstacles in a shopping mall (e.g., separating stands, public chairs, etc.). Unfortunately, we could not share pictures from the public environment due to policies and privacy concerns.

4.2 Trajectory Representation

We used the Asilla product to detect and extract the skeleton poses for humans in the collected videos. It include the following 10 poses: nose, neck, average ankles (right and left), average shoulders, average elbows, average wrists, average hips, average knees, average eyes, and average ears. To achieve a reasonable formulation of human trajectory using the detected poses from the videos, we analyzed trajectories in the collected data using each pose value (X, Y) separately, then compared the distribution of absolute positional noises (in terms of pixels) and absolute velocities (in terms of pixels/second) versus the overall average values for the whole body movement. The concept that we followed to

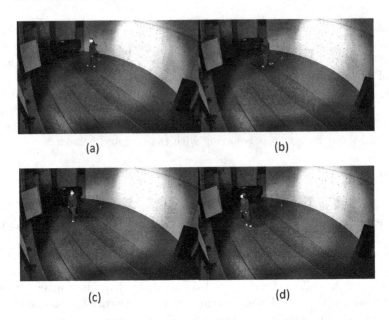

Fig. 2. Field experiment from different scenes (a, b, c, and d) in a closed environment where an actor is role-playing the UroKyoro behavior alone

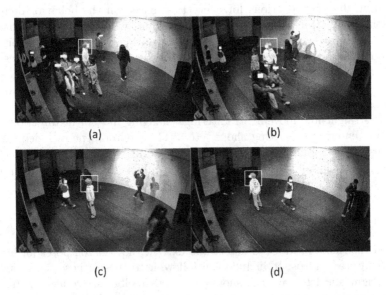

Fig. 3. Field experiment from different scenes (a, b, c, and d) in a closed environment where an actor (labelled in red) is role-playing the UroKyoro behavior with normal pedestrians moving around (Color figure online)

estimate trajectory noise (as shown in Fig. 4) is to calculate the relative distance between the middle points in the actual trajectory and the fake trajectory (straight line between the first and last point) every specific duration (e.g., 5 s).

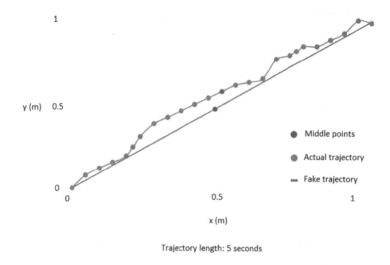

Trajectory length: 5 seconds

Fig. 4. Noise estimation process

Tables 1 and 2 show the average values for positional noise and velocities. The average noise ranges from neck poses show the closest value (29.86 pixels) to the overall average noise from all poses (31.26 pixels), while the absolute average velocities from hip poses (27.06 pixels/s) seem to show the closest value to the overall average velocity from all poses (27 pixels/s). However, the quality of the detected neck poses is better than that of hip poses due to the fact that humans upper body sections are almost visible and clear in most cases. In addition, the average absolute velocity ranges vary within a too small range [26.42 to 27.78 pixels per second], which makes it difficult to consider specific poses to represent the best velocity distribution. Based on that, we decided to use neck poses to formulate the human trajectory from our data. Figures 5 and 6 show a couple of 2D trajectory plots using neck poses for UroKyoro and normal behaviors (5 s per sample).

5   Results

We include in this section the training results following the LSTM training structure (explained in the next subsection). Based on our behavioral observations on UroKyoro and several training trials using different sample sizes, we found that 5 s is the minimum possible duration to include most of the related characteristics, and it showed acceptable results. Based on that, a series of five-second windows (26 frames per window) of the UroKyoro trajectory and the normal

Table 1. Average Positional Noise for All Poses, Ordered from Maximum to Minimum

Pose Name	Average Positional Noise (in pixels)
Eyes	37.07
Nose	36.68
Ears	35.99
Neck	29.86
Shoulders	29.52
Wrists	29.44
Elbows	29.29
Hips	28.57
Ankles	28.34
Knees	27.82
Average for All	31.26

Table 2. Average Velocity for All Poses Ordered from Maximum to Minimum

Pose Name	Average Velocity (in pixels/second)
Eyes	27.78
Nose	27.64
Ears	27.55
Hips	27.06
Knees	26.93
Wrists	26.77
Elbows	26.77
Ankles	26.67
Neck	26.44
Shoulders	26.42
Average for All	27

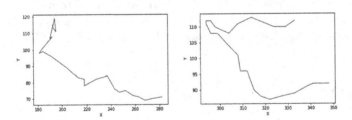

Fig. 5. a couple of 2D (X, Y in pixels) trajectory plots using neck poses for UroKyoro behavior (5 s per sample)

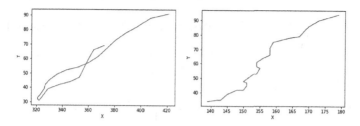

Fig. 6. a couple of 2D (X, Y in pixels) trajectory plots using neck poses for normal behavior (5 s per sample)

trajectory are fed to the network. For the UroKyoro class, we split the processed data from the videos with the single UroKyoro person into 90% for training and 10% for validation, while for evaluation (testing), we used the processed data from the videos, which include normal pedestrians moving around our targeted behavior. On the other hand, all normal class data is collected from a shopping mall and split for training, validation, and evaluation with the same size as the other UroKyoro class. In addition, to avoid over-fitting, a dropout of 0.1 is used after each LSTM layer. We also monitored the validation loss every 50 epochs to stop the training when there was no enhancement in performance.

5.1 Training Details

LSTMs demonstrated promising performance in various applications when trained with time series data [5,6,8]. Based on that, we followed a LSTM-supervised training structure as shown in Fig. 7. The training is performed using Python and PyTorch, where a series of 2D windowed trajectories (X, Y) are fed to the network with scaled samples of five seconds (26 frames per window) as a single window, where each window consists of the UroKyoro or normal pedestrian trajectory. The size of the data used for training is balanced (50% normal, 50% UroKyoro). The applied learning rate is 0.0001, while the optimizer is RMS. Two fully connected LSTM layers are used (512 units), while the classifier layer activation function is "RelU" (256 units) to finally distinguish between UroKyoro and normal behaviors (2 classes).

5.2 Baseline

The baseline is trained using only 2D (X, Y) positional data (406 windows) by following the presented LSTM network structure to be compared with the combined (i.e., considering additional training inputs, "physical parameters") and augmented (i.e., increasing data size) models, which are explained in the following subsections. The resultant testing accuracy is 87% (testing data in 300 windows).

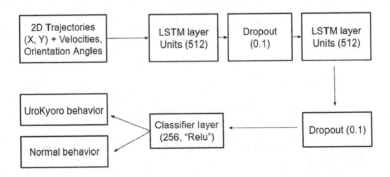

Fig. 7. The LSTM network structure distinguishes UroKyoro from normal behavior

5.3   Combined Features

To successfully detect complex behavioral characteristics, we considered training using combined input features by feeding absolute velocities (in pixels/second) and orientation angles (in degrees) along with 2D (X, Y) trajectory positional data to the training structure. Velocities and orientation angles are calculated based on the absolute position between every frame and the following one, so that finally every frame has its own 2D (X, Y) absolute position along with the absolute velocity and orientation angle. The results showed that orientation angle is a powerful factor to enhance the detection of the UroKyoro class. Also, combining all features together showed better evaluation performance, up to 90.33%. Table 3 shows the overall results achieved.

Table 3. Training Results Using Combined Features

Input	Training	Validation	Testing
X, Y	100%	97.50%	87%
X, Y, Velocity	100%	95%	88.66%
X, Y, Theta	98.09%	95%	89.66%
X, Y, Velocity, Theta	98.91%	92.50%	90.33%

5.4   Data Augmentation

We augmented the data by following five rounds of overlapping between the five-second samples with a step of 1 s for every round to check the effectiveness of increasing the data size on the detection performance. The total size of the augmented data is 2380 windows. In this case, the improvement in the evaluation (testing) performance is shown when considering training inputs as (X, Y, Theta) up to 91.33%. Table 4 shows the corresponding results.

Table 4. Training Results Using Augmented Data

Data Size	Training	Validation	Testing
406	98.09%	95%	89.66%
2380	99.35%	96.22%	91.33%

The lowest number of failure cases to detect UroKyoro behavior (7 samples) is shown from the model, which is trained using 2D positional data along with orientation angles (X, Y, and Theta). The confusion matrix for evaluated (tested) samples is shown in Fig. 8. It is obvious from the matrix results that the model detects UroKyoro behavior with good performance. The majority of failure cases are caused by normal pedestrians' confusing trajectories, which are similar to UroKyoro trajectory shapes on certain occasions, while a minority of failure cases are caused by UroKyoro trajectories, which are similar to those of normal pedestrians. Figure 9 shows a couple of trials of the failure cases.

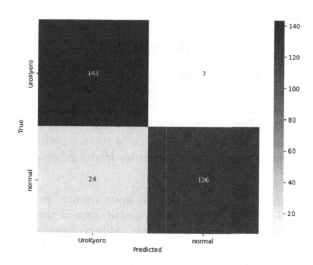

Fig. 8. Confusion matrix for evaluated data

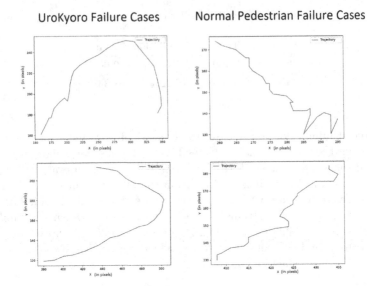

Trajectory Samples (5 seconds "26 frames" / each)

Fig. 9. Samples from failure cases

6   Discussions

Based on research findings and our UroKyoro case study, we confirmed that the proposed approach resulted in promising detection performance for rarely occurring behaviors by developing a trajectory learning model using combined training features:

- The proposed analysis of human skeleton poses resulted in precise trajectory formulation and confirmed the accurate distribution of the physical parameters based on the overall body movements. This resulted in a realistic representation of human trajectories from the collected video data.
- Velocity and orientation angle have a promising effect on enhancing the detection of rarely occurring behaviors. However, combining all parameters together for training could not be an effective approach to enhancing detection performance. This is due to the fact that related characteristics for every behavior differ from other ones. For instance, orientation angle seems to be the most powerful parameter to enhance the detection of UroKyoro behavior.

This is the first research study to focus on analyzing human skeleton poses to formulate precise trajectories with accurate distribution of the physical parameters and investigating the effect of trajectory-related physical parameters (e.g., velocities and orientation angles, etc.) on the detection performance of rarely occurring behaviors by following different combinations of training inputs along with 2D (X, Y) positional data. In this context, the research methodology and findings should generalize to other complex, rarely occurring behaviors if their characteristics are closely related to human movement. In addition, since the data are collected from different angles of view, the approach should generalize in the case of implementing security robots fitted with cameras in public places.

The limitations of the proposed method include:

- The detection accuracy of trajectory-learned models can be affected by the quality of the detected poses from videos.
- Behavioral trajectories may lack diversity in the data due to the collection of data in specific environments. Data collection from several environments may be needed based on the focused behavior.

Although the accuracy reported in [34] or [29] to detect abnormal actions is rather high (around and over 90%), most of the investigated behavioral characteristics do not relate to trajectory shape and are closely related to the whole skeleton (e.g., kicking, smoking, talking on the phone, etc.). Up to our knowledge, this is the first focused research on trajectory-related, rarely occurring behaviors. The accuracy reported from our case study is promising and reaches 91.33%. It shows the effect of trajectory-related physical parameters (velocity and orientation angle) on the detection performance of the studied case of UroKyoro behavior. Future work includes studying the effect of other physical parameters (e.g., acceleration, deceleration, etc.) on the detection performance and validating the research findings based on real-life case studies. Also, the Asilla team will consider collecting datasets using different scenarios of rarely occurring behavior, collecting data under similar conditions with different environmental shapes and sizes, training the network using these different datasets, and comparing the results.

7 Conclusions

We propose a new approach towards successful detection of rarely occurring behaviors in public places by strengthening human trajectory formulation from videos and developing trajectory learning models by following combined training inputs of 2D positional data and their associated physical parameters (e.g., velocity and orientation angle). To evaluate the proposed method, we studied a rare Japanese behavior in public places called UroKyoro. The behavior involves moving around while repeatedly looking in the right and left directions without clear intention or purpose. Since there is a lack of related data from real-life cases, we hired actors to role-play the behavior. The best detection performance of the studied behavior showed an accuracy of 91.33%. Also, we compared the detection performance by training using different inputs of physical parameters along with 2D (X, Y) positional data and confirmed that the performance may differ based on the focused behavioral characteristics.

Data Availability Statement. The datasets generated during and/or analyzed during the current study are available from the corresponding author on reasonable request.

Conflict of Interest. The authors declare that they have no conflicts of interest.

References

1. Beer, J.M., Fisk, A.D., Rogers, W.A.: Toward a framework for levels of robot autonomy in human-robot interaction. J. Hum.-Robot Interact. **3** (2014)
2. Nahavandi, S.: Trusted autonomy between humans and robots. IEEE Syst. Man Cybern. Mag. (2017)
3. Lin, P., Abney, K., Bekey, G.: Robot ethics: mapping the issues for a mechanized world. Artif. Intelli. J. **175** (2011)
4. Lee, N., Choi, W., Vernaza, P., Choy, C.B., Torr, P.H.S., Chandraker, M.: Desire: distant future prediction in dynamic scenes with interacting agents. In: Proceedings of the IEEE Conference on Computer Vision and Pattern Recognition, pp. 336–345 (2017)
5. Su, H., Zhu, J., Dong, Y., Zhang, B.: Forecast the plausible paths in crowd scenes. In: IJCAI, vol. 1 (2017)
6. Yang, F., Peters, C.: App-LSTM: data-driven generation of socially acceptable trajectories for approaching small groups of agents. In: Proceedings of the 7th International Conference on Human-Agent Interaction, pp. 144–152 (2019)
7. AI Guardman' system aims to cut shoplifting losses, JAPANTODAY. https://japantoday.com/category/features/kuchikomi/vigilant-%27ai-guardman%27-system-aims-to-cut-shoplifting-losses. Accessed 20 June 2018
8. Alahi, A., Goel, K., Ramanathan, V., Robicquet, A., Fei-Fei, L., Savarese, S.: Social LSTM: human trajectory prediction in crowded spaces. In: Proceedings of the IEEE Conference on Computer Vision and Pattern Recognition, pp. 961–971 (2016)
9. Sun, L., Yan, Z., Mellado, S.M., Hanheide, M., Duckett, T.: 3DOF pedestrian trajectory prediction learned from long-term autonomous mobile robot deployment data. In: IEEE International Conference on Robotics and Automation (ICRA), pp. 5942–5948 (2018)
10. Shi, K., Zhu, Y., Pan, H.: A novel model based on deep learning for Pedestrian detection and Trajectory prediction. In: IEEE 8th Joint International Information Technology and Artificial Intelligence Conference (ITAIC), pp. 592–598 (2019)
11. Xu, Y., Piao, Z., Gao, S.: Encoding crowd interaction with deep neural network for pedestrian trajectory prediction. In: Proceedings of the IEEE Conference on Computer Vision and Pattern Recognition, pp. 5275–5284 (2018)
12. Crivellari, A., Beinat, E.: LSTM-based deep learning model for predicting individual mobility traces of short-term foreign tourists. Sustain. J. **12**, 349 (2021)
13. Ono, T., Kanamaru, T.: Prediction of pedestrian trajectory based on long short-term memory of data. In: 21st IEEE International Conference on Control, Automation and Systems (ICCAS), pp. 1676–1679 (2021)
14. de Freitas, N.C.A., da Silva, T.L.C., de Macêdo, J.A.F., Junior, L.M., Cordeiro, M.G.: Using deep learning for trajectory classification. In: Proceedings of the 13th International Conference on Agents and Artificial Intelligence (ICAART 2021) (2021)
15. Brito, B., Zhu, H., Pan, W., Alonso-Mora, J.: Social-VRNN: one-shot multi-modal trajectory prediction for interacting pedestrians. arXiv preprint arXiv:2010.09056 (2020)
16. Zhang, Y., Zheng, L.: Pedestrian trajectory prediction with MLP-social-GRU. In: 13th International Conference on Machine Learning and Computing, pp. 368–372 (2021)

17. Helbing, D., Molnar, P.: Social force model for pedestrian dynamics. Phys. Rev. E J. **51** (1995)
18. Luber, M., Stork, J.A., Tipaldi, G.D., Arras, K.O.: People tracking with human motion predictions from social forces. In: IEEE International Conference on Robotics and Automation, pp. 464–469 (2010)
19. Mehran, R., Oyama, A., Shah, M.: Abnormal crowd behavior detection using social force model. In: IEEE Conference on Computer Vision and Pattern Recognition, pp. 935–942 (2009)
20. Wu, S.: Approach to auto-recognition of human trajectory in squares using machine learning-based methods-an application of the Yolo-v3 and the DeepSORT algorithm. CUMINCAD, CAAD research (2021)
21. Zamboni, S., Kefato, Z.T., Girdzijauskas, S., Norén, C., Dal Col, L.: Pedestrian trajectory prediction with convolutional neural networks. Pattern Recogn. J. **121** (2022)
22. Quan, R., Zhu, L., Wu, Y., Yang, Y.: Holistic LSTM for pedestrian trajectory prediction. IEEE Trans. Image Process. J. **30**, 3229–3239 (2021)
23. Zhong, Jianqi and Sun, Hao and Cao, Wenming and He, Zhihai: Pedestrian motion trajectory prediction with stereo-based 3D deep pose estimation and trajectory learning. IEEE Access **8**, 23480–23486 (2020)
24. Yi, S., Li, H., Wang, X.: Pedestrian behavior understanding and prediction with deep neural networks. In: Leibe, B., Matas, J., Sebe, N., Welling, M. (eds.) ECCV 2016. LNCS, vol. 9905, pp. 263–279. Springer, Cham (2016). https://doi.org/10.1007/978-3-319-46448-0_16
25. Ren, S., He, K., Girshick, R., Sun, J.: Faster R-CNN: towards real-time object detection with region proposal networks. Adv. Neural Inf. Process. Syst. J. **28** (2015)
26. Krizhevsky, A., Sutskever, I., Hinton, G.E.: Imagenet classification with deep convolutional neural networks. Adv. Neural Inf. Process. Syst. J. **25** (2012)
27. Tay, N.C., Connie, T., Ong, T.S., Goh, K.O.M., Teh, P.S.: A robust abnormal behavior detection method using convolutional neural network. In: Computational Science and Technology. LNEE, vol. 481, pp. 37–47. Springer, Singapore (2019). https://doi.org/10.1007/978-981-13-2622-6_4
28. Ribeiro, M., Lazzaretti, A.E., Lopes, H.S.: A study of deep convolutional auto-encoders for anomaly detection in videos. Pattern Recogn. Lett. J. **105**, 13–22 (2018)
29. Ko, K.-E., Sim, K.-B.: Deep convolutional framework for abnormal behavior detection in a smart surveillance system. Eng. Appl. Artif. Intell. J. **67**, 226–234 (2018)
30. Xu, D., Yan, Y., Ricci, E., Sebe, N.: Detecting anomalous events in videos by learning deep representations of appearance and motion. Comput. Vision Image Underst. J. **156**, 117–127 (2017)
31. Pennisi, A., Bloisi, D.D., Iocchi, L.: Online real-time crowd behavior detection in video sequences. Comput. Vision Image Underst. J. **144**, 166–176 (2016)
32. Nater, F., Grabner, H., Van Gool, L.: Exploiting simple hierarchies for unsupervised human behavior analysis. In: IEEE Computer Society Conference on Computer Vision and Pattern Recognition, pp. 2014–2021 (2010)
33. Lv, F., Nevatia, R.: Single view human action recognition using key pose matching and Viterbi path searching. In: IEEE Conference on Computer Vision and Pattern Recognition, pp. 1–8 (2007)
34. Du, K., Kaczmarek, T., Brščić, D., Kanda, T.: Recognition of rare low-moral actions using depth data. Sens. J. **20** (2020)

Improving of Robotic Virtual Agent's Errors Accepted by Agent's Reaction and Human's Preference

Takahiro Tsumura[1,2]([envelope]) [ID] and Seiji Yamada[1,2] [ID]

[1] Department of Informatics, The Graduate University for Advanced Studies, SOKENDAI, Tokyo, Japan
[2] Digital Content and Media Sciences Research Division, National Institute of Informatics, Tokyo, Japan
takahiro-gs@nii.ac.jp

Abstract. One way to improve the relationship between humans and anthropomorphic agents is to have humans empathize with the agents. In this study, we focused on a task between an agent and a human in which the agent makes a mistake. To investigate significant factors for designing a robotic agent that can promote humans' empathy, we experimentally examined the hypothesis that agent reaction and human's preference affect human empathy and acceptance of the agent's mistakes. In this experiment, participants allowed the agent to manage their schedules by answering the questions they were asked. The experiment consisted of a four-condition, three-factor mixed design with agent reaction, selected agent's body color for human's preference, and pre- and post-task as factors. The results showed that agent reaction and human's preference did not affect empathy toward the agent but did allow the agent to make mistakes. It was also shown that empathy for the agent decreased when the agent made a mistake on the task. The results of this study provide a way to influence impressions of the robotic virtual agent's behaviors, which are increasingly used in society.

Keywords: human-agent interaction · empathy agent · human's preference

1 Introduction

Humans use a variety of tools in their daily lives. They become attached to these tools and sometimes treat them like humans. The Media Equation claims that humans treat artifacts like humans [19]. It has been shown that humans have the same feelings toward artifacts as they do toward other humans. In fact, there are examples of people empathizing with artifacts in the same way that humans empathize with humans. Typical examples include cleaning robots [13], pet-type robots [13], characters in competitive video games [25], and anthropomorphic agents [6] that provide services such as online shopping and help desks. These robots, AI, and anthropomorphic agents are generally defined as agents. On the other hand, There are certain types of humans who cannot accept agents [10,11]. For example, Nomura et al. [9] conducted a field study to address the issue of children's violence against robots, interviewing visiting children with severely abusive behaviors, including physical contact, to determine the reasons for the abuse. As a result, the majority of the reasons for the abuse were either because they were interested in the robot's reactions or because they enjoyed the abuse and considered the robot to be a human-like being. About half of the children also believed that the robot could perceive their abusive behavior. Currently, such agents are already being used in human society and coexist with humans.

Agents used in society often perform tasks with humans. At times, an agent may get the task wrong. When an agent makes a mistake on a task, many humans lower their expectations and trust in the agent. However, we often develop agents so that they do not make mistakes, but rarely do we take an approach that preserves the human's impression of the agent when it actually makes a mistake. One way to do so is to have the human empathize with the agent. When agents are used as tools, they may not need empathy, but when they are used in place of humans, being empathized with by humans can help build a smooth relationship.

Humans and anthropomorphic agents already interact in a variety of tasks. For a human to develop a good relationship with an agent, empathy toward the agent is necessary. Empathy makes it easier for humans to take positive action toward an agent and to accept it [23–25].

Although various factors have been studied that cause empathy, including verbal and nonverbal information, situations, and relationships, this study focuses on situations in which the robotic virtual agent (RVA) gets the task wrong and experimentally examines how the agent's reaction and the agent's human's preference affect empathy. The empathy investigated in this study is human empathy toward the agent, and we investigated changes in impressions of the agent used in the experiment.

2   Related Work

In the field of psychology, empathy has been the focus of much attention and research. Omdahl [14] classified empathy into three main categories: (1) affective empathy, which is an emotional response to another person's emotional state, (2) cognitive empathy, which is a cognitive understanding of another person's emotional state, and (3) empathy that includes both of the above. Preston and De Waal [18] proposed that at the heart of empathic responses is a mechanism that allows the observer access to the subjective emotional state of the subject. The Perception-Action Model (PAM) was defined by them to unify the differences in empathy. They defined empathy as a total of three types: (a) sharing or being affected by the emotional states of others, (b) evaluating the reasons for emotional states, and (c) the ability to identify and incorporate the perspectives of others.

Various questionnaires are used as measures of empathy, but we used the Interpersonal Reactivity Index (IRI). IRI, also used in the field of psychology, is used to investigate the characteristics of empathy [4]. There is another questionnaire, the Empathy Quotient (EQ) [2], but we did not use it in our study because we wanted to investigate which categories of empathy were affected after experiencing the task.

In the fields of human-agent interaction (HAI) and human-robot interaction (HRI), empathy between humans and agents or robots is studied. The following studies have been conducted in various areas of HRI. Salem et al. [21] examined the effects of robot hand and arm gestures on attribution of typical human characteristics, robot liking, shared sense of reality, and future contact intentions after interaction with the robot. As a result, when the robot used gestures, the robot was more anthropomorphic, participants perceived the robot as more likable, reported that the robot shared more of their reality, and increased their future contact intentions than when the robot did not use gestures. This effect was particularly pronounced when the robot's gestures were partially mismatched with speech. Leite et al. [7] conducted a long-term study in elementary schools to present and evaluate an empathy model for a social robot that interacts with children over a long period of time. The empathy model developed had a positive impact on the long-term interaction between the child and the robot. Ratings of social presence, engagement, support, and self-awareness remained similar after 5 weeks.

Rossi et al. [20] hypothesized that the severity and timing of the consequences of the robot's various types of misbehavior during interaction may have different effects on users' attitudes toward household robots. They concluded that there is a correlation between the magnitude of errors made by the robot and the corresponding loss of trust in the robot by humans. They measured children's perceptions of social presence, engagement, and social support. Mathur et al. [8] present a first approach to modeling user empathy elicited during interaction with a robot agent. They collected a new dataset from a novel interaction context in which participants listen to a robotic storyteller. Johanson et al. [6] examined whether the use of verbal empathic statements and head nodding by a robot during video-recorded interactions between a healthcare robot and a patient could improve participants' trust and satisfaction. The results showed that the health care robot's empathetic statements significantly increased participants' perceptions of the robot's empathy, trust, and satisfaction, and reduced their distrust of the robot.

In addition, the following studies have been conducted in the field of HAI. Okanda et al. [13] focused on appearance and investigated Japanese adults' beliefs about friendship and morality toward robots. They examined whether the appearances of robots (i.e., humanoid, dog-like, oval-shaped) differed in relation to their animistic tendencies and empathy. Samrose et al. [22] designed a protocol to elicit user boredom to investigate whether empathic conversational agents can help reduce boredom. With the help of two conversational agents, an empathic agent and a non-empathic agent, in a Wizard-of-Oz setting, they attempted to reduce the user's boredom. Al Farisi et al. [1] believe that in order for chatbots to have human-like cues, it is necessary to apply the concepts of human-computer interaction (HCI) to chatbots and compare the empathy of two chatbots, one with anthropomorphic design cues (ADC), and one without. Tsumura and Yamada [23] focused on tasks between agents and humans, experimentally examining the hypothesis that task difficulty and task content promote human empathy. We also considered the design of empathy factors from previous studies of anthropomorphic agents using empathy. Tsumura and Yamada [24] focused on self-disclosure from agents to humans in order to enhance human empathy toward anthropomorphic agents, and they experimentally investigated the potential for self-disclosure by agents to promote human empathy. Tsumura and Yamada [25] also focused on tasks in which humans and agents engage in a variety of interactions, and they investigated the properties of agents that have a significant impact on human empathy toward them.

Paiva defined the relationship between human beings and empathic agents, referred to as empathy agents, as designed in previous HAI and HRI research. As a definition of empathy between an anthropomorphic agent or robot and a human, Paiva represented empathy agents in two different ways and illustrated them [15–17]: A) targets to be empathized with by humans and B) observers who empathize with humans. In this study, we use the empathic target agent to promote human empathy.

3   Experimental Methods

3.1   Experimental Goals and Design

The purpose of this study is to investigate whether human empathy toward an agent is affected by the agent's reaction and human's preference during interaction with an robotic virtual agent (RVA). It will then investigate whether agents can be forgiven when they make mistakes. We believe that this research will facilitate the use of agents in human society by influencing human empathy. In addition, knowing the factors that allow agents to make mistakes will be useful for future use of agents in society. For these purposes, we formulated two hypotheses.

H1: Agent's reaction and human's preference affect human empathy toward agents.

H2: Agent's reaction and human's preference affect human acceptance of agent mistakes.

We arrived at this hypothesis because previous studies have shown that agent reactions (facial expressions and gestures) affect human empathy [17,25]. The intent of the human preferences is also to examine whether the addition of personal preferences for agents by humans affects their empathy for agents and their acceptance of agents' task errors.

Similarly, this study focuses on whether agents' mistakes are acceptable. This study investigates an agent's relationship with a human in situations where the agent is wrong. If the agent's reaction and human's preference affect how a human accepts the agent's mistakes, then there is no need to incorporate empathy toward the agent in order to maintain the human's impression of the agent.

To test these hypotheses, an experiment was conducted with a three-factor mixed design with three factors: agent reaction, human's preference, and pre- and post-task. The levels between participants were 2 (available, not available) for agent reaction and 2 (available, not available) for human's preference. The within-participants level was 2 pre- and post-task. Participants participated in only one of the four different content conditions. The dependent variable was the questionnaire that participants responded to (empathy, acceptance for error, other).

3.2   Experimental Details

The experiment was conducted in an online environment. The environment used is already a common method of experimentation [3,5,12]. As mentioned earlier, the goal of this study is to promote human empathy toward RVA. A scheduling agent was also used in this study to measure the acceptance of the agent's mistakes. For this reason, we believed that the same effect as being face to face could be achieved even in an online environment.

Before performing the task, a questionnaire was administered to measure empathy toward RVA. At the same time, another questionnaire was administered to determine whether participants could accept the agent's mistakes. At this time, participants were not allowed to see the agent's reactions or to select the color of the agent. However, because it was necessary to display appearance for conducting a survey of the agents, agents of each color used in the experimental conditions were displayed side by side. This questionnaire was administered before the task in order to see the effect of participants' empathy toward the agent and the change in the acceptance of the agent's mistakes.

Participants selected an agent by color from among multiple differently colored agents before beginning the scheduling task. In the no human's preference condition, participants were told that the agent displayed would manage a schedule. The schedule consisted of 10 items: the participant's weekly schedule, waking time, sleeping time, and number of outings per week. Fig. 1 is a flowchart of the schedule entry order and up to the confirmation screen. During the scheduling task, the agent exhibited several reactions to the input information. The scheduling agent was designed to remember the participant's schedule but to make sure that the agent made a mistake when participant checked the schedule for the last time. There were three areas where mistakes were made: (1) the waking and sleeping times were reversed, the (2) Monday and Wednesday schedules were reversed, and (3) the schedules for Thursday and Saturday were reversed. Waking and sleeping times and the number of outings per week were selected from a list of options, and schedules from Monday to Sunday were answered in the form of free-text responses.

This was done to investigate how an agent's mistakes affect human empathy and acceptance. To screen out unfair participants, participants reported whether the schedule was correct or incorrect at the last confirmation of the schedule.

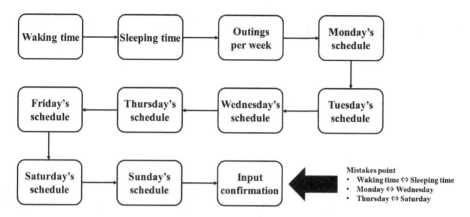

Fig. 1. Flowchart of the schedule

Only those participants who reported that the schedule was wrong were subsequently administered the same questionnaire about RVA as before the task. Two additional questions were also asked. Finally, they were asked to write their impressions of the experiment in free text.

3.3 Agent's Reactions

In this study, two levels of agent reactions were prepared. In the one with the agent's reaction, RVA responded with gestures and comments when the participant's schedule was sent. For the one without the agent's reaction, it did not respond to the participant's schedule and stayed upright. The three types of reactions actually seen by the participants are shown in Fig. 2. The three types were displayed three times equally and in the order in which they were displayed to the participants. Because the reactions were based on the content of the participant's schedule, RVA did not react to anything when the schedule was first entered.

There is a study by Tsumura and Yamada [25] as an example of how agent representations affected human empathy toward agents, but unlike reactions, which are very brief representations, they did not focus on detailed representations for a single action, as in this experiment.

3.4 Human's Preference

There were two levels for a human's preference factor. In this study, participants were asked to choose the color of the agent's appearance to investigate people's preferences. If a human's preference was had, the participants were required to choose one of three types of RVA: red, blue, or green. There was no difference in

Fig. 2. Types of agent reactions

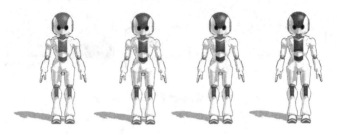

Fig. 3. Types of agent's color

the agent's personality or behavior based on human's preference. If no human's preference was had, the gray agent would manage the schedule. The color of each agent is shown in Fig. 3.

In this study, we did not consider bias in human's preference. The human's preference factor was chosen as a factor that allowed participants to interact with RVA. The purpose was to investigate whether the participants' impressions of RVA changed depending on the selection. Therefore, differences in participants' feelings towards particular colors and gender bias were ignored in this study.

3.5 Questionnaire

Participants completed a questionnaire before and after the task. In this study, human empathy for the agent was evaluated based on changes in human empathy characteristics. The questionnaire was a 12-item questionnaire modified from the Interpersonal Reactivity Index (IRI), which is used to investigate the characteristics of empathy, to suit the present experiment [4]. The modified questionnaire has already been used in several previous studies by Tsumura and Yamada [23–25]. The two questionnaires before and after were the same. Both were based on the IRI and were surveyed on a 5-point Likert scale (1: not applicable, 5: applicable). The questionnaire used is shown in Table 1. Q4, Q9, and Q10 are inverted items, so the scores were reversed when analyzing them.

Table 1. Summary of questionnaire used in this experiment

Affective empathy
Personal distress
Q1: If an emergency happens to the character, you would be anxious and restless
Q2: If the character is emotionally disturbed, you would not know what to do
Q3: If you see the character in need of immediate help, you would be confused and would not know what to do
Empathic concern
Q4: If you see the character in trouble, you would not feel sorry for that character
Q5: If you see the character being taken advantage of by others, you would feel like you want to protect that character
Q6: The character's story and the events that have taken place move you strongly.
Cognitive empathy
Perspective taking
Q7: You look at both the character's position and the human position
Q8: If you were trying to get to know the character better, you would imagine how that character sees things
Q9: When you think you're right, you don't listen to what the character has to say
Fantasy scale
Q10: You are objective without being drawn into the character's story or the events taken place
Q11: You imagine how you would feel if the events that happened to the character happened to you
Q12: You get deep into the feelings of the character.
Other questions than empathy
QA: If the scheduling agent makes a mistake, can you forgive the mistake?
QB: Did the scheduling agent express emotions?
QC: Would you like to use a scheduling agent in the future?

Three questions other than those related to empathy were prepared: QA, QB, and QC. QA was surveyed before and after the task, while QB and QC were surveyed only after the task. QA was investigated before and after the task to compare the difference between the participants' assumed acceptance of agent error and the actual agent error after it occurred. QB was prepared to investigate whether the agent's very brief reactions appeared emotional. QC was an item to investigate the impact of differences in factors on the participants' evaluations of the agent's future use. These three questions were also surveyed on a 5-point Likert scale (1: not applicable, 5: applicable). The questionnaire is shown in Table 1.

3.6 Experimental Environment and Participants

Participants were recruited for the experiment using a Yahoo! crowdsourcing company. They were paid 55 yen after completing all tasks as a reward for participating. A website was created for the experiment, which was limited to using a PC.

There were a total of 197 participants. The average age was 48.82 years (standard deviation: 11.08), with a minimum of 19 years and a maximum of 77 years. The gender breakdown was 144 males and 53 females. The number of participants in each condition is shown in Table 2. We then applied Cronbach's α coefficient to determine the reliability of the questionnaire responses, which was found to be between 0.4040 and 0.8190 in all conditions. Some participant groups had lower Cronbach's α values, but we also found several conditions with values between 0.7 and 0.8. Therefore, we used the questionnaire without any modifications.

Table 2. Number of participants in each condition

		Reaction	
		Yes	No
	Yes	50	50
human's preference	No	49	48

Table 3. Results of participants' statistical information

Category		Conditions	Mean	S.D.	Category		Conditions	Mean	S.D.
Empathy (Q1–Q12)	pre	reaction-preference	36.94	5.705	Agent's acceptance (QA)	pre	reaction-preference	2.660	0.8947
		reaction-no preference	38.78	5.363			reaction-no preference	2.837	0.7457
		no reaction-preference	36.90	6.370			no reaction-preference	2.880	0.8722
		no reaction-no preference	38.67	6.096			no reaction-no preference	2.563	0.9655
	post	reaction-preference	33.98	7.347		post	reaction-preference	2.560	0.9510
		reaction-no preference	34.94	6.710			reaction-no preference	2.755	0.7781
		no reaction-preference	34.72	6.716			no reaction-preference	2.600	1.107
		no reaction-no preference	35.71	6.694			no reaction-no preference	2.271	0.9618
Expressed emotions (QB)	post	reaction-preference	2.840	0.9116	Continued use (QC)	post	reaction-preference	2.140	0.9260
		reaction-no preference	2.674	1.068			reaction-no preference	2.286	0.9129
		no reaction-preference	2.000	0.8571			no reaction-preference	2.080	0.9223
		no reaction-no preference	1.896	0.7217			no reaction-no preference	1.979	0.8627

3.7 Analysis Method

The analysis was a three-factor analysis of variance (ANOVA). The between-participant factors were the two levels of agent's reaction and two levels of agent's human's preference. The within-participants factor consisted of two levels of empathy values before and after the task. On the basis of the results of the participants' questionnaires, we investigated how the agent's reaction and human's preference influenced the promotion of empathy as factors that elicit human empathy. The numerical values of empathy aggregated before and after the task were used as the dependent variable. Three of our own questions were also used as dependent variables. R (R ver. 4.1.0) was used for the ANOVA.

4 Results

All 12 questionnaire items were analyzed together. Table 3 shows the statistical results for each. Table 4 shows the results of each ANOVA.

To begin, as can be seen from Table 4, when the participants' empathy for the agent was examined, there were no significant differences other than the main pre- and post-task effects. Comparing the pre- and post-task empathy values in Table 3 for the ability to empathize with the agent, empathy decreased after the task (all pre-task: mean $= 37.81$, S.D. $= 5.921$; all post-task: mean $= 34.83$, S.D. $= 6.850$).

The results for agent acceptance showed an interaction between the agent's reaction factor and human's preference factor. Therefore, we analyzed the simple main effect in Table 5 and found that the agent's reaction more likely lead to acceptance to the agent's error when the participant did not make a human's preference. We also found that, although a significant trend, the human's

Table 4. Analysis results of ANOVA

	Factor	F	p	η_p^2
Empathy (Q1-12)	Reaction	0.1567	0.6926 ns	0.0008
	human's preference	2.606	0.1081 ns	0.0133
	Before/after task	94.11	0.0000 ***	0.3278
	Reaction × human's preference	0.0001	0.9909 ns	0.0000
	Reaction × Before/after task	1.817	0.1793 ns	0.0093
	human's preference × Before/after task	1.810	0.1801 ns	0.0093
	Reaction × human's preference × Before/after task	0.0064	0.9363 ns	0.0000
Agent's acceptance (QA)	Reaction	1.132	0.2887 ns	0.0058
	human's preference	0.3440	0.5582 ns	0.0018
	Before/after task	10.68	0.0013 **	0.0525
	Reaction × human's preference	4.725	0.0309 *	0.0239
	Reaction × Before/after task	2.864	0.0922 ns	0.0146
	human's preference × Before/after task	0.0008	0.9768 ns	0.0000
	Reaction × human's preference × Before/after task	0.0170	0.8964 ns	0.0001
Expressed emotions (QB)	Reaction	39.86	0.0000 ***	0.1712
	human's preference	1.116	0.2921 ns	0.0057
	Reaction × human's preference	0.0592	0.8080 ns	0.0003
Continued use (QC)	Reaction	2.012	0.1577 ns	0.0103
	human's preference	0.0302	0.8623 ns	0.0002
	Reaction × human's preference	0.9100	0.3413 ns	0.0047

p: *$p<0.05$ **$p<0.01$ ***$p<0.001$

Table 5. Analysis results of simple main effect

	Factor	F	p	η_p^2
Agent's acceptance (QA)	Reaction with preference	0.5613	0.4555 ns	0.0057
	Reaction with no preference	5.851	0.0175 *	0.0580
	human's preference with reaction	1.577	0.2122 ns	0.0160
	human's preference with no reaction	3.160	0.0786 +	0.0319

p: +$p<0.1$ *$p<0.05$ **$p<0.01$

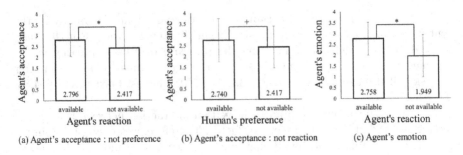

(a) Agent's acceptance : not preference   (b) Agent's acceptance : not reaction   (c) Agent's emotion

Fig. 4. Result of each main effect or simple main effect

preference made its mistake more acceptable when there was no agent reaction. These results are shown in Fig. 4(a) and (b).

The results for the agent's emotional expression showed a main effect for the agent's reaction factor. However, no main effect was found for the agent's human's preference factor. This indicated that the agent's reactions appeared to be emotionally charged. These results are shown in Fig. 4(c). Finally, there were no significant differences in the continued use of the agents in all conditions.

5   Discussion

5.1   Supporting Hypotheses

This experiment was designed to investigate the conditions necessary for humans to empathize with anthropomorphic agents. In particular, by investigating when an agent makes a mistake on a task, the goal was to identify factors that influence empathy between an agent who makes a mistake on a task and a human. To this end, two hypotheses were formulated, and the data obtained from the experiment were analyzed.

The results supported one hypothesis, but not the other. In **H1**, we thought that the agent's reaction and human's preference would affect the participants' empathy toward the agent, but this one was not supported. In the present experiment, there was a decrease in empathy after the task in all conditions. This was also the case in Tsumura and Yamada [23]. The reason for the decrease in empathy may be that the all agents made mistakes, as there was no significant difference in each factor. Therefore, as a future study, we will compare the results with those obtained when the agents did not make mistakes.

In **H2**, we thought that the agent's reaction and human's preference would affect the acceptance toward the mistakes the agent made, which was supported here. In each case, when the agent's reaction was absent, the agent's mistake was accepted when human's preference was present, and when it was absent, the agent's mistake was accepted when the agent's reaction was present. On the other hand, when both agent reaction and human's preference were present, there was no effect. A possible reason for the lack of acceptance of agent error when both conditions were included is discouragement toward the agent. Therefore, as a future study, we will compare the results with those obtained when the agent does not make mistakes.

In addition, we surveyed participants through questionnaire whether the agent's responses appeared to be emotional expressions. This was a survey conducted as a manipulation check of the agents' reactions. As a result, the agent's very short reactions seemed emotional to the participants. However, regardless of the agent's reaction, empathy toward the agent was reduced, indicating that even when the agent acts emotionally, it is unlikely to affect empathy in situations where the agent makes a mistake on the task.

5.2 Limitations

One limitation of this experiment is that by eliminating factors other than the agent's reaction and the human's preference, the task itself was perceived as tedious, and the simplicity of the task may have reduced empathy. By not allowing RVA to engage in conversation or introduce themselves beyond the scheduling task, participants may have decreased their impression of RVA. Also, RVA were silent in this experiment, which was also done to eliminate the effect of voice on empathy and thus simplified the agents' reactions.

Although there was no need for an in-person experiment in this experiment, an in-person experiment using actual equipment could have made a difference in the impact on participants' impressions. A scheduling task was used in this study to investigate whether humans empathize with RVA and accept their mistakes even when they make mistakes on a task. However, even when agents' mistakes are acceptable, it is necessary to investigate the extent to which they are acceptable.

6 Conclusions

In this study, we investigated agent reaction and human's preference, focusing on human-agent task error as a factor that causes humans to empathize with RVA. RVA was designed to be in charge of managing the human's schedule and to make some mistakes in the input information. Two hypotheses were formulated and tested. The results showed that empathy toward RVA decreased when RVA made a mistake on the task. In addition, agent reaction and human's preference were shown to be effective in helping humans accept agent mistakes. However, it was shown that the use of either factor was not effective. Future research should investigate empathy and acceptance toward agents when they do not make mistakes on a task since it was confirmed that empathy toward RVA decreases when they make mistakes on a task.

Acknowledgments. This work was partially supported by JST, CREST (JPMJCR 21D4), Japan. This work was also supported by JST, the establishment of university fellowships towards the creation of science technology innovation, Grant Number JPMJFS2136.

References

1. Al Farisi, R., Ferdiana, R., Adji, T.B.: The effect of anthropomorphic design cues on increasing chatbot empathy. In: 2022 1st International Conference on Information System and Information Technology (ICISIT), pp. 370–375 (2022). https://doi.org/10.1109/ICISIT54091.2022.9873008
2. Baron-Cohen, S., Wheelwright, S.: The empathy quotient: an investigation of adults with asperger syndrome or high functioning autism, and normal sex differences. J. Autism Dev. Disord. **34**(2), 163–175 (2004)
3. Crump, M.J.C., McDonnell, J.V., Gureckis, T.M.: Evaluating amazon's mechanical Turk as a tool for experimental behavioral research. PLOS ONE **8**(3), 1–18 (2013). https://doi.org/10.1371/journal.pone.0057410
4. Davis, M.H.: A multidimensional approach to individual difference in empathy. In: JSAS Catalog of Selected Documents in Psychology, p. 85 (1980)
5. Davis, R.: Web-based administration of a personality questionnaire: comparison with traditional methods. Behav. Res. Methods Instrum. Comput. **31**, 572–577 (1999). https://doi.org/10.3758/BF03200737
6. Johanson, D., Ahn, H.S., Goswami, R., Saegusa, K., Broadbent, E.: The effects of healthcare robot empathy statements and head nodding on trust and satisfaction: a video study. J. Hum.-Robot Interact. **12**(1) (2023). https://doi.org/10.1145/3549534
7. Leite, I., Castellano, G., Pereira, A., Martinho, C., Paiva, A.: Empathic robots for long-term interaction. Int. J. Soc. Robot. (2014). https://doi.org/10.1007/s12369-014-0227-1
8. Mathur, L., Spitale, M., Xi, H., Li, J., Matarić, M.J.: Modeling user empathy elicited by a robot storyteller. In: 2021 9th International Conference on Affective Computing and Intelligent Interaction (ACII), pp. 1–8 (2021). https://doi.org/10.1109/ACII52823.2021.9597416
9. Nomura, T., Kanda, T., Kidokoro, H., Suehiro, Y., Yamada, S.: Why do children abuse robots? Interact. Stud. **17**(3), 347–369 (2016). https://doi.org/10.1075/is.17.3.02nom, https://www.jbe-platform.com/content/journals/10.1075/is.17.3.02nom
10. Nomura, T., Kanda, T., Suzuki, T.: Experimental investigation into influence of negative attitudes toward robots on human–robot interaction. AI Soc. **20**(2), 138–150 (2006). https://doi.org/10.1007/s00146-005-0012-7
11. Nomura, T., Kanda, T., Suzuki, T., Kato, K.: Prediction of human behavior in human-robot interaction using psychological scales for anxiety and negative attitudes toward robots. IEEE Trans. Rob. **24**(2), 442–451 (2008). https://doi.org/10.1109/TRO.2007.914004
12. Okamura, K., Yamada, S.: Adaptive trust calibration for human-AI collaboration. PLOS ONE **15**(2), 1–20 (2020). https://doi.org/10.1371/journal.pone.0229132
13. Okanda, M., Taniguchi, K., Itakura, S.: The role of animism tendencies and empathy in adult evaluations of robot. In: Proceedings of the 7th International Conference on Human-Agent Interaction. HAI '19, pp. 51–58. Association for Computing Machinery, New York, NY, USA (2019). https://doi.org/10.1145/3349537.3351891
14. Omdahl, B.L.: Cognitive Appraisal, Emotion, and Empathy. Lecture Notes in Computer Science, 1st edn. Psychology Press, New York (1995). https://doi.org/10.4324/9781315806556
15. Paiva, A.: Empathy in social agents. Int. J. Virtual Real. **10**(1), 1–4 (2011). https://doi.org/10.20870/IJVR.2011.10.1.2794, https://ijvr.eu/article/view/2794

16. Paiva, A., et al.: Caring for agents and agents that care: building empathic relations with synthetic agents. In: International Joint Conference on Autonomous Agents and Multiagent Systems, vol. 1, pp. 194–201, January 2004. https://doi.org/10.1109/AAMAS.2004.82

17. Paiva, A., Leite, I., Boukricha, H., Wachsmuth, I.: Empathy in virtual agents and robots: a survey. ACM Trans. Interact. Intell. Syst. 7(3) (2017). https://doi.org/10.1145/2912150

18. Preston, S.D., de Waal, F.B.M.: Empathy: its ultimate and proximate bases. Behav. Brain Sci. 25(1), 1–20 (2002). https://doi.org/10.1017/S0140525X02000018

19. Reeves, B., Nass, C.: The Media Equation: How People Treat Computers, Television, and New Media Like Real People and Places. Cambridge University Press, Cambridge (1996)

20. Rossi, A., Dautenhahn, K., Koay, K.L., Walters, M.L.: How the timing and magnitude of robot errors influence peoples' trust of robots in an emergency scenario. In: Kheddar, A., et al. (eds.) ICSR 2017. LNCS, pp. 42–52. Springer, Cham (2017)

21. Salem, M., Eyssel, F., Rohlfing, K., Kopp, S., Joublin, F.: To err is human(-like): effects of robot gesture on perceived anthropomorphism and likability. Int. J. Soc. Robot. 5(3), 313–323 (2013). https://doi.org/10.1007/s12369-013-0196-9

22. Samrose, S., Anbarasu, K., Joshi, A., Mishra, T.: Mitigating boredom using an empathetic conversational agent. In: Proceedings of the 20th ACM International Conference on Intelligent Virtual Agents. IVA '20, Association for Computing Machinery, New York, NY, USA (2020). https://doi.org/10.1145/3383652.3423905

23. Tsumura, T., Yamada, S.: Agents facilitate one category of human empathy through task difficulty. In: 2022 31st IEEE International Conference on Robot and Human Interactive Communication (RO-MAN), pp. 22–28 (2022). https://doi.org/10.1109/RO-MAN53752.2022.9900686

24. Tsumura, T., Yamada, S.: Influence of agent's self-disclosure on human empathy. PLOS ONE 18(5), 1–24 (2023). https://doi.org/10.1371/journal.pone.0283955

25. Tsumura, T., Yamada, S.: Influence of anthropomorphic agent on human empathy through games. IEEE Access 11, 40412–40429 (2023). https://doi.org/10.1109/ACCESS.2023.3269301

How Language of Interaction Affects the User Perception of a Robot

Barbara Sienkiewicz[1]([✉])[iD], Gabriela Sejnova[2][iD], Paul Gajewski[3][iD], Michal Vavrecka[2][iD], and Bipin Indurkhya[1][iD]

[1] Cognitive Science Department, Jagiellonian University, Krakow, Poland
barbara.wzietek@student.uj.edu.pl
[2] Czech Institute of Informatics, Robotics and Cybernetics,
Czech Technical University, Prague, Czechia
[3] Institute of Computer Science, AGH University of Science and Technology,
Krakow, Poland

Abstract. Spoken language is the most natural way for a human to communicate with a robot. It may seem intuitive that a robot should communicate with users in their native language. However, it is not clear if a user's perception of a robot is affected by the language of interaction. We investigated this question by conducting a study with twenty-three native Czech participants who were also fluent in English. The participants were tasked with instructing the Pepper robot on where to place objects on a shelf. The robot was controlled remotely using the Wizard-of-Oz technique. We collected data through questionnaires, video recordings, and a post-experiment feedback session. The results of our experiment show that people perceive an English-speaking robot as more intelligent than a Czech-speaking robot ($z = 18.00$, p-value $= 0.02$). This finding highlights the influence of language on human-robot interaction. Furthermore, we discuss the feedback obtained from the participants via the post-experiment sessions and its implications for HRI design.

Keywords: Human-Robot Communication · Social Robots · perception of the robot · User-centered HRI design

1 Introduction

Social robots that interact with ordinary people are becoming increasingly commonplace. It is important that this interaction be facilitated naturally, similar to human-human communication [29]. Spoken language is one such natural medium of communication [15]. Speech-based interfaces allow a social robot to be used effectively and flexibly in many situations [3], such as tutoring children [15].

This research was supported in part by a grant from the Priority Research Area Digi-World PSP: U1U/P06/NO.02.19 under the Strategic Programme Excellence Initiative at the Jagiellonian University, and by the National Science Centre, Poland, under the OPUS call in the Weave programme under the project number K/NCN/000142.

A. Al. Ali et al. (Eds.): ICSR 2023, LNAI 14453, pp. 308–321, 2024.
https://doi.org/10.1007/978-981-99-8715-3_26

Towards this goal, we need to study how language and speech affect people's perception of a robot. This applies to all voice-based human-robot interfaces, whether they are on land, sea, air or in cyberspace. Some aspects of speech have already been investigated: for example, vocal prosody [7], the melody of speech [8], or formal/informal speech [26]. However, the effect of language itself (native language as opposed to a non-native language like English) has not yet been studied. We hypothesize that there is a difference in the perception of the robot when the interaction is in the native language or a familiar foreign language. We conducted an empirical study to study this effect. This article is an expanded version of a brief study that is published elsewhere [22]. In this article, we provide more details of the related research, experimental set up, and a more through data analysis and discussion.

2   State of the Art

2.1   Human Perception of a Robot

A user's perception of a robot depends on several factors, e.g. appearance [25], behavior [28], and their correlation [1]. However, these factors may vary with respect to the application area [21].

A user's perception of robots is influenced by the context of interaction: e.g., the perception differs when the robot is a teacher [18] as opposed to when the user is teaching the robot [30]. Moreover, people with a prior knowledge about robots tend to perceive them differently than those without [11]. Finally, cultural and social context also plays a role in the perception of robots: e.g., people in Japan have more positive attitudes towards robots than in Europe [24].

2.2   Speech, Language, and Ethnicity in HRI

Rapid advances in computer-based speech understanding (e.g., Apple's SIRI) suggest that it will become easier to command a robot using speech [21]. Marge *et al.* [15] propose directions for further development and improvement of spoken language interaction between humans and robots. Their recommendations cover topics such as multimodal communication, dialogue management, and user-centred design, aiming to create intuitive and effective communication systems. T. Takahashi et al. [27] argue that incorporating emotional expressions into a robot's speech makes it more human-like and easier to talk to. Cultural aspects play a dominant role in speech-based human-robot interaction. A study conducted in Qatar with native English and Arabic [20] speakers found that the Arabic-speaking participants held a more positive perception of the robot and anthropomorphized it more than the English-speaking participants. Another study [33] found that the Japanese prefer a Japanese robot and feel discomfort while interacting with an Egyptian robot, and the opposite is true for the Egyptians. Such results show the importance of robot ethnicity in improving human acceptance during human-robot social interactions.

Other studies show differences in interaction with robots when using different accents [2,32]. Language is one factor that contributes to ethnic differences; other factors include race, skin color, historical background, and religion [16]. A robot's perceived ethnicity has a significant effect on human trust and robot's perception [10]. Manipulating the robot's language allows us to change its ethnicity and how it is perceived by the user.

2.3 Role of Language in Human-Human Communication

Here we briefly comment on the effect of using the mother tongue or a foreign language on human-human communication. Language is a primary means of human communication, allowing individuals to express their thoughts, feelings, and ideas to others. When communicating with others, individuals typically use their mother tongue, which is the language they learned first as a child. Using one's mother tongue influences interaction, as it is often associated with a sense of familiarity, comfort, and cultural identity [23]. However, communicating in a foreign language can also have both positive and negative effects on the interaction. On one hand, using a foreign language can provide opportunities for cross-cultural communication and learning. On the other hand, it can create communication barriers and misunderstandings due to language proficiency and cultural differences [31]. In multicultural societies, English serves as a lingua franca, facilitating communication across diverse backgrounds [12]. However, due to its limited shared understanding, it can sometimes create confusion and uncertainty. Additionally, interacting in English lingua franca involves some vulnerability and potential risk that are not present when communicating within a shared linguistic community that shares social meaning [12]. Recent research has also shown that the phenomenon of false memory in bilingual people is affected by whether they are required to match the language in which the initial information was given and the language in which they were asked to recall the information [6].

Given all these factors related to how the language of interaction affects human-human communication, we would like to explore how the language of communication affects human-robot interaction.

3 Experiment

3.1 Objective

The research question we focused on was how a human's perception of a robot is influenced by the language of interaction. We compared the interaction in the native language of the speaker (Czech) with the interaction in a well-known foreign language (English). Participants were asked to teach a robot how to organize objects on a desk and shelves above it. Each participant interacted with the robot under two conditions (the order of the conditions was randomized):

– Condition A: The participant and the robot spoke to each other in English.
– Condition B: The participant and the robot spoke to each other in Czech.

We hypothesized that the participants' perception of the robot would differ depending on the language of interaction, and they would prefer interacting in their native language. The collected data combined our observations of the participants' behaviour during the interaction, the participants' self-reported answers to a questionnaire after each interaction, and post-test interviews with each participant.

3.2   Task

There is growing interest in the integration of robots into domestic environments [14], which poses a number of challenges. As each home and its inhabitants are unique, robots must be able to learn how to operate in different environments and non-expert users should be able to explain the robot its task.

To address these requirements, we designed a real-life scenario in which a user has to teach a robot how to organize objects to tidy up. By instructing the robot to clean and organize their desk, the participant would potentially be relieved of this responsibility in the future, which is a great motivation for accomplishing the task. Moreover, the task did not require specialized domain knowledge or technical jargon, making it easily comprehensible and feasible to demonstrate. Participants were instructed to treat the desk as their own and teach the robot the desired organization of the objects, considering their personal preferences (Fig. 1). The concept of *teaching* was defined as physically handling each object and placing it in the desired location while providing verbal descriptions of the actions, as it can be seen in Fig. 1. Furthermore, participants were informed that the robot would remain stationary throughout the interaction, observing but not performing any actions. Figure 2 (a) shows the setup before the interaction started for condition A.

To ensure the validity and reliability of the experiment, we employed two distinct sets of objects, one for each condition. In Condition A, the objects included a plant, a mug, a glass bottle and a tissue box (Fig. 2 (b). For Condition B, the objects consisted of a metal cookie tin, a watering can, a cup with pens, and a red paper cube.

There were several rationales behind using different sets of objects. Firstly, it prevented any references or comparisons to previous conditions, ensuring that participants approached each teaching session independently. This minimized potential biases or influences that could arise from participants' previous experiences.

Secondly, the use of diverse objects enhanced the realism of the scenario, making it more representative of real-life situations. In real-world contexts, individuals encounter various objects with different shapes, sizes, and functions. By replicating this diversity in the participants' experimental setup, we aimed to capture the complexity of teaching a robot to organize objects in a practical manner. Another reason for using distinct objects in each condition was to facilitate language consistency. As the *wizard* (the person operating the robot) was

Fig. 1. The user demonstrating to the robot where to place an object

physically present in the same room as the researcher and the participant, they could not ask clarifying questions or show emotions on their face. By associating specific objects with a particular language, it was easier for the wizard to recall and maintain the appropriate language throughout the interaction. This ensured clarity and minimized potential language-related errors or confusion during the teaching process.

3.3   Experiment Set up

The experiment took place in a room at the Czech Institute of Informatics, Robotics, and Cybernetics, where researchers frequently work.

Figure 3 provides a bird's eye view of the experimental setup. During the initial stage and questionnaire sessions, the participant was seated at Location 1, and was asked to stand at Location 2 for the interaction phase. The experimenter stood at Location 1 in the initial phase and at Location 2 in the interaction phase to give the participant freedom and privacy with the robot. There were two robot operators involved in the experiment: one was responsible for controlling the robot's speech, while the other operated its movement. Additionally, in the other part of the room (shown as white space on the right side of the figure), two other researchers were working on their computers. The participant did not expect the robot operators to be directly involved in the experiment, as several people were present in the room. Besides the participant and the experimenter, everyone else was quiet. The camera covered the desk at which the participant was sitting, the desk with the objects, and the robot.

(a) Objects used in condition A (interaction in English)

(b) Objects used in condition B (interaction in Czech)

Fig. 2. Set up of the experiment

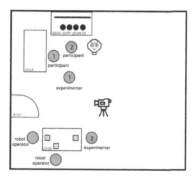

Fig. 3. Bird's eye view of the study setup

3.4   Robot Operation

First the humanoid robot used in the experiment is described with its hardware and software specifications. Then, we describe our program designed to operate the robot using the Wizard-of-Oz method.

Humanoid Robot. We used Pepper, a humanoid robot developed by SoftBank Robotics and released in June 2014 (see Fig. 2 (a)). Pepper is equipped with two identical video cameras on the forehead and a 3D video camera. It is capable of facial recognition and analysis of human expressions. In addition, four microphones in the robot's head allow it to analyze speech and vocal tones, and to detect the direction of incoming sounds.

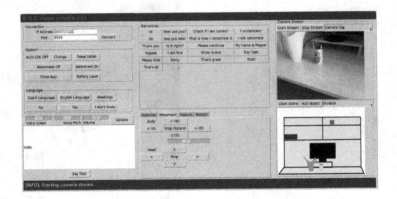

Fig. 4. GUI for operating the robot using the Wizard-of-Oz method. We control the language (left-middle), speaking (top-middle), and head movements (bottom-middle), and display the current scene on the tablet when needed (bottom-right). We can also watch the scene using the robot's head camera (top-right).

Pepper was controlled by the NAOqi operating system, which is a programming framework for developing applications on the robot. NAOqi addresses common robotics requirements such as parallelism, resource management, synchronization, and event handling. NAOqi functions can be called in C++ or Python, and a graphical environment called Choregraphe is available to create complex behaviors for Pepper. Our research team developed a Python API wrapper around the NAOqi framework, which was used in this study.

The Pepper class, the main component of our Python API, establishes a connection to the robot instance using a specified IP address and port. Once the connection is made, it provides tools to interact with the robot, such as moving its arms, legs, and head, changing its LED lights, playing sounds and speech, and accessing its sensors and cameras. The API also allows the creation of custom behaviors and applications using Python code that can be run on the robot.

Wizard of Oz. The Wizard-of-Oz method [19] was implemented using a GUI built on top of our Python API described above. After establishing a connection with the robot, we can control it by clicking the corresponding buttons in the GUI. Each button is mapped to a Python function in the Pepper class. The GUI overview is shown in Fig. 4. Its main components are as follows:

- Connection panel - to connect with the robot via its IP address
- System - to control the level of autonomous movement of the robot and reset any current process

- Language - enables to switch between Czech and English language and to control voice volume, speed and pitch
- Sentences - each button is mapped to a sentence that the robot says in the selected language
- Movement - enables head movement
- Camera Stream - displays what the robot sees using its top head camera
- Scene scheme - the operator can edit the current scene by adding objects as they are arranged by the participant. The "Show Scene" button then displays this image on Pepper's tablet

Though the robot can move around on its wheels, for this experiment, it remained in one place and only moved its head in a natural way to give the impression of observing the actions of the participant. Voice parameters (such as volume, speed, and pitch) remained fixed throughout the experiments. Besides its head, the robot moved its arms and hands to gesticulate while speaking. After each object shown by the participant, the robot confirmed that he understood ("Okay", "I see", "I understand") with appropriate gestures and head movements.

3.5   Questionnaires

We used the following questionnaires and tests:

- Pre-test: To collect demographic data and information about the participants' experience with programming and familiarity with robots.
- English test: To verify the level of English, each participant was asked to complete a short English test for B2/C1.
- Godspeed Questionnaire [4,5]: Standardised questionnaire to measure the perception of robot in 5 subscales: anthropomorphism, animacy, likeability, perceived intelligence, perceived safety.
- Post-interaction questionnaire: After each condition we asked the participant how easy it was to check the robot's knowledge, whether the robot made any mistakes, and whether the robot was capable of retaining the knowledge. This questionnaire was designed to explore the participant's reasoning. It also allowed us to compare the actual errors with the ones noticed by the participants. Each participant filled two questionnaires, one after each condition.
- Post-test questionnaire: This was designed to get the participant's overall feedback to evaluate the study methodology.

All questionnaires were in English and Czech, in order not to bias any language.

3.6   Participants

Twenty-three participants (9 women, 14 men), aged (14–72 yrs, M = 32.04, SD = 14.22), were recruited through emails and web announcements. Informed consent was obtained from all the participants above 18 yrs. and from their parents for those under 18 yrs. (four participants). To avoid language skills as a confounding factor, the requirement to participate in the study was proficiency in both English and Czech.

3.7   Procedure

Each participant interacted with the robot individually. The experiment took about 20–30 min. The procedure was as follows:

1. The participant was seated at a desk with their back to the robot. At first, the participant took the English test; they were told that their test performance would not impact their interaction with the robot. Then the participant read and signed the consent form, followed by filling the pre-test questionnaire. The English test was given first, and was followed by other tasks to maximize the gap between the test and the interaction for avoiding bias.
2. The participant was asked to move near the robot and the task was explained. If (s)he had any questions or hesitations, explanations were provided without disclosing the purpose of the study or how the robot works. The participant was asked to use a particular language (Czech or English) before each interaction. The order of conditions was random.
3. The camera was turned on, and the robot initiated the interaction, which lasted about 2–3 min. Then, the camera was turned off, and the participant returned to the desk to complete the Godspeed and post-interaction questionnaire, while the objects in the scene were changed.
4. The second round of interaction and questionnaires followed similarly to the first round, except that the language of interaction was switched and the objects to be arranged were different.
5. The participant was asked to provide feedback on the paper and was compensated 200 Czk (about 10 euros) for their participation. The participant was then debriefed about the purpose of the study and the Wizard-of-Oz methodology, revealing the robot operators. As this part was not recorded, participants' comments from this part were written down in a file after the participant was gone.

4   Results and Discussion

Data from one participant was excluded from the analysis due to numerous deficiencies in the questionnaires. One participant wrote in the survey his suspicions that the robot is controlled by a human, but the rest of 21 participants did not express any such doubts.

4.1 Pre-test

Most participants had no experience with humanoid robots, but some had knowledge of programming and robotics. The most common answers to questions about the robot's appearance were cute, friendly, child/childlike.

4.2 English Test

We conducted an English test to verify fluency in English. All participants received 8 or more out of a possible 13 points in an English-level test between B2 and C1.

4.3 Godspeed Questionnaire

The Godspeed Questionnaire was used to measure participants' ratings of the robot in five sub-scales. Table 1 shows the average scores, and the distribution of results is shown in Fig. 5. We are aware of the criticism regarding the use of intelligence as a dependent variable [34], but we still considered it as a relevant outcome measure for our study. This criticism refers to the evaluation of operator intelligence during the Wizard-of-Oz methodology, rather than that of the robot. In our study, the same operator employed a set of predetermined sentences (in translation), consistently supervising the robot's speech and movements.

Based on a previous study [9], we used a nonparametric test to evaluate the results. For our within-subjects study we used the Wilcoxon test. Only the subscale of perceived intelligence showed a significant result, $z = 18.00$, p-value $= 0.02$; an English-speaking robot is perceived as more intelligent than a Czech-speaking robot. A plausible explanation for the observed phenomenon is that when the robot communicates in a foreign language (English), participants may perceive it as more intelligent due to the increased difficulty in detecting errors compared to their native language. This language barrier could lead participants to allocate more cognitive capacity toward explaining the organization of objects, resulting in reduced attention toward the robot itself. Support for this hypothesis comes from the feedback questionnaire, where participants expressed their observations. For instance, one participant stated, "[...] when he speaks Czech, he was using words that I would never use in my daily life." Another participant remarked, "It seemed more lively when using English." Yet another participant commented, "For me, it was better in English as I could notice a slightly unusual wording or tempo of the sentences [in Czech]." These responses provide evidence supporting the notion that language choice influences participants' perceptions and attentiveness during human-robot interaction.

We investigated whether the sequential order of interactions influenced the ratings provided by the participants by comparing the results from the first interaction with those from the second, irrespective of the specific experimental conditions. Our analysis revealed no statistically significant differences between the two interactions. This suggests that the order of interactions did not have a significant impact on the outcomes observed in the study.

Table 1. Average Scores in Godspeed Questionnaire

Subscale	English	Czech
Anthropomorphisation	2.96	2.84
Animacy	3.16	3.15
Likeability	4.3	4.32
Perceived Intelligence	4.04	3.79
Perceived safety	3.44	3.60

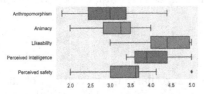 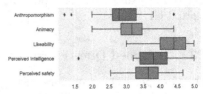

(a) Condition A: the English language   (b) Condition B: the Czech language

Fig. 5. Distribution of results in both conditions

This result suggests a potential advantage in utilizing English language during robot interactions, as it appears to yield more favorable outcomes, which is desirable in the design of social robots for widespread adoption. However, it is important to acknowledge that this approach could restrict the participant pool to individuals proficient in English, as speaking a foreign language often generates feelings of anxiety [13]. Hence, it is necessary to study this issue further: for example by conducting a study with native English speakers, and also with a larger sample.

4.4 Questionnaire After the Interaction

Based on the responses of the participants on a six-point Likert scale, the majority of the trials (37 of 44) were rated as easy (5) or very easy(6). Lower scores were observed in cases where the robot experienced technical issues, such as delays in response time or errors in visualization (6 out of 44 trials). Some participants considered the wrong orientation of the tissue box as an error, which was not expected. (The system was unable to display objects in different orientations.) This suggests that the system could be improved e.g. to rotate objects in future studies.

4.5 Insights from the Feedback Questionnaire

The feedback questionnaire proved valuable in comprehending the participants' perceptions of the research. Notably, a majority of responses focused on exploring the robot's capabilities and evaluating its usability in human-robot interaction, with only one participant highlighting language as the primary concern.

This suggests that the study effectively diverted attention from the language aspect, potentially influencing participants' expectations and perception of the research. It is important to note that bilingual individuals often encounter difficulty in recalling the language in which information was presented, without affecting their ability to recall the content. This phenomenon may have positively influenced the participant's response.

We included questions related to the experiment itself: clarity of instructions, areas of confusion, and potential improvements. Respondents expressed satisfaction with the study, frequently stating phrases such as "It was fun," "Everything was clear," and "I would like to have a robot like this at home." Two participants suggested that incorporating physical demonstrations of teaching the robot, rather than solely relying on verbal explanations, would have been beneficial. The deliberate omission of such demonstrations was intentional, as we aimed to observe participant attitudes without imposing specific instructional methods.

A participant commented that there were too many questionnaires, indicating the importance of appropriately adjusting the quantity to maintain participant engagement. When participants become excessively bored, they may not attentively read the questionnaires, resulting in uninformative data. To address this issue, we recommend including questionnaires in pilot studies to adjust their length and content. We also analysed the emotional aspects of the participants' responses. One participant expressed feeling nervous due to the presence of many people in the room. This suggests making the experiment venue less crowded for future studies. Another participant expressed fear toward the robot's hands, highlighting the significance of individuals' attention towards robot appendages [17]. Although sometimes subjective and specific to individual participants, it is crucial to recognize that participants are humans with emotions and needs, not merely sources of data. We must remember that the primary objective of HRI is to understand human-robot interaction, which includes comprehending the human user's emotional responses [15].

5   Conclusions

The results of the Godspeed questionnaire show that the participants perceived the English-speaking robot to be more intelligent than the Czech-speaking one. However, this result may be attributed to the fact that errors and unnatural behaviors are more difficult to be detected in a second language, as indicated by some participants in the feedback questionnaire. The limitations of the present study were: a small sample size, a diverse age range of the participants, and the absence of a comparison group comprising native English speakers fluent in Czech. We plan to address these issues in future research.

The importance of feedback questionnaires in HRI research has been highlighted by our research: they provide valuable insights into the participants' understanding and emotional responses towards the interaction and the study as a whole.

References

1. Matching robot appearance and behavior to tasks to improve human-robot cooperation. In: The 12th IEEE International Workshop on Robot and Human Interactive Communication, 2003. Proceedings. ROMAN 2003, pp. 55–60. IEEE (2003)
2. Andrist, S., Ziadee, M., Boukaram, H., Mutlu, B., Sakr, M.: Effects of culture on the credibility of robot speech: a comparison between English and Arabic. In: Proceedings of the Tenth Annual ACM/IEEE International Conference on Human-Robot Interaction, pp. 157–164 (2015)
3. Bainbridge, W.A., Hart, J.W., Kim, E.S., Scassellati, B.: The benefits of interactions with physically present robots over video-displayed agents. Int. J. Soc. Robot. **3**, 41–52 (2011)
4. Bartneck, C.: Godspeed questionnaire series: translations and usage (2023)
5. Bartneck, C., Kulić, D., Croft, E., Zoghbi, S.: Measurement instruments for the anthropomorphism, animacy, likeability, perceived intelligence, and perceived safety of robots. Int. J. Soc. Robot. **1**, 71–81 (2009)
6. Beato, M., Albuquerque, P.B., Cadavid, S., Suarez, M.: The effect of memory instructions on within- and between-language false memory. Appl. Psycholinguist. **44**, 1–25 (2023). https://doi.org/10.1017/S0142716423000140
7. Breazeal, C.: Emotive qualities in robot speech. In: Proceedings 2001 IEEE/RSJ International Conference on Intelligent Robots and Systems. Expanding the Societal Role of Robotics in the the Next Millennium (Cat. No. 01CH37180), vol. 3, pp. 1388–1394. IEEE (2001)
8. Fischer, K., Niebuhr, O., Jensen, L.C., Bodenhagen, L.: Speech melody matters-how robots profit from using charismatic speech. ACM Trans. Hum.-Robot Interact. (THRI) **9**(1), 1–21 (2019)
9. Gombolay, M.C., Shah, A.: Appraisal of statistical practices in HRI vis-a-vis the t-test for Likert items/scales. In: AAAI Fall Symposia (2016)
10. Gong, L.: The boundary of racial prejudice: comparing preferences for computer-synthesized white, black, and robot characters. Comput. Hum. Behav. **24**(5), 2074–2093 (2008)
11. Hall, J., Tritton, T., Rowe, A., Pipe, A., Melhuish, C., Leonards, U.: Perception of own and robot engagement in human-robot interactions and their dependence on robotics knowledge. Robot. Auton. Syst. **62**(3), 392–399 (2014)
12. Henderson, J.K., Louhiala-Salminen, L.: Does language affect trust in global professional contexts? Perceptions of international business professionals. J. Rhetoric Prof. Commun. Global. **2**(1), 2 (2011)
13. Horwitz, E.: Language anxiety and achievement. Annu. Rev. Appl. Linguist. **21**, 112–126 (2001)
14. Kim, J., et al.: Control strategies for cleaning robots in domestic applications: a comprehensive review. Int. J. Adv. Rob. Syst. **16**(4), 1729881419857432 (2019)
15. Marge, M., et al.: Spoken language interaction with robots: recommendations for future research. Comput. Speech Lang. **71**, 101255 (2022)
16. Nam, C.S., Lyons, J.B.: Trust in Human-Robot Interaction. Academic Press, Cambridge (2020)
17. Piazza, C., Grioli, G., Catalano, M., Bicchi, A.: A century of robotic hands. Annu. Rev. Control Robot. Auton. Syst. **2**, 1–32 (2019)
18. Polishuk, A., Verner, I.: An elementary science class with a robot teacher. In: Lepuschitz, W., Merdan, M., Koppensteiner, G., Balogh, R., Obdržálek, D. (eds.) RiE 2017. AISC, vol. 630, pp. 263–273. Springer, Cham (2018). https://doi.org/10.1007/978-3-319-62875-2_24

19. Riek, L.D.: Wizard of OZ studies in HRI: a systematic review and new reporting guidelines. J. Hum.-Robot Interact. **1**(1), 119–136 (2012)
20. Salem, M., Ziadee, M., Sakr, M.: Marhaba, how may I help you? Effects of politeness and culture on robot acceptance and anthropomorphization. In: Proceedings of the 2014 ACM/IEEE International Conference on Human-Robot Interaction, pp. 74–81 (2014)
21. Sheridan, T.B.: Human-robot interaction: status and challenges. Hum. Factors **58**(4), 525–532 (2016)
22. Sienkiewicz, B., Sejnova, G., Gajewski, P., Vavrecka, M., Indurkhya, B.: Native Czech speakers consider English-speaking robots more intelligent. In: Proceedings of the Eleventh International Conference on Human-Agent Interaction (2023)
23. Snow, C.E.: Rationales for native language instruction. Bilingual Education: Issues and Strategies, pp. 60–74 (1990)
24. Sone, Y.: Japanese Robot Culture. Springer, New York (2016). https://doi.org/10.1057/978-1-137-52527-7
25. Song, S., Yamada, S.: Expressing emotions through color, sound, and vibration with an appearance-constrained social robot. In: Proceedings of the 2017 ACM/IEEE International Conference on Human-Robot Interaction, pp. 2–11 (2017)
26. Steinhaeusser, S.C., Lein, M., Donnermann, M., Lugrin, B.: Designing social robots' speech in the hotel context-a series of online studies. In: 2022 31st IEEE International Conference on Robot and Human Interactive Communication (RO-MAN), pp. 163–170. IEEE (2022)
27. Takahashi, T., Tanaka, K., Kobayashi, K., Oka, N.: Melodic emotional expression increases ease of talking to spoken dialog agents. In: Proceedings of the 9th International Conference on Human-Agent Interaction, pp. 84–92 (2021)
28. Tan, H., et al.: Relationship between social robot proactive behavior and the human perception of anthropomorphic attributes. Adv. Robot. **34**(20), 1324–1336 (2020)
29. Thomaz, A.L., Breazeal, C.: Teachable robots: understanding human teaching behavior to build more effective robot learners. Artif. Intell. **172**(6–7), 716–737 (2008)
30. Thomaz, A.L., Hoffman, G., Breazeal, C.: Reinforcement learning with human teachers: understanding how people want to teach robots. In: ROMAN 2006-The 15th IEEE International Symposium on Robot and Human Interactive Communication, pp. 352–357. IEEE (2006)
31. Ting-Toomey, S., Dorjee, T.: Communicating Across Cultures. Guilford Publications, New York (2018)
32. Torre, I., White, L.: Trust in vocal human-robot interaction: implications for robot voice design. In: Voice Attractiveness: Studies on Sexy, Likable, and Charismatic Speakers, pp. 299–316 (2021)
33. Trovato, G., et al.: Cross-cultural study on human-robot greeting interaction: acceptance and discomfort by Egyptians and Japanese. Paladyn, J. Behav. Robot. **4**(2), 83–93 (2013)
34. Weiss, A., Bartneck, C.: Meta analysis of the usage of the godspeed questionnaire series. In: 2015 24th IEEE International Symposium on Robot and Human Interactive Communication (RO-MAN), pp. 381–388. IEEE (2015)

Is a Humorous Robot More Trustworthy?

Barbara Sienkiewicz$^{(\boxtimes)}$[ID] and Bipin Indurkhya[ID]

Cognitive Science Department, Jagiellonian University, Krakow, Poland
barbara.sienkiewicz@student.uj.edu.pl, bipin.indurkhya@uj.edu.pl

Abstract. As more and more social robots are being used for collaborative activities with humans, it is crucial to investigate mechanisms to facilitate trust in the human-robot interaction. One such mechanism is humour: it has been shown to increase creativity and productivity in human-human interaction, which has an indirect influence on trust. In this study, we investigate if humour can increase trust in human-robot interaction. We conducted a between-subjects experiment with 40 participants to see if the participants are more likely to accept the robot's suggestion in the Three-card Monte game, as a trust check task. Though we were unable to find a significant effect of humour, we discuss the effect of possible confounding variables, and also report some interesting qualitative observations from our study: for instance, the participants interacted effectively with the robot as a team member, regardless of the humour or no-humour condition.

Keywords: Human-robot interaction · Humour · Nao robot · Social robots · Three-card Monte · Trust

1 Introduction

In recent years, social robots are increasingly being deployed in various roles where they need to interact heavily with human users or play the role of a human. Some examples of such domains are military [29], medicine [11], consumer assistant [10], healthcare, and care for the elderly [28]. However, to have an effective and meaningful interaction with the robot, it is necessary that people consider them trustworthy and reliable [15].

This applies to all human-robot interactions, whether they take place on land, sea, air, or in cyberspace. Many factors can influence trust. In the research presented here, we explore the role of humour in facilitating trust in human-robot interaction (HRI, henceforth). Humour has been shown to increase creativity and productivity in human-human interaction; moreover it has an indirect influence

This research was supported in part by a grant from the Priority Research Area Digi-World PSP: U1U/P06/NO/02.19 under the Strategic Programme Excellence Initiative at the Jagiellonian University, and by the National Science Centre, Poland, under the OPUS call in the Weave programme under the project number K/NCN/000142.

A. Al. Ali et al. (Eds.): ICSR 2023, LNAI 14453, pp. 322–335, 2024.
https://doi.org/10.1007/978-981-99-8715-3_27

on trust in humans. We conducted a study with 40 participants, using a between-subjects design with humor and no-humor conditions, to determine whether participants would be more inclined to accept a robot's suggestions in the Three-card Monte game, which we considered as a measure of trust towards the robot. In this paper, we present the details of the pilot and the main studies, and discuss the results.

The structure of the paper is as follows. We present a review of the related research in Sect. 2. Then our experiment design and the pilot study is presented in Sect. 3, followed by the details of the main study in Sect. 4. Results and discussion are presented in Sect. 5, followed by the conclusions and suggestions for future research in Sect. 6.

2   Related Work

We provide here background and motivation for this research. First, we introduce into the concept of trust in human-robot interaction (HRI), which is a key to effective collaboration between humans and robots, with an emphasis on the potential pitfalls of over-trust and under-trust. Next, we explore trust in human-human communication, shedding light on the dynamic nature of trust judgments and the factors influencing them. We then discuss the role of humor in human-human communication, emphasising its subjectivity and its impact on trust in human interactions. Then we briefly describe the existing research on the role of humor in HRI, focussing on its potential to enhance trust and likeability. This motivates our main research question: Does the use of humor in human-robot interaction improve trust?

2.1   Trust in Human-Robot Interaction

Before we start discussing different aspects of trust, we need to define trust. Though there are many definitions of trust [12, 26], we use the following definition from [24]:

"Trust is a dyadic relation in which one person accepts vulnerability because they expect that the other person's future action will have certain characteristics; these characteristics include a mix of performance (ability, reliability) and/or morality (honesty, integrity, and benevolence)."

An inappropriate level of trust between a human user and a robot may lead to misuse or disuse of the robotic agent [16]. Misuse occurs when the user over-trusts the robot and accepts all its suggestions without questioning: for example trusting a GPS-based route assistant blindly while ignoring the actual situation on the road [6]. On the other hand, disuse appears when the human user rejects all the suggestions of a robot and questions its capabilities: for example when a senior with Alzheimer's disease does not believe the robot that she or he has not yet taken the medication. Both misuse and disuse undermine the effectiveness of human-robot interaction, and it is important to study how to maintain trust between a robotic system and its human user.

There are many factors that affect trust in HRI. Studies have shown that humans are more likely to trust robots that exhibit social cues, such as eye contact, appropriate facial expressions, and naturalistic movements [23]. Further, it has been found that people are more willing to trust a robot when it apologises and acknowledges that it made a mistake [14]. Another work of research has found that embodiment increases trust towards the robot [20]. Trust in HRI can be divided into two categories: performance-based trust and relation-based trust [24, pp. 28–32]. Performance-based trust centres on the robot being capable and competent for its task: for example, in autonomous cars or banking systems. This trust is based on rational arguments and beliefs. Relation-based trust focuses on the robot's role as a social agent, which is more important when the robot serves as a companion, in a nursing home, or in a school. The users may not be completely aware why and how they trust the robot; they just feel more secure and comfortable about relying on the robotic system beyond the available evidence [21].

Many of the factors mentioned in the earlier research are rooted in interpersonal behaviours. Therefore, it is important to consider what influences trust in human-human interaction, as this may provide clues to facilitating trust in HRI.

2.2   Trust in Human-Human Communication

Trust plays a key role in social interaction, and is crucial for effective cooperation. When two humans interact, whether they are strangers or close associates, each one has to decide how much to trust the other [4]. Furthermore, trust is dynamic: it changes as the interaction proceeds based on many conscious and subconscious factors. At first, we judge trustworthiness based on facial features [32]. As we get to know each other better, this assessment of trustworthiness changes [1]. Sometimes, the social position of a person, like being a doctor, increases the initial assessment of trust in her or him. Another factor that leads humans to trust another is similarity to themselves. Similarities can include common values (such as strong work ethics), membership in defined groups (local churches and even gender), and common personality characteristics (extroversion and ambition) [9].

2.3   Humour and Trust in Human-Human Communication

Humour is an activity that is largely subjective and hard to measure objectively [18]. Human brain is capable of taking into account many factors, such as the situation, atmosphere, and mood of the people around, to produce fun and bring smiles on people's faces. Everyone has a different sense of humour: some people like jokes, some gallows humour, and still others like pranks. Everyone reacts differently, even to the same joke. Due to the many variables and cultural conditioning, it is difficult to define humour precisely. For the this research, we consider a good sense of humour to be the ability to create jokes, riddles, and situations that make people laugh. Previous research has shown that humans with a good sense of humour are more intelligent [5]. Most relevant to our research is the finding that humour can increase trust between agents [13]. In teams, humour is found to increase productivity and creativity, reduce conflict, and decrease stress [8].

2.4 Research on the Role of Humour in HRI

Given that humour has such a positive influence on human-human interaction, it is useful to explore if it can also facilitate human-robot interaction. Anton Nijholt studied the specific role and use of humour in human-computer interaction, and demonstrated the potential of using humour with special attention on humour creation [25]. Another study found that humour helps robots to interact with humans in the same way as humans interact with each other [7, pp. 333–360]. Yet another study showed that the interaction with humour is more natural and flexible [22], and it might be correlated with trust. Humour can also help robots to be perceived as smarter: for example, when they tell clever jokes [33]. Francesco Vigni et al. argue that users perform better in a game when interacting with an agreeable robot [31]."

An empirical study of humour with Nao and iCat robots demonstrating different laughing behaviours showed higher likeability ratings for the robots when they use humour [19]; interestingly, the likeability ratings tended to converge when either robot laughed or when both robots laughed together. This suggests that it is not necessary for both participants in the interaction to have a sense of humour in order to yield a positive effect of humour, which is important as we are not able to manipulate the human's humour in the interaction. Another study on humour in HRI showed that using jokes during the initial greeting is effective in enhancing likeability and reducing awkwardness [30]. Our methodology in creating the study presented here is inspired by it.

Based on the existing literature, there is evidence to suggest that humour can indirectly affect trust by increasing the likeability and naturalness of interactions between humans and robots. However, the question remains whether the use of humour in HRI can also directly enhance trust between humans and robots. Therefore, the research question we explore in this study is: Does the use of humour in human-robot interaction improve trust?

3 Experiment Design

In this section, we present the main task for the participants in the experiment, introduce the robot and its software, and provide a detailed description of the obstacles we encountered during the pilot study.

3.1 Task

To investigate whether people consider a humorous robot more trustworthy, we designed an experiment where the participant is asked to team up with a robot while playing a version of the card game *Three-card Monte*. In our version of the game (Fig. 1b), the participant is shown three cards, two of which are black and one red. The cards are then turned face down and shuffled out of the sight of the participant and the robot (behind the back of the experimenter). The experiment was deliberately designed so that the robot did not have more information than the participant. This allows us to focus on relation-based trust, when both agents have the same information, and there is no rationale for trusting the robot.

The three cards are shown to the participant again, who is asked to point to the red card. The robot then offers a suggestion that is contrary to the participant's guess. We observe if the participant follows its advice, thereby showing that she or he trusts the robot: this measure is based on the experimental types for measuring trust in the book 'Trust in Human-Robot Interaction' [24].

We also use the Multi-Dimensional Measure of Trust (MDMT) questionnaire after the interaction to measure the subjective level of trust towards the robot [17].

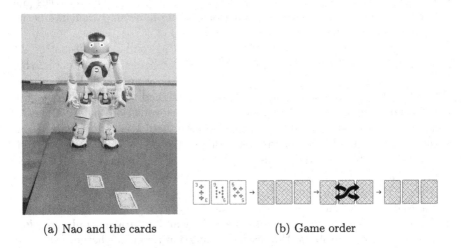

(a) Nao and the cards   (b) Game order

Fig. 1. Main task: Three-card Monte

To study the effect of humour, we compared humour and no-humour conditions. Three jokes were selected to be used in the humour (experimental) condition. All three jokes employed a form of wordplay in the Polish language. For example, one of the jokes used during the interaction is as follows: "What is the name of the cat that flies?" The punchline to this joke relies on a wordplay between the Polish words for cat ("KOT") and flies ("LECI'), resulting in the humorous response of "small cutlet" ("KOTLECIK").

It is important to note that the jokes were chosen to be neutral with respect to factors such as race, gender, and profession, in order to minimize the potential for offense or biases. The same jokes were used for the pilot study as for the main study. Additionally, one situational joke was included in the main study, where the robot humorously remarks, "Sweets are just for you, I'm on a diet."

In the no-humour (control) condition of the experiment, the robot engaged in a conversation with the participant about some neutral topic like the weather, before proceeding to the main task. This serves as a baseline for comparison against the conditions involving joke interactions.

Throughout the experiment, the same pre-selected jokes were consistently used during the interactions, with an additional joke available in case the participant expressed interest in hearing more.

3.2 Robot

We used the humanoid robot NAO from Aldebaran (Fig. 1a). Nao is 58 cm tall and has 25°C of freedom. The same NAO robot was used in both conditions. We used the methodology of Wizard-of-Oz [27]. The robot's voice and talking speed were also kept identical. Nao turned its face towards sounds, which made the interaction more natural when we modified the experimental setting after the pilot study, as explained below.

3.3 Pilot Study

We first conducted a pilot study with 12 participants to test our methodology. The study was conducted in the Social Robotics Lab at Jagiellonian University in Krakow, Poland. In this pilot study, we included another condition, namely using a video of the robot instead of an embodied robot. This led to a between-participants design where each participant was tested with one of the following four conditions: 1) A humorous robot; 2) a neutral robot; 3) a humorous robot displayed on a tablet; and 4) a neutral robot displayed on a tablet. We list below some problems observed in the pilot study and how they were fixed for the main study.

Rigid and unnatural movements of the robot: The robot moved unnaturally and stiffly, which resulted in some participants failing to notice it at all and talking only to the experimenter. To remedy this problem, we implemented animated speech for the main study, so the robot was constantly moving, gesturing, and making small talk (initiated by the operator), which did not depend on the input from the robot's operator.

Slow and delayed speech from the robot: To address slow speech and typing sounds, we pre-programmed certain robot responses, assigning each an index. During interactions, the operator only needed to input the corresponding index, allowing for quicker and more seamless communication. The operator could still type responses in real time for unexpected questions or comments from participants.

Unnatural communication with the avatar: Two conditions required the participants to talk to the avatar on the tablet and read messages on the screen. They found this interaction quite weird and did not feel comfortable. So, we decided to remove this condition (interaction with an avatar) from the main study.

Lack of eye contact: In the pilot study, the robot remained stationary but faced away from the participant while speaking due to the operator's limited view. This felt unnatural to participants. In the main study, we improved this by giving the operator a view of both the participant and the robot, using a second computer to control the robot's head orientation for better interaction.

4   Main Study

The main experiment was also carried out in the Social Robotics Lab at Jagiellonian University in Krakow, Poland. It was organized as a between-participants study, with each participant being assigned to one of the two conditions: 1) a humorous robot (experimental condition); and 2) a neutral robot (control condition).

4.1   Participants

Forty participants (F=17, M=22, Non-binary =1; Mean age = 28,97; SD=10,71) were recruited through social media and departmental email. During the recruitment, participants were asked if they ever met a humanoid robot (two participants had taken part in a previous study, so had met a humanoid robot before) and about their background (age, sex, educational background). The participants were randomly assigned to the experimental group or the control group. Each participant was paid 20 PLN (about 5 Euros) in cash for their participation.

4.2   Experimental Set up

The setup is shown in Fig. 3. The light in one part of the laboratory was turned off to hide the robot operator, and most participants did not see the operator. The participants were told at the beginning of the experiment that the robot is autonomous, and they did not show any indication of doubting this assumption.

The robot was operated by the same person for all the participants. The operator could see the participant through the camera on the robot's forehead (Fig. 2). The robot was stationary throughout the experiment but moved its head and arms naturally (live mode). All the conversation with the participant was conducted by the operator through the robot. The operator used two computers to control the robot: one running the Choregraphe program to control the robot's body movements and the view of the participant, and the other to control the robot's speech.

While filling out the questionnaire, the participant and the experimenter were near the door (position 1), during the initial small-talk phase, when the robot told jokes or commented on the weather, the participant was in position 2 and the experimenter in position 1, and during the game, both the participant and the experimenter were in positions 2. The interaction with the robot was recorded with the participant's consent.

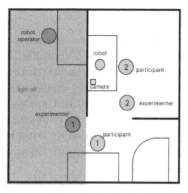

(a) Schematic of the study setup

(b) View of the robot's operator during the experiment.

Fig. 2. Experiment set up

4.3 Procedure

The participant entered the lab and was welcomed by the experimenter. Then they sat down at the table, and the participant was asked to sign the informed consent form. The participant was given a paper with the introduction to the experiment and the instructions. Then the participant was led to sit in front of NAO and wait for it to start the conversation. NAO welcomed the participant, introduced itself, and asked the participant's name and how he or she is. Then, for the experimental group, NAO made some small talk and told two jokes to the participant. The conversation always had the same structure, the jokes came at the same time for each participant and were only in this part of the experiment. For the control group, NAO made some remarks about the weather.

After the conversation, NAO explained the rules of the game, and then the researcher entered the space, showed the cards, turned them face down, and shuffled them out of the participant's sight. The researcher then spread the cards on the table face down, and asked the participant, 'Where is the red card?' After the participant made a guess, NAO suggested a card different than what the participant had chosen. If the participant asked why, NAO replied that it was its intuition. The researcher then stopped further interaction and asked the participant to choose a card without flipping it. The participant was asked to return to the first table and fill out the questionnaire. The researcher then let the participant reveal the card. Regardless of the colour of the card, the participant was offered a sweet as a prize. The participant was then given the participation fee. Finally, the robot operator was exposed and, depending on the interest of the participants, the study was explained, and the experimenter answered any questions. The entire procedure took 15 to 20 min.

4.4   Questionnaire

We used the Multi-Dimensional Measure of Trust (MDMT) questionnaire to measure the subjective level of trust in the robot [19]. The MDMT contains 16 elements to assess four differentiable trust dimensions. An agent can be trusted because it is reliable, competent, ethical, and/or sincere. These four dimensions are organized into two broader trust factors: Capacity Trust (Reliable, Capable) and Moral Trust (Ethical, Sincere). Moral trust is the subjective level of trust a person has in the robot's ethical and reliable behavior, while capacity trust is the subjective level of trust a person has in the robot's abilities or performance in executing its designated tasks.

Each of the 16 items was to be evaluated on an 8-point Likert scale from 0 (not at all) to 7 (very). They could also choose the option 'Does not fit', to avoid a forced answer. This questionnaire is widely used to measure trust in HRI and for comparison with other research. The original version is in English, which we translated into Polish for our study.

5   Results and Discussion

5.1   Objective Independent Variable

As shown in Table 1, about 75% of the participants followed the robot's advice. We conducted a Chi-square test to assess whether the proportion of participants who changed their decision differed significantly between the humour and the non-humour conditions. We did not find a significant difference ($p = 0.288$).

Table 1. Proportion of Participants Who Trusted the Robot

Condition	Followed the robot	Did not follow the robot
Humourous Nao	13	7
Non-humorous Nao	16	4
Total	**29**	**11**

For representativeness of the sample, we collected the age and gender of the participants before the study. We did additional analysis for the effect of age and gender on whether the participants accepted the suggestion by the robot in both the humour and the non-humour conditions (Fig. 3). We expected that more participants in the non-humour group would not accept the robot's suggestion, but we found that fewer participants (4 out of 20) did not change their decision. However, the mean age of these participants (43.5 yrs) was significantly higher than the other group (28.4 yrs). Though there were too few participants to make any generalizations (no statistical significance), this observation is consistent with the previous research that shows that older adults have a more negative attitude towards robots than younger adults [2]. We also noted that in the humour

Fig. 3. Effect of gender and age in humour and non-humour conditions

group, seven out of twenty participants did not accept the robot's suggestion, and only one of them described herself as a female. The present observation is in agreement with the prior study, which has suggested that women tend to place more trust in robots as compared to men [3].

Moreover, it is worth noting that two participants from the non-humorous group changed their decision to select a card that was neither suggested by the robot nor their initial preference. They might have chosen to deviate from the robot's recommendation while also wanting to avoid any potential conflict within the group. This possibility suggests that social dynamics and the desire to maintain positive relations within the team may have played a role in their decision-making process.

It should be emphasized that our study's outcomes may have been influenced by certain biases that could be attributed to both the nature of the task and the participants' prior knowledge of robots. For example, the experimenter shuffled the cards behind her back, which meant that the participant did not know where the red card was and had to guess. This might have created a negative attitude toward the task. In contrast, in the standard version of Three-card Monte, the three cards are moved around rapidly in the plain view of the participant. Moreover, the participants did not have any information about how the robot worked and what basis, if any, it might have to make its suggestion. Some participants reported after the study that theirs was a pure guess, that they decided to trust the robot because they thought it might have more information.

Another variable affecting the results is the participants' varying sense of humour. We prepared three jokes, two for the interaction and one just in case. The jokes were neutral according to race, gender, profession, and other factors that might be considered offensive; there was also one situational joke. However, participants could have had a different sense of humour and may not have liked the robot's humour.

5.2   Subjective Independent Variable

We conducted the Mann-Whitney U test on the results of the MDMT questionnaire to see if there was any difference between the humour and the non-humour conditions (Table 2). However, we did not find a significant difference either for the capacity trust (p=0.465) or for the moral trust (p=0.378).

Table 2. Average scores in MDMT

Condition	Capacity trust	Moral trust	Trust
Control condition	4.76	5.49	5.12
Research condition	4.98	5.70	5.34

Although we did not get significant differences in the Mann-Whitney U test, average scores in MDMT questionnaire had recurring differences. The participant who interacted with the humorous robot gave higher responses in the MDMT questionnaire than in the control group. This is visible on the capacity sub-scale and also in the moral sub-scale. The average score on the moral sub-scale trust is higher than the capacity trust in both conditions, suggesting relation-based trust. We also found a strong correlation between those sub-scales (r(39) = .794; $p < .01$), which explains the recurring differences.

It is worth examining the genesis of the questionnaire we used. The MDMT questionnaire was constructed by researchers who conducted open surveys and questionnaires with people recruited through Amazon Mechanical Turk. In one part of the creation, sorting trust words, participants were asked to consider 32 words or short phrases, 6–7 for each of the four hypothesized dimensions, as well as five filler items assumed to be unrelated to trust, which included the word 'humourous' [7]. Thus, this questionnaire assumed that humour is not related to trust. The MDMT questionnaire was constructed not for interaction with robots, but to distinguish different dimensions in trust, according to human, institutions, or robots. However, as far as we are aware, no studies have been conducted on humour and trust between humans with the MDMT questionnaire, so this area is still unexplored.

5.3   Relation of the Objective and Subjective Variables

We conducted a Mann-Whitney U test to see if the MDMT questionnaire results correspond to the decision to accept or not accept the robot's suggestion during the card game. We expected that the participants who changed their decision rated the robot higher in the MDMT questionnaire. However, we did not get a significant result in this regard ($p > 0.05$). This may be due to different personal attitudes of the participants, which requires further study [24, p.25]. Some participants trust robot less even if they accept the robot's suggestion, because their general baseline trust is lower.

5.4   Qualitative Analysis: Behavioural Observations

Analyzing the recording from the main study, we noticed some interesting behaviour patterns of the participants. For example, at the beginning of the interaction with the robot, many participants had their hands hidden under the table. But as time passed, and before they were asked to choose a card, they put their hands on the table. This suggests that these participants felt more comfortable with the robot as the interaction proceeded, and did not feel the need to keep a safe distance. (We excluded the possibility that the participants were cold as it was summer in Poland then, and the experimental room was at a comfortable temperature.)

Another observation was that some participants asked the robot why it thinks that the other card is red. Even though these participants asked for an explanation but did not receive it (the robot answered 'That is my intuition'), most of them followed the robot's suggestion.

Finally, a surprising behaviour was observed from most participants at the end of the interaction. After the participant selected the card, the experimenter asked them to go back to the table and complete the final questionnaire. As the participant stood up to leave, the robot conveyed its final message, "Thank you for the game, and see you later!" The participants consistently responded with a farewell remark such as "Thank you too, bye" or "It was nice to meet you". This suggests that the participants treated the robot as a social agent, a team member, or even a partner. This observation adds to the current understanding of human-robot interaction and highlights the need for further exploration of this phenomenon.

6   Conclusion

The primary objective of this study was to investigate the influence of humor on trust in the context of human-robot interaction (HRI). Despite not being able to confirm the main hypothesis, our study found some valuable insights by implementing a between-subjects study design. Our findings demonstrate that participants consistently engaged in effective teamwork with the robot, regardless of the presence or absence of humor.

Our study provides a notable contribution to the field of Human-Robot Interaction (HRI) by introducing a framework for using the Wizard-of-Oz methodology. This approach facilitated a controlled manipulation of humor in the robot's behavior while ensuring a realistic and interactive environment for participants. The pilot study played a crucial role in refining our methodology and improving the overall quality of the study. We believe that the comprehensive documentation of challenges encountered during the study serves as a valuable contribution to the field by highlighting potential pitfalls for future research endeavors.

The effect of humor on trust in human-robot interaction needs more research overcoming our limitations to be able to make further conclusions.

Acknowledgment. We thank Anna Kołbasa and Sharon Spisak for their help in conducting this study.

References

1. Alarcon, G.M., Lyons, J.B., Christensen, J.C.: The effect of propensity to trust and familiarity on perceptions of trustworthiness over time. Personality Individ. Differ. **94**, 309–315 (2016)
2. Chien, S.E., et al.: Age difference in perceived ease of use, curiosity, and implicit negative attitude toward robots. ACM Trans. Human-Robot Interact. **8**(2), 9:1–9:19 (2019). https://doi.org/10.1145/3311788
3. Gallimore, D., Lyons, J.B., Vo, T., Mahoney, S., Wynne, K.T.: Trusting robocop: gender-based effects on trust of an autonomous robot. Front. Psychol. **10**, 482 (2019)
4. Gladwell, M.: Talking to strangers. Gramedia Pustaka Utama (2020)
5. Greengross, G., Miller, G.: Humor ability reveals intelligence, predicts mating success, and is higher in males. Intelligence **39**(4), 188–192 (2011). https://doi.org/10.1016/j.intell.2011.03.006, https://www.sciencedirect.com/science/article/pii//S0160289611000523, publisher: JAI
6. Hansen, L.: 8 drivers who blindly followed their GPS into disaster (2015), https://theweek.com/articles/464674/8-drivers-who-blindly-followed-gps-into-disaster
7. Hempelmann, C.F., Samson, A.C.: Cartoons: drawn jokes? The primer of humor research pp. 609–640 (2008)
8. Holmes, J.: Making humour work: creativity on the job. Appl. Linguis. **28**(4), 518–537 (2007). https://doi.org/10.1093/applin/amm048, https://academic.oup.com/applij/article-lookup/doi/10.1093/applin/amm048
9. Hurley, R.F.: The decision to trust. Harv. Bus. Rev. **84**(9), 55–62 (2006)
10. Ivanov, S.H., Webster, C.: The robot as a consumer: a research agenda. SSRN Scholarly Paper ID 2960824, Social Science Research Network, Rochester, NY (2017), https://papers.ssrn.com/abstract=2960824
11. Joshi, S., de Visser, E.J., Abramoff, B., Ayaz, H.: Medical interviewing with a robot instead of a doctor: who do we trust more with sensitive information? In: Companion of the 2020 ACM/IEEE International Conference on Human-Robot Interaction, pp. 570–572. ACM, Cambridge UK (2020). https://doi.org/10.1145/3371382.3377441
12. Khavas, Z.R.: A review on trust in human-robot interaction (2021), arXiv:2105.10045
13. Kim, T.-Y., Lee, D.-R., Wong, N.Y.S.: Supervisor humor and employee outcomes: the role of social distance and affective trust in supervisor. J. Bus. Psychol. **31**(1), 125–139 (2016). https://doi.org/10.1007/s10869-015-9406-9
14. Larzelere, R.E., Huston, T.L.: The dyadic trust scale: toward understanding interpersonal trust in close relationships. J. Marriage Fam. **42**(3), 595–604 (1980)
15. Lee, J.D.: Review of a pivotal human factors article: humans and automation: use, misuse, disuse, abuse. human factors: J. Human Factors Ergonomics Soc. **50**(3), 404–410 (2008)
16. Lee, J.D., See, K.A.: Trust in automation: designing for appropriate reliance. Human Factors, p. 31 (2004)
17. Malle, B.F., Ullman, D.: A Multi-Dimensional Conception and Measure of Human-Robot Trust p. 21 (2019)
18. McDonald, P.: The Philosophy of Humour. Humanities-Ebooks (2013)
19. Mirnig, N., Stadler, S., Stollnberger, G., Giuliani, M., Tscheligi, M.: Robot humor: how self-irony and schadenfreude influence people's rating of robot likability. In: 2016 25th IEEE International Symposium on Robot and Human Interactive Communication (RO-MAN), pp. 166–171. IEEE (2016)

20. Moura Oliveira, P., Novais, P., Reis, L.P. (eds.): EPIA 2019. LNCS (LNAI), vol. 11805. Springer, Cham (2019). https://doi.org/10.1007/978-3-030-30244-3

21. Moussawi, S., Benbunan-Fich, R.: The effect of voice and humour on users' perceptions of personal intelligent agents. Behav. Inf. Technol. 40, 1603–1626 (2020). https://doi.org/10.1080/0144929X.2020.1772368, https://www.tandfonline.com/doi/full/10.1080/0144929X.2020.1772368

22. Mulder, M.P., Nijholt, A.: Humour Research: State of the Art. University of Twente, Centre for Telematics and Information Technology (2002)

23. Mutlu, B., Shiwa, T., Kanda, T., Ishiguro, H., Hagita, N.: Footing in human-robot conversations: how robots might shape participant roles using gaze cues. In: Proceedings of the 4th ACM/IEEE International Conference on Human Robot Interaction, pp. 61–68 (2009)

24. Nam, C.S., Lyons, J.B.: Trust in Human-Robot Interaction. Academic Press (2020), google-Books-ID: R8DvDwAAQBAJ

25. Nijholt, A., Niculescu, A.I., Valitutti, A., Banchs, R.E.: Humor in human-computer interaction: a short survey. Adjunct Proceedings of Interact, pp. 527–530 (2017)

26. O'Hara, K.: A general definition of trust. https://eprints.soton.ac.uk/341800/ (2012)

27. Riek, L.D.: Wizard of OZ studies in HRI: a systematic review and new reporting guidelines. J. Human-Robot Interact. 1(1), 119–136 (2012)

28. Schaefer, K.E., Chen, J.Y., Szalma, J.L., Hancock, P.A.: A meta-analysis of factors influencing the development of trust in automation: implications for understanding autonomy in future systems. Hum. Factors 58(3), 377–400 (2016)

29. Springer, P.J.: Military Robots and Drones: A Reference Handbook. ABC-CLIO (2013), ISBN: 978-1-59884-732-1

30. Tae, M., Lee, J.: The effect of robot's ice-breaking humor on likeability and future contact intentions. In: Companion of the 2020 ACM/IEEE International Conference on Human-Robot Interaction, pp. 462–464 (2020)

31. Vigni, F., Andriella, A., Rossi, S.: Sweet robot o'mine - how a cheerful robot boosts users' performance in a game scenario. RO-MAN Conference (2023)

32. Willis, J., Todorov, A.: First impressions: making up your mind after a 100-MS exposure to a face. Psychol. Sci. 17(7), 592–598 (2006)

33. Zhang, H., Yu, C., Tapus, A.: Why do you think this joke told by robot is funny? the humor style matters, pp. 572–577 (2022). https://doi.org/10.1109/RO-MAN53752.2022.9900515

A Pilot Usability Study of a Humanoid Avatar to Assist Therapists of ASD Children

Carole Fournier[1]([envelope]), Cécile Michelon[2], Arnaud Tanguy[1], Paul Audoyer[2], Véronique Granit[2], Amaria Baghdadli[2,3], and Abderrahmane Kheddar[4,1]

[1] CNRS -University of Montpellier, Laboratory of Computer Science, Robotics and Microelectronics of Montpellier, Montpellier, France
carole.fournier@lirmm.fr
[2] Centre Ressources Autisme Languedoc-Roussillon and Center of Excellence for Autism and Neurodevelopmental Disorders, CHU Montpellier, Montpellier, France
[3] Faculty of Medicine, University of Montpellier, Montpellier, France
[4] CNRS-AIST Joint Robotics Laboratory, IRL3218, Tsukuba, Japan

Abstract. In this article, we report on a pilot study consisting of an evaluation of the usability satisfaction and effectiveness of a preliminary telerobotic system to assist therapists of children with ASD. Unlike existing pre-programmed robotic systems, our solution beamed therapists in a humanoid robot (Pepper) to reproduce in real-time the therapist's gestures, speech and visual feedback aiming to embody the therapist in a humanoid robot avatar and be able to perform activities during an ESDM intervention. Evaluations of our system, used by eleven therapists in internal tests during mock session without children, are reported and suggest that future use in real therapy sessions with ASD children can begin.

Keywords: ASD therapists beaming · teleoperation · humanoid avatar

1 Introduction

Children diagnosed with autism spectrum disorder (ASD) have well-known difficulties in social communication. While the merit of behavioural methods for early social communication training in ASD is well documented, e.g., [23], that of robot-mediated social communication training is only emerging [19, 24]. Studies suggest that robots provide socialisation benefits for people with autism by increasing social engagement and attention, see examples in [22, 28]. These findings suggest that social robots could be therapeutic aids in ASD. For several years now, various studies have been conducted on the possibilities of interaction between humanoid robots and humans, especially with children with ASD, e.g., [9, 22, 28]. However, there are few studies evaluating or highlighting the effects over time of the beneficial contributions of robotic interventions [4, 32]. These perspectives imply new interdisciplinary studies for the design, development and implementation of new robotic observation and interaction systems.

According to a very recent study [38], approximately 1/100 people have an ASD and the recommendations of the French National Authority for Health

© The Author(s), under exclusive license to Springer Nature Singapore Pte Ltd. 2024
A. Al. Ali et al. (Eds.): ICSR 2023, LNAI 14453, pp. 336–349, 2024.
https://doi.org/10.1007/978-981-99-8715-3_28

highlight the value of early and personalised behavioural intervention models in ASD. One of these models is the Early Start Denver Model (ESDM) [16,31] which is a programme developed specifically to work with children with autism between the ages of 12 and 48 months (although the programme can be used up to a maximum age of 60 months, that is 5 y.o.). This method is employed for at least 20 h per week per child in some western countries such as the United States [3]. In France, the care time using this model is most often less than 5 h/week due to a lack of trained professionals in sufficient numbers, according to the Hospital of Montpellier, which limits the progress of children. Furthermore, one of the foundations of ESDM is the positive engagement between a child and a therapist built through the pleasure of play. Each intervention therefore consists of offering the child different activities that s/he can choose from, then playing with her/him and using every interaction opportunities: e.g., singing songs, approving what s/he is doing by vocal interaction, grabbing and asking for toys to interact with her/him as well, and so on. Through this intervention, therapists have to adapt to each child through play and their wishes. However, it can be difficult for a therapist to accurately and faith-fully collect and analyse all the socially adapted or expected behaviours of the child while being fully engaged in the interaction required by the behavioural intervention. An assistant in these tasks could reduce the therapist's workload and improve interventions. Therefore, it seems appropriate to use teleoperation technology in this case to assist the therapist in games and collecting data at the same time.

To both see how the robot can assist the therapist during an intervention with the Denver method,

1. we designed a complete humanoid (Pepper) teleoperation system to be operated (beamed) by therapists as own avatar;
2. we conducted a pilot study aiming to train therapists in the use of their social robot avatar Pepper as a tool for therapeutic mediation and assistance in routine care; and
3. assessed our results with respect to complement those found in [24] where virtual reality (VR) teleoperated robots are a relevant tool to deliver intervention with ASD children.

Our hypothesis is that an interactive teleoperated robot is indeed an effective tool for therapists, and is ready to use for future interaction with an ASD child during an ESDM intervention.

2   A Teleoperated Robotic Avatar

Teleoperation designates a robotic system that is remotely controlled by a user [20]. We choose to use the humanoid Pepper [29] a robot designed for assistive purpose, e.g., [39], as a therapist avatar to interact with children with ASD. Indeed, this robot is specifically targeted to interact with and assist people in social environments. The robot is 1.20 m high, weighs 28 kg, has 20 DoF and was already used to interact with children, e.g., [14,24,35].

To devise our telepresence system, we accounted for different criteria determined by therapists. We have based our technical specifications from two sources: (i) the study in [21] that includes collaboration between doctors, parents and ASD adults; and (ii) our multiple meetings and discussions with therapists of the Autism Resource Centre (CRA)[1] of the Montpellier hospital, that started two years ago.

The main robot functionality requirements we retained are: the appearance shall be "friendly"; the voice should be soft; the robot must be able to get down to the appropriate children's level; to interact with them with human-like gesture and be able to carry an object when given (e.g., carry a small toy to propose the child to play with it). The main requirements for the whole telerobotic system are: a minimal training phase (time) for therapists before the intervention; installation with minimalistic equipment for easy set-up on hospital premises.

The whole body control is made with our framework **mc_rtc**[2] and **mc_naoqi**[3] thanks to previous work carried out in [8].

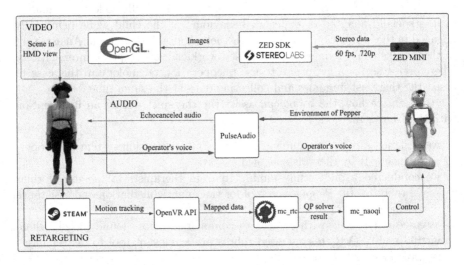

Fig. 1. The simplified system architecture to teleoperate Pepper through VR. The system is divided into three parts: (1) The video stream; (2) The audio stream; (3) The retargeting module.

To enable remote control of the robot, VR tools are integrated into the development of the remote operation system. As shown in Fig. 1, the whole architecture is structured between two main entities: the Pepper and the VR materials connected to the software `SteamVR`. An `HTC VIVE Pro` Head-Mounted Display (HMD) enables the teleoperator to display to the therapist the stereo video

[1] https://www.autisme-ressources-lr.fr/index.php.

[2] https://github.com/jrl-umi3218/mc_rtc.

[3] https://github.com/jrl-umi3218/mc_naoqi.

environment perceived by a ZED Mini camera mounted on the head of Pepper. Then, to transmit the sound environment between the therapist and the child, the internal microphone and loudspeaker of Pepper are connected to the HMD.

2.1 Retargeting

One of the main challenges is to have an intuitive anthropomorphic mapping between the therapist and the robot workspaces. This is particularly challenging due to the short size of this robot and the limited number of DoFs. Different methods have been proposed to solve this issue, e.g., [1,13,24]. To control the robot remotely in real-time, a first method trial is tested based on [13]. The idea is to base the whole retargeting on the orientation and angular velocity of each link and not to take into account the positions. This way, size and morphology factors are not an obstacle. However, the limited number of DoFs, 6 in each arm with the wrist and elbow yaw being redundant, leads to an over-constrained arm control. This method is therefore not suitable.

In the end we developed our method that we also implemented successfully in another context and another humanoid [11]. The user is equipped with an HTC VIVE VR headset, two controllers in the hands and one VIVE tracker on the lower back as shown in the Fig. 1. Each of these elements allows to track in real-time the position and the orientation of the following articulations: head, wrists, and lower back. End-effector hands tracking allows for easy and complete arm movements. Tracking hand posture in the workspace is sufficient to achieve "human-like" arm movements for the robot Pepper, due to the limited DoFs in each arm. Hand, lower back and head postures are tracked in the SteamVR reference world w with the transformation matrix at the origin O: T_{Ow}^{Hw}, T_{Ow}^{Bw} and T_{Ow}^{HEw} respectively.

As a difference with [11], a scaling ratio α is determined at the start of the controller's launch, to match the size of the therapist's arms to that of the controlled robot with a sensation of matching size. The position of the user's shoulder S relative to the tracker in the lower back is assessed a priori using a tape measure. The ratio α corresponds to the ratio between the length of the user's arm l_{human} (measure between the position of the shoulder and the beginning of the finger) and that of the robot l_{robot}, that is,

$$\alpha = \frac{l_{robot}}{l_{human}}, \qquad \alpha \in [0,1] \cap \mathbb{R} \tag{1}$$

The lower back tracker is used as the reference frame to sustain posture coherence between the robot and the operator if the latter moves during the teleoperation. The position of the hand for example, relative to the shoulder in the SteamVR world reference is:

$$T_{Sw}^{Hw} = T_{Ow}^{Hw}(T_{Bw}^{Sw}T_{Ow}^{Bw})^{-1} \tag{2}$$

Thus with the robot's wrists as end-effectors, the hands are directed into the robot's frame r through the position and orientation of the controllers. The ratio

α is applied to the relative position of the hand in the world frame of reference to obtain its posture relative to the shoulder in the robot frame of reference.

$$T_{Sr}^{Hr} = \begin{pmatrix} R_{Sw}^{Hw} & \alpha \cdot p_{Sw}^{Hw} \\ 0 \quad 0 \quad 0 & 1 \end{pmatrix} \quad (3)$$

As the reference frames are not oriented in the same way between the robot and SteamVR (designed as a world reference frame), a mapping is defined manually for each tracked body. Moreover, an offset is applied to correspond to the correct initial posture. Then, the position of the hand in the robot frame is determined by multiplying the matrix in eq. (3) by the transformation matrix of the shoulder in the robot frame, assuming that the robot and human shoulder are in the same posture. The same method is applied for the head, with only the orientation needed (head yaw and head pitch).

2.2   Perceptual Feedback

Visual Feedback. To display the view to the user, we render the scene (in practice, the child room environment) in the VR headset. To do this, a ZED Mini camera is mounted on the robot at the eye level. The camera is attached using a system that allows its height and orientation to be adjusted. Adjusting its orientation, notably slightly forward, allows the therapist to better see the robot hands in the reduced field-of-view of the camera and due to the anatomical proportion of the robot. Adjusting the height allows the therapist to be better embodied [2]. To render the view in the HMD, data from the robot camera are extracted by means of the ZED SDK with a 720 p resolution and at 60 fps; then they are rendered through a texture in a scene with OpenVR and OpenGL.

To help users become more aware of their ability to move in space, red bands appear around the visual field of the display point-of-view, as the mobile base approaches an obstacle. An obstacle is detected at a 50 cm distance. The sonars in Pepper's mobile base can be used to assess possible impacts to the front and rear, and the infra-red sensors for the right and left sides.

Sound Feedback. Real-time audio feedback is established between the robot and the teleoperator via the PulseAudio server and the FFmeg library as shown in Fig. 1. On the robot side, the loudspeaker and microphone are very close together, inducing an echo that will be heard on the user side. The echo-cancel module is then used to cancel this effect. The voice of the robot is then the one of the therapist who knows how to modulate her/his voice according to the child in front of her/him.

2.3   Adaptive Joint Stiffness

During teleoperation the hip actuator (between the torso and legs) is supporting the weight of all the upper body which is half of Pepper weight. The joint is in a quasi-static posture during 15 mn of intervention and has a tendency to overheat.

In NAOqi the stiffness is in %, 0 meaning the joint is free and 100 meaning the joint can use full torque power. When the stiffness of all joints is at 100% all the time, as our design control with mc_naoqi was before, the leg joint overheats in less than 15mn. Aldebaran Robotics proposes a *smart stiffness*[4] solution to adjust the torque power over time, proportional to the error. However, since the error is not considered as an absolute value, as soon as the error is negative, stiffness falls to 0. This means that during teleoperation, one may be locked in a position, by moving one's arm backwards for example. We decided to propose our own adaptive stiffness with a corrector as follow:

$$S = K_p \cdot |q_d - q_r| + K_i \cdot \text{EMA}_{\Delta t}(|q_d - q_r|) \tag{4}$$

where q_d (rad) is the joint target value provided by the QP controller; q_r is the real encoders value (rad); K_p is a positive proportional gain; K_i is the negative integral gain; and $\text{EMA}_{\Delta t}$ stands for exponential moving average along Δt s. We use the EMA filter instead of an integral value to reduce the stiffness if the average absolute error, over a time window, is too large. In this case, if the therapist pushes over one arm during teleoperation, the stiffness will grow proportionally and then decrease after a few seconds so it can avoid damaging the motors.

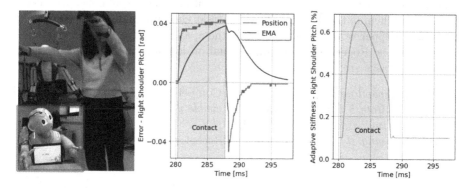

Fig. 2. Adaptive stiffness values (in light orange) on the right shoulder over time when the arm is pushed manually and the torque error increases (dark green). The EMA of the absolute error is in (dark blue). (Color figure online)

This is particularly useful because Pepper does not have a force sensor so it is not easy to implement haptic feedback [6,7]. So during teleoperation one could contact a table, for example on the side, without being aware of it and unintentionally push over the table which can damage the motors. With our method, the stiffness will decrease avoiding damaging the motors, see Fig. 2. The final value is then filtered with: (i) the robot's native method of reducing stiffness when it reaches a threshold according to four defined levels; (ii) a value

---

[4] http://doc.aldebaran.com/2-4/naoqi/motion/reflexes-smart-stiffness.html.

always between 10 and 100%, except when the temperature reaches level 4, in which case the stiffness is reduced to 0; (iii) a first-order low-pass filter with sampling period $dt = 0.012$ s and a cutoff period of $100dt$.

3   Use Case and Pilot Study

3.1   Early Start Denver Model: A Use Case

The ESDM is a behavioural therapy technique with a major advantage: its therapeutic methods are entirely play-based. This helps to improve the social and communicative skills of children with ASD. A list of skills is drawn up to assess the child's abilities, and learning objectives are written in collaboration with the parents. Each goal is divided into several progressive learning steps, from the basic skill, the one observed in the initial assessment, to complete mastery of the goal as defined in [34]. Several studies have shown the effectiveness of ESDM for autism, e.g., [33]. The study in [17] show a significant improvement in autism symptoms in children aged between 18 to 30 months. These improvements included language, IQ and social skills after two years of therapy.

For the purpose of this study we determined with two speech therapists, three tasks over 15 mn. This duration is chosen to represent the end of 1-hour sessions, during which children often lose attention. They would therefore need to re-engage them in the session. The three tasks chosen were determined in such a way that Pepper would be able to carry them, and which are part of the tasks proposed in the Rogers and Dawson manual on learning to communicate [34]. These three tasks are:

– Task 1: *responding to greetings* - Social Competencies, Level 1, item 8;
– Task 2: *imitate 5 movements involving visible parts of the body in song/play routines* - Imitation, Level 1, item 2;
– Task 3: *giving the requested object* - Receptive Communication, Level 1, item 13.

3.2   Preliminary Testing Scenario with Therapists

Population. To evaluate the acceptance of the guided robot in teleoperation as a therapy tool in the department of the CRA, we recruited 11 therapists (2 registered nurses, 2 child psychiatrists, 6 psychologists, 1 speech therapist), all are staff of the Montpellier Hospital and none of them is from the co-author list. We don't have the benefit of feedback from the psychomotor therapist, who lost interest in the issue after noticing that the robot has very little grip in the hands and lacks dexterity. We considered the following as inclusion criteria: work in the CRA team with children with autism syndrome, no history of epilepsy for visual feedback in VR. The group is constituted with 81.81% of women (9) and 18.18% of men (2), with 4 people under the age of 30, 2 between 31 and 40 and 5 over 41. This repartition is representative of the gender proportion in this department. Few of the participants in the study are familiar with new technologies: only one had already used a virtual reality headset (but not with ASD children); none had ever used a humanoid robot such as Milo [27], Kaspar [36] or Pepper [14], and only 4 out of the 11 participants said they were used to using digital tools during their work (such as eye tracking, tablets and external cameras), one 'always', two 'rather' and one 'sometimes'. The other participants are not used to working with digital tools (4 'at all' and 3 'rather not').

Study Protocol. During the preliminary study, each participant tries the system within the same conditions, in order to complete tasks needed during interventions.

1) Training: First, a period of 5 mn for each participant is dedicated to the training of the system, recognizing the button commands, understanding the goal and the movement possibilities. This first part of training is made in simulation with the robot displayed in an RVIZ scene.

2) Teleoperation trial: Then, a session of 10 mn of VR teleoperation is started with different goals to meets: (i) To see if they are able to move in space and be aware of their environment, they are asked to cross the hall from the teleoperation room to the intervention room (around 2 m away); (ii) greeting another person in the intervention room, as asked for the (Task 1); (iii), asking each user to reproduce different song routines they know, one at least, with gestures (Task 2), (iv) and finally we ask them to choose a game among many disposed in front of them, and try to ask for it and catch it (Task 3).

3) Teleoperation free time: At the end of the session we proposed to each participant if s/he wanted to test something else, and let them try to see if they succeeded in doing other tasks.

4) Feedback: After removing the VR material, each participant answered four questionnaires: (i) one overall questionnaire to know the profile of each of them (age, gender, career...); (ii) one *Usability* Metric for User Experience (UMUX) questionnaire which follows the definition of the ISO 9241-11 of usability [15], adapted to our design setup and evaluate with a 7-point Likert scale [25]; (iii) one *pragmatic* quality scale from AttrakDiff2 [18] which describes the usability of the system and determined if the user is able to meet her/his goal using it. It is used to complete and to compare with the previous one and is evaluated also with a 7-point Likert scale; (iv) an *acceptability* score to assess the views of therapists from CRA towards social robots as a tool for autistic children, this survey is inspired by the study of [30] with 5-point Likert scale. The questions are: Q1- In your opinion, is it acceptable for social robots to be used as assistants for care staff during interventions with ASD children? Q2- In your opinion, is it acceptable for social robots to be used to monitor the progress and help diagnose an ASD child? Q3- In your opinion, is it acceptable for information to be recorded and stored by a robot when it interacts with an ASD child? (assuming parental consent) Q4- In your opinion, would it be acceptable for some ASD children to perceive social robots as friends following their therapy? Q5- Do you think the risk that some children might become attached to social robots is acceptable? Q6- Do you think it's acceptable to use social robots that closely resemble humans? The original version of the questions is established in French.

4   Results

Each of the 11 participants succeeded in completing all the tasks during teleoperation: saying "hello" and "goodbye" using speech and gestures (Task 1); mime and sing a nursery rhyme (Task 2); managing to move the robot to another room along a hall in the hospital ward to go to the intervention room; and grabbing an object to play with (a rainstick and a ball) after asking for it (Task 3). These tasks took between 4 and 10 mn to complete, depending on the skill and willingness of each operator to complete the tasks quickly. Some of the therapists asked to try other activities: 3 decided to point their hand at another object they wanted to try and manipulate (maracas, for example); 1 therapist wanted to shake the hand of another therapist with whom the robot was interacting; and 5 therapists tried to return the ball by throwing it. However, due to the delay in opening the hand, the throws were unsuccessful. Some limitations of the system were raised. Almost all participants needed guidance to be able to move around the corridor and the slightly heavy rain stick tended to slip out of Pepper's hands.

The user experience (UX) is evaluated using two questionnaires: one usability score and one pragmatic quality score. The first questionnaire, adapted from methode UMUX, is evaluated following the method of System Usability Scale (SUS) score and the one presented in [15]. Each question is scored with a value between 0 and 6. The questions Q1, Q2, Q3 and Q5 are scored following the rule [score $-$ 1] and the Q4 and Q6 with [7 $-$ score]. To calculate the total score as a percentage, we divide the sum by 36 and multiply the result by 100. This score is calculated for each participant and we obtain a final average score of $\mu = 66.67\%$ and $\sigma = 10.83\%$. The pragmatic quality score is above 4 on average for each question, which is the minimum value to be acceptable.

The acceptability of the robot as a therapeutic aid for carrying out an ESDM session is obtained from the final questionnaire. The aim of this questionnaire is to understand the wishes and concerns of the therapists with regard to this new technology and the possibilities of working in the department. The first three questions concern the acceptability of using the tool. The second part is about the general use of humanoid robots. Responses to the questions 1 and 3, see Fig 3, have on average high scores (value out of 5 from 1-"Strongly disagree" to 5-"Strongly agree") and small standard deviation (std) as shown in Table 1. Whereas questions 2, 4 , 5 and 6 have lower average score with wider std.

5   Discussion

The results of the questionnaires and the feedback from the therapists and our observations show that *the system is usable* to perform a 15 mn ESDM session

Q1 - In your opinion, is it acceptable for social robots to be used as assistants for care staff during interventions with ASD children?

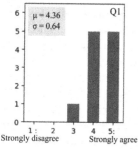

Q2 - In your opinion, is it acceptable for social robots to be used to monitor the progress and help diagnose an ASD child?

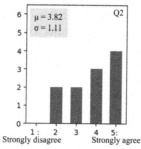

Q3 - In your opinion, is it acceptable for information to be recorded and stored by a robot when it interacts with an ASD child? (assuming parental consent)

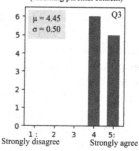

Q4 - In your opinion, would it be acceptable for some ASD children to perceive social robots as friends following their therapy?

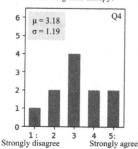

Q5 - Do you think the risk that some children might become attached to social robots is acceptable?

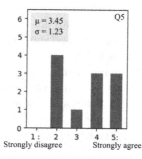

Q6 - Do you think it's acceptable to use social robots that closely resemble humans?

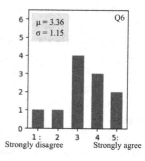

Fig. 3. Acceptability score data, mean and standard deviation (in grey boxes) for each question. The answer are evaluated with semantic differential questions and the answers : 1- Strongly disagree 2- Disagree 3- Neutral 4- Agree 5- Strongly agree. (Color figure online)

Table 1. The UX results for usability and pragmatic quality of the system.

UMUX questions (Scale score 1 to 7)	n	mean	std
1. Do you think this teleoperation system is a good intermediary for interacting with children with ASD?	11	4.72	1.35
2. Do you think this remote operation system is a good tool to assist you during interventions?	11	4.64	1.21
3. The system allows users to perform a 15 mn ESDM session	11	5.10	1.51
4. Using Pepper in teleoperation is a frustrating experience	11	2.91	1.97
5. This remote operation system is easy to use	11	5.18	0.75
6. I have to spend too much time correcting things with this teleoperation system	11	2.72	0.90
AttrakDiff2 - (Scale score 1 to 7) - The teleoperation system is rather :	n	mean	std
1. 1-Technical 7- Intuitive	11	4.64	1.63
2. 1-Complicated 7- Simple	11	5.18	0.98
3. 1-Not practical 7- Practical	11	4.64	1.03
4. 1-Cumbersome 7- Straightforward	11	4.00	1.00
5. 1-Unpredictable 7- Predictable	11	5.36	1.36
6. 1-Confusing 7- Clearly structured	11	5.73	1.01
7. 1-Unruly 7- Manageable	11	5.45	0.93

for three predefined tasks. The results of the UMUX-like survey of 66.67% highlights the correct usability of the system according to the SUS and UMUX score metrics: between "ok" and "good" on the scale, but also reveal paths of possible improvements. The score of the pragmatic quality questions validates this same hypothesis with scores slightly above the average (i.e., above 4). The main limitations put forward the therapists are: the lack of dexterity in the hands that prohibits fine manipulation of toys. Currently, a single actuator enables the hands to be opened and closed completely, making it impossible to point with the fingers (useful for expressive communication [5]). This lack of dexterity due to the design of the robot [29] means also that it is unable to grip objects that are too large or relatively heavy. And the absence of wrist flexion/extension actuator makes the gripping tasks more complicated. This clearly puts high-constraints on next-generation robotics design for ASD applications, notwithstanding the consequent impact on prices. During teleoperation, some therapists also discovered that due to the limitate workspace of Pepper [1] some postures are more complicated up to not possible to reproduce with Pepper than others. For example: clapping both hands, spinning both arms around one another or maintaining both hands in contact while moving. Two participants judged that a more important amount of time, i.e.,higher than 5 mn, is necessary to be trained with the system before manipulation, to be completely efficient during interventions.

Regarding *visual feedback in VR*, many therapists mentioned before teleoperation that they might have sickness and nausea, but only one participant mentioned a disorientation after removing the HMD. The reduced field of view means that therapists do not always have full confidence that the robot is perfectly replicating the gestures produced and do not feel completely aware of their environment (i.e., lack of embodiment [2]). However, when interacting and learning with ASD children, they want to make sure that the movements made are understandable to the child. We might consider having two point-of-views displayed on two different screens such as the setup of the Team Northeastern during the global competition ANA Avatar XPrize [26]: (i) in a first screen: a ZED 2 camera with a wide field-of-view and positioned high up to display a global view of the room, 2) in a second screen: the ZED Mini camera on Pepper displays the robot's point of view, and the operator wears 3D glasses. A VIVE tracker is then placed on the head to track the movement of the user instead of the HMD. The latest feedback on VR is to sit down during teleoperation so as to be more or less at the same height as the robot, and so be less disturbed in seeing the environment from below.

As raised by one participant of this study, the *acceptance* is subjective to each individual and requires a multidisciplinary approach. These results are only indicative in the context of the Montpellier CRA and our protocol.

According to the results, most of the therapists agreed that a social robot can be used as a tool to interact with ASD children as an assistant and for recording and collecting data. Although the average is high for diagnostic aid and assessment of the child's progress, the standard deviation is higher. Practitioners emphasise that the robot must remain in the field of assistance as it is also highlighted in [12]. However, as this department is a diagnostic unit, the feeling of being able to be replaced was often evoked and may have had an impact on the answers to this question. The responses from the 11 therapists show heterogeneous opinions on the acceptability of the *robot's appearance* in the case of it being a humanoid robot. The study in [30] reveals the same non-conclusive results regarding the acceptability of human-like robots. The lack of examples of this type of interaction may be a hindrance, and as one of the therapists pointed out, the look and ease with humanoid robots may be different for autistic children. A study carried out in [37] shows a positive appreciation by children of the Pepper robot. On the other hand, any other shape would have made it difficult to beam and teleoperate!

Another concern raised is that the child may interact with the robot and make progress in social communication with it. Yet, there is no guarantee that any progress can be reproduced when interacting with humans over time.

6   Conclusion and Future Work

This pilot study allowed us to assess that our system can effectively be used by and assist therapists during a short ESDM intervention with ASD children. It also shows that they are willing to try out new tools and agree to help design new ones to better assist them during therapy sessions. Obtained feedback revealed rooms of improvements for the teleoperation system with a view to setting up a future protocol at Montpellier University Hospital. The improvements will focus on visual feedback by adding SLAM [10] or two point-of-views on two screens [26] to increase therapists awareness of their environment, and on the implementation of haptic feedback to avoid collisions and complement sensory feedback for better interaction with the children. Another protocol beginning in fall 2023 will evaluate the quality of the robot as a tool during ESDM intervention with children aged between 18 to 30 months. This new study aims to evaluate the relevance of the solution during real interventions both for therapists and children. That is, whether this technology will enhance the learning effects of social communications according to the tasks defined above, and whether this will enable therapists to concentrate more on the session while the robot itself records the children's progress and proceed with predefined markings.

References

1. Alibeigi, M., Rabiee, S., Ahmadabadi, M.N.: Inverse kinematics based human mimicking system using skeletal tracking technology. J. Intell. Robot. Syst. **1485**, 27–45 (2017)
2. Aymerich-Franch, L., Petit, D., Ganesh, G., Kheddar, A.: The second me: seeing the real body during humanoid robot embodiment produces an illusion of bi-location. Conscious. Cogn. **46**, 99–109 (2016)
3. Bartolini Girardot, A.M., Chatel, C., Bessis, C., Avenel, E., Garrigues, M.H., Poinso, F.: Expérimentation de la prise en charge early start denver model (ESDM): les effets sur le développement de 4 jeunes enfants avec troubles du spectre de l'autisme. Neuropsychiatr. Enfance Adolesc. **65**(8), 461–468 (2017)

4. Beaumont, R., Sofronoff, K.: A multi-component social skills intervention for children with asperger syndrome: the junior detective training program. J. Child Psychol. Psychiatry **49**(8), 895 (2008)

5. Belmonte, M., Saxena-Chandhok, T., Cherian, R., Muneer, R., George, L., Karanth, P.: Oral motor deficits in speech-impaired children with autism. Front. Integrat. Neurosci. **7**, 47 (2013)

6. Bolotnikova, A., Courtois, S., Kheddar, A.: Compliant robot motion regulated via proprioceptive sensor based contact observer. In: IEEE-RAS International Conference on Humanoid Robots, pp. 1–9 (2018)

7. Bolotnikova, A., Courtois, S., Kheddar, A.: Contact observer for humanoid robot pepper based on tracking joint position discrepancies. In: IEEE International Symposium on Robot and Human Interactive Communication, pp. 29–34 (2018)

8. Bolotnikova, A., Gergondet, P., Tanguy, A., Courtois, S., Kheddar, A.: Task-space control interface for softbank humanoid robots and its human-robot interaction applications. In: IEEE/SICE International Symposium on System Integration, pp. 560–565 (2021)

9. Cabibihan, J.-J., Javed, H., Ang, M., Aljunied, S.M.: Why robots? a survey on the roles and benefits of social robots in the therapy of children with autism. Int. J. Soc. Robot. **5**(4), 593–618 (2013)

10. Chen, Y., et al.: Enhanced visual feedback with decoupled viewpoint control in immersive humanoid robot teleoperation using slam. In: IEEE-RAS 21st International Conference on Humanoid Robots, pp. 306–313 (2022)

11. Cisneros-Limon, R.,et al.: A cybernetic avatar system to embody human telepresence for connectivity, exploration and skill transfer. Int. J. Soc. Robot. (2024)

12. Coeckelbergh, M., et al.: A survey of expectations about the role of robots in robot-assisted therapy for children with ASD: ethical acceptability, trust, sociability, appearance, and attachment. Sci. Eng. Ethics **22**(1), 1353–3452 (2016)

13. Darvish, K., et al.: Whole-body geometric retargeting for humanoid robots. In: IEEE-RAS 19th International Conference on Humanoid Robots, pp. 679–686 (2019)

14. Efstratiou, R., et al.: Teaching daily life skills in autism spectrum disorder (ASD) interventions using the social robot pepper. In: Lepuschitz, W., Merdan, M., Koppensteiner, G., Balogh, R., Obdržálek, D. (eds.) RiE 2020. AISC, vol. 1316, pp. 86–97. Springer, Cham (2021). https://doi.org/10.1007/978-3-030-67411-3_8

15. Finstad, K.: The usability metric for user experience. Interact. Comput. **22**(5), 323–327 (2010), modelling user experience - An agenda for research and practice

16. Geoffray, M.M., et al.: Using ESDM 12 hours per week in children with autism spectrum disorder: feasibility and results of an observational study. Psychiatria Danubina (2019)

17. Geraldine, D., et al.: .: Early behavioral intervention is associated with normalized brain activity in young children with autism. J. Am. Acad. Child Adolesc. Psychiatry **51**(11), 1150–1159 (2012)

18. Hassenzahl, M., Burmester, M., Koller, F.: AttrakDiff: Ein Fragebogen zur Messung wahrgenommener hedonischer und pragmatischer Qualität, pp. 187–196. Vieweg+Teubner Verlag, Wiesbaden (2003)

19. Hijaz, A., Korneder, J., Louie, W.Y.G.: In-the-wild learning from demonstration for therapies for autism spectrum disorder. In: IEEE International Conference on Robot and Human Interactive Communication, pp. 1224–1229 (2021)

20. Hokayem, P.F., Spong, M.W.: Bilateral teleoperation: an historical survey. Automatica **42**(12), 2035–2057 (2006)

21. Huijnen, C.A.G.J., Lexis, M.A.S., Jansens, R., de Witte, L.P.: How to implement robots in interventions for children with autism? a co-creation study involving people with autism, parents and professionals. J. Autism Dev Disord **47**(06), 3079–3096 (07 2017)

22. Ivani, A.S., et al.: A gesture recognition algorithm in a robot therapy for ASD children. Biomed. Signal Process. Control **74**, 103512 (2022)

23. Kouroupa, A., Laws, K.R., Irvine, K., Mengoni, S.E., Baird, A., Sharma, S.: The use of social robots with children and young people on the autism spectrum: a systematic review and meta-analysis. PLOS ONE **17**(6), 1–25 (06 2022)

24. Kulikovskiy, R., Sochanski, M., Hijaz, A., Eaton, M., Korneder, J., Geoffrey Louie, W.Y.: Can therapists design robot-mediated interventions and teleoperate robots using VR to deliver interventions for ASD. In: IEEE International Conference on Robotics and Automation, pp. 3669–3676 (2021)

25. Likert, R.: A technique for the measurement of attitudes. Archives Psychol. **140**(55) (1932)

26. Luo, R., et al.: Team northeastern: Reliable telepresence at the ANA XPRIZE avatar final testing. In: IEEE International Conference on Robotics and Automation (2023)

27. Marinoiu, E., Zanfir, M., Olaru, V., Sminchisescu, C.: 3D human sensing, action and emotion recognition in robot assisted therapy of children with autism. In: Proceedings of the IEEE Conference on Computer Vision and Pattern Recognition (CVPR) (2018)

28. Mayadunne, M.M.M.S., Manawadu, U.A., Abeyratne, K.R., Silva, P.R.S.D.: A robotic companion for children diagnosed with autism spectrum disorder. In: International Conference on Image Processing and Robotics, pp. 1–6 (2020)

29. Pandey, A.K., Gelin, R.: A mass-produced sociable humanoid robot: pepper: the first machine of its kind. IEEE Robot. Autom. Mag. **25**(3), 40–48 (2018)

30. Robot enhanced therapy for children with autism disorders: measuring ethical acceptability. IEEE Technol. Soc. Mag. **35**(2), 54–66 (2016)

31. Peter, C., Mengarelli, F.: La prise en charge précoce en autisme avec le modèle ESDM. Le Journal des psychologues **1**(353), 19–22 (2018)

32. Puglisi, A., et al.: Social humanoid robots for children with autism spectrum disorders: a review of modalities, indications, and pitfalls. Children **9**(7), 953 (2022)

33. Raffaella, D., Vissia, C., Andrea, D., Giulia, B., Marco, C., Costanza, C.: Feasibility and outcomes of the early start denver model delivered within the public health system of the friuli venezia giulia italian region. Brain Sci. **11**(9), 1191 (2021)

34. Rogers, S.J., Dawson, G.: Early start denver model for young children with autism: Promoting language, learning, and engagement (2009)

35. Uluer, P., Kose, H., Landowska, A., Zorcec, T., Robins, B., Erol Barkana, D.: Child-robot interaction studies during COVID-19 pandemic

36. Wood, L.J., Zaraki, A., Robins, B., Dautenhahn, K.: Developing kaspar: a humanoid robot for children with autism. Int. J. Soc. Robot. **13**, 491–508 (2021)

37. Zehnder, E., Jouaiti, M., Charpillet, F.: Evaluating robot acceptance in children with ASD and their parents. In: International Conference on Social Robotics (2022)

38. Zeidan, J., et al.: Global prevalence of autism: a systematic review update. Autism Res. **15**, 778–790 (2022)

39. Zheng, Z., Das, S., Young, E.M., Swanson, A., Warren, Z., Sarkar, N.: Autonomous robot-mediated imitation learning for children with autism. In: IEEE International Conference on Robotics and Automation, pp. 2707–2712 (2014)

Primitive Action Recognition Based on Semantic Facts

Adrien Vigné[1]([✉])(ID), Guillaume Sarthou[2](ID), and Aurélie Clodic[1](ID)

[1] LAAS-CNRS, Université de Toulouse, CNRS, INSA, Toulouse, France
{adrien.vigne,aurelie.clodic}@laas.fr
[2] IRIT, Université de Toulouse, CNRS, Toulouse, France
guillaume.sarthou@irit.fr

Abstract. To interact with humans, a robot has to know actions done by each agent presents in the environment, robotic or not. Robots are not omniscient and can't perceive every actions made but, as humans do, we can equip the robot with the ability to infer what happens from the perceived effects of these actions on the environment.

In this paper, we present a lightweight and open-source framework to recognise primitive actions and their parameters. Based on a semantic abstraction of changes in the environment, it allows to recognise unperceived actions. In addition, thanks to its integration into a cognitive robotic architecture implementing perspective-taking and theory of mind, the presented framework is able to estimate the actions recognised by the agent interacting with the robot. These recognition processes are refined on the fly based on the current observations. Tests on real robots demonstrate the framework's usability in interactive contexts.

Keywords: Action Recognition · Human-Robot Interaction · Cognitive Robotics

1 Introduction

Where robots have been restricted for a while at performing complex tasks on their own in an autonomous way, or in coordination with other robotic agents, the field of Human-Robot Interaction brings the new challenge of robots performing shared tasks with humans. In light of the definition of joint action, this means that robots should be able to interact with humans and coordinate their actions in space and time to bring about a change in the environment [18]. Cooperation and collaboration tend to be key features to make robots more adaptative and thus flexible with respect to humans' actions.

As a prerequisite to joint action, Tomasello in [21] emphasized intentional action understanding, meaning that an agent should be able to read its partner's intentions. In this way, when observing a partner's action or course of actions, the agent should be able to infer its partner's intention in terms of goal and plan to achieve the goal. Where in a shared task one can assume a shared goal to

Fig. 1. A shared task example where the robot, performing its own part of the task, cannot monitor the human activity.

exist, a shared plan can only be estimated by both partners. As a consequence, during the entire realisation of a shared task, agents should continue to monitor others' actions to be able to adapt and coordinate their own actions.

Considering a shared task like cooking, when performing its own actions, a robot has to perceive the elements it has to interact with. Wanting to grasp a knife, the robot needs to look at the knife to estimate its position. However, when focused on such elements, monitoring others' actions can become unfeasible. Even having multiple visual sensors, we cannot assume that the human will perform its part of the plan in front of the robot, as illustrated in Fig. 1. In the same way, we cannot assume to act in a fully instrumented area allowing the robot to be omniscient. In such realistic applications, the need to detect human actions with as little visual information as possible is mandatory.

In the following, we will make the distinction between action and task considering a hierarchic task decomposition point of view. This means that a task can be decomposed into a set of sub-tasks and actions, where each sub-task can also be decomposed in such a way. We consider as actions the leaves of the resulting decomposition, meaning actions that can be directly executed by a robotic agent (i.e. pick, place, release, etc.). Reversing this assumption, a human task can be monitored through the detection of the underlying human actions. Task recognition is out of our current scope as requiring as a first step the recognition of actions.

In this paper, we present a lightweight method for action recognition based on a semantic knowledge flow. This knowledge is obtained through the use of the DACOBOT robotic architecture [16]. The main contribution of this work is the possibility to detect actions through the changes they brought to the environment. Such a contribution allows to pass over the general assumption of constant monitoring of the humans using visual sensors. The side contribution of this work, more related to the context of Human-Robot Interaction, is the ability to estimate the actions perceived by each agent it interacts with thanks to perspective-taking.

In Sect. 2, we discuss related work and how action recognition is generally performed. A detailed explanation of the approach is then provided in Sect. 3 before providing an overview of the knowledge flow in which it has been integrated in Sect. 4 and its application in Human-Robot Interaction in Sect. 5. Finally, Sect. 6 presents results on a dataset and Sect. 7 concludes the paper.

2   Related Work

Action recognition takes its application in various fields [2] such as health care, sports analysis, and robotics. It is used, for example, to monitor patients in healthcare in order to detect falls [19], or to anticipate human action for autonomous driving vehicles [7]. In robotics applications, action recognition is intensively used to learn tasks from video demonstrations [22]. In the field of Human-Robot Interaction, action recognition has become an important topic as detailed in [6], with applications such as gestures learning [25] or risk evaluation for decision making [26].

To date, two approaches coexist to recognise human actions: data-driven and knowledge-based. While data-driven approaches aim to directly deal with sensor data such as images, knowledge-based approaches rather focus on the analysis of semantic data either stated or extracted beforehand.

Data-driven approaches were initially based on 2D images with the use of pattern matching [1] or support vector machine [17]. The use of deep neural networks has then allowed the generation of more robust recognitions [24] but with the initial assumption of no occlusion. This concern has been later addressed in [23] to deal with real-world scenarios and thus environments like offices with desks and chairs. For finer estimations of the humans poses and thus more precise recognition, similar approaches but using 3D point clouds have been proposed [9].

The data-driven approaches also provide solutions to the problem of recognising human actions when the robot cannot perceive directly the human activity. A combination of RF-based (Radio Frequency) and vision-based detection has been used in [8] where the RF part can provide information when it is impossible for the vision. Other solutions aim at equipping the environment itself instead of the robot with multiple sensors like cameras [5] to provide the greatest vision and thus always keep track of the human's body. The main inconvenience of such solutions is the use of dedicated environments or specific robot hardware.

With regard to all the presented data-driven approaches, a general concern is that they mostly recognise humans' activities (i.e. drinking, sleeping, eating or humans' gestures) rather than primitive actions. In addition, as these approaches focus on the human body, the track of objects is not considered. Nevertheless, for human monitoring in a joint task, one would rather need low-level actions recognition (to maybe recognise higher level tasks on top of it) such as picking or placing and a track of the objects involved in the task.

On the other hand, knowledge-based approaches rely on data already processed by the robot in order to abstract its environment. All these data are thus centrally stored and formalised. One such formalism is ontology which can be formalised thanks to the Ontology Web Language (OWL). Riboni et al. in [11], explain that the human action recognition can be handled by an ontology-based approach with a result at the same level as the better data-driven algorithm. Nevertheless, they also specify that the ontology-based approach needs a way to have a time representation to reach this level of result. Thanks to [10], this time representation can be solved. In this work, they define a temporal Web Ontology Language (tOWL) as an extension to OWL with which it is possible to have a time representation of actions or events in the ontology. This enables to recognise actions thanks to ontology reasoning. However, it does not manage knowledge uncertainty or noise in the perception. To solve this, Rodriguez et al. in [12] propose to use a fuzzy ontology described and formalized in [20]. Thanks to their model and the use of a fuzzy ontology, Rodriguez et al. solve the problem of uncertainty and time representation, but their system does not detect low-level actions.

Finally, at the intersection of data-driven approaches and knowledge-based approaches, some hybrid approaches have been proposed [3,4]. In such works, the data-driven part is used to recognise the low-level activities while the knowledge-base part is used the recognise higher-level activities, based on the low-level actions. While still demonstrating the usability of knowledge-based methods, the need to continuously observe humans still exists.

3   Approach and Recognition

Let's consider an example of a robot and a human working together to prepare a meal in a kitchen. If we observe someone holding a fork, it must have been picked up somewhere. Similarly, if utensils appear on the workplace, someone must have placed them there. A human can infer which actions have caused these changes in the environment without seeing them, even if some parameters can remain unknown (e.g. who acted?).

This cognitive process allows the recognition of actions thanks to the observation of changes in the environment and also allows an estimation of the possible set of actions in a given situation [21]. For example, if we see Bob's hand approaching an apple on the workplace, we can estimate that Bob's next action will probably be related to the apple, but we cannot predict whether he will pick it up or push it. If we observe Bob grasping the apple, we can refine our estimation because the set of possible actions in this state is limited.

Taking inspiration from this human ability, we choose to represent actions as sequences of geometric changes in the environment. In this section, we thus present our method to recognise on-the-fly actions, based on symbolic facts.

3.1   A Dynamic State Machine to Handle the Recognition

To represent the recognition process introduced earlier, we have chosen State Machines (SM) where transition conditions represent the steps of the recognition process, i.e. the changes to be perceived. Thus, a pick action can be recognised by the following transitions of a SM: (1) the agent's hand approaches the object (2) the object is in the agent's hand (3) the object is no longer on its support.

These changes in the geometric situation of the environment can be abstracted using semantic facts, resulting in the following sequence:

1. *?A hasHandMovingToward ?O*
2. *?A isHolding ?O*
3. *NOT ?O isOnTopOf ?S*

To represent the unspecified entities involved in the sequence (i.e. the agent, the object, and the support), we use variables here represented by question marks followed by a literal. During a recognition process, these variables will be instantiated and will thus constrain the following facts of the sequence. For example, perceiving first Bob's hand approaching the object o_1 meaning the fact (bob hasHandMovingToward o_1), the variables A and O become instantiated and constrain the rest of the sequence. The next expected fact would thus be (bob isHolding o_1).

Even if sequence representation is convenient, some facts could be unperceived by the robot. We propose a way to specify the minimal set of facts to be perceived to recognise an action with the use of the tag *REQUIRED*. The resulting description of an action is provided in Listing 1.1.

Listing 1.1. Extract of the models file for a pick_over action

```
Pick_over:
   sequence:
      − ?A hasHandMovingToward  ?O
      − ?A isHolding  ?O
      − NOT ?O isOnTopOf  ?S  REQUIRED
```

As a consequence, our actions are no longer some purely linear sequences and could rather be transposed to state machines as illustrated in Fig. 2. We can see that the transition carrying the fact *?A isHolding ?O* connects both states *s0* and *s1* with state *s2*. These links mean that the transition between states *s0* and *s1* is not necessary to recognise the action. Not perceiving that the agent's hand approaches the object but perceiving that the agent is holding the object is sufficient to reach state *s2* and to start the recognition. Nevertheless, due to such a bypass, one could notice that triggering the transition from *s0* to *s3*, variable *A* will never be instantiated resulting in missing parameters.

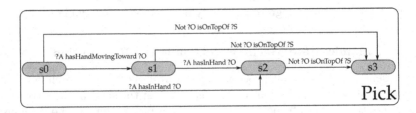

Fig. 2. State Machine for the detection of the pick action with only transition fact

3.2   Dynamically Created State Machines

In real-world situations in general and in human-robot interaction scenarios in particular, several agents can act simultaneously and even a single agent can do several actions at the same time, like picking two objects. An action recognition system must be able to handle the recognition of multiple actions in parallel that's why we designed **state machine factory**. When a semantic fact is submitted to a factory, if it allows to activate one of the transitions of the initial state, the factory will create an instance of the SM it is responsible for. Such a SM will be called an **active state machine**. The newly created SM will thus be in a different state than the initial one and some of its variables will already be instantiated.

When a new fact arrives in the recognition system, meaning a change in the environment has been perceived by the robot, this fact is first used to try to trigger a transition of all the active SMs. In the case the fact does not allow any of them to trigger any transition, then it is submitted to each factory to try to generate new SMs. Indeed, without this rule, multiple SMs recognizing the same action (in terms of instance) could exist at the same time. Nevertheless, several SMs coming from the same factory can exist simultaneously, that is to recognise the same action type performed by different agents simultaneously, or by the same agent on different objects.

When an active SM is finished, if all the variables used in the conditions of its transitions have been set, the SM is stated to be **complete**, otherwise, the SM is **incomplete**. Indeed, as not all transitions are required to recognise an action, some variables can stay unbounded.

Once a SM is finished, an action has been recognised. The finished SM is thus removed from the set of active SMs. In addition, as several SMs could have been created from the same semantic fact (based on the principle of progressive refinement when new facts arrive), all active SM involving facts used by the finished SM are also removed from the set of active SMs. The implicit hypothesis made here is that a fact can only be part of a single action performed by an agent.

4   Integration and Knowledge Flow

In order to be fed with meaningful semantic facts representing the changes in the environment, our Action Recognition System has been integrated into the DACOBOT [16] robotic architecture. In this section, we present the knowledge flow illustrated in Fig. 3.

4.1   Geometrical Situation Assessment

In this architecture, the geometrical Situation Assessment is handled by the software Overworld [14]. This software can be connected to any perception system to perceive objects, humans, or areas. As the same entity can be perceived through several systems, Overworld is first able to aggregate the data from all the used

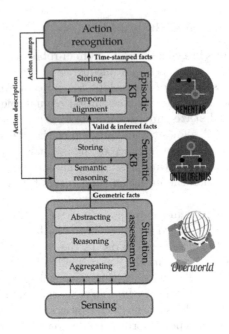

Fig. 3. Knowledge flow for Action Recognition System in the DACOBOT architecture

perception systems to create a unified 3D representation of the robot's environment. Thanks to geometrical reasoning based on the sensors' field of view, the entities' visual occlusions, and physics simulation, Overworld provides a coherent representation of the entire environment.

On the basis of the 3D representation, Overworld can then compute semantic facts. These facts can link objects together like with isOnTopOf or isInContainer. They can link objects or agents to areas with isInArea. They can also link agents to objects with facts such as hasInHand, isLookingAt, or hasHand-MovingToward. These facts are computed at every update of the system and are output on a ROS topic. A fact is generated when it starts to be perceived (ADD) and when it stops (DEL).

An important feature of Overworld, essential for HRI, is its ability to estimate the perspective of other agents and their representation of the world. From there, in the same way it is done from the robot's perspective, Overworld computes and generates semantic facts from the others' perspective allowing the use of the theory of mind.

4.2   Semantic Knowledge Base

The architecture used considers as a central component a semantic knowledge base. This latter contains both common sense knowledge (general concepts like object types, colors, ...) and anchored knowledge related to the current situation. This knowledge can be accessed by every component of the architecture allowing a unified and coherent representation among the entire architecture. This semantic knowledge base is managed by Ontologenius [15]. This software has been specially developed for robotic applications with good performances both on queries and dynamic updates. It is thus adapted to maintain the current state of the situation at a semantic level with online inferences resolutions. Regarding the knowledge stream, Ontologenius is directly connected to the output of Overworld. When new facts arrive in it, they are first analysed to verify their consistency regarding common sense knowledge, then once added to the knowledge, Ontologenius will reason on this knowledge in order to extract new facts. For example, from the fact ADD (cup_1 isInTopOf table_3), we can infer thanks to inverse ADD (table_3 isUnder cup_1).

As an output, Ontologenius sends on a ROS topic the validated facts as well as the inferred ones. However, as it does not deal with temporal aspects, the inferred facts cannot be stamped on the base of the used facts for the inference nor at the time of the inference. They are rather sent with an explanation about the facts involved in their inference.

Like Overworld, Ontologenius can maintain several knowledge bases in parallel, allowing theory of mind. Each output of Overworld (one per human agent in addition to the robot) is thus connected to a specific knowledge base.

4.3 Episodic Knowledge Base

As explained by Riboni et al. in [11], ontology-based action recognition is possible when linked to time representation. Regarding this temporal representation, the DACOBOT architecture proposes the software Mementar [13] as an episodic knowledge base. It is responsible for the organization of the semantic facts, provided by the ontology, on a temporal axis. While only the validated facts are already stamped, the inferred ones have to be aligned. To this end, Mementar finds the more recent fact among the ones used in the inference and aligns the inferred fact on this later. All the facts once correctly stamped are then republished on a ROS topic for the components (as the action recognition) needing continuous monitoring.

On the basis of this timeline, Mementar proposes a set of queries to retrieve past facts based on their timestamp, their order, or their semantics thanks to a link with the semantic knowledge base. In addition, Mementar allows to represent actions/tasks in the timeline with a start stamp and an end stamp. These actions can also be queried to retrieve the facts appearing during an action, the actions holding during an action, their stamps, or their type.

Finally, in the same way it has been done for the two previously presented components, Mementar can manage a timeline per agent allowing to manage theory of mind at a temporal level.

4.4 Action Recognition

The action recognition component described in this paper is connected to the output of Mementar where no distinction is made between the inferred facts and the others. As illustrated in Fig. 3, as an output, the action recognition sends the description of the recognised actions to the semantic knowledge base and temporally marks them in the episodic knowledge base.

This description of the recognised actions at the semantic level allows us to link the actions to their parameters as a relation reification. An example of such a description is presented in Listing 1.2. This description is stored in a description file and can reuse all the different variables used in the facts sequence linked to the action models. Here we reuse the variables A to provide the knowledge of who has acted. We also provide a way to symbolise the action itself with the specific variable?.

Actions are thus described both at the semantic and episodic levels, each providing a different view of them and thus different ways to retrieve them. For example, to know the agent having performed a given action, one can query the semantic knowledge base. On the contrary, to know the facts that took place during a given action or to know when has started an action, one would rather query the episodic knowledge base.

5   Multi-human Estimation and HRI

As described previously, all software used in the knowledge flow can manage in parallel multiple instances. This specificity provides multiple independent knowledge flows, one for each agent interacting with the robot in addition to the flow for the robot itself. Taking advantage of that, we can recognise actions from the knowledge flow of any available agent in order to estimate the actions they are aware of. In this way, the knowledge base of each agent can be updated independently which can lead to the generation of belief divergences.

To illustrate this divergence in beliefs, let's consider a robot and a human interacting together. The human temporarily leaves the room to pick up a tool. Meanwhile, the robot picks an object and places it in a drawer. When the human comes back, thanks to the actions recognition system, the robot can estimate that the human knows that it picked the object but can also estimate that he does not know that it placed the object in the drawer. Here a divergence in beliefs is raised between the knowledge bases of both agents.

Such piece of information could later be used by a decisional process, like a supervision component, to prevent future errors in the execution of a plan.

Listing 1.2. Description part of our model for the pick action

```
pick:
      description:
      - ?? isA PickAction
      - ?? isPerformedBy ?A
      - ?? isPerformedOn ?O
      - ?? isPerformedFrom ?S
```

In a similar way, actions with no visual effects on the environment, like scanning a bar code, can be estimated as unknown by the human partner and thus communication could be required to prevent a blockage in the execution of a plan.

6   Experimentations

To illustrate the possibilities offered by our action recognition system, we present here two scenarios tested on two different robots[1].

6.1   Scenario 1

In the first scenario, we use a Pr2 robot to pick a cube and to drop it in a box previously flipped by the human partner. Here we want to illustrate the recognition of the actions of the robot itself but also actions made by a human agent not perceived by the robot[2]. This case study thus demonstrates among others the recognition of incomplete action as the robot does not have access to all data needed to recognise all parameters of the action like who has performed the action.

In this scenario, our system has been able to recognise a pick and a place action of the robot but also a pick and a place action of an unknown agent. This illustrates the multiple recognition of actions even if some are incomplete and the capability to create and manage multiple SMs.

6.2   Scenario 2

In this second scenario, we use a Pepper as the robotic agent that is perceiving two human agents (a_1 and a_2) making some tabletop manipulation on cubes over boxes. Each human agent is equipped with a motion capture system to be perceived by the robot. The configuration of the scenario is represented in Fig. 4[3]. This scenario is decomposed into three parts.

In the first part of the scenario, each agent looks at the table, to initialise their knowledge base with the current state of the environment. After this initial step, one agent (a_2) turns around (Fig. 4a) and the other human agent (a_1) moves one cube. This later action is perceived by the robot and is also added to the estimated knowledge base of a_1 who has done the action. The pick is recognised between t0 and t2 for these two agents as it is presented in Fig. 5. Based on the estimation of the perspective of a_2, the action made by a_1 is not added to the knowledge base of a_2 as it could not be perceived by a_2. This part allows us to demonstrate the recognition of the actions from the point of view of different agents making a shared task.

---

[1] ROSbags: https://gitlab.laas.fr/avigne/action_recognition_dataset.
[2] The agent is not perceived because it has not been equipped to do this.
[3] Video: https://youtu.be/cwLLEAA_mCY.

Fig. 4. Representation of the situations used in scenario 2. At the left the situation where a_2 can't see the cubes. At the right the situation when a_2 turns around again to continue the task.

In the second part of the scenario, a_2 turns around again to see what has been done (Fig. 4b). With the estimation of his perspective, the robot now estimates that the agent has perceived that the cube has moved. This allows our system to recognise that a pick and a place action have been performed, from a_2 perspective, but with no additional information. Indeed, with the facts linked to this action (around t6), it's impossible from the point of view of a_2 to know who has done the action.

The last part of this scenario is a shared task between the two humans. They have to take at the same time one cube each and make a tower. In this part, we demonstrate the recognition of actions performed at the same moment on different objects and made by different agents. This simultaneous recognition is illustrated between the timestamp t11 and t12 in Fig. 5.

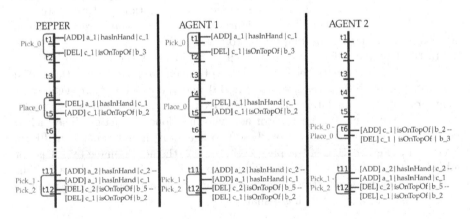

Fig. 5. Simplified view of the timelines maintained by Mementar for each agent of the scenario 2. Facts are represented at the right of the timeline and actions are at the left.

7   Conclusion and Future Work

In this paper, we present our Action Recognition system[4]. The recognition process uses state machines dynamically created and instantiated thanks to the semantic facts produced by the knowledge flow of the robotic architecture it has been integrated into. These state machines are easily configurable to be adapted to new actions. In addition, our system is also adapted to the HRI context thanks to the management of multiple knowledge flows in parallel relying on perspective-taking.

This system is a first step toward a larger system for task recognition based on Hierarchical Task Network (HTN), allowing us to validate and test all the requirements before handling this new challenge. Nevertheless, our action recognition system has some limitations that will have to be handled. The main limitation is due to the limited set of facts currently computed by the situation assessment. Indeed, we are aware that with the current set of facts, only pick and place can be detected. However, with the presented system, we can easily handle new sets of facts and thus describe and recognise new actions.

Another aspect that we want to develop would be a post-processing of detected actions to try to fulfil the incomplete actions and to remove false detection due to natural changes in the environment. Indeed, currently, an object falling on the ground would generate the recognition of a pick action and the presence of a single action at the place of action is not used to estimate who performed the action.

Acknowledgements. This work has been supported by the Artificial Intelligence for Human-Robot Interaction (AI4HRI) project ANR-20-IADJ-0006 and DISCUTER project ANR-21-ASIA-0005.

References

1. Aggarwal, J.K., Cai, Q., Liao, W., Sabata, B.: Nonrigid motion analysis: articulated and elastic motion. Comput. Vis. Image Underst. **70**(2), 142–156 (1998)
2. Al-Faris, M., Chiverton, J., Ndzi, D., Ahmed, A.I.: A review on computer vision-based methods for human action recognition. J. Imaging **6**, 46 (2020)
3. Díaz-Rodríguez, N., Cadahía, O.L., Cuéllar, M.P., Lilius, J., Calvo-Flores, M.D.: Handling real-world context awareness, uncertainty and vagueness in real-time human activity tracking and recognition with a fuzzy ontology-based hybrid method. Sensors **14**(10), 18131–18171 (2014)
4. Helaoui, R., Riboni, D., Stuckenschmidt, H.: A probabilistic ontological framework for the recognition of multilevel human activities. In: ACM International Joint Conference on Pervasive and Ubiquitous Computing (2013)
5. Iosifidis, A., Tefas, A., Pitas, I.: Multi-view human action recognition under occlusion based on fuzzy distances and neural networks. In: EUSIPCO. IEEE (2012)
6. Ji, Y., Yang, Y., Shen, F., Shen, H.T., Li, X.: A survey of human action analysis in HRI applications. Trans. Circuits Syst. Video Technol. **30**(7), 2114–2128 (2019)

---

[4] https://github.com/vigne-laas/Procedural.

7. Koppula, H.S., Saxena, A.: Anticipating human activities using object affordances for reactive robotic response. Trans. Pattern Anal. Mach. Intell. **38**(1), 14–29 (2015)
8. Li, T., Fan, L., Zhao, M., Liu, Y., Katabi, D.: Making the invisible visible: action recognition through walls and occlusions. In: ICCV (2019)
9. Li, W., Zhang, Z., Liu, Z.: Action recognition based on a bag of 3D points. In: Computer Society Conference on Computer Vision and Pattern Recognition-Workshops. IEEE (2010)
10. Milea, V., Frasincar, F., Kaymak, U.: tOWL: a temporal web ontology language. Trans. Syst. Man Cybern. **42**, 268–281 (2011)
11. Riboni, D., Pareschi, L., Radaelli, L., Bettini, C.: Is ontology-based activity recognition really effective? In: PERCOM Workshops. IEEE (2011)
12. Rodríguez, N.D., Cuéllar, M.P., Lilius, J., Calvo-Flores, M.D.: A fuzzy ontology for semantic modelling and recognition of human behaviour. Knowl.-Based Syst. **66**, 46–60 (2014)
13. Sarthou, G.: Mementar. https://github.com/sarthou/mementar
14. Sarthou, G.: Overworld: assessing the geometry of the world for human-robot interaction. Robot. Autom. Lett. **8**, 1874–1880 (2023)
15. Sarthou, G., Clodic, A., Alami, R.: Ontologenius: a long-term semantic memory for robotic agents. In: RO-MAN. IEEE (2019)
16. Sarthou, G., Mayima, A., Buisan, G., Belhassein, K., Clodic, A.: The director task: a psychology-inspired task to assess cognitive and interactive robot architectures. In: RO-MAN. IEEE (2021)
17. Schuldt, C., Laptev, I., Caputo, B.: Recognizing human actions: a local SVM approach. In: ICPR. IEEE (2004)
18. Sebanz, N., Bekkering, H., Knoblich, G.: Joint action: bodies and minds moving together. Trends Cogn. Sci. **10**, 70–76 (2006)
19. Sree, K.V., Jeyakumar, G.: A computer vision based fall detection technique for home surveillance. In: Smys, S., Tavares, J.M.R.S., Balas, V.E., Iliyasu, A.M. (eds.) ICCVBIC 2019. AISC, vol. 1108, pp. 355–363. Springer, Cham (2020). https://doi.org/10.1007/978-3-030-37218-7_41
20. Tho, Q.T., Hui, S.C., Fong, A.C.M., Cao, T.H.: Automatic fuzzy ontology generation for semantic web. Trans. Knowl. Data Eng. **18**, 842–856 (2006)
21. Tomasello, M., Carpenter, M., Call, J., Behne, T., Moll, H.: Understanding and sharing intentions: the origins of cultural cognition. Behav. Brain Sci. **28**, 675–691 (2005)
22. Ullah, A., Ahmad, J., Muhammad, K., Sajjad, M., Baik, S.W.: Action recognition in video sequences using deep bi-directional LSTM with CNN features. IEEE Access **6**, 1155–1166 (2017)
23. Weinland, D., Özuysal, M., Fua, P.: Making action recognition robust to occlusions and viewpoint changes. In: Daniilidis, K., Maragos, P., Paragios, N. (eds.) ECCV 2010. LNCS, vol. 6313, pp. 635–648. Springer, Heidelberg (2010). https://doi.org/10.1007/978-3-642-15558-1_46
24. Weinland, D., Ronfard, R., Boyer, E.: A survey of vision-based methods for action representation, segmentation and recognition. Comput. Vis. Image Underst. **115**, 224–241 (2011)
25. Yavşan, E., Uçar, A.: Gesture imitation and recognition using Kinect sensor and extreme learning machines. Measurement **94**, 852–861 (2016)
26. Zhang, H., Reardon, C., Han, F., Parker, L.E.: SRAC: self-reflective risk-aware artificial cognitive models for robot response to human activities. In: ICRA. IEEE (2016)

Two-Level Reinforcement Learning Framework for Self-sustained Personal Robots

Koyo Fujii[1] , Patrick Holthaus[2]([✉]) , Hooman Samani[2,3] ,
Chinthaka Premachandra[1] , and Farshid Amirabdollahian[2]

[1] Department of Electronic Engineering, Shibaura Institute of Technology,
3-7-5 Toyosu, Koto-ku, Tokyo 135-8548, Japan
{ag20045,chinthaka}@shibaura-it.ac.jp

[2] Robotics Research Group, University of Hertfordshire, College Lane, Hatfield AL10
9AB, UK
{p.holthaus,f.amirabdollahian2}@herts.ac.uk

[3] Creative Computing Institute, University of the Arts London, London SE5 8UF,
UK
h.samani@arts.ac.uk

Abstract. As social robots become integral to daily life, effective battery management and personalized user interactions are crucial. We employed Q-learning with the Miro-E robot for balancing self-sustained energy management and personalized user engagement. Based on our approach, we anticipate that the robot will learn when to approach the charging dock and adapt interactions according to individual user preferences. For energy management, the robot underwent iterative training in a simulated environment, where it could opt to either "play" or "go to the charging dock". The robot also adapts its interaction style to a specific individual, learning which of three actions would be preferred based on feedback it would receive during real-world human-robot interactions. From an initial analysis, we identified a specific point at which the Q values are inverted, indicating the robot's potential establishment of a battery threshold that triggers its decision to head to the charging dock in the energy management scenario. Moreover, by monitoring the probability of the robot selecting specific behaviours during human-robot interactions over time, we expect to gather evidence that the robot can successfully tailor its interactions to individual users in the realm of personalized engagement.

Keywords: Personalized interaction · Companion robots · Battery Management · Reinforcement learning

1 Introduction

As social robots become more and more integrated into everyday human life, their handling becomes an increasingly complex issue. One of the most important aspects to consider is managing the robots' battery life [5]. Especially during long-term human-robot interactions (HRIs), it would be cumbersome for users to continually monitor their robots' battery status to send them to the charging dock when the battery is close to depletion. Furthermore, robot adaption to user preference is certainly a key element of long-term interactions between humans and robots [7]. Hence, it would be beneficial if a robot could autonomously navigate to its charging dock and replenish its battery at an optimal time determined by its own algorithms, considering social interaction. At the same time, it would be advantageous if home robots could tailor their interactions to individual users, enhancing their utility and user experience.

In this paper, we present approaches that employ Q-learning [16] to combine both these aspects. The primary contributions of this paper include (1) determining the optimal timing for the robot to approach the charging dock using Q-learning in a simulated environment; and (2) enabling the robot to adapt to individual users over time during human-robot interactions by leveraging Q-learning with a real Miro-E robot. For that, we first present some existing approaches to battery management and personalized user engagement in Sect. 2 and introduce theoretical backgrounds about Q-learning in Sect. 3. After that, we present our method by describing our own implementation of Q-learning for self-sustained energy management and personalised user engagement in Sect. 4. We further provide an initial proof of concept of our approach in Sect. 5 before concluding the paper.

2 Background

In the field of battery management, a diverse range of methodologies have been established. Some approaches do not incorporate learning but rely on estimation functions [4], or model predictive control [10]. Many others instead [1,3,8,12] used strategies involving energy storage and decision-making frameworks using some form of reinforcement learning, allowing for dealing with uncertainties effectively. Likewise, our approach is based on a form of reinforcement learning (Q-learning, c.f. Sect. 3).

To personalize and adapt a robot's user engagement, frameworks have been proposed by [9], while [6] have presented designs, implementations, and assessments for socially assistive robots. [9] allows robots to understand children with ASD's emotions using physiological signals, while [6] motivates elderly users to exercise via a vision-equipped robot. However, the adaptation techniques vary. [9] utilizes random phrase selections during exercises to avoid repetitiveness, while [6] employs Support Vector Machine (SVM)-based modelling to interpret children with autism's physiological signals. The work presented here combines such reinforcement learning-based behavioural adaption systems (e.g. [11,14]) with reinforcement-based solutions for autonomous battery management.

Our approach extends our previous work [2] in which we effectively utilized Q-learning for "Energy Autonomy" and "User's Preferences" in a study involving an early version of the Aibo robot[1]. There, we demonstrated a robot that could

---

[1] See: https://electronics.sony.com/more/c/aibo.

operate for extended periods without depleting its energy source and had successfully learned an effective policy for engaging users through real-world interactions. Current work follows up on this study, replicating the original methods using a modern Miro-E^2 robot. Additionally, we have expanded and improved some methodological aspects of the original work, c.f. Sect. 4.

3   Theory

In this section, we will briefly introduce the theoretical background to the learning algorithm used in this work. Specifically, we discuss Q-learning [16], the epsilon-greedy [13], and the softmax [15] policies, which we consider in our implementation. The goal of Q-learning is to find optimal Q values, q_*, which means to find an optimal policy π_* as the policy $\pi(a|s)$ that maximizes the expected total reward from a given state. Q values are a measure of the expected return after taking a specific action in a specific state with a particular policy. The learned Q values directly approximate q_*, independent of the policy being followed [13] because Q-learning is an off-policy algorithm and its updates always reflect the maximum expected reward. This specifically enables early convergence of a chosen policy and the target policy can be deterministic, while the behaviour policy can continue to sample all possible actions [13]. Therefore, Q-learning is a simple way for agents to learn how to act optimally in controlled Markovian domains as articulated by Christopher [16]. The update for Q-learning is defined as follows:

$$Q(S_t, A_t) \leftarrow Q(S_t, A_t) + \alpha(R_{t+1} + \gamma \max_a Q(S_{t+1}, a) - Q(S_t, A_t)) \qquad (1)$$

In off-policy algorithms, the policy used to generate behaviour called the behaviour policy, may in fact be unrelated to the policy that is evaluated and improved, called the target policy. The Q-learning updates its Q-values to align with the optimal (or "target") policy. However, while the behaviour policy could in theory be any policy, it should be soft (i.e. it should consider all actions in all states with nonzero probability) in order to explore all possibilities [13].

In reinforcement learning, maintaining an appropriate balance between exploration and exploitation is a crucial aspect. A simple yet effective strategy for managing the exploration-exploitation trade-off is the epsilon-greedy action selection mechanism [13]. With this approach, the agent selects an action that maximizes its Q-value for a given state with a probability of $1 - epsilon$ and chooses an action randomly with a probability of $epsilon$. The epsilon-greedy policy treats the selection probability of all non-greedy actions equally, thereby neglecting the estimated Q-values for these actions.

However, softmax [15] uses action-selection probabilities which are determined by ranking the Q-value estimates using a Boltzmann distribution. In practical applications, to prevent overflow and ensure numerical stability, τ denotes a positive parameter known as the 'temperature':

---

^{2} See: https://miro-e.com/robot.

$$\pi(a|s) = Pr\{a_t = a|s_t = s\} = \frac{e^{\frac{Q(s,a) - \max_b Q(s,b)}{\tau}}}{\sum_b e^{\frac{Q(s,b)}{\tau}}} \qquad (2)$$

4   Method

In this section, we describe our implementation of Q-learning on the Miro-E robot to allow for self-sustained energy management and personalized user engagement. The goal of self-sustained energy management is to determine an optimal threshold for charging, thus enabling Miro-E to engage in extended periods of interaction for enhanced human-robot interaction. To this end, we extended the original approach with a negative reward system [2], which encourages Miro-E to engage in play and discourages battery depletion at the same time. In addition to the original approach [2], where the state dimension was one-dimensional, we introduced an additional dimension called "people's faces" in personalized user engagement. This addition is anticipated to facilitate more personalized interactions and provide flexibility in the learning process. By making these modifications to the original work, we aim to develop a robot that optimizes battery use and potentially offers personalized features for each user. To efficiently facilitate the training of self-sustained energy management in simulation and trial user engagement in the real world, this work addresses both aspects individually.

4.1   Self-sustained Energy Management

A robot must visit the battery charging dock to maintain autonomous movement. Ideally, it should be able to play around in a room for extended periods and approach the charging dock with optimal timing. To achieve this autonomous behaviour and expedite convergence as compared to on-policy learning methods such as SARSA [13], we employed Q-learning in a simulation environment.

Q-learning Implementation. For learning self-sustained energy management, we implemented an epsilon-greedy policy for the selection of actions to allow Miro-E to determine action probabilities based on epsilon, independent of Q values, which are updated to maximize the next Q value in Q-learning. We configured the reinforcement learning parameters as follows:

- State space (two-dimensional Q-table): "charging" or "playing", the battery level is divided into levels ranging from 6 (fully charged) to 0 (nearly empty). We designed this two-dimensional state space to enable Miro-E to select its next action based on its current engagement and battery level.
- Initial state: when the first dimension of the state space is "playing" and the second dimension (the battery level) is 6 (fully charged).
- Terminal state: either when the first dimension of the state space is "playing" and the second dimension (the battery level) reaches 0, or when the steps within a single episode reach 500.

- Action space: "play" or "go to charging dock".
- Reward: a reward of $+100$ is provided when Miro-E opts to play to incentivise longer playtime, and a reward of -100 is given when the robot decides to proceed to the charging dock to discourage unnecessary returns. If Miro-E depletes its battery, a penalty is assessed that is 100 times the number of steps taken, with this counter resetting once Miro-E returns to the charging dock. We have chosen this penalty structure to prevent the battery from running out, ensuring that the penalty magnitude exceeds the reward value associated with choosing to play.

Evaluation Environment. We used a simulation environment to determine whether the robot can change its behaviour from engaging a user to going to a virtual charging location using the above implementation. Figure 1a depicts the moment when Miro-E is playing while Fig. 1b captures the moment when Miro-E is moving to a predetermined position. We configured the following parameters for the Q-learning algorithm in the simulation: Learning rate at 0.1, Discount factor at 0.9, Initial epsilon for the epsilon-greedy method set to 0.3, Epsilon discount rate of 0.99, the maximum number of steps set to 500, and a total of 200 episodes.

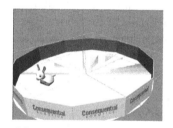

(a) example of "play" action

(b) example of "going to dock" action

Fig. 1. Examples of Miro-E actions in simulation.

4.2 Personalized Engagement

Individual preferences for behaviour vary and consequently, a robot should adapt to the specific person it is interacting with. To achieve this, we also employed Q-learning. In our use case, the robot interacted with an actual person in the real world, as it needs to adapt to existing individuals. We introduced a novel element to facilitate personalized engagement. Specifically, we enabled the robot to recognize a human face, allowing the robot to adapt to the specific preferences of the identified individuals. In the following section, we describe the implementation of Q-learning and outline the experimental setup and procedure.

Q-learning Implementation. For personalizing user engagement, we implemented a softmax policy for the selection of actions, allowing Miro-E to determine action probabilities based on their corresponding Q-values and to ensure that actions have a nonzero probability of being selected during an interaction. Additionally, our updating strategy aims to facilitate dramatic changes in Q values compared to on-policy methods like SARSA [13] to allow for faster user adaptation. We configured the reinforcement learning parameters as follows:

- State space (two-dimensional Q-table): the person's face, "tracking a ball", "responding to sound", "detecting a person's face" or a state of inactivity.
- Initial state: when the robot is not engaged in any actions.
- Terminal state: when the user sends a signal.
- Action space: "track a ball," "respond to sound," "detect a person's face".
- Reward: a reward of +10 when a person pats Miro-E on its head, indicating a preferred action, while no rewards are given for other actions.

Evaluation Environment. To evaluate our approach, we implemented an interactive learning routine using a real Miro-E robot as follows: At the beginning of each episode, the first state dimension is determined by recognizing a pre-registered person's face. Then, one of the actions is selected using the softmax method and executed.

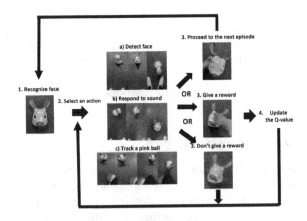

Fig. 2. Behaviour flow of Miro's interactive training routine.

If a reward is given by the user, the Q-value is updated and the subsequent action is chosen. If not, the next action is determined. If the user signals they want more adaptive actions by patting Miro-E on its body, the temperature parameter is adjusted by multiplying it with the discount factor before selecting the next action. Figure 2 summarises the interactive training steps for the behaviour adaption. We configured the following parameters for the Q-learning algorithm in the real world: learning rate at 0.5, discount factor at 0.9, initial temperature for the softmax method set to 100, and temperature discount rate of 0.9.

5   Proof of Concept

To determine whether our approach can function, we tested the energy management routine and the behaviour adaption separately. Firstly, we tested whether we could find a valid timing for the robot to approach the charging dock and secondly, whether the robot would adapt its behaviour to a user over time.

5.1   Self-sustained Energy Management

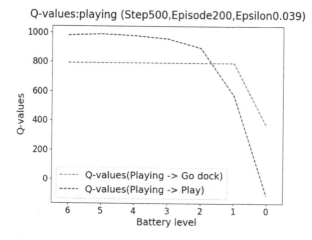

Fig. 3. Q value: Motion state "playing".

The objective of the first evaluation was to identify the optimal battery threshold that would enable the Miro-E robot to operate for extended periods. For that, we have investigated how the Q-values change when the motion state of the robot is "playing". Figure 3 illustrates that when the Miro-E robot was in a "playing" state, the Q-value for "play" exceeded the Q-value for "go to dock" until the battery level dropped between 2 and 1. Beyond this point, the Q-values inverted, indicating that "go to dock" became the more valued action. Based on the results, the optimal battery threshold appears to be between a battery level of 2 and 1. More precisely, the voltage corresponding to this threshold is 4.4 V, suggesting that the identified threshold is approximately 4.4 V.

5.2 Personalized Engagement

The second part of our evaluation looks at whether Miro-E would adapt its behaviour during an interaction. For that, we provided the system with different rewards in a test run lasting for approximately 60 min. Figures 4a and 4b depict the Q-values at episodes 10 (30 min) and 18 (60 min), respectively, while Figs. 4c and 4d show the probabilities of selecting each action at the same episodes and corresponding times, which show that the probabilities associated with each action evolve over time, indicating Miro-E's adaptation to a specific person's preferences. Consequently, Miro-E likely selects "respond to sound" following actions "detect a person's face" and "track a ball". Additionally, "track a ball" is probably chosen after "respond to sound" or at the episode's outset.

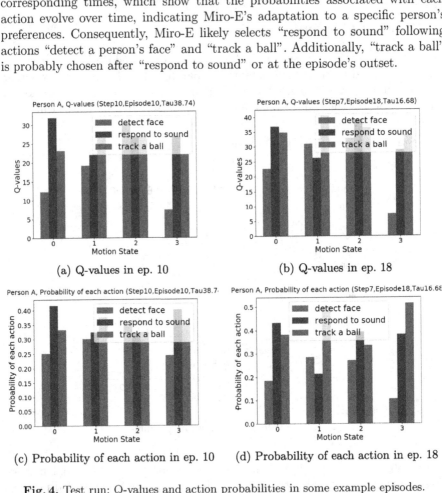

(a) Q-values in ep. 10   (b) Q-values in ep. 18

(c) Probability of each action in ep. 10   (d) Probability of each action in ep. 18

Fig. 4. Test run: Q-values and action probabilities in some example episodes.

Miro-E chose actions using the softmax formula outlined in Eq. 2. The temperature parameter was adjusted throughout each episode, especially when the user signaled a desire for more adaptive interactions by patting Miro-E. Initially, Q-values had minimal influence on action choices due to a high temperature parameter. But as episodes advanced and the temperature decreased, the influence of Q-values on action selection grew stronger. This behaviour is evident in

Fig. 4, which displays results for one person with the first state space dimension set to "1", Motion State "3" in Figs. 4a and 4b showing Miro-E inactive at the beginning of an episode. Here, Q(13, 0) remains unchanged between episodes 10 and 18. However, in Figs. 4c and 4d, despite static Q values, there's a growing difference in the likelihood of Miro-E choosing "track a ball" and "respond to sound" over "detect a person's face". This suggests Miro-E gradually refines interactions based on both exploring user preferences and leveraging past experiences.

Its adaptability to changing user preferences was enhanced by Q-learning. The Q-learning formula (Eq. 1) ensures that if an action was rewarded, the related Q value would adjust to improve future rewards. This could mean large increases in Q values for less-favored actions, thereby increasing their chances of selection and allowing Miro-E to quickly modify its interactions. Rapid changes in Q values across episodes can be observed, for instance, between episodes 9 and 10 in Figs. 5a and 5b. Notably, the test run depicted in Fig. 5 is unrelated to that in Fig. 4. Q values, such as Q(10,2), Q(11,2), and Q(13,2) exhibited significant changes within the span of just one episode.

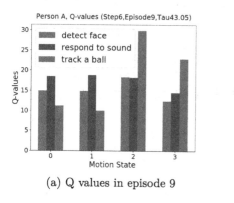
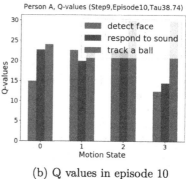

(a) Q values in episode 9   (b) Q values in episode 10

Fig. 5. Q values in episodes 9 and 10 during the second test run.

6   Conclusion

In this paper, we utilized Q-learning with the Miro-E robot to successfully attain self-sustained energy management and personalized engagement. For self-sustained energy management, we showed that the robot could determine the optimal timing for approaching the charging dock in a simulated environment. For personalized engagement, we anticipate that our method will adeptly adapt the robot's interactions over time to meet the preferences of an individual user during human-robot interactions.

Our future work is to evaluate these algorithms in an interactive trial involving different individuals with free choices of interaction, as offered by Miro-E and implemented additionally. Moreover, we consider the expansion of the state space, e.g. introducing an idling state to the self-sustained energy management component.

References

1. Cao, J., Harrold, D., Fan, Z., Morstyn, T., Healey, D., Li, K.: Deep reinforcement learning-based energy storage arbitrage with accurate lithium-ion battery degradation model. IEEE Trans. Smart Grid **11**(5), 4513–4521 (2020)
2. Castro-González, A., Amirabdollahian, F., Polani, D., Malfaz, M., Salichs, M.A.: Robot self-preservation and adaptation to user preferences in game play, a preliminary study. In: International Conference on Robotics and Biomimetics, pp. 2491–2498 (2011)
3. Chaoui, H., Gualous, H., Boulon, L., Kelouwani, S.: Deep reinforcement learning energy management system for multiple battery based electric vehicles. In: 2018 IEEE Vehicle Power and Propulsion Conference (VPPC), pp. 1–6. IEEE (2018)
4. Chellal, A.A., Lima, J., Gonçalves, J., Megnafi, H.: Battery management system for mobile robots based on an extended Kalman filter approach. In: 2021 29th Mediterranean Conference on Control and Automation, pp. 1131–1136. IEEE (2021)
5. Deshmukh, A., Aylett, R.: Socially constrained management of power resources for social mobile robots. In: International Conference on Human-Robot Interaction, pp. 119–120 (2012)
6. Fasola, J., Mataric, M.J.: Using socially assistive human-robot interaction to motivate physical exercise for older adults. Proc. IEEE **100**(8), 2512–2526 (2012)
7. Gockley, R., et al.: Designing robots for long-term social interaction, pp. 1338–1343, September 2005
8. Kuznetsova, E., Li, Y.F., Ruiz, C., Zio, E., Ault, G., Bell, K.: Reinforcement learning for microgrid energy management. Energy **59**, 133–146 (2013)
9. Liu, C., Conn, K., Sarkar, N., Stone, W.: Online affect detection and robot behavior adaptation for intervention of children with autism. IEEE Trans. Rob. **24**(4), 883–896 (2008)
10. Liu, Y., Zhang, J.: Self-adapting J-type air-based battery thermal management system via model predictive control. Appl. Energy **263**, 114640 (2020)
11. Mitsunaga, N., Smith, C., Kanda, T., Ishiguro, H., Hagita, N.: Adapting robot behavior for human-robot interaction. IEEE Trans. Rob. **24**(4), 911–916 (2008)
12. Natella, D., Vasca, F.: Battery state of health estimation via reinforcement learning. In: 2021 European Control Conference (ECC), pp. 1657–1662. IEEE (2021)
13. Sutton, R., Barto, A.: Reinforcement Learning: An Introduction. MIT Press, Cambridge (2018)
14. Tapus, A., Ţăpuş, C., Matarić, M.J.: User-robot personality matching and assistive robot behavior adaptation for post-stroke rehabilitation therapy. Intel. Serv. Robot. **1**, 169–183 (2008)
15. Tokic, M., Palm, G.: Value-difference based exploration: adaptive control between Epsilon-Greedy and Softmax. In: Bach, J., Edelkamp, S. (eds.) KI 2011. LNCS (LNAI), vol. 7006, pp. 335–346. Springer, Heidelberg (2011). https://doi.org/10.1007/978-3-642-24455-1_33
16. Watkins, C.J.C.H., Dayan, P.: Q-learning. Mach. Learn. **8**(3), 279–292 (1992)

Robot Companions and Sensors for Better Living: Defining Needs to Empower Low Socio-economic Older Adults at Home

Roberto Vagnetti[1]([✉]) [ID], Nicola Camp[1] [ID], Matthew Story[2] [ID], Khaoula Ait-Belaid[3] [ID], Joshua Bamforth[2], Massimiliano Zecca[3] [ID], Alessandro Di Nuovo[2] [ID], Suvo Mitra[4] [ID], and Daniele Magistro[1] [ID]

[1] Sport, Health and Performance Enhancement Research Centre, Department of Sport Science, Nottingham Trent University, Nottingham, UK
roberto.vagnetti@ntu.ac.uk
[2] Department of Computing and Advanced Wellbeing Research Centre, Sheffield Hallam University, Sheffield, UK
[3] Wolfson School of Mechanical, Electrical and Manufacturing Engineering, Loughborough University, Loughborough, UK
[4] Department of Psychology, Nottingham Trent University, Nottingham, UK

Abstract. Population ageing has profound implications for economies and societies, demanding increased health and social services. The global older adult population is steadily growing, presenting challenges. Addressing this reality, investing in older adults' healthcare means enhancing their well-being while minimizing expenditures. Strategies aim to support older adults at home, but resource disparities pose challenges. Importantly, socio-economic factors influence peoples' quality of life and wellbeing, thus they are associated with specific needs. Socially Assistive Robots (SARs) and monitoring technologies (wearable and environmental sensors) hold promise in aiding daily life, with older adults showing willingness to embrace them, particularly if tailored to their needs. Despite research on perceptions of technology, the preferences and needs of socio-economically disadvantaged older adults remain underexplored. This study investigates how SARs and sensor technologies can aid low-income older adults, promoting independence and overall well-being. For this purpose, older adults (aged ≥ 65 years) with low income were recruited, and a series of focus groups were conducted to comprehend how these technologies could address their needs. Thematic analysis results highlighted five key dimensions, specifically: 1) promote and monitor an active lifestyle, 2) help with daily errands and provide physical assistance, 3) reduce isolation and loneliness, 4) considerations regarding monitoring technologies, and 5) barriers affecting SARs and monitoring technologies usage and acceptance. These dimensions should be considered during SARs and sensors design to effectively meet users' requirements, enhance their quality of life, and support caregivers.

Keywords: older adults · social robots · socio-economic status · wearable sensors · environmental sensors

© The Author(s), under exclusive license to Springer Nature Singapore Pte Ltd. 2024
A. Al. Ali et al. (Eds.): ICSR 2023, LNAI 14453, pp. 373–383, 2024.
https://doi.org/10.1007/978-981-99-8715-3_31

1 Introduction

Population ageing is an important phenomenon since it impacts economy and society, bringing new challenges such as an increased demand of health and social services [1]. Older adults represent about 13% percent of the global population, increasing by 3% annually [2]. Ageing also impacts people's life as older adults could face loneliness and isolation [3]. With ageing people could have a decline of cognitive and physical abilities [4], with an increased risk of frailty and neurodegenerative disease, such as Alzheimer and Parkinsons [5], and of physical ailments, such as arthritis or osteoporosis [6]. According to this demographic reality, investing in health services for older adults is an important priority for countries, also in terms of economic burden [7]. Current intervention trends, known as "aging-in-place", aim to support older adults in their homes to foster their well-being and independence while reducing healthcare costs [8, 9]. Indeed, due to an imbalance between people requiring care and resources, providing an appropriate service is challenging [7], especially for those with impairing conditions [8]. Different strategies have been investigated to foster older adults well-being: for instance, an active lifestyle seems to reduce the cognitive decline this population could face as physical activity is associated with lower risk of cognitive and physical impairments, frailty and loss of independence [10]. However, factors such as socio-economic conditions are reportedly associated with health outcomes [11]. Older adults with low income are likely to have more need for personal and instrumental or environmental support, affecting their quality of life [12]; this status is also associated with frailty conditions [13]. Moreover, caregivers often informally provide various forms of support to older adults [14]. The need for instrumental and socio-emotional support can result in heightened stress and a decline in the physical and psychological well-being of the caregivers as well [12]. The impact on caregivers is linked to the extent of support needed [15]. Answering older adults' needs could alleviate their caregivers' burden as well. Socially Assistive Robots (SARs) have the potential to enable and support older adults with activity of daily living [16]. The acceptance of this technology depends on the perception of its usefulness [17], and it is worth noting that older adults could also be more accepting even than younger people regarding SARs [18]. Monitoring technologies, typically referred to as wearable and environmental sensors, have been also suggested as potential tools to monitor older adults and help them maintain their autonomy [19]. These technologies are considered an acceptable method for monitoring activities of daily living among older adults [19], and they could potentially offer valuable data to SARs. Consequently, older adults may display higher openness towards incorporating assistive technologies into their home when they address their specific needs [20] and could help to enable and support their independence [21]. Thus, even if the perception of robots and technology among older adults has been considered among literature, needs and preferences among older adults with low socio-economic status are still limited. This is particularly important because socio-economic status is related to people's health and lifestyle [22], thus causing specific daily needs as well. Individuals with low incomes may be sceptical about using SARs [23]; however, people's willingness to invest in SARs is associated with their perception of the technology's ability to adapt to their needs [24]. To reach and improve well-being for a broader audience, considering these aspects is relevant. For instance, in the UK, 2.1 million older adults live in relative poverty [25]. Indeed, from a biopsychosocial perspective, the well-being and quality of life of individuals during the aging process are influenced not only by biological factors but also by psychological and social factors [17, 26], therefore a systemic approach should be considered when developing assistive technologies as it could improve their usage [27, 28]. For these reasons, in performing a thematic analysis, the aim of the present study is to analyse and understand the perception and needs of low-income older adults regarding SARs, monitoring technologies and their use in home.

2 Method

2.1 Participants

A total of 17 (10 women and 7 males, mean age = 69.8 years, SD = 3.4) older adults were recruited via convenience sampling. Inclusion criteria were: a) age ≥ 65 years old and b) having a relatively low income as defined by [29]. Participants were divided in two groups and took part in two separate focus groups. All of the participants were informed about the nature of the study during the recruiting and before the beginning of each focus group; thus, all the participants provided their written informed consent to take part in the study, including to be audio recorded. Ethical approval for this study was provided by the institutional human research ethics committee (ID: 1726544).

2.2 Procedure

Each group session began with welcoming participants, explaining the aims of the focus groups, and establishing rules about the subsequent focus groups, and providing any further information on request.

Live Robot and Sensors Presentation. Subsequently, a live presentation of SARs and sensors was conducted to provide participants with a clearer and more tangible idea about the currently available SARs and monitoring technologies, along with providing examples of their capabilities. This procedure was used to elicit concrete ideas and associations related to these technologies in the subsequent interactions. The SARs were selected to present a range of different available types. For the presentation, 4 types of SARs that could showcase the widest possible range of variation in terms of type, functions, dimensions, movements, and other characteristics associated with this technology were selected. Specifically, the following robots were used: a) NAO, a humanoid robot of about 58cm equipped with various sensors and with gripped hands, its legs and feet contain motors and joints allowing NAO to walk; b) Pepper, a humanoid robot with a height of approximately 120 cm and a tablet-like display on its chest, contrary to NAO, Pepper moves thanks built-in omnidirectional wheels; c) MiRo-E, a more minimalistic appearance compared to humanoid robots, resembling a small animal with expressive LED eyes, and d) TurtleBot 4, a mobile robot featuring a differential drive base, sensors for perception, offering a versatile and affordable solution for robotics applications. These SARs are depicted in Fig. 1. During this phase the researchers described each robot main features, other than the main physical aspects; attention was given to robot's sensors and how they can be utilised to different aims (e.g., navigate the space, detect faces, recognise speech). Examples of functionalities were also provided, these included verbal interactions and demonstrations of robot movements capacities. The presentation followed a schedule led by the researchers. Likewise, participants received instructions about monitoring technologies through the display of sensor images and explanations of their functions. Participants were also informed that sensors could be utilised to provide information to the SARs. Additionally, actual sensors were showcased and described to the participants. Any uncertainties or questions were addressed to ensure a clear understanding of the concepts. The presentation lasted for about 30 min.

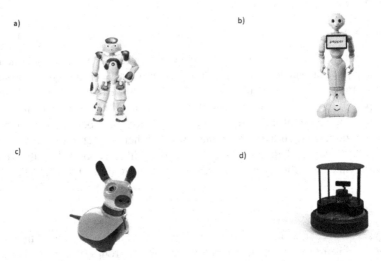

Fig. 1. SARs utilised during the presentation: a) NAO (SoftBank Robotics); b) Pepper (SoftBank Robotics); c) MiRo-E (Consequential Robotics); d) TurtleBot 4 (Open Robotics and Clearpath Robotics)

Focus Groups. The focus groups were conducted using a semi-structured interview approach, allowing participants to freely talk about the proposed topics. This technique was used as the collective discussion could elicit the development of ideas and concepts [30]. Two members of the research team, who were experts in this technique, facilitated the focus groups. Specifically, while one team member acted as the moderator, another member took note of the participants' non-verbal behaviours, managed the tools, and provided support to the moderator when necessary. The moderator facilitated group interaction through probing, balancing participant interactions, and encouraging the expression of personal viewpoints. The focus groups began with an engagement question, asking participants about their thoughts regarding robots. The main dimensions investigated during the discussion were related to thoughts about robots at home, everyday aspects where participants needed support and how robots could support them, features and functions that the robot should have, opinions and suggestions regarding the use of sensors, any possible concerns, and concluded with an exit question, asking if participants had anything else to add. Each focus group lasted approximately 90 min.

2.3 Data Analysis

Audio recordings were transcribed verbatim and were analysed using a thematic analysis approach [31]. This method involves becoming familiar with the data, creating codes, identifying, reviewing, and labelling themes, and compiling a final report. The analysis followed an inductive approach. A coding manual was developed and the fit between code and data was reviewed in a series of meetings; revisions were performed if necessary. The reliability of the coding process was established by a cross-coding comparison. Specifically, two members of the research team, who were not involved in the coding process, were trained on the developed code and asked to independently code a sample representing the 20% of the total focus groups. Inter-rater agreement was then carried out, indicating almost perfect agreement (Cohen's k = 0.87). If any dispute arose, it was settled through discussion between the researchers. Thus, codes were grouped and refined into themes, through an iterative and reflexive process. Then, to ensure consensus and agreement with the interpretation of the data, the entire research team discussed these themes and decided on their final definitions.

3 Results

Below are briefly reported the main themes emerged from the analysis, with meaning-ful sentences extracted from each theme to provide examples of participants opinions. The themes encompassed potential applications to 1) promote and monitor an active lifestyle, 2) help with daily errands and provide physical assistance, 3) reduce isolation and loneliness, along with 4) considerations regarding monitoring technologies and 5) barriers affecting SARs and monitoring technologies usage and acceptance.

3.1 Promote and Monitor an Active Lifestyle

Participants highlighted the potential of SAR as a tool to enhance aspects of their well-being by being more physically active. Indeed, they noted that the SAR could offer valuable support in engaging in physical daily activities, especially as they age and face limitations: "*As we get older, there are certain activities I don't do as before. Having assistance in those areas could really make a positive difference. Walking, for example, would be a key benefit...having something that could walk alongside you, and give assistance, that would be quite helpful.*"; "*I used to go walking. I can't do that now without someone with me, er, so I'm not very happy getting old but you can't do anything about it, you know*". In addition to aiding in physical activities, participants expressed the importance of reminders for such daily tasks: "*You could set it [the robot] to remind you, like, when the garden needs attention, and then I can go and take care of it,...*" In this context, the SAR's potential to provide motivation in performing physical activities was also acknowledged: "*I've seen people who lack the motivation to move and engage. I believe something like this could stimulate them, you know, having the robot act as encouragement...*".

The participants shared that an important feature would be the ability to monitor and provide feedback on daily activities and movements in order to further enhance them: "*if the robot could check and let me know if I'm doing enough or if I need to walk more could be useful,"* a participant pondered; *"if this thing [the robot] could actually recognise the way I move – well, that might be quite something. It could possibly let me know, you see, if I'm getting something wrong...or what if it could even give me a nudge about my posture?"*. Furthermore, participants highlighted a critical safety aspect, suggesting that the SAR could potentially detect any risky situations: *"if you are living on your own, and you need some help. If you have a fall and this can detect and ring the emergency, or get some help from someone, that would be very good for lonely people who are living on their own"* a participant emphasised.

3.2 Help with Daily Errands and Provide Physical Assistance

Participants indicated that they would like the SAR to help support them to go out and help them in errands and outdoor activities since *"I think one robot would integrate with things that could, you know, that if I'm going somewhere I could take it with me, and it could help me"*. Indeed, the participants indicated a current physical limitation as well: *"I believe my main challenge is strength. I'm quite physically able but I haven't got the strength...I wonder if [the robot] would provide any help"*. Consequently, they envisioned the SAR as a potential ally, especially when confronted with physically demanding tasks. Elaborating this idea a participant remarked: *"I can see that being useful where you could utilise a remote control to guide the robot to pick up items or handle mechanical lifting tasks,..."* This assistance would prove invaluable, especially during activities that require venturing outside for daily errands, such as grocery shopping: *"Erm, especially as you're getting older, you know,"* another participant reflected, *"tasks involving lifting and performing basic functions become increasingly challenging. Consider the simple act of shopping, getting to the stores and carrying the groceries back home."* In such situations, the participants envisioned interacting with the robot as a collaborator, saying things like *"Alright, you pick this shopping up and follow me"*.

3.3 Reduce Isolation and Loneliness

The SAR has emerged as a promising tool with the potential to alleviate the feelings of isolation and loneliness experienced by older adults. Participants in the study proposed innovative ways to harness the SAR's capabilities, suggesting that it could serve as an interactive companion: *"A lot of people have grown lonely, and having something intelligent to engage in meaningful conversations with could be quite comforting."* Another participant envisioned the SAR facilitating interactions beyond the confines of the home, saying: *"Imagine being able to step outside, perhaps into your garden, and engage in a conversation with the robot."* Moreover, the SAR could enhance interpersonal communication by offering features that enable more effective connections with others. For instance, it could assist in enabling and maintaining relationships by helping individuals reach out to their loved ones: *"Consider having a feature in there (indicating the robot) that reminds you to call your aunt, which I should have done yesterday. It could prompt me with a reminder: 'Remember to give your aunt a call.'"*

3.4 Considerations Regarding Monitoring Technologies

Participants generally indicated their acceptance of using sensors, *"If it can help gather useful information, I believe people would accept it."*. However, they also expressed a preference for a limited number of sensors rather than utilising too many, as stated by one participant: *"I'd rather avoid having a multitude of sensors around the house...I would limit their number, maybe have just one or two that can gather all the necessary information."*. Additionally, participants suggested that they would prefer to use wearable sensors due to their perceived ease of use, *"I'd like to have something that you can just take and wear, you know, something that you just take and that monitors you."* However, their main concern pertains to the possibility of forgetting or losing it, *"I am only concerned that I might forget it somewhere [laughs] and end up not using it."*

3.5 Barriers Affecting SARs and Monitoring Technologies Usage and Acceptance

Participants have expressed concerns regarding certain aspects related to SARs and sensors that could potentially hinder the adoption of these technologies. Primarily, these aspects pertain to participants' accessibility and usability of these technologies. Indeed, among these concerns, worries have arisen regarding the cost of SARs and sensors *"If you have got a robot to assist you in your home, well how much will it cost you. It would cost you more than probably what a home help would cost"* and *"People would use it depending on how much its cost, you know, can they afford? Because nowadays we are limited with resources, people are having a difficult time..."* and some of the participants reported that they are concerned about difficulties in utilise the SAR due ageing *"...they're very good but I'm a bit too old now to be taking all this in...um...I don't know if I can use it. I'll leave it to the younger ones."*, which could lead to demanding situations as expressed by another participant, *"...I generally, you know, don't have that much patience. You want an instant response."*

4   Discussion

This study aimed to investigate the needs of older adults with low income that SARs and monitoring technologies could address in their home-based everyday contexts. Their reports are meaningful, as socio-economic status could impact various aspects of people's lives. Therefore, gaining a better understanding of their needs could lead to enhanced SARs and monitoring technologies development and increased utility in addressing these aspects. As a result, this could contribute to improving their quality of life and alleviating caregivers' burden. The analysis of the data gathered from focus groups indicated five main themes that the SARs and sensors should respond to within this population. The first theme indicated that older adults face a reduction of daily physical activities, and the SAR could be a tool to enable physical activity. Overall, the SAR should support them in daily physical activities, motivate them, provide reminders, and consider solutions to monitor activities and provide feedback. Identifying risk situations is also considered an important aspect. Since participants emphasized the significance of physical support, we suggest the need to design or select SARs tailored for older adults to enhance this aspect.

This is in line with literature, as it is well-known that aging is characterised by a decline of physical abilities that are fundamental for daily activities [32, 33]. Moreover, participants indicated that the recognition of movements and daily activities is an important aspect that should be further considered and developed for this population, which further confirms the increasing trend and importance of monitoring activities of older adults through the use of technology [34–36]. Another theme emerged regarding the limitations older adults could face in daily errands and outdoor activities. They expressed a desire for a SAR that can assist them in these activities, especially in tasks like transporting objects, which would be particularly helpful in addressing the physical situations they may struggle with, as these situations could require too much strength. Reducing isolation and loneliness was identified as a prominent theme within the focus groups, which the SAR could help to alleviate. This is not surprising, as this is another issue consistently associated with aging [3], and it aligns with further evidence indicating that older adults rely on home-based technology to improve their social connections [19]. Interestingly, participants not only suggested solutions to improve communication with others but also expressed an acceptance of interacting with the SAR as a social partner to reduce loneliness. The fourth theme proposed specific considerations that should be taken into account during the design and implementation of monitoring technologies, which could also support SARs' functions. The last theme pertained to the barriers that could reduce SARs and monitoring technologies utilisation. Mainly, participants expressed concerns related to costs and their own skills in utilising SARs. This study that takes into consideration the needs of older adults in SARs and monitoring technologies design considering their socio-economic status. The results from low-income older adults confirm findings from previous research on older adults [37–39] and provide valuable insights and examples related to isolation and the need for physical assistance and support of daily living skills at home. Furthermore, before providing their interventions, they had the opportunity to observe SARs and sensors with different features and functions firsthand. As an additional perspective, it would be interesting to understand how the proposed themes are ranked according to priority for older adults. However, we should also consider some limitations. Participants were recruited through convenience sampling, and there are other aspects that could impact the quality of life and needs of older adults which this study did not consider, such as frailty conditions. Indeed, as a future perspective, the needs of older adults with frailty should be considered to address their growing demands.

In conclusion, the study has brought to light five primary themes that require attention during the design and implementation of SARs and monitoring technologies. These themes play a crucial role in enhancing the perceived usability of these technologies and consequently improving the quality of life for older users.

Funding. This work was supported by the EPSRC and NIHR (grant number EP/W031809/1, IMACTIVE).

References

1. Office for National Statistics: Living longer: is age 70 the new age 65? https://www.ons.gov. uk/peoplepopulationandcommunity/birthsdeathsandmarriages/ageing/articles/livinglonger isage70thenewage65/2019-11-19. Accessed 31 July 2023

2. The United Nations (UN): World population prospects: the 2017 revision. United Nations Econ SocAff, ed. WPN ESA/P/WP/248. United Nations, New York (2017)

3. Donovan, N.J., Blazer, D.: Social isolation and loneliness in older adults: review and commentary of a national academies report. Am. J. Geriatr. Psychiatry **28**(12), 1233–1244 (2020)

4. Park, D.C., Gutchess, A.H., Meade, M.L., Stine-Morrow, E.A.: Improving cognitive function in older adults: Nontraditional approaches. J. Gerontol. Ser. B: Psychol. Sci. Soc. Sci. **62**(Special_Issue_1), 45–52 (2007)

5. Hou, Y., et al.: Ageing as a risk factor for neurodegenerative disease. Nat. Rev. Neurol. **15**(10), 565–581 (2019)

6. Holland, G.J., Tanaka, K., Shigematsu, R., Nakagaichi, M.: Flexibility and physical functions of older adults: a review. J. Aging Phys. Act. **10**(2), 169–206 (2002)

7. Bloom, D.E., et al.: Macroeconomic implications of population ageing and selected policy responses. Lancet **385**(9968), 649–657 (2015)

8. Prince, M.J., et al.: The burden of disease in older people and implications for health policy and practice. Lancet **385**(9967), 549–562 (2015)

9. Zhou, W., Oyegoke, A.S., Sun, M.: Service planning and delivery outcomes of home adaptations for ageing in the UK. J. Housing Built Environ. **34**, 365–383 (2019)

10. Snowden, M., et al.: Effect of exercise on cognitive performance in community-dwelling older adults: Review of intervention trials and recommendations for public health practice and research. J. Am. Geriatr. Soc. **59**(4), 704–716 (2011)

11. Braveman, P., Gottlieb, L.: The social determinants of health: it's time to consider the causes of the causes. Publ. Health Rep. **129**(1_suppl2), 19–31 (2014)

12. Choi, N.G., McDougall, G.: Unmet needs and depressive symptoms among low-income older adults. J. Gerontol. Soc. Work **52**(6), 567–583 (2009)

13. Hayajneh, A.A., Rababa, M.: The association of frailty with poverty in older adults: a systematic review. Dement. Geriatr. Cogn. Disord. **50**(5), 407–413 (2022)

14. Bookwala, J., Zdaniuk, B., Burton, L., Lind, B., Jackson, S., Schulz, R.: Concurrent and long-term predictors of older adults' use of community-based long-term care services: the caregiver health effects study. J. Aging Health **16**(1), 88–115 (2004)

15. Wolff, J.L., Spillman, B.C., Freedman, V.A., Kasper, J.D.: A national profile of family and unpaid caregivers who assist older adults with health care activities. JAMA Intern. Med. **176**(3), 372–379 (2016)

16. Cavallo, F., et al.: Robotic services acceptance in smart environments with older adults: user satisfaction and acceptability study. J. Med. Internet Res. **20**(9), e9460 (2018)

17. Camp, N., et al.: Perceptions of socially assistive robots among community-dwelling older adults. In: Cavallo, F., et al. (eds.) Social Robotics: 14th International Conference, ICSR 2022, pp. 540–549. Springer, Heidelberg (2022). https://doi.org/10.1007/978-3-031-24670-8_48

18. Arras, K.O., Cerqui, D.: Do we want to share our lives and bodies with robots? A 2000 people survey: a 2000-people survey. Tech. Rep. **605** (2005)

19. Camp, N., et al.: Perceptions of in-home monitoring technology for activities of daily living: semistructured interview study with community-dwelling older adults. JMIR Aging **5**(2), e33714 (2022)

20. Tinker, A., Lansley, P.: Introducing assistive technology into the existing homes of older people: feasibility, acceptability, costs and outcomes. J. Telemed. Telecare **11**(1_suppl), 1–3 (2005)

21. Pain, H., Gale, C.R., Watson, C., Cox, V., Cooper, C., Sayer, A.A.: Readiness of elders to use assistive devices to maintain their independence in the home. Age Ageing **36**(4), 465–467 (2007)

22. Wang, J., Geng, L.: Effects of socioeconomic status on physical and psychological health: lifestyle as a mediator. Int. J. Environ. Res. Public Health **16**(2), 281 (2019)

23. Smakman, M.H., Konijn, E.A., Vogt, P., Pankowska, P.: Attitudes towards social robots in education: enthusiast, practical, troubled, sceptic, and mindfully positive. Robotics **10**(1), 24 (2021)

24. Fracasso, F., Buchweitz, L., Theil, A., Cesta, A., Korn, O.: Social robots acceptance and marketability in Italy and Germany: a cross-national study focusing on assisted living for older adults. Int. J. Soc. Robot. **14**(6), 1463–1480 (2022)

25. Age UK: Briefing Poverty in later life. https://www.ageuk.org.uk/globalassets/age-uk/doc uments/reports-and-publications/reports-and-briefings/money-matters/poverty-in-later-life-briefing-june-2023.pdf. Accessed 09 Oct 2023

26. Candela, F., Zucchetti, G., Magistro, D.: Individual correlates of autonomy in activities of daily living of institutionalized elderly individuals: an exploratory study in a holistic perspective. Holist. Nurs. Pract. **27**(5), 284–291 (2013)

27. Scherer, M.J.: The change in emphasis from people to person: introduction to the special issue on assistive technology. Disabil. Rehabil. **24**(1–3), 1–4 (2002)

28. Pino, M. C., Vagnetti, R., Tiberti, S., Valenti, M., Mazza, M.: Involving autism stakeholders in identifying priorities for interventions based on augmented reality. Disabil. Rehabil.: Assist. Technol., 1–9 (2022)

29. Francis-Devine, B.: Poverty in the UK: Statistics. (2022). https://commonslibrary.parliament. uk/research-briefings/sn07096/. Accessed 31 July 2023

30. Acocella, I.: The focus groups in social research: advantages and disadvantages. Qual. Quant. **46**, 1125–1136 (2012)

31. Braun, V., Clarke, V.: Using thematic analysis in psychology. Qual. Res. Psychol. **3**(2), 77–101 (2006)

32. Magistro, D., Candela, F., Brustio, P.R., Liubicich, M.E., Rabaglietti, E.: A longitudinal study on the relationship between aerobic endurance and lower body strength in Italian sedentary older adults. J. Aging Phys. Act. **23**(3), 444–451 (2015)

33. Candela, F., Zucchetti, G., Ortega, E., Rabaglietti, E., Magistro, D.: Preventing loss of basic activities of daily living and instrumental activities of daily living in elderly. Holist. Nurs. Pract. **29**(5), 313–322 (2015)

34. Camp, N., et al.: Technology used to recognize activities of daily living in community-dwelling older adults. Int. J. Environ. Res. Public Health **18**(1), 163 (2021)

35. Magistro, D., et al.: A novel algorithm for determining the contextual characteristics of movement behaviors by combining accelerometer features and wireless beacons: development and implementation. JMIR Mhealth Uhealth **6**(4), e8516 (2018)

36. Candela, F., Zucchetti, G., Magistro, D., Ortega, E., Rabaglietti, E.: Real and perceived physical functioning in Italian elderly population: associations with BADL and IADL. Adv. Aging Res. **3**, 349–359 (2014)

37. Ciuffreda, I., et al.: Design and development of a technological platform based on a sensorized social robot for supporting older adults and caregivers: GUARDIAN ecosystem. Int. J. Soc. Robot. (2023)

38. Liu, B., Tetteroo, D., Timmermans, A., Markopoulos, P.: Exploring older adults' acceptance, needs, and design requirements towards applying social robots in a rehabilitation context. In: 2022 31st IEEE International Conference on Robot and Human Interactive Communication (RO-MAN), pp. 1077–1084. IEEE (2022)

39. Cesta, A., Cortellessa, G., Fracasso, F., Orlandini, A., Turno, M.: User needs and preferences on AAL systems that support older adults and their carers. J. Ambient Intell. Smart Environ. **10**(1), 49–70 (2018)

Large-Scale Swarm Control in Cluttered Environments

Saber Elsayed[1(✉)] and Mohamed Mabrok[2]

[1] School of Systems and Computing, University of New South Wales, Canberra, Australia
s.elsayed@unsw.edu.au
[2] Mathematics Program, Department of Mathematics, Statistics and Physics, College of Arts and Sciences, Qatar University, P.O. Box 2713, Doha, Qatar

Abstract. In the evolving era of social robots, managing a swarm of autonomous agents to perform particular tasks has become essential for numerous industries. The task becomes more challenging for large-scale swarms and complex environments, which have not been fully explored yet. Therefore, this research introduces a methodology incorporating multiple coordinated robotic shepherds to effectively guide large-scale agent swarms in obstacle-laden terrains. The proposed framework commences with deploying an unsupervised machine-learning algorithm to categorise the swarm into clusters. Then, a shepherding algorithm with coordinated robotic shepherds drives the sub-swarms towards the goal. Also, a path planner based on an evolutionary algorithm is proposed to help robotic shepherds move in a way that minimises the dispersion of each sub-swarm and avoids potential hazards and obstructions. The proposed approach is tested on different scenarios, with the results showing a success rate of 100% in guiding swarms with sizes up to 3000 agents.

Keywords: Swarm Control · Robotic Shepherding · Large-scale · Path Planning

1 Introduction

Swarm intelligence (SI), a branch within artificial intelligence (AI), focuses on decentralised systems. Within such systems, individual agents work in synergy with each other and their immediate environment to achieve specific objectives [2,8]. As we progress into an era of social robots and multi-domain human-robot collaboration, the principles of SI have been witnessed across various sectors, from defence and Internet of Things to proactive crowd control [10]. Imagine this: a team of small drones zips through the skies during an emergency, like a fire or flood. There is another drone that leads them all using advanced techniques to guide the swarm safely and quickly where help is needed. The leading drone sees the big picture and navigates the swarm around obstacles or dangers while

---

This research is supported by UNSW Rector's start-up grant (No. PS48058) and the U.S. Office of Naval Research-Global (ONR-G).

the swarm follows, carrying supplies or helping locate people in need. They all communicate, ensuring the swarm reach people efficiently, delivering aid, and providing real-time information back to emergency services.

However, steering a swarm agent (i.e., robots) remains challenging. Over time, various methodologies have emerged, with shepherding emerging as a notably effective.

In SI, shepherding is a paradigm that emulates the canonical interaction observed between shepherds and sheep. This dynamic involves a swarm of autonomous agents, analogous to sheep, that reactively adjust their behaviors in response to guiding agents (shepherds) [12,14]. On the contrary, shepherd's actions are characterised by repulsion and attraction dynamics, allowing for proactive maneuvering of the flock to guide them towards a predetermined location [1,11]. The shepherding paradigm has been integrated into diverse domains, such as crowd management, military operations, wildlife conservation, unmanned aerial vehicle applications, and environmental remediation, including oil spill cleanup [1,11]. Recent research indicates that implementing shepherding algorithms within robotic systems may enhance task efficiency [15].

However, factors such as sheep spatial density, swarm size, number of shepherd robots, and complex environmental settings (i.e., cluttered environments) can influence shepherding efficiency [5,8]. While specific models, such as the Strombom model [14], have shown promise, they falter in scalability. Furthermore, despite extensions and adaptations, they remain untested in expansive scenarios. In a recent shift, deep learning, particularly reinforcement learning, has been applied to these challenges. Instances include Zhi et al.'s deep reinforcement learning for obstacle navigation [18] and Hussein et al.'s curriculum-based reinforcement learning for herding guidance [10]. However, most existing solutions thrive only with limited agent numbers, exhibiting deficits with larger groups.

Our recent study [6] was successful in scaling up the Strombom model. However, the study was tested only in obstacle-free environments and used only one shepherd. Also, the model was not able to achieve a 100% success rate in controlling swarms of sizes 2000 and 3000.

Motivated by these research gaps, this study introduces a framework for controlling large-scale autonomous agents in cluttered environments. The approach involves using more than one synchronised robotic shepherd to steer large clusters of agents through environments replete with obstacles. The framework uses an unsupervised machine-learning algorithm to divide the swarm into groups. The two shepherd robots coordinate on which sub-swarm each one can drive to the goal. If one of the shepherds drives the allocated sub-swarm, it moves to help the other shepherd robot drive its sub-swarm. Shepherd robots keep collaborating until they complete the whole mission. A path planner grounded in an evolutionary algorithm is also introduced to aid robotic shepherds in their navigation and reduce swarm dispersion while evading potential threats. The efficacy of the suggested approach is examined across diverse settings, demonstrating a perfect success rate in controlling swarms encompassing up to 3,000 agents.

The contributions of this work are as follows:

- Assessing the current shepherding models for large-scale control in cluttered environments
- Development of a shepherding model with multiple coordinated robotic shepherds for large swarm control in cluttered environments.
- The design of an evolutionary framework to optimise the robotic shepherds' paths to the herding points that can minimise sub-swarm dispersion and avoid obstacles.
- Illustrating the significance of the proposed model with detailed experiments and analysis.

This manuscript's structure entails a subsequent review of related literature (Sect. 2), followed by a description of the proposed approach in Sect. 3. The discussion of results is presented in Sect. 4 while the concluding remarks are articulated in Sect. 5.

2   Brief Review

Although shepherding has shown success in many domains, limited work on large-scale shepherding exists. Below is a brief review of related work on large-scale shepherding

As previously mentioned, shepherding as an approach within SI has seen considerable popularity, with studies including creating robotic shepherds, guidance mechanisms, real-world simulations of shepherding, and swarming conduct [11]. If relevant, initialising a shepherding model may require several assumptions, such as a predetermined goal, environmental boundaries, the initial autonomous herd locations, and obstacles. Specific applications may introduce additional constraints, such as agent behavior. For example, unmanned aerial vehicles (UAVs) can disregard obstacles.

Strombom presented foundational work in this area [14], classifying flocking as gathered or scattered according to the central mass. The model formulated sheep (autonomous herd) and sheepdog movements using attractive and repulsive forces, considering various factors such as collision avoidance and attraction to the local centre of mass. Further details of the Strombom model will be elaborated in Sect. 3.

Recently, there has been significant growth in distributed methods, leading to research on distributed shepherding [2]. These studies used multiple sheepdogs to steer the flock while maintaining coordination to prevent conflicts. Despite these advancements, certain methods encountered inefficiencies with the collaboration of multiple sheepdog agents [13,16]. An intriguing model was developed in [9] that controlled each sheep agent through a feedback consensus technique.

Investigating large-scale shepherding has remained somewhat limited, focusing primarily on small to medium-scale problems. Although practical, only a handful of studies have explored large-scale scenarios. For instance, [3] put forth an animal herding method for extensive areas (70 ha), but without addressing large numbers (10 to 50 animals). In another attempt, Zhang *et al.* proposed an edge-following and shrink behavior mechanism in [17], emphasising local distribution density, but it was only tested on small-scale issues. In [4], the authors applied the Random Finite Set (RFS) theory to represent the state of the swarm and used predictive control of the model to guide the swarms. The research measures the distance between swarm RFS and desired distribution through information divergence. However, information on the size of the swarm was missing, and there were no obstacles.

3 Large-Scale Swarm Control Framework in Cluttered Environments

This section presents our proposal for large-scale swarm control in cluttered environments.

3.1 Proposed Framework

As previously detailed, the proposed method aims to effectively employ multiple shepherd robots to direct a substantial number of autonomous robots within an environment cluttered with obstacles.

The methodology begins with dividing the flock into groups (refer to Sect. 3.3). Subsequently, an analysis is performed to determine the mean distance from the goal for each sheep within these clusters. As we are using two shepherds, the two groups positioned furthest from the destination are then selected as the first targets for the shepherds. A strategic aim drives this selection: moving the furthest group towards the goal might inadvertently guide other sheep closer to the target [6]. The shepherds coordinate among them to select the group to drive, i.e., the shepherd drives the cluster close to it.

Given that the environment is filled with obstacles, the shepherd must navigate carefully to minimise the scattering of the autonomous herd. To aid in this, an evolutionary algorithm has been crafted to chart the path for each sheepdog to its herding point, which is positioned behind the cluster and aligns with the route to the goal. This optimal path planning takes into account the environment's obstacles and establishes a safety zone around each sheep, ensuring that they do not stray too far from the shepherd robot. When reaching its herding point, each shepherd robot begins exerting forces on the entire cluster to guide them to the destination bearing in mind avoiding obstacles.

Enhanced collaboration is facilitated between the two shepherds by enabling them to assist each other based on their progress. Specifically, if one shepherd successfully guides its cluster to the goal before the other, it shifts its focus to aid the remaining shepherd in directing its cluster. Note that when a shepherd moves to help the other shepherd, the path planner is utilised to find the best path. This cooperative approach ensures more efficient and synchronised execution of their shared task.

Algorithm 1: Large-scale Shepherding Framework with Coordination

---

Input : sheep (Π) and shepherds ($B = 2$) locations, initial algorithm
              parameters
Output: The location of herd agents
Divide Π into Z groups (Section 3.3)
while $k = 1 : 2 : Z$ **do**
  | Collaborate between shepherds to select which furthest group to drive
  | Find a path for each shepherd (avoid obstacles and ensure a safety zone
  | around each sheep))
  | **while** *agents have not reached goal* **do**
  | | Drive each cluster to the goal (refer Section 3.2)
  | | **if** *one shepherd completes the task before the other* **then**
  | | | Redirect it (using a path planner) to assist the other shepherd
  | | **end**
  | **end**
  | Recluster the remaining Π into $q - k$ groups
end

Once both clusters have successfully reached the destination, the method reinitiates the clustering process for any remaining sheep, and the guiding procedure resumes. The sheepdogs systematically steer the groups towards the goal, adhering to the described process until either all the subgroups have arrived at the destination or other predetermined termination conditions are satisfied.

The detailed steps are shown in Algorithm 1.

3.2   Shepherding Algorithm

The framework provides a solution to herding problems of an autonomous herd using shepherd robots, outlining the relationships and rules governing their movement within their environment [8,14]. Through a calculated combination of weights, the dynamics of the autonomous herd movement are defined, accounting for the influences of various entities.

Let us denote the set of autonomous herd agents as $\Pi = \pi_1, ..., \pi_i, ..., \pi_n$ and the set of shepherd robots as $B = \beta_1, ..., \beta_i, ..., \beta_m$, with a set of behaviors $\alpha_1, ..., \alpha_i, ..., \alpha_k$. The primary interactions and behaviors are:

1. Driving: The shepherd robot guides the autonomous herd towards a specific path or ray that connects the centre of mass to the target, represented by the normalised force vector $F^t_{\beta_j cd}$.
2. Gathering: If a member of the autonomous herd strays, the shepherd robot brings it back using the same force vector $F^t_{\beta_j cd}$. In this study, the gathering behavior is only triggered if the furthest agent is not between the flock and the goal, as introduced in [8].
3. Random Influence on Shepherd Robot: Random force $F^t_{\beta_j \epsilon}$ and angular noise $W_{e\beta_j}$ are introduced to avoid stalemate situations. The total force for the shepherd robot is given by

$$F_{\beta_j}^t = F_{\beta_j,cd}^t + W_{e\beta_j} F_{\beta_j\epsilon}^t. \tag{1}$$

4. Repulsive Forces in Autonomous Herd: Each member is subject to a repelling force from the shepherd robot ($F_{\pi_i\beta}^t$) and from other members ($F_{\pi_i\pi_{i1}}^t$ where $i \neq i1$).

5. Centre Attraction in Autonomous Herd: The herd is attracted to its local centre of mass. This is quantified by $F_{\pi_i\Lambda_{\pi_i}^t}^t$.

6. Autonomous Herd's Angular Noise: Denoted by $F_{\pi_i\epsilon}^t$.

Therefore, the total force in the autonomous herd is the total sum of all forces.

$$F_{\pi_i}^t = W_{\pi_v} F_{\pi_i}^{t-1} + W_{\pi\Lambda} F_{\pi_i\Lambda_{\pi_i}^t}^t + W_{\pi\beta} F_{\pi_i\beta_j}^t + W_{\pi\pi} F_{\pi_i\pi_{-i}}^t + W_{e\pi_i} F_{\pi_i\epsilon}^t. \tag{2}$$

Here, W signifies specific weights for each force.

After each movement, the total forces for both the autonomous herd and shepherd robots are updated as:

$$\begin{aligned} P_{\pi_i}^{t+1} &= P_{\pi_i}^t + S_{\pi_i}^t F_{\pi_i}^t, \\ P_{\beta_j}^{t+1} &= P_{\beta_j}^t + S_{\beta_j}^t F_{\beta_j}^t, \end{aligned} \tag{3}$$

3.3 K-Means Clustering

The K-means algorithm remains a significant method in machine learning and is selected for its straightforward and efficient characteristics. Let $X = \{x_1, x_2, ..., x_n\}$, $x_n \in R^d$ be the data set. The goal is to partition the data into Z disjoint clusters $C_1, ..., C_Z$, where Z is a predetermined number of clusters. The mean squared error (MSE) is commonly employed as a quality metric.

The K-means algorithm randomly selects the initial centres and then iteratively reassigns clusters to minimise the MSE until convergence. Despite its simplicity, it can be sensitive to initial centre placements and requires a predefined number of clusters, Z, which might not always be optimal.

In this study, clustering is influenced by the shepherd robot's capability, and the number of clusters is dictated by the quantity of the autonomous herd a shepherd robot can manage. If any cluster size is bigger than a predefined shepherd robot's capacity (200 agents), another trial of the K-means algorithm is applied (with a maximum number of trials of 20).

3.4 Evolutionary-Based Path Planner

This study leverages the capabilities of Differential Evolution (DE) [8] to optimise the waypoint locations in path planning. Initially, a random population of size PS is generated, wherein each member symbolizes a path $A =$

$[w^1, w^2, \ldots, w^D]$ consisting of D waypoints. Each waypoint comprises x and y coordinates, constituting a two-dimensional array. Though the following discussion focuses only on the x values, the described evolutionary processes equally apply to the y-coordinates.

The potential solutions denoted as $\vec{x}_z$ for $z = 1, 2, \ldots, PS$, are initialised within the defined search space.

Evaluation of each individual (i) considers both the objective function value and constraint violation ($f_i = L_i + \gamma \psi_i$, where γ is a penalty factor, while L_i and ψ_i are computed as in Eqs. 4 and 5). At every population assessment, the current fitness evaluations cfe are incremented. Subsequently, DE operators (mutation and crossover) evolve the entire population. Due to their efficiency, ϕ-to-current mutation and binomial crossover are used.

After creating the new solutions, a pairwise comparison between each new solution and its parent determines which one survives to the next generation. The evaluation phase entails assessing the quality of each solution, gauging both the fitness value and any constraint violation. In this context, the primary objective function is the total length L of a path leading from the start point to the target destination. The procedure involves the following stages for each solution $\vec{x}_i$:

1. Define the x-coordinate vector as $XS \leftarrow [\underline{x}, x_{i,1}, \ldots, x_{i,D}, \bar{x}]$;
2. Construct the y-coordinate vector as $YS \leftarrow [\underline{y}, y_{i,1}, \ldots, y_{i,D}, \bar{y}]$;
3. Divide a line into $k = D + 2$ points, creating equal intervals, as $TS \leftarrow$ split;
4. Generate a vector $LS \leftarrow$ space comprising $p_{\max} = 100$ uniformly distributed points between 0 and 1;
5. Perform cubic spline interpolation on XS and YS over unevenly-spaced sample points, producing vectors $\overrightarrow{XI}$ and $\overrightarrow{YI}$, respectively. The path from start to target, represented by $[\overrightarrow{XI}; \overrightarrow{YI}]$, consists of points XI_p and YI_p for $p = 1, 2, \ldots, p_{\max}$;
6. Compute the length L of the path as:

$$L_i = \sum_{p=1}^{p_{\max}-1} \sqrt{(XI_{p+1} - XI_p)^2 + (YI_{p+1} - YI_p)^2} \tag{4}$$

The extent of constraint violation (or overlap with obstacles) is quantified mathematically, with a value of 0 indicating no overlap:

1. Compute the Euclidean distance between each path point and each obstacle's centre O, given by $d_{p,s} = \sqrt{(XI_p - O_{x,s})^2 + (YI_p - O_{y,s})^2}$, where $O_{x,s}$ and $O_{y,s}$ define the centre coordinates of O;
2. Determine the violation for the i-th solution as:

$$\psi_i = \sum_{p=1}^{p_{\max}} \sum_{s=1}^{N} \max\left(1 - \frac{d_{p,s}}{O_{s,\text{radius}}}, 0\right) \tag{5}$$

where $O_{s,\text{radius}}$ is the radius of the s-th obstacle.

Table 1. The set of parameters used

Parameter	Value
Total number of autonomous herd (m)	[1000, 2000, 3000, 5000]
Total number of shepherd robot (n)	2
Length of the environment	300
Goal Location	(0, 0)
Goal radius R_H	$\sqrt{m} * 3$
Maximum step size of shepherd	4.5
Maximum step size of sheep	1
Shepherd's Sheep sensing radius	30
Repulsion strength from sheep	1.75
Repulsion strength from shepherdt	1
Attraction strength to the local centre of mass	1.05
Strength of sheep angular noise	0.3
Strength of shepherd angular noise	0.3
Maximum number of steps	$630 + 20 \times m$

3. Remember, each agent within the flock is considered an obstacle, functioning to create a safety zone that the shepherd must avoid. This safety zone is defined by a radius equal to the shepherd's repulsion strength, ensuring that a protective distance is maintained around every individual agent in the flock.

4 Experiments

In this section, the experimental results of the proposed model are discussed and compared to another well-known algorithm.

Mutation and crossover factors in DE are self-adaptively controlled, as in [7]. The stopping criterion for DE is 200 iterations. In this paper, we assume the environment is occupied by nine obstacles (with a radius of 5) placed outside the initial locations of the flock and the target area. Throughout all iterations of the simulation, these obstacles remain in their fixed positions. The algorithm is tested on different sizes of the herd 1000, 2000 and 3000. Ten simulation runs are considered with the remaining settings shown in Table 1. For such experiments, the sheep agents were initialised as one large cluster in the top right corner of the environment. The stopping criteria used are (1) the sheep agents have reached the goal or (2) the maximum number of steps for shepherds has been reached.

In the simulation environment, nine fixed obstacles are strategically located outside both the initial flock positions and the target region, each with a radius of 5 units. These obstacles maintain their designated locations throughout each iteration of the simulation process. The model's efficacy was evaluated in various herd sizes, specifically, 1000, 2000, and 3000. A total of ten individual simulation

Table 2. Comparison between the proposed approach, ISMLS and Strombom

Herd size	Algorithms	Steps			Success Rate		
		Best	average	std	Best	average	std
1000	Proposed	1.9110E+03	2.9576E+03	6.4494E+02	100%	100%	0.000E+00
	ISMLS	5.0970E+03	6.3017E+03	1.8927E+03	100%	100%	0.000E+00
	Strombom	–	–	–	–	–	–
2000	Proposed	4.0520E+03	6.2804E+03	1.6077E+03	100%	100%	0.00E+00
	ISMLS	1.1674E+04	1.3132E+04	2.2406E+03	100%	99.3%	2.143E-02
	Strombom	–	–	–	–	–	–
3000	Proposed	4.6780E+03	7.6088E+03	1.8624E+03	100%	100%	0.000E+00
	ISMLS	1.8726E+04	2.8813E+04	5.3376E+03	100%	94.5%	4.1533E-02
	Strombom	–	–	–	–	–	–

runs were executed, and the remaining settings are shown in Table 1. During these experimental procedures, the autonomous agents were initially grouped into a single large cluster in the upper right section of the domain. The simulation ends when either of two conditions is met: (1) the sheep agents have successfully arrived at the goal, or (2) the shepherd has reached the predefined maximum number of steps.

4.1 Comparative Analysis

To evaluate the robustness of the proposed method, the proposed approach is compared against the baseline model (Strombom) [14] and the methodology presented in [6], referred to herein as ISMLS. Note that, for a fair comparison, ISMLS was adapted to use the same gathering behaviour used in the proposed approach. Comparative analysis is conducted by examining the number of iterations (time ticks) required by the sheepdogs to herd all the sheep to the designated goal. We also evaluate the success rate of the shepherd robot, specifically focusing on how often it successfully guides all agents to the designated goal. This assessment will be based on a series of ten trials(runs). Table 2 presents a comparative analysis of these algorithms in terms of their performance on different herd sizes, that is 1000, 2000 and 3000.

From Table 2, the following observations are found:

- For each herd size, the proposed algorithm consistently reports the best performance with respect to the number of steps taken to complete the mission. Note that the table reports the total steps taken by both shepherds. If we consider the number of generations as a criterion, this number of total steps will be halved. It is also noted that the algorithm's performance is more stable, as noted by the standard deviation results.
- ISMLS is the next in terms of performance, with higher step counts across all measures. In particular, as the size of the herd increases, the gap between the proposed algorithm and ISMLS in terms of steps widens. This indicates the potentially better scalability of the Proposed method.

- Strombom was unsuccessful in completing the tasks for all herd sizes.
- In terms of success rate, both proposed and ISMLS have the best success rate of 100% for all herd sizes. However, while the proposed algorithm maintains a consistent 100% average success rate, the ISMLS sees a slight deterioration as the herd size increases, dropping to 99. 3% for 2000 and further to 94.5% for 3000. The standard deviation for the ISMLS success rate also increases as herd size grows.

A statistical comparison was performed using the Wilcoxon rank sum test with a significance level of 5%; the results demonstrated that the proposed method was statistically better than the other two algorithms.

4.2   Effect of Using the Path Planner

This subsection aims to determine whether the algorithm derived any benefits from using the path planner. In essence, would it be sufficient to use two shepherd robots without coordinating them in terms of path planning?

To do so, the algorithm was run under the same settings mentioned earlier, but no path planning was performed. The results presented in Fig. 1 demonstrate that using a path planner reduces the number of steps to complete the mission.

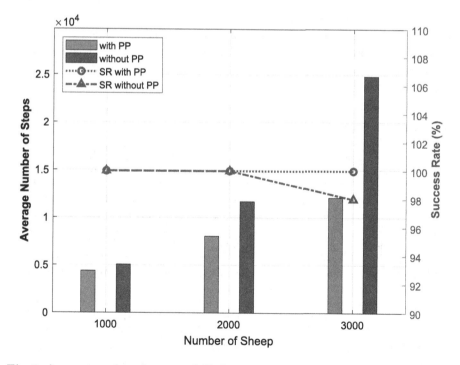

Fig. 1. Average number of steps and SR for the proposed algorithm with and without using a path planner (PP)

For a herd size of 1000 agents, the reduction is about 13%. Interestingly, this efficiency increases when the herd size increases, reaching more than 50% for 3000 agents. In addition, for the herd size of 3000, the SR, when not using path planning, deteriorates by 2%. This indicates that path planning is beneficial when the herd size increases.

5   Conclusion

This study introduced an approach to control large-scale agent swarms in cluttered environments. We used an unsupervised machine learning algorithm to decompose the swarm into clusters. Subsequently, coordinated robotic shepherds guide these sub-swarms. An evolutionary algorithm-based path planner aided these shepherds, ensuring minimal sub-swarm dispersion and safe navigation around obstacles.

In summary, the proposed algorithm appears to outperform existing algorithms in terms of both the number of steps required and the consistent success rate. The performance gap is more pronounced with increasing herd size, hinting at the superior scalability of the proposed method. While the proposed algorithm achieved a 100% success rate, the baseline algorithms failed in all scenarios. In addition, the results demonstrated that path planning could lead to better results when the herd size increases.

Future work should focus on testing the algorithms on more scenarios with more types and sizes of obstacles. Another possibility is to provide more coordination between shepherd robots; for example, coordination on which shepherd can collect the furthest sheep while the other focuses on driving the flock to the goal.

References

1. Abbass, H.A., Hunjet, R.A. (eds.): Shepherding UxVs for Human-Swarm Teaming. UST, Springer, Cham (2021). https://doi.org/10.1007/978-3-030-60898-9
2. Campbell, B., El-Fiqi, H., Hunjet, R., Abbass, H.: Distributed multi-agent shepherding with consensus. In: Tan, Y., Shi, Y. (eds.) ICSI 2021. LNCS, vol. 12690, pp. 168–181. Springer, Cham (2021). https://doi.org/10.1007/978-3-030-78811-7_17
3. Cimler, R., Doležal, O., Kühnová, J., Pavlík, J.: Herding algorithm in a large scale multi-agent simulation. In: Jezic, G., Chen-Burger, Y.-H.J., Howlett, R.J., Jain, L.C. (eds.) Agent and Multi-Agent Systems: Technology and Applications. SIST, vol. 58, pp. 83–94. Springer, Cham (2016). https://doi.org/10.1007/978-3-319-39883-9_7
4. Doerr, B., Linares, R.: Control of large swarms via random finite set theory. In: 2018 Annual American Control Conference (ACC), pp. 2904–2909. IEEE (2018)
5. El-Fiqi, H., et al.: The limits of reactive shepherding approaches for swarm guidance. IEEE Access 8, 214658–214671 (2020)
6. Elsayed, S., Hassanin, M.: Improved shepherding model for large-scale swarm control. In: 2023 International Conference on Smart Computing and Application (ICSCA), pp. 1–6. IEEE (2023)

7. Elsayed, S., Sarker, R., Coello, C.C.: Enhanced multi-operator differential evolution for constrained optimization. In: IEEE Congress on Evolutionary Computation, pp. 4191–4198. IEEE (2016)
8. Elsayed, S., et al.: Path planning for shepherding a swarm in a cluttered environment using differential evolution. In: 2020 IEEE Symposium Series on Computational Intelligence (SSCI), pp. 2194–2201. IEEE (2020)
9. Hu, J., Turgut, A.E., Krajník, T., Lennox, B., Arvin, F.: Occlusion-based coordination protocol design for autonomous robotic shepherding tasks. IEEE Trans. Cogn. Dev. Syst. 14(1), 126–135 (2020)
10. Hussein, A., Petraki, E., Elsawah, S., Abbass, H.A.: Autonomous swarm shepherding using curriculum-based reinforcement learning. In: AAMAS, pp. 633–641 (2022)
11. Long, N.K., Sammut, K., Sgarioto, D., Garratt, M., Abbass, H.A.: A comprehensive review of shepherding as a bio-inspired swarm-robotics guidance approach. IEEE Trans. Emerg. Top. Comput. Intell. 4(4), 523–537 (2020)
12. Mohamed, R.E., Elsayed, S., Hunjet, R., Abbass, H.: A graph-based approach for shepherding swarms with limited sensing range. In: 2021 IEEE Congress on Evolutionary Computation (CEC), pp. 2315–2322. IEEE (2021)
13. Pierson, A., Schwager, M.: Controlling noncooperative herds with robotic herders. IEEE Trans. Rob. 34(2), 517–525 (2017)
14. Strömbom, D., et al.: Solving the shepherding problem: heuristics for herding autonomous, interacting agents. J. R. Soc. Interface 11(100), 20140719 (2014)
15. Van Havermaet, S., Simoens, P., Landgraf, T., Khaluf, Y.: Steering herds away from dangers in dynamic environments. Roy. Soc. Open Sci. 10(5), 230015 (2023)
16. Varava, A., Hang, K., Kragic, D., Pokorny, F.T.: Herding by caging: a topological approach towards guiding moving agents via mobile robots. In: Robotics: Science and Systems, pp. 1–9 (2017)
17. Zhang, S., Pan, J.: Collecting a flock with multiple sub-groups by using multi-robot system. IEEE Robot. Autom. Lett. 7(3), 6974–6981 (2022)
18. Zhi, J., Lien, J.M.: Learning to herd agents amongst obstacles: training robust shepherding behaviors using deep reinforcement learning. IEEE Robot. Autom. Lett. 6(2), 4163–4168 (2021)

Alpha Mini as a Learning Partner in the Classroom

Oliver Bendel[(✉)] and Andrin Allemann

School of Business FHNW, 5210 Windisch, Switzerland
`oliver.bendel@fhnw.ch`

Abstract. Social robots such as NAO and Pepper are being used in some schools and universities. NAO is very agile and therefore entertaining. Pepper has the advantage that it has an integrated display where learning software of all kinds can be executed. One disadvantage of both is their high price. Schools can hardly afford such robots. This problem was the starting point for the project described here, which took place in 2023 at the School of Business FHNW. The aim was to create a learning application with an inexpensive social robot that has the same motor capabilities as NAO and the same knowledge transfer capabilities as Pepper. The small Alpha Mini from Ubtech was chosen. It was possible to connect it to an external device. This runs a learning game suitable for teaching at primary level. Alpha Mini provides explanations and feedback in each case. Three teachers tested the learning application, raised objections, and made suggestions for improvement. Social robots like Alpha Mini are an interesting solution for knowledge transfer in schools when they can communicate with other devices.

Keywords: Social Robots · Learning Application · Classroom

1 Introduction

In the classroom, whether in school or in university, robots have always had a certain importance [5]. They have been the subject of study and contemplation, assembled and disassembled, programmed, and integrated into settings of all kinds. Finally, social robots entered the classroom and with them came new possibilities and stimuli. They functioned as teachers, tutors, coaches, peers, or avatars, supporting teaching and learning. Their model was based not so much on the Lego Mindstorms-type kits as pedagogical agents that were already accessible in virtual learning environments in the 1990s [6]. Now, however, a physical presence was available, and the machine could enter and leave the classroom (usually with human assistance).

Nowadays, social robots such as NAO, Pepper, and Robin are repeatedly used in the classroom [3, 5, 9, 15, 20]. NAO has impressive motor skills, and Pepper has satisfactory gestural skills. Both provide natural language capabilities needed for knowledge transfer and praise and blame. NAO can serve as an avatar of pupils or as a coach for students [5]. Its movements are entertaining or serve as a model for children's and young people's movements. Pepper is a teacher, tutor, coach, and peer. Its great advantage is that it

© The Author(s), under exclusive license to Springer Nature Singapore Pte Ltd. 2024
A. Al. Ali et al. (Eds.): ICSR 2023, LNAI 14453, pp. 396–409, 2024.
https://doi.org/10.1007/978-981-99-8715-3_33

has an integrated tablet in its chest area. Educational software of all kinds can be run from there, such as learning games with text and images. The robot itself can then guide the execution and progress. It can explain questions and answers and motivate students through its physical and vocal presence [20].

One disadvantage of both robots is their high price [4]. Only universities with healthy budgets can afford Pepper, or more precisely the Robo Labs or didactic centers, from which the specimens can then be borrowed only temporarily. Schools are usually not in a position to purchase the models. There are alternatives such as Alpha Mini. It seems more convincing as a teacher or tutor than Cozmo or Vector, which are also on the market and which, despite their abilities, seem like toys. It can easily be ordered in Europe and costs only about $1,000 to $1,400, a fraction of the price of NAO and Pepper. It is comparable to NAO in terms of mobility. Unlike Pepper, however, it has no display or tablet, which is an enormous limitation in the context of knowledge transfer.

This problem was the starting point for the project described here, which took place at the School of Business FHNW from February to August 2023 [1]. The first author was the initiator and supervisor, the second author the developer. The research question was: Is it possible to combine an inexpensive social robot with a screen to create a complex learning application with text- and image-based learning software and verbal and gestural feedback? Alpha Mini was to become a learning partner in a school, in the role of a tutor who teaches, praises, and reprimands the child. To this end, it would interact with educational software that would run on an external display or tablet. Together, this would result in a learning application comparable to what Pepper is capable of [21]. The educational software would have to be as simple as possible and primarily serve demonstration purposes, i.e., to prove that it forms a functioning learning application together with the social robot.

This article discusses social robots in the classroom in the second section. Then, in the third section, it describes the implementation of the project at the School of Business FHNW. It also discusses the efforts and challenges that arose during integration. The fourth section summarizes the tests with Alpha Mini and the learning software that were conducted with three teachers.

2   Social Robots in the Classroom

The Educa report, "Digitization in Education", shows that almost 20% of students in Switzerland at all levels of education never use digital devices for school [10]. In primary schools, this is even more prevalent. One can find this questionable, especially since, according to Hillmayr et al., classes in which digital media are used consistently show better performance test results than those with traditional teaching methods [11]. According to Mou and Li, artificial intelligence (AI) robots have a great impact because they can represent abstract concepts in different ways and provide students with timely learning feedback [16]. Westlund and Breazeal [19] also describe that such robots can maintain engagement over many sessions.

Social robots that find their way into the classroom often have a human- or animal-like shape [5]. Some are only about 20 to 30 cm high, others as tall as an primary school child. They sometimes have the ability to move, either with wheels or legs. They have one or two arms, elaborated as in humans or in a reduced form, or lack extremities. Advanced models have an extensive arsenal of cameras, speakers, microphones, and sensors, coupled with systems for facial, speech, and voice recognition, and, in some cases, emotion recognition. Other AI systems can also play a role, for example, for learning.

An integrated dialog system, with a text-to-speech engine and speech-to-text engine, allows the social robot to communicate with teachers, students, and pupils in natural language [5]. At times, it is not simply an integrated voice assistant, but rather an application synchronized with facial expressions and gestures, contributing significantly to lifelikeness and believability. Most facial expressions are not generated by motors, as is the case with humanoid robots in the vein of Sophia and Harmony, but via a display [4]. It is important with an appropriate orientation that not only normal small talk is possible, but that technical discussions can be held just as well. In addition, some models – where the learning setting requires it – should be able to judge learners' answers as correct or incorrect.

The social robot can simulate empathy and emotions if necessary [17]. In turn, it can do this via facial expressions, gestures, and natural speech. In addition, human and non-human sounds, tones, and certain movements (such as head nodding) are important. Showing empathy and emotions – which is often discussed and sometimes vehemently rejected regarding machines – seems to be quite important in this context. If the student solved or said something correctly, the social robot can express praise; if something was solved incorrectly, it can encourage the student to try again. All in all, it is possible to create closer bonds, build trust, etc. [17]. The aforementioned emotion recognition can be useful for this end.

Social robots can be integrated into the classroom – whether it be a school or university – in a variety of ways: as a teacher, tutor, coach, or therapist, or even as a companion or peer, i.e., a fellow student [18]. These roles can be combined. Thus, a social robot may serve not only as a lecturer, but also as a tutor, as in the usual operation. It thus provides knowledge, exercises, and feedback. Another use is as an avatar. In this case, a social robot represents the sick, disabled, or incapacitated child. He or she participates in the events in the classroom via the robot and goes outside with it, to the schoolyard or the park, where he or she can follow the play and conversations of his or her classmates.

Social robots of all kinds can succeed in the classroom: medium to larger ones like NAO and Pepper, smaller ones like Alpha Mini, Cozmo, and Vector, and models specialized in empathy and emotions – also quite small – like QTrobot and Moxie [4]. One example is the use of Pepper for children with autism [13]. The focus here is on student well-being, which can be improved with the robot. QTrobot and Moxie are also applied specifically for autistic children. Pepper has also been used beyond the classroom to impart knowledge, for example in a children's hospital in Bern. There, it was available to children with diabetes and practiced estimating carbohydrate values at meals with them [7, 21].

3 Realization of the Alpha Mini Project

3.1 Foundations of the Project

The initiator had specified in his announcement of the project that it should be a learning application with Alpha Mini for school. This was further crystallized at the kick-off meeting in February 2023. The learning application with Alpha Mini and the learning software would be aimed at pupils in German-speaking Switzerland. The majority of these speak dialect. However, the language of instruction is officially High German. The focus is on the second cycle of Swiss primary school. The children are 8 to 12 years old. According to the curriculum, suitable topics for the educational software would be, for example, biology or geography [12].

Alpha Mini was designed as a tutor for the children. The crucial purpose of this didactic aid is to give the children an incentive to learn [16]. The robot responds to inputs from the children and shows appropriate reactions. Although Alpha Mini already has a high number of pre-existing capabilities – so-called "behaviors" (acts and speech acts) – more can be added. Since, apart from the eyes, it has no display of its own, it would be programmed to communicate with an external device, such as a tablet or laptop. The learning software – a learning game that essentially consists of a quiz – is displayed and executed on the external device.

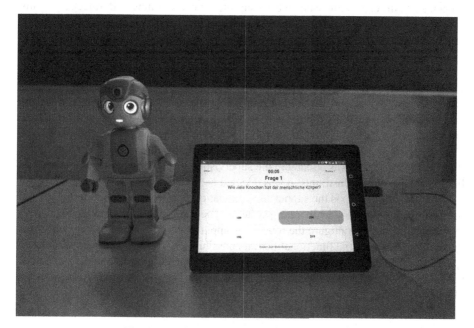

Fig. 1. Alpha Mini with the external end device

The additional end device must be able to receive user input, display outputs, and share data with the robot. In addition, it must provide the capability to develop and use custom programs and applications. These can also be executed directly via the device.

Thus, the solution concept consists of at least two hardware components, Alpha Mini and an additional end device (see Fig. 1). The social robot does not act autonomously but has pre-programmed sequences that it can call up.

3.2 Analysis Phase

This phase involved analyzing the technical components and making decisions with a view to design and implementation. In addition, a requirements analysis took place.

Analysis of Alpha Mini and the Alpha Mini Application

Alpha Mini was specifically designed as a learning robot that offers various ways of interacting and communicating with its environment. It looks human-like – cartoon-like like NAO and Pepper – and has natural language capabilities, with speech input and output. It has two small displays for eyes and a mouth that can be illuminated and change color. With numerous degrees of freedom in the arms, legs, feet, and head area, it has compelling motor skills. It has various sensors like a camera connected with face recognition, a touch sensor on the head, infrared sensor, gyroscope, accelerometer, and four microphones with sound source localization. For connectivity and communication, WLAN, Bluetooth, and sim card (2G/3G/4G) are available.

Through the two head displays mentioned, the social robot can show its eyes and adapt them to the environment and the current situation. According to Bartneck et al., this gaze and eye control is important for achieving similar effects to human communication and interaction: interest, comprehension, attention, and active conversation tracking [2]. In addition, Alpha Mini can display states and emotions through the eyes. Furthermore, it can display characters in the displays, such as dollar signs or stars. This can have a semantic and an emotional purpose.

The model of Alpha Mini used in the project speaks English. On inquiry with the company, it turned out that Chinese and English are offered, and it is impossible to change the language after the purchase of the robot. Before buying, one could have asked for a TTS engine for German. However, one then must manually enter the German sentences. So Alpha Mini, which was already in the supervisor's inventory and on loan, was set to English. Due to time constraints, it was decided not to use external libraries.

The Alpha Mini app is the supporting application for the social robot. It is available for Android and iOS mobile operating systems. The app is required for setup to connect to the internet and to configure the robot. The app has pre-programmed "behaviors" for the robot that show initial functionalities and possibilities. These include certain dances, sports, emotion displays, or testing voice commands. In addition, "behaviors", such as the social robot's own movement sequences or speech sequences, can be created using block programming (https://www.ubtrobot.com). The possibilities of the app are not sufficient for the purposes of the project.

Analysis of Implementation and Programming Possibilities

All of Alpha Mini's implementation and programming capabilities are built on an open-source SDK platform: the UBT ROSA system. ROSA stands for "Robot Operating System Android" and is a modular system with a hierarchical architecture that integrates all social robot functions. The components in the system are loosely coupled so that the functionalities are extensible and reusable. This includes software functionalities such as volume control, camera trigger, or checking of the system status. It also allows access to the hardware and control of the servo motors. With this platform, custom applications can be developed for Alpha Mini. This is exactly what is needed in the project to integrate learning software and robots.

The individual SDKs (Software Development Kits) provide the tools and information developers need to access Alpha Mini functions. A Python SDK and an Android SDK are available. The Python SDK is based on the Python programming language. The SDK is freely available and a demo exists that can be downloaded and installed from Github. UBTECH chooses PyCharm from JetBrains as the development environment. The company's Android SDK is based on the Java programming language. The entire SDK can be downloaded from Github with a program demo. After that, one can integrate this collection into the app. UBTECH suggests that the app is developed using the official Android development environment, Android Studio. A utility analysis in the project showed that the Android SDK suited given problems better.

Requirements Analysis
With the help of 15 use cases (UC), the developer defined the basic requirements for the learning application after consultation with the initiator and supervisor [1]. Table 1 shows one such use case for answering the quiz questions.

Table 1. Use case 102 [1]

UC: 102	Classification	Explanation
	Name	Answer quiz questions
	Short Description	The learning application must allow users to answer quiz questions
	Trigger	The user wants to answer the question
	Precondition	The topic has been selected and the question is displayed
	Postcondition	The user's answer is logged and the correct answer is shown
	Typical process	1. The quiz question is displayed 2. The user selects an answer option
	Type	Functional requirement

In the same way, the functions of Alpha Mini were defined. Table 2 shows the use case named "Alpha Mini responds to answers".

Other use cases for the social robot include "Alpha Mini explains answers" (UC 110) and "Alpha Mini reacts to points scored" (UC 111). This already shows how the learning game and the social robot were intertwined within the learning application.

Table 2. Use case 109 [1]

UC: 109	Classification	Explanation
	Name	Alpha Mini responds to answers
	Short Description	The learning application must allow users to receive feedback from Alpha Mini on the answers
	Trigger	The correct answer was displayed
	Precondition	The user selected an answer and the correct answer was displayed
	Postcondition	–
	Typical process	1. The correct answer is displayed 2. Depending on the selected answer Alpha Mini gives feedback 3. If the answer is correct, the feedback is positive 4. If the answer is incorrect, the feedback is negative
	Type	Functional requirement

3.3 Conceptual Phase

The conceptual phase focused on the requirements of the learning application specifically for the school context, the elaboration of the questionnaire, as well as design and language.

Requirements for the Learning Application

The target group of the learning application were children in primary school. Accordingly, social robots and learning software needed to be set up. As already described, the goal of this project was not to program a fully comprehensive learning application. Rather, it was to show that Alpha Mini can communicate with an external device and learning software on it. Therefore, the learning game in particular was limited to a few contents and functions.

The learning game needed a simple operation and appealing design and be appropriate for children of this age. In addition, it needed to be clearly structured and understandable so that the learning process would be clearly comprehensible. It needed to present questions to which answers could be given. For this purpose, the correct answer would be displayed after an answer selection and an explanation would be given in text form (German) and in spoken language (English).

To achieve this, a quiz was programmed that contained questions with four answer options each. One of these four answer options is correct. If the question is answered correctly, one point is collected. The final score is displayed after the quiz is completed. In addition, the progress of each question is displayed so that it is always clear how many questions are still open. A timer is implemented as an element of the learning game. For each question, the user has 30 s to answer. If he or she does not manage this in time, the answer counts as wrong. After each answer, whether correct or incorrect, an explanation of the correct answer is given.

Alpha Mini gives feedback on a correct or incorrect answer and on the score achieved. It explains the correct answer in English. This is a reproduction or summary of the text form. It behaves and moves accordingly, for example, by shaking its head or raising its arms. In addition, the user can specify a username. Alpha Mini can then address the user directly and individualize the user experience. Overall, the learning application belongs to the drill and practice programs, which provide opportunities for students to work on questions one at a time and then receive feedback on their performance. It is based on the use cases of the analysis phase.

Elaboration of the Questionnaire
The questions asked in the learning game had to be at the appropriate level for primary school pupils. To ensure this, the Lehrplan 21 (Swiss curriculum 21) was used [12]. In the learning software, it should be possible to select learning topics. The project team decided that questions should be defined for at least two topics from the Lehrplan 21. The subject area "Nature, Man, Society" lent itself best to being able to query theoretical basics. The topics chosen were "geography" and "humans and animals" (biology).

The developer defined three sample questions for each of these two topics, based on Curriculum 21 [12]. He then worked out four possible answers to each question. Only one of them is correct. As a final step, a short explanation of the correct answer was written and displayed in the learning game.

Design of the Learning Game
For the design, the developer followed the catalog of Liebal and Exner, which knows a total of 110 recommendations for the design of user interfaces for children's software [14]. These are divided into three categories: screen design, control or interaction, and content. In addition, the individual recommendations are coded according to children's developmental stages. Appealing colors, age-appropriate language, a cheerful atmosphere, and easy navigation are all important for the specific age group in question [8]. The developer created corresponding mockups, i.e., digital designs of a website or app, which were needed in the conception phase to visualize ideas and concepts.

Language of the Learning Application
German was chosen as the language of the learning application. Thus, it is easy to understand for children at the Swiss primary school level in the German-speaking part of Switzerland. Although dialect is spoken in everyday life, at school lessons must be taught in High German, even if this is not always adhered to.

The Alpha Mini model used only speaks English, as already mentioned. The only other language available was Chinese, which would not have been helpful in this context. However, this is of no further concern for the demonstration. Moreover, the learning application could be seen as a cross-competency learning application in which the children receive explanations and feedback from the social robot in English.

3.4 Implementation Phase

The implementation phase was about the technical realization of the learning application. The "behaviors" of Alpha Mini and the app development and integration played a central role. The results of the implementation of the educational software are shown in this section. The entire project can be found at the following URL: https://github.com/and rinallemann99/alphamini-learningapp.

"Behaviors" of Alpha Mini

Various "behaviors" were created for Alpha Mini based on the requirements outlined. These acts (movements of the body and the head, animation of the eyes, change of the color of the mouth, etc.) and speech acts would come into play when the application is started, when the application is exited, when a quiz is started, when the timer expires, when the results are obtained, and when the questions are answered.

The developer also programmed different "behaviors" in relation to the answering of questions. These are initiated depending on whether the answer was correct or incorrect. There are three different "behaviors" each for a correct answer or for a wrong answer, which are played randomly. This creates a kind of surprise effect that is intended to maintain curiosity and motivation.

App Development

With the mentioned utility analysis, it was determined that the app development would be done with the Android SDK. Thus, the learning application was developed with Java and in Android Studio. A total of three user interface layouts were created, one for the home screen, one for the quiz screen, and one for the results screen. These were defined in Android Studio as XML files. For the learning application, graphics from Flaticon (https://www.flaticon.com) were used to create an icon for the application. The icon was created by the developer himself.

Once the application was completed, it had to be installed on the robot. This enabled the application to access the files stored in the robot and execute "behaviors". The installation of the application on Alpha Mini could be done with Android Studio. The robot needed to be connected to the computer via a USB cable and the application could then be run on the robot. The application once installed, the robot was ready to be used.

Mirroring the Operating System with the App

As mentioned, the manufacturer UBTECH offers its own operating system, ROSA, which is based on the Android operating system. For this reason, it is possible to treat the social robot as an Android device and mirror the operating system (along with the app), thus allowing access to the application. However, to achieve this, a computer is required. The screen-sharing program is installed on the computer and the robot is connected to the computer via a USB cable. After that, the program can mirror the robot's operating system.

For this work, therefore, a computer was used that is mobile and can install screen-sharing programs. To simulate an app, a computer with a touchscreen was necessary. It also had to be easy to use and have Windows, MacOS, or Linux as its operating system. In this project, the given requirements led to the choice of the Microsoft Surface Go 3 – basically an intermediate form between a tablet and laptop. With its price of about $450 – $500, it is also attractive for schools.

UBTECH suggests that one uses Vysor for mirroring. The screen sharing program offers simple operation and can be downloaded for free. One drawback, however, is that

Table 3. Learning game [1]

Screenshot	Explanation
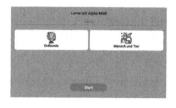	This is the start page of the learning application. The user can enter his or her name here and select a learning topic. Clicking on "Start" starts a quiz on the selected learning topic.
	The quiz is built with one question and four answer options. The username, timer and accumulated points are displayed at the top. In addition, the progress bar is displayed and updated for each question.
	The player can choose an answer and click on it. If the answer is wrong, it is highlighted in red, and the correct answer is highlighted in green.
	If the selected answer is correct, it is highlighted in green. If the timer has expired (it is then marked red), the correct answer is highlighted in green, but the answer is not counted as a point.
	If the user touches the screen after the correct answer is displayed, a short explanation is given. This explanation can be ended by clicking on the screen.
	Once all questions have been answered, the results are displayed. It is visible how many questions were answered correctly. In addition, the user has the option to start a new game.

the image quality is artificially lowered. Only with a paid pro-membership can a good image quality be secured. As an alternative, the open-source program Scrcpy (https://github.com/Genymobile/scrcpy) was used in this project. It offers many features for free, such as good image quality and changing the display via keyboard shortcuts. One disadvantage is that there is no user interface, so the program must be started via the command line.

Implementation of the Learning Software

In the following, the implementation of the learning software is illustrated. Screenshots of the individual pages are used, which are identical to the final mockups (Table 3). At this point it may be added that in the end a ten-year-old girl successfully went through the learning application. This is captured in this video: https://www.youtube.com/watch?v=c7tTmYQZPqo. The actual tests are presented in Sect. 4.

4   Tests with Experts

After the successful implementation of the learning application, internal tests took place. The last errors were identified and eliminated. Afterwards, the developer carried out external tests. Since it was during school vacations, no tests with pupils could take place. It was decided to involve as many teachers as possible. In the end, three were engaged. They were able to test the application independently without prior explanations and gather their first impressions. Their feedback was collected and recorded in writing. For this purpose, the developer had designed a template with open-ended questions, with the aim of obtaining the test subjects' impressions. This template consisted of the following questions: 1. How is the operation of the application itself?, 2. How is the concept evaluated?, 3. Is there added value and if so, what is it?, 4. How is the installation of the application?, 5. Can the application be integrated into the classroom?, 6. Can the application be technically implemented?.

1. The usage was rated as intuitive, clear, and simple by all test persons. There are no distractions, and the application is not overcrowded with elements that could lead to sensory overload. The fact that the handling was described positively throughout may also be since the learning application in this form contains only a few elements and functions.
2. There were mixed responses to this question. One test person would not purchase the robot for this use case, although it could promote motivation to learn. The other test subjects would include the robot in their lessons if it had more functions and was more versatile. Furthermore, two test persons see difficulties in the implementation, since the teachers would presumably have to invest a lot of time and effort in the competence development of the new teaching tool.
3. All testers agreed on this question. They feel that the concept can have a positive impact on learning. It is something new and exciting, which arouses curiosity in the children. In addition, according to one tester, there is a surprise effect because it is not clear what the robot will do next. This suggests that the robot offers added value within the learning application (whereby the physical and vocal presence in itself also adds value, as has already been pointed out).

4. The evaluation of the installation and the execution was negative for all test persons. The execution is still too complicated for children to be able to use the learning application independently. Above all, teachers need to acquire new knowledge about the execution so that they can help in case of problems. According to one test person, detailed instructions could help here. In addition, the need for a computer is an obstacle. The pupils of all three teachers have their own tablet with which they can already do many school activities. It would therefore be an advantage if no new computer had to be purchased and the learning application would run directly on the tablets.

5. According to all three test persons, the concept could be integrated into lessons. However, there are different views on how this could be done. On the one hand, the children could use the learning application as an additional offer that they handle independently. On the other hand, according to one test person, the robot could be used for the whole class, for example, for introductions to new topics. However, one test person saw it differently, as she thinks that the robot is primarily suitable for 1:1 lessons and not for the whole class.

6. All test persons are of the opinion that the setting could be technically implemented in the school. However, it must be clarified what happens in case of technical difficulties. There must be a contact person who is familiar with the application and the problems. However, the test persons did not have any concerns about the implementation with the children, as they already have a lot of experience with digital devices from an early age.

In addition, the developer asked the test persons what suggestions for improvement (7) and ideas for implementation (8) they had. For reasons of space, these cannot be listed here. However, they are contained in a document that can be accessed via https://studierendenprojekte.wirtschaft.fhnw.ch/view/2647.

5 Summary and Outlook

The project showed that a relatively inexpensive social robot, like Alpha Mini, can be connected to external devices, in this case an external tablet or laptop. In this way, a learning application with an artificial learning partner and learning software is created that can achieve something similar to much more expensive options such as Pepper and others. Schools in particular can benefit from this, as they usually have limited options when it comes to procuring social robots and digital learning tools in general. The research question could thus be answered in the affirmative.

The tests with teachers have shown that such a setting can in principle be implemented in a school. In a follow-up project, the learning software could be expanded, for example, by extending the question catalog to the existing topics and adding new ones. It would also be interesting to design the learning application so that the robot could interact with a group of children. The different settings should then be tested with primary school pupils.

Ethical and legal aspects could not be addressed in this paper. Whether social robots in the classroom promote or inhibit social skills and whether the temporary replacement of teachers and tutors poses a problem has already been answered in the literature [4, 18].

In this specific case, it will be particularly important to investigate whether a Chinese robot complies with the data protection regulations of Switzerland or other countries. It may be necessary to look for alternatives. It would also be possible to restrict the functions of the robot to satisfy this problem.

References

1. Allemann, A.: Alpha Mini in der Schule. Bachelor Thesis. School of Business FHNW, Olten (2023)
2. Bartneck, C., et al.: Mensch-Roboter-Interaktion: Eine Einführung. Hanser, München (2020)
3. Belpaeme, T., Kennedy, J., Ramachandran, A., Fumihide, T.: Social robots for education: a review. Sci. Robot. **3**, eaat5954 (2018)
4. Bendel, O. (ed.): Soziale Roboter: Technikwissenschaftliche, wirtschaftswissenschaftliche, philosophische, psychologische und soziologische Grundlagen. Springer Gabler, Wiesbaden (2021)
5. Bendel, O.: Soziale Roboter in der Moral: Ethische Betrachtungen am Beispiel des Unterrichts. In: Bendel, O. (ed.) Soziale Roboter: Technikwissenschaftliche, wirtschaftswissenschaftliche, philosophische, psychologische und soziologische Grundlagen, pp. 149–167. Springer Gabler, Wiesbaden (2021). https://doi.org/10.1007/978-3-658-31114-8_8
6. Bendel, O.: Pädagogische Agenten im Corporate E-Learning. Difo, St. Gallen (2003)
7. Bendel, O., Zarubica, S.: Pepper zu Besuch im Spital. In: Gransche, B., Bellon, J., Nähr-Wagener, S. (eds.) Technik sozialisieren? Metzler, Heidelberg und Berlin (2023)
8. Bhagat, V.: Designing websites for kids: trends & best practices (2020). https://www.fee dough.com/designing-websites-for-kids/. Accessed 14 Oct 2023
9. Csala, E., Németh, G., Zainkó, C.: Application of the NAO humanoid robot in the treatment of marrow-transplanted children. In: 2012 IEEE 3rd International Conference on Cognitive Infocommunications (CogInfoCom), Kosice, Slovakia, pp. 655–659 (2012)
10. Educa: Digitalisierung in der Bildung (2021). https://www.educa.ch/sites/default/files/2021-10/Digitalisierung_in_der_Bildung.pdf. Accessed 14 Oct 2023
11. Hillmayr, D., Reinhold, F., Ziernwald, L., Reiss, K.: Digitale Medien im mathematisch-naturwissenschaftlichen Unterricht der Sekundarstufe: Einsatzmöglichkeiten, Umsetzung und Wirksamkeit. Waxmann, Münster, New York (2017)
12. Lehrplan 21: Willkommen beim Lehrplan 21 (w. d.). https://www.lehrplan21.ch. Accessed 14 Oct 2023
13. Lemaignan, S., Newbutt, N., Rice, L., Daly, J.: "It's important to think of pepper as a teaching aid or resource external to the classroom": a social robot in a school for autistic children. Int. J. Soc. Robot. (2022)
14. Liebal, J., Exner, M.: Usability für Kids: Ein Handbuch zur ergonomischen Gestaltung von Software und Websites für Kinder. Vieweg und Teubner, Wiesbaden (2011)
15. Mendoza, N.: Emotional support robot robin headed to UCLA Mattel children's hospital. In: TechRepublic, 29 June 2020. https://www.techrepublic.com/article/emotional-support-robot-robin-headed-to-ucla-mattel-childrens-hospital/. Accessed 14 Oct 2023
16. Mou, X., Li, R.Y.M.: The impact of artificial intelligence educational robots in the field of education: a PRISMA review. In: Li, R.Y.M., Chau, K.W., Ho, D.C.W. (eds.) Current State of Art in Artificial Intelligence and Ubiquitous Cities, pp. 63–77. Springer Nature, Singapore (2022). https://doi.org/10.1007/978-981-19-0737-1_4
17. Schulze, H., et al.: Soziale Roboter, Empathie und Emotionen. Zenodo, Bern (2021). https://zenodo.org/record/5554564. Accessed 14 Oct 2023

18. Sharkey, A.J.C.: Should we welcome robot teachers? Ethics Inf. Technol. **18**(4), 283–297 (2016). https://doi.org/10.1007/s10676-016-9387-z
19. Westlund, J., Breazeal, C.: the interplay of robot language level with children's language learning during storytelling, pp. 65–66 (2015). https://doi.org/10.1145/2701973.2701989. Accessed 14 Oct 2023
20. Woo, H., LeTendre, G.K., Pham-Shouse, T., Xiong, Y.: The use of social robots in classrooms: a review of field-based studies. Educ. Res. Rev. **33** (2021). https://www.sciencedirect.com/science/article/pii/S1747938X21000117. Accessed 14 Oct 2023
21. Zarubica, S.: Entwicklung einer auf dem humanoiden Roboter Pepper lauffähigen Lernsoftware für Kinder. Bachelor Thesis. FHNW, Olten (2022)

Comprehensive Feedback Module Comparison for Autonomous Vehicle-Pedestrian Communication in Virtual Reality

Melanie Schmidt-Wolf[(✉)] [ID], Eelke Folmer [ID], and David Feil-Seifer [ID]

University of Nevada, Reno, 1664 N. Virginia Street, Reno, NV 89557 -0171, USA
mschmidtwolf@nevada.unr.edu, efolmer@unr.edu, dave@cse.unr.edu

Abstract. Autonomous driving technologies can minimize accidents. Communication from an autonomous vehicle to a pedestrian with a feedback module will improve the pedestrians' safety in autonomous driving. We compared several feedback module options in a Virtual Reality environment to identify which module best increases public acceptance, legibility, and trust in the autonomous vehicle's decision, and to identify preference. The results of this study show that participants prefer symbols or text over lights and road projection with no significant difference between symbols and text. Further, our results show that the preferred text interaction mode option when the vehicle is not driving is "Walk," "Safe to cross," "Go ahead" and "Waiting", and the preferred symbol interaction mode option is the walking person as on a traffic light, with no significant preference between the cross advisory symbol and the pedestrian crossing sign.

Keywords: Autonomous Vehicle · Virtual Reality · Legibility · Public Acceptance · Trust

1 Introduction

Traffic accidents are a leading cause of death and injury worldwide [1], with a substantial majority caused by human error [2]. In the year 2019, around 6,205 pedestrians were killed in the U.S., among which almost half of the accidents were caused by failure to yield right of way [3]. External displays can reduce the risk for pedestrians and make the pedestrian feel safe to cross when the

Supported by Nevada NASA Space Grant Consortium (80NSSC20M00043). This material is based upon work supported under the AI Research Institutes program by National Science Foundation and the Institute of Education Sciences, U.S. Department of Education through Award # 2229873 - AI Institute for Transforming Education for Children with Speech and Language Processing Challenges. Any opinions, findings and conclusions or recommendations expressed in this material are those of the author(s) and do not necessarily reflect the views of the National Science Foundation, the Institute of Education Sciences, or the U.S. Department of Education.

A. Al. Ali et al. (Eds.): ICSR 2023, LNAI 14453, pp. 410–423, 2024.
https://doi.org/10.1007/978-981-99-8715-3_34

(a) Left: Question widget during simulation. Middle: Pedestrian crossing. Right: Approaching vehicle with feedback module

(b) Perspective of the participant as a pedestrian

Fig. 1. Virtual Reality environment example.

vehicle is yielding [4]. However, it is uncertain how many pedestrian accidents were caused by lack of communication and miscommunication. A considerable amount of the attributed "failure to yield right of way" factor by the National Highway Traffic Safety Administration of fatal pedestrian accidents was caused by communication problems [3,5]. Autonomous driving will be introduced in everyday life in the future. However, since there is no driver for communication with vulnerable road users, safety of all road users is a growing concern. A fully autonomous vehicle can create a lack of nonverbal communication due to missing eye contact or hand signs with the driver [6]. This is a decisive moment to communicate intent [6]. The lack of possibility to communicate intent can result in confusion for both pedestrian and autonomous vehicle (AV) regarding whether to approach or wait for the other person first to continue moving forward.

In this paper, we conducted a Virtual Reality (VR) study validating for a virtual environment that leverages more realistic results than we obtained in an on-screen questionnaire study [7] to identify which visual feedback module increases public acceptance, legibility, and trust the most in the autonomous vehicle's decision. The feedback module options used in this study are based on our prior work [7] regarding visual communication between pedestrians and autonomous vehicles. The fundamental reason for validating the results of the on-screen user study in VR was the difference in the presentation of the feedback module options in embedded video simulations compared to immersive VR simulations.

2   Background

The safety and efficiency of pedestrians crossing the road can be increased if autonomous vehicles display their intention with an external human-machine interface for pedestrian interaction [4]. Developers and researchers of AV technologies have proposed different display types to communicate intent to pedestrians, such as digital road signs, text, audible chimes and voice instructions [4,8–10]. In this user study we use VR since VR tests have the advantage of high flexibility, safety certainty, cost-effectiveness, and acceptable ecological validity in comparison to real-world tests [11,12]. Tran et al. reviewed VR studies on autonomous vehicle-pedestrian interaction [11]. In the review, between 2010 and 2020, 31 VR-based empirical studies were identified for both implicit and explicit AV-pedestrian communication.

In the following you can find a description of selected papers on studies of autonomous vehicle-pedestrian-communication-feedback modules that used VR.

In Deb et al. [13] the efficacy of external features on a fully autonomous vehicle was investigated. In this VR study four visual and four audible features were used. The four visual features considered were an animated pedestrian silhouette, the flashing text "Braking," a flashing smile by bending a straight line, and no feature. The walking silhouette or the text "Braking" were significantly favored compared to the other considered features [13]. In a follow-up study Deb et al. [14] investigated seven features in VR: No feature, a green text message displaying "walk," a white walking silhouette, a red upraised hand, a red stop sign, music, and a verbal message saying "safe to cross". Pedestrians significantly preferred the combination of "walk" in text and the verbal message saying "safe to cross" [14]. Further, participants preferred the written features with the text message "walk" and the stop sign over the image signal of a walking silhouette and the upraised hand [14].

Löcken et al. [15] studied five features in VR: a smile by bending a straight line, a text message combined with a light strip, a road projection which changes from a wave to a zebra crossing, virtual eyes, and a smart road concept. The results indicate that the smart road concept was preferred, followed by the road projection which changes from a wave to a zebra crossing, the smile, the text message combined with a light strip, and the virtual eyes [15].

Holländer et al. [16] investigated a smile by bending a straight line, traffic light symbols, a gesturing robotic driver, and no feature in VR. The results of this study showed that participants preferred the traffic light symbols consisting of symbols of a green man and a yellow hand [16].

In De Clercq et al. [4], the following features were studied in VR: baseline without feedback module, front brake lights, Knight Rider [17] animation (a light bar moves from left to right), smiley by bending a straight line, a text which displays "WALK." The results of this study showed no significant differences between the four considered display options [4].

Stadler et al. [12] investigated a walking man, arrow, check, LED strip, and traffic light, each with a corresponding "Cross" and "Don't Cross" symbol. In this study the hypothesis is that VR is a suitable tool to evaluate the usability of feedback modules between AVs and pedestrian communication as an alternative for real-life tests [12]. The results of the different feedback module features did not show significant differences regarding efficiency, effectiveness, and satisfaction, but showed significant differences to the baseline without feedback module.

Thus, although there were several previous studies that investigated vehicle-to-pedestrian communication feedback modules, the amount of analyzed features studied in VR were limited. Further, there is no clear indication about which feedback module would increase the public acceptance and trust in the autonomous vehicle's decision the most. In this paper, we present a VR study that aims to replicate the results from our prior work [7], in which participants preferred a symbol as feedback module. We expand on previous studies by comparing feedback module options via VR to identify which visual feedback module would increase public acceptance, legibility, and trust the most in the autonomous vehicle's decision, and to identify preference.

3 Method

In this study we will validate the results of our prior work [7] with immersive VR instead of video simulations that were embedded in the questionnaire to check if we obtain the same results. Since VR establishes the possibility to create immersive environments, we expect the VR study to be more accurate than the 2-D online study while being safe to the user.

3.1 On-Screen Study

In previous research, we conducted an online on-screen user study with the target group pedestrians [7]. For the perspective of the illustrations the pedestrian view was situated in the front of the autonomous vehicle since it is most likely that pedestrians cross the road in front of the vehicle. For simplicity, and to not confuse participants with several perspectives, one perspective was selected to display the different interaction modes to the participants. The questionnaire used Qualtrics XM, an online survey tool. The participants were asked to watch different sections of videos and choose their most likable option. The results of this study showed that participants preferred symbols over text, lights and road projection. Further, the results showed that the text interaction mode option "Safe to cross" should be used combined with the symbol interaction mode option that displays a symbol of a walking person.

3.2 Research Question

The research question is: Which visual feedback module increases legibility, public acceptance, and trust the most in the autonomous vehicle's decision?

The message displayed on an autonomous vehicle should be **legible**, i.e., intuitive, concise and easy to understand since pedestrians have limited time to detect and interpret it [9,18]. **Public acceptance** is essential for the extensive adoption of autonomous vehicles considering that the biggest obstacle might not be technological, but public acceptance [19–21]. **Trust** has been identified as crucial to the successful design of autonomous vehicles [22]. According to the American Automobile Association (AAA), only one in ten U.S. drivers would trust to ride in an AV, while 28% of U.S. drivers are uncertain [22,23].

3.3 Study Design

This section describes the VR study setup to identify a feedback module for communicating between a pedestrian and an AV, which increases legibility, public acceptance and trust the most in the autonomous vehicle's decision.

Instruments. For the simulation environment we used the open-source autonomous driving simulator CARLA [24], which is based on Unreal Engine. In Unreal Engine 4, it is possible to create and modify objects, such as vehicles and the feedback displays. We used a HTC Vive Pro Eye headset. The HTC Vive Pro Eye headset has integrated Tobii eye trackers enabling head and eye-tracking. It is equipped with a resolution of 1440×1600 pixels per eye and offers a refresh rate of 90 Hz.

Visualizations. We used the same displays as in in our previously conducted on-screen study [7]. The different concepts stem from [4, 9, 10, 18, 25–33]:

- Text options: Accelerating, Driving, Don't Walk, Do not walk, Go, Go ahead, I'm in automated driving mode, I'm about to yield, I'm resting, I'm about to start, On my way, Safe to cross, Slowing Down, Stop, Waiting, Walk
- Symbol options: Cross advisory, Don't cross advisory, Moving eyes, Pedestrian crossing traffic sign, Static Eyes, Smiley, Stop traffic sign, Traffic light: Upraised hand, Traffic light: Walking person
- Light options: Green front brake lights, LED moves from left to right, Slow pulsating LED, Smiley Bar: Smiley, Smiley Bar: Line, Static LED
- Road projection options: Arrows indicating path, Arrows fading, Lines: Lines far apart, Lines: Lines close together, Zebra crossing

Virtual Reality Setup. In Fig. 1, you can see an example of the VR environment in which the pedestrian wants to cross the road to go to a bus stop. For the perspective of the participant as a pedestrian, we chose to situate the view in the front of the autonomous vehicle or in the front left if the distance to the AV is small to simulate a pedestrian road crossing in front of the vehicle (see Fig. 1b). In the study, the participants crossed the road by walking approx. 10 ft (3m) from a traffic island in the middle of the simulated road to the bus stop. We decided to let the participants physically walk instead of moving forward with motion controllers to create a more immersive environment. A demo video of the VR environment is provided at https://youtu.be/u5sU1-c9nz4.

Questionnaire. Similar to our previous work [7] we asked the following questions that are partially based on Schaefer's "Trust Perception Scale-HRI" [34] with a 5-point Likert scale for the different considered feedback module concepts:

- Question 1: I believe the ___ interaction mode protects people from potential risks in the environment
- Question 2: I believe the ___ interaction mode looks friendly to the pedestrian
- Question 3: I believe the ___ interaction mode communicates clearly
- Question 4: I prefer the ___ interaction mode over human-driver interaction.

Those questions were asked immediately after showing the corresponding feedback module in the VR simulation and were displayed as a widget in the VR headset (see Fig. 1a, left). The participant selected the Likert scale answers by navigating with the HTC Vive controller. To reduce bias we added randomization to the order of displaying the feedback module options.

Subsequent to the VR simulations we asked participants to rank the interaction modes Text, Symbols, Lights and Road Projections regarding preference, legibility, public acceptance and trust:

- Please rank the interaction modes from the most legible interaction mode (1) to the least legible interaction mode (4)
- Please rank the interaction modes from the interaction mode you trust the most (1) to the interaction mode you trust the least (4)
- Please rank the interaction modes from the interaction mode you accept the most (1) to the interaction mode you accept the least (4)
- Please rank the interaction modes in order of preference from your most preferred (1) to your least preferred (4).

The demographic questions included age, gender, ethnicity and current level of education.

3.4 Participants

40 participants were recruited via flyers and social media to participate in the IRB-approved (IRBNet ID: 1897708-1) VR study. The user study had a duration of about 30 min. Eleven participants identified as female and 29 participants identified as male. Further, the participants' age ranged between 18 and 67 (M=29.13, SD=11.2). None of the participants reported motion sickness.

4 Results

In this section we present the results studying the quality of potential feedback modules to enable an autonomous vehicle to communicate with pedestrians, which increases legibility, public acceptance and trust the most in the autonomous vehicle's decision, and to identify preference.

Since the Likert questions are ordinal we tested for normality with the Shapiro-Wilk's normality test. Since the result of the Shapiro-Wilk's normality test achieved a p-value that is less than $p < 0.05$ we cannot assume normality. Due to this result we used non-parametric tests and show the results of the questions with frequencies/percentages.

4.1 Legibility, Public Acceptance, Trust, and Preference

To identify the feedback module which most increases legibility, public acceptance, and trust in the autonomous vehicle, and to identify the preferred feedback module, we analyzed the ranking questions. Each question "Please rank the interaction modes in order of preference from your most preferred (1) to your least preferred (4)," "Please rank the interaction modes from the most legible interaction mode (1) to the least legible interaction mode (4)," "Please rank the

interaction modes from the interaction mode you trust the most
(1) to the interaction mode you
trust the least (4)," and "Please
rank the interaction modes from
the interaction mode you accept
the most (1) to the interaction
mode you accept the least (4)"
resulted in the following average rank order: Symbol, Text,
Projection, Light. Figure 2 shows
a visualization of the ranking questions results and the
results of the pairwise comparisons with the Mann-Whitney
U test. The Mann-Whitney U
test shows a significant difference
between symbols and the interac-

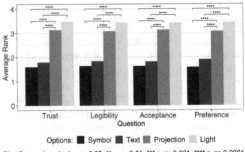

Fig. 2. The result of ranking questions regarding trust, legibility, acceptance and preference
shows that symbols or text should be selected
as interaction mode due to significant differences
between the interaction mode options symbols
and text to the interaction mode options lights
and road projection (lower is better).

tion mode options light and road projection as well as between text and the interaction mode options light and road projection. Symbols are ranked the highest.
However, there is no significant difference between symbols and text.

We analyzed the Likert questions sorted by interaction modes (see Fig. 3).
Regarding question 1, participants agreed with the text interaction mode the

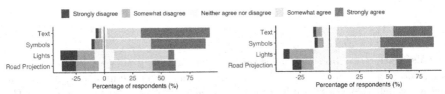

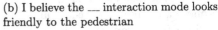

(a) I believe the ___ int. mode protects people from potential risks in the environment

(b) I believe the ___ interaction mode looks
friendly to the pedestrian

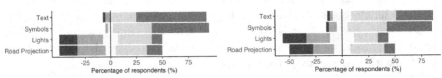

(c) I believe the ___ interaction mode communicates clearly

(d) I prefer the ___ interaction mode over
human-driver interaction

Fig. 3. Assessment by participants of the questions (a), (b), (c) and (d) with a 5-point
Likert scale for the four interaction modes text, symbols, lights and road projection
with resulting ranking in descending order: (a) Text, symbols, road projection, lights
(b) Symbols, text, road projection, lights (c) Symbols/text, road projection, lights (d)
Symbols, text, road projection, lights. Overall, participants preferred symbols and text,
followed road projection and lights.

most (90.00%), followed by the symbol interaction mode (87.5%), road projection interaction mode (57.5%) and light interaction mode (52.50%). Question 2 led to the greatest agreement for the symbol interaction mode (82.50%) and text interaction mode (80.00%), followed by the road projection interaction mode (55.00%) and light interaction mode (47.50%). Question 3 led to the greatest agreement for the symbol interaction mode (92.50%) and text interaction mode (92.50%), followed by the road projection interaction mode (45.00%) and light interaction mode (42.50%). Further, question 4 led to the greatest agreement for the symbol interaction mode (80.00%) and the text interaction mode (77.50%), followed by the road projection interaction mode (42.50%) and light interaction mode (32.50%). The pairwise comparisons with the Mann-Whitney U test showed significance between symbols and the interaction mode options light and road projection as well as between text and the interaction mode options light and road projection. There is no significant difference between symbols and text. Further, there is no significant difference between lights and road projection.

Taking all results together which feedback module increases most legibility, public acceptance and trust in the AV's decision, and to identify preference, participants selected symbols and text, followed by road projection and lights.

4.2 Supplemental Data

Amount of Messages. Also, we checked how many messages participants preferred to have displayed on the AV. The options for this question were the following:

- 1 message: Only to show the pedestrian that she/he is allowed to cross
- 2 messages: One message to show the pedestrian that she/he is allowed to cross and one message that it is not safe to cross
- 4 messages: Vehicle slowing down, vehicle is not driving, vehicle accelerating, vehicle driving
- Other

Table 1. The question results "How many messages would you prefer to be displayed?" shows that most participants would prefer to have two interaction modes displayed.

One	Two	Four	Other
27.50%	45.00%	20.00%	7.50%

From Table 1, we concluded that the option that participants selected most is to have two messages displayed (45.00%): One message to show the pedestrian that she/he is allowed to cross and one message that it is not safe to cross. The chi-square goodness of fit test shows no significant difference between one and two messages.

Specific Interaction Mode Options. Thus far, we have analyzed the rankings of Text, Symbols, Lights and Road Projections regarding our research question and determined that participants prefer symbol and text interaction modes. We now want to look at specific symbol and text options, which support our research question. For this we analyzed the 5-point Likert scale questions (see Fig. 4).

We will further consider the interaction mode options which are not significant with the highest rated option via the Mann-Whitney U test. Question 1 led to the result that the text options "Safe to cross," "Walk," "Waiting" and "Go ahead," and the symbol options "Traffic light walking person," "Cross advisory" and "Pedestrian crossing sign" are not significantly different. Question 2 showed that the considered text options are not significantly different, and the symbol options "Smiley," "Traffic light walking person," "Cross advisory" and "Pedestrian crossing sign" are not significantly different. Further, question 3 showed that the text options "Walk," "Safe to cross," "Go ahead," "Waiting"

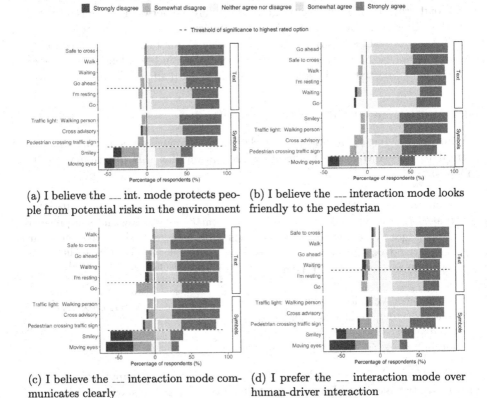

(a) I believe the ___ int. mode protects people from potential risks in the environment

(b) I believe the ___ interaction mode looks friendly to the pedestrian

(c) I believe the ___ interaction mode communicates clearly

(d) I prefer the ___ interaction mode over human-driver interaction

Fig. 4. Assessment by participants of the questions (a), (b), (c) and (d) with a 5-point Likert scale for the text and symbol interaction mode not driving options. This shows that "Walk," "Safe to cross," "Go ahead" and "Waiting" are the highest rated options for the text interaction mode, and for the symbol interaction mode the walking person as on a traffic light and the cross advisory symbol are the highest rated options with no significant difference. The threshold of significance to the highest ranked option is visualized by a dashed line.

and "I'm resting," and the symbol options "Traffic light walking person," "Cross advisory" and "Pedestrian crossing sign" are not significantly different. Question 4 showed that the text options "Safe to cross," "Walk," "Go ahead" and

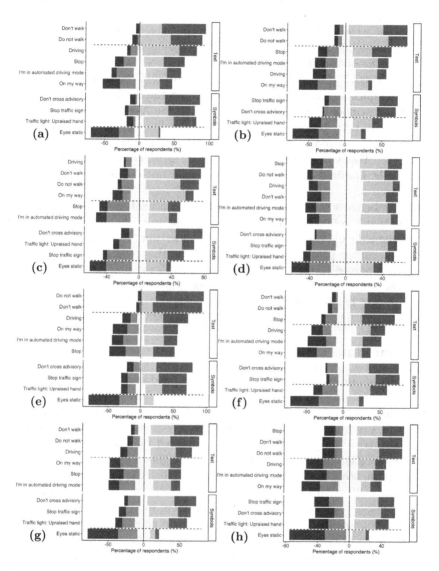

Fig. 5. Assessment by participants of the questions (a), (b) I believe the ___ interaction mode protects people from potential risks in the environment, (c), (d) I believe the ___ interaction mode looks friendly to the pedestrian, (e), (f) I believe the ___ interaction mode communicates clearly and (g), (h) I prefer the ___ interaction mode over human-driver interaction for the text and symbol interaction mode driving options. (a), (c), (e) and (g): VR study. (b), (d), (f) and (h): On-screen study.

"Waiting," and the symbol options "Traffic light walking person," "Cross advisory" and "Pedestrian crossing sign" are not significantly different. Altogether, the preferred text interaction mode option when the vehicle is not driving for the 5-point Likert scale questions is "Walk," "Safe to cross," "Go ahead" and "Waiting" with no significant difference, and the preferred symbol interaction mode option is the walking person as on a traffic light, the cross advisory symbol and the pedestrian crossing sign with no significant difference. In Sect. 4.2 we found that the option that participants selected most is to have two messages displayed (45.00%). Consequently, you can see in Fig. 5 the results of the 5-point Likert scale questions for both the VR study and the on-screen study regarding the text and symbol interaction mode options if the AV is driving. Both studies show that the text interaction modes "Don't walk" or "Do not walk" should be used and the symbol interaction modes "Don't cross advisory," "Stop traffic sign" or the "Traffic light upraised hand," (see Fig. 5). In the on-screen study, the "Traffic light upraised hand" symbol had significant differences to the options "Don't cross advisory" and "Stop traffic sign" regarding the questions if the participant believes that it protects people from potential risks in the environment and that it communicates clearly (see Subfigures 5(b) and 5(f)). Regarding the "Traffic light upraised hand" symbol the question "I believe the ___ interaction mode protects people from potential risks in the environment" showed that participants agreed in the VR study with 75.00% vs. 40.00% in the on-screen study. The question "I believe the ___ interaction mode communicates clearly" regarding the "Traffic light upraised hand" symbol resulted in agreement of the participants with 62.50% in the VR study vs. 51.02% in the on-screen study.

5   Discussion

The results of our previous study [7] of the modified trust questionnaire showed that the text interaction mode option "Safe to cross" or "Walk" should be used or the symbol interaction mode option that displays a symbol of a walking person. In this VR study and the on-screen study, the results of the legibility, public acceptance, trust and preference questions showed that participants prefer the symbol interaction mode, followed by the text, lights and road projection interaction modes, see Subsect. 4.1. It is noticeable that the light interaction mode has less favorable results in the VR study than in the on-screen study. This could be a cause of less visibility of the lights in a more immersive environment such as VR due to more distractions or additional light effects from the surrounding.

The results of the non-driving options for the text and symbol options are also very similar (see Fig. 4). In both the VR and the on-screen study, the results of the modified trust questionnaire show that the text interaction mode option "Safe to cross" or "Walk" should be used (with no significant difference to "Go ahead" and "Waiting" in the VR study), or the symbol interaction mode option that displays a symbol of a walking person. Further, when comparing the results of the VR study and the on-screen study for the considered text and symbol driving options, the results are similar: Both studies show that the text interaction modes "Don't walk" or "Do not walk" should be used, and the symbol interaction modes "Don't cross advisory," "Stop traffic sign," or the "Traffic light upraised hand," (see Fig. 5).

In contrast to the on-screen study, the VR study showed no significant differences between the highest ranked symbol option "Don't cross advisory" and the upraised hand as displayed on a traffic light. In the on-screen study, the participants selected that the upraised hand as displayed on a traffic light protects people from potential risks in the environment less and communicates less clearly than the highest ranked option. A possible reason is that the upraised hand is a less universal symbol than the symbols "Don't cross advisory" and "Stop traffic sign." We found similar results in the immersive VR study and the on-screen study, which validated the on-screen study results [7].

6 Limitations and Future Work

The VR study presented in this paper has several limitations due to complexity and time constraints. In this user study, we asked about general concepts and therefore omitted, e.g., current law requirements, location, color or size of a possible vehicle-to pedestrian communication feedback module. Another limitation is that, despite our efforts to minimize bias through randomization and careful selection of options, it cannot be considered completely eliminated.

The results of this user study will be used in further research regarding a vehicle-to pedestrian communication feedback module to develop a communication capability between an autonomous vehicle and a pedestrian. We will also validate our study regarding a vehicle-to bicycle communication feedback module [35] in VR. In additional user studies, we will use the results in another VR user study to create and simulate the selected interaction modes in more detail. As a subsequent step, we will verify the VR user study results in the real world on a vehicle. This research aims to create hardware that displays the selected feedback module on an autonomous vehicle. The hardware should remain visible regardless of various weather and light conditions that may otherwise hinder visibility. Developing this technology will improve the safety of vulnerable road users, such as pedestrians.

7 Conclusion

We presented a Virtual Reality study to identify a feedback module for communicating between a pedestrian and an autonomous vehicle, which increases most legibility, public acceptance and trust in the autonomous vehicle's decision. The results of this VR study validate the on-screen study questionnaire results from our previous work [7] since the results are very similar. In both studies, the results showed that participants prefer the symbol interaction mode, followed by the text interaction mode. In both studies, the results of the modified trust questionnaire show that the text interaction mode option "Safe to cross" or "Walk" (with no significant difference to "Go ahead" and "Waiting" in the VR study) should be used or the symbol interaction mode option that displays a symbol of a walking person.

References

1. World Health Organization. Road traffic injuries (2022). https://www.who.int/news-room/fact-sheets/detail/road-traffic-injuries
2. Singh, S.: Critical reasons for crashes investigated in the national motor vehicle crash causation survey. Technical Report (2015)
3. National highway traffic safety administration. pedestrians killed, by related factors - State : USA (2019). https://www-fars.nhtsa.dot.gov/People/PeoplePedestrians.aspx
4. De Clercq, K., Dietrich, A., Núñez Velasco, J.P., de Winter, J., Happee, R.: External human-machine interfaces on automated vehicles: effects on pedestrian crossing decisions. Hum. Factors 61(8), 1353–1370 (2019)
5. Stanciu, S.C., Eby, D.W., Molnar, L.J., St. Louis, R.M., Zanier, N., Kostyniuk, L.P.: Pedestrians/bicyclists and autonomous vehicles: how will they communicate? Transp. Res. Rec. 2672(22), 58–68 (2018)
6. Rothenbücher, D., Li, J., Sirkin, D., Mok, B., Ju, W.: Ghost driver: a field study investigating the interaction between pedestrians and driverless vehicles In: 2016 25th IEEE International Symposium on Robot and Human Interactive Communication (RO-MAN). IEEE (2016)
7. Schmidt-Wolf, M., Feil-Seifer, D.: Vehicle-to-pedestrian communication feedback module: A study on increasing legibility, public acceptance and trust In: Cavallo, F., et al. International Conference on Social Robotics, vol. 13817. Springer, Cham (2022). https://doi.org/10.1007/978-3-031-24667-8_2
8. Urmson, C.P., Mahon, I.J., Dolgov, D.A., Zhu, J.: Pedestrian notifications. US Patent 8,954,252, 10 Feb 2015
9. Clamann, M., Aubert, M., Cummings, M.L.: Evaluation of vehicle-to-pedestrian communication displays for autonomous vehicles, Technical Report (2017)
10. Rover, J.L.: The virtual eyes have it (2018). https://www.jaguarlandrover.com/2018/virtual-eyes-have-it
11. Tran, T.T.M., Parker, C., Tomitsch, M.: A review of virtual reality studies on autonomous vehicle-pedestrian interaction. IEEE Trans. Hum.-Mach. Syst. 51(6), 641–652 (2021)
12. Stadler, S., Cornet, H., Novaes Theoto, T., Frenkler, F.: A Tool, not a Toy: using virtual reality to evaluate the communication between autonomous vehicles and pedestrians. In: tom Dieck, M.C., Jung, T. (eds.) Augmented Reality and Virtual Reality. PI, pp. 203–216. Springer, Cham (2019). https://doi.org/10.1007/978-3-030-06246-0_15
13. Deb, S., Strawderman, L.J., Carruth, D.W.: Investigating pedestrian suggestions for external features on fully autonomous vehicles: A virtual reality experiment. Transp. Res. Part F: Psychol. Behav. 59, 135–149 (2018)
14. Deb, S., Carruth, D.W., Hudson, C.R.: How communicating features can help pedestrian safety in the presence of self-driving vehicles: virtual reality experiment. IEEE Trans. Hum.-Mach. Syst. 50(2), 176–186 (2020)
15. Löcken, A. Golling, C., Riener, A.: How should automated vehicles interact with pedestrians? a comparative analysis of interaction concepts in virtual reality. In: Proceedings of the 11th International Conference on Automotive User Interfaces and Interactive Vehicular Applications (2019)
16. Holländer, K., Colley, A., Mai, C., Häkkilä, J., Alt, F., Pfleging, B.: Investigating the influence of external car displays on pedestrians' crossing behavior in virtual reality'. In: Proceedings of the 21st International Conference on Human-Computer Interaction with Mobile Devices and Services (2019)

17. Larson, G.A.: Knight Rider [TV series], 1982–1986
18. Rasouli, A., Tsotsos, J.K.: Autonomous vehicles that interact with pedestrians: a survey of theory and practice. IEEE Trans. Intell. Transp. Syst. **21**(3), 900–918 (2019)
19. Yuen, K.F., Wong, Y.D., Ma, F., Wang, X.: The determinants of public acceptance of autonomous vehicles: an innovation diffusion perspective. J. Cleaner Prod. **270**, 121904 (2020)
20. Shariff, A., Bonnefon, J.-F., Rahwan, I.: Psychological roadblocks to the adoption of self-driving vehicles. Nat. Hum. Behav. **1**(10), 694–696 (2017)
21. Newcomb, D.: You won't need a driver's license by 2040. Autopia, Wired. com (2012)
22. Raats, K., Fors, V., Pink, S.: Trusting autonomous vehicles: an interdisciplinary approach. Transp. Res. Interdisc. Perspect. **7**, 100201 (2020)
23. AAA, "Self-driving cars stuck in neutral on the road to acceptance," AAA Newsroom (2020). https://newsroom.aaa.com/2020/03/self-driving-cars-stuck-in-neutral-on-the-road-to-acceptance/
24. Dosovitskiy, A., Ros, G., Codevilla, F., Lopez, A. and Koltun, V.: CARLA: an open urban driving simulator. In: Proceedings of the 1st Annual Conference on Robot Learning (2017)
25. Lagström, T., Malmsten Lundgren, V.: "AVIP-autonomous vehicles' interaction with pedestrians-an investigation of pedestrian-driver communication and development of a vehicle external interface", Master's thesis (2016)
26. Daimler, A.: Autonomous concept car smart vision EQ fortwo: welcome to the future of car sharing-Daimler global media site (2017)
27. Eisma, Y.B., van Bergen, S., Ter Brake, S., Hensen, M., Tempelaar, W.J., de Winter, J.C.: External human-machine interfaces: the effect of display location on crossing intentions and eye movements. Information **11**(1), 13 (2020)
28. Carmona, J., Guindel, C., Garcia, F., de la Escalera, A.: eHMI: review and guidelines for deployment on autonomous vehicles. Sensors **21**(9), 2912 (2021)
29. Risto, M., Emmenegger, C., Vinkhuyzen, E., Cefkin, M. and Hollan, J.: Human-vehicle interfaces: the power of vehicle movement gestures in human road user coordination. In: Driving Assessment Conference, vol. 9 (2017)
30. Fridman, L., Mehler, B., Xia, L., Yang, Y., Facusse, L.Y., Reimer, B.: To walk or not to walk: Crowdsourced assessment of external vehicle-to-pedestrian displays. arXiv preprint arXiv:1707.02698 (2017)
31. Semcon: The smiling car (2016). https://semcon.com/smilingcar/
32. Rasouli, A., Tsotsos, J.K.: Joint attention in driver-pedestrian interaction: from theory to practice. arXiv preprint arXiv:1802.02522 (2018)
33. Rover, J.L.: Jaguar land rover lights up the road ahead for self-driving vehicles of the future (2019)
34. Schaefer, K.E.: Measuring trust in human robot interactions: development of the *Trust Perception Scale-HRI*. In: Mittu, R., Sofge, D., Wagner, A., Lawless, W.F. (eds.) Robust Intelligence and Trust in Autonomous Systems, pp. 191–218. Springer, Boston, MA (2016). https://doi.org/10.1007/978-1-4899-7668-0_10
35. Schmidt-Wolf, M., Feil-Seifer, D.: Comparison of vehicle-to-bicyclist and vehicle-to-pedestrian communication feedback module: a study on increasing legibility, public acceptance and trust. In: 2022 31st IEEE International Conference on Robot and Human Interactive Communication (RO-MAN). IEEE (2022)

Author Index

© The Editor(s) (if applicable) and The Author(s), under exclusive license
to Springer Nature Singapore Pte Ltd. 2024
A. Al. Ali et al. (Eds.): ICSR 2023, LNAI 14453, pp. 425–428, 2024.
https://doi.org/10.1007/978-981-99-8715-3

Printed in the United States
by Baker & Taylor Publisher Services